Moving On

Moving On
The American People Since 1945

Third Edition

George Donelson Moss

PEARSON

Prentice
Hall

Upper Saddle River, NJ 07458

Library of Congress Cataloging-in-Publication Data
Moss, George
   Moving on: the American people since 1945/George Donelson Moss.—3rd ed.
      p. cm.
   Includes bibliographical references and index.
   ISBN 0-13-189825-6
      1. United States—History—1945–I. Title.

E741.M673 2005
973.92—dc22

2004040013

Editor-in-Chief: Charlyce Jones Owen
Acquisitions Editor: Emsal Hasan
Editorial Assistant: Adrienne Paul
Marketing Manager: Heather Shelstad
Marketing Assistant: Jennifer Bryant
Production Editor: Laura A. Lawrie
Manufacturing Buyer: Tricia Kenny
Art Director: Jayne Conte
Cover Design: Bruce Kenselaar
Composition: This book was set in 10/12 Times Roman by Pine Tree Composition, Inc.
Printer/Binder: The interior was printed by Phoenix Book Tech.
The cover was printed by Phoenix Color.

Credits and acknowledgments borrowed from other sources and reproduced, with
permission, in this textbook appear on appropriate page within text.

Pearson Education LTD.   Pearson Education Australia PTY, Limited
Pearson Education Singapore, Pte. Ltd.   Pearson Education North Asia, Ltd.
Pearson Education Canada, Ltd.   Pearson Educación de Mexico, S.A. de C.V.
Pearson Education—Japan   Pearson Education Malaysia, Pte. Ltd.

10 9 8 7 6 5 4 3 2 1
ISBN 0-13-189825-6

For the "baby boomers" and their descendants:
This is the story of their America.

Contents

Preface   *xiii*

Acknowledgments   *xiv*

1   The American People in 1945   1

    War as Social Revolution   2

    Demographic Change   3

    Economic Transformations   5

    Women in Wartime   7

    African Americans at War   9

    Hispanic Americans in Wartime   12

    Native Americans in Wartime   13

    Asian Americans in Wartime   13

    The Politics of War   17

    The Election of 1944   18

    War and Culture   19

    Hollywood Goes to War   20

    Wartime Radio   22

    World War and Its Legacies   23

    Brief Bibliographic Essay   25

    Web Sites   25

2   The Rise of the Cold War   26

    Origins of Cold War   26

    The Truman Doctrine   37

The Marshall Plan   39
NATO   40
The Chinese Revolution   44
Vietnam: The Beginnings   46
NSC-68   47
War in Korea   47
The Cold War Consensus   53
Brief Bibliographic Essay   54
Web Sites   55

3   Postwar America   56
Postwar Politics   56
Labor Troubles   58
The Election of 1946   59
The 80th Congress   60
Women   61
Civil Rights   62
The Election of 1948   65
The Fair Deal   68
Cold War at Home   69
Brief Bibliography Essay   76
Web Sites   76

4   The American People at Mid-Century   77
Demographic Patterns   78
An Economy of Abundance   78
The Car Culture   79
Growth Industries   80
The Mixed Economy   81
Labor at Mid-Century   82
Poverty Amidst Plenty   83
The Rise of Suburbia   84
Class and Status   86
The Culture of Affluence   87
Women: Family Life and Work   89
Religion Revived   92
Social Critics   93
The Advent of Television   94
Rock 'N' Roll   97
Rebels   99
Brief Bibliographic Essay   100
Web Sites   100

5   The Politics of Consensus   101
The Election of 1952   101
Dynamic Conservatism   103

McCarthy: Zenith and Ruin   104
The Politics of Consensus   106
Civil Rights   106
The New Look   109
Vietnam: Getting in Deeper   111
The China Crisis   113
At the Summit   115
The CIA at Work   115
Trouble in Suez   116
Sputnik   118
Cuba and Castro   120
Controversy in Europe   122
End of an Era   122
Brief Bibliographic Essay   124
Web Sites   124

6   New Frontiers   126
The Election of 1960   126
The Cold Warrior   130
The Bay of Pigs   131
The Third World   132
Berlin   132
The Missile Crisis   134
Vietnam: Raising the Stakes   138
The Space Race   140
Social Reform   141
The Economy   143
Let Freedom Ring   144
Tragedy in Dallas   148
The Legacy of Camelot   150
Brief Bibliographic Essay   152
Web Sites   153

7   Great Society and Vietnam   154
The Tall Texan   154
The Election of 1964   155
Great Society   157
An Activist Court   161
Continuing the Cold World   163
Vietnam: Going to War   166
The American Way of War   168
War at Home   171
Tet-68 and Its Consequences   172
Brief Bibliographic Essay   175
Web Sites   175

8   Rebellion and Reaction   176
        Young Radicals   176
        The Greening of America   179
        The Fire This Time   183
        Black Power   185
        Red and Brown Power   187
        Gay-Lesbian Liberation   188
        The Rebirth of Feminism   188
        Backlash   191
        The Election of 1968   192
        Summing Up the Sixties   197
        Brief Bibliographic Essay   199
        Web Sites   199

9   Calming Down   201
        Pragmatic Centrism   201
        The Southern Strategy   203
        Activists and Reformers   207
        Ecology and Consumerism   209
        The Election of 1972   210
        Watergate   212
        Decline and Fall   215
        Brief Bibliographic Essay   221
        Web Sites   221

10   Detente, China, and Vietnam   223
        Detente   223
        Opening China   226
        A War to End a War   228
        The Middle Eastern Dilemma   233
        Chaos in Chile   236
        Troubles in Europe   237
        The Emergence of Japan   238
        Diplomacy in Perspective   238
        Brief Bibliographic Essay   240
        Web Sites   240

11   Era of Limits   241
        A Ford, Not a Lincoln   241
        Economic and Energy Woes   242
        Extending Detente   244
        Vietnam: The End   245
        The Election of 1976   247
        Mr. Carter Goes to Washington   249
        The Decline of Detente   251
        Debacle in Iran   255

The Election of 1980   257
A Time of Troubles   260
Brief Bibliographic Essay   261
Web Sites   261

12   The American People in the 1970s   262
A Demographic Profile   262
Economic Stasis   263
Cars and Computers   265
New Immigrants   267
African Americans: A Dual Society   269
Women: Changing Attitudes and Roles   272
Education   276
The Rise of the Religious Right   277
The "Me" Decade   279
Popular Culture   280
A Dismal Decade   284
Brief Bibliographic Essay   284
Web Sites   285

13   America Revived   286
The Advent of Reaganomics   287
Recession and Recovery   290
The Cold War Revived   291
The Pacific Rim   293
Disaster in Lebanon   294
Policing the Western Hemisphere   296
The Election of 1984   298
Centrist Conservatism   300
The Go-Go Economy   302
Judicial Conservatives   306
Containing Terrorism   307
The Iraqi-Iranian War   308
Central America   309
Iran-Contra   309
The Sleaze Factor   314
Thawing the Cold War   314
The Election of 1988   316
Brief Bibliographic Essay   318
Web Sites   319

14   Going Global   320
The Demographics of Diversity   321
Bust, Boom, and Bust   321
TV and Cyberspace   324
Black and White, but not Together   324

A Fragmented Society   327
Culture Wars   328
Women and Work   331
The Good Earth   332
The Presidency of George H. W. Bush   333
The Supreme Court in the 1990s   334
Ending the Cold War   335
Post–Cold War Diplomacy   337
War in the Persian Gulf   339
The Election of 1992   343
Return of the Democrats   344
A Republican Earthquake   347
The Election of 1996   348
A President Impeached   348
Clintonian Diplomacy   352
War in Kosovo   353
Terrorism Abroad and at Home   355
Brief Bibliographic Essay   356
Web Sites   357

15   The New Millennium   358
The 2000 Census   359
Economic Disparities   361
A Multicultural Society   362
Children of the New Millennium   365
Election 2000   365
Thirty-Six Days   367
Compassionate Conservatism   369
Judicial Warfare   371
9/11/01 and the War on Terrorism   371
The Iraq War   378
Brief Bibiographic Essay   384
Web Sites   385

Appendices   387
Appendix A The Declaration of Independence   387
Appendix B Amendments to the United States Constitution
          Since 1945   390
Appendix C Presidential Elections Since 1944   393
Appendix D Population of the United States Since 1940   395

Index   397

Preface

Moving On: The American People Since 1945 covers the sixty years of American history from the end of World War II to the present; it endeavors to explain how the American nation has become what it is today and how the American people have become what they are today. It represents my best efforts to probe the deeper meanings of the recent historical experiences that have shaped our nation and forged the social character of our people. Recent American history is a compelling saga of human struggle, achievement, and failure; it is filled with irony, tragedy, and comedy.

It has been an exciting book to write and revise for a third edition, because our recent past has been, and no doubt will continue to be, supercharged with energy, conflict, and drama. The book has been throughly revised for this new edition. Each chapter has been carefully reworked. For some chapters, new material has been added. For others, material has been abbreviated or deleted. Chapters 13 and 14 covering the 1980s have been shortened and combined, as have Chapters 15 and 16 covering the 1990s. The new Chapter 14 encompassing the significant events of the 1990s also has been redesigned and largely rewritten.

A new chapter, Chapter 15, has been added that covers the momentous events occurring during the first years of the twenty-first century, including the terrorist attacks on the United States that we know as 9/11/01. It contains accounts of the ongoing war on terrorism including the military interventions into Afghanistan and Iraq. This new edition also puts the war on terrorism into a larger historical context and provides an analytic framework. The ongoing war on terrorism is rooted in developments that occurred during the late 1970s and early 1980s.

At the conclusion of each chapter, I have appended a short bibliographic essay. Each essay contains brief descriptions of carefully selected works chosen for their currency, accessibilty, and literary quality to assist students in selecting the best available books on topics that attract their interest. The bibliographic essays have all been revised and updated for this new edition. This edition also includes carefully selected Internet Web sites to help readers make their way through the proliferating online resources on recent U.S. history.

The era that began amidst the storm of the planet's largest war and continues to the present global war against terrorism forms a coherent unit of study. It is no wonder that students have made recent U.S. history courses among the most popular currently being offered on the nation's college and university campuses. Paradoxically, most students, even the best and the brightest who have had good high school survey courses in U.S. history, are unlikely to know well the recent history of their country—even though it is that recent history that most usefully illuminates the present and suggests the shape of the future rapidly exploding upon us.

For most young people, Watergate and the Warren Commission are merely rhetorical labels, names for events that scarcely one student in ten can discuss meaningfully. Students often know more about the Spanish-American War than they do about the Persian Gulf War. Having scant historical understanding of recent events, they have little sense of causation or consequences. They lack the experience of constructing meaningful patterns of explanation and interpretation that creates out of these recent events an intelligible, usable past.

Did the upheavals of the 1960s have an enduring impact on the status of minorities, women, and gay-lesbian people? How has the legacy of the Vietnam War influenced subsequent American diplomatic and strategic policies? Does the ongoing war against terrorism derive from a long U.S. involvement in the Middle East, and if so, what are the particular sources of this conflict? Two of the most significant and challenging questions to try to answer is how did the global economy evolve and how did the United States come to play a dominant role in the emergent global village. Only a close study of the past sixty years can provide answers to these and the myriad of other questions that thoughtful students bring to the recent U.S. past.

The year 1945 is an appropriate one to begin our story of recent America. World War II signified one of the most profound turning points in the history of the Republic. Out of that horrific conflict came America's involvement in the postwar world, giving rise to the long Cold War struggle with the Soviet Union that dominated U.S. foreign policy for nearly fifty years. Out of World War II came a revitalized, transformed American economy that undergirded the remarkable prosperity that most American families enjoyed for nearly thirty years. Forged within the terrible crucible of war, a new, more egalitarian society emerged that influenced the historical experience of Americans for decades.

During the late 1960s, Americans found themselves embroiled in twin convulsions, full-blown political and cultural crises. These crises occurred because of American involvement in a controversial war in Indochina and because of the rise of domestic insurgencies, of which the militant civil rights movement was the most powerful. War and domestic rebellions combined to polarize Americans in 1968. Political activists clashed with defenders of traditional values and institutions. During the presidential election of 1968, Richard Nixon rallied traditional forces, which then defeated the forces of reform and social activism, ushering in a more conservative era that has stretched from the 1970s to the opening years of the twenty-first century.

Moving On retains what is most valuable from traditional public policy approaches to U.S. history: It incorporates political history, economic history, military history, and foreign policy history. These kinds of histories are usually told from the top down, from the perspectives of elite groups that have dominated governmental and economic institutions. While retaining some elements of these traditional approaches, I also have integrated much demographic, ecological, social, and cultural history.

During the past sixty years, Americans have developed a vital popular culture. Its most important forms reach most Americans through the mass media of radio, movies, television, and the Internet. Sections of many chapters chart the rise of a multimedia-saturated popular culture that is flourishing in the opening years of the twenty-first century.

I have also devoted a good deal of space to the new social history that has enriched our historical literature and greatly expanded our understanding of what constitutes mainstream American history. Much of this new social history, with its focus on issues of class, gender, race, and ethnicity, is told from the perspective of those groups that in the past were either ignored or were perceived as passive objects of more powerful historical agents. Social history is often told from the ground up. Thus you will find that I have given much attention to immigration history, labor history, women's history, gay-lesbian history, African-American history, Hispanic-American history, Asian-American history, and Native American history. The story of recent America includes the stories of all individuals and groups who have played active roles in the unfolding drama.

My inclusive approach amounts to a work of restoration. I aim to restore to the recent past all its diversity and complexity. Within the traditional framework of public policy history, I have crafted innovative multicultural structures as diverse and dynamic as American society itself. Moving On is a book for everyone, for traditionalists and multiculturalists alike. If I have created the book that I intended, it will be the first study of the recent American past that one reads, not the last. If historical study represents a kind of journey, consider *Moving On* a point of departure, not a destination.

ACKNOWLEDGMENTS

One of the many features of the historian's profession that makes it so rewarding is the incredible generosity of others who so willingly give their time, energies, talents, and knowledge. In the creation and two revisions of *Moving On*, I am profoundly grateful for so much help from so many fine people: my students and colleagues at City College of San Francisco and the University of California, San Diego, and other scholars who also contributed in ways that improved the content, organization, and writing of this book and its various revisions. They are too numerous to cite individually, and I want to assert as emphatically as I can that my not mentioning them by name is not in the slightest way an indicator of ingratitude. I also want to thank the reviewers of this book: Yanek Mieczkowski, Dowling College, and Margo J. Anderson, University of Wisconsin, Madison.

Special thanks go to Charles Cavaliere and Emsal Hasan, my editors at Prentice Hall who have given me an opportunity to create a third edition of *Moving On*. My only hope is that it at least comes reasonably close to meeting their expectations. I also am exceedingly grateful to Laura Lawrie, who expertly took charge of the production process.

A special, special thanks goes to the lovely Linda, who, forsaking all others, has hitched her team to my wagon. Together it is a grand ride!

George Donelson Moss

Moving On

1

The American People in 1945

On August 14, 1945, the Japanese government announced Japan's unconditional surrender, bringing history's largest war to a triumphant conclusion for the United States and its allies. Across America, its people erupted in frenzied victory celebrations. Tumultuous parades occurred in New York, Chicago, San Francisco, and in other great cities. In the American heartland, in small towns and villages everywhere, citizens joined in spontaneous, joyous victory parades. All Americans rejoiced at the final destruction of the Axis menace and the advent of peace throughout a battered world.

In Blythe, California, an agricultural community of perhaps 2,500 people, amidst the honking cars and trucks, a ten-year-old boy, astride his chestnut pony, shouted, "We won! We won!" Leading the parade, the high school marching band played "The Star-Spangled Banner," "America the Beautiful," and John Philip Sousa's rousing "Stars and Stripes Forever." Immediately behind the band came a black car draped with a large gold star. Inside of the car, their grief and loss temporarily masked as they waved to bystanders gathered along Main Street, rode three women whose sons had died in battle.

The parade constituted a motley column of vehicles, cowboys on horseback, pedestrians, Native Americans from a nearby reservation, and soldiers from an air base at the edge of town. At the tail end of the parade, riding in their wagon pulled by a team of mules, came an African-American couple whose son had been fighting in the great war to preserve democracy.

The mood of the paraders was exultant. Americans had just won history's greatest war! At last the killing and dying would stop. Husbands, fathers, brothers, and sweethearts could come home. Wartime shortages and rationing would soon end. Thirty miles north of Blythe, Japanese Americans interned at Camp Poston quietly observed the end of the war. They too could go home.

After the paraders had traversed Main Street, they turned onto a side road that led to the fairgrounds, which also served as a rodeo arena and a football stadium. As they reached the fairgrounds, the paraders dispersed. George Donelson Moss, tired but immensely proud to be an

1

Figure 1.1   Americans celebrating V-J day in Times Square. All across the country, people erupted into spontaneous celebrations of victory.   *Source:* Bettmann Archive.

American on that long-ago, glorious summer day, his little boy's imagination fired by the sense that he had played a small part in a great historical drama, rode his pony home. It was dinner time.

WAR AS SOCIAL REVOLUTION

At war's end, the United States was vastly changed from the nation that had been thrust suddenly into the cauldron of war by the Japanese surprise attack on Pearl Harbor on December 7, 1941. During the intervening three years and nine months of fighting and winning World War II, America had undergone profound transformations that forever changed the social landscape and created new possibilities for its people.

During the war years, huge military forces were raised and sent to fight on the land, on the sea, and in the air around the globe. The most productive economy the world had ever seen sustained America's large civilian population and simultaneously supplied its and its allies' military forces fighting the Axis powers. The war revitalized the American economy, extricated the American people from the lingering clutches of the Great Depression, and inaugurated a cycle of affluence that stretched into the 1970s. War enhanced the power and reach of the federal government. War thrust America irrevocably into the center of world affairs and destroyed forever isolationist tendencies that had lingered tenaciously until the morning that Japanese aircraft bombed Pearl Harbor.

War transformed the nation's social structure. Well-paying jobs in war industries located in coastal cities triggered a vast folk migration that rapidly depopulated the countryside. War opened up unprecedented economic opportunities for women, African Americans, and Hispanic Americans. War, hysteria, and race prejudice combined to harm gravely the Japanese-American population that lived along the West Coast when America entered the war. Army troops uprooted 120,000 people from their homes and interned them in desolate camps in isolated desert regions for the duration of the war.

Demographic Change

In 1945, approximately 140,000,000 Americans inhabited the nation and its territories and served overseas in the armed forces. World War II had had a dramatic impact on the lives of nearly all Americans—on where they lived and what kind of work they did. It also affected family life and patterns of leisure and recreation. The war experience established demographic patterns that would persist for the rest of the twentieth century.

Between 1941 and 1945, approximately sixteen million men, about 95 percent of whom were drafted, and 250,000 women served in the armed forces. About half of those who went into the military during the war never left the Continental United States. But many of those servicemen who never left the states were assigned to bases in different parts of the country that they had never before seen. After the war ended and they had been discharged, they often returned with their families to become permanent residents of the locales where they had performed military service. In addition to service personnel, millions of civilian war workers moved from rural areas to the cities, where jobs in war industries could be found. In many cases, those transplanted civilian war workers, refugees from rural poverty and isolation, did not go home after the war. They and their families joined the burgeoning postwar urban and suburban populations.

Several important population shifts occurred in wartime that would shape the demographic contours of postwar America for decades. Population flowed from the rural interior of the country outward toward the cities along the Pacific, Atlantic, and Gulf coasts. People also left inland farms and villages for the cities of the Upper Midwest, because it was in the coastal and Midwestern cities that the major military installations, shipyards, aircraft assembly plants, and other war industries were located. Population also made a major shift westward, particularly to California. California's population increased by 40 percent from 1940 to 1945, and millions of the military personnel and war workers who came to California in wartime remained or returned after the war to become permanent residents of the Golden State. The Sunbelt, that southern rim of states stretching from South Carolina to Southern California, also began to grow rapidly during the war years. The Sunbelt states, especially Florida, Texas, and Southern California, would become the nation's most dynamic centers of population growth and economic expansion in the postwar decades.

Another important demographic trend, induced by World War II, was the well-paying jobs in war industries that lured over 1 million African Americans out of the Old South and on to New York, Chicago, Philadelphia, Detroit, and the rapidly growing cities along the West Coast. Most African Americans and their families also remained in these new locales after the war,

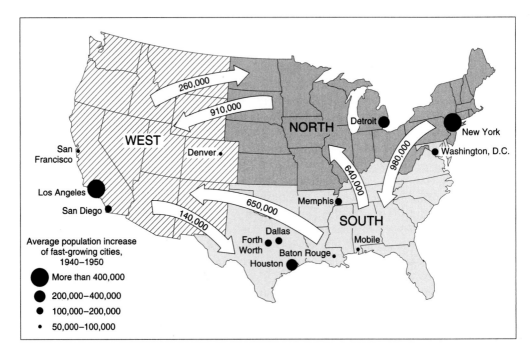

Figure 1.2   Internal migration in the United States during World War II.   *Source:* Statistical Abstract

becoming permanent residents of New York, Ohio, Pennsylvania, Illinois, Michigan, and California. The geographic mobility induced by the war resulted in permanent relocations for millions of American families. Rural America declined, regional differences among Americans diminished; and the demographic foundations for the postwar surge of urban and suburban communities were laid.

Despite the mobilization of the nation's vast human and economic resources for the war effort, there occurred more social reform affecting the quality of American lives during the war than had occurred during the previous years of New Deal reforms. Medical and dental care improved dramatically. Prepaid health insurance for working people became available for the first time. Millions of young men from disadvantaged backgrounds drafted into the armed forces enjoyed a nutritious diet and adequate medical and dental care for the first time in their lives. Even with the nation at war and with the dangers inherent in war work, the overall health of the nation's population improved dramatically. The birthrate rose rapidly; the death rate sharply diminished. Median life expectancy increased by five years.

A huge increase in the size of the American middle class was the most significant demographic transformation of the war years. The United States became, for the first time in its history, a middle-class nation in the sense that a statistical majority, more than half of its families, enjoyed middle-class incomes and lifestyles. Real personal income more than doubled during the war years, and national income was more equitably distributed than ever before. Perhaps one-third of the nation's families remained poor, but even poor families often enjoyed relative improvements in their living standards. It was during the early 1940s that prosperity levels that had been reached in this country during the late 1920s before the Great Crash were finally eclipsed.

ECONOMIC TRANSFORMATIONS

In addition to raising a vast military force, the United States had to gear its economy for global war. America's factories had to produce arms for itself and its major allies, the British, the Soviets, and the Chinese. During the first half of 1942, the federal government placed orders for over $100 billion in war contracts, more goods than the economy had ever produced in a year. Converting the economy to a war footing challenged American industrials and government officials. Initial government efforts to organize the war economy proved ineffective. But by 1943, the Office of Economic Stabilization, headed by James F. Byrnes, brought order to the gigantic wartime industrial effort. Byrnes used the immense powers granted his office to weave together the various strands of America's domestic war effort into a relatively efficient system.

Fueled by vast federal expenditures, total productivity increased at the remarkable rate of 25 percent per annum, a growth rate never approached before or since World War II. The gross domestic product more than doubled during the war years, from $95 billion in 1940 to more than $211 billion by 1946. During those years, economic expansion added ten million new jobs. The federal government during World War II spent more than twice as much money than all previous governments combined had spent since the creation of the Republic in 1789.

To help pay for these prodigious wartime expenditures, Congress broadened and deepened the tax structure. The Revenue Acts of 1942 and 1943 created the modern federal income tax system. Most Americans had never filed an income tax return before World War II, because the income tax, on the books since 1913, had been a small tax on upper-income families and corporations. Starting in 1942, anyone earning $600 or more annually had to file an income tax return. A withholding tax went into effect in 1943, which made employers the nation's principal tax collectors. Income tax revenues rose from $5 billion in 1940 to $49 billion in 1945, a tenfold increase. Even with the huge increase in federal income taxes, the largest federal tax increase in U. S. history, tax revenues paid only 41 percent of the cost of the war. The government paid the rest of the war bills by borrowing. War bonds, peddled by movie stars, war heroes, and professional athletes, added $135 billion. But ordinary citizens bought only about one-third of these bonds; large institutional investors purchased the bulk of them. By war's end, the national debt had climbed to $280 billion, up from $40 billion when it began. And by war's end, the national debt was larger than the economy, that is, the debt exceeded the gross domestic product.

Vast federal spending for war ended the lingering depression that had afflicted Americans for a decade. The New Deal had failed to find a cure for economic depression. On the eve of war, over seven million Americans were out of work, or 14 percent of the labor force. Real wages in 1941 were below 1929 levels. By New Year's Day in 1943, unemployment in America had vanished. Wartime economic expansion, fueled by unprecedented levels of government spending, combined with mass conscription to create severe labor shortages. By war's end, the nation's workers enjoyed full employment at the highest wages in history.

The discovery that government spending could banish the specter of depression appeared to confirm the claims of the world's foremost economist, England's John Maynard Keynes. Keynes had contended that government spending could cure economic depression. If private sector investment proved inadequate, government could cut taxes and begin large-scale spending programs to stimulate demand and restore the business cycle. During the New Deal of the mid-1930s, government spending was not large enough and taxes were generally regressive, so Keynes's theories could not be tested until the war years.

Their wartime success in eliminating the depression also gave American political leaders a confidence that they could regulate the business cycle, a confidence that would last for the next thirty years. They believed that they now possessed the fiscal tools to monitor spending levels, maintain prosperity, keep unemployment low, and prevent the recurrence of recession, all the while controlling inflation. Americans also looked to government after the war to maintain a prosperous, growing, and full-employment economy.

Farmers and industrial workers, two classes devastated by the depression, prospered during the war years. Farm output rose 20 percent, even though the farm population declined more than 50 percent and farmers struggled with chronic labor shortages, fuel shortages, and worn-out machinery. Big labor prospered along with big business in wartime. Congress created the War Labor Board in 1942, which set guidelines for wages, hours, and collective bargaining. Employers, unions, and government officials generally cooperated during the war. Union membership grew from 10.5 million in 1941 to over 15 million in 1945, one-third of the nonfarm workforce. During the war, trade union leaders consolidated their new status as members of the nation's political and economic elites.

There were some labor problems that the War Labor Board could not resolve. The American Federation of Labor and the Congress of Industrial Organizations engaged in bitter, sometimes violent, jurisdictional disputes. Although organized labor had given a no-strike pledge for the duration of the war, it could not be enforced. In 1943, over 3 million workers went out on strike, although most work stoppages during the war years lasted only a few days. These strikes never caused serious production delays in the industries that cranked out the huge amounts of war materials required by the armed forces.

Vastly increased federal spending also unleashed powerful inflationary forces. The shift from peacetime to wartime production sharply reduced the amount of consumer goods available to buy just at the time when people had significantly more money to spend. By 1943, the production of new cars and other durable goods had ceased. A giant inflationary gap generated by too much money chasing too few goods threatened to drive prices way up and to rob Americans of their wartime economic gains. To clamp a lid on inflation, the government imposed price controls, joining them to a rationing system that used coupon allotments to consumers for scarce items such as sugar, butter, coffee, beef, tires, and gasoline.

Roosevelt created the Office of Price Administration (OPA) to administer the control apparatus nationally. The OPA had a daunting task. Business lobbyists, farm bloc politicians, and union leaders waged unceasing "guerrilla warfare" against the OPA for the duration of the war. Consumers chafed under rationing restrictions, particularly those on beef and gasoline. A ban on all "pleasure driving" and a 35 mph speed limit accompanied gasoline rationing. The average motorist received three gallons of gas a week. Most people walked to work or took public transportation. Auto touring practically vanished. Black markets in gasoline flourished; racketeers had not had it so good since Prohibition. At times, motorists could not obtain any gas, legal or illegal. Service stations often closed, stranding motorists and truckers. When a station could get gas, customers lined up their cars for miles waiting to buy it.

Beef rationing caused the worst problems. Butcher display cases were frequently empty. Frustrated shoppers often abused butchers and occasionally rioted. Despite grievances and injustices, the universally unpopular OPA maintained a semblance of price stability and distributed scarce goods reasonably fairly. Most people complied with the system of controls, considering it both a wartime necessity and to their economic advantage. The cost of living rose only 3 percent in 1944 and 1945. Government controls and rationing effectively contained inflation in wartime.

Even as ordinary citizens chafed under the restrictions of rationing and price controls, purchased war bonds, and saved grease, scrap metals, and used tires, a quite remarkable redistribution of income occurred. During the war years, real wages for workers employed in manufacturing rose over 50 percent, from $24 dollars to $37 dollars a week. The share of national wealth owned by the richest 5 percent of American families dropped from 23.7 percent to 16.8 percent. The number of families earning less than $2,000 annually declined by 50 percent from 1941 to 1945, and the number of families earning $5,000 or more quadrupled during the same time span. World War II was the most successful war on poverty in American history; it also created the social foundations for the affluent society that flowered during the postwar era.

Despite annoying shortages and rationing, people with money to spend in wartime found ways to spend it and to enjoy it. Wartime prosperity strengthened materialistic values and revived consumerism, which largely had been suspended during the Depression decade. Americans spent money on entertainment, on going to the movies, and on going out to dinner. People resorted to black markets when rationed goods could not be found. Many people saved their money for new cars, new homes, new appliances, and new radios that they would buy after the war. Advertisers promised consumers new and better goods when civilian production patterns were restored following victory over the Axis powers. Consumerism, reborn amidst war, would become a powerful engine driving the postwar affluent economy.

WOMEN IN WARTIME

Between 1941 and 1945, over six million women entered the labor force, about half of whom worked in the manufacturing sector. Women also joined the branches of military service open to them. They served in the WACS (Women's Auxiliary Army Corps) and in the WAVES (Women Accepted for Voluntary Emergency Service). They also served in women's units in the Coast Guard and Marine Corps, and thousands of women became noncombat military pilots.

Married women, many with children, made up three-quarters of working women in wartime. By 1945, more than half of working women had married, and their median age was thirty-seven. Before the war, women had been excluded from most manufacturing jobs. Employers considered women unsuitable for heavy labor amidst the masculine atmosphere prevailing in factories. Acute wartime labor shortages quickly changed those attitudes. Women learned skilled trades, joined unions, and earned high wages. They performed certain jobs better than men, such as those requiring close attention to detail and manual dexterity. Women worked in munitions factories and foundries. They also became riveters, welders, crane operators, tool and die makers, and iron workers. They operated heavy equipment, drove trucks, and became train engineers. Women increased their geographic and occupational mobility tremendously in wartime. Black women quit work as domestics to join the factory labor force. Millions of women moved from the rural South and Midwest to coastal cities where the war-generated jobs were located. In Southern California, hundreds of thousands of women went to work in aircraft assembly plants.

A government propaganda agency, the Office of War Information (OWI), mounted publicity campaigns to persuade women to join the war labor force. These media campaigns portrayed women's work in shops and factories as both noble and absolutely necessary to the war effort. A fictional "Rosie the Riveter" became a popular wartime symbol of women working in war industries. She was celebrated in a hit tune of the era, and her picture appeared on posters and magazine covers. "Do the Job HE Left Behind" exhorted the billboards.

Traditional patterns of gender discrimination persisted in wartime. Surveys showed that women in manufacturing earned about 60 percent of what men received for comparable work. Factories offered limited promotional opportunities and supervisorial positions for women. Even though the war emergency opened up hitherto closed occupations to women, most jobs in the sex-segregated labor market remained classified as "male" or "female" work. Where women worked in factories, they often worked on all-female shop floors, under male supervisors. Women resented the unequal pay and working conditions, and the sexual harassment from

Figure 1.3   Over six million women entered the labor force during World War II. Many of them worked in the aircraft industry such as these two "Rosie the Riveters."   *Source:* National Archives.

chauvinistic males. But they loved the opportunity to do important work that contributed to winning the war, and they also enjoyed the camaraderie and support of their female co-workers.

The most serious problem faced by working mothers in wartime was the almost complete absence of child care centers. During the war, juvenile delinquency, venereal disease, and teenage pregnancies rose sharply. "Latchkey children," children left alone while their mothers worked their shifts at a factory, became a national scandal. Children roamed the streets, were put in all-day movie houses, or were locked in cars outside of defense plants. Police arrested many teenage girls for prostitution and apprehended boys for theft and vandalism.

Because so many men went to war, millions of women found themselves the *de facto* heads of single-parent households. They had a much greater range of responsibilities than just working full-time shifts in factories and shipyards. They became the centers of family life. Many also found time for neighborhood volunteer work. They served on civil defense committees, attended club meetings, went to PTA meetings, gave blood, and worked as hostesses at USO (United Service Organizations) centers.

Increasing numbers of women got married at the same time they went to work in war industries. Many young couples got married to spend time together before the man got shipped overseas. The birthrate also climbed sharply. Many births enabled men to qualify for military deferments. Others conceived "good-bye babies" to perpetuate the family, even if the fathers were killed in the war. Returning prosperity provided the main reason for the increase in marriages and the rising birthrate. The baby boom that would be one of the most significant demographic trends of the postwar decades had begun.

Women's wartime factory work was considered only a temporary response to a national emergency. Once victory was achieved and the soldiers returned, women were expected to surrender their jobs to returning GIs. The president of the National Association of Manufacturers intoned, "Too many women should not stay in the labor force. The home is the basic American institution." But surveys showed that most women wanted to continue working after the war. After the war, with their war contracts canceled, employers fired their female employees. Others were pressured by their husbands to quit and return to the kitchen. Single working women continued to work. But often they could find only low-paying jobs in domestic service, restaurants, and department stores. Many of these women felt a keen sense of personal defeat over having to resume work in low-status, low-paying fields from which they had temporarily escaped for a few years during the war.

But the roots of the modern feminist movement can be found in the work experience, financial independence, and attitudinal changes achieved by millions of women during World War II. They had found new opportunities and met new challenges that traditionally had been denied women. Many women derived a larger sense or their own worth and felt a strong sense of empowerment. Many reared their daughters to have greater self-esteem and to demand much more from life than their own mothers had taught them to expect.

AFRICAN AMERICANS AT WAR

World War II proved a mixed blessing for African Americans: It provided both unprecedented economic opportunities and continuing encounters with the hardships of segregation and racism. About 1 million black men and women, nearly all of the men draftees, served in the armed forces during the war, entering all branches of military service. Even though the American military was still segregated during World War II, African Americans attained far more opportunities than had been available during World War I. The Army Air Corps trained black pilots who flew in all-black squadrons. African American Marines, fighting in all-black units, fought heroically in savage island battles in the Pacific war.

Black–white race relations within the military reflected the racist society it served. Many race riots occurred on military bases. White civilians often attacked African-American soldiers stationed in the South. The morale and motivation of black soldiers frequently suffered from encounters with racist whites. African-American soldiers often found themselves serving in menial positions in wartime. African-American soldiers sometimes found enemy prisoners of war treated better than they were. But most black soldiers found reasons to fight the Axis powers, even if at times they could see little difference between German racism and the home-grown kind. They also kept up steady pressures for better assignments, fairer treatment, and improved statuses. African Americans planned to trade their wartime military service for improved

Figure 1.4   African Americans made a major contribution to American victories during World War II. Here the Army Air Force's all-black 99th Fighter Group assembles at the beachhead of Anzio, Italy, in 1944.   *Source:* National Archives.

educational and job opportunities after the war. Leading the war with its "Double V" campaign, the National Association for the Advancement of Colored People (NAACP) encouraged blacks to fight for a double victory: over the Axis powers abroad and Jim Crow at home. A more militant organization, The Congress of Racial Equality (CORE), founded by activist minister James Farmer in 1942 employed the "sit-in" tactic in demonstrations held in Northern cities that broke down racial varriers.

The war also opened up many new employment opportunities for African Americans. In January 1941, A. Philip Randolph, angered because employers with war contracts refused to hire African American workers, threatened to stage a march on Washington to protest both employer discrimination and segregation in the armed forces. President Roosevelt, wanting to avoid the embarrassment of a protest march and possible violence, persuaded Randolph to call off the proposed march in return for an executive order establishing a President's Fair Employment Practices Committee (FEPC), which ordered employers in defense industries to make jobs available "without discrimination because of race, creed, color, or national origin." The FEPC was understaffed and underfunded, and it had limited enforcement powers. It was a symbolic gesture that proved to be of little use during the war. Acute labor shortages far more than government policy opened up war employment opportunities for African Americans.

Over two million African-American men and women left the South to find work in the industrial cities of the North and West. Many joined Congress of Industrial Organizations (CIO) unions. Black voters in Northern cities became an important constituency in local and state elections. Most African American families who left the South during the war remained a permanent part of the growing Northern urban population in the postwar era. Southern black migrants often encountered racist hostility as they struggled to adapt to their new lives in Northern cities. They discovered that there was little difference between Northern and Southern white racial attitudes. Many Northern whites hated blacks for competing with them for housing, jobs, and schools for their children. They resented coming into contact with African Americans at parks, beaches, and other public facilities.

These racial antagonisms flared violently during the summer of 1943. About 250 race riots occurred in nearly fifty Northern cities; the largest riots were in Detroit and Harlem, but the worst violence was in Detroit, where it had been building for years. The immediate provocation had been an angry struggle for access to a public housing project demanded by both African-American workers and white workers during a time of acute housing shortages for everyone. One hot night in June, things got out of control. A full-scale race riot exploded, which lasted several days. Before order could be restored, twenty-five African Americans and nine whites lay dead.

Despite these outbreaks of homefront racial violence, World War II proved to be a watershed for African Americans; the war experience aided the black struggle for civil rights and full citizenship. Military service gave most African-American veterans greater self-esteem and a sense of empowerment. It also raised expectations. Many black veterans did not return to the rural South after the war but chose to settle in one of the Northern or Western states, perhaps one in which they had spent time while in the military. Others took advantage of the GI Bill to go to college, learn a skilled trade, or start a business after the war. These black professionals, technicians, and businessmen formed a new and much larger African-American middle class. A combination of vastly improved economic opportunities and continuing encounters with racism generated a new militancy among black people. They were determined not to accept second-class citizenship after the war. These African-American veterans and their children took the lead in challenging Jim Crow and racism in the postwar era. The roots of the modern civil rights movement can be found in black experiences during World War II.

HISPANIC AMERICANS IN WARTIME

According to the 1940 census, about 2.7 million Hispanic people lived among the American population. Most were of Mexican descent living in California, Texas, and the Southwest. Much of this predominantly rural population endured poverty, discrimination, and segregation. These people lacked decent jobs, housing, and educational opportunities and had no political influence. However, World War II created opportunities for Hispanics; thousands of Mexican Americans moved to urban areas to find work in war industries. About 350,000 went into the armed forces, nearly all of them draftees. Mexican-American warriors joined elite units such as the airborne rangers, and they often volunteered for dangerous missions. Eleven Mexican Americans won the nation's highest military award, the Congressional Medal of Honor.

Because so many Hispanic Americans moved to the cities or went into the armed forces, farmers faced acute shortages of workers. American growers persuaded the government to make arrangements with Mexico to import farm workers from Mexico. Under a program established in 1942, nearly two million Mexican *braceros* (laborers) entered the United States. Because of lax government supervision, employers often ruthlessly exploited these imported contract laborers.

Hispanics in the war labor force often suffered discriminations similar to those encountered by African Americans and women. They sometimes got paid less than "Anglo" employees for doing the same work. They found their problems most acute in the crowded cities. Many young Mexican Americans belonged to neighborhood gangs. They called themselves *pachucos* and favored a distinctive style of dress called a "zoot suit." The "zoot suit" consisted of baggy trousers that flared at the knees and were fitted tightly around the ankles, complemented by a wide-brimmed felt hat. These costumes were an assertion of a distinct cultural identity and a defiance of Anglo values.

In June 1943, at a time when black-white racial tensions were erupting in cities, ethnic relations in Los Angeles also were strained. Hundreds of sailors and Marines on leave from bases in Southern California assaulted Mexican Americans on the streets of Los Angeles and tore off their "zoot suits." Police either looked the other way or arrested only Mexican-American youths during these encounters. The local media supported the attacks on the *pachucos*. Only after the president of Mexico threatened to cancel the *bracero* program did President Roosevelt intervene to stop the violence.

Despite the zoot-suit incidents, Hispanic-American wartime experiences brought some advances. As was the case for African Americans, military service gave thousands of Mexican Americans an enhanced sense of self-worth. They returned from the war with greater expectations and enlarged views of life's possibilities. Many Hispanic veterans took advantage of the GI Bill. In the postwar years, Mexican-American veterans and their sons assumed leadership roles in organizations that challenged discrimination against Hispanic people in Southwestern states.

NATIVE AMERICANS IN WARTIME

Approximately 25,000 Native Americans served in the armed forces during World War II. One group of Navajos performed invaluable service during combat operations against the Japanese. These "code-talkers" communicating via radio in their tribal dialect, transmitted crucial battlefield information about enemy operations that could not be decoded by the Japanese. Thousands more Native Americans left their reservations to work in war industries around the country. Most of these mobile people did not return to their reservations after the war. They remained in the cities and became part of the rapidly growing postwar urban and suburban population. Some of those who returned to the reservations brought with them new ideas, technologies, and plans for the future.

In 1944, in California, lawyers representing a group of Native Americans filed suit in federal court for $100 million as compensation for lands taken illegally from Native Americans' ancestors during the 1850s. Congress enacted legislation to pay them for their lands, but President Roosevelt vetoed the bill. Litigation on this matter continued on and off for the next thirty-five years, until finally, both parties reached a compromise. The Native Americans accepted a settlement that brought them about 47¢ per acre.

ASIAN AMERICANS IN WARTIME

During the spring and summer of 1942, about 120,000 Japanese Americans, two-thirds of them native-born American citizens, were uprooted from their homes along the Pacific Coast and taken to internment centers in remote, desolate interior regions of the country. There they lived in tar paper barracks behind barbed wire for three years. The internment of Japanese Americans for the duration of World War II represented the worst violation of civil liberties in wartime in American history.

The initiative was taken by the military commander in charge of security along the West Coast, General John Dewitt. Dewitt and other officials claimed that the relocation of Japanese Americans was necessary to guarantee military security along the West Coast. They argued that if the Japanese Americans were not relocated, some of them would aid the enemy in case of attack. Their accusations were false. FBI agents admitted later that they never discovered a single proven act of disloyalty committed by any Japanese American. The real reasons for their removal included anti-Japanese prejudice, wartime hysteria, and greed. The claim of military necessity was based on unfounded suspicion, not on evidence. The relocation of Japanese Americans in wartime also was the culminating act of a half-century of anti-Japanese agitation and assaults in California, Oregon, and Washington.

Japanese-American spokesmen asserted their loyalty, to no avail. No political leaders or newspaper editors defended the Japanese. Earl Warren, California's attorney general in 1942, strongly advocated removal. The removal order, Executive Order No. 9066, came from President Roosevelt and could not be challenged. In 1944, the Supreme Court sustained the relocation of Japanese Americans. In the case of *Fred Korematsu v. the United States,* the Court accepted the claim of army lawyers that relocation was a wartime military necessity. A 5 to 3

Figure 1.5   Three Native American Marine Corps Woman Reservists at Camp Lejuene, North Carolina, October 1943. They are (from left to right): Minnie Spotted Wolf (Blackfoot), Celia Mix (Potawatomi), and Viola Eastman (Chippewa). *Source:* National Archives.

majority ruled that in time of war, individual rights could be sacrificed to military necessity. Associate Justice Frank Murphy filed a powerful dissenting opinion, stating that the relocation of Japanese Americans fell "into the ugly abyss of racism."

Following the advice of their leaders, virtually the entire Japanese-American population complied with the relocation order without resistance or protest. They submitted in accordance with the spirit of *Shikata Ga Nai* (realistic resignation). Because they were given little time to gather at assembly centers and were allowed to take only what they could carry to the camps, families lost homes, businesses, farms, and personal property worth an estimated $400 million. They arrived at the camps to find hastily built tar paper barracks amidst bleak desert landscapes that would be their homes for three years. The internment centers were *de facto* prisons. People were not free to come and go. The camps were under continuous surveillance by armed guards and enclosed by barbed wire fencing. During the war, some internees were allowed to leave the camps, provided that they agreed to settle in Eastern states. By war's end, all were allowed to leave. A few fortunate families had friends who had saved their homes or businesses for them while they were incarcerated. But many internees had no homes or businesses to return to. They found that interlopers now resided in their former residences and owned their former businesses.

Even though their families were imprisoned in camps, thousands of young Japanese-American men volunteered for military service. They were determined to prove their loyalty to a government that had betrayed them. Japanese-American soldiers contributed much to the war effort. They fought in the European theater, and many served in the Pacific war as translators, interpreters, and intelligence officers. One Japanese-American unit, the 442nd Regimental Combat Engineers, was the most decorated unit in American military history.

Figure 1.6   U.S. soldiers uprooted about 120,000 Japanese Americans, most of them U.S. citizens, from their homes in early 1942 and imprisoned them in various internment centers. The move, spawned by panic and prejudice, was both unnecessary and wrong. Here a family awaits a bus to haul them away.   *Source:* National Archives.

Ironically, the government refused to relocate Japanese Americans living in Hawaii. Thousands of them continued to work for the American military at Pearl Harbor and other installations following the Japanese attacks. They were not removed because of military necessity. They made up one-fifth of the Hawaiian population and their labor was essential. And there was no place to put them or ships to transport them.

Loyal Americans were the victims of an egregious injustice, a vicious example of the tyranny of the white majority in wartime. Congress authorized token restitution for Japanese Americans in 1948, and a total of about $38 million was paid to claimants during the 1950s. These payments totaled about 10¢ for each dollar of loss claimed. Years later, after much litigation and quiet political pressure, Japanese Americans belatedly received vindication and additional restitution. In 1983, U.S. District Court Judge Marilyn Hall Patel vacated Fred Korematsu's conviction. Judge Patel's action came after Korematsu's attorneys discovered secret government documents proving that government officials knew that Japanese Americans posed no dangers to national security in wartime, and they withheld this evidence from the Supreme Court. On August 10, 1988, President Ronald Reagan signed legislation authorizing $20,000 in reparations to each of the estimated 60,000 survivors of wartime relation. As he signed the historic legislation, President Reagan, speaking for all Americans, apologized to the Japanese American community: "We admit a wrong. Here we affirm our commitment as a nation to equal justice under the law."

Although some embittered victims dismissed the money as "too little, too late," others were grateful and appreciated the symbolic significance of the gesture. Ten years later, in the summer of 1998, after paying out over $1.6 billion to survivors, their heirs, and to some people whose property had been confiscated by the government, the government closed the books on the matter of compensating the internees.

After the war, Japanese Americans did not protest the gross injustices that they were forced to endure in wartime. They internalized the anger, shame, and humiliation associated with the relocation experience and rarely talked about those experiences, even among close friends and family. Instead, Japanese Americans vowed to put their wartime experiences behind them and to go forward—to prove to the government and to the white majority that had abused them that they were good citizens and productive members of society.

Their postwar record of achievement has been astonishing. Japanese Americans, by any measure, are among the most successful groups in the country. They have integrated themselves into mainstream society and have achieved distinction in the sciences, the arts, medicine, law, engineering, academic life, business, finance, athletics, and politics. They are among the leaders in the amount of education attained and in annual per capita income.

In contrast to the brutal mistreatment of Japanese Americans during wartime, Chinese Americans fared comparatively well. Chinese Americans enjoyed the sympathy and goodwill of most Americans, because China was a wartime ally of the United States. Americans also felt much sympathy for the Chinese people, who were suffering terribly at the hands of Japanese soldiers during the war. Because of their status as allies and because of acute labor shortages in war industries, unprecedented opportunities for Chinese workers suddenly opened up. By the thousands, Chinese families streamed out of the Chinatown ghettos into the mainstream of American life. Most of these mobile families never returned to the ghettos, and in the years following World War II, they headed for the suburbs.

In 1943, Congress at long last repealed the Chinese Exclusion Act, that artifact of anti-Asian racism that had been in place since 1882. For the first time in over sixty years, it was now possible for people to emigrate from China to the United States. In addition, the government finally extended citizenship to thousands of Chinese, many of them quite elderly, longtime residents of the United States who had hitherto been ineligible for citizenship.

THE POLITICS OF WAR

War moved the country toward the Right. Resurgent Republicans gained seventy-seven seats in the House and ten seats in the Senate in the 1942 midterm elections. A conservative coalition of Northern Republicans and Southern Democrats, which had emerged following the 1938 elections, consolidated its control of Congress. Roosevelt, sensing the political drift and preoccupied with the immense task of running history's largest war, put social reform on the back burner. Conservatives snuffed out many New Deal agencies in 1942 and 1943, on the grounds that wartime economic revival had rendered them obsolete. Among their most prominent victims were the WPA (Work Progress Administration) and the CCC (Civilian Conservation Corps).

Antitrust activity ceased. Businessmen poured into Washington to run new wartime bureaucracies. They regained much of the popularity and prestige that they had lost during the 1930s. Depression-bred popular resentment of business greed and social irresponsibility gave way to a new image of businessmen as patriotic partners providing the tools needed to win the war. Roosevelt, needing business cooperation for the war effort, cultivated a cordial relationship among his former adversaries. Populistic, antibusiness rhetoric vanished from public discourse. Many corporate leaders abandoned their bitter criticisms of Roosevelt and New Deal policies, having discovered that they could profit from the policies of the welfare state turned warfare state. Businessmen switched their political strategy from one of trying to dismantle big government to trying to use it to their advantage. Corporate executives would continue these new political strategies in the postwar era.

The war effort further centralized the corporate economy, because 90 percent of the billions of dollars the government spent on war contracts went to 100 large corporations. Big business got bigger in wartime, and most companies enjoyed historic high profits. Wartime politics showed that the positive state, erected by liberals to fight the Great Depression and to promote social reform, could be manned by conservatives who would use its power to promote business interests, curtail reform, and attack trade unions—while winning a war.

The huge increase in the size and scope of the federal government, particularly of the executive branch, represented the most important wartime political development. As government spent more and more money, it became far more centralized than ever before. Federal bureaucracies assumed many economic functions previously performed by the private sector. The number of federal employees rose from 1 million in 1940 to 3.8 million in 1945, the most ever in the nation's history. Wartime agencies proliferated. The most powerful politicians in the country, after Roosevelt, were the men he appointed to run the war agencies. The president recruited most of these "war lords" of Washington from the ranks of business.

As the executive branch made a quantum leap in size and power, Congress suffered a relative decline in power and prestige. Through his active participation in foreign conferences and various domestic agencies coordinating the gigantic war effort, Roosevelt significantly enhanced the powers of the presidency. He became by far the most powerful president in U.S. history and set an example followed by all postwar presidents. The "imperial" presidency had its origins in World War II.

The Supreme Court, dominated by Roosevelt's eight liberal appointees, refused to review any cases involving wartime extensions of federal power into economic affairs, an arena in which it had been especially active during the New Deal years. The Court also refused to intervene in cases involving wartime violations of civil liberties, except to affirm the relocation of Japanese Americans from the Pacific Coast. The FBI, in wartime, acquired enhanced authority to spy on Americans and to tap telephones in national security cases.

The war multiplied the points of contact between the federal government and its citizens. Millions of names were added to the Social Security rolls, and everyone who worked had to pay federal income taxes. War experiences strengthened the tendency of people to look to Washington for solutions to their problems. This trend weakened social bonds and undermined state and local governments. People traded some of their personal freedom for greater government control and an enhanced sense of social security. This tradeoff, of liberty for security, carried into the postwar era.

Washington became the biggest of all war boomtowns. In 1942, the Pentagon, the world's largest office building, opened. It housed over 35,000 bureaucrats, and its offices consumed thirty tons of paper annually. Lobbyists stalked the corridors of political power seeking ever-larger shares of the vast wartime expenditures flowing outward from Washington into corporate coffers. The broker-state, a creation of New Dealers, was much refined and significantly expanded in wartime. The government also subsidized the creation of new industries required by the necessities of war. With supplies of natural rubber from Southeast Asia cut, Washington spent nearly $1 billion to create a synthetic rubber industry to provide substitute products.

Much basic research for new weaponry and war industries had come from universities and colleges, which became committed to meeting the needs of military research. Most colleges and universities suffered no loss of enrollment during the war, despite massive conscription, because the government utilized their campuses for training enlisted men and officers. After the war, the GI Bill, which paid for millions of veterans' college educations, ensured the continuing growth and expansion of higher education.

World War II created a wartime partnership among businesses, universities, Congress, and the Pentagon, engaged in the procurement of war contracts. This "military-industrial complex," as President Eisenhower would later call it during his famed farewell address, nurtured during the war, came of age during the Cold War. It became a powerful lobby for creating a kind of permanent war economy in the postwar decades. The military-industrial complex guaranteed that the vastly enhanced authority of government in American economic and scientific affairs would continue after the war.

THE ELECTION OF 1944

During the 1944 election, President Roosevelt faced the challenge of Republican New York Governor Thomas E. Dewey. Roosevelt, to keep his party unified in wartime, dumped his vice president, Henry Wallace. Wallace, a fervent New Dealer, had alienated powerful big-city bosses and conservative Southerners within the Democratic Party. Roosevelt replaced Wallace with a candidate acceptable to all factions within the party, Missouri Senator Harry Truman. Truman had rendered valuable service to the country in wartime, heading a watchdog committee that had investigated government war contracts. Senator Truman's scrupulous efforts saved taxpayers billions of dollars and expedited the delivery of crucial war materials. Despite his wartime service, Truman was still a relative unknown in 1944, an undistinguished political journeyman acceptable to all powerful factions within the Democratic Party.

The contest between Roosevelt and Dewey was a rather dull, one-sided affair. In the eyes of many observers, Dewey did not appear presidential. He was a short, neat little man who came across as rather aloof, cold, and stiff. He also did not cultivate good relations with the media: Socialite Alice Roosevelt Longworth asked, "How can we be expected to vote for a man who looks like the bridegroom on a wedding cake?"

Newly empowered, organized labor played a major role in the 1944 campaign. The CIO, through its Political Action Committee, circumvented laws restricting union activities and funneled millions of dollars into the campaign for the Roosevelt ticket and many liberal congressional candidates. It also registered voters, circulated campaign literature, and got out the vote on Election Day.

Dewey's campaign strategy differed from previous Republican efforts. He accepted the New Deal welfare state but accused New Dealers of waste and inefficiency. He endorsed U.S. membership in a postwar United Nations. He also refused to make Roosevelt's foreign policy a campaign issue, not wishing to revive isolationist issues amidst the war. By embracing the welfare state and internationalism, Dewey placed both the New Deal and the war beyond partisan debate.

Roosevelt, who did not campaign much, exploited his prestige as wartime commander-in-chief of a vast military effort that was winning everywhere. He called attention to legislation benefiting veterans, including the G.I. Bill of Rights. Ominously, Roosevelt had aged dramatically by 1944. Friends and close political associates noticed that he had grown frail and thin. His hands trembled, and there were dark circles under his eyes. His doctors knew that he was suffering from heart disease and hypertension. In accordance with the journalistic practices of the era, reporters, even those hostile to Roosevelt, did not call attention to his rapidly deteriorating health.

Roosevelt easily won his fourth presidential election victory in November. His electoral vote count was 432 to 99, but his popular vote tally was only 25.6 million to 22 million for Dewey. The 1944 vote revealed that the Democratic Party was becoming more urban as a result of the wartime migration that had lured millions of workers from rural regions into the cities. The Democrats regained twenty-two of the seats in the House that they had lost in 1942, but they lost another Senate seat. The bipartisan conservative coalition retained its control of Congress.

WAR AND CULTURE

During the war, television had not yet come of age. Print journalism, radio, and "movies" flourished in vigorous variety. People spent hours each week listening to radio programs in their homes or while driving their cars. They also read one or two daily newspapers, subscribed to several magazines, and went to the movies on the average of twice a week.

Sales of books, both fiction and nonfiction, increased sharply in wartime. People had more money to spend on books and more time available for reading. In 1943, Ayn Rand wrote *The Fountainhead,* a best-seller that praised individualism over collectivism. Friedrich Hayek, an expatriate Austrian economist living in the United States, wrote *The Road to Serfdom,* a conservative tract that argued that modern liberalism was the path to tyranny. Although a difficult book to read, *The Road to Serfdom* enjoyed wide sales.

By no means did most Americans read serious fiction or nonfiction books in wartime. By far the most popular literary genre was comic books. One-third of young adults read comic books regularly; some adults read only comic books. Special editions of the most popular comic books were made available to soldiers.

An emerging generation of young writers found in World War II the defining experience of their lives, among them Saul Bellow, Irving Shaw, and John Hersey. Many war novels and journalistic accounts of the war made the best-seller charts. The best and most popular war correspondent was Ernie Pyle, a quiet Midwesterner who wrote with great insight and accuracy about ordinary soldiers in combat. His *Brave Men,* published in 1945, after he had been killed covering the Okinawa campaign, is the finest account of GI life ever written.

Ballroom dancing also flourished during the war. The popularity of jitterbugging continued unabated, especially among young people for whom it offered a distinctive world with its own clothes, language, and ritualistic behaviors. Energetic, athletic youngsters spun, whirled, and tossed their partners to the pulsing rhythms of hot jazz. Older couples enjoyed the more sedate pleasures of fox trots and waltzes. Night life, particularly New York night life, sparkled. Patrons of the Copacabana or the Latin Quarter could spend $100 on an evening of drinking, dancing, and enjoying the singing of young crooners such as Frank Sinatra or the sounds of big bands such as Tommy Dorsey's or Frankie Carle's.

Professional spectator sports drew large crowds, and racetracks enjoyed historic high attendance in wartime. Since most of its outstanding players were in military service, major league baseball continued its pennant races and annual World Series using mostly teenagers, castoffs, and overage players. A women's professional baseball league started up and, after a rugged start, flourished in wartime. The women's league continued its run into the 1950s before disbanding, mainly because of a lack of fan interest.

HOLLYWOOD GOES TO WAR

Hollywood prospered in wartime, even though the major studios produced far fewer movies a year than they had during the late 1930s. Attendance at the nation's 18,000 movie houses trebled between 1941 and 1945. About 75 percent of all Americans went to the movies. The typical moviegoer patronized a neighborhood theater at least twice a week during the war years. Millions of moviegoers also avidly read Hollywood fan magazines and newspaper stories about prominent movie stars.

Hollywood had to adapt to wartime conditions. Most top male stars either were drafted or they enlisted, and thousands of technicians and production personnel went off to war. Jimmy Stewart flew bombing missions over Germany. Henry Fonda joined the Navy and served in the South Pacific. Clark Gable joined the Army Air Corps. A lesser star from Warner Brothers,

Ronald Reagan, was assigned to an Army Air Corps motion picture unit in Hollywood that made training and propaganda films. Many actors not in the armed forces including Bob Hope and Bing Crosby as well as top women stars such as Dorothy Lamour, Rita Hayworth, and Betty Grable entertained the troops both in the States and around the world.

Even though the major studios continued to turn out the standard genres—Westerns, detective thrillers, adventure films, romances, gangster pictures, and musicals, wartime Hollywood mostly made war movies. The studios churned out a flood of war and spy stories. Many Chinese actors got work in Hollywood films for the first time, playing Japanese villains in war movies. John Wayne starred in a series of war epics glorifying various branches of the military service— *Flying Tigers, Fighting Seabees,* and *The Sands of Iwo Jima,* the last about the U.S. Marine Corps.

The best war film was *The Story of GI Joe,* adapted from Ernie Pyle's reporting. It contained no preaching, no propaganda, no hateful enemy stereotypes, and no heroes. It depicted American soldiers as skilled professionals doing a dirty job, trying mainly to survive and return home after the war. Hollywood also made several excellent war documentaries, the best ones a series produced by Frank Capra and John Huston. Another wartime film genre was the "canteen film." It was a celluloid USO show, hosted by a big-name star featuring celebrity guests who sang, danced, and told jokes—all promoting the war effort.

Hollywood films in wartime continued to project cultural stereotypes onto the silver screen. African-American soldiers occasionally appeared in war films, usually as "happy Negroes," jiving, dancing, grinning, and laughing. Jewish soldiers were portrayed as guys named "Brooklyn" who looked forward to returning to Ebbets Field after the war and jeering at the Giants. Women were usually portrayed as the "weaker sex," dependent upon men and totally involved with their homes, children, and marriage. Native Americans continued to be depicted as primitive and duplicitous savages. The Japanese were portrayed as depraved, cruel, and vicious, with many references to "slant-eyed rats," "little yellow monkeys," and "beasts."

Responding to governmental pressure applied through the Office of War Information, war films portrayed American allies such as the Chinese, the British, and the French as heroic. Wartime movie Russians were hearty, simple people and gallant fighters. In *Mission to Moscow,* an American diplomat goes off to Moscow to meet the Russians. He is tailed by two jolly KGB agents who cheerfully inform the American star that the infamous purge trials of the 1930s were necessary to save the Soviet Union from a Fascist coup.

Wartime Hollywood had to continue to conform to strict moral codes and observe political limits as well. Churches, especially the Catholic Church's Legion of Decency, functioned as moral watchdogs for the movie industry. The major studios were scrupulous in placating these powerful censors, especially the Legion of Decency, which purportedly spoke for the nation's Catholics, representing 20 percent of the national movie audience. The major film factories also resorted to considerable self-regulation to placate the self-appointed guardians of movie morality. Criminals could never escape unpunished in a Hollywood film. Sexual contact was carefully limited to gentle kissing between fully clothed adults. Homosexuality was never mentioned, much less displayed. Profanity was forbidden. Characters were statically portrayed either as total villains with no redeeming features or as heroic figures with no faults or weaknesses. Ideas were censored, as was moral conduct. Films had to stay within mainstream ideological boundaries. Radical ideas or serious social criticism were excised from Hollywood pictures. Serious political discourse rarely found its way into Hollywood films, and when it did, it usually parroted the bland patriotic liberalism emanating from Franklin Roosevelt's wartime White House.

Most wartime movies were mediocre, but a few qualified as cinematic art. In 1945, Billy Wilder directed *Lost Weekend,* a story about an alcoholic, starring Ray Milland and Jane Wyman. It was a serious, sensitive treatment of alcoholism and its ruinous effects upon the lives of people. *Lost Weekend* won an Academy Award for best picture, and both Milland and Wilder also received Oscars. One World War II film became a classic. In 1942, Warner Brothers brought out a low-budget melodrama set in Morocco. It told a tale of an American nightclub owner, Rick Blaine, who hides patriotic idealism beneath a hard-boiled surface. In the end, Blaine sacrifices both his business and the woman he loves to rescue an anti-Nazi resistance fighter. Humphrey Bogart played Blaine in *Casablanca,* becoming a cult hero to millions of moviegoers in the postwar era.

WARTIME RADIO

Radio became more popular than ever in wartime. The most popular radio programs during World War II were musical shows. One of the top musical shows was the *Lucky Strike Hit Parade.* Other popular musicals featured well-known singers such as Kate Smith and Bing Crosby. For aficionados of serious music, there was the NBC symphony orchestra, sponsored by Standard Oil, and the New York Metropolitan Opera, sponsored by Texaco.

After musicals, the second most popular programs were drama, including the daytime dramas or "soap operas," whose large audiences consisted mostly of women. Prime-time programming featured a variety of action-adventure dramas with a cast of heroic detectives, cowboys, and space warriors who overcame villains and upheld law and order. Other genres included quiz programs and situation comedies. The longest-running and one of the most popular of these weekly comedies in 1945 was *Amos 'n Andy.* The show highlighted the hilarious adventures of two African Americans from the South, now living in Harlem, but the characters of Amos and Andy were played by two white actors.

Radio was a prime source of news about the war. World War II was the first war that was ever given live media coverage. War correspondent Edward R. Murrow described the Battle of Britain for American radio audiences in the summer of 1940. People listened to his deep, solemn voice, hearing shrill air raid sirens and the roar of exploding bombs in the background, as Murrow vividly described the "blitz" of London. He brought the European war into American living rooms. Throughout the war, foreign correspondents in Europe and Asia often risked their lives to go everywhere the soldiers went and to transmit firsthand accounts of battles to the folks back home. Radio correspondents hit the beaches at Normandy with the invading forces. Many of these correspondents were killed or wounded in action. Never had war journalism been so direct or authentic.

But censors often edited the news. Broadcasters frequently sacrificed factual accuracy for dramatic effect. War news had entertainment as well as informational value. Wartime radio remained essentially an entertainment medium, always accompanied by incessant commercial messages urging listeners to buy cigarettes, soap, and chewing gum. Radio often appeared to be little more than a conduit through which advertisers poured their commercials for the myriad of products they manufactured. Advertisers also had great influence on the contents of the shows that they sponsored, including news and news commentaries. Sponsors favored the largest possible audiences and frowned upon any programming that was artistically or politically controversial, because they feared it might alienate viewers. The biggest single purchaser of airtime, Proctor and Gamble, the giant cleaning products company, had a policy of never offending a single listener. During the war, good radio often was subordinated to good salesmanship.

WORLD WAR AND ITS LEGACIES

World War II was an intense, transforming experience for most Americans. These war-induced changes were more profound and permanent than any occurring in this country since the Industrial Revolution. On the eve of war, Americans suffered from the lingering effects of the Great Depression—high unemployment, low productivity, and massive poverty—accompanied by lurking doubts about the vitality of American institutions and the purpose of national life. Americans looked out at a threatening world engulfed in war, a world in which their nation played only a peripheral role. Within the nation, Isolationists and Interventionists quarreled bitterly among themselves over President Roosevelt's conduct of foreign policy, until the bombing of Pearl Harbor abruptly ended the debate.

Four years later, a unified and powerful nation emerged victoriously from war. Its armed forces and industrial might had played decisive roles in destroying Fascism, militarism, and imperialism around the globe. America had won the largest war in human history. War revitalized the American economy; it emerged far more productive and prosperous than ever. More Americans lived better than they ever had before, and the proportion of poor Americans had been reduced to historic lows. American faith in capitalism and democratic institutions had been restored. Compared to other nations at war, American casualties had been light. American civilians had been spared the devastations and terrors of a war fought outside of its continental boundaries. Fewer than 12 percent of the nation's population had served in the armed forces; over half of those who did never left the States, and the majority of those who got sent overseas never experienced a moment's combat.

The day the war against Japan ended, the United States strode the world as an international colossus; its armed forces, linked to its nuclear monopoly, made it the most powerful nation-state in the history of the planet. Its statesmen took the lead in creating a new international agency to preserve peace in the postwar era. Fittingly, the United Nation's permanent home would be New York, the financial and cultural capital of the new imperium.

The war was a watershed from which emerged the dominant patterns of postwar life. It forced Americans to accept involvement with the world beyond national boundaries; there could be no reversion to isolationism after 1945. Their war experiences gave Americans new confidence that they could solve all serious problems, both internal and external. They had proved that they had both the will and the means to lick depression at home and aggression abroad.

The major contours of post–1945 American history originated in the war experience. The long Cold War with the Soviet Union that dominated international affairs for decades after the war stemmed from the tensions and conflicts that strained the Grand Alliance in wartime. Soviet leader Joseph Stalin distrusted the Western leaders, whom he suspected of deliberately delaying the opening of a second front against the Germans. Postwar economic policies were derived from the awareness that federal spending in wartime had finally ended economic depression. Political leaders during the postwar era assumed that similar fiscal practices could stabilize the business cycle and promote economic growth. A new understanding of the role of consumerism in sustaining economic growth meant that government would promote spending instead of saving after the war. The struggles and achievements of women and minorities in wartime planted the seeds of their postwar drives for equal access to the American Dream.

The war shifted American politics to the Right. Americans generally became more conservative, fundamentally because the restoration of prosperity gave most Americans more to conserve. The Republican Party made a significant comeback during the war years, and the informal conservative coalition of Southern Democrats and Northern Republicans consolidated its control of the legislative process. Leviathan was the most important political legacy of World War II. Big government became the foundation of the modern social welfare/warfare state that would dominate national politics in the decades following the war. Washington regulated the economy and was the conservator of the natural environment. In the postwar era, huge federal bureaucracies became a fourth branch of the national government; most of the actions taken by the federal government directly affecting the lives of its citizens were taken by the legions of bureaucrats staffing these large federal agencies. The organizational society, a society increasingly dominated by large public and private sector bureaucracies that characterized the postwar era, came of age during World War II.

The war left a mixed environmental legacy. On the one hand, it heightened awareness that the American economy was becoming less self-sufficient and increasingly dependent on foreign sources for strategic minerals and oil. On the other hand, the crash production programs of wartime to outproduce the enemy accelerated the depletion of natural resources. During the war, energy sources, technology, and industrial capacity were all maximally utilized. Trees were cut down. Air and water were polluted. Farmers made far greater use of chemical fertilizers and pesticides to enhance output. Ecological awareness and conservation issues were neglected in wartime; these were seen as luxuries that a nation engaged in total war for its survival could not afford. Trends established in wartime continued into the postwar era. Deteriorating environmental conditions finally brought about a surge of interest in the environment, which surfaced during the 1960s.

The war restored America's philosophic birthright, an optimistic sense of individual and national potential that would shape the national experience for decades to come. The Axis powers were destroyed, the Soviet Union was exhausted, and Western Europe was depleted. But America was strong, prosperous, and free. Its people felt ready for the "American Century" they felt lay ahead. America's economy was powerful, its resources were abundant, and it had the scientific and technological talent to use them. Success in wartime gave Americans confidence and great expectations for a future that appeared to stretch limitlessly before them.

Americans also soberly confronted a future that they feared could bring a recurrence of the Great Depression. Could prosperity, growth, and full employment be sustained in the postwar era without the stimulus of a war economy? Could jobs be found for the millions of returning veterans and displaced war workers? Americans also worried about threats to their peace and security posed by the Soviet Union, an expanding Communist power. Perhaps the war had not made the world safe for democracy. Perhaps there was not going to be an American Century. Most of all, Americans were alarmed by the nuclear shadow that they had cast over the postwar era.

And so, Americans, in the summer of 1945 faced the future with mixed feelings: feelings of pride, confidence, and hope, but also feelings of fear—of the return of depression, of expanding Soviet power, and of a nuclear Armageddon.

Brief Bibliographic Essay

Many fine studies of America during World War II are available. The following is a select list of those books that are especially well written and easily accessible. They will make informative, enjoyable reading for students who want to learn more about the prominent individuals and major events that dominated the war years and influenced the course of recent American history. Most of these books are available in paperback editions and can be found in any good college, university, or public library.

The best studies of the home front are Richard Polenberg's *War and Society: The United States, 1941–1945* and John Morton Blum's *"V" Was for Victory: Politics and American Culture during World War II*. The best social history of the United States at war is Geoffrey Perrett's *Days of Sadness, Years of Triumph*. Roland Young's *Congressional Politics in the Second World War* is a good political history. Susan M. Hartmann's *The Homefront and Beyond: American Women in the 1940s* is an account of women and the war. Another fine account of women's experiences during the war is Karen Anderson's *Wartime Women*. See also Sherna B. Gluck's *Rosie the Riveter Revisited: Women, the War, and Social Change*. Neil A. Wynn's *The Afro-American and the Second World War* has recorded the crucial experiences of black people in wartime. The best account of the wartime relocation of Japanese Americans is Edward Spencer's *Impounded People: Japanese Americans and World War II*. See also Peter Irons's *Justice at War: The Story of the Japanese-American Internment Cases*. Jeanne Wakatsuki Houston's and James D. Houston's *Farewell to Manzanar* is a compelling story of a Japanese family interned for the duration of the war. Richard R. Lingeman's *Don't You Know There's a War On?* is a general account of popular culture in wartime. Joel Greenberg's *Hollywood in the Forties* is an account of wartime movies and their effects on the populace. James L. Baughman's *The Republic of Mass Culture* has an informative chapter about the major mass media—print journalism, radio, and movies—during the war years. John Brooks's *The Great Leap: The Past Twenty-Five Years in America* is an important book highlighting the immense changes brought about in this country by World War II that shaped the postwar era. The best novel about the war experience in this country is Harriet Arnow's *The Dollmaker,* which movingly describes its disruptions and dislocations.

Web Sites

Chapter 1 is mainly concerned about the Home Front experiences of the American people during World War II, 1942–1945. For readers who want to learn more about that vast world calamity called "World War II," log on to <http://www.worldwar2history.net>. Students interested in particular topics such as the internment of Japanese Americans can consult <www.ericfacility.net/ericdigests/ed447066.html>. There is a rich collection of materials on women and the Home Front during World War II at <http://www.teacheroz.com/WWIIhomefront.htm>.

2

The Rise of the Cold War

World War II left a large part of Europe and many nations of Asia and elsewhere in ruins and shattered the old balance of power. Even most of the victors had fared badly. The Soviets had lost thirty million people, and much of their economy had been ruined by war. The British, depleted economically and militarily, faced the imminent loss of much of their vast empire. After 1945, Britain's ability to play a major role in world affairs would depend mainly on American friendship and support. France had been humiliated by defeat and occupation during the war. The French economy was weak, its government was unstable, and the French Communist Party was a rising force.

The war had so weakened the British, French, and Dutch nations that they could no longer control many of their rebellious colonies in Asia, Africa, and the Middle East. Throughout the postwar era, the decolonization process that had begun during World War II accelerated, presenting challenges to the United States in what became known as the Third World. In the Far East, China was sinking into the chaos of civil war, dashing any hopes that Americans still entertained that it would be a major factor in postwar Asian diplomacy. Only the United States emerged from the devastation of global war with its wealth and power enhanced and with most of its citizens better off than they had ever been before.

Postwar American celebrations of victory and expectations of a peaceful and prosperous world order dominated by the United States quickly gave way to conflicts between America and its erstwhile ally, the Soviet Union. A multitude of challenging postwar political problems generated over forty years of tension, ideological warfare, and a thermonuclear arms race that historians called the Cold War. The Cold War would remain the dominant international reality shaping the conduct of U.S. foreign policy for over forty years. Cold War preoccupations also exerted a powerful influence on domestic politics and culture during this era.

ORIGINS OF COLD WAR

Immediately after the war, the United Nations (UN) provided relief to the war-ravaged populations of Europe and Asia. The United States funneled billions of dollars through the UN agencies for food, clothing, and medicines for needy people in Germany, Japan, China, and eastern

Europe. The British borrowed $3.75 billion from the United States in 1946, much of which was used to pay for food imports. Postwar Germany faced economic disaster. German industrial and agricultural production had shrunk to pitiful fractions of prewar levels.

The United States shared occupation responsibilities in Germany with the Soviets, the British, and the French, but it had sole authority in Japan. In the American occupation zone in Germany, U.S. officials worked hard to root out all traces of Naziism. Special courts punished over 1,500 major Nazi offenders and over 600,000 minor Nazi officials. The most famous trial occurred at Nuremberg, the former site of huge Nazi Party rallies during the 1930s. An international tribunal put twenty-two former high Nazi officials on trial, nineteen of whom were convicted and twelve hanged for "war crimes and atrocities." In Japan, U.S. officials, under the command of the American proconsul General Douglas MacArthur, staged a Tokyo equivalent of Nuremberg. Twenty-eight former high Japanese officials were tried, and all were convicted of war crimes. Seven were hanged, including former Premier Hideki Tojo.

Americans also completely refashioned Japanese society. They broke up industrial monopolies, abolished feudal estates, and implemented land reform. They introduced political democracy and established independent trade unions. They forced the Japanese to destroy all military weapons and to renounce war as an instrument of national policy. The Japanese have depended on America's nuclear shield to protect their national security ever since. Most important for the future of Japan, American engineers modernized Japanese industry, introducing new management and quality control techniques and modern industrial technology. From the ashes of war, with help from their conquerors, the Japanese fashioned a working system of political economy. By the early 1970s, Japan had become both a major trading partner and a potent commercial rival of the United States.

During 1945 and 1946, American and Soviet leaders clashed over many postwar political issues. Their wartime alliance deteriorated. Even before war's end, the Allies had quarreled over the opening of a second front in Western Europe and the future political status of Eastern European countries. The proximate origins of the Cold War conflict lay in these wartime strains within the Grand Alliance. Historians, concerned with putting the origins of the Cold War into a larger framework, have traced the roots of the Cold War to the American response to the 1917 Bolshevik Revolution and Lenin's profound hatred of Western liberal capitalist culture. From 1917 until 1933, a succession of American presidents refused to recognize the Soviet state. Even after the normalization of U.S.–USSR relations in 1933, friendly relations between the two nations did not evolve. When Stalin concluded the nonaggression pact with Hitler in August 1939, most Americans equated the Soviet Union with Nazi Germany. It was the wartime alliance between the Americans and the Soviets, born of strategic necessity, that represented a departure from the historic norm of mutual distrust and ideological hostility.

During the war, the leaders of the major allies, the Big Three—Roosevelt, Stalin, and Churchill—met on occasion to discuss political problems and to plot grand strategy. The most famous meeting of the Big Three took place at Yalta, a resort on the Black Sea coast, on February 4, 1945, to February 11, 1945. At Yalta, Roosevelt, Churchill, and Stalin charted the final drives of the European war, discussed the Pacific war, talked about the postwar political status of Eastern European countries, planned for occupying Germany, and arranged for the creation of a proposed United Nations.

It was at Yalta that the Big Three agreed to divide Germany into four occupation zones, with France assigned the fourth zone. They also agreed to a joint occupation of Berlin, which lay deep within the Soviet zone in Eastern Germany, an arrangement that both sides deeply regretted after the rise of the Cold War. Berlin became one of the recurring flash points of the Cold War in Europe for thirty years. All parties accepted the principle of German reparations for the Soviet Union and referred the matter to an appointed commission to determine specific amounts.

Roosevelt initiated discussions at Yalta on the pending formation of the United Nations. Vigorous American participation in an international organization armed with power to maintain peace by using economic sanctions or military force was Roosevelt's chief concern at Yalta. He wanted Stalin, without whose cooperation it could not succeed, to commit himself to full support for the new agency to be created at San Francisco in April 1945. To ensure Soviet cooperation, he accepted Stalin's demand for three votes in the General Assembly.

The postwar political status of Poland caused the most controversy at the Yalta conference, particularly the composition of its new government. There were, at the time, two governments claiming to represent all Poles, one headquartered in London, championed by the British, and one in Lublin, backed by the Soviets. Stalin, making it clear that Poland was a vital Soviet interest, proposed that the Communist-controlled government at Lublin become the government of a new Poland. Roosevelt proposed a government comprised of representatives of Poland's five major political parties. The Soviets rejected it, but Stalin agreed to add "democratic elements" to the Lublin regime. To avoid letting differences over Poland undermine conference harmony, the Allies worked out an agreement that papered over significant differences with vague, elastic language. Stalin agreed to "free and unfettered elections" at an unspecified time in the future. Roosevelt settled for a reorganized Lublin regime that included "other" political leaders, language susceptible to differing interpretations.

At Yalta, Roosevelt also wanted to commit the Soviets to entering the Asian war against Japan as soon as possible. On February 10, Stalin and Roosevelt signed a secret treaty in which the Soviet Union agreed to enter the war within three months following Germany's surrender. In return, the Soviets were given several concessions: a Soviet-controlled satellite in Outer Mongolia; the guaranteed return of the southern portion of Sakhalin Island; the internationalization of the port of Darien; a lease for the use of Port Arthur as a naval base; the establishment of a joint Chinese-Soviet consortium to operate the Manchurian railways; and the Japanese transference of the Kurile Islands to them.

President Roosevelt and his advisers considered the price of Soviet entry into the Asian war reasonable at the time. The expectation that an atomic bomb would be ready in August did not alter Roosevelt's goal of getting the Soviets into the war. His military advisers told Roosevelt that Soviet participation at the earliest possible moment would ensure the defeat of Japanese forces in Manchuria, and that Soviet air raids on Japan flown from Siberia would ensure the disruption of Japanese shipping from the Asian mainland. Most important, Soviet intervention would shorten the war and save thousands of American lives.

The atmosphere at Yalta was cordial, as befitted members of a wartime coalition who still needed one another to achieve victory over their enemies. Both sides made compromises and concessions. Controversies and disagreements were covered over or deferred; they were not allowed to disrupt proceedings. But the Soviets achieved more important diplomatic victories at

**Figure 2.1   The Big Three.
Prime Minister Winston
Churchill of Great Britain,
President Franklin Roosevelt of
the United States, and Premier
Joseph Stalin of the Soviet
Union held several wartime
conferences. At Yalta, a Black
Sea resort in the Crimea, they
met for the last time in
February 1945.** *Source:* U.S.
Army Photo.

Yalta than the United States. Stalin used the military situation favoring the Soviet Union at the time to achieve his objectives. The role of the Allied military in the ultimate defeat of the Germans was relatively minor compared to the Soviet effort. Hundreds of Soviet divisions fighting the best Wehrmacht armies in the Soviet Union and Eastern Europe eventually broke the spine of German power. As Red forces overran Eastern and Southern Europe, Stalin used military occupation to gain political control of countries within these strategic regions. Stalin also used the American desire for Soviet entry into the war against Japan to exact major diplomatic concessions in the Far East. Roosevelt did not "sell out" China to the Soviets at Yalta as Republican critics later charged, but the Yalta agreements amounted to a significant diplomatic victory for the Soviet Union.

Cordiality among the Allies began to dissipate soon after the Yalta conference. In March 1945, President Roosevelt perceived Soviet efforts to impose a Communist regime on Poland as a violation of the Yalta agreements and protested to Stalin. Truman, who succeeded Roosevelt in April, was inexperienced in the craft of diplomacy and lacked FDR's poise and style. Truman also believed that Roosevelt had been too easy on Stalin and that he would stand up to the Soviets. Truman personally rebuked Soviet Foreign Minister V. M. Molotov over Yalta violations. Truman's outburst shocked and angered the Soviet foreign minister, but Truman's tough words to the Soviet diplomat had no effect on Soviet foreign policy. Stalin made it bluntly clear that maintaining a security zone in Eastern Europe was much more vital to Soviet interests than maintaining cordial relations with wartime allies. Besides, military force gave the Soviet Union control of Eastern Europe's political destinies. In 1945 and 1946, Soviet military forces installed puppet Communist regimes in Poland, Bulgaria, and Rumania. In 1947 and 1948, the Soviets used local Communist forces to install Communist regimes in Hungary and Czechoslovakia. Stalin, determined to protect his empire and its Communist system from future security threats, and perhaps also from Western cultural influences and U.S. investment, erected a ring of submissive client states along the Soviet Union's western periphery.

American political leaders and prominent journalists strongly condemned Soviet domination of Poland and other Eastern European countries. American statesmen would not concede, at least for the record, that the new Soviet empire in Eastern Europe constituted a legitimate "sphere of influence," for several reasons: besides the sense of betrayal felt over Yalta, there were domestic political considerations. Millions of Americans of East European background were enraged at the Soviet Union's brutal domination of their ancestral homelands. Americans also anticipated having trade and investment opportunities in Eastern European countries in the postwar era until Communist control sealed them off. American leaders also felt a sense of righteous, missionary power, that they could move Eastern Europe toward democratic capitalism. Soviet intrusions frustrated American intentions and imposed an abhorrent system of political economy on the region that many Americans equated with Fascism.

At a time when American–Soviet relations were strained because of Stalin's intrusions into Eastern Europe, the Soviets applied for a $6 billion loan from the United States to rebuild their wrecked economy. American officials tried to apply pressure on the Soviets to make them more receptive to American goals for Eastern Europe. The State Department refused to consider the loan unless, as U.S. Ambassador to the Soviet Union Averill Harriman put it, the Soviets "work cooperatively with us on international problems in accordance with our standards." The Soviets refused, and Americans rejected the loan request. A later Soviet request for $1 billion was made, contingent upon the Soviets permitting American trade and investment in Eastern Europe. Stalin refused to accept those terms and the loan was denied. The Soviets rebuilt their economy using their own resources, plus whatever they could extract from Germany and Eastern Europe. Although U.S. efforts to extract Soviet concessions in exchange for credits had failed to change Soviet behavior in Eastern Europe, they angered Stalin, reinforcing his distrust of Western capitalist powers. Stalin also resented America's refusal to accept Soviet domination of Eastern Europe while excluding the Soviets from Italian and Japanese occupations.

But there were clear limits to what actions the Truman administration would take to prevent Soviet domination of Eastern Europe. It could denounce Soviet actions and apply economic and diplomatic pressures, but the United States never threatened the Soviets with military action. In the judgment of American leaders, the freedom of Eastern Europe from Soviet domination was not worth a war with the Soviet Union. When Stalin forcibly incorporated the eastern half of Europe into the Soviet empire between 1945 and 1948, the United States grudgingly accepted the creation of a *de facto* Soviet sphere of influence.

The Potsdam conference, held in late July 1945, the final wartime meeting of leaders of the United States, Great Britain, and the Soviet Union, revealed the strains within the Grand Alliance. The leaders often quarreled—over German boundaries and reparations, over the composition of the new Polish government, and over when the Soviet Union would enter the Pacific war against Japan. At Potsdam, a suburb north of Berlin, the Soviets pressed their demand, made at Yalta, for $20 billion of reparations to be taken from the German occupation zones. The Americans and British again refused to fix a dollar amount for reparations, but they permitted the Soviets to remove some industry from their zones.

But in May 1946, the American military governor suddenly halted all reparations shipments from the U.S. zone. The angry Soviets denounced this U.S. unilateral action that canceled an agreement vital to Soviet postwar reconstruction. Continual conflicts between the Soviets and the Western powers over occupation policy in occupied Germany were major causes of the

Cold War. Conflicts among former allies over Germany were the core causes of the Cold War, which originated in the heart of Europe.

It was at Potsdam that President Truman learned of the first successful testing of an atomic device. The U.S. atomic bomb project was history's most expensive scientific undertaking. Between 1941 and 1945, American and British scientists, engineers, and technicians, many of them émigré European Jews who had fled Nazi tyranny, labored intensively to build atomic bombs. U.S. Army Corps of Engineers General Leslie Groves headed the secret, top-priority program, code-named the "Manhattan District Project." A brilliant scientific team, gathered under the leadership of Dr. J. Robert Oppenheimer and working at Los Alamos, New Mexico, eventually solved the complex theoretical and technical problems involved in creating the immensely powerful new weapons.

The Manhattan Project was so secret that Congressmen who appropriated the vast sums of money for the bomb had no idea what the money was for. Harry Truman came to the presidency ignorant about the project. He was astonished to learn from Secretary of War Stimson, a few days after becoming president in April 1945, that the United States would soon have "the most terrible weapon ever known in human history, one bomb of which could destroy a whole city." In July, the world's first atomic device was exploded in the desert near Los Alamos at a site called Trinity. An awed Dr. Oppenheimer, witnessing the enormous fireball created by the explosion, was reminded of a passage from Hindu scriptures: "I am become Death, destroyer of worlds."

Before the weapon was completed, Stimson convened an Interim Committee that recommended unanimously to the president that the atomic bomb, when ready, be used without warning against Japan. Truman concurred. Some scientists who had worked on the project opposed this recommendation at Committee hearings and proposed instead that the United States invite Japanese observers to witness a harmless demonstration of the bomb's power, perhaps inducing their surrender. Committee members unanimously rejected their recommendation, and Truman never learned of their proposal. Other high-ranking officials also urged holding back and trying to get Japan to surrender without having to use atomic weapons, perhaps by offering them better surrender terms. Truman consistently rejected such advice.

Meanwhile, a new government took power in Japan. Its peace faction sought a way to end the hopeless war. Unaware of the secret Yalta agreements that would soon bring the Soviet Union into the war against Japan, a member of the peace faction sought Soviet mediation to get a modification of the unconditional surrender terms that would permit the Japanese to keep their emperor. The Soviets rebuffed the Japanese approach and informed Washington. American officials already knew of the Japanese peace feelers, because U.S. military intelligence personnel had been intercepting and decoding Japanese messages. They also knew that Japanese army officers, controlling the government, meant to fight on.

After discussions with his advisers at Potsdam, Truman issued a final warning to Japan before dropping the bombs. The message urged Japan to surrender unconditionally, or face "the utter devastation of the Japanese homeland." It made no mention of atomic weapons. The divided Japanese government, rejecting the ultimatum as "unworthy of public notice," ignored it.

Interpreting their silence as rejection, Truman saw no need to rescind an order given on July 30 to proceed with the atomic bomb attack. Early on the morning of August 6, 1945, three B-29s lifted off the runway at Tinian, bound for Hiroshima, Japan's eighth largest city. The lead aircraft, the *Enola Gay,* carried a five-ton atomic bomb in its specially configured bomb bay. The other two planes were escorts; they carried cameras and assemblages of scientific recording instruments.

At 8:45 A.M. local time, the sky exploded over Hiroshima. The world's first atomic bomb struck with the force of 12,000 tons of TNT. It killed or seriously wounded about 80,000 people instantly, many of them vaporized by the intense heat that exceeded fifty million degrees Fahrenheit at the center of the huge fireball. By the end of the year, 60,000 more people had died a dog's death from burns, wounds, and radiation poisoning. A thriving city of 350,000 inhabitants was reduced to instant rubble. A few hours after the bombing, Truman announced to the world the existence and first use of the atomic bomb. He also warned the Japanese that, unless they surrendered unconditionally, immediately, "they may expect a rain of ruin from the air, the like of which has never before been seen on earth." The Japanese did not surrender. Military leaders urged death over defeat.

Bad weather delayed for a few days the dropping of the second bomb. On August 8, Red Army units invaded Manchuria and Korea. The day after the Soviet Union entered the Asian war, a second atomic bomb was dropped on Nagasaki, as previously planned. Originally the city of Kokura had been selected for the second bombing, but stormy weather made bombing that target impossible. Nagasaki was an alternative target. The bomb that devastated Nagasaki was a plutonium one that yielded about 20,000 tons of TNT. It destroyed large sections of the city and killed 45,000 people. It would have killed far more people and done far greater damage had it not fallen off target.

Even after the atomic bombings and Soviet entry into the war, Japanese military leaders wanted to fight on. Only the personal intercession of Emperor Hirohito induced them to surrender. On August 10, the Japanese offered to surrender if they could keep their emperor. Truman accepted surrender unconditionally on August 14, although he did offer veiled assurances that the Japanese could retain their emperor, providing that he was stripped of his status as a divinity. Surrender ceremonies occurred on September 2 aboard the battleship USS *Missouri,* anchored in Tokyo Bay, with General Douglas MacArthur presiding.

Most Americans have accepted President Truman's justification for using the atomic bomb: "We have used it in order to shorten the agony of war, in order to save the lives of thousands and thousands of young Americans." But since the 1960s, a few radical critics have contended that the Japanese, perceiving their cause as hopeless, would have surrendered soon, without the atomic bombings. They argue that Truman had other, more important motives for using nuclear weapons besides ending the war—he wanted to enhance American postwar diplomatic leverage against the Soviet Union. They accuse him of practicing "atomic diplomacy," of dropping the bombs on the already beaten Japanese to hasten their surrender in order to keep the Soviets from venturing too far into China and from sharing in the postwar occupation of Japan. Critics further contend that Truman also intended the bombings to make the USSR more agreeable to American solutions to postwar political problems.

It is impossible for any scholar, after examining the extensive available evidence, to determine, with any degree of certainty, Truman's exact motives for ordering the two atomic bombings. Truman never debated with his senior advisers over whether to use atomic weapons on the Japanese. The atomic bomb project, initiated by Franklin Roosevelt years earlier, was nearing completion at the time Truman assumed the presidency. FDR had understood that the bomb, when available, would be used on the Germans and the Japanese if the wars were still raging. Since Germany surrendered on May 8, 1945, Truman assumed that atomic bombs would be used on Japan as soon as they became available.

Truman and his advisers discussed where, when, and how to use atomic weapons; they did not debate over whether to use them or not to use them. No one in Truman's circle considered the morality, wisdom, or strategic necessity of using those incredibly destructive weapons. Truman's role in the decision-making process was essentially a decision not to interfere with existing plans for the bombs' uses. Truman himself said later, "I regarded the bomb as a military weapon and never had any doubt that it would be used." There were additional considerations. U.S. leaders feared *post hoc* criticisms if they did not use the weapons. Suppose it came out after the war that they had wasted $2 billion on a giant atomic boondoggle that was developed and never used? Suppose it came out that they had developed a powerful weapon that might have shortened the war and saved thousands of U.S. soldiers' lives and failed to use it?

Although there can be no certainty in discerning Truman's motivation, it appears that his primary concern was to try to shorten the war and save American soldiers' lives, just as he always claimed. He hoped to avoid a protracted, bloody campaign to conquer the Japanese home islands. Truman had solicited the views of many senior advisers; they all had agreed that an invasion of the Japanese home islands would be necessary and it could result in hundreds of thousands of U.S. casualties. Many of them shared Truman's fervent hope that dropping the atomic bombs might shock Japan into surrendering and thereby avoid a bloodbath. Truman also hoped that American use of the powerful new weapon would make the Soviets more cooperative, that it would give the United States additional bargaining leverage with them. And he hoped that use of the bombs might induce Japanese surrender before the Soviet Union entered the war, but the Soviets intervened between the dropping of the bombs. Truman also was disappointed to discover that U.S. possession and use of atomic bombs did not soften Soviet diplomacy. Whenever the Americans brought up the matter of atomic bombs with the Soviets, Stalin's response was to become more intractable, not less.

American willingness to use the atomic bombs in war along with Washington's failure to keep Stalin informed of the progress of the Manhattan District Project and American refusal to share any broad scientific information about nuclear weaponry with the Soviets were contributing causes of the Cold War. At a garden party held one afternoon following a Potsdam conference session, Truman told Stalin informally that the United States had recently tested an extremely powerful new weapon. He did not tell the Soviet dictator that it was a nuclear device. Stalin merely smiled and said that that was fine, and that he hoped that it would soon be used on Japan. Truman did not have to tell Stalin that the United States had developed an atomic bomb; the Soviet leader understood instantly what Truman was referring to. As soon as Truman walked away, Stalin hastily conferred with his aides and decided on the spot to speed up a Soviet atomic weapons project that had been curtailed in wartime. The nuclear arms race began at that moment at a garden party in Potsdam.

FBI files, subsequently made public, proved that a spy ring working for the Soviet Union, whose most prominent members included an English physicist Klaus Fuchs and Americans David Greenglass, Harry Gold, and Julius Rosenberg, had penetrated the Manhattan District Project. By the time Americans had atomic bombed two Japanese cities, the spy ring had already delivered about 10,000 pages of classified documents to their Soviet masters. These secret data significantly helped the Soviet atomic bomb project. Experts have estimated that espionage accelerated the Soviet bomb project by as much as two years. At war's end, Soviet scientists already understood much of the technology required to process fissionable materials; they would build their own bombs within four years.

Perhaps the Japanese should have been forewarned. Perhaps a demonstration explosion should have been made. Perhaps the unconditional surrender terms should have been modified before the bombs were used in order to strengthen the peace party within the Japanese government. Any or all of these measures might possibly have induced Japanese surrender before the bombs were used, although no one can know for sure how the Japanese might have responded to any of these initiatives or when they might have surrendered.

It is also important to remember that even if Japan could have been induced to surrender without having to endure the horrors of two atomic bombings, the conceivable alternative scenarios would have in all probability been worse. Had the war gone on for even for a few weeks more, the continuing firebomb raids over Japanese cities would have killed more people and destroyed more property than did the two atomic bombs. And had invasions by U.S. forces been necessary (the first was scheduled for November 1, 1945), there would have been massive losses on both sides. While continued fighting went on in Japan between the Americans and the Japanese, Soviet armies would have annihilated the Japanese armies in Korea, Manchuria, and northern China.

At war's end, the United States was overwhelmingly the world's preeminent economic and military power. With about 5 percent of the world's population, the United States produced over 60 percent of the world's goods and controlled over half of the world's wealth. Its $14 billion in gold reserves stored at Fort Knox represented about 75 percent of the world's gold supply in 1945. Despite its great wealth and power, the United States could not prevent the growing division of Europe nor bring stability to the Far East. When American, British, and Soviet foreign ministers met in London in September 1945, they quarreled bitterly over who threatened whom. Mutual suspicion and hostility rendered diplomacy impossible. The Western powers demanded that the Soviets ease their control of Eastern Europe. In response, the Soviet leaders accused the West of capitalist encirclement and atomic blackmail. The former allies appeared to be on a collision course: the Soviets were determined to dominate the lesser states of Eastern Europe in order to erect a security sphere around their nation; the United States was determined to break down international trade barriers and to rebuild Germany. In the postwar era, America intended to build a prosperous new world order, one based on free governments and free trade. In the world's family of nations, given its great wealth and power, America would be *primus inter pares* (first among equals). From the American perspective, neither its great wealth nor its atomic monopoly guaranteed U.S. security in the postwar era.

The destruction of German and Japanese power had removed historic barriers to Soviet expansion in Europe and Northeastern Asia. Anticolonial rebellions against lingering Western imperialism also gave the Soviet Union opportunities to expand its influence. Expanding American influence in Europe and Asia alarmed the Soviet leaders. They were fearful of the vastly superior American wealth, technology, and military power. Instinctively, Stalin tried to isolate the Soviet Union and its newly acquired empire in Eastern Europe from contact with the Western powers.

In early 1946, both sides escalated their rhetoric. On March 5, 1946, former Prime Minister Winston Churchill, visiting in the United States, declared, "From Stettin in the Baltic to Trieste in the Adriatic, an iron curtain has descended across the continent." He then called for a joint Anglo-American effort to roll back the Soviet Iron Curtain. Stalin promptly accused Churchill of calling for war against the Soviet Union. U.S. public opinion polls showed widespread disapproval for Soviet actions in Germany and Eastern Europe. Stalin had also given a speech previously in which he reasserted the Leninist doctrine of the incompatibility of capitalism and socialism, and the necessity of revolutionary conflict in the world. Following Churchill's belligerent speech, the Soviets rejected an American offer to join the World Bank and the International Monetary Fund (IMF), the two principal agencies for promoting free trade and stable currencies in the postwar world. The Soviets refused to join because they saw the Bank and the IMF as instruments through which the United States intended to dominate the postwar world economy.

American possession and use of nuclear weapons had spurred the Soviets to accelerate their own nuclear weapons development projects. Scientists knew that the U.S. monopoly was temporary; it was only a matter of time until the Soviets produced a bomb. The scientists, unaware of the extensive Soviet espionage, predicted that it would take the Soviets about five years. The world would then be at the mercy of a costly and dangerous arms race without precedent in human history. They urged political leaders to implement a system of international control of nuclear weapons technology to fend off the looming nuclear arms race.

In an atmosphere of growing hostility and suspicion, Truman and his advisers tried to work out a plan for the international control of nuclear weapons through the UN. Bernard Baruch, the American delegate, proposed a plan calling for the international control of atomic weapons to be achieved in stages, during which the United States would retain its nuclear monopoly. His plan called for inspections within the Soviet Union by a UN commission to ensure compliance. The Soviets, working feverishly to develop their own nuclear weapons, rejected onsite inspections within their territory. They proposed an alternative plan calling for the destruction of American nuclear weapons before any control system would be devised. The Americans rejected the Soviet plan. Each side insisted on its plan or nothing, and they got nothing. The United States then opted for its own internal control mechanisms. In 1946, Congress enacted the Atomic Energy Act, which empowered the newly created Atomic Energy Commission (AEC), a civilian agency, to control all atomic energy research and development in the nation under tight security restrictions.

Thus vanished the world's only chance, admittedly a slim one, to eliminate the nuclear arms race before it became a major feature of the Cold War. It was the nuclear arms race that added a terrifying dimension to the U.S.–USSR rivalry, making it unlike any previous great power conflict in history. By 1955, both sides possessed the technical capability to destroy the other, and much of the rest of the world. Ironically, nuclear weapons also functioned to keep the Cold War cold. Had it not been for nuclear weapons, the Americans and the Soviets would probably have had a war long ago, for there was enough provocation on both sides. But neither dared attack the other because it knew the other side would resort to nuclear weapons before it would accept defeat. Mutual terror deterred both sides from full-scale war during the Cold War. The great redeeming irony of the Cold War era was that the most terrible weapons ever developed by the perverse technological genius of mankind prevented World War III between the United States and the Soviet Union.

The failure of Washington and the Kremlin to find a mutually acceptable formula for controlling nuclear weapons technology highlighted the dawn of the Atomic Age. At about the same

Figure 2.2   On October 31, 1952, the first hydrogen bomb exploded over the Pacific Ocean with a force of ten megatons—more than 800 times the power of the atomic bomb that destroyed Hiroshima. Photo by Joint Task Force One.   *Source:* AP/Wide World Photos.

time the UN was debating the weapons issue, the United States conducted a series of atomic bomb tests in the South Pacific at Bikini atoll. Radio accounts and dramatic photos of the tests forced Americans to the horrific realization that humankind had produced weapons of mass destruction that could destroy the world. Some jaunty folks tried to make light of the matter, to laugh it off. Later that year, a French designer brought out a new type of women's bathing suit, which he named the "bikini." It had an explosive impact on women's swimwear fashion, because the new-style swimsuits exposed much more of the female body than did any previous model. Despite these brave efforts to laugh it away, the fear of a nuclear holocaust had rooted itself in the American collective psyche. American imagination in the postwar era was haunted for decades by the twin symbols of catastrophe—the mushroom cloud and nuclear missiles striking America's great cities. According to historian Paul Boyer, "A primal fear of extinction pervaded society." The Atomic Age ushered in the age of anxiety that continuously undercut celebrations of the affluent society.

There were many other conflicts and misunderstandings arising in the period 1945–1946 that poisoned the postwar U.S.–USSR diplomatic atmosphere. The major conflicts—over the postwar political status of Eastern Europe, over occupation policy in Germany, and over international control of atomic weapons—drove the United States and the Soviet Union apart. They were the major causes of the Cold War.

These disputes between America and the Soviet Union grew out of the war and the power vacuum created by the smashing of German power, a vacuum into which rushed the two expansionist powers: the United States, a global power, its leaders motivated by a sense of right-eous power based on America's prosperous economy and atomic monopoly, strong ideological convictions, and important economic interests; and the USSR, a strong regional power, its lead-ers motivated by a fervent Communist ideology, an urgent desire to protect vital security inter-ests, and a pressing need to rebuild its shattered economy. The two "superpowers" collided at many points in Central and Eastern Europe. Emotions flared as leaders on both sides struggled to solve challenging and frustrating problems. Given their fundamental differences, their differ-ing beliefs and perceptions, the intrinsic difficulties of their many problems, the pressures and antagonisms inherent in their many disputes, and their clashing goals and ambitions, in retro-spect, it appears that conflicts between the Americans and the Soviets were inevitable.

Cold War also was inevitable. It occurred because of the failure of the two most powerful nations emerging from World War II to resolve their major disputes through the traditional processes of diplomacy, by negotiations and compromise. Instead, the leaders of the two na-tions, ready to read the worst intentions into the actions of their rivals and to habitually antici-pate worst-case scenarios, believed themselves compelled to resort to over four decades of ideological warfare. They also felt compelled, "like two apes on a treadmill," in Paul Warnke's phrase, to engage in a costly and dangerous thermonuclear arms race without precedent in his-tory. The Cold War evolved as an interlocking, reciprocal process, involving genuine differences of principle, clashes of interest, and a wide range of misperceptions and misunderstandings.

THE TRUMAN DOCTRINE

To Washington in early 1947, the world appeared to be sinking into chaos. A nearly bankrupt Great Britain prepared to abandon India, Palestine, and Greece. The Vietnamese refused to ac-cept the return of French colonialism, and Indochina was engulfed in war. Likewise, the Indone-sians refused to accept the return of the Dutch and ignited a war. In China, a civil war raged between the Nationalists and Communists. Amidst rubble-strewn cities and ruined economies, the Japanese and Germans struggled to avoid famine. American leaders feared that the Soviet Union would try to exploit the severe political and economic problems of Europe and Asia.

In 1947, crises arose in the Balkans involving Greece and Turkey. Greece was engulfed in a civil war that pitted Communist-led insurgents against a Rightist government backed by the British. Simultaneously, the Soviets were pressuring the Turkish government to grant them joint control of the Dardanelles, a strait between the Black Sea and the Mediterranean. The Turks re-buffed the Soviets, and Stalin threatened to take action against them. The British also were backing the Turks in their dispute with the Soviets over control of the waterway. On February 21, 1947, citing economic problems, the British government informed Washington that it could no longer provide support to the Greek and Turkish governments.

President Truman wanted the United States to replace the British in the Mediterranean and to help the Greeks and Turks, but he had to convince the Republican-controlled and economy-minded 80th Congress that his initiative served the national interest. The principal architect of the American aid program to Greece and Turkey was Undersecretary of State Dean Acheson. Acheson evoked an early version of the "domino theory" to stress the need for American aid to the two countries. He stated that if Greece fell to the Communists and the Soviets gained control of the Dardanelles, North Africa and the Middle East would be endangered. Morale would sink in Italy, France, and western Germany; all would then be more vulnerable to a Communist takeover. Three continents would be opened to Soviet penetration. Acheson's alarmist presentation persuaded Senator Arthur Vandenberg, chairman of the Senate Foreign Relations Committee to support Truman's proposed aid bill for Greece and Turkey. George Kennan, a brilliant State Department Soviet expert, also furnished arguments supporting Truman's interventionist policy. Kennan wrote of the need to develop

> a policy of firm containment, designed to confront the Russians with unalterable counter-force at every point where they show signs of encroaching upon the interests of a peaceful and stable world.[1]

His analysis coincided with Truman's views of Soviet behavior: His recommendations accorded with the president's desire to get tough with the Soviet leaders. Containment, stopping the spread of Communist influence in the world, soon became the chief operating principle of American foreign policy in the postwar era. It would remain the cornerstone of U.S. foreign policy for more than forty years.

Truman also actively promoted the proposed aid bill for Greece and Turkey. In a speech given at Baylor University on March 6, 1947, he said that the American system of free enterprise could survive only if it were part of a free world economic system. He contended that American aid to Greece and Turkey was part of his strategy for preserving economic freedom in the world. Only a peaceful and prosperous world ensured American security in the Cold War era. He warned his audience that the "seeds of totalitarian regimes are nurtured by misery and want."

Truman's Baylor University speech preceded his major address before a joint session of Congress on March 12 to ask Congress to appropriate $400 million for Greek and Turkish aid. In the most important foreign policy speech of his presidency, mostly written for him by Acheson, Truman told the American people that the Communist threat to Greece and Turkey was Hitler and World War II all over again. Truman then spoke the famed words that soon became known as the Truman Doctrine. The anti-Communism of the Truman Doctrine became, in the words of historian Thomas G. Paterson, "the commanding guide to American foreign policy in the Cold War."

> At the present moment in world history, nearly every nation must choose between alternative ways of life.
>   One way of life is based upon the will of the majority, and is distinguished by free institutions . . . and freedom from political oppression. The second way of life is based upon the will of a minority forcibly imposed on the majority . . . and the suppression of personal freedom.
>   I believe that it must be the policy of the United States to support free peoples who are resisting attempted subjugation by armed minorities or by outside pressures. . . . If we falter in our leadership, we may endanger the peace of the world—we shall surely endanger the welfare of our own nation.[2]

Truman's speech amounted to a declaration of ideological warfare against the Soviet Union. He depicted a world engaged in a struggle between the forces of freedom and the forces

---

[1]George Kennan, *American Diplomacy* (New York: New American Library, 1952), p. 104. (Reprinted with permission of the editor from *Foreign Affairs,* xxv, No. 4 (July 1947), pp. 566–582.)

[2]Taken from a printed copy of Truman's speech found in Armin Rappaport, ed., *Sources in American Diplomacy* (New York: Macmillan, 1966), pp. 329–330.

of tyranny. The political fate of mankind hung on the outcome. In this mortal struggle, American aid to Greece and Turkey would serve the American mission of preserving freedom in the world and preventing World War III. Polls, which had been negative before his speech, soon showed a large majority favoring the aid program.

Not everyone accepted Truman's eloquent invitation to join the anti-Communist crusade. Both liberal and conservative critics opposed aid to Greece and Turkey. Henry Wallace denounced the aid bill as a waste of money and provocative to the Soviets. Walter Lippmann, the nation's most influential political journalist, also opposed it, observing that the United States could not police the world. But after a brief debate, large bipartisan majorities in both houses of Congress supported the aid bill. Truman's powerful rhetoric had carried his cause.

The Truman Doctrine defined a new American postwar foreign policy. Isolationism had been abandoned and the United Nations bypassed. Truman had committed America to resist actively Soviet expansionism in Southern Europe. The Truman Doctrine proclaimed that the era of the containment of Communism had begun. Although the first application of the new containment policy was limited, the doctrine justifying it was unlimited. During the early 1950s, American foreign policy based on the containment of Communism would inevitably expand to become a global commitment.

Congress fashioned several new government agencies to implement the containment policy. The National Security Act (1947) created the Department of Defense and established the Joint Chiefs of Staff. The act also made the Air Force a separate branch of military service and put the administration of the Army, Navy, and Air Force under a single department. The first Secretary of Defense was a hard-line Cold Warrior, James Forrestal. The National Security Act also created the National Security Council (NSC), a Cabinet-level advisory body to coordinate military and foreign policy for the president. The creation of the NSC indicated the growing influence of strategic considerations in the conduct of American foreign policy. The National Security Act also created the Central Intelligence Agency (CIA) as an agency directly under the authority of the National Security Council. The CIA, a child of the Cold War, became a covert arm of American foreign policy during the early 1950s. The National Security Act institutionalized the Cold War.

THE MARSHALL PLAN

In 1947, European recovery from the devastation of war was flagging. Washington feared that continuing hardships could force cold and hungry Europeans to turn to Communism, particularly in France and Italy, which had strong and popular Communist parties. A prostrate Europe also endangered American prosperity because of a huge "dollar gap" that had emerged. The dollar gap, totaling about $8 billion in 1947, represented the difference between the value of U.S. exports and the amount of dollars that European customers had on hand to pay for them. The dollar gap threatened to undermine American overseas trade and to erode U.S. postwar economic growth and prosperity.

Europeans could not buy American products unless they received dollars from the United States. To offset the lure of Communism and the possibility of Soviet intervention in Western Europe and to pump dollars into the impoverished European economy, U.S. officials drafted a comprehensive European recovery program. On June 5, 1947, Secretary of State George Marshall announced the plan directed against "hunger, poverty, desperation, and chaos," that came to bear his name. Truman urged Congress to back the proposed Marshall Plan with a $27 billion appropriation.

The Marshall Plan called for a cooperative approach in which Europeans would plan their recovery needs collectively and the United States would underwrite a long-term recovery program. All European nations were invited to participate in the Marshall Plan, including the Soviet Union and the East European nations. With the British and French leading the way, Europeans responded immediately and enthusiastically. A general planning conference convened in Paris on June 26, 1947, to formulate an European reply. But the Soviets walked out of the conference, denouncing the Marshall Plan as an American scheme to dominate Europe. Stalin also may have feared that American economic aid would undermine his control of Eastern Europe, so he forced these nations to abstain from the recovery program. On July 16, Europeans established a Committee on European Economic Cooperation, which drew up plans for a four-year recovery effort.

Within the United States, Senator Vandenberg led a bipartisan effort to get congressional approval for the plan. Support for the aid program increased when Americans learned of a Communist takeover in Czechoslovakia that occurred as Congress debated the bill. Stalin ordered the Czech coup as a response to the increasing integration of the West German economy into the liberal capitalist order. Congress passed a slimmed-down version of the aid plan. The legislators appropriated $5.3 billion to implement the Marshall Plan in the summer of 1948. When the Marshall Plan ended in 1952, the United States had provided over $13 billion for European economic recovery.

The Marshall Plan worked. European industrial production increased 200 percent from 1948 to 1952. The foundations for the West's later affluence were firmly laid. The appeal of Communism in the West dropped sharply. The program worked mainly because of its planned, long-term, cooperative approach. It also succeeded because Europe possessed the industrial base and skilled manpower needed to use the aid funds effectively. European economic recovery restored a region of crucial importance to the United States. It also proved to be a major stimulus to American economic activity and was in accord with Cold War ideological goals. George Marshall expected American economic aid to permit the "emergence of political and social conditions in which free institutions can exist." The Marshall Plan gave the U.S. policy of containment of Communism in Europe a sound economic foundation.

NATO

While furnishing the means for Europe's economic reconstruction, America also concerned itself with rebuilding Western Germany. With the rise of Soviet power in Eastern Europe, there was a power vacuum in Central Europe that America wanted to fill with a democratic and capitalistic Germany. Near the end of 1946, the Americans and British merged their German occupation zones and began to assign administrative responsibilities to German officials. By mid-1947, the effort to rebuild Germany's industrial economy had begun.

The Soviets reacted to Western efforts to rebuild the German economy and incorporate it into the European recovery plan by tightening their control of Eastern Europe. Perceiving that he had failed to prevent the restoration of a West German state, Stalin also tried to squeeze the Western powers out of Berlin. In June 1948, the Soviets suddenly shut down all Western access routes to their Berlin sectors, which lay deep inside the Soviet zone. The Berlin Blockade confronted the Truman administration with a serious crisis. Choices, at first, appeared only to include surrender or to risk World War III. Truman ordered sixty U.S. strategic bombers with the capability of hauling nuclear weapons to targets in the Soviet Union to fly to bases in England. The Western powers also devised an Anglo-American airlift that flew food and fuel to 2.5 million West Berliners. Around the clock, British and American pilots flew food and fuel into West Berlin. Pilots, harassed by Soviet fighters and often flying in bad weather with poor visibility, risked their lives to deliver their precious cargoes to the isolated men, women, and children of West Berlin. The Soviets, not wanting to start World War III, did not try to interdict the airlift. After 324 days, the Soviets canceled the blockade. It had failed to dislodge the Allies, and it had failed to prevent the integration of the West German economy into the European recovery program. And the Berlin airlift had raised the morale and hopes of the beleaguered people of West Berlin.

In American eyes, the airlift symbolized Western resolve to maintain an outpost of freedom in the heart of Soviet tyranny. Truman had outmaneuvered the Soviets and forced them to rescind the blockade. The airlift also confirmed George Kennan's contention that only force, or a credible threat of force, could contain Communist expansionism. The Western powers created the Federal Republic of Germany (West Germany) soon after the blockade ended. In retaliation, the Soviets erected the Democratic Socialist Republic of Germany (East Germany). The Berlin Blockade represented the first major American–Soviet conflict of the Cold War. It also was the paradigmatic conflict that established the pattern of U.S.–USSR confrontations that would continually recur until the Cold War ended.

The Czech coup, the Berlin Blockade, and other Soviet actions hostile to Western interests convinced Washington officials that containment required military as well as economic measures. The germ of the North Atlantic Treaty Organization (NATO) appeared in a Senate resolution passed in 1948, expressing America's resolve to defend itself through collective security if necessary. The Truman administration began planning for the defense of Western Europe.

NATO came to life on April 4, 1949; ten European nations, Canada, and the United States signed the treaty. The heart of the mutual security pact could be found in Article 5: "An armed attack against one or more members . . . shall be considered an attack against them all." Attack any NATO member and you have to fight them all. With the establishment of NATO, Soviet aggression against Western Europe would mean World War III. The Senate ratified the treaty 82 to 13 on July 21, 1949, with little debate.

Congress followed its approval of American membership in NATO by voting to grant military aid to its allies and to contribute American troops to NATO defense forces. By early 1950, a NATO command structure had been created. American forces stationed in Europe would function as a "tripwire" in case of Soviet aggression, guaranteeing that U.S. strategic bombers would attack the Soviet Union if Western Europe were invaded. The Soviets responded to the creation of NATO by creating the Warsaw Pact among East European countries.

Because U.S. forces were not sent to Europe until 1952, the creation of NATO did not immediately alter the strategic balance of power in that critical region. At the time of NATO's creation, there was no imminent threat of war in Europe. Few senior American civilian or military advisers believed that the Red Army was poised to invade Western Europe. The United States

Figure 2.3   Beleaguered West Berliners eagerly await the arrival of an airplane carrying precious food and fuel during the Berlin Airlift.   *Source:* Getty Images/Time Life Pictures.

appeared to be winning the Cold War in Western Europe and Japan. The Marshall Plan nations and the Japanese were both well on the road to economic recovery. The new state of West Germany, under the leadership of Konrad Adenauer, had been firmly established. Soviet efforts to keep Japan and Europe weak and divided and isolated from the United States had obviously failed.

Given the geopolitical situation in Europe, it is evident that NATO had other uses besides giving containment of Communism in Europe military muscle. NATO was less about giving Europeans arms and more about giving them the confidence to combat internal subversion and the will to resist Communist aggression. NATO conveyed a sense of security that encouraged West European economic recovery under the Marshall Plan. NATO also served as a means to bind Western Europeans more tightly into an American sphere of influence and to discourage any separatist tendencies to make deals with or to appease the Soviets. Ironically, NATO later proved useful in providing a way to rearm West Germany. By integrating the new West German military forces into NATO, the United States could allay French alarm at a rearmed Germany.

From 1947 to 1949, American leaders made many crucial decisions that shaped American Cold War policy for decades. First came the formulation of containment ideology, the declaration of principles embodied in the Truman Doctrine. It represented a contemporary reformulation of the traditional doctrine of American mission: Americans had a special mission to protect

Figure 2.4   Division of Europe, 1945–1955.   *Source:* George D. Moss, *Moving On, 1st ed.* (Englewood Cliffs, N.J.: Prentice Hall, 1994), p. 38. Public Domain Map.

free nations from expansionist Communism in the Cold War era. The Marshall Plan offered economic aid enabling Western Europeans to stay clear of the Iron Curtain and to rebuild their war-shattered economies. NATO added a strategic component. NATO also represented a historic departure for the United States: America joined its first binding military alliance in modern history. Foreign entanglements now appeared necessary to ensure U.S. security in the nuclear age.

Soon after Senate ratification of NATO came the alarming news that the Soviets had developed an atomic bomb. The American nuclear monopoly, which had functioned as a security blanket to dampen Cold War anxieties, had vanished. The atomic "genie" had escaped from its bottle. Soviet possession of nuclear weapons prompted President Truman to consider ordering the development of a hydrogen fusion weapon, a "superbomb" many times more powerful than atomic fission weapons. In January 1950, an intense secret debate occurred between scientific supporters of the H-bomb, led by Dr. Edward Teller, and its opponents, led by J. Robert Oppenheimer. Teller carried the debate with his argument that if the United States failed to develop the weapon and the Soviets did develop it, the Kremlin could blackmail the United States. Truman agreed with Teller and ordered the hydrogen bomb to be built.

U.S. scientists exploded a hydrogen bomb in October 1952. But the American technological edge in the spiraling arms race against the Soviet Union proved to be short lived. The Soviets tested their own hydrogen bomb in August 1953, less than a year later. These thermonuclear weapons were a thousand times more powerful than the bombs dropped on Hiroshima and Nagasaki in 1945. With the advent of the hydrogen bomb, an ominous threshold had been crossed; the potential thermonuclear threat to world survival had taken a quantum leap.

THE CHINESE REVOLUTION

Since the Cold War began, the Truman administration had pursued an Europe-oriented foreign policy. But the collapse of the Chinese Nationalist government in October 1949, after years of civil war between its forces and Communist troops, brought American Asian policy to the fore. As the Communist leader Mao Zedong established the People's Republic of China, the American people were disheartened at the loss of a favored ally, and conservative critics of the Truman administration went on the political warpath.

America's China policy had been in disarray since the end of World War II. The long civil war between the Nationalists and the Communists, suspended during the war against Japan, resumed soon after the Japanese surrendered. Between 1945 and 1949, the United States had given Jiang Jieshi's Nationalist government $2 billion in economic and military assistance. In 1946, Truman had sent General George C. Marshall to China to try to arrange a political compromise between the warring parties. But both sides, each believing that it could win a military victory over the other, refused to share power. Marshall gave up his futile efforts in January 1947, pronounced a plague on both of their houses, and returned to America.

In 1947, Nationalist leader Jiang Jieshi, using American logistical support, launched a major offensive designed to destroy his Communist foes. His armies captured the major cities of China, but in doing so, Jiang's forces spread themselves thin. The Communists controlled the countryside that contained over 85 percent of the vast Chinese population and provided food for the cities. The Maoist armies besieged the Nationalist troops in the cities. By the summer of 1949, Nationalist forces had lost their will to fight and surrendered en masse. As 1949 ended, Jiang, with remnants of his army and government, sought refuge on the island of Formosa (Taiwan).

Washington cut itself loose from the failing Nationalist government in August 1949, a few months before Jiang fled China. A State Department report, known as the China White Paper,

Figure 2.5   In homage to Mao Zedong, crowds filled the streets of China's cities in 1949, celebrating the triumph of the Communist revolution.   *Source:* AP/Wide World Photos.

condemned Mao for being a Soviet puppet, but the paper maintained that the United States had done all it could for the Nationalists; they had lost the civil war because they had not used U.S. assistance properly.

The Communist victory in China triggered an intense debate within the United States over foreign policy in general and Asian policy in particular. Bipartisanship, which had prevailed during the years of containing Communism in Europe, disintegrated as Republican leaders attacked Truman's Far Eastern policy. The Asia-first wing of the Republican Party and the China Lobby, led by Senator Styles Bridges and Congressman Walter Judd, charged the Democratic-controlled Congress and the Truman administration with responsibility for Jiang's fall. They insisted that U.S. military involvement in the Chinese civil war could have saved Jiang's government.

But China was not America's to lose. If anyone could be saddled with the responsibility for losing China, it would be Jiang and his corrupt, inept government. The American failure in China was not providing insufficient aid or lack of concern. American leaders never understood the dynamic force of a peasant society ripe for change and the strong appeal of the Maoist land reform program among the Chinese peasants. The mistake the Truman administration made was to continue to cling to Jiang until it was much too late. As the historian Barbara Tuchman observed, "There is little virtue in a client being anti-Communist if he is at the same time rotting from within."

However, millions of Americans believed the charges brought by the Asia firsters and the China Lobby. Such beliefs stemmed from a false assumption many Americans made about U.S. foreign policy during the early Cold War era—that the rich and mighty United States could control political events around the globe if only leaders took the right actions. They could see no limits to American power. If China had fallen to Communism, millions reasoned that such a catastrophe could occur only because U.S. leaders had blundered, or worse, as Senator Joseph McCarthy and others charged, because disloyal U.S. officials, secretly favoring the Communist forces, had subverted America's China policy.

If the Chinese revolution could have been thwarted, it would have taken a massive, sustained American military intervention for years. In 1949, the United States lacked the ground troops to intervene in China. Had Truman confronted Congress and the American people with the hard choices of either a large-scale military intervention or a Communist victory in China, they probably would have opposed direct American involvement in an Asian civil war. But Truman tried to hide the declining status of the Nationalist regime until near the end, hence its collapse came as a sudden shock. His own actions made him vulnerable to Republican accusations that he had lost China. Containment of Communism had worked in Europe and in Japan; it had failed in China. The Maoist victory in China was a devastating diplomatic defeat for the United States and a political disaster for the Truman administration.

After the Maoist victory, the United States implemented a policy of nonrecognition and clamped a trade boycott on the world's most populous nation. U.S. officials insisted that Jiang's government now ensconced in Formosa constituted the legitimate government of China. Nonrecognition toward mainland China would represent official U.S. policy for the next 20 years, until Richard Nixon made his famous journey to Beijing in February 1972.

VIETNAM: THE BEGINNINGS

The success of the Chinese Communist revolution also had a major influence on U.S. foreign policy in Southeast Asia. Since 1946, the French had been trying to reimpose colonialism on the Vietnamese people. The Vietnamese, led by Ho Chi Minh and General Vo Nguyen Giap, leaders of a Nationalist front organization known to the West as the Viet Minh, refused to accept the return of their former imperial masters and waged a guerrilla war that the French could not suppress. American policy toward the war in Indochina had been ambivalent. Publicly, the United States took a neutral stance; the Americans did not wish to align themselves with European colonialism in Southeast Asia, and they were skeptical that the French could defeat the Vietnamese Nationalists. But since Ho and Giap and most of the other Vietnamese leaders were Communists, Americans strongly opposed the idea of another country joining the Communist world. Hence, Americans covertly supported the French effort in Vietnam. The United States also supported the French war in Vietnam because Washington feared that a French defeat in Indochina might weaken Paris's resolve to resist Soviet expansionism in Europe. In 1949, the French made their cause in Southeast Asia more palatable to the Americans when they set up a puppet government in Saigon under the nominal leadership of Bao Dai, a descendant of the last Vietnamese royal family. Now the French could claim, disingenuously, that they were fighting to preserve Vietnamese national independence from the threat of Communism.

The Communist victory in China had a major impact on the Indochinese war. Hitherto the Vietnamese had been fighting alone against the French. Now they had a powerful friend and ally in the Chinese Communists, with whom they shared a long common border. Soon Chinese economic and military aid flowed to the Viet Minh, and the war began to go badly for the French. In February 1950, China and the Soviet Union formally recognized Ho's revolutionary government. Alarmed, the French appealed to the United States for help. Dean Acheson, who had become Secretary of State in 1949, succeeding Marshall, responded by formally recognizing Bao Dai's pseudogovernment. In May 1950, the United States began to send economic and military aid to the French forces fighting in Vietnam. A small group of U.S. military advisers arrived in Vietnam during the summer of 1950. On a modest scale, the Truman administration began an American involvement in Vietnam during the summer of 1950 that would last for twenty-five years, include a major war, and would ultimately end in disaster for the United States and the people in Southeast Asia whom it tried to help.

NSC-68

Truman, responding to the news that the Soviets had developed atomic weapons and the fall of China, directed Secretary of State Acheson to conduct a full-dress review of American foreign policy. Under Acheson's guidance, the review was conducted by the State and Defense Departments, and coordinated by the National Security Council. Six months later, analysts produced National Security Council Document Number 68 (NSC-68), an important top-secret paper that shaped American foreign policy for the next 20 years.

Truman received NSC-68 in April 1950. It assumed continual conflict in the world between the United States and the Soviet Union. It depicted this struggle in stark terms—what was at issue was no less than the survival of America, its free institutions, and its ideals. It assumed that the Soviets would achieve the nuclear capability to destroy the United States within a few years. Hence, NSC-68 called for a massive buildup of American military force to resist the Soviet menace anywhere in the world that it might arise. It recommended defense budgets of $50 billion a year, a fourfold increase over the $13 billion for 1950. NSC-68 called these huge expenditures "the necessary price of freedom." The outbreak of the Korean War would give President Truman the opportunity to implement many of the recommendations contained in NSC-68, which militarized containment and transformed it from a regional into a global policy.

WAR IN KOREA

After the fall of China, the Administration forged a new Asian policy. Secretary of State Acheson delineated a new defense perimeter in the Far East, incorporating Japan, Okinawa, and the Philippines. It excluded Formosa, Korea, and Southeast Asia. The new line suggested that nations located within the excluded regions would have to defend themselves against Chinese aggression, or they would have to seek help from the United Nations. Republican leaders vigorously attacked Truman's Asian policy.

As controversy over American Asian policy continued, the Truman administration confronted another Far Eastern crisis—North Korea's invasion of South Korea. The invasion was rooted in divisions within the country stemming from World War II. As the war ended, Soviet and American troops had occupied the Korean peninsula, which had been a Japanese colony since 1910. The two nations arranged for Soviet soldiers to accept the surrender of Japanese troops north of the 38th parallel of north latitude and for American soldiers to accept the surrender of Japanese forces south of that line. Efforts to unify Korea failed, and the nation remained divided at the 38th parallel. North of the boundary, the Soviets created a Communist state and trained an army to defend it. South of the border, the United States supervised the creation of a government headed by Syngman Rhee. The Soviet Union and America removed their troops from the divided land in the late 1940s. Both Rhee and Kim Il-Sung, the North Korean leader, sought to unify Korea—one under capitalism and the other under Communism.

Kim moved first. On June 25, 1950, with direct assistance from the Soviet Union, North Korean forces invaded the South in an effort to unify Korea under Communist control. Kim expected to win an easy victory, having calculated that the United States would not intervene given the recent policy statements out of Washington that Korea lay outside of the boundary of U.S. vital interests. Kim evidently had received Stalin's permission to invade South Korea, and Mao Zedong concurred. They anticipated a quick victory for the North Koreans and saw the move as advancing their national interests in Northeastern Asia.

President Truman, surprised by the invasion, immediately conferred with his advisers. He understood that if the United States did not intervene quickly, North Korea would overrun the South. He quickly decided to send U.S. troops to try to save South Korea from Communism. He called Korea "the Greece of the Far East." He compared Communist aggression in Korea to Fascist aggression during the 1930s. He said that if the United States let aggression go unchallenged, as the democracies had done in the 1930s, "it would mean a third world war." Truman viewed the conflict in global terms. He assumed that the Soviets had masterminded the attack, and he believed that U.S. national security and world peace were threatened. Truman also believed that the Soviets might be using the invasion as a feint to suck American troops into Korea, leaving Western Europe vulnerable to Soviet attack, just at the time NATO was being implemented. He further shared a concern about Japanese security. The conquest of South Korea would give the Communists airfields within thirty minutes' flying time of Japanese cities. Finally, Truman dared not serve up the loss of Korea to the Republicans in an election year that followed so soon after the "loss" of China.

When Truman committed the U.S. troops to the Korean War, he did not seek a declaration of war from Congress. He claimed that he lacked time, and he relied on what he called his "inherent war-making powers" as commander-in-chief of the Armed Forces. But the United States did obtain UN endorsement for its Korean intervention. The Security Council approved American military intervention because the Soviet delegate was absent from its sessions. The Soviet representative had been boycotting the Security Council sessions to protest its refusal to replace the Chinese Nationalist delegate with a Communist delegate following Mao's victory. Officially, the Korean War was a United Nations "police action" to repel aggression against South Korea. In reality, the UN sanction furnished a multilateral cover for what was mainly an American unilateral effort. The United States provided 90 percent of the ground forces and all of the sea and air power aiding the South Koreans. All battlefield commanders came from the United States. General MacArthur, whom Truman appointed to head the Korean campaign, took orders from the U.S. Joint Chiefs of Staff.

The was nearly lost at its beginning. North Korean troops overran most of South Korea, except for a small area around Pusan, a seaport at the southern tip of the peninsula. For a time, Washington feared that the defenders would be pushed into the sea. But U.S. and South Korean forces finally halted the invaders at Pusan in August 1950. General MacArthur then turned the war around with a brilliantly executed amphibious landing at Inchon 150 miles north of Pusan. U.S. forces moved south from Inchon as other forces broke out at Pusan and headed north. They caught the North Koreans in a giant pincers, and a rout was on. By the end of September, the UN forces had pushed the retreating North Koreans back across the thirty-eighth parallel.

Within three months, the UN mission had been accomplished. The aggressors had been cleared from South Korea. With the North Korean army in disarray, and the USSR and China apparently not inclined to intervene, Truman decided to go north across the 38th parallel. General MacArthur enthusiastically approved. Truman's decision to cross the line transformed the war. Containment became rollback, an effort to liberate North Korea from Communism. UN forces set out to destroy a Communist satellite and to unify Korea under a pro-Western government. The Security Council endorsed Truman's decision to transform the war.

At first, all went well. The U.S. forces drove their foes north. Meanwhile, the general American military buildup in accordance with NSC-68 continued. The draft had been reinstated. Congress doubled the Pentagon's budget, from $13 billion to $26 billion. Additional troops were earmarked for NATO. The Seventh Fleet was stationed between the Chinese mainland and Formosa to shield Jiang's forces from a possible Communist attack. Both the rapid military buildup and the war in Korea enjoyed strong bipartisan support and broad popular approval. The UN forces appeared to be headed for victory. The North Korean army was on the verge of destruction.

As the UN forces advanced northward, Chinese leaders issued a series of warnings. When General MacArthur ignored their warnings, Chinese officials stated publicly that if the U.S. forces continued their advance, they would intervene. On October 15, 1950, President Truman flew to Wake Island in the mid-Pacific to confer with General MacArthur. MacArthur assured the President that the Chinese would not intervene, and if they did, they would be slaughtered. He also told Truman that he would win the Korean War and "have the boys home by Christmas." Truman accepted MacArthur's assessment and discounted the Chinese warnings. MacArthur launched what he thought would be the final offensive of the Korean War on November 24. UN forces advanced along two widely separated routes toward the Yalu River border with China and toward Pyongyang, the North Korean capital. Two days later, the Chinese sent more than 300,000 troops swarming across the frozen Yalu. Fighting in icy winter weather, the Chinese armies split the UN forces and sent them reeling backward. In two weeks they drove MacArthur's forces back across the 38th parallel and down the Korean peninsula.

U.S. officials, who had walked into disaster together, were now divided over how to respond to it. General MacArthur wanted to expand the war and strike at China. He was supported by many conservative Republicans and some Democrats, including a young Congressman from Massachusetts, John F. Kennedy. MacArthur believed that the Chinese made the decision to invade Korea on their own. Truman and Acheson assumed that the Chinese were carrying out Soviet policies. If they were correct, going to war with China meant going to war with the Soviet Union in Asia. Truman opted for a return to the original limited UN mission of restoring the prewar status quo in Korea and for continuing the U.S. military buildup in accordance with NSC-68.

Figure 2.6   The Korean War, 1950–1953. *Source:* Public Domain Map.

    In December, the U.S. field commander in Korea, General Matthew Ridgway brought in reinforcements and rallied the U.S. forces. Heavy artillery slaughtered the Chinese forces that were advancing in massed formations. U.S. naval and air forces helped blunt the Chinese drive. Ridgway's Eighth Army fought its way back to a point near the 38th parallel and held that line for the rest of the war. Truce negotiations began on July 10, 1951, but they were unproductive for a long time. A seesaw war of trenches and fortified hills would continue for two more years and claim thousands of American lives.

    During the first months of 1951, as Ridgway's troops held the line in Korea, Truman continued his implementation of NSC-68. Annual military spending reached $50 billion. The United States committed additional forces to NATO and obtained additional overseas bases. The U.S. Army expanded to 3.6 million men, six times its size when the Korean War began. Military aid was sent to Jiang's Nationalist forces on Formosa. The United States also began to supply military aid going to the French forces fighting in Indochina. Washington signed a peace treaty with Japan that ended the occupation and restored Japanese sovereignty. However, the treaty permitted America to maintain military bases in Japan. The Truman administration embraced the general strategy of ringing China and the Soviet Union with U.S. military might. Containment had become a global commitment, and now packed potent military muscle.

The rapid U.S. military buildup did not satisfy Republican critics supporting General MacArthur's proposal to take the war to China. He did not want to hold the line at the 38th parallel and negotiate; MacArthur wanted a military victory over China and a unified, pro-Western Korea. Ordered by Truman to make no public statements, he defied his commander in chief. On April 5, House Republican leader Joseph Martin read a letter from MacArthur to Congress calling for an alternative foreign policy. If victory in Asia required bombing Manchurian bases, blockading Chinese ports, using nuclear weapons, and employing Nationalist forces from Taiwan, so be it: "In war there is no substitute for victory." MacArthur's letter also stated: "Here in Asia is where the Communist conspirators have elected to make their play for global conquest." MacArthur rejected Truman's Europe-first orientation, his effort to achieve limited political goals in Korea, and his containment policy. He had issued a fundamental challenge to the Administration's foreign policy.

Truman dismissed MacArthur from his command and ordered him home. Truman's actions provoked one of the great emotional events of recent American history. The White House was swamped with letters and phone calls, mostly supporting MacArthur. Polls showed that 75 percent of the people supported the general. Republican supporters of MacArthur heaped abuse upon the embattled Truman. Many newspaper and magazine editors called for his impeachment.

Much of the uproar over Truman's firing of MacArthur reflected popular disenchantment with the Korean War. Many Americans neither understood nor accepted the concept of limited war for particular political objectives. After all, when an easy military victory appeared possible, Truman himself had tried to take all of Korea, only to revert to the original, limited objective following Chinese intervention. The President wanted to avoid a major war that he feared could escalate into World War III, but MacArthur's contempt for half measures and his stirring call for victory appealed to a nation of impatient idealists. The United States obviously had the military power to destroy North Korea and China. Why not use it?

MacArthur returned to America to a hero's welcome. 500,000 people turned out to greet him when he arrived in San Francisco on April 16, 1951. Three days later, he addressed a joint session of Congress. His moving speech was interrupted thirty times by applause.

As MacArthur basked in public acclaim, Congress investigated the circumstances of his removal. Hearings were held before the combined Senate Armed Services Committee and Foreign Relations Committee. At first, the senators favored MacArthur, but the testimony of the Joint Chiefs, particularly of General Omar Bradley, put the case for containment in Korea forcibly and clearly: the Soviet Union, not China, was America's main enemy; Europe, not Asia, was the most important region of American interest. General Bradley stated that fighting China in Asia "would be the wrong war in the wrong place at the wrong time against the wrong enemy." There also was MacArthur's refusal to follow orders and his efforts to make foreign policy over the President's head. The constitutional principle of civilian control of foreign policy and military strategy was at stake. Truman had fired an insubordinate general. Gradually, the tumult subsided, and MacArthur faded into quiet retirement.

Figure 2.7   U.S. soldiers in the 2nd Infantry Division, fighting in Korea near the Chongchon River, December 1950. The Korean War was the first war in American history in which soldiers fought together in racially integrated combat units.   *Source:* Moss, *America in the Twentieth Century, 3rd ed.* CORBIS. Photo by Dept. of Defense/Acme/UPI.

Meanwhile in Korea the truce talks between the Americans on the one side and the North Koreans and Chinese on the other side dragged on inconclusively, and fighting continued. Fighting and talking would continue until July 1953. The main reason for the impasse at the talks was Chinese insistence that captured North Korean and Chinese soldiers be returned to them, even though these soldiers wanted to remain in South Korea. The United States refused to return them against their will. An armistice was finally reached on July 27, 1953, when President Eisenhower threatened the Chinese with an expansion of the war. The Chinese yielded, and the prisoners remained in the South. The 38th parallel was restored as the boundary between North and South Korea. To appease Syngman Rhee, who was unhappy with the settlement, the United States furnished his government with military aid and kept 50,000 American troops in South Korea.

Although it has been forgotten by many Americans, Korea was a major land war in Asia. It lasted for three years and involved over three million American military personnel. Its costs exceeded $100 billion; only World War II and the Vietnam War cost more. About 37,000 Americans died in Korea, and another 150,000 were wounded. Millions of Koreans and Chinese perished during the war. Korea proved to be an unpopular war that ended in a draw. No celebrations greeted its end. Returning Korean veterans melted into society to became part of the 1950s "silent generation."

The Korean War significantly influenced U.S. foreign policy. Containment was transformed from a regional policy to a general global stance. U.S. foreign policy shifted from its Eurocentric focus toward increasing involvement in the the Far East. War with the People's Republic of China ensured that the United States and China would remain bitter Cold War adversaries for decades. The image of an aggressive Soviet Union commanding a centralized, worldwide Communist movement fastened itself on the American mind. China was seen as an extension of Soviet power. Truman incorporated the defense of Formosa and French interests in Southeast Asia into the larger framework of U.S. containment of Communism in the Far East.

The Korean War transformed the Cold War from a political and an ideological conflict into a military struggle. Prior to the war in Korea, containment primarily represented an effort to eliminate the political and economic conditions that spawned Communism. After Korea, containment consisted of setting up military frontiers behind which free societies would have an opportunity to develop. The United States committed itself to maintaining a huge permanent military force in peacetime, although given the crisis atmosphere prevailing during much of the Cold War, the traditional distinction between peace and war was blurred. The military-industrial complex expanded rapidly as a major component of the permanent war economy. Foreign aid was militarized, and the power of the presidency to conduct foreign policy was expanded. Although it failed to imprint itself indelibly on the national memory, the Korean War transformed the Cold War and influenced American foreign policy for decades.

THE COLD WAR CONSENSUS

From war's end to the spring of 1947, containment of Communism evolved as the major American foreign policy response to the rise of the Cold War. Beginning as a response to perceived Soviet threats to the security of small nations in Southern Europe, containment expanded to include the periphery of East and Southeast Asia in 1950 following the Maoist triumph in China, the U.S. decision to support the French in Indochina, and the outbreak of the Korean War.

As the world split between the former allies widened, most Americans came to support President Truman's "get tough" approach to the Soviet Union. Influenced by the media, Americans increasingly viewed the Soviet Union as the aggressive successor of the destroyed Third Reich. Communism was equated with Fascism, and Stalin was seen as a "Red" Hitler, a despotic ruler with megalomaniacal ambitions to dominate the new postwar world order. Soviet leaders were depicted as Marxist-Leninist zealots in the service of a master plan for imposing Communism on the world. The great lesson of World War II appeared to be that aggressors could not be appeased. As the Soviet leaders came to be seen as the new Nazis in the world, American leaders vowed to contain them, to prevent aggression and ensure that there would be no World War III.

Some Americans dissented from Truman's new foreign policy approach. They opposed the enormous costs of rearmament and foreign aid. They disliked the new internal security controls clamped onto American life, the complexities and tensions of great power rivalries, and the domination of public life by foreign policy issues. Some idealistic Americans did not relish having to support reactionary regimes just because they appeared to be threatened by Communism. Liberals such as Henry A. Wallace and conservatives such as Senator Robert Taft of Ohio were articulate critics of the Truman Doctrine, the Marshall Plan, and NATO.

But the dramatic events of the early Cold War years—the Soviet takeover of Eastern Europe, Soviet pressures on Turkey, the civil war in Greece, the Communist coup in Czechoslovakia, the Berlin Blockade, Soviet acquisition of nuclear weapons, the "fall" of China, the war in Vietnam and the Korean War—collectively worked on the American public consciousness to create a consensus supporting the Truman administration's policy of containment. During World War II, cooperation with the Soviets had been a strategic necessity. By 1947, the world had changed dramatically. A revolution in world affairs brought about by World War II necessitated a revolution in U.S. attitudes and approaches to foreign policy. Containing the expansionist tendencies of the Soviet Union everywhere in the world had become the new American geopolitical imperative.

Despite continuing criticism from both the Left and the Right, a bipartisan consensus in support of the main direction of U.S. foreign policy had emerged in this country by 1947. There was broad agreement spanning all but the fringes of the political spectrum that the major objective of American foreign policy would be the containment of Communism. The American bipartisan foreign policy consensus in support of the containment of Communism would remain intact until the Vietnam War cracked it during the late 1960s and provoked the first serious debates over American foreign policy goals in nearly twenty years.

BRIEF BIBLIOGRAPHIC ESSAY

Dean Acheson's *Present at the Creation* is a superb account of the origins of the Cold War by a former high State Department official who was one of the principal architects of U.S. Cold War foreign policy. Stephen Ambrose's *Rise to Globalism: American Foreign Policy, 1938–1980* contains an excellent account of the origins of the Cold War. Another good study of the genesis of the Cold War is John L. Gaddis's *The United States and the Origins of the Cold War.* Gaddis, America's most eminent diplomatic historian, has recently written an important new study of the origins of the Cold War, *Now We Know: Rethinking Cold War History.* The book, based on materials recently accessed in Soviet archives, makes a convincing case that Stalin is primarily responsible for provoking the Cold War. See also Daniel Yergen's *A Shattered Peace: The Origins of the Cold War and the National Security State.* Walter LaFeber's *America, Russia, and the Cold War* is a classic account of the Cold War conflict between the United States and the Soviet Union. A fine, recent, interpretive study of the Cold War is Thomas J. McCormick's *America's Half-Century: United States Foreign Policy in the Cold War.* Another magisterial recent account of the Cold War is Melvyn Leffler's *A Preponderance of Power.* Problems in Germany that were the major causes of the Cold War are carefully analyzed in John Gimbel's *The American Occupation of Germany: Politics and the Military, 1945–1949.* Thomas Parrish's *Berlin in the*

Balance, 1945–1949: The Blockade, the Airlift, the First Major Battle of the Cold War is an excellent recent study of the first major U.S.–USSR confrontation of the evolving Cold War. John Gimbel's *The Origins of the Marshall Plan* and Robert E. Osgood's *NATO: Entangling Alliance* are two important studies of major American postwar foreign policy initiatives in Europe. Akira Iriye's *The Cold War in Asia* is a good account. See also Michael Schaller's *The American Occupation of Japan: The Origins of the Cold War in Asia.* Another fine study of the origins of the Cold War in Asia is Robert M. Blum's *Drawing the Line.* The best short history of the Korean War is Burton I. Kaufman's *The Korean War.*

WEB SITES

Readers interested in further study of the Cold War can start with `<http://www.dirs.educationworld.net/cat/17514/>`. It's a resource that includes a comprehensive survey of the Cold War, studies of its origins with hyperlinks to definitions of Cold War terminology, and links to Web sites covering documents and bibliography. `<http:www.askeric.org/Virtual/Lessons/crossroads/sec5/Unit_11L1R4.html>` is a document-based approach to the origins of the Cold War. It contains excerpts from primary source documents. An excellent analysis of the origins of the Cold War between the United States and the Soviet Union is `<http://www.mars.acnet.wnec.edu/~grempel/courses/wc2/lecture/coldwar.html>`. A uniquely valuable Web site is `<http://www.ecfs.org/projects/fieldston57/since40/units/unit1/supplements/html>`. It sets up a debate over the origins of the Cold War among the leading historians of the Cold War, journalists, and students.

3

Postwar America

As they emerged from the tumultuous experiences of World War II, most Americans believed that they were entering a new era, that postwar America would be a very different nation from the one that had gone to war on December 7, 1941. At the same time that they looked ahead to new opportunities and new experiences, Americans yearned for a return to the normal routines and rhythms of everyday life. They wanted to put the disruptions and dangers of the wartime crisis behind them. But for many Americans, the road back to normality in the years immediately after the war proved rocky. The immediate postwar years were dominated by hyperinflation, bitter strikes, continuing shortages of housing and consumer goods, fierce partisan political divisions, and racial conflict. Compounding the many problems inherent in adapting to the new postwar world, the Cold War struck home with a special fury: America was convulsed by a Second Red Scare and the rise of the politics of anti-Communism that reached intense levels during the Korean War.

POSTWAR POLITICS

Harry S Truman had come to the presidency on April 12, 1945, ill-prepared and nearly unknown. He had difficulties early in his presidency because of his inexperience and because he inherited an administration, many of whose members viewed him as an inferior successor to Roosevelt. Prominent New Dealers departed, and Truman replaced them with more conservative advisers recruited from the ranks of big business, corporate law firms, Wall Street brokerage houses, and the senior ranks of the military. Honest and able himself, Truman tolerated a crowd of political hacks who had followed him to Washington. Most of these camp followers belonged to the "Missouri gang," led by an obese politician, Harry Vaughn.

When the war ended, Truman's first major domestic issues involved demobilizing the armed forces and reconverting the war economy to peacetime production. The rush to disarm after the war was irresistible. The Armed Forces were quickly dismantled. When the Army and Navy could not bring servicemen home fast enough, they rioted overseas. A force that had numbered twelve million at its peak quickly shrank to 1.5 million, and the draft was canceled. As the Cold War heated up in 1946 and 1947, the United States had only a small arsenal of nuclear weapons with which to protect Europeans or Asians from Soviet expansion.

During his campaign for reelection in 1944, Roosevelt had promised the American people that after the war he would craft an economic bill of rights for all Americans, including jobs, decent housing, adequate health care, and a good education. Roosevelt's proposals convinced many of his liberal followers that the president planned to revive the New Deal reform tradition that had been placed on hold for the duration. Truman appeared to share his predecessor's reform commitments when he proposed to Congress in the fall of 1945 a sweeping program of social legislation. Truman called upon the legislators to enact a national housing program, to raise the minimum wage, to extend Social Security benefits, and to pass a full employment bill.

The proposed full employment bill was the centerpiece of Truman's reform package. It called for the federal government to assume responsibility for full employment by enhancing purchasing power and spending for public works. As the nation demobilized its military forces and shut down its war industries, most Americans shared a persistent fear that the American economy, no longer stimulated by war spending, would regress to massive unemployment and even depression. They feared that millions of suddenly released war workers and discharged veterans could not be absorbed by a peacetime economy.

But after making his bold proposals, Truman vacillated, allowing Congress to enact a measure in 1946 called the Employment Act. It called for "maximum employment" rather than full employment. It established the government's responsibility for maintaining prosperity without prescribing the means to achieve it. It was more a statement of principles than a program of action. The act's most significant reform was the creation of a Council of Economic Advisers (CEA) to provide policy recommendations to the president and to assist in long- range economic planning. Congress failed to enact any of Truman's other reform proposals.

With the creation of the economic council, the Truman administration and all subsequent U.S. presidencies, committed themselves to relying on economic theory and quantifiable measurements for direction. Economists became the nation's high priests. Henceforth, the starting point of every administration's economic policies would be growth: how to achieve it and for whose benefit. Generally, Democratic administrations focused on liberal demand-side economics and Republican administrations focused on conservative supply-side economics. Democratic presidencies generally used tax cuts to accelerate growth in order to expand the size of he middle classes and to eliminate poverty. Republican presidencies generally used tax cuts to promote growth in the private sector, undermine the welfare state, and limit the reach of government.

The economy shrank during the first year after the war, mainly because the government abruptly canceled $35 billion in war contracts. The gross domestic product (GDP) for 1946 was slightly smaller than for 1945, the last year of the war. Unemployment, which had vanished in wartime, rose to 4.5 percent in 1946. But the feared reversion to depression never happened; most war workers and veterans were absorbed into the postwar economy. Many factors accounted for the economy's unexpected resiliency. The GI Bill provided low-interest loans to help veterans buy homes, farms, and businesses. It granted billions of dollars of educational benefits, permitting millions of veterans, many with families, to attend colleges and trade schools. Tax cuts strengthened consumer purchasing power and stimulated business activity. Government also aided the business sector by transferring over $15 billion worth of government-owned plants to the private sector, adding some 20 percent to industrial capacity. Further, government spending, although much reduced from wartime levels, remained far higher than prewar levels. But the most important reason for the economy's transition from war to peace without recession or depression lay in an unforeseen powerful force. American consumers came out of the war with billions of dollars in savings and with long-frustrated desires to buy new clothes, homes, cars, radios, and appliances. Unleashed consumer spending kept factories humming and people working after the war ended, and it staved off recession or depression.

But unleashed consumer demand ignited hyperinflation as the economy was decontrolled. By early 1946, the Office of Price Administration had removed most rationing restrictions, but it had kept wage, price, and rent controls. Inflation soared. Desired goods like new cars and refrigerators remained scarce. Businessmen, farmers, and trade unionists demanded the removal of all remaining restrictions on their economic activity. A rash of strikes broke out in the auto, meat packing, electrical, and steel industries, idling productive capacity and delaying fulfillment of consumer demands. President Truman tried and failed to ensure a gradual, orderly phaseout of controls by restraining all interest groups.

In the spring of 1946, the bipartisan conservative coalition controlling Congress battled the President over extending the life of the OPA. Congress enacted a weak control measure that Truman vetoed, causing all controls to expire on July 1. There followed the worst surge of inflation since 1919. Congress, deluged with angry complaints, hastily passed another, even weaker bill, which Truman signed. Consumer prices continued to soar amidst the politics of confusion. Thereafter, the OPA lifted all remaining controls and faded away. The cost of living rose 20 percent in 1946, and acute shortages persisted.

LABOR TROUBLES

Organized labor had grown powerful during wartime. Union membership surpassed 15 million, as almost every major industry had been unionized. The CIO's political arm, the Political Action Committee (PAC), was committed to working with the liberal factions of the Democratic Party to institutionalize the welfare state in America. Some liberal labor leaders such as Walter Reuther, head of the United Auto Workers (UAW), and David Dubinski, leader of the International Ladies' Garment Workers' Union (ILGWU), hoped to forge new labor-management industrial partnerships in the postwar era: representatives from the unions and corporations would jointly determine workplace policies. But liberal labor aspirations soon foundered amidst economic dislocations and the more conservative postwar political climate. Trade unions found themselves on the defensive, trying to preserve wartime gains. Real industrial wages and consumer purchasing power fell during 1945 and 1946 because of skyrocketing inflation.

As runaway inflation degraded their incomes and purchasing power, frustrated workers went on strike. Waves of strikes swept through important industrial sectors. Over 200,000 General Motors workers walked off the job on November 20, 1945. They were soon joined by striking electrical and steel workers. During the first year after the war, over five million men and women went on strike, tying up most of the nation's major industries. Reflecting their primary concern with inflation that was eroding incomes and living standards, strikers' demands focused on pay increases and job security.

Many of these strikes lasted for months, as management resisted union demands and the workers refused to back down. Eventually most were settled on terms that resulted in significant pay increases for workers and substantial price increases for companies' products. Corporations passed their increased costs of production onto their customers, thereby retaining high profit margins but adding to the inflationary spiral. The settlement of the UAW strike against General Motors set the pattern for postwar industrial relations. After a bitter 113-day strike that hurt both sides, they agreed on a new contract, which granted workers substantial pay increases over the life of the contract and tied wage levels to increases in the cost of living. The new contract also strengthened job security for senior workers and contained more generous pension plans. In addition, the new agreements signaled that union leaders and management representatives in the postwar era would confine negotiations to the traditional issues of wages and hours, working conditions, fringe benefits, and job security. Union leaders quickly abandoned their social agenda for restructuring industrial relations or remaking society. Henceforth, they focused on "bread-and-butter" issues.

Strikes also threatened in railroads and coal, two primary industries. Walkouts in both of these industries could have paralyzed the U.S. economy. The railroad strike was averted, but not before the President had asked Congress to grant him authority to draft striking railroad workers into the Army. Congress refused. John L. Lewis took his coal miners off of the job in April 1946 over wage and pension fund disputes with mine owners. Industrial production dropped. Efforts to settle the strike failed. On May 21, with the nation's supplies of coal exhausted, President Truman ordered the federal government to seize the mines. The coal mines were administered by Julius Krug, Secretary of the Interior, who promptly began negotiations with Lewis. They reached an agreement within two weeks, and the coal strike ended. The mines were returned to their owners. Truman's bold actions hurt him politically; he and his party lost support among resentful workers, which affected the upcoming elections.

THE ELECTION OF 1946

As the 1946 midterm elections approached, Truman and his party faced serious political trouble. The Democrats had split into their Northern and Southern wings, with Southern conservative Democrats often joining Northern Republicans to block liberal measures. Many liberal Democrats still yearned for Roosevelt, dismissing Truman as an inept successor. Truman and his party were damned both for shortages and for skyrocketing prices. Organized labor, sullen over Truman's threat to draft strikers, made only token efforts to support the Democrats.

Republican congressional candidates attacked the failures of Truman's price control program. They jeered "to err is Truman." When beef disappeared from meat markets, housewives rioted. When beef was back on the shelf a week later, the women were shocked to discover that prices had doubled. "Had enough?" chorused Republicans. On the eve of the elections, polls showed that Truman's popularity had dropped to 32 percent.

The election results mirrored the popular mood. Republicans scored substantial victories, winning control of the new House of Representatives by 246 to 188, and they would hold a 51 to 45 majority in the new Senate. For the first time since before the Great Depression, the

Republicans won control of both houses of Congress. Many working-class voters deserted the Democrats, shattering the labor bloc that had been solidly Democratic since 1932. The election results also confirmed the new conservative mood of the electorate and doomed liberal hopes for a revival of the New Deal spirit or the enactment of social reforms in the postwar era.

THE 80TH CONGRESS

A lot of new faces appeared in Washington as members of the 80th Congress. Many were war veterans, representing a new generation of politicians that had come of age. This new breed of politico tended to be less idealistic, less liberal, and more pragmatic in its approach to public policy. One congressional rookie, Republican Richard Nixon, hailed from Southern California. Another, Democrat newcomer, John F. Kennedy, represented a working-class district of south-side Boston. A conservative Republican from Wisconsin, Joseph McCarthy, went to the Senate. McCarthy would soon propel himself into the center of the Communists-in-government controversy that rocked Washington and made his name a household word.

So long out of power, the Republicans set out to reassert the authority of Congress and to trim the executive branch. They proposed the Twenty-Second Amendment, which limited future presidents to two elected terms. They wanted to ensure there would be no more presidential reigns such as Franklin Roosevelt's. The 80th Congress tore to shreds Truman's liberal domestic program to extend the welfare state and rejected all of his important proposals. Although it did not abolish basic New Deal programs, the 80th Congress certainly trimmed its edges.

Senator Robert Taft of Ohio, son of a former president and the intellectual leader of the GOP, spearheaded the Republican assault on the New Deal. Taft, who had been in the Senate since 1938, hoped to create a record that would vault him into the White House one day. Taft believed that the voters had given the Republicans a mandate to curtail the New Deal. He believed that most Americans wanted lower taxes, less governmental interference in business, and curbs on the power of organized labor. Twice in 1947, Congress enacted tax cuts. Truman vetoed both measures. A third tax cut was passed over his veto in 1948.

In 1947, Taft led the fight to enact a measure, passed over Truman's veto, modifying the National Labor Relations Act (Wagner Act), the nation's basic labor law and centerpiece of the Second New Deal. The new law, the Labor Management Relations Act, popularly called the Taft-Hartley Act, made many changes in the Wagner Act. It extended the concept of "unfair labor practices," previously confined to management, to unions. Among forbidden union practices were the closed shop, which required a worker to join a union before working. It required unions to file annual financial statements with the Department of Labor. Cold War concerns could be seen in the requirement that all union officials file affidavits showing that they were not members of the Communist Party or any other subversive organization. It prohibited union contributions to national political campaigns, and it forbade strikes by federal employees. In cases of strikes that "affected the national welfare," the Taft-Hartley Act empowered the attorney general to seek a court injunction ordering an eighty-day delay in the strike. During this eighty-day "cooling-off period," federal mediators would try to settle the conflict. If, after eighty days, union members rejected the mediator's final offer, the strike could occur. One section of the new law, Section 14(b), permitted states to legalize the open shop, making union membership voluntary.

Figure 3.1   Class of 1946. A group of freshman Congressmen introduces themselves in January 1947. Standing to the right rear of this gathering of rookies are two future presidents, John F. Kennedy and Richard M. Nixon.
Source: National Archives.

Organized labor vigorously attacked the Taft-Hartley Act. William Green, head of the AFL, charged that the bill was forged "in a spirit of vindictiveness against unions." Many workers condemned what they called the "slave labor law." President Truman claimed that it was both unworkable and unfair. In addition to general denunciations, labor leaders attacked particular provisions of the new law, such as the mandatory eighty-day strike delay feature. For years, repeal of the Taft-Hartley Act was the major political goal of organized labor.

The Taft-Hartley Act was the most important social legislation enacted during Truman's presidency. It did not undermine the basic strength of American trade unions that conservatives hoped and liberals feared would happen. The Communist registration requirement was nullified by the Supreme Court. Union membership increased from 15 million at the time of passage to 17 million five years later. During the 1950s, collective bargaining between teams of labor and management representatives generated wage increases and improved fringe benefits that made American industrial workers members of the most affluent working class ever. Later Congresses never repealed the Taft-Hartley law, nor even amended any of its major provisions.

WOMEN

The postwar era proved disappointing to millions of women who had hoped to consolidate and build upon their wartime achievements in the nation's workforce. Women were subjected to tremendous pressures from industry, government, and influential media to surrender their well-paying jobs and to return to their "rightful" places in the homes of America. Ads placed in mass circulation magazines implied that any woman who resisted the propaganda campaigns aimed at driving her out of the workplace and back to the kitchen was being selfish, greedy, and a poor wife and mother as well.

As factories converted from war to peacetime production, women by the hundreds of thousands were fired. Under the provisions of the Selective Service Act, returning veterans had priority over civilian war workers in competition for factory jobs. In the auto industry, which during the war years made jeeps, army trucks, and tanks, women had constituted 25 percent of the workforce in 1944. A year after the war, as automakers began producing new cars for civilian consumers for the first time since 1942, only 7 percent of auto workers were women. Sometimes, older married women workers ran afoul of newly imposed, or reimposed, age requirements or restrictions on the hiring of married women. In the immediate postwar years, as women were swept out of jobs in the mass production industries, the percentage of women members in many industrial unions also declined sharply.

Overall, female employment did not decline in the postwar years. By 1950, women made up 32 percent of the workforce, compared to 27 percent at war's end. But women had been forced out of high-paying jobs in manufacturing to resume work in occupations traditionally reserved for women such as waitresses, maids, and service jobs. Women welders and riveters now washed dishes and scrubbed floors for a lot less money. Women's median earnings had reached 66 percent of what men were paid in wartime manufacturing jobs. Studies in the postwar era showed women earning 53 percent of what men earned for comparable work. Although more women than ever before were working in the postwar era, most found themselves back in low-paying jobs, with little possibility of promotion.

Professional opportunities for middle-class women also deteriorated in postwar America. The number of women doctors, lawyers, and college professors declined. Medical schools and law schools imposed quotas on women's admissions, usually in the 5 to 10 percent range. The Equal Rights Amendment, which had been introduced in every congressional session since the 1920s, did not come close to garnering enough votes for passage. Prominent women leaders continued to oppose the amendment on the grounds that retaining laws providing special protections for women in the workforce was more important than establishing a constitutional principle of equal rights. Organized feminism did not exist in postwar America; no one challenged traditional definitions of masculinity and femininity. Neither the Truman administration nor any government agency showed the slightest concern about declining opportunities for women in the job markets. Women's issues were simply not part of the public discourse in the postwar era.

CIVIL RIGHTS

African Americans emerged from the war years with an enhanced pride in themselves. Despite their encounters with racism, black soldiers had fought well; over 1 million African-American men and women had worked in war industries to produce the ships, tanks, and guns that had enabled the Allied forces to triumph over their Axis foes. African-American leaders sensed a new spirit of militancy in the land. Returning veterans would lead the assault on Jim Crow in the South; they would fight for full citizenship and equal access to housing, jobs, and schools.

Blacks achieved some successes in the postwar years. The number of African Americans eligible to vote rose slightly in some Southern states. Attorneys from the NAACP pushed court cases that chipped away at the judicial foundations of segregation. But everywhere in the post-war South, black insurgents encountered massive, and often violent, resistance to change. No Southern white political leader voiced any support for African American aspirations; most loudly asserted their unstinting support of black disfranchisement and systemic segregation, a kind of American apartheid that kept African Americans locked in separate and unequal statuses.

Sometimes violence and intimidation were employed by Southern whites determined to confine African Americans to traditional subservient roles, but often more subtle methods worked just as effectively. Ninety-five percent of blacks in the South worked for white people. African Americans brave enough to show up on the voting rolls risked losing jobs, having insurance policies canceled, being evicted from rented farms or businesses, or having lines of credit revoked. Literacy requirements for voting, discriminatorily applied, meant that black college graduates sometimes failed to qualify for the vote, while illiterate whites happily signed on. Poll taxes continued to disqualify masses of poor Southern African Americans (and poor whites and Hispanic Americans) from the ballot.

A dramatic breakthrough occurred in 1947, when Branch Rickey, the general manager of the Brooklyn Dodgers, broke the color line of major league baseball by adding a gifted black athlete, Jackie Robinson, to his team's roster. Robinson quickly became an all-star player and future hall of famer on a team that won six National League pennants in the next ten years. His success paved the way for other gifted African American athletes, previously confined to segregated black leagues, to play major league ball, including Larry Doby, Henry (Hank) Aaron, and the legendary Satchel Paige.

The Cold War brought additional pressure for integrating African Americans and other nonwhite minorities into the mainstream of American life. The United States was now seeking the support of African and Asian nations whose leaders resented American mistreatment of its racial minorities. Jim Crow laws also made the United States vulnerable to Soviet propaganda that sought to highlight the inequities of American democracy in order to win influence among Third World people.

Truman was the first modern president to promote civil rights causes. His involvement came from both moral and political considerations. He passionately felt a strong need for justice for African Americans. He also was aware of the growing importance of the black vote in Northern cities, and he wanted to offset efforts by Republicans to regain African American support that they had enjoyed before the Great Depression. Truman had supported the creation of the Fair Employment Practices Commission (FEPC) in 1941, and he wanted to extend it after the war, but Congress refused to renew it.

Responding to the concerns of African-American leaders, Truman created a Committee on Civil Rights in December 1946. The committee issued a report entitled "To Secure These Rights," in which it recommended a series of actions to eliminate racial inequality in America. Among its recommendations were: the creation of a civil rights division within the Justice Department, the creation of a Commission on Civil Rights, the abolition of the poll tax,

Figure 3.2   Jackie Robinson in action during a World Series with the New York Yankees. Robinson was the first African American to play major league baseball in modern times.   *Source:* CORBIS.

the desegregation of all government agencies, the desegregation of the Armed Forces, and the enactment of a permanent FEPC. In a special message to Congress, Truman endorsed the committee's recommendations. Black leaders, delighted by Truman's statements, lavishly praised him.

But the President's rhetorical support for civil rights did not produce any positive legislative results. Congress rejected all of the committee's proposals, Republicans generally ignored them, and Southern Democrats denounced them. The Justice Department did not investigate Southern efforts to prevent African Americans from registering to vote, although Justice Department attorneys began to submit friends-of-the-court briefs on behalf of civil rights cases involving public schools and housing. Truman became the first president ever to address a civil rights organization when he spoke at an NAACP convention in 1948.

In February 1948, the president made an important contribution to the cause of racial equality when he issued an executive order barring discrimination in all federal agencies. In July of that year, Truman also ordered the desegregation of the Armed Forces. At first progress was slow in desegregating the military, particularly the Army, which had more African Americans than the other branches of military service. Segregation persisted in the Army until the Korean

War. Integration of the Army occurred during that conflict when Army officers discovered that African-American soldiers fought more effectively in integrated units than in segregated ones. It was Truman's most important civil rights victory. Within a few years, the Army became the most integrated American institution, and many African Americans found opportunities in the military during the 1950s and 1960s that were not available to them in civilian life. Truman played a major role in bringing civil rights issues to the center of the American political stage; it was his greatest domestic political achievement.

THE ELECTION OF 1948

As the 1948 election approached, Truman appeared to have no chance for reelection. At times he was discouraged by his inability to lead the country and by his low ratings in the polls. In the fall of 1947, he had even sent a member of his staff to talk to General Eisenhower, then Army Chief of Staff, to see if Ike might be interested in the Democratic nomination for 1948. Eisenhower was not. Truman then decided to seek reelection. At the Democratic Convention, held in Philadelphia in July, delegates, convinced that Truman could not win, tried to promote a boom for Eisenhower; it fizzled. Disappointed Democrats then held up signs that read, "I'm just mild about Harry."

To add to his political woes, the Democratic Party was fragmenting. Factions formed on the Left and on the Right. At the convention, Northern liberals forced the adoption of a strong civil rights plank over the furious objections of Southern leaders. Fearing a party rupture, Truman's supporters had tried to soften the language of the civil rights plank. But when it passed unsoftened, Truman boldly endorsed it and praised the convention for adopting it.

With its adoption, delegates from Mississippi and Alabama marched out in protest. These renegade Southerners later formed their own party, the States' Rights, or "Dixiecrat" Party. At their convention, delegates from thirteen states nominated South Carolina Governor J. Strom Thurmond as their candidate for president. The "Dixiecrats" did not bother to craft a platform. They had a single issue: "We stand for the segregation of the races . . ." These Southern defections appeared to remove any remaining Democratic hopes for success. The Solid South, a Democratic stronghold since the end of Reconstruction, had vanished.

The left wing of the Democratic Party also threatened to split off. Back in 1946, Truman had fired his Secretary of Commerce Henry Wallace for publicly criticizing his "get tough" foreign policy toward the Soviet Union. In 1948, Wallace became the presidential candidate of a leftist third party, the Progressive Party. Many New Dealers considered Wallace, whom Truman had replaced as Roosevelt's vice president in 1944, the true heir to the Roosevelt legacy and supported his candidacy. Polls taken that summer showed that Wallace could cost Truman several Northern industrial states. It appeared that the remnants of his party had given Truman a worthless nomination. But the gutsy leader accepted their unenthusiastic endorsement in a fighting spirit. He told them, "I will win this election and make those Republicans like it—don't you forget that." Few believed him.

The confident Republicans, eager to regain the White House after a sixteen-year Democratic hold on the presidency, again nominated New York Governor Thomas E. Dewey and adopted a moderate program. Dewey, soundly beaten by Roosevelt in 1944, was determined to avenge that defeat this time around. Polls taken at the outset of the electoral campaign in September showed Dewey running far ahead of Truman. It appeared that Truman might get only about one-third of the popular vote, and that Dewey could coast to an easy landslide victory. Dewey opted for a safe political strategy to carry him to the executive office. He spoke in platitudes and generalities, raised no controversial issues, and never mentioned his opponent by name. Dewey's manner conveyed an air of absolute confidence that he would soon be president of the United States.

But Truman, aided by former Roosevelt adviser James Rowe, had devised an electoral strategy that he believed could win. Truman would stress his adherence to the New Deal tradition, advocating an advanced program of liberal reform to appeal to urban voters, unionized workers, and minorities. As soon as he got the nomination, he called the 80th Congress into special session and reintroduced all of his reform programs that Congress had failed to pass in regular sessions. Again, Congress rejected them. This bold move set the tone for the campaign.

Truman took off on a transcontinental train tour in search of an electorate. He traveled over 32,000 miles and made hundreds of speeches, talking directly to about 12 million people. He repeatedly blasted what he called the "do nothing, good for nothing" 80th Congress, blaming all of the ills of the nation on the Republican-controlled legislature. He called the Republicans "gluttons of privilege" who would destroy the New Deal if elected. He depicted Dewey as Hoover redux and insisted that a Republican administration would bring back the grim days of the Great Depression. Speaking in an aggressive, choppy style, he delighted his crowds: "Give 'em hell, Harry!" they would yell. "I'm doin' it!" Truman would yell back.

Despite his strenuous grass-roots campaign, Truman apparently faced certain defeat. As the election date neared, he continued to trail badly in the polls. Dewey was far ahead, and Wallace's support had dwindled to a few percentage points. Two weeks before the election, fifty political experts unanimously predicted that Dewey would win; most predicted that Dewey would score a landslide victory. Pollsters stopped interviewing a week before the election, assuming that Dewey already had it wrapped up.

On Election Day, Truman pulled off the biggest upset in American political history. He beat Dewey in the popular vote, 24.2 million to 22 million, and 303 to 189 in the electoral college. His party also regained control of Congress by a 54 to 42 margin in the Senate and a whopping 263 to 171 margin in the House. It was a significant victory for the party as well as for the man at the top of the ticket. Wallace's campaign fizzled. Most liberals ended up voting for Truman. The Dixiecrats carried only four Deep South states, enabling Truman and the Democrats to win most of the South.

How could Truman score such a surprising victory? How could the experts all be wrong? Republican complacency and overconfidence helped. Many Republicans, assuming victory, did not bother to vote. Truman's spirited, grassroots campaign effort was a factor, but mainly, Truman won because he was able to hold together enough of the old New Deal coalition of labor, Northern liberals, blacks, and farmers to win. Black voters provided Truman with his margin of victory in key states such as California, Ohio, and Illinois. Many independent voters opted for Truman, blaming an obstructionist Republican-controlled Congress rather than the President for the legislative gridlock. Many Southern whites, although offended by Truman's advocacy of

**Figure 3.3   How sweet is was! A jubilant Harry Truman holds up a
Republican paper whose prediction of victory for Thomas Dewey was to
say the least a bit premature.**   *Source:* St. Louis Mercantile Library. Used
with permission.

civil rights, nevertheless voted for Truman out of party loyalty and perhaps because they did not
want to waste their votes on a protest candidate who had no chance to win. A trend toward Truman had surfaced in the final week of the campaign, but the pollsters missed it, since they had
already quit taking opinion samples.

Truman successfully pinned an anti-New Deal label on the Republicans and identified
them with Depression memories. He effectively identified the Progressives with Communism
and support for the Soviet Union at a time of rising Cold War tensions. A commentator suggested that "Roosevelt had won a fifth term." Ironically, the splits within his party worked to
Truman's advantage. They sheared off the Democratic Left and Right and allowed Truman to
concentrate on the political center, where most of the votes were.

There was a larger significance to the 1948 election. It was a transitional election during
which American liberalism was reconfigured. Party-based voting declined and issue-based voting increased. Two relatively new issues became prominent in the election, as Truman embraced
both civil rights and anti-Communism. With Truman's victory in 1948, the South and The Left
both shrank in importance to the Democrats in national elections. The party gravitated from the
Left toward the Center. Henceforth, most Democratic Party leaders would abandon New Deal
liberalism and embrace a more Centrist variety.

THE FAIR DEAL

In the fall of 1945, President Truman had sent an ambitious package of legislative proposals to Congress, only to see them shunted aside during the political scrambling over decontrol and inflation. Now president in his own right, his January 1949 program began: "Every segment of our population and every individual has a right to expect from our government a fair deal." Truman's Fair Deal proposals included price controls, tax increases, improving civil rights, expanding public housing, raising the minimum wage, expanding Social Security, repealing the Taft-Hartley law, supporting farm prices, providing federal aid to education, and implementing national health insurance.

The 81st Congress enacted only a small portion of the Fair Deal. They rejected his proposals for tax hikes and price controls; refused to repeal the Taft-Hartley law; and refused to implement his agricultural program embodied in Secretary of Agriculture Charles F. Brannan's plan for high fixed supports for commodity prices. Truman's civil rights proposals were thwarted by the threat of a Southern filibuster in the Senate. Federal aid to education was opposed by the Catholic Church for not including funds for parochial schools. Truman's controversial proposal for compulsory health insurance provoked opposition from the American Medical Association (AMA), a powerful doctor's lobby that defeated what it called "socialized medicine."

Nevertheless, the president succeeded in getting some Fair Deal measures passed during his second term, although most of the measures enacted only extended existing programs. The minimum wage was raised from forty cents to seventy-five cents an hour. Social Security coverage was extended to 10.5 million additional workers, and benefits were increased on an average of 77 percent. The most important Fair Deal measure to pass in 1949, with the help of Senator Taft, was the National Housing Act, which provided funds for slum clearance and for the construction of 810,000 units of low income housing over a period of six years.

Truman's efforts to expand the boundaries of the welfare state were defeated by a combination of lobbyists, the congressional bipartisan conservative coalition, an apathetic citizenry, and his own ineffective leadership. But he succeeded in updating and expanding many existing programs, and Truman thereby helped assimilate the New Deal into the vital center of American life. The Fair Deal was a centrist variant of liberal reformism that presaged the New Frontier and Great Society reforms of the 1960s.

During the midterm elections of 1950, the Republicans picked up twenty-eight seats in the House and gained five senators. Although still nominally controlled by the Democrats, the 82nd Congress saw the bipartisan conservative bloc grow more powerful than it had been in the 81st. The Fair Deal lost momentum, and no new social legislation of any consequence was enacted in 1951 or in 1952. Social reform was submerged by Cold War concerns and growing public complacency about domestic institutions. Truman spent much of the last two years of his presidency focused on foreign policy and the Korean War. He also was on the defensive much of the time, trying to defend his floundering government against mounting Republican charges that his administration had been infiltrated by Communists and was riddled with corruption.

Republican charges that corruption was rampant in the Truman administration stemmed from irregularities unearthed in several government agencies that involved minor officials. The "mess in Washington" never reached Truman personally, but one of the accused "influence peddlers" turned out to be Harry Vaughn, the head of the notorious Missouri gang and military aide to the president. Vaughn had been given a home freezer allegedly for using his influence on behalf of clients who had business with federal agencies. The wife of an official with the Reconstruction Finance Corporation (RFC), which loaned money to banks and insurance companies, was given a mink coat. The coat was a gift from an executive with a company that borrowed funds from the RFC on very favorable terms. Scandals in the Internal Revenue Service (IRS) forced several officials to resign from their positions and led to an administrative overhaul of the agency.

It may have been true that the Truman presidency was the most corrupt since Harding's, but the corruption infesting Truman's administration appeared to be confined to a handful of low-level officials at the periphery of power and influence. Nevertheless, when the wrongdoing was exposed, the American people were shocked and angry. Republicans got a lot of partisan political mileage out of the Truman scandals. In the wake of these damaging exposés, public support for the Truman administration, never very high, plummeted to historic lows. One Gallup Poll gave Truman an approval rating of only 23 percent, the lowest rating ever given to a sitting president. Truman's approval rating was even lower than Richard Nixon's had been on the eve of his forced resignation from office, and it was much lower than Bill Clinton's had been during his impeachment trial.

COLD WAR AT HOME

As a result of the growing hostility between the United States and the Soviet Union, frustrations, tensions, and anxieties gripped the American people. The Cold War hit home in early 1950, when millions of Americans were alarmed by charges that Communists had infiltrated their government and many other institutions. Fears of internal threats posed by Communists long preceded the Cold War era. They first surfaced in the decade of the 1850s and flared periodically during times of social tension and political upheaval. Following World War I, jittery Americans worried that a Bolshevik-style uprising would occur in America. The Red Scare of 1919 and 1920 had culminated in government raids on the homes and meeting places of suspected revolutionaries, followed by mass deportations of radical aliens. In 1938, Southern opponents of New Deal agricultural policies established the House Committee on Un-American Activities (HUAC), chaired by Martin Dies. Dies and his colleagues accused New Deal farm officials of marching to Moscow's beat. In 1940, Congress enacted the Smith Act, which made it a federal crime for anyone to advocate the overthrow of the government.

Neither the Palmer raids nor HUAC's accusations of the late 1930s were justified, but fears of Communist subversion arising after 1945 had a basis in reality. During the late 1930s and early 1940s, U. S. government security procedures had been lax. Communists had infiltrated virtually all important federal agencies, hundreds of whom spied for the Soviets. Unfortunately, during this Second Red Scare, opportunistic politicians exploited the popular fear of Communism to enhance their power. They exaggerated the Communist menace, harmed innocent people, confused and divided Americans, and threatened basic political freedoms.

The drive to root Communists out of government agencies began in 1945. The Office of Strategic Services (OSS), a wartime intelligence agency, discovered that some of its classified documents had been delivered to Soviet agents. In February 1946, a Canadian investigating commission exposed the operation of Soviet spy rings within Canada and the United States that had given the Soviets military and atomic secrets. Investigators documented subversion that had occurred during the war.

These spy revelations, coming at a time when United States–Soviet relations were deteriorating, energized Washington. President Truman issued an executive order on March 21, 1947, establishing a loyalty program for federal employees. Truman also directed the Attorney General to publish a list of ninety organizations that were considered disloyal to the United States. Truman's efforts resulted in 2,900 resignations and 379 dismissals from various federal agencies. Although federal investigators found no spies, the Truman loyalty program heightened rather than calmed public fears of subversion.

Congress also actively hunted subversives. In October 1947, HUAC, with rookie Congressman Richard Nixon as its junior member, launched a sensational two-week-long investigation of Hollywood to see whether the film industry had been subverted by Reds. The actor Ronald Reagan, president of the Screen Actors Guild (SAG), appeared before the committee to defend the loyalty of the film industry. For anyone familiar with the ways of Hollywood, the notion that Communist party members had inserted Communist propaganda into movies that brainwashed the children of America as they sat innocently in their corner neighbor theaters munching popcorn on Saturday afternoons was absurd. No doubt, a few Communists and fellow travelers were working in Hollywood during the 1940s, but they worked for studio heads, not for Moscow. As writer Murray Kempton observed, it was Hollywood that corrupted the Communists, not vice versa.

Nevertheless, HUAC's investigation of the movie colony made for great political theater, and it generated tremendous national attention. Although they found little evidence of celluloid Communism, HUAC subpoenaed a group of ten writers, directors, and actors who were or had been members of the Communist Party USA. They refused to answer any questions about their political beliefs and lectured committee members about civil liberties. Such political grandstanding proved to be poor tactics; the "Hollywood Ten's" confrontational tactics confirmed committee suspicions that they were disciplined Stalinists determined to disseminate agitprop through the movies. The studio heads, already worried about dropping box office receipts for their films, panicked. They considered the Congressional investigation and the performance of the Hollywood Ten a public relations disaster. The moguls blacklisted the ten radicals. No studios would hire them until they agreed to cooperate with HUAC. They refused, and all went to jail for contempt of Congress.

During the early 1950s, the blacklist grew dramatically and extended to Broadway, radio, and television. For several years, government investigators, private vigilante groups, and political conservatives working within the entertainment industry continually accused various actors, writers, and directors of past membership in the Communist Party or in Communist front organizations. Fearing box-office disaster, loss of advertising revenue, and drops in audience ratings, Broadway producers and network executives were no more willing than the film bosses had been to resist political pressures and protect the accused performers.

Those who were accused came under tremendous pressures to repudiate their radical pasts. They confronted a Hobson's choice: They could defy the inquisitors and risk being blacklisted, or they could cooperate with the authorities by recanting their radical beliefs and naming names, that is, providing investigators with the names of individuals they had known from party or front activities. Some defied the committee and were blacklisted. Others such as Elia Kazan and Burl Ives named names and continued to work in the entertainment business. Altogether, about 250 people were blacklisted; many of these blacklistees never worked again in show business.

In the aftermath of Truman's loyalty program and HUAC's Hollywood investigations, a powerful fear of anyone thought to be disloyal spread across the land. In such a paranoid atmosphere, teachers and professors were fired for expressing dissenting views. Books were removed from library shelves. PTA leaders were attacked as subversives. The Boy Scouts and Campfire Girls came under suspicion for their advocacy of world peace and understanding. Liberal ministers were harassed. School districts required teachers and administrators to sign loyalty oaths. Many states enacted legislation denying public employment to Communists or to anyone affiliated with any organization that showed up on the Attorney General's list.

Those who waged the domestic Cold War in the name of national security often undermined the democratic rights and intellectual freedoms for whose sake the United States waged the Cold War against the Soviet Union. The idea that a free society, tolerant of wide-ranging discussions and rigorous criticisms of American institutions, might be the best defense against the spread of Communism in the United States, appeared to be an alien notion to those engaged in the urgent quest for internal security. During the early 1950s, to many an enthusiastic Red hunter of that era, it had become necessary to destroy freedom in order to save it.

The domestic Cold War also engulfed the trade union movement. Within the ranks of the CIO, Communist Party members or individuals supportive of the Communist Party program held leadership positions in many of the affiliated unions. Often these Communist labor leaders had been skilled organizers who had helped build the CIO unions. The Communists had risen to positions of power within the ranks of labor because they were committed trade unionists. Most of the rank-and-file members of these Communist-led unions were either indifferent or hostile to Communism. In 1948, Philip Murray, head of the CIO, fearing his organization's vulnerability to attack by powerful anti-union forces for having Communist leaders, began to purge the CIO of its Communist influences. Within a year, eleven unions had been expelled from the CIO. CIO membership fell from 5.2 million to about 3.7 million.

In 1949, the Truman administration went after the leadership of the American Communist Party. The Justice Department put the top leaders of the party on trial for violating the Smith Act. They were convicted, and the Supreme Court upheld the verdicts. After the Court had sustained the convictions of the top leaders, the Justice Department prosecuted dozens of lesser figures within the Communist movement over the next several years.

Truman's loyalty program did not quiet popular fears of Communist subversion, nor did it prevent Republicans from exploiting the Communists-in-government issue. One event severely damaged the reputation of the Truman administration. In 1949, after the most famous political trial in American history, Alger Hiss was ostensibly convicted of perjury, but in the public mind, he had been convicted for having been a Communist spy.

Hiss, allegedly a participant in a Soviet espionage ring during the late 1930s, had risen to become an assistant secretary of state. He had been an adviser at Yalta and had chaired the founding sessions of the United Nations in San Francisco. He left the State Department in 1947 to become director of the prestigious Carnegie Endowment for International Peace. Outwardly,

Hiss's public career had been that of a model New Deal bureaucrat. However, prior to leaving government service, he had already come under suspicion.

Hiss's downfall came in 1948, when Whittaker Chambers, a confessed former courier in the same spy ring to which Hiss allegedly had belonged, appeared before HUAC. In a closed session, he accused Hiss of having been a Communist spy while working for the State Department in 1937 and 1938. Chambers offered no evidence to substantiate his charges. In a later closed HUAC session, Hiss confronted Chambers and threatened him with a libel suit if he dared make his accusations public. Chambers appeared on a television show *Face the Nation* and repeated his charge that Hiss was a former Communist spy. Hiss denied the charge and filed his libel suit. Many prominent public figures, including Secretary of State Dean Acheson, backed Hiss and dismissed the charges against him. Among HUAC members, only Richard Nixon, who believed that Hiss was lying, initially backed Chambers's unsubstantiated charges.

To defend himself against Hiss's libel suit, Chambers produced evidence: microfilm copies of sixty-five classified State Department documents, which Chambers claimed Hiss had passed to him in 1937 and 1938 to give to Soviet agents. A federal grand jury could only indict Hiss for perjury, because the statute of limitations on espionage had expired. Hiss was tried twice, his first trial having ended with a hung jury. During the second trial, the prosecution established that many of the documents had been copied in Hiss's handwriting and others had been typed on a typewriter that had belonged to Hiss at the time. Hiss was convicted and sentenced to five years in prison for perjury.

Hiss was HUAC's greatest catch and vaulted Richard Nixon into national prominence. Many liberals believed that Hiss was innocent, that he had been framed by a conspiracy of vindictive conservative political forces. But the Hiss conviction, more than any other event of the domestic Cold War, convinced millions of Americans that there was truth to the oft-made Republican charges that Roosevelt and Truman had not been sufficiently alert to the dangers of Communist espionage. Americans worried about other undetected Communist agents who might still be working at the State Department and other government agencies.

Other events shook the Truman administration. In March 1949, the FBI caught Judith Coplon, a Justice Department employee, passing information to a Soviet agent. In September 1949, the Soviets exploded an atomic device, ending the American nuclear monopoly. A month after this shock came the Communist victory in China. The stage was set for the emergence of a demagogue: Widespread fear of a hidden enemy thought to be everywhere, and frustration that victory in the Second World War had brought not eternal peace but only the tensions and setbacks of the Cold War, and the nightmare possibility of a nuclear holocaust.

Enter Senator Joseph McCarthy. In 1950, casting about for an issue that might get him reelected, he decided to see if he could get any political mileage out of the Communists-in-government issue. He had previously used the issue effectively in Wisconsin political battles. McCarthy was by no means the only politician who practiced the politics of anti-Communism, in fact, he was something of a latecomer to the issue. But McCarthy quickly became the political star of the domestic Cold War, and he retained his top billing until his Senate colleagues destroyed him politically in 1954.

McCarthy opened his anti-Communist campaign on February 9, 1950, in Wheeling, West Virginia. He told the Ladies' Republican Club of Wheeling that the United States found itself in

Figure 3.4   The Red Scare of the late 1940s gave Richard Nixon, an obscure young Congressman from California, his chance to become nationally prominent. Here he is shown with Robert Stripling, chief investigator for the House Committee on Un-American Activities, examining some of the microfilm evidence that led to Alger Hiss's perjury convictions. *Source:* Bettmann Archive.

a weak position in the Cold War because of the actions of disloyal officials in the State Department. Holding up a piece of paper in his right hand, he told his fascinated audience that, "I have in my hand" a list of 205 names of Communists working at the State Department. Further, he charged that some of them were in policy-making positions and that their names were known to the Secretary of State. The media carried McCarthy's sensational charges of Communists working in the State Department. Quickly this obscure, young politician captured the limelight; soon the whole nation knew of his accusations.

The Democratic leadership in the Senate, responding to McCarthy's sensational charges, convened a subcommittee chaired by a distinguished Maryland Senator, Joseph Tydings, to investigate McCarthy's accusations. The Tydings Committee quickly demonstrated that McCarthy not only did not have 205 names, he did not have even the name of one Communist employed in the State Department. Undaunted, McCarthy then accused Owen Lattimore, a prominent expert on Far Eastern affairs, of being the leader of "the espionage ring in the State Department." At the time McCarthy accused him, Lattimore did not work for the State Department. Lattimore denied under oath that he was or had ever been a Communist or had ever espoused the Communist line. The charges against Lattimore also collapsed. In a public report issued in July, the Tydings Committee dismissed McCarthy's charges as a "fraud and a hoax."

Such setbacks at the outset of his campaign might have derailed a less nervy politician, but McCarthy persisted. Most Republican members of Congress backed McCarthy. They sensed that the "Communists in government" issue could pay political dividends. Frustrated and embittered by their losses in the 1948 elections, Republicans hoped that the politics of anti-Communism could be the vehicle that would carry them to power in 1950 and 1952. Conservative Democrats from the South and the West also took up the politics of anti-Communism.

Congress enacted the McCarran Internal Security Act in September 1950 over President Truman's veto. The act required that all Communist and Communist-front organizations register with the Attorney General's office. It also forbade Communists from working in defense factories and prohibited them from traveling abroad on an American passport. Congress enacted another strong anti-Communist measure in 1952, again, over Truman's veto, the McCarran-Walter Act, which forbade Communists and other "undesirables" from entering the United States.

The 1950 elections confirmed the Republicans' hunch that they had found a popular issue. In California, Richard Nixon won a seat in the Senate by calling his liberal Democratic opponent, Helen Gahaghan Douglas, "the pink lady." Several prominent liberal Democrats went down in defeat, including Senator Joseph Tydings. McCarthy quickly became one of his party's most popular campaigners.

McCarthy and his fellow practitioners of the politics of anti-Communism soon acquired a vast following among a public primed by the Hiss case and frustrated by the Korean War. McCarthy stayed on the political offensive. He kept making unsubstantiated charges and naming names. He implied guilt by association, and he told outright lies. It was impossible to keep up with his accusations or to pin him down. He could never be put on the defensive. If one set of charges was dismissed as bogus, he was soon back with another. He called Secretary of State Acheson the "Red Dean of the State Department." He denounced George Marshall, a man with a distinguished record of public service, as a liar and a traitor. McCarthy was always careful to make his charges when shielded by his senatorial cloak of immunity that prevented his victims from suing him for libel. His smear tactics and his use of the "big lie" technique added a new word to the American political lexicon—"McCarthyism."

Several factors accounted for McCarthy's spectacular success. The ground had been prepared by years of Cold War conflict with the Soviet Union, and by politicians who had dramatized the issue, frightening Americans with their accounts of the hidden enemy within. J. Howard Mcgrath, Truman's Attorney General, had alarmed the nation in 1949 with his vivid warning:

> Communists . . . are everywhere—in factories, offices, butcher shops, on street corners, in private business. . . . At this very moment (they are) busy at work—undermining your government, plotting to destroy the liberties of every citizen, and feverishly trying, in whatever way they can, to aid the Soviet Union.[1]

---

[1]Quoted in Athan Theoharis, *Seeds of Repression: Harry Truman and the Origins of McCarthyism* (Chicago: Quadrangle Books, 1971), p. 136.

Alarms raised by politicians were seconded by prominent media editorials. McCarthy's sense of timing, his ruthless tactics, and his demagogic ability to voice the fears of many ordinary American citizens all strengthened his cause. He made skillful use of the news media. Radio and television newscasts carried his charges. Newspapers headlined his accusations. Millions of Americans, frightened by revelations of real espionage, found McCarthy's lies plausible. McCarthy's popularity also came from his being the man with a simple, plausible explanation for America's Cold War setbacks: Communists and liberals who secretly supported the Communists had undermined American foreign policy from within. Traitors working within the State Department and other government agencies were responsible for Communist Cold War triumphs.

Events also played into McCarthy's hands. Two weeks after his Wheeling speech, British intelligence agents discovered an Anglo-American spy ring that had penetrated the atomic bomb project in New Mexico during 1944–1945. The key man in the ring had been a nuclear physicist, Dr. Klaus Fuchs, a German-born, naturalized British citizen assigned to the bomb project. He was arrested and confessed everything. He told the British that he had succeeded in delivering complete information on the bomb to Soviet agents. Using information from Fuchs's confession, FBI agents arrested his American accomplices, Harry Gold and David Greenglass. They in turn implicated Julius and Ethel Rosenberg. The Rosenbergs were tried for espionage, convicted, and executed in 1953. The stalemated Korean War also aided McCarthy significantly. As American morale sagged, he attacked those whom he called "the traitors and bunglers in the State Department who were losing the Cold War to the Communists."

When the Republicans regained control of the Senate as a result of the 1952 elections, McCarthy, now more powerful than ever, became the chairman of his own investigating committee. He continued his rampages in the State Department and other federal agencies. But in 1954, he overreached when he attacked the United States Army for allegedly harboring subversives. It was the beginning of the end for the nation's most formidable practitioner of the politics of anti-Communism.

Figure 3.5   The preeminent practitioner of the politics of anti-Communism, Senator Joseph McCarthy of Wisconsin. For a few years during the early 1950s, this ruthless and clever demagogue was the second most powerful politician in Washington. *Source:* National Archives.

BRIEF BIBLIOGRAPHIC ESSAY

Alonzo L. Hamby's *Beyond the New Deal: Harry S. Truman and American Liberalism* is the most comprehensive account of postwar politics. Eric Goldman's *The Crucial Decade and After: America, 1945–1960* is a lively account of the Truman and Eisenhower years. Samuel Lubell's *The Future of American Politics* remains an informative, interpretive account of changing postwar politics. William Berman's *The Politics of Civil Rights in the Truman Administration* is the most complete account of Truman's civil rights policies. An excellent recent study, Thomas Borstelmann's *The Cold War and the Color Line: American Race Relations in the Global Arena,* convincingly demonstrates that from 1945–1960 government officials working to end white supremacy were driven more by geopolitical considerations than by a quest for social justice. An excellent recent study of postwar economic policy is Robert M. Collins, *The Politics of Economic Growth in Postwar America.* David Brody's *Workers in Industrial Society* is the best account of postwar labor history. By far the best biography of the controversial Senator from Wisconsin is *A Conspiracy So Immense: The World of Joe McCarthy* by David Oshinsky. Allen Weinstein's *Perjury: The Hiss-Chambers Case* is a brilliant study that argues persuasively that Hiss was a secret member of the Communist Party and was guilty of espionage. Richard Freeland's *The Truman Doctrine and the Origins of McCarthyism* is a good account of the origins of the Second Red Scare. Stephen J. Whitfield's *The Culture of the Cold War* recreates the atmosphere of the 1950s, when fear of international Communism pervaded American culture. The best account of the general issues of anti-Communism during the domestic Cold War is Earl Latham's *The Communist Controversy in Washington.*

WEB SITES

An excellent new Web site encompassing all the major events of the Truman years and containing much information on the life and political career of Harry Truman is <http://www.whistlestop.org>. The site presents hundreds of documents, photographs, cartoons, and audio files from the Harry S Truman Library in Independence, MO. It includes an in-depth treatment of Truman's controversial decision to authorize the atomic bombings of Hiroshima and Nagasaki. For those readers with a special interest in HUAC's investigations of Hollywood and the resultant blacklisting of hundreds of writers, directors, and performers, see <http://www.english.upenn.edu/~afilreis/50s/blacklist.html>. There is an informative collection of materials that illumine the life and political career of Senator Joseph McCarthy at <www.foxvalleyhistory.org/mccarthy/menu.htm>.

4

The American People At Mid-Century

At the middle of the twentieth century, a majority of American families enthusiastically participated in a culture of abundance and leisure. The world's most productive economy generated a cornucopia of consumer goods that crowded the shelves and display racks of supermarkets and stores everywhere. Millions of working-class families owned those twin symbols of American affluence—a home in the suburbs and a gleaming new automobile. Americans at mid-century were the most mobile people on the planet. By the millions, families moved from the cities to the suburbs. From the Northeast and the Upper Midwest, they moved to the dynamic states of the Sunbelt region.

Americans had evolved into an affluent middle-class society, based on consumerism fueled by credit buying on an unprecedented scale. The children of affluence created their own teen variant of the consumer culture, buying adolescent staples such as chewing gum, Cokes, hamburgers, clothes, and phonograph records. During the 1950s, television quickly established itself as the dominant mass medium, drastically reducing the sizes of audiences for radio and Hollywood movies. Religion enjoyed a major revival, as America remained the most religious nation in the Western world.

During the 1950s, legions of critics developed a scathing critique of the culture of affluence: Millions of American families were mired in poverty amidst plenty. Many young people were growing up alienated and rebellious. They did not fit easily into the niches of the consumer society. As to the large majority who did fit in, critics found them to be suffering from a herd mentality; America had reared a generation of mindless conformists. Looking through the picture windows of suburban homes, critics could see that millions of middle-class. Americans, displaying all of the outward trappings of affluence, found achieving the 1950s' version of the American Dream insufficient. Some of these troubled souls sought solace and meaning in religion; some sought escape in popular music, sports, alcohol, and a frenetic social life. Others worried about the possibility of nuclear war and continued to live lives of quiet desperation. For many Americans in the 1950s, the age of affluence also generated an age of anxiety.

DEMOGRAPHIC PATTERNS

The postwar "baby boom" caused a tremendous population increase, as returning veterans and their wives made up for lost time. The American population grew from 153 million in 1950 to 179 million in 1960, the second-largest decennial increase ever. In 1957, 4.3 million births were recorded, the highest one-year total in American history. That year, demographers discovered that over fifty million Americans were age fourteen or younger. These young baby boomers created powerful demands for new houses, appliances, bicycles, toys, and diapers. During the decade of the 1950s, the number of youngsters enrolled in schools grades K–12 increased from twenty-eight million to forty-two million. More new schools were constructed during the 1950s, mostly in the burgeoning suburban communities surrounding central cities, than had been built during the first fifty years of the twentieth century. As the U.S. birthrate shot up, the death rate fell. Americans added five years to their median life expectancy during the 1950s, and death rates among young people declined dramatically as well. New "miracle drugs" such as penicillin and cortisone took much of the pain and misery out of life. Polio vaccines tamed a cruel childhood disease that often left its victims crippled and helpless for life.

Suburban growth, underway in the late 1940s, exploded during the 1950s. Millions of families seeking new homes and jobs or just fleeing from myriad urban problems moved from metropolitan centers to outlying communities. By the end of the decade, the suburban population of sixty million equaled that of the rest of urban America. During the 1950s, most large cities within the United States lost population. Of cities with more than one million people, only Los Angeles grew significantly during the decade. The flight to the suburbs transformed living patterns for millions of middle-class families at mid-century.

Americans in the 1950s were not only the richest and healthiest generation ever, they also were the most mobile. Regionally, the American population continued its shift west and south. Families poured into the South, the Southwest, and the West. California, Florida, and Texas added millions of new residents. Soon the Sunbelt encompassed most of the southern rim of the nation, from Southern California to Florida. Americans moved in search of better jobs and business opportunities and the more spacious lifestyles that were possible in Sunbelt suburbs. The economic foundations of the Sunbelt's spectacular population boom included agribusiness, aerospace, electronics, oil, real estate, and a large infusion of military spending. Low taxes and right-to-work laws also attracted industry to the Southern Rim. Rural America continued to lose population during the 1950s. The depopulation of the countryside, a demographic trend that had accelerated during the years of World War II, continued into the 1950s.

AN ECONOMY OF ABUNDANCE

War spending restored American prosperity in the early 1940s, ending a decade of depression and beginning an era of sustained economic expansion and rising living standards that stretched into the 1970s. Between 1945 and 1960, the GDP doubled. During the 1950s, the American economy grew at an average rate of 4.0 percent per year, despite enduring periodic recessions. Between 1946 and 1960, the American workforce grew from 54 million to 68 million jobholders. Median wages in manufacturing industries rose 60 percent, and median family income rose from $3,000 to $5,700 during that same period. Since the rate of inflation remained low, about 2 percent per annum for the decade of the 1950s, wage increases translated into significant gains in purchasing power and rising standards of living. Unemployment rates remained low, averaging around 4 percent in the 1950s. During this decade, millions of Americans could afford goods and services that would have been beyond their means previously. The rapidly growing American economy generated a widespread abundance that became the envy of the world. During the 1950s, the United States, with about 5 percent of the world's population, consumed over one-third of its goods and services.

Credit significantly enhanced consumer purchasing power. Short-term installment credit, mainly for new cars, increased fivefold from 1946 to 1960. A revolution in spending patterns got underway in 1950, when the Diners' Club introduced the general credit card, soon followed by American Express. During this decade, oil companies and department stores issued millions of revolving credit cards. Private debt within the affluent society climbed from $73 billion to $200 billion during the decade of the 1950s. Consumer demand stimulated huge private sector investment in new plant capacity and new technology, an average of $10 billion per year. Automation, the use of self-regulating machines to control manufacturing operations, enhanced the nation's industrial productivity and improved the quality of products.

Big business grew bigger during the postwar era. Another wave of mergers swept the industrial economy. By 1960, America's 200 largest industrial corporations owned over half of the nation's industrial assets. But unlike the merger waves of the 1890s and 1920s, which joined businesses within the same economic sectors, the 1950s' mergers brought together businesses in unrelated fields. Conglomerates such as International Telephone and Telegraph (ITT) linked a car rental company, a home construction company, a retail food outlet, a hotel chain, and an insurance company under the same corporate roof.

THE CAR CULTURE

The manufacture of automobiles remained the most important American industry during the 1950s. New car and truck sales averaged seven million units annually during the decade. By 1960, there were seventy million vehicles on the nation's roads and highways. Two-thirds of the nation's employees commuted to work by car. The number of service stations, garages, motels, and the size of the oil industry all expanded with autos.

The growth of suburbia and the automobile boom occurred together. Suburbia required automobiles. Mothers driving station wagons, piled full of kids on their way to school, shopping centers, or team practice, became the reigning symbol of the 1950s' suburban lifestyle. In the late 1950s, the federal government began constructing an interstate highway system funded mainly by gasoline taxes. Summer traveling vacations became the great American pastime. The huge highway building project also included the construction of thousands of miles of freeways connecting the new suburbs to the central cities. Government road building amounted to a subsidy for the American car culture that promoted suburban growth and urban decay.

As the numbers of cars on the roads multiplied, they became longer, wider, more powerful, and gaudier. Detroit reached its pinnacle in the late 1950s. Automakers outdid themselves, creating chromium ornaments, two- and three-tone color combinations, soaring tail fins, and

Figure 4.1   A big gleaming new car was one of the supreme status symbols of the affluent society. Here a 1954 Buick Super Riviera shines in all of its glory.
Source: National Archives.

gas-guzzling V-8 engines. The buying public was delighted with Detroit's offerings, which also included wrap-around windshields, power steering, automatic transmissions, air conditioning, and hi-fi radios. Advertisers stressed the power, the flashiness, and even the sex appeal of these elaborate machines. Dinah Shore appeared on television to sing, "See the U.S.A. in your Chevrolet." Advertisers linked owning a new car to participating in the very essence of what it meant to be a successful American: what was more American than apple pie, mom, and your new Chevrolet? Domestic automakers had the American market all to themselves; imports accounted for less than 1 percent of sales in 1955. Gas was cheap and plentiful at 25¢ to 30¢ per gallon. A big, gleaming new car was one of the supreme status symbols of the affluent society, a shining testament to America's technological world supremacy. It would be left to later generations of urban planners to worry about the decay of mass transit, the decline of smog-choked inner cities, and freeway gridlock.

GROWTH INDUSTRIES

The chemical industry grew even faster than the auto business during the 1950s. Du Pont's slogan, "Better things for better living through chemistry," became known to every television viewer. Du Pont, Dow, and the other chemical giants turned out a never-ending feast of new synthetic products—aerosol spray cans, Dacron, and new plastics like vinyl and Teflon.

Electricity and electronics also grew rapidly in the postwar era. A horde of new electric appliances sprang forth—air conditioners, electric blankets, automatic clothes washers, clothes dryers, and hair dryers. The electronics industry expanded mainly because of the advent of television. By the early 1950s, dealers were selling six million new TV sets each year. Other popular electronic products enjoyed wide sales during the 1950s. Almost every one of the nearly sixty million new cars sold in the decade had a radio. Transistors made possible the development of new computer technologies. International Business Machines (IBM) marketed its first main-frame computers, inaugurating the postindustrial age. In 1960, the Xerox corporation marketed its 914 copier, thereby inaugurating a revolution in document copying. The aerospace industry kept pace with other growth industries, stimulated by multibillion dollar contracts to supply the Pentagon with sophisticated military hardware. Air travel increased rapidly after 1945 and took a quantum leap forward in 1958 with the introduction of regularly scheduled commercial jet travel.

Although postwar growth industries flourished, some traditional heavy industries and manufacturing declined such as railroads, coal mining, and textiles. Long-haul trucking and air travel cut heavily into railroad freight and passenger business. Coal could no longer compete with oil, natural gas, and electricity. Cotton and woolen manufacturers succumbed to synthetic fibers spun out by the chemical companies. Americans increasingly wore clothes made of nylon, orlon, and polyester. Industrial decline brought permanent depression to New England mill towns and to Appalachia, creating pockets of poverty amidst general affluence.

Agriculture changed drastically in the postwar years. Farmers produced more food than consumers could buy, and commodity prices dropped. Profits could be made in farming only

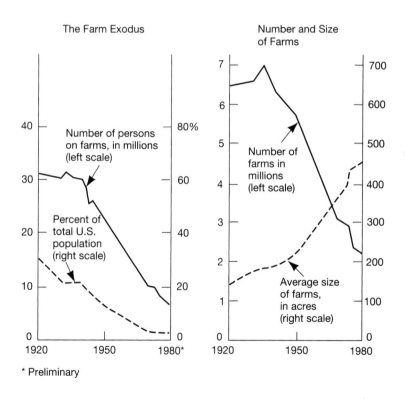

* Preliminary

Figure 4.2   In the postwar period, the trends toward fewer but larger farms and a much smaller rural population accelerated. By 1980, three out of every four Americans lived in a metropolitan area.   *Source:* Public Domain.

by reducing unit costs of production through intensive use of fertilizers, pesticides, expensive farm machinery, and sophisticated managerial techniques. Larger farms prospered from a combination of greater efficiency and government subsidies. Small farmers got squeezed out and joined the rural exodus to the cities. The nation's farm population dropped from twenty-five million at the end of the war to fourteen million in 1960. The number of agricultural workers dropped to just 6 percent of the workforce. In regions of Arizona, Florida, and California, huge corporate farms replaced family farms.

THE MIXED ECONOMY

The federal government stimulated economic growth during the 1950s in many ways. Washington dispensed billions of dollars annually as welfare payments, Social Security checks, and farm subsidies. Congress funded over half of the nation's industrial research and development and over half of all university scientific research. The Federal Reserve Board regulated the money supply and interest rates. Other government bureaucracies regulated the securities and communications industries, interstate transportation, and aviation. During the 1950s, military budgets pumped $40 billion to $50 billion a year into the economy, and government spending as a percentage of the GDP increased steadily. The number of Americans working for government at all levels increased by 50 percent during this decade. The prosperity of many locales became dependent on government purchases or government payrolls.

Americans at mid-century celebrated what they were fond of calling the "American free enterprise system." But economic reality was more complex and ambiguous than their simplistic rhetorical labels implied. Out of their efforts to battle the Great Depression and to produce the materials needed to win World War II, Americans had fashioned a mixed economy that blended public and private enterprise. Government spending and regulatory activities had become integral elements of the mixed economy. The mixed economy conformed to no economic model or theory. Most Americans did not understand its nature or how it worked, but they were delighted with its prime creation—the culture of abundance.

LABOR AT MID-CENTURY

Organized labor prospered during the 1950s, as trade unions won significant wage increases and new fringe benefits from corporate employers. The United Auto Workers and General Motors agreed to a clause in their contract calling for automatic annual cost-of-living adjustments in wages. That agreement set a pattern soon copied in other industries and occupations. Corporate managers discovered that it was more profitable to negotiate wage increases with union representatives and to pass their increased costs on to consumers rather than to engage in lengthy strikes with strong unions. Organized labor remained a powerful force within the Democratic Party that normally controlled Congress during the 1950s. George Meany declared in 1955, "American labor never had it so good." Labor's major achievement was to bring about the merger of the AFL and CIO in 1955. The creation of the AFL-CIO brought 90 percent of America's eighteen million trade unionists into a single national labor federation, headed by Meany.

Although unions generally prospered during the 1950s, they also faced serious problems. Corruption riddled several of them. Senator John McClellan of Arkansas chaired a Senate committee that investigated union racketeering in 1957. The McClellan committee exposed widespread corruption in the Teamster's Union. Robert "Bobby" Kennedy served as chief counsel for the committee and his brother Senator John F. Kennedy also served on the committee. They found that Teamster officials had involved themselves in a wide range of crooked activities, including the misappropriation of union funds, rigged elections, extortion, and association with members of organized crime. Committee investigations led to the enactment of the Landrum-Griffin Act in 1959. This moderate labor reform measure imposed new legal restrictions on unions, and expanded the list of union unfair labor practices. It also contained anticorruption provisions to safeguard democratic election procedures within unions and to make misuse of union funds a federal crime.

Trade unions also confronted a more fundamental problem than racketeering during the late 1950s. Union membership peaked in 1956 at 18.6 million and declined thereafter. The proportion of the workforce that belonged to unions declined mainly because of the loss of jobs in heavy industry. The American economy continued to grow and prosper after 1958, but organized labor could not keep pace. Many industries moved to the South to take advantage of lower wage levels and nonunion workers. But even where unions remained strong, workers were less inclined to join them than before, primarily because, without joining, they received the higher wages and benefits that union negotiators had obtained. Most important, the economy was shifting from a production-oriented to a service-oriented one, which meant a shift from blue-collar occupations to white-collar jobs.

Most of the new job growth in the 1950s economy occurred in the service, clerical, and managerial sectors. In 1956, for the first time in American economic history, white-collar workers outnumbered blue-collar workers in the workforce. White-collar workers generally resisted the efforts of union organizers in the 1950s. As white-collar jobs multiplied in the growth sectors of the economy, technological innovations eliminated jobs in mining, manufacturing, and transportation. A few unions did manage to organize categories of white-collar employees, the most successful being the American Federation of State, County, and Municipal Employees (AFSCME), whose members worked for various state and local government agencies. Since the 1950s, the most dynamic sectors of the trade union movement have been the public employee unions, whose leaders constitute the most important power bloc within the Democratic party in the early years of the twenty-first century.

Poverty Amidst Plenty

Although the majority of American families were eager participants in the culture of abundance, millions of their fellow citizens were mired in poverty. In 1960, according to the Bureau of Labor statistics, forty million Americans representing approximately 25 percent of the population were poor. The elderly, people over sixty-five, made up one-fourth of the poor. One-fifth were nonwhite, including 45 percent of the black population. Two-thirds of the poor inhabited households headed by a person with an eighth-grade education or less. One-fourth of poor people lived in a household headed by a single woman.

The poor congregated in the inner cities, as middle-class people fled to the suburbs. Between 1945 and 1960, over 3 million black people, most of them unskilled and many of them illiterate, moved to Northern and Western cities from the rural South. Poor whites from Appalachia joined blacks in this migration from the country to the cities. Many poor people also inhabited rural America in the 1950s. Both white and black tenant farmers and sharecroppers were trapped in a life cycle of poverty and hard work. A famous television documentary shown in 1960, *The Harvest of Shame,* narrated by Edward R. Murrow, depicted the poverty and hopelessness of migrant farm workers.

One of the major causes of poverty in America lay in the fact that wealth in America remained highly concentrated. In 1960, the richest 1 percent of the population owned one- third of the national wealth. The wealthiest 5 percent of America's families owned over half of the nation's wealth. At the same time, half of the nation's families had no savings. Some of the poverty in mid-century America could be attributed to the failure of the welfare state forged during the New Deal era to provide for poor people. Its benefits had mostly gone to groups that were organized to make demands on the broker state. The Wagner Act did nothing for nonunion workers. Minimum wage laws and Social Security benefits did not extend to millions of low-income workers in dozens of occupations. Welfare programs available to poor people maintained them at subsistence levels and perpetuated a demoralizing lifestyle based on dependency.

Women made up a large percentage of poor Americans at mid-century. Few well-paying jobs were open to them in the 1950s. A greater portion of women's jobs than men's jobs was not covered by minimum wage or Social Security protection. Also, divorced women usually were saddled with major child-rearing responsibilities. Ex-husbands often failed to make child support payments, and many divorced women with children slipped into poverty.

Few government officials or anyone else showed much interest in the plight of poor Americans during the 1950s. Publicists focused on celebrating the achievements of the affluent majority. The poor themselves were silent. They lacked organizations and articulate leaders to call attention to their problems. They inhabited another America outside the boundaries of affluence.

THE RISE OF SUBURBIA

America experienced the greatest internal population movement in its history in the fifteen years following World War II, when forty million Americans fled the cities for the suburbs. Young white middle-class people led the flight to the suburbs. Many factors combined to create this mighty exodus from metropolis to suburbia. Families fled traffic jams, high taxes, polluted air, contact with racial minorities, overcrowded schools, high real estate prices, and high crime rates. Suburbia beckoned for many reasons: the obvious attraction of open country where land could be acquired and spacious houses could be built for a fraction of what big-city construction would cost. People wanted homes with yards where, as one father put it, a kid could "grow up with grass stains on his pants." Suburban homes also promised the privacy and quiet not found in crowded city apartments. Many suburbanites sought a community of like-minded people and accessible local government.

Government subsidies permitted millions of families to move into suburbia who otherwise could not have afforded to. Low-interest mortgages requiring little or no down payments and tax subsidies produced a postwar housing boom. During the 1950s, contractors built an average of two million new homes a year. Across the country, developers busily tossed up new housing tracts, replacing forests, bean fields, fruit orchards, and grazing lands. By 1960, over 60 percent of American families owned their homes, the most significant accomplishment of the affluent society. Businesses also moved to the suburbs in response to the growing demands of suburbanites. Suburban shopping centers multiplied; by 1960, there were 3,840 such centers sprawled across the nation, transforming shopping patterns throughout the nation. Suburban dwellers no longer needed to shop in the central cities; they bought whatever they needed in suburban stores. New freeways connected the suburbs to the central cities creating commuter lifelines.

Some suburban developments were tossed up virtually overnight. Using mass production and merchandising techniques, William Levitt built Levittown, Long Island. Soon, a flourishing community of some 16,000 homes built on 5,100 acres existed where only a few months earlier farmers had raised potatoes. Other Levittowns soon appeared in Pennsylvania and New Jersey. Penn Kimball, a New York Times Magazine writer, vividly described the process of Levittown's instant community formation:

> Starting from scratch the Levitts have converted eight square miles of open farm country into a densely populated community of 70,000. Paved streets, sewer lines, school sites, baseball diamonds, shopping centers, parking lots, new railroad stations, factory sidings, churches, trunk arteries, newspapers, garden clubs, swimming pools, doctors, dentists, and town hall—all conceived in advance, all previously planned in one of the most colossal acts ever of moral creation.[1]

The Levittowns were immediate successes primarily because of their affordable prices. Levitt's mass production techniques lowered the prices of homes and brought them within reach of tens of thousands of young families, many of them headed by veterans. These families left their urban neighborhoods and joined the rush to the suburbs. But social critics made Levittown stand as a metaphor for the postwar failings of suburban society. They condemned Levittown for its uniform houses lined up on uniform streets in a treeless communal waste. According to cultural critic Lewis Mumford, Levittown homes represented a culture of "ticky-tacky." They were inhabited by people of the same class, watching the same pallid fare on television, and eating the same prefabricated foods.

Mumford's elitist indictment, was not so much incorrect as it was beside the point. Levittown appealed to the mass of ordinary American families, precisely because it was safe and reassuring as well as affordable. Levitt observed that "critics don't live in Levittowns, people do." Although suburbs tended to be internally homogeneous, they were typically differentiated along social and economic lines. Suburbs were identified as working class, middle class, or elite enclaves of upper-middle-class families. Analysts of suburban culture observed that ethnic identities attenuated in suburbia; in that sense, suburbs tended to make people more homogeneous.

While ethnicity declined in mid-century America, suburbanization separated Americans racially. Most African American and Hispanic families remained in large cities as white families

---

[1]Quoted in Dewey W. Grantham, *Recent America, The United States Since 1945* (Arlington Heights, Ill.: Harlan Davidson Inc., 1987), pp. 60–61.

Figure 4.3   Levittown, Long Island, New York, USA, during the 1950s.
Source: National Archives.

headed for the suburbs. The national metropolitan pattern became one of predominantly black cities encircled within white suburbs. The 1960 census showed that suburbia was 98 percent white; it also showed that some of the nation's larger cities—Washington, D.C., Newark, Richmond, and Atlanta—had black majorities. As the white middle classes moved out, the central cities declined. Urban tax bases shrank, social services shriveled, and crime rates soared. A consequence of the white flight to suburbia that left African Americans trapped in deteriorating inner cities was the fiery urban riots during the hot summers of 1965 to 1968.

CLASS AND STATUS

Sustained postwar economic growth and prosperity allowed millions of Americans to increase their incomes, advance their occupational statuses, and improve their standards of living. During the 1950s, most Americans believed that their society offered hard-working individuals abundant opportunities—a better job, a higher income, more profitable business ventures, or a college education. They believed that enhanced occupational and social mobility operated to diminish social distinctions and to distribute income more evenly in mid-century America.

While it was undoubtedly true that 1950s' American society was highly mobile and that many people found opportunities to enhance their wealth, status, and influence, it also remained in many important ways a class society. Wealth remained concentrated in the hands of a relatively small number of families at the top. Below the wealthy elite classes, Americans aligned themselves in strata markedly differentiated by wealth, status, culture, ethnoracial identities, political clout, legal protections, education, health, and patterns of recreation and leisure. At the bottom rungs of American society were the masses of poor people, who had little money, status, power, and only meager opportunities to acquire them.

Champions of the affluent society believed that it provided the ultimate counter to the ideological challenge posed by Communism during the Cold War. These pundits believed that Americans had eliminated class conflict, that ancient problem that had riven capitalistic societies for centuries. In the America of the 1950s, they argued, the "bourgeois" society included nearly everyone. Industrial workers were members in good standing of that vast middle class that constituted nearly the entire American society. By becoming a nation of middle-class families, Americans had attained social equality and had done so while maintaining an unprecedentedly high level of material well-being. Within America, it had not been necessary to dispossess the wealthy or to redistribute wealth, merely to let the solvents of economic growth and social mobility work their magic. The pie was so large that all could share in the abundance.

It was certainly true that unionized workers employed in the mass production industries made striking gains in job security and economic well-being during the 1950s. Many senior skilled workers earned larger incomes annually than many traditional middle-class office workers, teachers, and those in the service trades. Yet achieving middle-class incomes, buying a new car, and moving into Levittown did not mean that industrial workers adopted middle-class manners, attitudes, and values. The great American middle class remained split, if no longer along class lines, then along cultural lines. Working-class lifestyles in many instances remained distinct from middle-class suburban lifestyles.

THE CULTURE OF AFFLUENCE

A vast increase in the size of the middle classes was the defining characteristic of the affluent society. The postwar class structure resembled a diamond instead of a pyramid, with the bulge of the diamond representing the 60 percent of the population that had joined the middle classes. A large increase in college enrollments accompanied the growth in numbers of middle-class households. A college education became accessible to young people from average American families. As the 1950s ended, nearly four million young people were enrolled at more than 2,000 colleges and universities across the land. Most individual members of this large college population sought the conventional goals of family, career, and a home in the suburbs. Students shunned politics, radicalism of any kind, and intellectual adventure. Observers labeled these careful young men and women of the 1950s the "silent generation."

American teenagers often set popular cultural trends during the 1950s. A teen culture flourished with money to spend and clear consumer preferences. Merchandisers responded synergistically to these teenage consumers. Ray Kroc, a traveling salesman from Chicago, observed a drive-in restaurant in San Bernardino, California, that was doing a thriving business. It sold only hamburgers, french fries, and milk shakes, and it sold them cheap and fast. Its owners, Dick and Mac McDonald, had applied assembly-line, mass production technology to the preparation of food, and in the process they had invented the fast-food restaurant. With borrowed money, Kroc concluded a business arrangement with the McDonald brothers that permitted him to establish a chain of fast-food restaurants using their name and modeled on their format. The first McDonald's, complete with twin golden arches, sprang out of the prairie soil of Des Plaines, Illinois, a suburb of Chicago, on April 15, 1955. By the end of the decade, there were hundreds of McDonalds' restaurants rapidly spreading across the country selling hamburgers for fifteen cents, french fries for a dime, and milk shakes for twenty cents. Ray Kroc was rapidly becoming rich.

In the same year that Ray Kroc opened the first McDonald's fast-food restaurant in the Midwestern heartland, Walt Disney offered Disneyland, the first theme park, to American consumers. Disney sponsored a lavish telecast the night before Disneyland opened to the public. One of the hosts of the telecast was a screen actor, television personality, and future President of the United States, Ronald Reagan. Disneyland, located in Anaheim, a suburb of Los Angeles, California, immediately attracted hordes of visitors, mostly families with children. It featured combinations of fairy-tale images derived from Disney's earlier animated masterpieces and sanitized historical images from his live-action films.

The Autopia ride was meant to be the major magnet when Disneyland first opened. Autopia was a miniature freeway with small cars for child drivers. Disney believed that it would not only be fun for kids but also would teach youngsters to be responsible adults behind the wheel. Within six weeks after opening, only six of the cars were drivable, the rest battered wrecks. Rather than drive safely and responsibly, young scofflaws had turned their vehicles into bumper cars, happily chasing and slamming into one another at high speeds. Autopia was shut down and redesigned. When it reopened, the cars could only go slow and were fastened to tracks.

Some areas of the park—Main Street, Frontierland, and Adventureland—featured a vast display of the icons of Americana. Young people could take a Jungle Cruise and conquer Africa, the "dark continent." They also could take a cruise on the steamboat Mark Twain down a manmade river and they could be inspired by a larger-than-life robotic Abraham Lincoln who, in a deep, rumbling voice, declaimed the virtues of constitutional democratic governance.

Much of the 1950s' popular culture can only be explained by recapitulating the American historical trajectory since the Great Depression of the 1930s. As Franklin Roosevelt famously observed, the dominant reaction to the financial collapse and severe economic downturn of the early 1930s was fear, "stark unreasoning terror." Add to that decade of depression the disruptions of the 1940s—the horrors of World War II and the rise of the Cold War. Americans had to endure nearly twenty years of frightening historical experiences before they could enjoy the prosperity and popular culture of the 1950s. Finally, Americans could once again believe that the conventional order of things could be relied upon and that American institutions and core values were fundamentally sound. Americans could once again feel safe and secure. The awful fears caused by economic collapse, global war, and the rise of the Soviet menace could be banished as Americans took refuge in a culture of conformity and mass consumerism. Disneyland epitomized this popular culture of reassurance.

**Figure 4.4   Affluent Americans at mid-century had more money to spend and more
leisure time to enjoy than any previous generation. Here people flock to the beach at Coney
Island for a day of sun and surf.**   *Source:* National Archives.

WOMEN: FAMILY LIFE AND WORK

The postwar years were a time of transition, frustration, and confusion for many American
women. Life magazine ran a feature in 1947 entitled "The American Woman's Dilemma." Its
author found that many women were torn between the traditional expectation of staying home
and the desire to work outside of the realm of domesticity. Millions of women continued to
work outside of the home, mostly because they had to. Whether they wanted to work or not,
more and more women married and gave birth to children in the postwar era. During the late
1940s and the decade of the 1950s, the family was the most rapidly growing American social institution. These new families held down well-paying jobs, purchased suburban homes, reared
children, and made the consumer purchases that kept the mighty U.S. economy growing and
prospering.

American families became more child oriented after the war. Dr. Benjamin Spock published the first edition of his *Baby and Child Care* in 1946, which strongly influenced child-
rearing practices in the postwar era. He advised women to make child rearing their most
important task, to put their children's needs first. Early editions of Spock's book also advised
women to stay at home and not to work outside of the home so that they would be available to
meet all of their babies' needs.

Some psychiatrists, influenced by Sigmund Freud's writings, criticized working women. To these writers, the independent woman was an oxymoron. They claimed that women could only be fulfilled and happy through domesticity. Dr. Marynia Farnham's influential *Modern Woman: The Lost Sex* considered women who held jobs outside the home to be neurotic feminists trying ot be "imitation men." Farnham and other writers assumed that a woman's gender determined her role in life. Anatomy was destiny. At the core of this "feminine mystique" was the idea that women constituted the foundation of society. Women made the home a haven from the stress of the competitive business world. Women in their roles as wives and mothers did necessary and noble work, and in the process they fulfilled their feminine destinies.

In 1956, *Life* published a special issue on American women. It profiled housewife Marjorie Sutton as a successful woman who fulfilled her feminine potential. She was mother, wife, home manager, and hostess. She was active in the PTA, the Campfire Girls, and charity work. Sutton had four children, and she did all of the cooking, cleaning, and sewing for her family. She chauffeured her large brood of children wherever they needed to go. She also helped her husband's career by entertaining his business clients. Marjorie Sutton fulfilled the official feminine ideology of the 1950s, the suburban wifely counterpart to her husband, the organization man.

Films of the 1950s highlighted sex symbols such as Marilyn Monroe or wholesome heroines such as Doris Day. They became role models for women. Women's fashions stressed femininity at the expense of practicality or comfort. There were strong pressures on women to conform to the prevailing sexual stereotype. During the decade, no organized feminist movement existed to challenge the prevailing feminine mystique.

Mid-century women were caught in a dilemma. According to the prevalent ideology, the ideal role for women was found in the home. Her fulfillment lay in creating an island of love and security for her children and husband, with scant regard for her own needs. But studies of women, especially college-educated women, showed that many were unhappy with the constraints and lack of fulfillment in their lives, as defined by domesticity. They especially resented the lack of mental stimulation, the lack of any outlet for their academic skills and intellectual energies. The rise of social pathologies—of alcoholism, divorce rates, and anomie among women who supposedly had it all, who had fulfilled the cultural ideal of wife and mother—furnished additional evidence of their widespread stress and confusion.

Compounding the confusion over women's roles in mid-century society was the fact that millions of middle-class women had entered the labor markets. The female labor force expanded from seventeen million in 1946 to twenty-two million in 1958. By 1960, 40 percent of women were employed full time or part time. During the decade of the 1950s, female employment increased at a rate four times faster than male employment. By 1960, 30 percent of married women worked outside of the home. Despite the burgeoning cult of motherhood, most new entrants to the female job market during the 1950s were married women with children. Most of these married women workers were not pursuing full-time careers, were not competing with men, and certainly were not seeking equality in the workplace. Many worked part time, and most did "women's work," that is, they took positions in clerical and other white-collar fields traditionally reserved for women, where pay and status were low and the prospects for promotion were slim.

Figure 4.5   An office in New York City. Women at work during the 1950s.   *Source:* Brown Brothers.

In many instances, these married, middle-class women worked to supplement their families' incomes. Their contributions ensured a solid, middle-class status and lifestyle for their families that was not attainable from their husbands' earnings alone. A sizable proportion of middle-class family incomes in the $12,000 to $15,000 per annum range during the 1950s was made possible by having two income earners. The wife's income made possible the purchase of a split-level suburban home in a fashionable neighborhood and the purchase of a second car or station wagon. These hardworking 1950s' middle-class women did not see a conflict between working outside of the home and maintaining their duties as wives and mothers. Most worked for a few years until their children were born, then quit their jobs until their children had become teenagers. They then reentered the workforce. They were not careerists competing with their husbands or seeking independence; they were helping their families achieve a higher status and a better standard of living. These women, of course, deviated from the norms prescribe by the feminine mystique, from the roles played to perfection by the Marjorie Suttons of the 1950s. According to the historian William Chafe, these working women "were carving out one of the only paths available within the existing culture for resolving the contradiction between traditional and modern definitions of women's 'place.' "

Another factor strongly influencing family life and the roles of women during the 1950s was a consequence of American social history. Millions of American families during the 1950s were headed by men and women who had grown up amidst the economic deprivations of the Great Depression of the 1930s. They had been young adults during World War II, experiencing the loneliness and physical separation from friends and family inherent in military service in wartime. After experiencing fifteen years of economic and emotional insecurity, they were determined to enjoy the material security of the affluent society, and they were equally determined to have the emotional security found in a cohesive family life. These men and women made the baby boom and championed "togetherness." The term togetherness first appeared in a 1954 *McCalls* article. It meant a happy family melded into a team, specifically the woman fusing herself with her husband and children. Family life was oriented around shared activities—television watching, backyard barbecues, outings to parks and beaches, and traveling vacations.

RELIGION REVIVED

Religion enjoyed a revival during the 1950s. President Eisenhower tied religion to patriotism when he observed that recognition of God was "the first, the most basic, expression of Americanism." With America locked in a Cold War with godless Communists, religious worship became one of the defining characteristics of Americanism. Atheism was associated in the popular mind with Communism and disloyalty; a mix of religious worship, free enterprise, and political democracy epitomized the American way. Religion also was promoted as bonding family members together in worship: "The family that prays together stays together." The Bible topped the best-seller charts every year during the 1950s. Congress inserted the words "under God" in the Pledge of Allegiance to the American flag, recited in classrooms, and it put the motto "In God We Trust" on paper money.

Thousands of new suburban churches appeared during the 1950s. From 1945 until 1960, church attendance in this country increased by 50 percent. The Baptist evangelist Billy Graham emerged as the major leader of a mass movement back to Bible fundamentalism. Bishop Fulton Sheen became a prominent television personality, speaking to millions of people about ethical and spiritual issues. A minister with training in psychology, Dr. Norman Vincent Peale was the most popular preacher of the 1950s. His book *The Power of Positive Thinking* sold millions of copies. Blending religion with pop psychology, Peale preached a gospel of reassurance. He told his anxious listeners that God watched over Americans, assuring individual success in careers and ultimately national victory over Communism in the Cold War.

A public opinion poll taken in 1955 showed that 97 percent of Americans believed in God and that two-thirds of the population claimed to attend church regularly. America remained the most religious nation in the West. Religion played a serious role in the lives of millions of American families. Most Americans appeared unconcerned over doctrinal differences among the various religions or with serious theological issues. For most Americans, religious commitments had little, if any, intellectual content. Rather than reorient their lives to God, most Americans considered religious observances essentially a social activity. For others, religious belief got intermixed with patriotism, family togetherness, and Thursday night bingo. High school and college athletic events began with a prayer or a moment of meditation. Religion also could serve as a means of establishing one's social identity, of becoming a member of a suburban community. Religion in the 1950s suffused most American social and public affairs, adding a sense of goodness and appropriateness to these activities.

SOCIAL CRITICS

Although the decade of the 1950s is remembered mainly as a time of conformity and complacency, an era of pervasive intellectual blandness when Americans took a holiday from thinking to indulge in the pleasures of affluent consumerism, it also produced a number of independent thinkers who espoused a lively critical discourse about the foibles and failures of mid-century Americans. While most 1950s' social critics agreed that Americans had created an affluent society, that most Americans no longer needed to concern themselves with basic questions of economic survival, they also observed that pockets of poverty, concentrations of wealth and power, class distinctions, and social injustice persisted in mid-century America. Others raised questions about the lack of meaning in lives based on work, consumerism, and social conformity.

William Whyte, author of the best-selling *Organization Man,* claimed that Americans no longer followed the traditional individual success ethic. They embraced what Whyte termed an organizational ethic, which stressed belonging to a group and being a team player. Corporations employed more and more Americans. Within these large companies, bureaucratic management styles prevailed. Businesses encouraged their employees to look, dress, and act alike. Each appeared to be The Man in the Gray Flannel Suit, the title of a best-selling 1950s' novel by Sloan Wilson. Whyte raised serious questions about the energy, drive, and productivity of corporate executives whose highest ambition was to belong to a group and "fit in."

The urge to conform spread to the general society. David Riesman's *Lonely Crowd,* a classic study of the postwar social character, highlighted the lonely individual lost within mass society. Riesman observed that mobility had uprooted people from their traditional ethical moorings. Old values no longer offered guidance or meaning. People were cast adrift morally. Young people adapted to the new social environment by embracing peer group norms and turning to television for guidance. They consumed their values as they did their breakfast cereals. Unpopularity with peers was more to be feared than violations of personal standards, which often were confused. People valued success in the personality market more than retaining their integrity.

Riesman called this new American character type "other-directed" in contrast to the traditional "inner-directed" American who internalized individualistic success values early in life from his parents and thereafter followed his destiny. Other-directed men preferred to join the lonely crowd, not lead it. They would rather fit in than stand out. Other-directed workers were better adapted to fill the niches of the 1950s consumer economy. The American workforce at mid-century was predominantly white collar. New jobs were mostly generated in the service sectors—sales, advertising, customer service, clerical, accounting, and the like. Organization men, whose tickets to employment were high school diplomas or college degrees instead of union cards, proliferated.

Critics of the 1950s also attacked the rampant consumerism of the age; they questioned whether a fulfilling life could be based on earning money only to spend it on the proliferating goods and services churned out by the productive American economy. Other mid-century critics raised serious questions about the quality of suburban life. They wrote about hastily built, shoddy developments teeming with haggard men, frustrated women, and demanding children. The economist John Kenneth Galbraith, in *The Affluent Society,* while praising the triumphs of the private sector, wrote about the squalor of the public sector and the persistence of poverty. One radical critic of the 1950s, Columbia sociologist C. Wright Mills, argued in his book *The Power Elite* that American political democracy was a facade. In reality, a small group of powerful military, political, and corporate leaders controlled America within a political framework that left most Americans relatively powerless. The anarchist Paul Goodman, in *Growing Up Absurd,* leveled a withering criticism at public schools for stifling the individualism and creativity of America's children. Probing beneath the bland surface of 1950s' complacency about society, perceptive social critics understood that America's problems had not disappeared. They were simply being ignored by the nation's political leaders, influential mass media, and most of its people.

THE ADVENT OF TELEVISION

Americans not only fashioned an affluent society at mid-century, they also evolved a flourishing popular culture. Americans, especially young Americans, were vigorous participants in the 1950s' popular culture: they watched hours of television daily, went to movies, participated in numerous recreational activities, and listened to popular music.

The most remarkable aspect of television was how quickly it became a mass medium. Regularly scheduled telecasts began in this country in 1947. As late as 1948, fewer than two million households owned a television set. That year, most people watched television in bars and taverns, or perhaps stood in front of a department store window gazing in wonderment at the new electronic marvel that broadcast pictorial imagery. Some skeptics were unimpressed by the new electronic gadgetry called television. They dismissed it as "radio with pictures" and predicted it would be merely a passing fad. But within five years, half of America's households had a television set, and by 1960, 90 percent of homes had at least one black-and-white set. No new household technology had ever spread so wide or so fast nor acquired such a tight hold on the entire culture. By the mid-1950s, studies revealed that the average American spent more time watching television than he or she spent in school or on the job.

Prime-time evening television viewing became the social focus of family life during the 1950s. It displaced listening to the radio, playing records, attending movies, reading magazines and books, playing cards and board games, and conversation. A comedian joked that after-dinner conversation in the typical television-saturated American household of the 1950s consisted of two phrases: "What's on the tube tonight?" and "Good night."

As television fastened itself onto the American imagination during the early 1950s, programming was dominated by the "Big Two," NBC and CBS. The prime-time television fare that Americans watched during the 1950s was mostly dictated by a bicoastal duopoly: NBC's programs produced in New York and CBS's shows emanating from Television City in Los Angeles. Both national networks owned many of the nation's 240 television stations, especially those broadcasting in the larger metropolitan markets. By the mid-1950s, those stations earned a high return on their investments, often in the 30 percent to 35 percent per annum range. So lucrative had television broadcasting become by the mid-1950s that getting a license from the Federal Communications Commission (FCC) to operate a television station amounted to getting a government permit to print money.

Initially the producers of television shows borrowed from all established popular cultural forms for their programs, particularly vaudeville and radio. Many of the early television stars such as Jack Benny, Burns and Allen, Red Skelton, Groucho Marx, and Arthur Godfrey had previously been popular performers on radio. Some TV performers reached heights of stardom in the new visual medium, far surpassing anything that they had achieved in radio. Milton Berle, a second-rate nightclub comedian, became NBC's biggest TV star. As the star of the variety show *The Texaco Comedy Hour,* "Uncle Miltie," often appearing in drag, became known as Mr. Television. Another top variety show host, CBS's Ed Sullivan, could neither sing nor dance. A New York newspaper gossip columnist, Sullivan's awkward posture, mechanical gestures, and slurred speech became the standard fare of nightclub impressionists for twenty years.

As radio and Hollywood had done previously, 1950s' television programming relied on standard formats or genres. In addition to variety shows, popular TV genres included thirty-minute situation comedies (sitcoms), dramatic series, musicals, and Westerns. The most popular TV sitcom of the 1950s, *I Love Lucy,* starred Lucille Ball. She played Lucy Ricardo, the bubble-headed wife of Cuban-born band leader Ricky Ricardo, played by Desi Arnaz, Ball's real-life husband. Another popular situation comedy, *The Honeymooners,* starred Jackie Gleason as bus driver Ralph Cramden and his good buddy, sewer-pipe repairman Ed Norton, played by Art Carney. Other 1950s' sitcom stars included Phil Silvers as *Sergeant Bilko,* Eve Arden as the quick-witted schoolmarm in *Our Miss Brooks,* and Sid Caesar, Carl Reiner, and Imogene Coca in *The Show of Shows.*

In the late 1950s, Westerns became the most popular television genre. At one time there were thirty-nine Westerns on each week. CBS showed most of these top-rated shows, including *Have Gun Will Travel,* which starred Richard Boone as "Palladin," a hired gunman from San Francisco who killed wicked men in the Old West. The most durable of the 1950s' television Westerns turned out to be *Gunsmoke,* starring James Arness as U.S. Marshall Matt Dillon, enforcing the law in Dodge City, Kansas.

Many factors accounted for the enormous popularity of the 1950s' TV horse operas. Children, especially young boys, loved to watch them. They afforded viewers the opportunity to watch gunplay and violence. The charismatic actors who starred in the leading shows had vast appeal. More important, Westerns evoked the frontier myth of national origins. Each show recapitulated, in melodramatic style, a chapter in the saga of how the West was won—the taming of the wild frontier, the suppression of the Indians, and the triumph of law and order over villainy and anarchy. Westerns were a highly romanticized, didactic genre that celebrated the triumphalism of America's democratic national culture.

The appeal of Westerns also connected with America's Cold War with the Soviets that raged with great intensity during the 1950s. Westerns reaffirmed the American national identity in a time of ideological conflict with Communism. Just as Marshall Dillon's steady hand maintained the rule of law and morality in a violent frontier cattle town, so too would America's nuclear-carrying bombers maintain law and order in the violent world frontiers of the 1950s. Westerns reigned supreme in the late 1950s, while the Cold War consensus remained intact. The genre vanished precipitously amidst the cultural crisis attendant among the American disaster in

Vietnam. As disillusioned Americans rejected the frontier as a viable national myth, Westerns quickly disappeared from the nation's television screens.

In addition to the programs produced in studios, television covered many live events during the 1950s. Sporting events quickly became a staple of live television: professional wrestling, auto races, boxing, and roller derby were early favorites. Football, baseball, and basketball, all of which had been covered extensively on radio, also received television coverage. Initially, because of technological limitations, neither National Football League games nor major league baseball games telecast particularly well. An innovation that greatly increased the size of the audience for televised football games was the introduction in 1960 of instant replay. In the early years of TV, baseball was an especially difficult game to telecast. One camera stationed behind home plate tried to cover all of the action. The single camera gave a static, one-dimensional aspect to the game; it also foreshortened the distances that balls were hit and players had to run. Owners of professional sports franchises in the early years resisted television coverage. They claimed that it cut into their attendance. Many minor league baseball teams and entire leagues folded during the 1950s, in part the victims of the advent of television coverage of major professional sports.

During television's early years, many hours were devoted to live coverage of public affairs and news features. United Nations sessions at Lake Success, New York, received extensive live coverage. Starting with the 1948 conventions, television quickly established the tradition of live coverage of the major political parties' quadrennial presidential nominating conventions. Controversial Congressional hearings were telecast during the 1950s, the most famous being the Army-McCarthy hearings of 1954. The major networks all inaugurated nightly newscasts of a fifteen-minute duration. In retrospect, it appears that during the 1950s television had limited impact on American politics. There was no evidence that television altered political behavior in any significant way nor had any impact on voting patterns. Millions of Americans continued to rely on radio for political commentary, for news, and for listening to presidential speeches.

Serious scandals rocked the world of television in the late 1950s. During the mid-1950s, quiz shows that awarded winning contestants rich cash prizes became very popular. The *$64,000 Question* and *Twenty-One* were the two most popular shows. *Twenty-One* was especially dramatic. Contestants, sweating in isolation booths under the glare of studio lights, answered lengthy, complex, and very difficult questions about a wide range of topics. In 1956, Charles Van Doren, a young English instructor at Columbia, and the bearer of a distinguished literary pedigree, became a celebrity performer on *Twenty-One*. Week after week, Van Doren demonstrated encyclopedic knowledge, a phenomenal memory, and grace under pressure, winning a total of $129,000. He was celebrated in the media and became a role model. *Time* featured him on its cover. Educators hailed Van Doren's inspiring example for young people and contrasted his influence with the supposedly baneful influence of rock 'n' roll stars such as Elvis Presley.

Alas, Van Doren turned out to be a fraud. One of the contestants that Van Doren had defeated complained that Van Doren had been fed answers to questions in advance. A congressional subcommittee investigated *Twenty-One* and other game shows. Van Doren admitted under oath that he had cheated. He claimed that he had been corrupted by the lure of wealth and fame. He also admitted that he had even been given acting lessons to appear more convincing as he feigned to struggle to answer questions. Disgraced, Van Doren lost his academic job and quickly faded from public view. The networks canceled the big-money quiz shows. A wave of angry dis-illusionment swept the nation. The print media devoted much space to soul-searching and to asking rhetorical questions about the sources of corruption in American life. Critics of television used the quiz show scandals to indict the new mass medium as a cultural wasteland and cor-rupter of youth.

Corrupt wasteland or not, television had surely become an all-encompassing cultural force as the 1950s ended. An estimated two-thirds of the nation's sixty million households watched television on an average of six hours a day. Network executives aimed their fare at the largest possible audiences, treating their viewers as though they were an undifferentiated mass with identical tastes and preferences. In reality, the mass audience consisted of diverse viewing groups, differentiated by age, lifestyle, gender, class, education, ethnicity, and race. Although during the 1950s no one was interested in studying them, these distinctive groups probably had different perceptions of and ascribed different meanings to the programming they watched. Their particular understandings and preferences simply got overridden during the heyday of crude demographics and mass marketed national network shows.

Television programming during the 1950s generally reinforced official values and estab-lished hierarchies of power, wealth, and status. Popular programs such as *Father Knows Best* portrayed the warm inner life of a typical, middle-class, white suburban family. It celebrated to-getherness and the domestic destinies of women. Television functioned as a conservative cul-tural instrument. It never challenged the powers that be nor their official views. Racial minorities hardly appeared on television; when they did, they were cast in traditional servile roles and depicted as demeaning stereotypes. Mostly television served up popular entertainment and commercials. It functioned primarily as a commercial instrument, an advertising conduit, the most intrusive yet invented. Television quickly became the vital center of the consumer cul-ture. It was a vast educational enterprise teaching Americans about the latest styles of con-sumerism and creating desires to purchase the vast array of goods and services constituting consumer civilization.

ROCK 'N' ROLL

A teen culture flourished, with money to spend and clear consumer preferences, centered around fads and pop music. Affluent teenagers constituted a vast new market that the recording companies and record stores hastened to exploit. Before rock music made its appearance in the mid-1950s, mainstream pop music was a diverse mélange of somewhat bland musical styles. Novelty songs, ballads, waltzes, celebrations of teenage love, and an occasional significant song such as Les Paul's and Mary Ford's beautifully rendered "Vaya Con Dios" topped the charts. African-American music, although supercharged with religious and sexual energies, remained largely unknown to white audiences and off of the pop charts.

In the early 1950s, a white Cleveland disc jockey, Allen Freed, began airing African-American music, which he called "rhythm-and-blues." In 1954, Freed moved to New York, where he continued to promote rhythm-and-blues recordings. That same year, a white band, Bill Haley and the Comets, recorded "Rock Around the Clock," the first rock 'n' roll hit.

In 1956, a sullenly handsome nineteen-year-old truck driver from Tupelo, Mississippi, Elvis Presley, became the first rock 'n' roll superstar. Presley, who developed his unique blend of black rhythm-and-blues and country-and-western idioms, shot to the top of the hit parade in 1956 with a series of monster hits, including "Heartbreak Hotel," "Blue Suede Shoes," and "Hound Dog." Crowds of teenage girls screamed hysterically at Presley's highly suggestive stage performances, particularly his gyrating hips keeping time with the frenetic chords he banged out on his acoustic guitar. He made a famous appearance on the *Ed Sullivan Show,* where the cameras focused discreetly on Presley's midsection to conceal his suggestive pelvic thrusts from the huge television audience. Over the next two years, Presley released an amazing string of fourteen consecutive hit recordings. His incredible success helped bring African-American music into the pop mainstream and also helped win white acceptance of African-American recording artists such as Chuck Berry, Little Richard, Ray Charles, and Fats Domino.

Presley's performing style became a symbol of youthful rebellion. His concerts provoked criticism from parents, teachers, and ministers, who encouraged youngsters to listen to the recordings of Pat Boone, a devoutly religious, wholesome performer with a rich baritone voice. The Presley rebellion was implicit in his music, in its rhythms, which excited youngsters and provoked sexual fantasies. Presley himself was anything but a rebel. He was an artist and a showman, a champion of traditional values and a political conservative. When the Army drafted Presley in 1958, he dutifully served his two-year stint without fanfare or incident. Student radicals of the 1960s outraged him.

Figure 4.6   Elvis Presley with fans.
Source: St. Louis Mercantile Library.
Used with permission.

Controversy over the moral threat to young people posed by rock 'n' roll music in the late 1950s was closely linked to a taboo subject, sexual behavior. An Indiana biology professor, Dr. Alfred Kinsey, had published *Sexual Behavior in the Human Male* (1948) and its sequel *Sexual Behavior in the Human Female* (1955). Kinsey interviewed thousands of subjects and used statistical analyses to produce the first scientific study of American sexual behavior. Among his most important findings, Kinsey discovered that premarital sexual relations, adultery, and homosexuality were more widespread than previously thought. Subsequently, investigators would discredit many of Kinsey's findings, particularly his use of statistical data that significantly exaggerated the number of homosexuals inhabiting American society.

REBELS

Not everyone was caught up in the culture of conformity during the 1950s; rebels, especially young people, rejected the manners and mores of the affluent society. Juvenile delinquency increased, and violent gangs of brawling teenagers staged gang fights in the streets of New York and Chicago. Bands of motorcyclists roamed the streets of big cities, back roads, and highways. Some middle-class youngsters dropped out of the college-career "rat race." They joined Bohemian enclaves in Greenwich Village and in San Francisco's North Beach district. Herb Caen, a San Francisco columnist, dubbed these dropouts "beatniks"; they preferred to call themselves the "beat generation." "Beats" confronted the apathy and conformity of American society; they went out of their way to defy prevailing norms of respectability. They abandoned materialistic values to embrace poverty; and they lived in cheap flats, did not work or study, listened to jazz, smoked marijuana, and indulged in a casual sexuality. The Beats were harbingers of the hippie rebellion of the 1960s.

Beat writers wrote poems and novels espousing the values of their rebellious generation. Jack Kerouac wrote the best Beat novel, *On the Road* (1958), which told the tale of two young men, Sal Paradise and Dean Moriarty, who had no money, traveling across America and into Mexico in frantic search of emotionally engaging adventures, what Kerouac and his buddies called "kicks." Poet Allen Ginsberg wrote the most famous beat poem, "Howl," which scathingly indicted a materialistic age that destroyed sensitive souls:

> I saw the best minds of my generation destroyed by madness, starving hysterical naked, dragging themselves through the negro streets looking for an angry fix, . . . burned alive in their innocent flannel suits on Madison Avenue amid blasts of leaden verse & the tanked-up clatter of the iron regiments of fashion.[2]

In addition to the Beat writers, individual authors expressed their alienation from the conformist culture. J. D. Salinger expressed the theme of personal alienation in *Catcher in the Rye*. Salinger's hero, Holden Caulfield, was a schoolboy trapped in a world populated by adults with whom he could not communicate and who did not understand him. Caulfield rebelled, ran away, and had a weekend fling in New York, desperately trying to find an island of integrity amidst a

---

[2]From George Donelson Moss, *America in the Twentieth Century* (Englewood Cliffs, N.J.: Prentice Hall, 1987), p. 282.

sea of conformity. His efforts failed and Caulfield returned to home and school. Salinger's novel was especially popular among 1950s' college students, for he expressed their discontent with a culture that masked a painful reality—not everyone easily fit into the society of would-be organization men and women.

BRIEF BIBLIOGRAPHIC ESSAY

There are many fine books written about American economic, social, and cultural history during the 1950s. Landon Y. Jones's *Great Expectations: America and the Baby Boom Generation* is the best study of the most important demographic development of postwar America. Recently, David Halberstam has written a fine general study of the 1950's focusing on social and cultural history, called *The Fifties.* John Kenneth Galbraith's *The Affluent Society* is a good analysis of postwar prosperity. John B. Rae's *The American Automobile* describes the car culture the 1950s. Kenneth Jackson's *Crabgrass Frontier: The Suburbanization of the United States* is an excellent study of suburbia. A path breaking recent book by Catherine Jurca, *White Diaspora: The Suburb and the Twentieth Century American Novel* demonstrates that fictional treatments of suburbia and its inhabitants have been negative virtually from the moment suburbs came into existence. For women's roles during the 1950s, see Betty Friedan's famed *Feminine Mystique.* Elaine T. May's *Homeward Bound: American Families in the Cold War Era* is a fine recent study. Will Herberg's *Catholic-Protestant-Jew* stresses the important role of religion in mid-century American society. The role of churches in suburban America is well treated in Gibson Winter's *The Suburban Captivity of the Churches.* C. Wright Mills's *White Collar: The American Middle Class* and *The Power Elite* are two very good accounts of the affluent society by a radical critic. For two classic studies of the social and cultural history of the 1950s, see *The Lonely Crowd: A Study of the Changing American Character,* by David Riesman et al. and *The Organization Man,* by William H. Whyte Jr. The popular culture of the 1950s is analyzed critically in *Mass Culture* by Bernard Rosenberg and D. M. White, eds. Erik Barnouw's *Tube of Plenty* is the classic study of television during its "golden age." Another good study of television during the 1950s is Alexander Kendrick's *Prime Time.* Bruce Cook, in *The Beat Generation,* writes about the "beat" writers who flourished in the late 1950s.

WEB SITES

There is an excellent Web site on the social and cultural history of the 1950s compiled by Jessamyn Neuhaus, which includes links to many related topics, at `<http://www.home.earthlink.net/~newhausj/1950s>`. There also is an excellent Web site devoted to the Beat literary movement with many links to individual Beat writers including Jack Kerouac, Allen Ginsberg, and William S. Burroughs, plus topics of interest to them such as jazz and Buddhism, which can be found at `<http://www.charm.net/~brooklyn/LitKicks.html>`.

5

The Politics of Consensus

In the larger world, the Cold War conflict between the United States and the Soviet Union raged unrelentingly throughout the 1950s. The focus of the U.S.–Soviet rivalry shifted to the Third World, to those nations of Africa and Asia emerging from long periods of colonial domination by fading European imperial powers. At home, a bipartisan consensus spanning the American political spectrum supported the American global commitment to contain Communism.

The domestic Cold War climaxed in 1954, when the Eisenhower administration combined with the Senate leadership to destroy the power of the preeminent Red hunter in Washington, Senator Joseph McCarthy. After 1954, the Cold War at home receded; fears and tensions calmed. As the domestic Cold War cooled, the drive by African Americans for full citizenship and dignity in America intensified. In a historic decision, the Supreme Court nullified school segregation and undermined the legal basis of the entire segregationist regime. Heartened by the Court's decision, black people accelerated their drive for freedom and equality, and for inclusion in the mainstream of American life.

President Dwight D. "Ike" Eisenhower was the dominant political leader and icon for the 1950s. He projected an image of confidence and optimism. Ike also was a determined anti-Communist, committed to maintaining American strength during continuing Cold War conflicts with the Soviets. British writer Godfrey Hodgson wrote that Americans in the 1950s were "confident to the verge of complacency about the perfectibility of American society, anxious to the point of paranoia about the threat of Communism." Americans embraced a consensus in the 1950s, that America was the greatest nation in the world, and the American Dream required thermonuclear defenses in the Cold War era.

THE ELECTION OF 1952

The Republicans swept to power in 1952. The Korean War had boosted their chances. The Republicans also capitalized on many scandals unearthed within Truman's administration. As the Republican presidential race shaped up in 1952, Senator Robert Taft, leader of the conservative

Midwestern heartland, appeared to have the inside track to the nomination. But the powerful Eastern internationalist wing of the party promoted the candidacy of popular war hero General Dwight Eisenhower, at the time the commander of NATO forces in Europe. At the Republican Convention, held in Chicago in July, Eisenhower won a close first ballot nomination. He chose thirty-nine-year-old Senator Richard Nixon, a fast-rising political star who had nailed Alger Hiss to be his running mate. When Truman declined to seek reelection, the Democrats chose Illinois governor Adlai Stevenson to challenge Eisenhower.

Eisenhower launched the Republican drive for the White House by announcing a "great crusade" for honest, efficient government at home and for freedom abroad. Nixon and Senator Joseph McCarthy turned their rhetorical siege guns on the Democrats. They convinced millions of voters that Communist infiltration of government agencies posed a serious threat to internal security, for which the Democrats were mainly responsible. Eisenhower's genial smile caused crowds to shout, "We like Ike!" He proved to be an adroit campaigner. His most dramatic move came when he took up the Korean War, the chief issue of the campaign. In a speech given in Detroit, he declared that "an early and honorable" peace required a personal effort, and he pledged, "I shall go to Korea."

In September, a hitch developed that threatened briefly to derail the smoothly running Republican campaign machine. Reporters discovered that Richard Nixon had benefited from a secret fund raised by wealthy Southern California businessmen to pay his political expenses. The party that had been scoring points from its moral crusade against its scandal-plagued opposition suddenly had a scandal of its own. A wave of anti-Nixon sentiment swept the land. Stevenson had a glimmer of hope. Pundits raised the possibility that Eisenhower might have to dump Nixon from the GOP ticket.

But the Republican National Committee purchased air time and gave Nixon the opportunity to go on television and radio to defend himself before the bar of public opinion. Nixon convinced most of his huge television audience that he had not broken the law or done anything wrong. The emotional high point of his speech came when he referred to a cocker spaniel puppy that a supporter had sent the family, which one of his daughters had named "Checkers."

> And you know the kids, like all kids, love the dog, and I just want to say this right now that regardless of what they say about it, we're going to keep it.[1]

The "Checkers" speech outmaneuvered the Democrats and turned a potential disaster for Nixon's party into political advantage. He stayed on the ticket, and the Republican campaign resumed its march toward victory.

On Election Day, Eisenhower scored a lopsided victory. Ike received 33,824,351 votes (55.4 percent) to Stevenson's 27,314,987 votes (44.4 percent). Eisenhower carried the electoral college, 442 to 89. Stevenson carried only nine Southern and border states. The Eisenhower-Nixon ticket lured millions of voters from the Democratic coalition that had given Truman his 1948 triumph—Catholics, working-class voters, and Southerners. Victory was in large measure a personal triumph for the popular general. The Republicans also regained control of Congress, but only by narrow margins: 221 to 214 in the House, and 49 to 48 in the Senate, with Vice

---

[1]Quoted in Stephen E. Ambrose, *Nixon: The Education of a Politician, 1913–1962* (New York: Simon & Schuster, 1987), p. 289.

President Nixon voting. In defeat, the Democratic Party showed considerable strength, and election returns indicated that a majority of the electorate still thought of themselves as Democrats. The Democratic majority coalition had crumbled, but no new Republican majority emerged to replace it. Issue differences between the parties appeared slight. The politics of consensus prevailed.

DYNAMIC CONSERVATISM

President Eisenhower projected an image of bland, moderate nonpartisanship. He came across as the amateur in politics, a disinterested leader serving the nation while relying heavily on subordinates. In reality, Ike embraced a strong conservative philosophy. He believed in fiscal restraint, balanced budgets, and devout anti-Communism. Beneath the bland mask was an able, effective politician who controlled his administration and its policies. Eisenhower also was a skilled, precise writer. Both his best-selling book, *Crusade in Europe,* which made him rich, and his memoirs, written after his presidency, show a talent capable of lucid, exact, and occasionally elegant prose. His writing stands in sharp contrast to the rambling, incoherent utterances characteristic of his press conference responses to reporters' questions. Liberal pundits made fun of Eisenhower's apparent muddleheadedness without realizing that they had fallen for one of his ploys. Eisenhower often feigned ignorance or resorted to gobbledygook to avoid premature disclosures of information or policy decisions. His frequent hunting and fishing trips, and his passion for golf masked a hard-driving, domineering chief executive.

Eisenhower began his presidency proclaiming a new "dynamic conservatism," which he said meant "conservative when it comes to money, liberal when it comes to human beings." Most of his leading advisers came from the ranks of business. Charles E. Wilson, the president of General Motors, became Secretary of Defense. The Treasury Department went to George Humphrey, a wealthy Ohio industrialist. Secretary of State John Foster Dulles was a wealthy corporation lawyer.

The new Administration tried to implement conservative policies in several important areas. Humphrey put conservative fiscal policies in place. Income taxes and federal spending were both cut by 10 percent. Interest rates were raised, and credit was tightened to reduce inflation, which had averaged 10 percent between 1950 and 1953. Republicans tried hard to balance the budget, but they usually failed. Republican efforts to reduce the role of the federal government and to strengthen local and state governments also failed. For agriculture, the Administration pushed for more flexible and lower price supports for farmers. Crop production increased, farm income dropped, and farmers angrily protested the new policies.

But it soon became evident that "dynamic conservatism" was not an effort to repeal the New Deal. Although a fiscal conservative, Eisenhower accepted the expansion of several New Deal programs. Congress expanded Social Security coverage, raised the minimum wage, and extended unemployment insurance. It also created a new Department of Health, Education, and Welfare to coordinate government social programs. The size and scope of the authority of the federal government continued to expand during the Eisenhower years. State and local governments also grew rapidly throughout the years of Eisenhower's presidency.

Eisenhower proposed the largest domestic spending program in American history in 1955, a vast federal-state highway construction program. Congress enacted the Interstate Highway Act in 1956, setting in motion the largest public works project in U.S. history. The federal government provided 90 percent of the costs through the Highway Trust Fund, financed by users' taxes on cars, trucks, buses, gasoline, tires, lubricants, and auto parts. It projected a 42,000-mile network of freeways linking all major urban areas. Construction of mammoth freeway systems continued into the 1970s, and the government spent billions of dollars annually on them. These road-building projects had an enormous impact on American life. Annual driving mileage increased fourfold. Shopping centers, linked by the new roads, sprang up to serve rapidly growing suburban communities. By the 1970s, the new freeways covered as much land as the nation's central business districts. Every suburb had a highway strip mall replete with drive-in movies, bowling alleys, gas stations, and fast-food restaurants.

Eisenhower's moderation accorded with the public mood of the 1950s. Most Americans felt smugly complacent about their society. They believed that economic growth would solve all social problems, gradually enlarging the economic pie until poverty vanished. There was no need for higher taxes, special programs, or sacrifices by anyone. The 1950s were a time for holding the line against inflation, recession, and social disorder—of balancing liberty and security within a moderate framework acceptable to all.

The New Deal was legitimated during the reign of Ike. It became the status quo undergirding consensus politics. Despite its business orientation and its conservative ideology, the Eisenhower administration supported the welfare state and managed the economy much as Truman had done. The pragmatic accommodation that the conservative Eisenhower made by protecting and expanding the welfare state signaled the breakdown of traditional political categories. Politicians no longer battled one another over fundamental issues; they merely quarreled over which interest group got how much. Previously, big government had been linked to liberalism and limited government to conservatism. In the 1950s, except for a few traditional ideologues on the Left and the Right, the real issue was no longer whether government was large or small, but whose interests it served. Conservatives often voted for huge spending programs such as defense budgets, highway programs, and Social Security extensions. Liberals often voted for huge defense budgets in the name of Cold War bipartisanship and to protect national security in the nuclear age.

McCARTHY: ZENITH AND RUIN

National alarm over Communist infiltration of government agencies persisted well into Eisenhower's presidency. Joseph McCarthy quickly resumed his investigations of alleged subversion in government. For eighteen months, McCarthy was the second most powerful politician in Washington, dominating the news with his spectacular accusations. A 1954 poll showed that 50 percent of Americans approved of his activities, and only 29 percent opposed them. Many of his Senate colleagues, knowing that he was a fraud, despised him. But they feared him even more, and they refused to challenge him openly, having seen what McCarthy could do to an opponent at election time. Eisenhower also refused to confront him because he did not want a party rupture over the controversial demagogue.

The State Department continued to be McCarthy's favorite hunting ground, even though it was now controlled by Republicans. In 1953, McCarthy went after the State Department's overseas information service. Secretary of State John Foster Dulles ordered department personnel to cooperate fully with McCarthy's investigation. Supposedly subversive books were dutifully removed from the shelves by State Department functionaries, and some of the books were burned.

In 1954, McCarthy attacked the U.S. Army. His subcommittee investigated alleged Communist subversion at Fort Monmouth, New Jersey, the site of sensitive communications technology. During the inquiry, McCarthy discovered that the Army had promoted a dentist, Irving Peress, to the rank of major and had then given him an honorable discharge when it learned that he had once invoked the Fifth Amendment when asked about Communist affiliations. An angry McCarthy bullied and humiliated General Ralph Zwicker, Peress's commanding officer, when he refused to give him Peress's file.

The Army mounted a counterattack against McCarthy, accusing him of trying to blackmail the Army into giving preferential treatment to G. David Schine, a former McCarthy staffer who had been assigned to Fort Monmouth. McCarthy retorted that the Army was holding Schine hostage to keep his committee from investigating the Army. McCarthy's subcommittee voted to hold hearings on the charges made by the two adversaries, with Senator Karl Mundt of South Dakota temporarily assuming the chairmanship. On April 22, 1954, the famed Army-McCarthy hearings began. For six weeks, they were telecast daily to fifteen million fascinated viewers.

McCarthy himself starred in the televised political drama. He bullied and harried witnesses. He interrupted the proceedings frequently, made threats, and shouted "point of order, Mr. Chairman, point of order!" Some committee members, particularly Senator Stuart Symington of Missouri, gave as well as took from McCarthy. Symington was especially adept at taunting McCarthy and annoying him. The hearings also made a star out of Joseph Welch, a soft-spoken trial lawyer who was the Army's chief counsel. At one point, Welch left McCarthy temporarily speechless by asking rhetorically, "At long last, sir, at long last, have you left no sense of decency?" The hearings ended inconclusively. Neither the Army nor McCarthy won. It is not true that television exposure or Welch's dramatic remark undermined McCarthy's popularity. Polls taken shortly after the hearings showed that McCarthy still retained his 50 percent approval ratings.

It was McCarthy's methods, his unruly behavior, that provoked his downfall. He went too far when he attacked the Army. In August 1954, the Senate established a committee to study a set of censure charges brought against McCarthy by Republican Ralph Flanders of Vermont. Chairing the committee was conservative Republican Arthur Watkins of Utah. The committee recommended that the Senate censure McCarthy. After noisy hearings, the full Senate voted 67 to 22 to "condemn" McCarthy on two counts: for contempt of the Senate and for abuse of Watkins' committee members.

Senate condemnation effectively destroyed McCarthy. He still made accusations, but his attacks no longer commanded headlines. He had lost the spotlight even faster than he had found it. His health failed, and he died in May 1957, of infectious hepatitis, aggravated by heavy drinking. McCarthy could perform only as long as his Senate colleagues were willing to tolerate his behavior. Anti-Communist liberals have insisted that McCarthy's greatest disservice to the nation was to give anti-Communism a bad name, thereby enabling the Old Left and the New Left in later years to claim that any concern about Communism was just another McCarthyite smear.

THE POLITICS OF CONSENSUS

1954 was the last election year in which the Communist-in-government issue had any force. Anti-Communism as a major issue in American domestic politics died with McCarthy. Americans became less obsessed with paranoid fantasies about Communist subversives threatening the nation's internal security. But anti-Communism remained a staple of American political culture, far outliving its foremost practitioner. Intolerance, fear, and suspicion of dissent persisted. Most Americans regarded as axiomatic the notion that the Soviet Union headed a vast international conspiracy unrelentingly hostile to the United States. The Cold War bipartisan consensus on the conduct of American foreign policy remained intact.

Political alignments during the 1950s remained unstable. Eisenhower's 1952 victory signaled the breakup of the Roosevelt coalition of labor, farmers, ethnics, and Southerners, forged during the 1930s; but the Republicans could not form a majority coalition to replace it. As traditional political allegiances declined during the 1950s, a large independent "swing" vote emerged, varying in size with each election. Millions of citizens voted a split ticket, supporting a man or an issue instead of a party, and shifted sides in response to particular situations. The two major parties attained a rough equality for the first time since the early 1890s. An unstable equilibrium prevailed. National elections held during the 1950s reflected the unstable balance of political forces. Except for 1952, the Democrats won the Congressional elections and the Republicans the presidential elections.

The 1956 election was a dull replay of 1952. Ike was at the peak of his popularity and almost immune to criticism. Stevenson campaigned tentatively, groping for an issue and never finding one. He tried to make issues of Ike's age and health. Eisenhower had suffered a serious heart attack in September 1955 and had been incapacitated for weeks. But he recovered, and in 1956 the sixty-five-year-old leader enjoyed good health and was obviously fit to run again. In 1956, the Democratic arsenal contained no political weapons to match the Republican slogan of "four more years of peace and prosperity." Eisenhower won reelection by a larger margin than his 1952 victory. But the Democrats carried both houses of Congress. The year 1956 was the first time in American political history that a party won both Houses while losing the presidency. Eisenhower was the first president to begin a term with Congress controlled by the opposition.

But the nominal Democratic congressional majorities were undercut by the conservative bipartisan coalition of Southern Democrats and Northern Republicans who could gut or block most liberal legislation. During the 1950s, moderate Texas politicians led the Democrats in Congress. Speaker Sam Rayburn led the House, and his protege Lyndon Johnson led the Senate. Both leaders pursued a strategy of compromise and cooperation with the Republican White House.

CIVIL RIGHTS

Soon after taking office, President Eisenhower appointed Governor Earl Warren of California as Chief Justice of the Supreme Court. The Court had been chipping away at the constitutional foundations of racial discrimination since the 1940s in two areas—denial of voting rights and school segregation. It was in the realm of education that the Court chose to nullify the "separate but equal" principle that had provided the constitutional basis of Jim Crow.

Several cases challenging school segregation came before the Court. With Warren providing the leadership that spurred his associates to action, the justices decided a representative case, *Brown v. the Board of Education* of Topeka, on May 17, 1954. A unanimous Court ruled that *de jure* (legal) public school segregation was unconstitutional under the Fourteenth Amendment, reversing the "separate but equal" doctrine established in *Plessy v. Ferguson* (1896). The Court's decision incorporated much of the legal brief filed by Thurgood Marshall, chief counsel for the NAACP:

> In the field of public education, the doctrine of "separate but equal" has no place. Separate educational facilities are inherently unequal.[2]

On May 31, 1955, the Supreme Court issued its enforcement decree directing federal district courts to order school desegregation to begin in their areas and to require "good faith compliance with all deliberate speed." Having destroyed the legal basis of school segregation, the courts proceeded to undermine institutional segregation everywhere. Federal court decisions nullified segregation in public housing, recreational facilities, and interstate commerce. The *Brown* decision was the most controversial and most important Supreme Court decision of modern times.

White Southerners defied the *Brown* decision and refused to implement it for many years. In 1956, a group of 101 Congressmen and Senators from eleven Southern states that had comprised the Confederacy almost a century before, signed the Southern Manifesto. It pledged to "use all lawful means to bring about a reversal of this decision which is contrary to the Constitution." The Southern Manifesto also encouraged Southern officials to try to prevent implementing desegregation. All across the segregated South, white officials called for "massive resistance" to prevent the integration of public schools.

The crucial confrontation between federal and state authority over school desegregation came at Little Rock, Arkansas, in September 1957 where Eisenhower faced the most serious domestic crisis of his presidency. The Arkansas chapter of the NAACP endeavored to implement the *Brown* decision by enrolling nine African American students in Central High School.

Arkansas Governor Orville Faubus prevented integration by ordering National Guardsmen to block the school entrance. A federal court ordered the troops to leave, and the African-American students enrolled. But white students threatened them, and school officials, fearing for their safety, removed them from the school. Faced with clear defiance of the law, Eisenhower acted. For the first time since Reconstruction, a president sent federal troops into the South to protect the rights of African Americans. Paratroopers entered Central High, and the National Guardsmen were placed under federal command. Guarded by soldiers with fixed bayonets, the nine teenagers enrolled again at Central High. Governor Faubus then ordered all Arkansas public schools to shut down rather than allow further integration.

There is a close relationship between the Supreme Court decision outlawing segregation and the Southern civil rights campaigns of the mid-1950s. Civil rights activists were tremendously

---

[2]Quoted in Anthony Lewis, *Portrait of a Decade: The Second American Revolution* (New York: Bantam Books, 1965), p. 26.

Figure 5.1   A fifteen-year-old African-American student, Elizabeth Eckford, is shown outside Central High School in Little Rock, Arkansas, being jeered by a white student, Hazel Massery. Massery later apologized to Eckford and spoke out publicly against racism. *Source:* AP/Wide World Photos.

encouraged by the Court's rulings. They responded by escalating their attacks on racial injustice. When state and local jurisdictions refused to obey the *Brown* decision, activists took to the streets in an effort to pressure white Southerners into compliance with the law or else provoke federal interventions to enforce it. Civil rights activists often resorted to radical tactics such as civil disobedience and boycotts to bring about enforcement of federal laws.

As the Court struck down the legal foundations of segregation, African Americans stepped up their attacks on racial injustice. Eighteen months after the *Brown* decision, in Montgomery, Alabama, Rosa Parks refused to surrender her seat at the front of a bus to a white man and ignited the modern civil rights movement. A charming myth has risen about Parks as the seamstress who was simply too tired to move to the back of the bus and whose arrest set off a spontaneous demonstration that ended happily with integrated bus service. That appealing story misrepresents a carefully planned and well-organized movement for social change. It also omits Parks's and other men and women's long prior careers as community leaders and social activists. The boycott was initiated by the Montgomery chapter of the NAACP working closely with the Women's Political Council in which Rosa Parks had long been a leader. These organizations brought a young Baptist minister on board to lead the boycott, who, for the rest of his tragically short life, would be the foremost leader of the civil rights revolution. He was Dr. Martin Luther King Jr., who declared:

Integration is the great issue of our age, the great issue of our nation and the great issue of our community. We are in the midst of a great struggle, the consequences of which will be world-shaking.[3]

Helped by a Supreme Court decision declaring bus segregation unconstitutional, and after an arduous campaign lasting 381 days, the boycott eventually forced the city to integrate its bus service. The company also agreed to hire African-American drivers and mechanics.

At the same time, the NAACP mounted an intensive legal campaign against segregation everywhere African Americans encountered it. Victorious in forty-two of forty-six appeals to the Supreme Court, the NAACP advanced voting rights and integrated housing, transportation, public accommodations, and schools in many parts of the South. While Thurgood Marshall and the NAACP fought their civil rights battles in the courts, King and his followers fought theirs in the dusty streets of Southern towns and cities.

A drive to guarantee African-American voting rights also began. The Senate Majority Leader Lyndon Johnson masterfully shepherded The Civil Rights Act of 1957 through the Senate. It created a Civil Rights Commission and gave the Attorney General power to take local officials to court in cases where they denied African Americans the right to vote. Congress enacted a stronger civil rights law in 1960; it provided legal penalties against anyone interfering with the right to vote.

The civil rights movement made a powerful start during the 1950s. Most progress came from efforts by African Americans themselves. They were aided by Supreme Court decisions that nullified the legal foundations of segregation and by Congressional legislation that strengthened the gathering forces of the black revolution. These actions set the stage for the spectacular gains of the early and mid-1960s.

THE NEW LOOK

During the 1952 presidential campaign, Republicans charged that the Truman-Acheson policy of containing Communism had failed, especially in Asia with the loss of China and the stalemate in the Korean War. John Foster Dulles insisted that the United States, instead of pursuing containment, should make it "publicly known that it wants and expects liberation to occur." But in office, Eisenhower and Dulles, continued the containment policies, with some minor alterations, which they had condemned during the 1952 campaign. They had no choice. The logic of liberation led inescapably to one conclusion—Americans would have to fight to free the captive nations, because the Communists would never voluntarily set them free. Freedom for Eastern Europe meant war with the Soviet Union. Further, Eisenhower had committed himself to cutting military expenditures. Liberation, far more costly than containment, could never be carried out by fiscal conservatives. Republicans hid their failure to liberate anyone from Communism behind tough talk.

Republicans called their foreign policy the New Look. It relied on strategic air power to destroy the Soviet Union with nuclear bombs if Communist aggression occurred anywhere in the world. Dulles believed that the threat to obliterate the Soviets would "deter" them from hostile

[3]Quoted in *ibid.*, p. 62.

Figure 5.2   The Montgomery, Alabama, bus boycott ignited the modern civil rights movement in the South. The boycott began in December 1955 when Rosa Parks, here shown sitting in the front of a city bus, refused to surrender her seat to a white man and return to the back of the bus.   *Source:* National Archives.

actions. The New Look strategy allowed the Administration to reduce outlays for conventional forces. Dulles described their approach as *massive retaliation.* Secretary of Defense Wilson observed that the New Look provided "more bang for the buck." Eisenhower insisted that cuts in defense spending were necessary to preserve the American way of life. In a speech given on April 16, 1953, he said,

> Every gun that is made, every warship launched, every rocket fired signifies, in the final sense, a theft from those who hunger and are not fed, those who are cold and are not clothed.[4]

Critics of the New Look strategy charged that *massive retaliation* had locked the United States into an all-or-nothing response to Communist aggression. A Communist-led uprising in a small country would not warrant an attack on the Soviet Union, hence the revolution would probably succeed. The Soviets also could see the limitations of massive retaliation and would not be deterred from promoting small-scale insurrections in Third World countries. Freedom would be nibbled away at the periphery.

Ike defended his New Look foreign policy by contending that the United States could not afford to police the entire world, that it must concentrate on defending its vital interests. If NATO nations or Japan were attacked, the U.S. response would be swift and overwhelming. Dulles also tried to compensate for the limitations of the New Look strategy by forging regional

---

[4]Charles C. Alexander, *Holding the Line: The Eisenhower Era, 1952–1961* (Bloomington, Ind.: Indiana University Press, 1975), p. 164.

security pacts with allies in which the United States would furnish the military hardware and the allies the troops if the Communists attacked. By 1960, as a result of "pactomania," the United States had committed itself to defend forty-three countries.

VIETNAM: GETTING IN DEEPER

Dulles described his diplomatic method as the willingness to go to the brink of war to achieve peace. "Brinkmanship" was more threatening as rhetoric than as action. Dulles never used brinkmanship on the Soviets, nor did the United States become embroiled in any major wars during the Eisenhower-Dulles tenure. Brinkmanship was tried mainly in Asia, with mixed results. It worked in Korea to phase out a war. The President told Dulles to warn the Chinese that if they did not accept a settlement, the United States might use nuclear weapons in the war. That threat broke a two-year-old deadlock and ended the conflict on American terms.

Dulles then applied brinkmanship to Southeast Asia, where, since 1946, the French, trying to reimpose colonialism in Indochina, had been fighting Vietnamese guerrillas. In 1950, the Truman administration began sending economic and military aid to support the French efforts to contain Communism in Asia, following the Maoist triumph in China. Eisenhower expanded American aid to the French; by 1954, the United States was paying 78 percent of the cost of the war. Eisenhower, like Truman before him, applied Cold War ideology to this struggle between Asian nationalists and European imperialists. Washington viewed the Indochina War as part of the global conflict between Free World forces and Communism.

Despite U.S. help, the French were losing the war. By 1954, Viet Minh forces held most of Vietnam. French generals tried to retrieve the military initiative. They put 11,000 of their best troops in a remote fortress deep within guerrilla-held territory at Dien Bien Phu and challenged them to fight an open battle. The French believed that Asians could not defeat European forces in a conventional battle. Vietnamese forces besieged the garrison. Within weeks, it was on the verge of surrender. With war weariness strong in France after eight years of war, the fall of Dien Bien Phu would mean victory for the Vietnamese Nationalists and the end of French Indochina.

Facing imminent ruin in Southeast Asia, the French appealed to the Americans to save them. President Eisenhower considered air strikes to relieve the siege around Dien Bien Phu, but he insisted that American allies join the effort and that Congress support it. Prime Minister Winston Churchill rebuffed Dulles's efforts to enlist British support. Senate leaders told the President that without British involvement, the Senate would not approve U.S. military intervention. Lacking support from allies or Congress, Eisenhower rejected the French request. On May 7, 1954, Dien Bien Phu fell to the Communists.

Meanwhile, an international conference previously convened in Geneva sought to find a political solution to the Indochina War. Conferees worked out a settlement in July 1954. By its terms, the French and Viet Minh agreed to a cease-fire and a temporary partition of Vietnam at the 17th parallel of north latitude, with French forces withdrawing south of that line and Viet Minh forces withdrawing to the north. Free elections were to be held within two years to unify the country. During the interim, the French were to help prepare Southern Vietnam for independence and then leave.

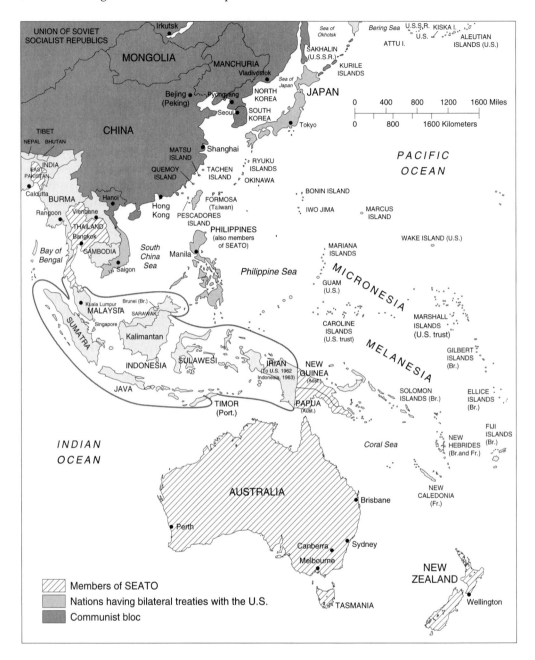

Figure 5.3   The Alliance System in the Far East.   *Source:* Moss, *Moving On, 1st ed.,* p. 119.

The United States opposed the Geneva Accords but could not prevent the conferees from adopting them. The U.S. delegate refused to sign them, but he agreed to accept them and pledged not to use force to upset the arrangements. But at the time, President Eisenhower announced that the United States "has not been party to or is bound by the decisions taken by the conference." Ho Chi Minh, whose forces verged on taking all of Vietnam, settled for just the northern half of the country at Geneva, because he was confident of winning the forthcoming elections over the French-backed regime in the south and because he was pressured by his allies, the Soviets and the Chinese, who wanted an end to the fighting in Vietnam.

After Geneva, Dulles salvaged what he could from what Washington regarded as a major Communist victory that threatened all of Southeast Asia. In September 1954, Dulles arranged for Great Britain, France, Australia, New Zealand, Thailand, Pakistan, and the Philippines to create the Southeast Asia Treaty Organization (SEATO). SEATO members agreed to "meet and confer" if one of them were attacked. A separate agreement covered Laos, Cambodia, and "South Vietnam," that is, Vietnam south of the seventeenth parallel. SEATO tried to project American power into Indochina in the aftermath of the French defeat and to provide a legal basis for subsequent American interventions in Southeast Asia.

The United States also supported a new government emerging in southern Vietnam, headed by Ngo Dinh Diem. Americans trained and equipped Diem's army and security forces. The Eisenhower administration promoted the diplomatic fiction that the seventeenth parallel had become a national boundary separating two states, "South Vietnam" and "North Vietnam." Washington also backed Diem when he refused to allow the scheduled elections to unify the country to take place in 1956.

Eisenhower believed that if Southern Vietnam fell to the Communists, all of Southeast Asia would be imperiled. He compared the nations of Southeast Asia to a row of dominoes: knock one over, and the rest would fall quickly. After Geneva, the United States committed itself to creating a new nation in Southern Vietnam that would "serve as a proving ground for democracy in Asia." The survival of the new South Vietnam would sabotage the Geneva settlement that assumed the emergence of an unified, Communist-controlled Vietnam within two years.

With U. S. support during the late 1950s, Diem attempted to suppress all opposition to his regime. His repressive actions provoked violent opposition. Local officials and Diem informers were assassinated by Communist and non-Communist opponents, all of whom Diem called "VietCong," meaning Vietnamese who are Communists. The Viet Minh infiltrated men and supplies south of the seventeenth parallel to take control of the anti-Diem insurgency. Small-scale civil war had begun. By 1959, the second Indochina War was underway. It would eventually involve the United States in its longest war.

THE CHINA CRISIS

While Americans were trying to build a nation in Southeast Asia, they faced a confrontation with mainland China over Formosa (Taiwan). Nationalist Chinese pilots, flying from Formosan bases in U.S. planes, had bombed mainland shipping and ports since 1953. The U.S. Seventh Fleet patrolled the waters between China and Formosa, protecting the Nationalists from Communist reprisals. In September 1954, Communist Chinese artillery began shelling Nationalist defenders of Quemoy and Matsu, two small islands held by Nationalist forces sitting in the mouths of two mainland ports about 100 miles from Formosa. Eisenhower was determined to hold these islands that he believed were essential to the defense of Formosa.

Figure 5.4   In the dense jungle terrain of Vietnam, South Vietnamese nationalist forces were unable to defeat the Viet Minh. *Source:* National Archives.

Washington reacted to the shelling by increasing the American military presence in the Taiwan Strait, strengthening Nationalist forces, and issuing stern warnings to Beijing. In December 1954, Washington and Taiwan signed a mutual defense treaty. The following year, Congress gave President Eisenhower the authority to use military force if necessary to defend Taiwan and the offshore islands. The Chinese, lacking nuclear weapons and getting no help from the Soviets, reduced the shelling and offered to negotiate a "relaxation of tensions." The United States, which did not recognize the mainland Chinese government, refused to negotiate with the Communist Chinese. However, it stopped its war preparations, and the situation calmed. Beginning quietly at Geneva in the summer of 1955, Chinese and U.S. officials held talks about Taiwan, trade, and other topics.

U.S. problems in Asia highlighted the emergence of Third World nations as a major force in world affairs during the 1950s. These nations, many of them recently independent former European colonies, increasingly became the focus of the Cold War conflict between the USSR and the United States. Third World nations were sources of raw materials, they attracted foreign investment, and they provided markets, particularly for American exports. Many Third World nations wanted to remain neutral in the Cold War. But to U.S. Secretary of State Dulles, neutralism in a bipolar world dominated by two superpowers, one of which was "immoral," was wrong. He opposed a conference of twenty-nine African and Asian nations held at Bandung, Indonesia, in April 1955, during the height of the Quemoy-Matsu crisis. Leaders of the Afro-Asian nations called for these nations to form an alternative to the two superpowers and their alliance systems. Chinese Premier Jou En-lai played a prominent role at Bandung; China moved to assert leadership of the emerging Third World nations.

AT THE SUMMIT

When the United States considered using nuclear weapons during the Formosan crisis, it highlighted a frightening world reality. Thermonuclear weapons of the mid-1950s were a thousand times more powerful than the two bombs that had devastated Hiroshima and Nagasaki in 1945. Both the Soviets and Americans possessed hydrogen bombs, and both were developing intercontinental missiles. Both sides had to face the possibility of a nuclear exchange if they went to war. They agreed to hold a "summit conference" to try to reduce the possibility of nuclear catastrophe.

The conference convened at Geneva on July 18, 1955. President Eisenhower, Premier Nikolai Bulganin of the Soviet Union, Prime Minister Anthony Eden of England, and Premier Edgar Faure of France attended. Geneva signaled a turning point in the Cold War. Both sides conceded in effect that the Cold War could not be won militarily. The atmosphere at the summit was cordial. A "spirit of Geneva" emerged, symbolized by a photograph of Eisenhower shaking hands with Bulganin. Eisenhower also scored a propaganda victory when he offered, and the Soviets rejected, his "Open Skies" proposal that would permit aerial surveillance of both countries' nuclear development and testing facilities. The conference yielded no substantive agreements, and the arms race continued after the summit ended. But a thermonuclear stalemate had forced the superpowers to a relaxation of tensions. The Cold War thawed a little. Both sides agreed to begin arms control negotiations and later suspended atmospheric testing of nuclear weapons.

THE CIA AT WORK

In 1953, Ike appointed Allen Dulles, younger brother of the Secretary of State, as director of the CIA. Dulles recruited Cold Warriors eager to fight Communism, many of whom were liberal intellectuals from Ivy League universities. Under his leadership, paramilitary covert operations became a secret arm of U.S. foreign policy. The CIA's first major triumph came in Iran in 1953. A Nationalist government, led by Mohammed Mossadegh, had nationalized oil fields controlled by the British and forced the young Shah of Iran into exile. The United States, fearing that Mossadegh might sell oil to the Soviets and align himself with Iranian Communists, sent CIA operatives to Iran. Working with the British and Iranian army officials, they helped overthrow Mossadegh and restored the Shah to power. Iran then made a deal that gave U.S. oil companies 40 percent of Iranian oil production, the British 40 percent, and the Dutch 20 percent. The CIA had helped to subvert a popular government and the United States subsequently controlled a major share of Iranian oil production.

The CIA also helped overthrow a Leftist government in Central America. Jacob Arbenz Guzman had been elected president of Guatemala in 1951. Arbenz was not a Communist, but

Communists supported his government and held offices within it. In 1953, the Arbenz government expropriated 234,000 acres of land belonging to an American corporation, the United Fruit Company, for a land reform program.

The United States cut off economic aid and sent CIA forces to Guatemala to overthrow Arbenz. CIA officials recruited an army of exiles in neighboring Honduras, led by Colonel Carlos Castillo Armas. When Armas's forces were ready for attack, CIA pilots airlifted their supplies and bombed the Guatemalan capital. Arbenz, facing military defeat, fled into exile. Armas established a military dictatorship and returned the expropriated lands to the United Fruit Company. Bouyed by their success in toppling a Leftist government perceived to be hostile to U.S. economic and strategic interests in Guatemala, CIA officials would try to replicate their efforts in Cuba in 1961 with disastrous results.

TROUBLE IN SUEZ

The Cold War spread to the Middle East after World War II, deeply involving the United States in a strategically significant region that had previously been of only peripheral interest. In the 1950s, the Middle East was a compound of many parts: Arab nationalism, regional rivalries, weak and unstable governments, the world's richest oil reserves, feudal societies, religious extremism, superpower penetration, and most of all, the intractable Arab-Israeli conflict. It was the presence of a Jewish state on land that was formerly part of Palestine that lies at the core of many Middle East conflicts.

The Arab-Israeli conflict dated from the end of World War II. Most of the European Jews who survived the Holocaust wanted to go to Palestine, where a sizable Jewish population had been built up since 1900. Palestine was administered by the British, who tried to prevent Zionist refugees from entering Palestine in order to safeguard their Anglo-Arabian oil interests. But the British, weakened by losses in World War II, withdrew from Palestine in 1947, turning its problems over to the United Nations. At that time, the United States and the Soviet Union united to carve an Israeli homeland out of the western portion of Palestine. The United Nations partitioned Palestine to create a Jewish state, Israel, along the Mediterranean coast. On May 14, 1948, Israel proclaimed its independence. America recognized Israel immediately and the Soviet Union soon afterward.

Instantly, Arab armies attacked, determined to drive the Jews into the Mediterranean Sea, to destroy the new Jewish state, and to preserve all of Palestine for the Palestinian Arabs. At first, the outnumbered Israelis were driven back. They asked for a truce, and the Soviets and Americans imposed one. During the cease-fire, the Soviets flew in quantities of heavy arms, violating the truce. When fighting resumed, the Israelis routed the Arab forces. Israeli forces also advanced far beyond the original boundaries assigned by the UN partition. The beaten Arabs sued for peace in 1949.

An African American diplomat, Ralph Bunche, arranged an armistice ending the first Arab-Israeli war. Israel survived because of Soviet arms and U.S. diplomatic support. Its inflated borders included thousands of Palestinians. Another 700,000 Palestinians fled or were driven from their homes by the advancing Israeli forces, creating a Palestinian refugee problem that has never been resolved. The Soviets supported Israel until 1955, when they switched to the Arab side. The United States has continued to be Israel's major supporter, while trying to maintain friendly relations with moderate Arab nations.

With U.S. assistance, Gamal Abdul Nasser came to power in Egypt in 1952, the first of a new generation of Arab Nationalist leaders. America offered him $270 million to build a dam on the Upper Nile to control flooding and to generate hydroelectric power. The aid money for the Aswan Dam represented an American effort to tilt its Middle East policy in an increasingly pro-Arab direction. In 1955, Dulles arranged the signing of the Baghdad Pact, linking Britain, Turkey, Iran, Iraq, and Pakistan. The pact's main objective was to keep the Soviets out of the Middle East. The pact angered Nasser, who viewed it as an effort to bring the Cold War to the Middle East and to strengthen Iraq, Egypt's rival for Arab leadership. The USSR reacted to the signing of the Baghdad Pact by becoming more active in Arab affairs, particularly in Egypt and Syria.

Egyptian and Israeli forces clashed along the Gaza Strip, territory that both nations claimed, inhabited mainly by Palestinian refugees. The Israelis suddenly attacked in force in 1955, inflicting a major defeat on the Egyptians. Nasser, angry and humiliated, asked the United States for arms. Washington refused him. Nasser then turned to the Soviet bloc and concluded an arms deal with the Communists. Dulles, fearing that Egypt might become a Soviet client, withdrew U.S. aid for the Aswan Dam. Nasser responded by nationalizing the Suez Canal, owned by an Anglo-French consortium. He used its $30 million of annual revenues to finance the Aswan Dam. He also closed the canal to Israeli shipping.

Britain and France, dependent on Persian Gulf oil shipped through the Suez Canal, proposed overthrowing Nasser and returning the canal to its former owners. The United States, afraid such actions could bring the Soviets into the fray and even lead to World War III, rejected the Anglo-French proposal. The British and French decided to overthrow Nasser, and incorporated the Israelis into their plans. On October 29, 1956, Israel invaded Egypt. A week later, the French and British landed troops in Egypt to seize the canal. The United States condemned the Anglo-French-Israeli actions before the United Nations. The United States also cut off oil shipments to France and Britain and threatened to wage financial war against the British pound sterling. The French and British, reeling from a combination of U.S. and UN opposition, Soviet threats to intervene, and an Arab oil boycott, withdrew without occupying the canal. The Soviets used the occasion to provide funds for the Aswan project; in return the Egyptians granted the Soviets use of a former British military base at Suez.

U.S. efforts to avoid war in the Middle East had mostly negative consequences for American foreign policy interests. Administration efforts weakened NATO, humiliated America's major European allies, alienated Nasser, angered the Israelis, helped the Soviets get a military base in Egypt, and failed to improve relations with other Arab countries. But Nasser eventually paid the French and British $81 million for the Suez Canal, and Middle Eastern oil supplies remained in Western hands.

While the Suez crisis raged, crises erupted in Eastern Europe. Early in 1956, the new Soviet leader, Nikita Khrushchev, promised to ease Soviet restrictions in satellite countries. Ferment spread quickly throughout Eastern Europe. Riots in Poland forced the Soviets to grant the Poles substantial concessions. Hungarian students and workers overthrew a Stalinist puppet. He was replaced by Imre Nagy. Nagy demanded the removal of Red Army forces and the implementation of democracy; the Soviets acceded to both of these demands. Dulles promised the Hungarians economic aid if they broke with the Soviets. On October 31, Hungary announced that it was leaving the Warsaw Pact. Liberation appeared to be at hand; a captive people were freeing themselves from Communist tyranny.

Soviet leaders, unwilling to let the Warsaw Pact disintegrate, invaded Hungary. Soviet tanks crushed the Hungarian revolution and killed 30,000 Hungarians. Radio Budapest pleaded for help, but none came from America or elsewhere. Eisenhower had never considered sending troops, nor would he have had there not been a Suez crisis. Neither he nor any other U.S. president would ever risk World War III to help liberate an East European country from Soviet clutches. American talk of liberation for Eastern Europe had always been a sham. U.S. forces were not strong enough to defeat the Red Army in Hungary, except with the use of nuclear weapons that would have ruined the country and killed millions of people.

After the Suez crisis, Washington announced the Eisenhower Doctrine to try to offset Soviet influence and militant Arab nationalism in the Middle East. It offered military aid to any country requesting it to resist Communist aggression. The Eisenhower Doctrine extended containment to the Middle East region. Twice it was implemented. In the spring of 1957, U.S. troops were sent into Jordan to protect its government from Egyptian threats. In 1958, about 14,000 marines landed in Lebanon to protect its pro-Western government from an insurgency supported by Nasser.

As the 1950s ended, America enjoyed good relations with traditional Arab states such as Saudi Arabia, the region's major oil producer, which had become a U.S. client through economic aid and arms sales. Middle Eastern oil continued its flow through the Suez Canal. But U.S. influence in the Middle East was declining. Arab nationalism and Soviet influence were growing. Arab hostility toward Israel, combined with U. S. support of the Jewish state allowed the Soviets to champion Arab nationalism. American efforts to balance Arab and Israeli interests largely failed during the 1950s. But it was already clear by the end of the 1950s that no conceivable diplomatic formula promised a long-term solution to Middle East conflicts unless the Arab-Israeli impasse was overcome. It was this seemingly intractable and long-running Arab-Israeli conflict that was one of the prime causes of the rise of Islamic fundamentalism and the terrorist attacks on Israeli and U. S. interests that began in the 1970s and have continued to the present.

SPUTNIK

After the Suez crisis, the strategic balance appeared to shift toward the Soviet Union. In September 1957, the Soviets test-fired an intercontinental ballistics missile (ICBM) over a year ahead of the United States. One month later, they launched the first space satellite, which they called *Sputnik*. *Sputnik's* strategic implications were ominous, proving that the Soviets had powerful booster rockets and had solved guidance problems essential to delivering a thermonuclear warhead to its target. The United States appeared to face both a missile "gap" and a space "lag" with the Soviet Union.

At first, President Eisenhower played down the Soviets' achievements, trying to reassure anxious Americans. But he was not convincing. He offered no new programs to catch the Soviets in either the arms or space race. For the first time, Ike was vigorously attacked in Congress and in the media. The attacks were reinforced by the sluggish performance of the economy, which had slipped into recession, and the revelation of a scandal in the administration. Eisenhower's special assistant, Sherman Adams, was forced to resign for accepting favors from a businessman who needed a favor from the federal government. The Soviets had scored a

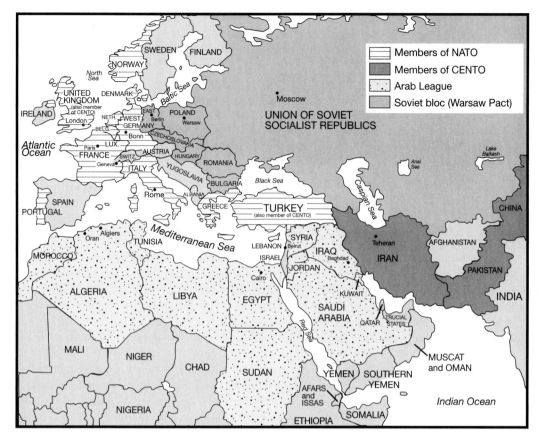

Figure 5.5   Postwar alliances: Europe, North Africa, and the Middle East in the 1950s.   *Source:* Litwack & Jordan, *The United States: Becoming a World Power,* Vol. 2, 7th ed. (Englewood Cliffs, N.J.: Prentice Hall), p. 416.

tremendous ideological victory over their rivals. U.S. technological superiority over the supposedly backward Soviets, a source of security during the Cold War, had been swiftly wiped away. Lyndon Johnson conducted a thorough investigation of the nation's missile and space programs, thereby establishing the Democrats as favoring stronger national defense and space efforts than the Republican Administration.

Critics faulted American public schools for not demanding excellence from students and for stinting on basic education, math, and science training. There had been persistent criticisms of public schools preceding *Sputnik.* Dr. Rudolf Flesch, in his best-selling *Why Johnny Can't Read* (1955), had attacked overcrowded schools that used obsolete teaching methods and offered diverse, aimless curricula to bored students. After *Sputnik,* educational shortcomings became a national security issue. Educators insisted that Americans must put greater emphasis on mathematics, foreign language study, and science in order to regain its technological edge over the Soviets. Congress responded in 1958 by enacting the National Defense Education Act

(NDEA), which funded high school math, language, and science programs, and offered fellowships and loans to college students entering these fields.

Initial American efforts to match Soviet rocketry embarrassed the nation. Two months after *Sputnik's* launching, a U.S. rocket blew up on its launch pad; a journalist promptly dubbed it "kaputnik." Not until January 1958 did an Army rocket team manage to get a small American satellite into orbit. But the Soviets then hurled aloft a 3,000-pound satellite. Khrushchev claimed that Soviet leadership in rocketry demonstrated the superiority of socialism over capitalism. In the wake of *Sputnik,* Congress enacted legislation creating the National Aeronautics and Space Administration (NASA), which during the 1960s surpassed the Soviets and put a man on the moon.

CUBA AND CASTRO

Eisenhower, preoccupied with conducting Cold War diplomacy in Europe, Asia, and the Middle East, usually gave relations with Latin America a low priority. Latin American politics during the 1950s swung between the extremes of Leftist democracies and Rightist military dictatorships. Washington, while paying lip service to democracy, preferred military regimes that maintained order, protected private property, supported U.S. foreign policy, and suppressed Communists. Latin Americans envied U.S. wealth, feared U.S. power, and resented U.S. diplomacy.

In the 1950s, U.S. economic interests dominated the Cuban economy, a result of the neo-colonial relationship between the countries that had evolved in the aftermath of the Spanish-American War. U.S. companies owned Cuba's oil industry, 90 percent of its mines, 80 percent of its utilities, 50 percent of its railroads, 40 percent of its sugar plantations, and 40 percent of its cattle ranches. Most of Cuba's major export crop, sugar, was sold on U.S. markets, and two-thirds of Cuban imports came from the United States.

At the end of 1958, Fidel Castro overthrew Fulgencio Batista, a corrupt dictator who had protected U.S. economic interests in Cuba. Castro quickly implemented a social revolution. He broke up the large cattle ranches and sugar plantations, giving the land to peasants. He established summary courts that condemned former Batista supporters, thousands of whom were shot or imprisoned. Communists took over Cuban trade unions and infiltrated Castro's army.

Although alarmed by Castro's radical actions, the United States quickly recognized his regime. Castro had considerable popular support within the United States; he was viewed as a liberal reformer who would restore Cuban democracy. He visited the United States in April 1959. In meetings with American officials, he spoke reassuringly about future relations with the United States. He promised that any future expropriations of American property would be legal and the owners compensated, but these were pledges that he failed to keep. He tried to borrow money from U.S. bankers but rejected their terms because they conflicted with his plans for Cuban economic development. He then returned to Cuba and began nationalizing more U.S. property.

Relations between the United States and Cuba continued to deteriorate as Castro's revolution continued its left-wing tack. Cuban liberals, many of them former Castro supporters, fled Cuba for Florida. Castro had come to power with only vague notions about implementing

Figure 5.6   Cuban President Fidel Castro jabs two fingers together during a lengthy address before the United National General Assembly on September 26, 1960.   *Source:* AP/Wide World Photos.

an economic program. Once in power, he joined the Communists. By the end of 1959, his government had confiscated about $1 billion in U.S. properties. In February 1960, Castro signed an agreement with the Soviet Union in which the Soviets traded oil and machinery for sugar. The Soviets also loaned Cuba $100 million. Washington responded by ending all economic aid to Cuba and by sharply cutting the import quota on Cuba's sugar.

Eisenhower decided by mid-1960 that Castro would have to be removed from power. The President preferred to work through the Organization of American States (OAS), but that route proved ineffective. Castro had supporters among OAS members; they admired him as a nationalist who had defied the United States. Others were afraid to oppose Castro, lest he foment unrest among their people. Frustrated by OAS inaction, Ike approved a CIA project to train Cuban exiles for an invasion of Cuba to overthrow Castro. The CIA established a training camp at a remote site in Guatemala and began preparations. The United States then embargoed all trade with Cuba and severed diplomatic relations.

Cuban agents meanwhile spread Castroism elsewhere in Latin America, and Washington tried to blunt Castro's appeal by promoting social reform. Administration officials, working through the OAS, promoted a reform agenda including tax reform, improved housing and schools, land reform, and economic development. Congress appropriated $500 million to launch the ambitious program.

CONTROVERSY IN EUROPE

During the late 1950s, the Cold War in Europe intensified, erasing any lingering "spirit of Geneva." The Soviets used the psychological advantage gained by their space exploits to put pressure on the United States. In November 1958, Khrushchev, unhappy with the integration of West Germany into NATO, and with the unresolved German question, announced that within six months he would sign a separate peace treaty with East Germany. Such actions would nullify Western occupation rights in West Berlin. Another Cold War crisis was at hand.

Ike refused to abandon West Berlin, but he also used diplomacy to avoid a confrontation with the Soviets. Khrushchev extended the Berlin deadline following Eisenhower's invitation to him to visit the United States. Khrushchev spent two weeks in the United States in the summer of 1959, the first Soviet leader ever to set foot in America. Following meetings with Eisenhower at Camp David, an ebullient Khrushchev announced the cancellation of his Berlin ultimatum. At the same time, Eisenhower suggested that the troubling question of West Berlin ought to be speedily resolved. A month after Khrushchev's American tour, Eisenhower announced that there would be another summit meeting in Paris scheduled for May 1960, and he invited the Soviet leader to attend. Khrushchev accepted and invited the President to visit the Soviet Union following the summit. Ike accepted Khrushchev's invitation. The Cold War appeared to be thawing once again.

But the Paris summit never occurred. On May 1, 1960, a Soviet V-750 surface-to-air missile shot down an American U-2 spy plane over Soviet soil. Initially Eisenhower lied; he stated that a weather reconnaissance plane had flown off course and had inadvertently violated Soviet air space. An angry Khrushchev then revealed that the aircraft had been shot down 1,200 miles into the Soviet Union and that the Soviets had captured the pilot, Francis Gary Powers, who admitted that he had been on a spy mission. When Eisenhower took full responsibility for the flight and refused to repudiate it, Khrushchev angrily canceled the summit. He subsequently withdrew his invitation to the American president to visit the Soviet Union. Eisenhower deeply regretted the breakup of the summit, seeing all of his efforts for peace dashed because of the U-2 incident. A few months later, U.S. spy satellites equipped with high resolution space cameras began to overfly the Soviet Union.

END OF AN ERA

The U-2 incident, the launching of Sputnik, and the seemingly endless crises of the Cold War took their toll on the American people. A sense of declining power to control events in the world spurred a rising debate in this country over national purpose. Social critics wondered if Americans retained the same drive to achieve goals that had motivated previous generation. Did they have the will to face future Soviet challenges? Had Americans gone soft from technology and affluence? Adlai Stevenson said that the nation suffered from a "paralysis of will"; Americans appeared committed only to "pleasure and profit" and the "pursuit of ease."

In the spring of 1960, both *Life* and the *New York Times* published a series of commentaries on the national purpose. All the writers agreed that something was lacking in the national spirit. President Eisenhower established a National Goals Commission to develop national

Figure 5.7   On July 7, 1959, Vice President Richard Nixon, accompanied by Soviet leader Nikita Khrushchev, made an official visit to the American pavilion at an exhibit in Moscow. Moments later, the two leaders staged their famous "kitchen debate," arguing over the merits of their respective systems of government. The debate was one of the dramatic moments of the Cold War. *Source:* National Archives.

objectives. The Commission brought out a book, *Goals for Americans,* in which it recommended an increase in military spending to meet the Soviet challenge, a government commitment to an expanding economy, a college education to be made available for all, the promotion of scientific research and the arts, and a guaranteed right to vote for all citizens. The commission's suggested goals expressed a need felt by many Americans to reaffirm the American identity in a dangerous world; and to point the direction in which American society should be heading.

As Eisenhower prepared to leave office, the United States faced crises in Cuba, Berlin, and Southeast Asia. On January 17, 1961, Ike spoke to the American people for the last time as president. His Farewell Address consisted of a series of warnings to his countrymen, as had George Washington's famed address of 1797. Eisenhower warned of the Communist menace, of squandering the nation's resources, and of spending too much on either welfare or warfare. The most famous part of Ike's valedictory warned about the power of the military establishment and its corporate clients:

> we must guard against the acquisition of unwarranted influence, whether sought or unsought, by the military-industrial complex.[5]

Ike asserted that the military-industrial complex could endanger basic liberties and democratic processes. In light of Vietnam and Watergate, the old general's caveats proved to be prophetic. He understood more clearly than any other modern president the dangers that the Cold War posed to his people's wealth and freedom.

Eisenhower presided over a peaceful and prosperous interlude in U.S. history. But as he exited public life, the nation faced many foreign crises and unsolved domestic problems. The

---

[5]Quoted in *ibid.,* p. 289.

civil rights movement was gathering momentum, and other disadvantaged groups would soon challenge the status quo. Although the United States remained the world's wealthiest, most powerful nation, its prosperity and power had suffered relative decline in the late 1950s. Western Europe and Japan prospered. Soviet military power and diplomatic influence were expanding. Anti-Western nationalism had intensified among Third World countries.

BRIEF BIBLIOGRAPHIC ESSAY

There exists a sizable bibliography on domestic politics and foreign policy in the 1950s. Stephen E. Ambrose's *Eisenhower: The President* is the best account of the Eisenhower presidency. There is a good collection of contemporary appraisals of the Eisenhower presidency by Dean Albertson, ed., *Eisenhower as President.* Some of Eisenhower's former staffers have written accounts of his presidency. One of the best is by Emmet John Hughes, *The Ordeal of Power: A Political Memoir of the Eisenhower Years.* An important work is Fred I. Greenstein's *The Hidden Hand Presidency: Eisenhower as Leader.* Greenstein persuasively argues that Eisenhower was an effective leader on both domestic and foreign policy issues who "hid his hand" to achieve his goals. The best general political history of the 1950s is Charles C. Alexander's *Holding the Line: the Eisenhower Era, 1952–1961.* Juan Williams's *Eyes on the Prize: America's Civil Rights Years, 1954–1965,* is a stirring account of the civil rights movement. James T. Patterson's recent *Brown v. Board of Education: A Civil Rights Milestone And Its Troubled Legacy* is a lucid and evenhanded account of the most important Supreme Court decision of modern times and its consequences. Robert A. Divine's *Eisenhower and the Cold War* is the best diplomatic history of the Eisenhower years. H. W. Brands Jr.'s *Cold Warriors* also is excellent. Samuel P. Huntington's *The Common Defense: Strategic Programs in National Politics* is the best study of Eisenhower's strategic policies. Michael A. Guhin's *John Foster Dulles: A Statesman and His Times* offers the fullest treatment of Eisenhower's energetic Secretary of State. Using recently released records, Keith Kyle, in *Suez,* has written a good account of that crucial episode in American Middle Eastern diplomatic history. Richard H. Immerman's *The CIA in Guatemala* is a well-done account of the CIA's subversion of the Arbenz government. A recent study, Robert R. Bowie and Richard Immerman's *Waging Peace: How Eisenhower Shaped An Enduring Cold War Strategy,* makes a strong case for Eisenhower;s devising the strategy for victory over the Soviet Union in the Cold War.

WEB SITES

The Harvard Project on Cold War Studies at `<http://www.fas.harvard.edu/~hpcws/>` offers a rich variety of Cold War materials including recently declassified U.S. and Soviet documents and an Internet guide to Cold War studies. It also contains a history of the nuclear arms race and nuclear weapons testing, which reached their most dangerous levels during the 1950s. The Eisenhower Center located on the campus of the University of Kansas at `<http://www.uno.edu/~eice>` is a rich resource that includes links covering Dwight D. Eisenhower's life, military career, and political career. There also are hyperlinks to other resources including the Eisenhower presidential library. Two excellent sites concerning important leaders of the Civil Rights movement of the 1950s include (1) The Martin Luther King, Jr.

Papers Project operated by Stanford University at <http://www.stanford.edu/group/king>, and (2) a Rosa Parks portal directing users to all the Rosa Parks Web sites online at <http://www.e-portals.org/Parks/>. There is a new Web site just made available to students "Remembering Jim Crow" at <http://www.americanradioworks.org/features/remembering/index.html>. It is an excellent site that contains a wealth of material on the segregation and disfranchisement of African Americans from Reconstruction through the modern civil rights movement.

6

New Frontiers

In the early 1960s, Americans regained the confidence in their national destiny that had faltered in the late 1950s, when the economy went slack and the Soviets appeared to have gained a strategic advantage in the Cold War. The economy revived. Most middle-class American families enjoyed unprecedented affluence, and their children's prospects never looked brighter. An energetic, articulate young president kindled this resurgent optimism. John Fitzgerald Kennedy voiced national goals in language that Americans, particularly young Americans, could understand and accept. He told Americans that they could face the challenges of mid-century life, hold their own in world affairs, beat the Soviets in the space race, and solve nagging social problems at home. A new activist spirit surged across the land. For a few years, a spirit of "Camelot" reigned, a belief that anything was possible, that nothing was beyond the grasp of Americans.

THE ELECTION OF 1960

A Democratic resurgence began with the 1958 midterm elections. A series of events had shaken public confidence in the Eisenhower administration: Sputnik and the apparent missile and space race gaps, crises in the Middle East, and a sharp recession at home, which had driven unemployment above 7 percent, the highest level since 1941. Also, the Sherman Adams scandal tarnished the antiseptic image that the Republicans had enjoyed since coming to office. The Democrats increased their majorities in the Senate, sixty-four to thirty-four, and in the House, 283 to 153. These were their largest majorities since the New Deal heyday of 1936. In Massachusetts, John Kennedy won a lopsided reelection victory. His impressive performance made him the Democratic front-runner for 1960.

Many Democratic leaders entered the race for their party's 1960 presidential nomination. With the popular Ike forced to resign because of the twenty-second Amendment, prospects for a

Democratic victory looked better than anytime since the glory days of FDR. Other candidates included Senators Hubert Humphrey and Stuart Symington and Senate Majority Leader Lyndon Johnson. Adlai Stevenson was still a contender, even though he had lost twice to Eisenhower.

Two obstacles blocked Kennedy's path to his party's presidential nomination. First, he would have to dispel the myth that a Catholic could never be elected president. The second obstacle was the candidacies of his powerful rivals, all of whom had longer, more distinguished political careers than he. Kennedy was an upstart among seasoned veterans of the political wars.

Victories in the early primaries gave him momentum that carried him to the nomination. Kennedy chose Lyndon Johnson, who had come in second to him in the convention balloting for president, to be his vice-presidential running mate. He needed Johnson to win Texas and to hold the South if he were to have any chance of winning the presidency in November.

Figure 6.1   John and Jacqueline Kennedy. Photo by Peskin HY.
Source: FPG International L.L.C.

When the Republicans gathered in Chicago a week later, Richard Nixon had the nomination sewn up. The nearest thing to a challenge came from Nelson Rockefeller, governor of New York. He had no chance and withdrew long before the convention. But Rockefeller influenced the drafting of the party platform. The Republican platform came out similar to the Democratic one and amounted to an implicit indictment of Eisenhower administration policies for stinting on defense spending and allowing the economy to nosedive. Conservative Republicans reacted angrily to the Rockefeller platform. Arizona Senator Barry Goldwater called it "the Munich of the Republican Party."

Despite the candidates' dramatically different backgrounds—Nixon, the poor boy from rural southern California who had fought his way up the political ladder and Kennedy, the child of privilege whose political career depended largely on his father's wealth and influence—they shared similar political views. Nixon was a moderate conservative with liberal tendencies. Kennedy was a moderate liberal with conservative tendencies. Both were Cold Warriors. Both accepted the basic structure of the New Deal welfare state. Both advocated civil rights and believed in a strong presidency. Both were young men, Nixon, forty-seven, and Kennedy, forty-three. Because they shared similar political views, the campaign featured few substantial debates over the issues. Because the electorate perceived their views to be so similar, the outcome of the election turned on personal image and the voter's feel for one or the other.

Kennedy linked Nixon to what he called "the horse-and-buggy" policies of Eisenhower that had let the nation fall behind the Soviets in missile and space technology and had allowed the economy to stagnate. Kennedy promised "to get the country moving again" by providing strong leadership. He reminded audiences that although Richard Nixon might act the role of statesman in 1960, behind that facade lurked the "real Nixon," the mudslinger of the early 1950s, the man who belonged to the party of Lincoln, but unlike Lincoln, showed "charity to none and malice toward all."

Nixon began the campaign with some liabilities. The sagging economy was the most serious. The Cold War setbacks that the Eisenhower administration suffered also hurt the candidate's chances. Eisenhower gave Nixon only lukewarm support. Ike made matters temporarily worse for the candidate when a reporter asked him what decisions Nixon had helped him make and the old general quipped, "If you give me a week, I might think of one." Even so, the early advantage clearly lay with Nixon. He was far better known to the American people because of his active role in Eisenhower's administration. Eisenhower's quip notwithstanding, September public opinion polls gave Nixon the lead. The election appeared to be Nixon's to lose.

Kennedy's religious affiliation was an important campaign issue, and he met his detractors forthrightly. He clearly stated his views: there was nothing in his religion that would prevent him from obeying his constitutional oath and governing the nation; he supported the First Amendment's separation of church and state; he opposed federal aid to parochial schools; and he favored birth control. He appeared before a gathering of prominent Protestant leaders in Houston, and he told the ministers, "I am not the Catholic candidate for president, I am the Democratic party's candidate for president, who also happens to be a Catholic." When he finished, the ministers gave him a warm, standing ovation. His performance could not remove anti-Catholicism from the campaign, but it defused the religious issue and freed Kennedy to concentrate on attacking Nixon and the Republican record.

The highlight of the campaign occurred when the candidates staged four nationally televised debates between September 26 and October 21. They were the first televised debates between presidential candidates, and they reflected the growing influence that television was now playing in the nation's political life. The first debate was decisive, and Kennedy won it. Nixon looked haggard; he was weakened by a knee infection and tired from a long day of campaigning. He was victimized by a poor makeup job that did not hide his dark stubble. On camera, under hot lights, the makeup powder streaked as Nixon sweated noticeably. Kennedy, in contrast, was fresh and primed for the encounter. He had rested that day, pouring over his notes like a college student cramming for an examination. He exuded cool, cheerful confidence, displayed a sure grasp of the issues, an agile intelligence, and a sharp wit; Kennedy dispelled any lingering doubts about his maturity or ability to be president. Nixon did much better in the three subsequent debates and had a slight advantage overall, but he could not completely overcome the disadvantage of his appearance and performance during that crucial first debate. In none of the televised debates did the candidates explore issues in depth, and no clear issue distinctions between them surfaced. The debates were essentially popularity contests.

October polls showed Kennedy taking the lead for the first time. In the final month of campaigning, Kennedy attracted large, excited crowds. He appeared along a beach in Southern California and was mobbed by excited followers who were behaving like rock 'n' roll or movie star fans. Kennedy had momentum, and the Democrats could smell victory.

But in the final week of the campaign, the Republicans almost pulled it out. Nixon strongly defended the Eisenhower record and hammered away at Kennedy's inexperience in international affairs. Republicans staged a media blitz across the nation. Eisenhower finally entered the fray and campaigned energetically for Nixon. Ike nearly eliminated Kennedy's lead.

Kennedy's 303 to 219 edge in electoral votes masked the closest presidential election in American history. In some states, the outcome was in doubt for days. Kennedy, by narrowly winning populous states such as New York, Pennsylvania, Michigan, and Texas, squeezed out victory. Out of a record sixty-eight million votes cast, Kennedy's margin of victory was 118,574. Kennedy received 49.7 percent of the popular vote to Nixon's 49.5 percent. In congressional elections, Republicans picked up twenty-two seats in the House and two seats in the Senate, leaving the Democrats with large majorities in both. Most Democratic candidates ran better than Kennedy

It is impossible to say precisely what factor determined Kennedy's hairline victory. In such a close election, many variables could have determined the outcome, and there are too many imponderables involved. Suppose Eisenhower had entered the campaign a week earlier? Kennedy's religious affiliation cut both ways: in rural Protestant areas of the South, Southwest, and West, it cost him votes, but in Northeastern, Midwestern, and Western urban states, it gained him votes. On balance, he may have gained more votes than he lost because of his religion, for the states where people voted for him because of his religious affiliation contained the largest clusters of electoral votes. Kennedy benefited from the televised debates, particularly the first. The winner also ran well among black voters. Kennedy had followed a bold strategy during the campaign of relying on Johnson to hold white Southerners while he appealed for black voters. He responded to an appeal to help Dr. Martin Luther King Jr. gain release from a Georgia jail, where his wife feared he would be killed. Kennedy also promised to sign an executive order forbidding segregation in federally subsidized housing. Black votes provided his winning margin in Texas and North Carolina, and he received most of the Northern black inner-city vote.

The 1960 election demonstrated that sectional, class, and party loyalties continued to erode. Many voters split their tickets in 1960. Millions of Republicans, many of them Catholics, voted for Kennedy. Millions of Democrats, mostly Protestants, voted for Nixon. The 1960 election further blurred the distinctions between the major parties and their candidates. The politics of consensus still prevailed.

THE COLD WARRIOR

Kennedy believed in a strong, centralized presidency that operated free of the restraints of Congress, public opinion, and the media. He also believed that managerial competence was more important than dedication to a cause or commitment to ideological dogma. He thought that the major problems he had inherited from the outgoing administration—a sluggish economy at home and Cold War crises abroad—stemmed from Eisenhower's failure to assert his power and to streamline the executive office for action. Kennedy was determined to energize the presidency. He would be at the center of action.

Kennedy recruited his top advisers from a far wider talent pool than had his predecessor, who had drawn most of his senior advisers from the upper echelons of the corporate world. Secretary of State Dean Rusk came from the Rockefeller Foundation. For Secretary of Defense, Kennedy chose Robert S. McNamara, the president of Ford Motor Company. McGeorge Bundy, an administrator from Harvard, was appointed National Security Adviser, managing foreign policy. Kennedy's talented young staffer who had served with him in the Senate, Theodore Sorensen, took charge of domestic issues and wrote many of his speeches. Kennedy's younger brother Robert became Attorney General and his closest adviser on all issues. He appointed several Republicans to be his top advisers to try to reassure the business community that his administration would not be antibusiness.

Kennedy gave top priority to the conduct of American foreign and military policy that centered on America's global rivalry with the Soviets. His administration sought to contain the Soviet Union and prevent revolutionary change in the Third World. Cold War ideology shaped Kennedy's view of the world. He viewed the Communist system itself as the Free World's main enemy.

> . . . implacable, insatiable, unceasing in its drive for world domination. For this is not a struggle for supremacy of arms alone—it is also a struggle for supremacy between two conflicting ideologies: Freedom under God versus ruthless, godless tyranny.[1]

Kennedy and his advisers made their major foreign policy goal the development of policies and means to restore American primacy in world affairs. They would reverse the decline that they believed had occurred under the cautious leadership of Eisenhower. They viewed the Third World as the primary arena and the key to winning the Cold War. It was among the underdeveloped countries of Asia, Africa, and Latin America where the battle against Communism would be joined and won. He had a bold vision, rooted in a deep faith in the American system, confident that American technology and expertise could prevail in the long, twilight struggle with the Soviet menace.

---

[1]Quoted in Herbert Parmet, *Jack: The Struggles of John F. Kennedy* (New York: Dial Press, 1980), p. 301.

THE BAY OF PIGS

The new administration encountered its first Cold War crisis in Cuba. Kennedy no more than his predecessor could tolerate the existence of a Communist state in the Caribbean. The CIA project to overthrow Castro, begun by Eisenhower six months earlier, readied for action. Anti-Castro Cuban exiles, many of them former liberal supporters of the Cuban dictator, had been trained for an amphibious assault on Cuba at a secret camp set up in the Guatemalan mountains. CIA officials believed that an invasion of Cuba would activate a general uprising within Cuba that would overthrow Castro. Kennedy, after consultations with senior advisers, all of whom assured him that the planned invasion would succeed, gave the operation the green light.

About 1,450 invaders, debarking from a Nicaraguan port in ships provided by the CIA, landed before dawn at the Bay of Pigs, a remote area on the southern Cuban coast. Castro quickly deployed his army to meet them. Cuban gunners sank many of the landing craft. Attackers who made it ashore were hit by tanks and tactical aircraft. Lacking adequate artillery support and air cover, the invaders were quickly overwhelmed. Within three days, the Cuban Army had captured 1,189 of the invaders and killed 114. (About 150 were able to escape.) The invaders never made contact with Cuban underground elements, and the expected anti-Castro uprising never occurred.

The Bay of Pigs disaster humiliated the Kennedy administration. The United States' European allies sharply criticized its actions, and Third World spokesmen took turns condemning the United States at the United Nations. Within the United States, liberals attacked Kennedy for undertaking the invasion, and conservatives condemned him for failing to overthrow Castro.

The U.S.-backed invasion had violated the OAS charter that prohibited any Western Hemispheric nation from intervening in another's affairs. Latin American nations, resenting the thinly disguised American reversion to gunboat diplomacy, refused the U.S. request to quarantine Cuba from inter-American affairs. Both Soviet aid to Cuba and the pace of Cuban socialization accelerated in the aftermath of the failed invasion.

The invasion project had been ill-conceived and mismanaged from the start. The CIA underestimated Castro's military strength and exaggerated the extent of anti-Castro sentiment in Cuba. Kennedy ensured the mission's failure when he curtailed CIA air strikes preceding the landings and then refused all requests for naval air support as Castro's forces overwhelmed the invaders. Kennedy did not want a war with Cuba, and he tried to preserve the fiction that the invasion was an all-Cuban affair.

The President assumed full responsibility for the fiasco, but afterward he ordered an investigation of the CIA. He forced its aging director, Allen Dulles, who had assured him that the Bay of Pigs operation would succeed, into retirement, and he replaced him with John McCone, a conservative California oil man. Kennedy also made an aggressive speech before a convention of newspaper editors in which he made it clear that he remained determined to get rid of Castro despite the spectacular failure of the invasion.

According to the findings of a special Senate investigating committee that later examined CIA covert operations, Kennedy ordered the CIA to "eliminate" Castro following the failure of the Bay of Pigs invasion. Robert Kennedy took charge of Operation Mongoose, which included efforts to disrupt the Cuban economy and to support anti-Castro elements. During 1961 and 1962, CIA operatives tried to kill the Cuban dictator; their efforts included cigars laced with explosives and deadly poison and an attempt to spear him with a harpoon while he was snorkeling at a Caribbean resort. CIA agents even plotted with Mafia elements to get rid of Castro, but they had to abandon the project because of opposition from FBI Director J. Edgar Hoover. Castro knew about Operation Mongoose and was aware of some of the CIA plots to assassinate him. He appealed to his allies in Moscow for help. The Soviets responded by sending troops. Later they would try to station nuclear-capable, intermediate-range missiles in Cuba, which provoked the most dangerous crisis of the Cold War.

THE THIRD WORLD

During his campaign for the presidency, Kennedy had repeatedly criticized the Eisenhower administration for failing to promote economic development and the growth of political democracy among the nations of Latin America, Asia, and Africa. He insisted that such neglect had given the Soviet Union opportunities to get ahead of the United States in the race for influence among the strategically important developing nations of the Third World. Kennedy pledged to help these nations modernize their societies and restore American influence among them.

For Latin America, the Kennedy administration developed a multifaceted assistance program called the Alliance for Progress. Kennedy proposed the alliance in a dramatic speech given in Mexico City in May 1961. The alliance built upon and expanded Eisenhower's previously announced aid program for Latin America. Congress appropriated $500 million to start the program, which was designed to eradicate poverty and social injustice in the Western Hemisphere. Over the life of the program, billions of dollars in loans and grants from both public and private sources were fed into the Alliance for Progress. In most Latin American countries, the results were disappointing. Conservative governments refused to reform their tax systems, grant land reform, or democratize their politics. The elite classes who held power in these nations feared Castroism as much as Kennedy, but they preferred to rely on repression rather than take their chances with social reform. If the Alliance for Progress could have succeeded, it would have required far more funds than were made available, and mechanisms would have to have been created to bypass the governing elites and get money directly to the people most in need.

In the summer of 1961, the Kennedy administration launched the Peace Corps, a much more successful initiative to help people in Third World countries. The Peace Corps derived from the same Cold War concern to involve the United States more directly in Third World countries and to give idealistic young Americans an opportunity for public service. Over the next two years, about 7,500 mostly young Peace Corps volunteers were sent to forty-four nations in Asia, Africa, and Latin America. Most worked as teachers; others found jobs in health care, agricultural reform, and community development. For many of the young people who served in the Peace Corps, they not only found an opportunity to help poor people, but they also returned to America with a greater appreciation of the diversity of the world's cultures.

BERLIN

At the beginning of his presidency, Kennedy and Secretary of Defense McNamara began a crash program to expand and diversify America's military forces. They believed that Eisenhower's reliance on massive retaliation and his refusal to engage the Soviets in a missile race had set dangerous limits on the American ability to counter Soviet-backed insurgencies in Third World countries. The United States rapidly increased its strategic nuclear forces, which included ICBMs, missile-launching Polaris submarines, and long-range bombers. They also built up conventional war capabilities, adding a Kennedy favorite, counterinsurgency forces. The president sought strategic versatility, which he termed "flexible response"—the ability to intervene anywhere in the world with flexible force levels in response to Soviet or Soviet-backed initiatives.

The Kennedy military buildup had broad bipartisan congressional and popular support. At the same time the United States expanded its military capacities, Kennedy repeatedly urged the Soviets to join in arms limitation talks aimed at reducing the arms race. But Khrushchev responded by increasing Soviet military spending for more ICBMs, the backbone of the Soviet strategic system. The American arms buildup had triggered another upward spiral in the nuclear arms race.

Having been burned badly by the Bay of Pigs fiasco, Kennedy was more determined than ever to respond strongly to Communist threats. He worried lest his administration appear weak willed and lose prestige in the eyes of the world and its own people. Three months after the invasion, he met for a series of private talks with Khrushchev in Vienna in June 1961. The two leaders exchanged views on a wide range of issues and used the occasion to size each other up. Kennedy was calm, rational, and polite in these conversations. Khrushchev's moods varied. At times he talked warmly of peaceful coexistence between Communism and capitalism. At other times he became angry, even threatening. He turned into an ideologue, asserting the inevitable triumph of socialism in the world. He bullied the young president, coming away from these meetings with the mistaken impression that Kennedy could be pressured. Khrushchev misread Kennedy's civility as weakness. His misjudgment would later contribute to the most dangerous moment in modern history.

The major issue discussed in Vienna was the long-standing problem of Berlin. The German question had never been formally settled after World War II because of Cold War conflicts. At war's end, Germany had been divided into occupation zones by the victorious nations. In 1948 and 1949, the Western zones were merged into one zone, which became the Federal Republic of Germany (West Germany), a Western liberal state. The Soviet zone in Eastern Germany became the Socialist Democratic Republic of Germany (East Germany), on which the Soviets imposed a Communist system. By 1950, there existed two *de facto* German states.

Berlin, lying deep within East Germany, also remained divided between East and West, causing periodic crises during the Cold War. Tensions had flared in 1948, when the Soviets had tried to drive the Western nations out of Berlin and Truman had thwarted them with the Berlin Airlift. Khrushchev had pressured Eisenhower in 1958 about Berlin and then backed off when Ike stood firm. Now, with Kennedy in office, the Soviet leader pressed for a peace treaty between the two German states that would legitimate the *de facto* division of the country, remove the possibility of reunion, and deprive the West of any legal basis for its occupation of West Berlin. Khrushchev told Kennedy that he wanted the Berlin issue settled by year's end; if it was not settled, he threatened to conclude a separate peace treaty with East Germany, forcing the West to negotiate with a government that none of the Western states recognized. Khrushchev and the East German rulers also wanted to stop the flow of East Germans into West Berlin. Thousands of East Germans fled poverty and tyranny each month to enter free and prosperous West Germany through West Berlin.

Kennedy rebuffed Khrushchev's proposals and reaffirmed the Western presence in West Berlin. He also asked Congress to increase military appropriations by $3 billion, tripled draft calls, called up reserves, and extended enlistments of military personnel on active duty. He also asked for $207 million from Congress to expand civil defense fallout shelters, dramatizing the terrifying implications of the Berlin crisis.

The Soviet response came on August 13, when East German workers suddenly erected a concrete, barbed wire wall across Berlin, imprisoning East Germans in their own country and stanching the flow of refugees into West Berlin. Nearly three million East Germans had escaped to the West since 1945. During the first twelve days of August 1961, about 46,000 had fled Communism.

To reassure West Berliners that accepting the wall did not presage eventual Allied withdrawal from the divided city, Kennedy sent an additional 1,500 combat troops to West Berlin. In June 1963, he visited West Berlin and told a huge crowd, "Ich bin ein Berliner" ("I am a Berliner") to dramatize the United States' determination to stay. The Berlin Wall quickly became a potent Cold War symbol of the impasse between East and West, and of the division of Germany and its major city. It also was a stark admission of Communism's failure to win the hearts and minds of East Germans.

But the Wall also provided a practical solution to the Berlin question. It stopped the flow of refugees, which was Khrushchev's immediate goal, and it allowed West Berlin to remain in the Western orbit, which was Kennedy's main goal. German reunification was deferred to the indefinite future. Khrushchev announced in October that he would no longer insist on Western withdrawal from West Berlin. The crisis ended, and Berlin was never again a major source of Cold War conflict. But the Wall endured for nearly thirty years as the most vivid symbol of European Cold War divisions—until the people of East Germany themselves breached the wall in November 1989 as they began to dismantle the Communist system imposed on them after World War II.

THE MISSILE CRISIS

Following the Bay of Pigs, the Soviets sent soldiers and weapons to Cuba to protect that Communist satellite from U.S. hostility. Castro also supported guerrilla actions in other Latin American countries. Republicans, looking for election-year issues, attacked the Kennedy administration for allowing the Soviet arms buildup in Cuba. Kennedy opposed attacking or invading Cuba as long as the Soviets placed only defensive weapons in Cuba that posed no threat to the United States or any other hemispheric nation. But Khrushchev and Castro decided on a daring move to deter any further U.S. action against Cuba. The Soviet Union secretly tried to install medium-range and intermediate-range nuclear missiles and bombers in Cuba. These missiles and bombers were offensive weapons capable of carrying nuclear payloads to U.S. cities and military installations.

On October 14, 1962, a U-2 reconnaissance plane photographed a launching site for an intermediate-range missile nearing completion in western Cuba. Kennedy immediately determined that the missiles and bombers must be removed from the island. His sense of strategic and political reality told him that they had to go. But how to get the missiles out of Cuba? How without triggering a nuclear war? The most dangerous Cold War crisis ever had begun.

Figure 6.2   Medium-range ballistic missile base in Cuba. The United States detected Soviet efforts to install missiles in Cuba when reconnaissance aircraft photographed missile bases under construction on the island. Here is an example of the photographic evidence shown to President Kennedy in October 1962. *Source:* U.S. Air Force.

Kennedy convened a special executive committee consisting of thirteen senior advisers, which met secretly for the next twelve days. Their assignment was to propose tactics that would force the Soviets to remove the missiles from Cuba without igniting World War III. The president's brother and closest adviser, Robert, chaired the committee sessions.

Beginning with their initial session, all members of the committee agreed that the missiles had to be removed, but they disagreed on tactics. Some members, led by the chairman of the Joint Chiefs of Staff, Army General Maxwell Taylor, wanted to take the missile sites out with surprise air strikes that were likely to kill both Soviet technicians and Cuban soldiers. Robert Kennedy, who proved to be the most influential member of the executive committee, rejected that idea, saying he wanted "no Pearl Harbors on his brother's record." The Taylor-led faction then proposed an invasion to get rid of both the offensive weapons and the Castro regime. The president rejected this suggestion as being too risky; it could involve a prolonged war with Cuba, provoke a Soviet attack on West Berlin, or even bring nuclear war. Secretary of Defense McNamara proposed a naval blockade to prevent further shipments of weapons to Cuba. The blockade would allow both sides some freedom of maneuver. The United States could decide to attack or negotiate later, depending on the Soviet response to the blockade. A majority of the committee members endorsed McNamara's proposal and the president accepted it.

President Kennedy attended few of the committee sessions. With the 1962 midterm elections only three weeks away, he was on the campaign trail, acting as though everything was normal. He campaigned mostly about domestic issues. Neither the media nor the public had any inkling of the serious crisis that was building. The Soviets did not know that the missile sites had been detected, nor that Kennedy and the Executive Committee were planning the U.S. response.

On October 22, the blockade began. That evening, Kennedy went on television to inform the nation and the Soviets about the missile crisis. He bluntly announced, "Unmistakable evidence has established the fact that a series of offensive missile sites is now in preparation on that imprisoned island." He spoke of the naval blockade, which he called a "quarantine," that was in place around Cuba. He demanded that the Soviets dismantle and remove all missile bases and bombers from Cuba immediately, and he stated that the quarantine would remain in place until all offensive weapons had been removed. Then he spoke these chilling words:

> It shall be the policy of this nation to regard any nuclear missile launched from Cuba against any nation in the Western Hemisphere as an attack by the Soviet Union on the United States, requiring a full retaliatory response upon the Soviet Union.[2]

Kennedy confronted Khrushchev with the risk of nuclear war if he did not remove the missiles. For the next five days, the world hovered at the brink of catastrophe. Khrushchev denounced the United States and denied that he was installing offensive weapons in Cuba. Meanwhile, work on the missile sites continued around-the-clock. The first sites would be operational in a few days. The Air Force prepared strikes to take them out before they could be used to fire missiles at targets in the United States. Soviet merchant ships hauling more weapons continued to steam toward Cuba. The U.S. Navy positioned its blockade fleet to intercept them. American invasion forces gathered in Florida. B-52 strategic bombers took to the air with nuclear bombs on board. U.S. strategic missiles went to maximum alert. The moment of supreme danger would come if a Soviet ship tried to run the blockade, because U.S. ship commanders had orders to stop them.

The first break in the crisis came on October 24. Soviet ships hauling offensive weapons turned back. Two other Soviet freighters, hauling no offensive weapons, submitted to searches and were permitted to steam on to Cuba. Two days later, Khrushchev sent a letter to President Kennedy offering to remove all offensive weapons from Cuba in exchange for a U.S. pledge not to invade Cuba. Kennedy accepted the offer, but before he could send his reply, Khrushchev sent a second letter raising the stakes: America would have to give a no-invasion of Cuba pledge plus remove its Jupiter missiles that were stationed in Turkey, which were targeted at the Soviet Union. Kennedy refused to bargain. It was his view that Khrushchev's reckless initiative had threatened world peace, and it was the Soviet leader's responsibility to remove the missiles from Cuba quickly.

---

[2]Quoted in Elie Abel, *The Missile Crisis* (New York: Bantam Books, 1966), p. 106.

As the point of no return neared, Kennedy, heeding the advice of his brother, made one last try to avoid the looming cataclysm. The president sent a cable to Khrushchev accepting the offer in the first letter and ignoring the second letter. The next night, Robert Kennedy met with the Soviet ambassador to the United States, Anatoly Dobrynin, to warn him that the United States had to have "a commitment by tomorrow that those bases would be removed." He told Dobrynin this was the Soviets' last chance to avoid war: if the Soviets "did not remove those bases, we would remove them." He also indicated to Dobrynin that the American missiles in Turkey, although not part of any *quid pro quo,* would be removed soon after the Cuban missiles were removed.

While these tense negotiations were in progress, a U-2 spy plane was shot down over Cuba and the pilot, U.S. Air Force Major Rudolph Anderson, was killed. Angry hawks on the Executive Committee wanted to launch air strikes and invade Cuba, not only to destroy the missile sites but to overthrow Castro's regime and send the Soviet troops back home. Robert Kennedy, McNamara, and others restrained them, pleading that a few more days were needed to allow the president to work out a diplomatic solution to the crisis.

U.S. officials learned years later that their restraint may have avoided nuclear war with the Soviet Union. Unbeknownst to Washington at the time, the Soviet field commander in Cuba had six tactical nuclear surface-to-surface missiles in his arsenal. He is on record as having stated that if the Americans had invaded, he would have used the nuclear missiles on them. Secretary of Defense McNamara has stated that if any U.S. troops had been killed by Soviet nuclear missiles, "It is a 100 percent certainty" that the United States would have retaliated with their own nuclear weapons.

The next morning, on October 28, Khrushchev agreed to remove the missiles and bombers in return for the president's promise not to invade Cuba. He claimed that he had achieved his goal of protecting Cuba from U.S. attacks. The United States suspended its blockade. The United Nations supervised the dismantling and removal of the Soviet missiles. American missiles were removed from Turkey a few weeks later. The missile crisis had been resolved, without war. Kennedy received high praise for his actions. The Democrats gained in the fall elections. Kennedy's standing in the polls soared. Americans, who had been on the defensive in the Cold War for years, were elated. Americans had stood up to the Soviets and had forced them to back down.

While Kennedy was lavishly praised for his handling of the missile crisis, Khrushchev was humiliated. The Russian leader fell from power within a year, and his actions during the crisis contributed to his demise. The missile crisis had exposed the Soviets as strategic inferiors to the Americans. The Soviets responded by embarking on a crash program to expand their navy and to bring their missile forces up to parity with the United States.

Foreign policy analysts have raised serious questions about the missile crisis. Why had Khrushchev tried to put the missiles in Cuba? Had he really believed that Washington would acquiesce in the stationing of nuclear missiles ninety miles from U.S. territory? Surely Khrushchev and his colleagues on the Politburo would not expose the Soviet Union to annihilation just to protect Castro's regime. Historians who have examined documents found in Soviet archives recently made accessible to Western scholars state that what Khrushchev hoped to achieve by placing the missiles on Cuban soil was to use them as bargaining chips. He would offer to withdraw them in exchange for U.S. concessions on Berlin. He hoped to extract a German peace treaty from the West and possibly an Allied withdrawal from Berlin.

Khrushchev had not anticipated Kennedy's strong response, having previously sized him up as being weak under pressure. From Krushchev's vantage point, it appeared that during the Bay of Pigs invasion, Kennedy had backed off from a war with Cuba, let the invasion fail, and allowed Castro to consolidate a Communist revolution right in the United States' backyard. He had let the Berlin Wall stand rather than risk a confrontation with the Soviets. These acts of restraint had sent the wrong signals to the adventurous Soviet ideologue. Khrushchev was not looking for a confrontation with the United States when he tried to put the missiles in Cuba, and he certainly did not want a war.

The missile crisis forced both sides to tone down their Cold War rivalry and rhetoric. Khrushchev shifted back to emphasizing peaceful coexistence. Kennedy stressed the need for arms reductions. Direct communication, a "hot line," was established between Moscow and Washington so that the two leaders could communicate with each other in time of crisis in order to reduce the chances of miscalculation and war.

President Kennedy, endeavoring to move arms negotiations forward, spoke at American University on June 10, 1963. He called peace between the superpowers "the necessary end of rational men." He spoke of "making the world safe for diversity," conceding that every world problem did not require an American solution. Following the speech, he sent Under-secretary of State Averill Harriman to Moscow to negotiate an agreement. The Soviets proved eager to conclude a treaty. The agreement, signed on July 25, banned all atmospheric and underwater testing of nuclear weapons. The Senate promptly ratified the Nuclear Test Ban Treaty. It was the first agreement that imposed a measure of control on the nuclear arms race. Soon after signing the treaty, the United States and the Soviet Union concluded an agreement for Soviet purchases of U.S. wheat. A year after the showdown in Cuba, Americans and Soviets enjoyed friendlier relations than at any other time since World War II.

VIETNAM: RAISING THE STAKES

Throughout the Kennedy years, the United States continued its growing involvement in Indochina. The President first turned his attention in that region to Laos, which had been the scene of conflict for years. Neutral under the terms of the 1954 Geneva Accords, Laos was engulfed in a three-way civil war among pro-Western, pro-Communist, and neutralist forces. Kennedy, inheriting the conflict from Eisenhower, sought a political solution involving the Soviets that guaranteed a "neutral and independent Laos." Another Geneva conference worked out a settlement. On June 12, 1961, the leaders of the three Laotian factions formed a neutralist coalition government. But in South Vietnam, Kennedy significantly escalated U.S. involvement in response to the Communists' stepped-up efforts to topple the American-backed government of Ngo Dinh Diem.

Kennedy viewed the civil war in South Vietnam as a crucial part of the global Cold War struggle between the United States and Soviet Union. Kennedy failed to understand that Ho Chi Minh, although a Communist revolutionary ideologue, for millions of Vietnamese personified their nationalism and their desire to be free of all Western domination. Kennedy also did not understand that millions of Vietnamese citizens viewed the U.S. presence in Vietnam supporting

Figure 6.3   President Kennedy inherited the conflicts in Indochina from the Eisenhower administration. Here, at a press conference held in April 1961, he tells the American people about his policy for Laos, which was then engulfed in civil war.   *Source:* National Archives.

Diem as a continuation of Western imperialism. Kennedy also applied the domino theory to Vietnam:

> Vietnam represents the cornerstone of the Free World in Southeast Asia. . .Burma, Thailand, India, Japan, the Philippines and obviously, Laos and Cambodia are among those whose security would be threatened if the Red tide of communism overflowed into Vietnam.[3]

Kennedy shared with Eisenhower and Truman the ideological foundations of the Cold War. They believed that it was imperative to contain Communist expansionism in Southeast Asia. The legacy of McCarthyism also stalked the Democrats in power. Since the early 1950s, they had been vulnerable to charges that they were "soft on Communism," at home and abroad. Kennedy dared not appear irresolute in Southeast Asia, lest his administration suffer political reprisals at the hands of Republican critics in subsequent elections.

Further, Kennedy shared a faith in American power, technical expertise, and national goals. He and his senior advisers believed that the Americans would succeed in southern Vietnam where the French had failed. To them, Vietnam furnished a bright opportunity for nation building. They believed that aid programs, military support, and the use of America's counterinsurgency forces would show the world that Moscow-backed wars of national liberation could not succeed. Kennedy also deployed the U.S. Army Special Forces, the Green Berets, in Southeast Asia. They represented a key component of the flexible response capability to counter Communist insurgencies in peripheral regions without risking confrontations with China or the Soviet Union.

[3]Quoted in George C. Herring, *America's Longest War, 2d ed.* (New York: Knopf, 1986), p. 43.

In 1961, there were about 600 U.S. military advisers in South Vietnam assisting Diem's force. During the next eighteen months, Kennedy sent some 16,000 additional U.S. troops to South Vietnam. Even though the soldiers went officially as advisers, some units occasionally engaged VietCong forces in combat. Despite the huge increase in U.S. support, Diemist forces were losing the civil war to the insurgents and their North Vietnamese backers in 1962 and 1963. U.S. officials tried to persuade Diem to implement social reforms, including land reform, and to curb his repressive police forces. Diem refused to do either. Diem's decline stemmed mainly from the inability of his military forces to fight effectively and his failure to win the loyalty of the peasants, who constituted 85 percent of the South Vietnamese population.

Diem provoked a political crisis in June 1963 that led to his downfall when he ordered Buddhists to obey Catholic religious laws. When they refused and took to the streets of Hue to protest, Diem's security forces brutally crushed their rebellion. In response to this repression, an elderly Buddhist monk immolated himself by fire at a busy intersection in downtown Saigon. Other monks followed suit as opposition to Diem's government mounted. Observing that Diem's political base had been reduced to family members and a few loyal generals and bureaucrats, and fearing that his army was losing the civil war, Washington decided that Diem had to go. On November 1, an army coup, acting with the foreknowledge and support of the CIA, overthrew Diem. U.S. officials backed a directorate of generals who formed a new government and continued the war. Three weeks later, Kennedy was assassinated.

At the time of Kennedy's death, U.S. Vietnam policy was in disarray, and his advisers were divided over what to do. Kennedy had inherited a deteriorating situation in Southeast Asia; his actions ensured that the United States would remain there a long time. Historians can never know for sure what Kennedy might have done in Vietnam had he not been assassinated and there is much scholarly controversy on this matter. Robert Dallek, a distinguished biographer of Kennedy, suggests that had he lived he was prepared to withdraw U.S. forces and avoid war. Your textbook author, who has written books and articles about the U.S. war in Vietnam, believes that if Kennedy had lived and been reelected in 1964, he would probably have reacted much as Lyndon Johnson did in 1965 and committed the United States to full-scale war in Vietnam.

Kennedy's foreign policy approach fitted that of an orthodox Cold Warrior. Undeniably, Kennedy had the intelligence and the insight to see that the world was changing, that Third World independence movements were redrawing the map of the world. He also understood that the old bipolar world was being replaced by a more polycentric one. He understood that the U.S.–Soviet rivalry had to be replaced by *détente*. But the main thrust of his foreign policies was to escalate the arms race, sustain a tense relation with the Soviet Union for most of his presidency, and, at one terrifying point, push the world perilously close to nuclear disaster. He built up the U.S. presence in Vietnam, assuring the debacle that followed. In the summer of 1963, he improved relations with the Soviets, and the two powers signed a nuclear test ban treaty.

THE SPACE RACE

In mid-April 1961, Yuri Gagarin became the first human to orbit the earth. Once again the Soviets boasted of their accomplishments in space technology; the rest of the world was impressed, and Americans were dismayed. Even though NASA scientists assured the president that American space science was superior to Soviet efforts, it had been the popular perception in this country since *Sputnik* that the United States trailed the Soviets. Media editorialists fretted that the United States had fallen behind in the Cold War and was losing the ideological battle to the Soviets.

Not according to President Kennedy. He was determined to beat the Soviets in the space race; he also was determined to rally the American people to face a Cold War challenge that he believed America could win. He put Vice President Lyndon Johnson in charge of the Space Council and told him to do whatever had to be done to defeat the Soviets. Kennedy also persuaded Congress to vote for a large increase in NASA's budget to develop a space program "to put a man on the moon in ten years." To fulfill Kennedy's vision, NASA created the Apollo program. Soon, complexes of aerospace facilities mushroomed from Southern California to Texas to Florida. NASA employed thousands of technicians, engineers, and scientists. Private-sector subcontractors hired thousands more. Within five years, upwards of a half-million people were employed on the vast multibillion-dollar Apollo project.

As scientists worked toward the goal of putting a man on the moon, they also tried to match the Soviet Union's space achievements. Seven military test pilots were recruited for Project Mercury, and they became the nation's first astronauts. After months of rigorous training, the astronauts readied for their flights. On May 5, 1961, a cocky, wise-cracking Navy Commander, Alan B. Shepard Jr., strapped into a space capsule fastened to the nose of an Army Redstone rocket, was fired from a launch pad at Cape Canaveral, Florida, into a fifteen-minute suborbital flight 116 miles aloft. On February 20, 1962, nearly a year after the Soviets had put a man in space, Marine Colonel John H. Glenn Jr. was blasted into orbit aboard his space capsule Friendship 7. During his five-hour flight, Glenn orbited the earth three times. Americans were delighted by Glenn's remarkable achievement. After his epic flight, President Kennedy invited Glenn to the White House. Glenn also addressed a joint session of Congress and later received a frenzied ticker tape parade down Manhattan's famed Broadway. Following Glenn's flight, other astronauts rocketed into space and orbited the earth. At the time of Kennedy's death, the American space program was gaining momentum, the seven Mercury astronauts had all become national heroes, and Project Apollo was ahead of schedule.

SOCIAL REFORM

President Kennedy had more successes in the diplomatic arena than in the realm of domestic reform legislation. He failed to persuade Congress to enact most of his ambitious New Frontier program of medical care for the elderly, tax reform, federal aid to education, housing reform, aid to cities, and immigration reform. In Congress, the bipartisan conservative coalition could block any effort to expand the welfare state and could often dilute measures designed to broaden existing programs. Kennedy's thin electoral victory in 1960 carried with it no mandate whatsoever for social reform. The Democrats had lost seats in both the House and the Senate.

Two years later, Kennedy tried to focus the 1962 midterm elections on New Frontier issues, but the dangerous Cuban missile crisis forced him to curtail his campaign efforts. The new Congress of 1962 was similar to its predecessor. Public opinion in the early 1960s reflected the complacency toward unsolved social problems that had been characteristic of the 1950s.

**Figure 6.4   Three American heroes.
Project Mercury astronauts John
Glenn (left), Gus Grissom (center), and
Alan Shepard (right) are shown during
their training for manned space flights.**
Source: NASA Headquarters.

Kennedy's efforts to make most Americans share his sense of urgency for social reform through televised speeches and remarks at press conferences failed. Most New Frontier proposals never made it out of committee. The few that did were either defeated on the floor of the House or cleared Congress in diluted form.

Kennedy also failed to assert effective legislative leadership. Congress questioned the depth of his commitment to social reform, understanding that he gave higher priority to foreign policy, military matters, world trade, and strengthening the economy. In addition, Kennedy wanted to maintain bipartisan support for American foreign policy initiatives, and he was reluctant to strain the unity of Congress with divisive battles over reform measures. When he could see that the votes simply were not there for many New Frontier measures, he thought it unreasonable to battle for losing causes.

A major defeat came early when Congress rejected Kennedy's $2.3 billion education bill. It foundered over the issue of federal aid to parochial schools. A Catholic himself, Kennedy knew that he would be accused of showing favoritism toward his co-religionists if he favored federal aid to Catholic schools. His bill excluded federal aid for private schools with a religious affiliation. He claimed that such aid would violate the First Amendment principle of separation of church and state. Opposition to the bill from the Catholic lobby was intense. The education bill never got out of the House Rules Committee. Members of Congress, observing that

Kennedy had little leverage with its members, understood that they could go their own political ways on other important White House measures without fear of reprisal. The failure of the education bill foreshadowed the defeat of the rest of the New Frontier agendum.

Although Kennedy did not come close to achieving his broad program of social reform, he scored a few victories. Congress enacted an Area Redevelopment Act in 1961 to provide funds for economically depressed areas. The Manpower Retraining Act of 1962 provided $435 million over three years to train unemployed workers in new job skills. Congress raised the minimum wage from $1.00 to $1.25 per hour and extended coverage to 3.6 million more workers.

THE ECONOMY

When Kennedy took office, the American economy was suffering from a lingering recession. The new president tried to work with the business community to restore prosperity. He held meetings with corporate leaders to obtain their policy suggestions. He tried to reassure them that he was a pragmatic centrist not a liberal ideologue. He told them that the age of ideology had ended and the time had come for government, business, labor, and academic leaders to combine their expertise in seeking solutions to complex technical problems that afflicted the economy. Corporate leaders refused their cooperation. They rejected Kennedy's technocratic approach to problem solving and blamed all of their problems on his administration.

A major confrontation with business came in the spring of 1962. Earlier in the year, a strike in the steel industry had been averted when Secretary of Labor Arthur Goldberg had persuaded the steel workers to accept a modest pay increase that eliminated the need for a steel price rise. At the time, the president had praised both labor and management for their "industrial statesmanship." Ten days later, Roger Blough, the CEO of United States Steel, announced that his company was raising the price of steel by six dollars a ton. Other major steel producers promptly announced identical increases.

Kennedy, feeling betrayed, denounced the steel companies. He promptly mobilized all the powers of the federal government to force the steel companies to rescind their price hikes. The Federal Trade Commission (FTC) announced that it would investigate the steel industry for possible price fixing. Robert Kennedy hinted that he might open antitrust proceedings against the steel industry. Under assault from the White House, the steel companies quickly surrendered. U.S. Steel and the other companies canceled their price increases. Kennedy had won, but he paid a political price for winning: the business community remained intensely hostile toward his administration.

Kennedy proposed innovative economic policies to end the business slump of the early 1960s. Aware that huge budget deficits during World War II had promoted prosperity, he reasoned that deficit financing also would work in peacetime. In June 1962, he proposed a deliberately unbalanced budget to promote economic growth. Six months later, he asked Congress to enact a $13.5 billion cut in corporate and personal income taxes over the next three years. The tax cuts, coupled with increases in spending for military and space programs already in place, would guarantee budget deficits. Kennedy insisted that these applied Keynesian economic strategies would generate capital spending that would stimulate economic growth, create new jobs, and provide increased tax revenues—all without rampant inflation. But Kennedy's tax bill never cleared Congress.

Even though Kennedy failed to get his new economic policy enacted, the economy recovered from recession and in 1962 began an extended period of growth. Recovery mainly occurred because the Kennedy administration sharply increased military and aerospace spending. Kennedy's first defense budget called for spending $48 billion, a 20 percent increase over Eisenhower's final budget. Kennedy's foreign economic policies also contributed to the economic rebound. Most of his foreign aid requests were approved, including increased spending for technical assistance and economic development for Third World countries.

The Senate ratified a treaty in 1961, making the United States a member of the newly created Organization of Economic Cooperation and Development (OECD), made up of the United States, Canada, and eighteen European nations. Congress also enacted Kennedy's proposed Trade Expansion Act in 1962, his most important legislative victory. This legislation enabled the United States to establish closer ties with European Common Market countries. The Trade Expansion Act also allowed the President to reduce tariffs on commodities in which the United States and European nations accounted for most of the world's trade. American overseas trade increased significantly during the years of Kennedy's presidency.

LET FREEDOM RING

In order to maintain the momentum of the civil rights struggle during the late-1950s, Martin Luther King Jr. brought together nearly 100 black religious leaders to found the Southern Christian Leadership Council (SCLC). The SCLC called upon African Americans to continue their nonviolent resistance to segregation and disfranchisement. The creation of the SCLC also signaled that henceforth the southern black churches would lead the fight, replacing the northern elite that had focused on legal action and judicial directives. However, the next great surge in the civil rights struggle came not from activist ministers; it came from courageous black college students. Four freshmen from North Carolina Agricultural and Technical College in Greensboro, North Carolina, sat down at the whites-only lunch counter in Woolworth's and ordered coffee and doughnuts. They were refused service but they stayed until closing time. News of their actions spread quickly. The next day they returned with dozens of supporters. Within a few days scores of supporters, including a few white people, clogged the counters at Woolworth's and other stores in the downtown area. The sit-ins continued for months. The events in Greensboro made the national news. When police arrested forty-five students for trespassing on April 25, outraged African Americans boycotted major downtown businesses. Merchants, losing money, pressured Greensboro city leaders to reach a settlement with the protesters. On July 25, 1960, the first African American ate lunch at the now famous Woolworth's lunch counter.

The victorious Greensboro sit-in activated young African Americans all across the South. During the next eighteen months, thousands of college students, most of them black, staged sit-ins against segregation in dozens of cities. The most significant of these sit-in campaigns occurred in Atlanta, Georgia, the South's largest city. Beginning in March 1960, students from the all-black colleges comprising Atlanta University staged large-scale sit-ins in department stores; they also picketed and boycotted downtown merchants. The campaign went on for more than year, during which hundreds of protesters were jailed. The city's white establishment finally conceded defeat; Atlanta was desegregated in September 1961.

During the 1960 presidential campaign, civil rights had not been a central issue, although Kennedy praised the sit-in movements as an example of the revival of a national reform spirit. He also promised to issue an executive order ending racial segregation in federally funded housing. During the campaign, he helped to get Dr. King released from jail. African Americans appreciated these gestures from the candidate and gave Kennedy a large black majority in 1960, which helped him win his narrow victory.

But the very closeness of his victory imposed limits on Kennedy's support of the civil rights struggle. He proved to be a cautious leader on civil rights for most of his presidency. He delayed introducing civil rights legislation, fearing that it would fail and also that it would alienate Southern Democrats, whose votes he needed on other measures. He appointed dozens of African Americans to federal offices, the first president to do so. Robert Weaver became head of the Housing and Home Finance Agency, and Thurgood Marshall became a Circuit Court judge. But Kennedy also appointed many segregationist judges to Southern courts, and he delayed issuing his promised housing desegregation order for nearly two years.

At the beginning of his administration, the lead in civil rights was taken by the President's brother, Attorney General Robert Kennedy. Robert Kennedy energized the Civil Rights Division of the Justice Department, which had been created by the Civil Rights Act of 1957. He recruited a team of committed attorneys headed by Burke Marshall. They worked to end discrimination in interstate transportation and supported the voting rights of African Americans in the South. But the Kennedy administration could not solve the central political dilemma: how to move forward on civil rights issues without alienating powerful southern Democratic Congressional leaders.

But from the outset of his presidency, Kennedy had to respond to pressures created by confrontations between civil rights activists and their violent segregationist foes. In the spring of 1961, the Congress of Racial Equality (CORE) sponsored "freedom rides." Groups of black and white travelers rode through the South deliberately entering segregated bus terminals and restaurants. Local mobs often attacked the "freedom riders." In Anniston, Alabama, the Greyhound bus in which one group had been riding was burned. Black and white passengers fleeing the burning bus were attacked by a white mob. A newly-formed civil rights organization, the Student Nonviolent Coordinating Committee (SNCC) also sponsored "freedom rides." On May 20, 1961, a Greyhound bus carrying SNCC "freedom riders" pulled into the bus station at Montgomery, Alabama. As the passengers got off the bus, they were attacked by hundreds of whites. People were clubbed to the ground and beaten with chains. A journalist and a Justice Department official observing the violent scene were also beaten.

Responding to the freedom riders and their violent encounters, the Interstate Commerce Commission (ICC) ordered bus companies to desegregate all of their interstate routes and facilities. The companies complied, and black passengers began entering previously "whites-only" restaurants, waiting rooms, and restrooms. The Justice Department persuaded thirteen of the nation's fifteen segregated airports to desegregate and filed suits against the two holdouts.

The following year, Mississippi became a civil rights battleground. In September 1962, an African American, James Meredith, attempted to enroll at the all-white University of Mississippi. Although he met the university's entrance requirements, university officials refused to admit him. Meredith then obtained a court order from Supreme Court Justice Hugo Black enjoining the university to admit him, whereupon Governor Ross Barnett personally intervened to prevent his enrolling. President Kennedy responded to Barnett's defiance of federal authority by sending 500 federal marshals to the university. They were met by a mob of several thousand whites, many of them armed, who reacted to them as if they were foreign invaders. On the night of September 30, violence reigned on the university campus. Two men were killed and 160 marshalls were injured. Vehicles were burned and the stench of tear gas covered the campus. President Kennedy ordered 5,000 U.S. Army troops onto the campus to restore order. A contingent of troops remained on campus to protect Meredith after the riots were suppressed.

Another violent confrontation occurred on April 12, 1963, Good Friday, when Martin Luther King Jr. and the SCLC led demonstrations in Birmingham, Alabama. Birmingham was the most segregated big city in America. African Americans endured total segregation in schools, restaurants, movies, city parks, and shopping. Although they constituted over 40 per cent of the population, they represented only about 10 percent of the registered voters. The SCLC sought to end segregation and end discrimination in employment and hiring policies.

Their protests were nonviolent; the city's response was not. City leaders directed Public Safety Commissioner Eugene "Bull" Connor to forcibly put an end to the demonstrations. During the next month, Birmingham police arrested over 2,000 African Americans, many of them schoolchildren. Connor ordered his police force to use high-pressure fire hoses, electric cattle prods, clubs, and police dogs to break up the demonstrations. Newspapers and television news

Figure 6.5   Dr. Martin Luther King Jr. led demonstrations into the heart of the segregated South—Birmingham, Alabama—in April 1963. Local authorities fought back hard. Here, firemen use high-pressure fire hoses to disperse civil rights demonstrators.   *Source:* AP/Wide World Photo.

broadcasts conveyed to a shocked nation the brutal white police assaults on nonviolent black people. King himself was jailed. While locked up in solitary confinement, he composed his famed *Letter from Birmingham Jail,* an eloquent defense of the tactic of nonviolent civil disobedience.

The Justice Department intervened during the Birmingham demonstrations. On May 10, federal officials and city leaders worked out an agreement. The SCLC agreed to end the protests. City leaders agreed to desegregate municipal facilities and hire African Americans. A biracial committee was formed to keep open the channels of communication between the races. King claimed victory, but Governor George Wallace denounced the agreement. A thousand Ku Klux Klansmen burned a cross in a Birmingham park. Bombs rocked the local headquarters of the SCLC. Interracial harmony in Birmingham remained a distant dream.

A few months after the Birmingham encounter, two young African Americans, Vivian Malone and James Hood, tried to enroll at the University of Alabama. Governor George Wallace stood at the entrance to Carmichael Hall on the campus of the university. With television cameras rolling and over 200 reporters looking on, Wallace raised his hand and refused to allow the two black students to enter the school. Two hours later, the crisis was over. President Kennedy, hoping to avoid a replay of the Mississippi violence, federalized the Alabama National Guard. He confronted Wallace with an overwhelming show of force, using native Alabama white and black soldiers. Wallace had stood in the doorway only long enough to have his picture taken for the papers and to ensure that his actions made the nightly television and radio news. He then stepped aside. Malone and Hood enrolled at the university, peacefully.

That night, on June 11, 1963, John Kennedy gave the first civil rights speech ever delivered by a president. Part of his speech was extemporaneous, and he conveyed a sense of moral urgency, an emotional concern for civil rights:

> One hundred years of delay have passed since President Lincoln freed the slaves, yet their heirs, their grandsons, are not fully free. They are not yet free from the bonds of injustice; they are not yet freed from social and economic oppression. And this nation will not be fully free until all its citizens are free.[4]

A week later, Kennedy proposed the most comprehensive civil rights bill in American history. It called for the desegregation of all public accommodations, the protection of voting rights for African Americans, and the end of job discrimination.

To show support for the pending legislation, civil rights leaders organized a march on Washington. Over 200,000 people, including 50,000 whites, gathered on the mall in front of the Washington monument on August 28. Black and white people joined in a peaceful, festive occasion. With most people holding hands in an extraordinary show of interracial unity, folksinger Joan Baez led the massive crowd in singing the anthem of the civil rights struggle, "We Shall Overcome." The highlight of an exhilarating day of speeches came when the last speaker, Martin Luther King Jr. passionately affirmed his faith in the decency of humanity and in victory for his cause:

> I have a dream that one day this nation will rise up and live out the true meaning of its creed: We hold these truths to be self-evident; that all men are created equal. I have a dream that one day on

[4]From the transcript of Kennedy's televised speech over the three major networks on June 11, 1963.

the red hills of Georgia, the sons of former slaves and the sons of former slaveowners will be able to sit together at the table of brotherhood.[5]

King's passionate oratory marked the apogee of the civil rights struggle.

Immediately following the demonstration, King and other civil rights leaders met with President Kennedy. But Southern Senators threatened to filibuster any civil rights bill to death. Three weeks after the march on Washington, Ku Klux Klan terrorists bombed a Sunday school in Birmingham, killing four little girls. Two months later, President Kennedy was assassinated, his civil rights legislation still pending. King's dream remained only a distant hope.

TRAGEDY IN DALLAS

President Kennedy traveled to Texas in late November to mend some political fences. With the help of Vice President Johnson, who accompanied him on that fateful rendezvous, he came to unify warring factions of Texas Democrats who had feuded over policies and patronage. Texas was a populous state with a large bloc of electoral votes that Kennedy and Johnson had carried

[5]Quoted in Anthony Lewis, *Portrait of a Decade* (New York: Bantam Books, 1965), pp. 218–219.

Figure 6.6   On August 28, 1963, supporters of the pending civil rights bill staged a march on Washington to show their support. Over 200,000 people rallied in front of the stately Washington Monument to sing songs and hear speeches. *Source:* National Archives.

narrowly in 1960 and hoped to win again in 1964. Kennedy arrived at the Dallas airport on the morning of November 22. Governor John Connally and his wife Nellie joined the president and his wife Jacqueline in an open-air limousine for the trip into the city. The presidential motorcade proceeded from the airport into downtown Dallas. Thousands of people lined the motorcade route, most of them smiling, waving, and cheering the president as he passed by. Kennedy responded warmly to their enthusiasm, waving, frequently flashing his million-dollar smile, and stopping the motorcade twice to shake hands with well-wishers.

At 12:30 P.M., the motorcade turned onto Elm Street and drove by the Texas Book depository building. At 12:33 P.M., three shots rang out. The president clutched his neck with both hands and slumped downward. One bullet had passed through his throat and another struck the back of his head, blowing off part of his skull. Texas Governor John Connally, sitting beside the president, also had been hit. The president's limousine quickly pulled out of the motorcade and raced the mortally wounded leader to nearby Parkland Hospital, where, in its emergency room, Kennedy was pronounced dead at 1:00 P.M.

Within two hours of the shooting, police captured the apparent assassin, Lee Harvey Oswald, who worked in the book depository building. Oswald was a drifter with a troubled past. He had recently moved to Dallas after spending two years working in the Soviet Union. He was married to a Russian woman whom he had met while living in the Soviet Union. He was a Marxist sympathizer. Earlier in the year, he had tried to go to Cuba, but the Cuban Embassy in Mexico City, after consultations with Soviet officials, had refused to grant Oswald a visa.

Aboard the presidential plane, still on the ground at Dallas's Love Airport, ninety-nine minutes after Kennedy's death, Lyndon B. Johnson was sworn in as the thirty-sixth president of the United States. The former president's widow, Jacqueline, stood at Johnson's side. Two days later, a Dallas nightclub owner, Jack Ruby, shot and killed Oswald at point-blank range in the basement of the Dallas police station in full view of a national television audience. Ruby's murder of Oswald eliminated the possibility of ever discerning Oswald's political beliefs, his motives for killing the president, and whether he was part of a conspiracy.

From the moment of Kennedy's death, many people doubted that Lee Harvey Oswald had acted alone. A public opinion poll, taken within a week of the president's murder, showed that only 29 percent of Americans believed that Oswald was a lone killer. Within two weeks of Kennedy's murder, President Johnson appointed a special commission, headed by Chief Justice Earl Warren, to investigate the assassination and to report its findings to the American people. Ten months later, the commission published its conclusion: "The Commission has found no evidence that anyone assisted Oswald in planning or carrying out the assassination."

The commission's findings failed to satisfy those who felt others had to be involved in a plot to murder the president. Critics undermined the credibility of the Warren Commission's analysis of evidence and its findings, which were flawed and limited. Many people have proposed conspiracy theories to account for Kennedy's death, and millions of people have found them credible. These theories have implicated both pro- and anti-Castro Cubans, Texas oilmen, segregationists, Vietnamese, rogue elements within the Pentagon, the FBI and the CIA, the Mafia, the KGB, and Lyndon Johnson. The few responsible journalists and scholars who believe that it is possible that a conspiracy was involved in the assassination of the President think that Cubans and elements within organized crime were involved.

The most important critique of the Warren Commission came in 1979, when a special congressional investigating committee released the results of a two-and-one-half-year examination of the deaths of both President Kennedy and Martin Luther King Jr. Its key finding: "The scientific evidence available to the committee indicated that it is probable that more than one person was involved in the president's murder." But FBI experts demonstrated that the committee's evidence was flawed.

In all of the time that has passed since Kennedy's murder, no tangible evidence has been found that proves that the Warren Commission's conclusion was incorrect, despite its flawed investigation of the murder. Nor has any evidence turned up that links any particular group to the assassination. If a group of conspirators killed the President, their identities remain unknown and probably unknowable.

The persistence of the belief, especially among young people, that a conspiracy killed Kennedy, mainly represents an effort to make sense out of a horrific act. The notion that a sociopath, an utterly insignificant wretch acting alone, could bring down a great leader and wreak such havoc made the crime appear senseless and devoid of any political meaning. Novelist Norman Mailer has suggested that many Americans cling to conspiracies to explain the president's death because they cannot recognize the absurdity of historical events. The belief that a great and good man had been destroyed by powerful evil forces lurking within the dark underside of the American political system made sense in a bleak, rueful sort of way to many people: the man was too good, therefore the evil "theys," who really run things in this country, indeed the world, had to get him. Belief in a conspiracy theory also reflects a need for balance. Put an admired president of the United States at one end of the scale and that waif Oswald at the other— it does not balance. Add a conspiracy, especially one engineered by powerful persons in high places to Oswald's end of the scale—it balances.

In the years following Kennedy's death, Americans watched other leaders die at the hands of assassins—Malcolm X, Martin Luther King Jr., and Robert Kennedy. These assassinations reinforced a growing sense among Americans in the 1960s that they inhabited a violent, dangerous country where criminal conspirators thought nothing of snuffing out the lives of idealistic leaders. For many Americans, the age of innocence ended on November 22, 1963, and they have found it difficult to trust government leaders ever since.

People around the world wept openly at the terrible news. Explorers, hiking in a Colombian rain forest, came upon a little makeshift shrine honoring the murdered president's memory. A stricken nation watched numbly the solemn aftermath of the absurd tragedy. The president's body lay in state on the rotunda of the Capitol on the same catafalque that had held the body of Lincoln. Kennedy's funeral was held on November 25, on a clear, cold day in Washington. At St. Matthews Cathedral, Kennedy's friend, Richard Cardinal Cushing, archbishop of Boston, gave the funeral Mass. The funeral train slowly wound its way past national monuments to Arlington Cemetery. On a grassy knoll overlooking the capital of the nation, John Fitzgerald Kennedy was buried.

THE LEGACY OF CAMELOT

Kennedy's untimely death instantly transformed the man into a myth. After conversations with Kennedy's widow, Theodore White wrote an essay in which he compared Kennedy's presidency to the legend of Camelot. Camelot had recently been popularized in this country by the successful Broadway run of a musical of that same name. Kennedy had seen Camelot, and he loved to

Figure 6.7   Jacqueline Kennedy, dressed in black mourning attire, holds Caroline and John Jr.'s hands as they prepare to descend a flight of stairs during President Kennedy's funeral, Washington, D.C., November 26, 1963.   *Source:* Archive Photos.

listen to the sound track. Camelot referred to the Arthurian legend, to the mythical kingdom of Arthur and the Knights of the Round Table. Because the United States, soon after Kennedy's death, got caught up in a full-scale war in Southeast Asia and in violent domestic rebellions, followed in a few years by the sordid Watergate scandals, people came to view the Kennedy years as a brief golden age. Those who came of age during his reign felt an especially painful loss. For them, the Kennedy years had been a glorious interlude between the dull days of Eisenhower and the dark days of Johnson and Nixon.

For those who believed in Camelot, Kennedy had been the democratic prince whose achievements epitomized the American dream of success. His family history had been a saga of upward mobility from humble immigrant origins to the upper reaches of wealth, power, and fame. Then, in an instant, a loser's bullets had turned spectacular achievement into tragic loss.

The historical record belies the myth. Kennedy's record of accomplishment is mixed. Much of his New Frontier agenda failed to pass in his lifetime. He was mostly a cautious leader on civil rights issues. He only belatedly sensed the moral passion that motivated civil rights activists such as Martin Luther King Jr. He got only a portion of his economic program enacted. Posthumous revelations about his extramarital affairs, drug use, a myriad of serious health problems, and other Kennedy family scandals have tarnished his moral stature and diminished his reputation.

His foreign policy achievements were more significant. The Peace Corps and the Trade Expansion Act succeeded. But the Alliance for Progress flopped, neither undercutting the appeal of Castro nor promoting democracy and economic growth in most Latin American countries. Kennedy's "crisis managing" in Cuba was a disaster at the Bay of Pigs, and he risked nuclear war to pry Soviet missiles out of Cuba. The Berlin issue was defused after years of tension, but its resolution owed more to Khrushchev's Berlin Wall than to any initiatives taken by Kennedy. The test ban treaty and *détente* with the Soviets in 1963 decreased the danger of nuclear war, but Kennedy had previously ordered major increases in American military spending, particularly for strategic thermonuclear weapons, which had escalated the arms race. Kennedy also significantly expanded American involvement in Vietnam, putting the country on course for war in Southeast Asia.

Kennedy's best speeches proved that he had the imagination and courage to see beyond the confines of the Cold War, but he spent his presidency waging it. The man who could see the need for developing new relations with Third World people nevertheless applied counterrevolutionary Cold War ideologies to all nationalistic insurgencies. He remained until the end a Cold Warrior at heart.

Any accounting of his leadership must include intangible dimensions. Kennedy was a superb politician. His intelligence, wit, and personal charm set a high tone for his presidency. For most Americans, he embodied all that was good about the nation that he had been elected to lead. His beautiful First Lady, Jacqueline Bouvier Kennedy, became an iconic figure as the charming hostess who redecorated the White House. She also exuded high fashion, stylish good taste, and appreciated fine art and literature. John Kennedy was devoted to the ideal of national service. He paid high tribute to science and scholarship. He sought always to bring out the best in Americans, to challenge them to seek excellence in all things, especially young people, with whom he felt a special bond. Whatever the failings of the private man, the public image that Kennedy cultivated was positive, energetic, and effective. Always there must be the rueful speculation, what if he had lived? Any fair historical judgment must take into account the brutal fact of his abruptly abbreviated career, a man in his prime cut down before he could make his full mark on history.

BRIEF BIBLIOGRAPHIC ESSAY

A vast literature has accumulated on John Fitzgerald Kennedy, his family, and all facets of his political career. Robert Dallek, a distinguished biographer of presidents, has recently done *An Unfinished Life, John F. Kennedy, 1917–1963,* which promises to be the best general biography yet of John F. Kennedy. Two highly favorable insider accounts of his presidency are Arthur M. Schlesinger Jr.'s *A Thousand Days* and Theodore C. Sorensen's *Kennedy.* Bruce Miroff's *Pragmatic Illusions: The Presidential Politics of John Kennedy* and Garry Wills's *The Kennedy Imprisonment* are both negative assessments of his presidency. A controversial work by investigative reporter Seymour M. Hersh, *The Dark Side of Camelot,* amounts to a lengthy catalogue of the sins of the president. Much the best account of the election of 1960 is found in Theodore H. White's *The Making of the President, 1960.* Carl M. Brauer's *John F. Kennedy and the Second Reconstruction* is a favorable assessment of the president as civil rights leader. See also Peter Wyden's *Bay of Pigs: The Untold Story,* the best account of Kennedy's most embarrassing foreign policy venture. *The Kennedy Tapes: Inside the White House during the Cuban Missile Crisis,* edited by Ernest R. May and Philip D. Zeilkow, allows the reader access to history as it was being made by the Executive Committee. Two critical accounts of Kennedy's conduct of foreign policy include Richard J. Walton's *Cold War and Counterrevolution* and David Halberstam's *The Best and the Brightest.* A fine, recent study of Kennedy's foreign policy is Michael R. Beschloss's *The Crisis Years: Kennedy and Khrushchev, 1960–1963.* For Kennedy's space policy, see Walter A. McDougall's *The Heavens and the Earth: A Political History of the Space Age.* Anyone who cares to know about Kennedy's assassination must start by reading the Report of the *Warren Commission on the Assassination of John F. Kennedy.* Readers who want to read a fine historical treatment of Kennedy's assassination can access Michael L. Kurtz's *Crime of the Century: The Kennedy Assassination from a Historian's Perspective.* Gerald Posner's *Case Closed: Lee Harvey Oswald and the Assassination of JFK* does an effective job of demolishing the leading conspiracy theories and providing plausible answers to many of the lingering questions about the assassination.

WEB SITES

In the CNN.com series on the Cold War, there is fascinating section (Episode 10) on Kennedy, Castro, and Cuba. Among its many riches is an account of the Missile Crisis that includes the ExComm files, interviews with Castro and Anatoly Dobrynin, the Soviet Ambassador to the United States at the time.

See <http://www.africanaonline.com/civil_rights_birmingham.htm> for a unique approach to the Birmingham, Alabama, civil rights protests during April 1963. The protests, and the violent responses of white officials, are set within a historical context that conflates the history of Birmingham with a history of black-white race relations in that gritty industrial city.

7

Great Society and Vietnam

Lyndon Johnson deftly took charge of the nation's political life following President Kennedy's shocking assassination. He skillfully steered stalled New Frontier legislation through Congress. Following his landslide election victory in November 1964, he presided over the flowering of the Great Society, a multidimensional reform program that promised to fulfill the social vision of the New Deal and improve the quality of life for all Americans.

At the same time that Johnson asserted effective leadership as a domestic reform leader, he had to manage America's far-flung international commitments. Johnson was inexperienced in foreign policy realms. The knowledge and skill that made him an effective domestic legislative leader could not be applied to the conduct of foreign policy.

Johnson inherited a series of difficult world situations: The NATO alliance showed signs of strain, pressures for social and political change were rising in many Latin American nations, and the Middle East remained a powder keg that could blow at any time. Most of all, Johnson inherited a growing U.S. involvement in the Vietnam War. President Johnson met his nemesis in Vietnam. Vietnam undermined his credibility, strangled his beloved Great Society, and eventually forced him from office. The triumphs of the Great Society would be overwhelmed by the tragic losses of the Vietnam catastrophe.

THE TALL TEXAN

The new president assumed office under horrendous circumstances. The nation's papers all carried the photograph of a somber Lyndon Johnson being sworn into office by a federal judge on board Air Force One, parked at the Dallas airport less than two hours after John Kennedy had been murdered.

Johnson's immediate duty was to preside over an orderly transition of power that ensured continuity in government and restored the people's shattered confidence in the political order.

He handled this delicate task with great skill and remarkable sensitivity. He persuaded almost all of Kennedy's key White House staff and cabinet officials to remain at their jobs. His first speech to Congress and to the American people, given five days after the assassination and probably the most important speech of his presidency, demonstrated that a sure hand was at the helm. Johnson pledged to continue what Kennedy had started. He made it clear that stalled New Frontier legislation would be the top priority on his domestic agenda. He called specifically for Congress to enact swiftly the stalled civil rights act and tax reduction bill.

THE ELECTION OF 1964

As Lyndon Johnson took control of the reins of power during the first six months of 1964, the Republicans sought a candidate to run against him. Within Republican ranks, conservatives, unhappy with their party's tendency, ever since the New Deal, to nominate nonideological centrists for the presidency, were determined this time to nominate one of their own. Conservatives represented diverse groups: Midwesterners, Southerners, Westerners, far-right groups such as the John Birch Society, and New Right newcomers to the GOP, such as the former screen actor Ronald Reagan and an activist attorney from Illinois, Phyllis Schlafly. These

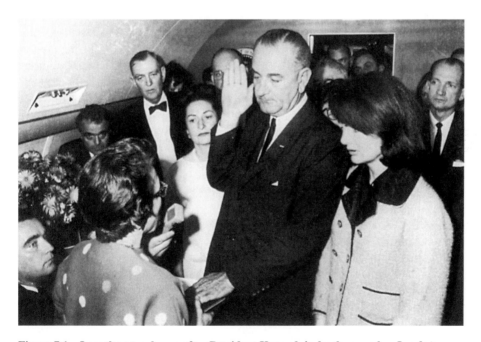

Figure 7.1   Less than two hours after President Kennedy's death, a somber Lyndon Johnson was sworn into office aboard *Air Force One,* **still parked on the ground at Dallas Airport. He is flanked by Kennedy's widow Jacqueline and his wife Lady Bird.**   *Source:* AP/Wide World Photo.

aggressive conservatives supported the candidacy of Arizona Senator Barry Goldwater. Goldwater's political philosophy blended traditional conservatism with New Right ideological discontent with the restraints imposed on the American system by the welfare state and the Cold War. Goldwater called for both free enterprise at home and unilateral military action against the Communists.

Moderate Eastern Republicans mounted an all-out effort to stall Goldwater's drive for their party's nomination in the California primary in June. Nelson Rockefeller challenged Goldwater in a bruising battle that split the California Republican Party. Goldwater scored a narrow victory, and with it he secured his party's nomination.

In the election campaign that followed, Goldwater never had a chance. From its outset, pollsters predicted an overwhelming victory for the Democrats. Early in the campaign, Goldwater urged that NATO field commanders be given control of tactical nuclear weapons. His proposal frightened most Americans, who thought it made nuclear war more likely. Goldwater often did not need Democratic help to drive away voters, as he insisted on waging an ideological rather than a pragmatic campaign. He told an audience of elderly people in Florida that he favored making Social Security voluntary. He chose Memphis, Tennessee, the cotton capital, to attack farm subsidy programs. He then journeyed to Knoxville, located in the center of a region made prosperous by the Tennessee Valley Authority (TVA), to tell voters that the TVA must be sold to private power companies. In Charleston, West Virginia, located at the edge of Appalachia, one of the poorest regions in the nation, he announced that the impending war on poverty was unnecessary.

Johnson refused to debate Goldwater on television. Because all of the polls showed him holding a big lead, Johnson did not campaign until the final month. When he did enter the fray in October, he campaigned as a unifier and peace maker. He forged a broad electoral consensus, including much of the business community, trade unions, farmers, most middle-class voters, liberals, intellectuals, the elderly, the poor, blacks, and other minorities. A sizable part of Johnson's support came from Republican voters who were fleeing Goldwater's extremist campaign. Goldwater showed strength among white Southerners, his true-believer followers, and hard-core Republicans.

On Election Day, Johnson won by a landslide. In the popular vote, he received forty-three million votes to Goldwater's twenty-seven million, and 486 electoral votes to Goldwater's 52. Johnson carried forty-four states and received 60.7 percent of the popular vote. Democrats added thirty-seven House seats and two more seats in the Senate. The new House of Representatives would have 295 Democrats to 140 Republicans. The new Senate would have sixty-eight Democrats to only thirty-two Republicans.

In the aftermath of the Goldwater debacle, some analysts spoke of the impending demise of the Republican Party as a major political force. Such epitaphs proved premature; it turned out that Goldwater was merely ahead of his time. Ronald Reagan, inheriting Goldwater's cause, would ride it to the White House in 1980. While celebrating their landslide victories, some Democratic Party leaders nervously took note of the fact that five of the six states carried by Goldwater were Southern. The Solid South was disintegrating as white voters, perceiving the Democratic Party to be increasingly identified with the drive by African Americans for full participation in American public life, abandoned their historic political allegiances and voted Republican. Goldwater's failed candidacy also signaled the permanent shift of African-American voters from the Republicans to the Democrats. Whereas Richard Nixon had polled nearly a third of the black vote in 1960, Goldwater got only 6 percent in 1964. Thirty-six years later, George W. Bush polled just 8 percent of the African-American vote.

GREAT SOCIETY

During his first six months in office, President Johnson used a successful strategy for getting Congress to enact much previously blocked New Frontier legislation. He evoked memories of the deceased Kennedy as a moral lever to pry bills out of congressional committees. He also sought to overcome conservative resistance to social reform by insisting on balanced budgets and reducing government expenditures. Johnson was both a liberal social reformer and a fiscal conservative. He obtained congressional passage of Kennedy's long-stalled tax cuts, which reduced personal and corporate income taxes about 5 percent across the board. Enactment of these tax cuts represented the first deliberate use of Keynesian fiscal policy to stimulate demand and to promote investment to keep the economy prosperous and expanding, thereby generating the tax revenues to pay for proposed reforms. Johnson's fiscal conservatism made many of his social reform measures palatable to conservatives in Congress.

Johnson also persuaded Congress to enact the most comprehensive civil rights bill in American history. The civil rights bill passed in the House in February 1964, but it ran into a Southern filibuster in the Senate that delayed its passage until June. The Civil Rights Bill of 1964 went far beyond Kennedy's original proposal. It was the most sweeping affirmation of equal rights and the strongest commitment to their enforcement ever made by the federal government. Its key provision guaranteed equal access to all public accommodations such as restaurants, bars, hotels, resorts, theaters, and casinos. Other provisions strengthened federal machinery for combatting discrimination in hiring and promotions. The bill also empowered the federal government to file school desegregation suits, and it further strengthened voting rights. It further required corporations and trade unions to ensure equal employment opportunities to all applicants.

In addition to promoting tax cuts and civil rights, Kennedy was considering an antipoverty program at the time of his death. Johnson immediately adopted it as his own. In his first State of the Union address delivered in January 1964, Johnson declared "unconditional war on poverty in America." Congress, a few months later, enacted the Economic Opportunity Act, authorizing the spending of $1 billion over three years, beginning in 1965. The act created an umbrella agency called the Office of Economic Opportunity (OEO) to administer the various antipoverty programs.

Soon after his overwhelming victory, Johnson, backed by the most liberal Congress since 1936, set out to complete what New Dealers had begun during the 1930s; he would create his Great Society. He organized task forces made up of his staffers, social scientists, bureaucrats, and activists to draft legislative proposals to send to Congress. Johnson and his liaison people also worked closely with Congress during all stages of the legislative process to get passage of the program. Among the most important measures enacted during 1965 was the Appalachian Regional Development Act. Appalachia, a mountainous region extending from Pennsylvania to northern Alabama, contained seventeen million people and was a vast pocket of poverty. The act provided over $1 billion in subsidies for a variety of projects stressing economic development of the region.

Congress also attacked the problem of America's decaying central cities. The Housing and Urban Development Act of 1965 provided funding for 240,000 units of low-rent housing. It also authorized spending $2.9 billion over four years for urban renewal projects. Federal rent supplements for low-income families were added in 1966. Congress also created a new Cabinet-level Department of Housing and Urban Development (HUD). President Johnson appointed Robert Weaver to head the new agency; Weaver became the first African-American Cabinet member.

In addition to attacking urban problems, Congress enacted both the Medicare and the Medicaid programs in 1965. Medicare provided health care for people age sixty-five and over, while Medicaid provided health care for low-income people not eligible for Medicare. Both programs would be funded through Social Security. At the time of the passage of these programs, the United States was the only industrial democracy in the world without some form of national health insurance. Organized physicians, working through their powerful lobby the AMA, had blocked all efforts to enact national health insurance since Truman had first proposed it in 1945. President Johnson overcame the opposition of the AMA and conservative legislators by limiting the insurance program to the elderly and to the poor, and by funding it through the Social Security system. Funding Medicare and Medicaid through the Social Security system was another example of Johnson's fiscal conservatism that won conservative support for social reform measures.

One of the most important achievements of Great Society was the enactment of federal aid to education. The Elementary and Secondary Education Act of 1965 ended a long debate in Congress over the use of federal funds to support public schools. President Kennedy had made federal aid to public schools a top New Frontier priority and had suffered a serious defeat because of Catholic opposition to his bill, which did not fund parochial schools. By contrast, Protestant and Jewish leaders strongly opposed funding parochial schools. Kennedy could never resolve the impasse. President Johnson, believing that education was the primary way in which the federal government could promote equality of opportunity in America, overcame the religious roadblock. He persuaded religious leaders to accept an aid program that provided federal funds for states based on the number of low-income students enrolled in their schools. The funds would be distributed to both private and public schools to benefit all children in need.

Johnson rescued another stalled New Frontier reform when he secured congressional passage of the Immigration Act of 1965, the first comprehensive overhaul of U.S. immigration policy in forty years. The new law abolished the discriminatory national origins quota system implemented during the 1920s, which had restricted immigration to this country on the basis of ethnic and racial background. These ethnoracial restrictions had proved embarrassing in the context of the Cold War struggle for friends in the Third World. Under the new legislation, each country would have an annual quota of about 20,000 immigrant slots. Eligibility to fill these slots would be based upon the skills and education of the individual immigrant plus close family ties to people already here.

The family unification provisions of the new immigration law allowed a naturalized immigrant to bring to the United States not only spouses and children, but also siblings. These siblings, upon becoming citizens, could in turn bring over their spouses and children, thus creating chain migrations. These family unification provision of the new immigration law had the unintended consequence of reviving immigration as a major social force shaping recent American history. Since 1970, an estimated thirty-five million immigrants have entered the United States, of which approximately twelve to fifteen million have entered illegally.

Additional civil rights legislation joined the Great Society agenda in 1965. Many African Americans could not yet vote in the Deep South states, despite the enactment of three previous civil rights bills and voter registration drives by civil rights groups. Hundreds of student volunteers working in Mississippi in the summer of 1964 to register African-American voters encountered stubborn, and often violent, opposition from white segregationists. In the spring of 1965, Martin Luther King Jr. prepared to lead a fifty-mile march of demonstrators from Selma, Alabama, to the state capitol in Montgomery to publicize continuing denial of African-American voting rights. A few days before the march was scheduled to begin, President Johnson made a nationally televised speech to a joint session of Congress calling for a voting rights bill that would close all remaining loopholes in civil rights laws. Near the end of his speech, Johnson raised his arms in the style of a country preacher and recited the words from the old black spiritual that had become the anthem of the civil rights movement: "And . . . we . . . shall . . . overcome." The demonstrators in Selma, poised to begin their march, listened to his speech through tears of joy.

As the demonstrators began their march for the right to vote, they were attacked by Alabama state troopers who gassed, clubbed, and whipped them. These vicious attacks on nonviolent protesters marching on behalf of a fundamental democratic right were televised nationally to a shocked nation. An angry president, viewing the attacks, federalized the Alabama National Guard and ordered it to provide protection for the marchers all the way to Montgomery. Johnson then pushed the voting rights bill through Congress. The Voting Rights Act of 1965 gave the Attorney General the power to appoint federal registrars to register voters in districts where historic patterns of disfranchisement prevailed. Empowered by the new law, federal officials registered hundreds of thousands of African-American and Hispanic voters in six Southern states during the next three years. The 1966 election was the first one held in this country in which most adult Southern African Americans could vote.

In addition to voting rights for African Americans, the Great Society also was committed to the cause of conservation. Congress enacted the National Wilderness Preservation Act in 1964, which incorporated all federally owned wilderness areas into a national wilderness system. It also established a program for meeting the nation's future wilderness preservation and recreation needs. Conservation and wildlife preservation laws were enacted. In early 1965, Congress passed the Highway Beautification Act, a cause pushed by First Lady Claudia "Lady Bird" Johnson. It also enacted the Water Quality Act and the Clean Air Act; these important measures provided federal funds for assisting state and local governments to set up air and water purification programs.

Congress enacted many more Great Society measures in 1965 and 1966. Two important pieces of consumer protection legislation passed, a "truth-in-packaging" bill and a "truth-in-lending" act. The former required sellers to label accurately the contents of packages sold for household use; the latter required detailed information about the true rate of interest charged on bank loans and credit purchases. Congress added a new Cabinet-level Department of Transportation in 1966 and enacted a series of highway safety laws. Consumer advocate Ralph

Nader did more than anyone to secure the passage of these new safety laws. His book, *Unsafe at Any Speed,* documented hazardous design defects in Detroit-made automobiles, promoting public awareness of these problems.

Great Society measures enacted between 1964 and 1966 represented the most far-reaching assault ever mounted on a vast array of social problems by the federal government. Reform measures left over from the New Deal and Fair Deal eras were enacted during the mid-1960s. Most of the problems Great Society tried to solve had been around for years, but they were challenged during the mid-1960s because of a confluence of circumstances that gave liberal reformers opportunities normally unavailable within the American political system. The nation was prosperous, and there existed a widespread sense that Americans could afford the costs of social reform. Large liberal majorities prevailed in both houses of Congress, breaking the bipartisan conservative bloc's power to veto or water down reform legislation. Johnson's smashing victory in the 1964 election had given activist liberal reform leaders a mandate for social change. Most of all, Johnson's concern for the welfare of ordinary citizens and his extraordinary political skills made Great Society a reality. He formed broad-based coalitions incorporating conservatives in support of social reform, and he steered complex legislation through congressional "minefields" of special interest groups.

For a time, many Great Society programs worked. The GDP increased by 25 percent from 1964 to 1966, providing billions of dollars of additional tax revenues to fund the new programs without incurring budget deficits, raising interest rates, or igniting inflation. Unemployment dropped below 4 percent in 1965, the lowest rate since World World II. The number of poor people declined by millions; this reduction came from both antipoverty programs and new jobs generated by the strong economy. Medicare and Medicaid improved the quality of health care available to the elderly and to the poor. Students at all educational levels benefited from federal programs. African Americans in the South at long last had the vote.

But the Great Society immediately incurred a flurry of criticism from both the Left and the Right. Conservatives assailed its high costs, its centralization of government authority, and its proliferation of new federal bureaucracies. They insisted that social problems could not be solved by creating new federal bureaucracies and by throwing money at them. A few Leftist radicals charged that most Great Society programs did not address "structural" problems.

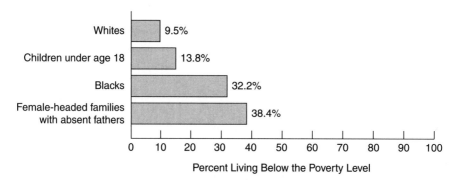

Figure 7.2   Poverty, 1969.   *Source:* U.S. Bureau of the Census, Current Population Reports, Series P-60, No. 194, and unpublished data.

Johnson's war on poverty, which was launched in 1965 with much fanfare, came under heavy fire. Some of its programs worked well, particularly those that helped prepare poor minority youngsters for school and the Job Corps, which furnished job training for disadvantaged young men and women. But a few radical critics insisted that if government officials were serious about eradicating poverty in America, then a few billion dollars could not begin to meet the needs of the nation's forty million poor people. In their view, the poverty program was both oversold and underfunded. It generated unrealistic expectations among poor African Americans and fierce resentments among working-class whites, who perceived antipoverty programs as favoring militant protesters over hard-working people. Michael Harrington, whose book *The Other America* (1962) had helped President Kennedy discover poverty in America, observed: "What was supposed to be a social war turned out to be a skirmish, and in any case, poverty won."

After 1966, Congress, concerned about rising crime rates, violence, and inflation, was reluctant to vote more funds for reform and social programs. Johnson had expected to finance the Great Society from increased tax revenues derived from an expanding economy. He believed that affluent Americans could continue to prosper without having to make any sacrifices to help the poor. He believed that the Great Society would enable the one-fourth of Americans who were disadvantaged to join the affluent three-fourths without requiring any tax increases or redistribution of wealth. He promised more than the Great Society could deliver. He both exaggerated American wealth and underestimated the profound structural barriers to achieving affluence for all. He believed that America could both fight a costly, large-scale war in Vietnam and continue to build the Great Society at home. The leader who wanted to achieve his place in history as the man who fulfilled the social vision of the New Deal, escalated the war in Vietnam and thereby strangled his beloved Great Society. The man who most wanted to extend the New Deal presided over its collapse and prepared the way for a profound shift to the Right in American politics. By 1967, except for token gestures, the Great Society was dead. The fight for civil rights, the struggle to save the cities, the efforts to improve the public schools, and efforts to clean up the environment—all were starved for the sake of the escalating war.

AN ACTIVIST COURT

Led by energetic Chief Justice Earl Warren, the activist liberal majority controlling the Supreme Court during the 1960s rendered a series of landmark decisions that struck down the last remnants of the segregation system. The Court also protected the right of dissent, expanded the freedom of the press, regulated obscene materials, and restricted the role of religion in public schools. It further altered criminal legal procedures, expanded the right to privacy, and made the American political system more inclusive.

In *Bond v. Floyd* (1966), the Court ordered the Georgia House of Representatives to admit an elected representative, civil rights activist Julian Bond, who had been denied his seat because of his opposition to the Vietnam War and the conscription system that sustained it.

In *The New York Times v. Sullivan* (1964), the Court ruled that people in the public eye—elected officials and celebrities—could not win a libel suit against a publication solely because its editors had published untrue statements. Under the Court's reading of libel laws, plaintiffs had to prove that the statements were "recklessly false" and made with "malice aforethought." Since motivation was extremely difficult to establish within a court of law, the practical effect of *The New York Times v. Sullivan* was to make it unlikely that a public figure could win a libel suit against a newspaper or a magazine publisher.

In *Roth v. United States* (1957), the Court defined obscenity as material "without any redeeming social importance." The Court also defined as obscene material that "the average person, applying community standards, regarded as appealing to prurient interests." However, the Court found it impossible to come up with objective criteria to determine what materials were obscene under its definitions.

The Court also broadened the First Amendment's ban on the establishment of religion as a part of the state. In *Engel v. Vitale* (1962), the Court banned prayer in public schools. In a later decision, the Court banned Bible readings from public school classrooms. The Court also nullified an Arkansas law mandating the teaching of "creation science" as an alternative to Darwinian evolutionary theory. The cumulative effect over the years of these decisions was to remove religious observances from public schools.

In two controversial 5 to 4 decisions, the Supreme Court also enhanced the procedural rights of citizens accused of crimes. In the first case, *Gideon v. Wainwright* (1963), the Court ruled that Clarence Gideon, a career criminal, had never gotten a fair trial because he had never had an attorney to defend him in court. The Court, in effect, ruled that the right to a fair trial included the right to be represented in court by a lawyer. As a consequence of the Court's rulings in *Gideon v. Wainwright,* all cases in the country where defendants had been convicted of felonies without the benefit of attorneys to represent them had to be retried. If the defendant could not afford an attorney, the state, at taxpayers' expense, had to furnish one. In the second case, *Miranda v. Arizona* (1966), the Court enhanced citizens' Fifth and Sixth Amendment rights against self-incrimination and affirmed the right of citizens to have a lawyer present during questioning. In this case, the Court ruled that Ernesto Miranda, a suspect charged with kidnapping, robbery, and raping an eighteen-year-old retarded girl, had been coerced by Phoenix police into confessing. The police questioning Miranda had told him that if he did not confess, the judge would give him a longer sentence. According to the new rules implemented in *Miranda v. Arizona,* police were required to inform suspects of their rights at the time of arrest: their right to remain silent, their right to have an attorney represent them in court, that anything they said could and would be used against them in court, and, in the event that they could not afford a lawyer, the state would provide them with one free of charge. Subsequently, Miranda was retried and convicted with other evidence of the same crimes.

In 1965, the Warren Court struck down a Connecticut law that forbade the sale or use of contraceptives. In *Griswald v. Connecticut,* Associate Justice William O. Douglas, writing for the majority, found the law an unwarranted invasion of privacy. Nowhere in the Bill of Rights is there delineated a specific right to privacy; Douglas apparently inferred a right of privacy. Years later, another Supreme Court justice, Harry Blackmun, would ground the right of women to have an abortion on demand during the first trimester of pregnancy on that same inferred right of privacy.

Warren Court rulings also affected political practices in this country. In *Baker v. Carr* (1962), the Court declared that it could determine whether state legislative districts had been fairly drawn. The principle that the courts used during the 1960s to determine whether state legislative districts had been fairly drawn was "one person, one vote," derived from the equal protections clause of the Fourteenth Amendment. During the 1960s, as a consequence of *Baker v. Carr,* several states, in which rural voters were overrepresented in state legislatures at the expense of urban residents, had to redraw the boundaries of their legislative districts to make them equal in population.

The cumulative effects of these landmark court decisions were to enhance significantly the rights of individuals, curtail the arbitrary powers of government, and make the political system more democratic. The least democratic branch of the federal government, and the only one beyond the reach of the voting majority, had strengthened American democracy and validated the growing pluralism of the political culture. In doing so, the Warren Court provoked many powerful enemies. Conservatives were enraged by what they considered judicial usurpations of the lawmaking process. Law enforcement officials complained that Court decisions made their jobs more difficult, allowed obviously guilty people to avoid punishment, and seemed to place the law on the side of criminals rather than on the side of law-abiding victims. Devoutly religious people were offended by the Court's proscriptions of religious observances in public schools. Loud calls to impeach Earl Warren resounded across the South and the Midwest. As the conservative revolt gathered momentum in this country during the 1970s, one of their salient issues was curtailing the judicial activism of the Supreme Court.

CONTINUING THE COLD WAR

Johnson's early ventures in world affairs met with mixed results. In time, his efforts to achieve a U.S. military victory in Vietnam would destroy his presidency and bring his nation, and those whom he had tried to help in Southeast Asia, to disaster.

In Europe, Johnson could not prevent relations with NATO allies from deteriorating. His chief difficulties came with Charles de Gaulle, who wanted France and Western Europe to rid themselves of U.S. domination. The French leader spurned Johnson's offer to create a multilateral nuclear force and directed France to accelerate development of its own nuclear forces. In early 1966, the French withdrew their forces from NATO and ordered the United States to remove all of its military installations and personnel from France. France's dramatic actions signaled that de Gaulle believed that the Cold War in Europe was waning. European countries no longer feared Soviet aggression, hence they no longer felt dependent on U.S. support.

As de Gaulle challenged American influence in Europe, tensions in the Middle East caused Johnson persistent problems. He perceived Egyptian leader Gamal Abdul Nasser's efforts to promote Arab nationalism to be the chief threat to American Middle Eastern interests. The Soviet Union, backing Nasser, was gaining influence in the region. Then came another Arab-Israeli war. It occurred in June 1967, following border clashes between the Israelis and Syrians in the Golan Heights area. Nasser, backing Syria, mobilized his forces and blockaded Israel's Red Sea port of Elath. Egypt also worked out an agreement with Jordan that placed its forces under Egyptian command.

Arab leaders appeared united in their determination to demolish the Jewish state. Their military forces comprised 900 combat aircraft, five thousand tanks, and half a million soldiers. The outnumbered Israelis possessed about 250 aircraft, one thousand tanks, and 275,000 soldiers. The Israelis, concluding that an Arab attack was imminent, launched a preemptive strike on June 5. Israeli forces quickly destroyed the Egyptian air force, decimated Jordan's army, and defeated Syrian forces. Israeli tanks routed the Egyptian army. Israel won the war in six days. The key to Israel's remarkable victory: it quickly established decisive air superiority.

When a UN-proposed cease-fire went into effect, Israel occupied the Sinai and that part of Jordan west of the River Jordan (the West Bank). Israeli forces also occupied Gaza, East Jerusalem, and Syrian territory in the Golan Heights. Egyptian military power was shattered, Nasser was humiliated, and Soviet interests suffered a setback. Israel, now the major power in the region, kept all occupied territories, determined to use them to enhance its territory and to guarantee its security. Israel now controlled a land area nearly four and a half times its prewar size. Israeli imperialism intensified already-powerful Arab anti-Zionist animosities.

The most important outcome of the war from Israel's perspective was that no responsible Arab leader would ever again seriously contemplate the military destruction of the Jewish state. Israel, now secure strategically, entered fully into the Middle Eastern World. Anti-Americanism increased among Arabs because Arab leaders perceived the United States to be the main backer of Israel and responsible for its smashing victory. And in the wake of the Israeli victory, U.S.-Israeli relations improved and thousands of Jews emigrated from the United States to Israel, further inflaming Arab anti-American feelings. The aftershocks of the Six Day War have echoed all the way to the present and the seething small-scale war between the Israelis and the Palestinians.

Aware of the dangers inherent in the U.S.–USSR competition for influence and strategic advantage in the Middle East and elsewhere in the Third World, President Johnson invited Soviet Premier Alexei Kosygin to the United States for another summit conference. The two leaders made limited progress toward controlling the spiraling thermonuclear arms race. Johnson and Kosygin agreed that negotiations would begin soon on limiting the number of strategic bombers that each side possessed. They also announced plans to hold regular summit meetings to discuss arms control and other issues of paramount importance to both. But there would be no more summits. Johnson had planned to go to Moscow in the fall of 1968, but the Soviet Union sent its tanks into Czechoslovakia on August 20, 1968, to crush efforts by the Czechs to establish a social democratic government. Johnson canceled the impending meeting.

Johnson also had to face crises in the Caribbean, where he made preventing further Castro-like insurgencies his top priority. His first crisis came in Panama, which had long been a U.S. protectorate. Violent conflicts erupted between Panamanians and American citizens living in the Canal Zone in January 1964. The violence began when Panamanian students demanded that their national flag be flown alongside the American flag at a high school located in the Canal Zone. U.S. authorities rejected the students' demand. U.S. soldiers killed twenty-one Panamanians, and three Americans died in riots. The OAS mediated the dispute. U.S. and Panamanian negotiators then produced a series of agreements, allowing Panamanian participation in the management of the Panama Canal and granting Panama a share of canal revenues.

A more serious crisis erupted in the Dominican Republic, which also had a long history of U.S. domination. A right-wing dictator, Rafael Trujillo, was overthrown in 1961 by a military coup, ushering in years of political instability in that impoverished island country. President Kennedy, delighted to see Trujillo go, sought free elections. The elections brought Juan Bosch to power in 1962. Bosch, a social democrat, was overthrown by another military coup seven

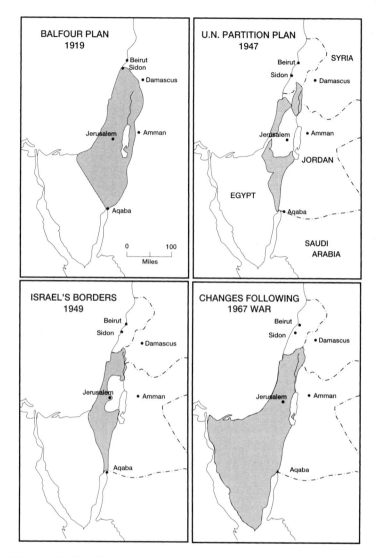

Figure 7.3   Israeli expansion.   *Source:* Yahya Armajani, *Middle East: Past and Present,* 1970, p. 323. Reprinted with permission of Prentice Hall, Englewood Cliffs, N.J.

months later. In early 1965, a coalition of liberals, radicals, and young army officers launched a revolution to restore Bosch to power.

President Johnson, fearful that pro-Castro elements might come to power and turn the country into another Cuba, sent U.S. troops to suppress the insurgency. U.S. Marines and Army infantrymen prevented Bosch's return to power. Administration spokesmen announced that U.S.

intervention had prevented a Communist takeover of the Dominican Republic. An occupation force was set up to maintain order. Elections were held in 1966, and Joaquin Balaguer defeated Bosch.

Balaguer established a government that protected U.S. interests, and Johnson withdrew the U.S. forces. But the Bosch movement was an independent, nationalistic movement, not a Communist conspiracy. U.S. intervention violated the OAS charter and canceled the U.S. pledge not to intervene militarily in the internal affairs of other Western Hemisphere countries. U.S. public opinion supported Johnson's military intervention. Liberals and foreign critics attacked his actions, but he ignored them. The campaign was limited in duration, and few American lives were lost. Johnson achieved his objectives, and his success silenced his critics. Success in the Dominican operation encouraged Johnson to try more of the same in Vietnam, expecting U.S. military success there to also silence any domestic or foreign detractors who might emerge.

VIETNAM: GOING TO WAR

The roots of U.S. intervention in Southeast Asia could be traced back to Truman's presidency, but it was not until the Kennedy years that the United States became inextricably involved in a war in Vietnam. At the time Johnson replaced Kennedy, the political situation in South Vietnam was deteriorating. A succession of inept military governments had followed Diem, none of which governed or fought effectively. National Liberation Front forces, the "VietCong," supported by supplies and troops from North Vietnam, extended their control in southern Vietnam.

Johnson did not concern himself greatly with Vietnam during his first year in office; he continued Kennedy's policy of supporting the South Vietnamese government. He retained Kennedy's top advisers, sharing their commitment to contain the spread of Chinese Communism into Southeast Asia. LBJ, just as Truman, Eisenhower, and Kennedy had before him, embraced the Cold War ideology. His primary foreign policy objectives were to contain the two Communist powers, the Soviet Union and the People's Republic of China, and to prevent revolutionary change in the Third World. Johnson dismissed any possibility of a U.S. withdrawal from Vietnam or any political solution that did not guarantee the survival of an independent, non-Communist state in southern Vietnam. He increased both the number of American advisers in South Vietnam and the level of economic aid. He also approved a series of covert operations against North Vietnam, including commando raids along the North Vietnamese coast and infiltration of CIA operatives into the North. This subtle shift toward the North opened the way to a wider war.

In the summer of 1964, as the presidential campaign was getting underway in the United States, there occurred a relatively minor event in the war that was developing in Vietnam that had major consequences. On August 1, while engaged in electronic espionage off the coast of North Vietnam, the U.S. destroyer USS *Maddox* was attacked by North Vietnamese torpedo boats. The *Maddox* returned the fire and repulsed the attackers with the aid of U.S. naval aircraft. It resumed its spy operations and it was joined by another destroyer, the *Turner Joy.* On the night of August 4, as they operated in heavy seas about fifty miles off the coast of North Vietnam in the Gulf of Tonkin, both ships reported that they were under attack. No one on either ship sighted any attackers; their initial reports were based on radar and sonar contacts. Later, the

Maddox's captain reported that weather effects and a misreading of sonar data may have been responsible for the reported attacks.

Even though evidence of a second attack was not certain, Johnson authorized retaliatory air strikes against North Vietnamese naval bases. He also asked Congress to approve a resolution, authorizing him to take "all necessary measures to repel any armed attack against the forces of the United States and to prevent further aggression." Johnson's use of force, coupled with his appeal for public support, silenced his Republican challenger, Barry Goldwater, who earlier had called for the bombing of North Vietnam. In presenting their case for the resolution, administration officials misled the Congress. Congressmen and senators were not told that the *Maddox* was on a spy mission when it was attacked, nor that the second attack may not have occurred. Secretary of Defense McNamara characterized both incidents as unprovoked acts of aggression against U.S. ships on routine patrol in international waters. Congress quickly gave the president what he wanted. The House passed the resolution unanimously, and the Senate enacted it by a vote of 88 to 2.

During the final month of the 1964 presidential campaign, Johnson said little about the war in Vietnam. Goldwater did not make an issue out of it, and most Americans did not concern themselves with a dirty little war in a faraway place. But at times Johnson did appear to be telling the American people that Americans would not be sent to fight there. In Akron, Ohio, on October 21, he stated "we are not about to send American boys nine or ten thousand miles away from home to do what Asian boys ought to be doing for themselves."

At the time he made those remarks, Johnson had not yet committed himself to the further bombing of North Vietnam, nor had he decided to send U.S. combat troops there. But he knew the situation in southern Vietnam was deteriorating, despite his own public assurances to the contrary. He also was involved with advisers who had developed contingency plans that could be implemented in the future, including bombing North Vietnam and sending U.S. combat forces to South Vietnam. During his reelection campaign, he deliberately misled the American people, conveying the impression that he would limit U.S. efforts in Vietnam to helping one side in a civil war. He offered himself as a peace candidate who did not seek a wider war in contrast to the hawkish Goldwater, who called for an unlimited U.S. military effort in Vietnam.

As 1965 began, the South Vietnamese government was on the verge of defeat, and Johnson confronted a dilemma that was largely of his own making. Since he had ruled out U.S. withdrawal from Southeast Asia, there remained only the options of negotiation or escalation. But negotiations with Hanoi in early 1965, given the military realities in southern Vietnam, could only mean having to accept a neutral coalition government for South Vietnam, with National Liberation Front (NLF) participation. Johnson knew that such a government would soon be dominated by the NLF, since the Saigon regime could only survive with strong U.S. support. He therefore ruled out negotiations until the military situation was more favorable, and he made his decision to escalate the war.

Johnson authorized a sustained, gradually expanding bombing campaign against North Vietnam beginning on February 13, called Operation ROLLING THUNDER, and he significantly expanded the much larger air war in southern Vietnam. There was a direct connection between the air war against North Vietnam and Johnson's decision to send combat forces to South Vietnam. Within two weeks, General William Westmoreland, the U.S. commander in Vietnam, requested Marine combat units to defend a large U.S. Air Force base at Danang because he could not rely on South Vietnamese security forces. Johnson quickly approved his request. On March 8, two Marine battalions in full battle gear waded ashore at beaches south of Danang.

In July 1965, Johnson and his advisers made a series of fateful decisions that set the United States on a course in Vietnam, from which it did not deviate for nearly three years and from which also began seven years of war. They approved General Westmoreland's requests for saturation bombing in southern Vietnam and for expanding the air war against North Vietnam. They also authorized sending an additional 100,000 combat troops to South Vietnam. Most important, President Johnson gave General Westmoreland a free hand to assume the major burden of fighting in the South. These decisions, made during the last week of July, represent a conscious decision to conduct an American war in Vietnam.

When he committed the United States to war in Southeast Asia, Johnson refused to tell the American people what he had done, and he refused to seek a formal declaration of war against North Vietnam. He claimed that the Gulf of Tonkin resolution granted him the authority to wage war. Since the Supreme Court never ruled on the matter, it remains a moot question whether the resolution amounted to a declaration of war against North Vietnam. Senator Fulbright, along with other legislators who later turned against the war, believed that Johnson had tricked them into supporting a war. At the time, Johnson felt confident that he could win the war in a few years and persuade Congress and most Americans to support it.

The Johnson administration's decisions for war were based on two fundamental errors in judgment. The United States seriously underestimated the capacity of the NLF and the North Vietnamese to resist large-scale applications of U.S. military power over a long period of time. Johnson and his advisers assumed that within a year or two, North Vietnam would probably "break" from the ever-increasing punishment inflicted by U.S. bombers, and that they would accept U.S. terms for settlement. Johnson did not believe that a poor Asian country about the size of New Mexico could stand up to U.S. military power. The second error, related to the first, was to underestimate drastically the cost of the war, in both lives and dollars, and to overestimate the willingness of Americans to go on passively paying those costs year after year.

THE AMERICAN WAY OF WAR

The United States relied heavily on air power to win the war. Air Force and Navy pilots had two primary missions—to check infiltration of men, equipment, and supplies coming south from North Vietnam along the "Ho Chi Minh Trail," and to punish the North Vietnamese from the air until they abandoned the insurgency in the South and came to the bargaining table on U.S. terms. Bombing failed to achieve either objective, even though the United States waged the largest aerial war in history. The bombing slowed the rate of infiltration down the Ho Chi Minh Trail, although never enough to seriously hampered the NLF war effort. Bombing disrupted North Vietnam's agriculture, destroyed its industry, and severely damaged some of its cities. Thousands of civilians were killed or wounded. But bombing never appreciably reduced North Vietnam's war-making ability, nor broke the morale of its people.

U.S. ground combat operations also escalated drastically between July 1965, and the end of 1967, when the United States had deployed nearly 500,000 troops. General Westmoreland used a strategy of attrition against the enemy. He believed that "search and destroy" operations

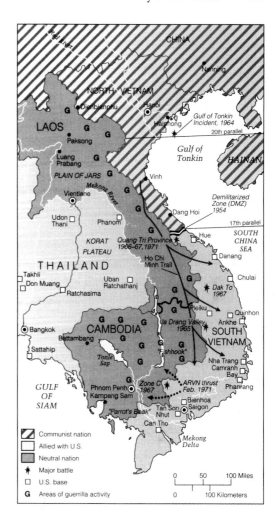

Figure 7.4   South Vietnam and Cambodia.
Source: Public Domain Map.

would eradicate the enemy and force them to the negotiating table. U.S. troops used their technological superiority to counter the enemy's guerrilla warfare tactics. Herbicides were used on a wide scale to deprive the VietCong of forest cover and food crops. These chemicals, especially Agent Orange, caused widespread ecological devastation and posed health hazards within southern Vietnam. Americans also relied on artillery, helicopter gunships, and bombing to destroy enemy bases and to drive the guerrillas into open country. Since all of South Vietnam became a combat zone, U.S. soldiers found themselves fighting an unconventional war without fronts or territorial objectives. The only measure of progress toward victory in a war of attrition was the number of enemy supplies captured or destroyed, the number of enemy weapons and ammunition captured or destroyed, and most of all, the number of enemy soldiers captured, wounded, or killed.

The American takeover of the war in early 1965 had prevented certain South Vietnamese defeat. But the United States could only achieve a stalemate not a victory. The attrition strategy was based on the assumption that U.S. forces, using their superior firepower, could inflict irreplaceable losses on the enemy while keeping their own casualties low. Even though the Americans inflicted heavy casualties, both the NLF and the North Vietnamese replaced their losses and matched each American escalation with one of their own during the period 1965 to 1967. They retained the strategic initiative, and the NLF political structure in the South remained intact.

U.S. artillery and bombing campaigns below the 17th Parallel disrupted the southern Vietnamese economy. Large numbers of civilians were killed, and millions more were driven into the arms of the VietCong, or became refugees. The violent U.S. assault undermined the social fabric of a fragile nation and alienated villagers from the South Vietnamese regime. The U.S. takeover of the war further weakened the resolve of the South Vietnamese forces, who became more dependent than ever on U.S. combat forces.

In 1967, the South Vietnamese government, headed by General Nguyen Van Thieu, attempted to build popular support among the rural population. It focused on pacification and rural development. Government cadres moved into villages, providing medical supplies and social services. They tried to insulate the villagers from both VietCong appeals and reprisals, and they sought to promote a national rebirth while U.S. forces tried to defeat the Communists militarily. These pacification efforts sometimes succeeded, but they more often failed. Americans occasionally bombed or shelled pacified villages by mistake. VietCong terrorists assassinated many rural development leaders. Often the cadres were inept or corrupt. The inability of the South Vietnamese military government to solve their country's massive social problems was a major reason for the eventual failure of the U.S. effort in Vietnam.

The Thieu government survived not because it was strong, because it was popular with most South Vietnamese, or because its soldiers fought well, but because it was backed by massive U.S. firepower. But relations between U.S. advisers and their Vietnamese clients often were ambivalent. The Vietnamese resented the Americans' arrogance and inability to understand them. The Americans were frustrated by pervasive Vietnamese corruption and inefficiency. U.S. soldiers, fighting in the steamy jungles and swamps of an alien land, and not always able to tell a friendly Vietnamese from a deadly enemy, often expressed hostility and mistrust toward the people they were defending.

The steady escalation of the war between 1965 and 1967 generated both international and domestic pressures for a negotiated settlement. But the continuing stalemate on the battlefields ensured that neither side wanted negotiations. For political reasons, both sides had to appear responsive to peace initiatives, but neither side would make concessions necessary to get serious negotiations started. Hanoi's strategy was to get maximum propaganda value out of peace initiatives, while matching U.S. escalations until the Americans tired of the war and pulled out. President Johnson believed that the steadily expanding U.S. military effort would eventually break Hanoi.

Hanoi maintained that the U.S. military presence in South Vietnam violated the 1954 Geneva Accords and that the bombing of North Vietnam was criminal aggression. The North Vietnamese refused to negotiate until the United States ceased all acts of war against their country and withdrew its forces. Hanoi also insisted that the government in Saigon would have to be replaced by a coalition government dominated by the NLF. The United States refused to

Figure 7.5   The helicopter war: The Vietnam War was the first in which helicopters were used extensively to airlift men into combat. Here, riflemen of the 25th Infantry Division prepare to board a squadron of "Hueys" (Bell UH-1Ds) for an assault on Communist positions. *Source:* U.S. Army Photo.

withdraw its forces until a political solution could be reached in the South that excluded the VietCong. It also refused to stop the bombing, which Washington insisted was necessary to keep the Communists from overrunning the South. The United States remained committed to achieving a non-Communist South Vietnam. So the war went on, and numerous peace initiatives from various sources failed in 1966 and 1967.

WAR AT HOME

While the expanding military stalemate in Vietnam continued, within the United States, supporters and opponents of the war engaged in debates of rising intensity. On one side were the Hawks, mostly conservative Republicans and Democrats, strongly supportive of the war, who wanted to increase the U.S. war effort. On the other side were the Doves, challenging both the effectiveness and the morality of the war. The Doves represented a more diverse group: old-line pacifists, student radicals, civil rights leaders, some college professors, and liberal politicians. The most prominent Dove was Senator Fulbright. Initially a supporter, Fulbright had turned against the war by 1966.

Opposition to the war took many forms. Senator Fulbright held hearings on the conduct of the war before his Senate Foreign Relations Committee, providing a forum for war critics and helping to legitimate opposition to the war. The Doves staged many rallies and protest demonstrations during 1967, the first year of extensive antiwar activity. On October 21, about 50,000 opponents of war demonstrated in front of the Pentagon. Many young men resisted or evaded the draft. Thousands fled America and its war for Canada or Sweden.

Most Americans in 1967 were neither Hawks nor Doves. Nearly all citizens had supported the initial escalations that Americanized the Vietnam war. Confident of quick victory, they had rallied around the flag. But after two years of rising costs and casualties, popular frustration with the Vietnam War had mounted. Polls taken in August showed for the first time that a majority of Americans believed that sending U.S. combat troops to Vietnam had been a mistake. But opponents of Johnson's war policy in 1967 formed no consensus on Vietnam. They were divided over whether to escalate the war drastically and win it, or to negotiate an American withdrawal. But the growing divisiveness, combined with declining confidence in the integrity and competence of government officials, strained the social fabric.

The president, trying to dampen growing criticism within the Congress of his war policy, brought General Westmoreland to Washington in November. Speaking before the National Press Club on November 21, Westmoreland gave an optimistic appraisal of the war. He said that pacification was going so well that the VietCong could no longer mount a major offensive anywhere in South Vietnam. He stated, "We have reached an important point where the end begins to come into view." Popular support for the war increased as the year ended.

Tet-68 and Its Consequences

Then came Tet. On January 30, 1968, choosing the Lunar New Year, the most important Vietnamese holiday, as a time to strike in order to catch their opponents by surprise, about 80,000 NLF and North Vietnamese troops suddenly brought the war to the cities and towns of South Vietnam. They simultaneously attacked provincial capitals, district towns, and a dozen major U.S. military bases all over the country. At most attack sites, the VietCong were beaten back within a few hours or few days and sustained heavy losses. Within a month, they had lost all of the cities they had originally taken.

Communist strategists had planned the Tet Offensive carefully. They designed it to give their forces a smashing victory over the Americans, demoralize the Army of the Republic of Vietnam (ARVN) forces, and bring the urban population of South Vietnam over to their side. They would show the urban populations of the South that neither the U. S. nor the South Vietnamese forces could protect them. The Communists hoped that their assaults would provoke popular uprisings against the South Vietnamese government, forcing the Americans to leave and hastening the end of the war. But Tet turned out to be a major defeat for the Communists; they failed to achieve most of their goals and suffered heavy losses.

Within the United States the Tet Offensive had a tremendous impact. It turned out to be a crucial political victory for the Communists. It had caught the South Vietnamese and Americans by surprise, although they had responded quickly to counteract it.

Although General Westmoreland spoke confidently about having anticipated and suppressed the Tet offensive, while inflicting heavy losses on the enemy, he soon requested an additional 206,000 troops to be able to follow up and win the war. The Chairman of the Joint Chiefs, General Earle Wheeler told the President that the Americans could lose the war unless the requested reinforcements were sent. Johnson, confused by events and conflicting military

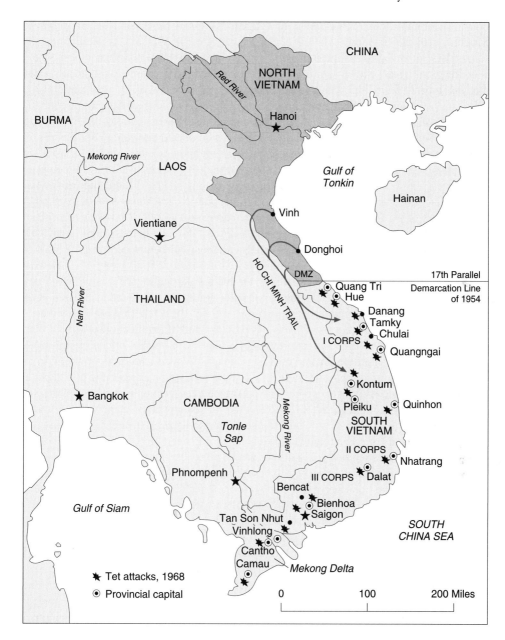

Figure 7.6   The Tet-68 Offensive.   *Source:* U.S. Army Map.

opinions, asked his new Secretary of Defense Clark Clifford to conduct a thorough review of the troop request before the president responded to the military's request for more troops. Clifford had replaced Robert McNamara, one of the principle architects of the U.S. war policy, who having lost faith in the policy, had resigned.

Clifford formed a committee whose investigations ranged far beyond the troop request issue; it conducted the first full review of the U.S. war effort in Vietnam. Clifford demanded precise answers to fundamental questions: What were the ultimate objectives of the United States in Vietnam? How would additional forces contribute to attaining these goals? What would be the impact of a major escalation of the war on the public and on the economy?

The answers he got from both military and civilian officials in the Pentagon discouraged him. To provide 206,000 more troops for Vietnam required further reductions of U.S. military commitments elsewhere. Meeting these troop requests would necessitate calling up reserves, increasing draft calls, and raising taxes. Casualties would rise, and domestic opposition would intensify. Civilian analysts in the Pentagon told Clifford that the current war strategy could not bring victory, even with the proposed escalation. They recommended that the United States start phasing back its military involvement and work for a negotiated settlement. They also proposed turning over more of the fighting to the South Vietnamese forces. Clifford subsequently recommended to Johnson that he reject Westmoreland's request for additional troops, assign the ARVN a greater fighting role, and seek a negotiated settlement rather than continue his futile efforts to win the war.

The Tet Offensive also influenced the way the media, particularly television news, covered the Vietnam War. Previously, television had usually presented a well-ordered vision of the war: On-the-scene reports of combat operations that usually were reported as U.S. victories, along with periodic analytical reports of the war's progress and of pacification programs. With Tet, viewers saw for the first time saw the results of a major Communist offensive striking all over South Vietnam. A rush of violent and confusing images flooded television—fighting in the streets of Saigon and Hue. The chaos in Vietnam viewed on television appeared to contradict all of the official reports and media coverage of the past three years, which had conveyed the idea of steady progress toward military victory. The fact that the enemy could stage surprise attacks all over South Vietnam caused a growing number of Americans to wonder if all that was achieved after three years of escalating war in Vietnam was an unending stalemate.

Congressional opposition to the war also escalated after Tet. Antiwar sentiment on Capitol Hill boosted the candidacy of an obscure Minnesota Senator, Eugene McCarthy, who had announced in December 1967 that he would challenge Lyndon Johnson for the presidency as an antiwar candidate. In the New Hampshire primary, held on March 12, 1968, McCarthy received 42 percent of the vote, almost as many votes as Johnson, indicating more widespread opposition to Johnson's war policy than previously thought. Johnson appeared to be politically vulnerable. Four days after the New Hampshire primary, a more formidable antiwar candidate, Robert Kennedy, announced that he too would seek the Democratic nomination.

At the White House, Johnson convened a panel of distinguished civilian and military advisers who had previously endorsed his war policy. But in March these "wise men" told the president that the Vietnam War could not be won, "save at unacceptable risk" to national interests at home and abroad. Their advice influenced Johnson. He accepted Clark Clifford's recommendations to scale back the war. On March 31, 1968, Johnson told the American people that he would reduce the bombing of North Vietnam in an effort to get negotiations underway. As he neared the end of his speech, he stunned the nation by stating, "I shall not seek, nor will I accept, the nomination of my party for another term as your president." To restore unity to America, he would remove himself from politics and seek peace in Vietnam.

BRIEF BIBLIOGRAPHIC ESSAY

Robert Caro has completed three volumes of his ongoing massive biographical study of Lyndon Johnson, *The Path to Power, Means of Ascent,* and *Master of the Senate.* Caro's research has given him encyclopedic knowledge of the details of Johnson's life, and he writes well. Robert Dallek has written a substantial two-volume biography of Johnson, *Lone Star Rising: Lyndon Johnson and His Times, 1908–1960* and *Flawed Giant: Lyndon Johnson and His Times, 1961–1973.* Dallek's work is balanced and more sophisticated than Caro's. Doris Kearns's *Lyndon Johnson and the American Dream* is an insightful study of Johnson's political career. Eric Goldman's *The Tragedy of Lyndon Johnson* is a sympathetic account of his presidency. James M. Sundquist's *Politics and Policy: The Eisenhower, Kennedy, and Johnson Years* offers a good account of the Great Society programs. Michael Harrington's analysis of poverty in the United States, *The Other America,* helped start the war on poverty. James C. Harvey's *Black Civil Rights During the Johnson Administration* is a good account of this important issue. Bernard Schwartz, in *Super Chief: Earl Warren and His Supreme Court,* offers a good study of the many landmark decisions of the Warren Court and of the man who led it. Johnson's foreign policy is studied by Philip L. Geyelin in *Lyndon B. Johnson and the World.* Michael B. Oren has written a remarkably good book, *Six Days of War: June 1967 and the Making of the Modern Middle East,* which places the Six Day War into its world and Middle Eastern contexts. A good general military and diplomatic history of U.S. involvement in Vietnam is George Donelson Moss, *Vietnam: An American Ordeal, 4th ed.* George C. Herring's *America's Longest War: The United States and Vietnam, 1950–1975,* 3rd ed., is a concise diplomatic history of the war. Larry Berman's *Planning a Tragedy* is an acute study of the Johnson administration's decision to go to war in Vietnam. Neil Sheehan, in *A Bright Shining Lie: John Paul Vann and America in Vietnam,* offers a fine study of a capable official who gave ten years and finally his life to the American cause in Vietnam. It also is a finely crafted history of American involvement in Vietnam.

WEB SITES

An excellent new Web site *Lyndon Baines Johnson Library and Museum* at `<http://www.lbjlib.utexas.edu/>` is created and maintained by the Lyndon Baines Johnson Library and Museum located on the University of Texas campus in Austin. The site is part of the National Archives and Records Administration, and it covers the life and political career of Johnson, focusing on his presidency. The best part of the site is its collection of primary source documents concerning the major events of Johnson's presidency.

`<http://www.students.vassar.edu/~vietnam/overview.html>`, "The Wars of Vietnam: An Overview" offers an extensive overview of military conflicts in Vietnam from 1945 through the U.S. engagement. This site offers full text of historical documents including the Tonkin Gulf resolution and excerpts from U.S. presidential speeches. "Vietnam, Online" at `<http://www.pbs.org.wgbh/amex/vietnam/index.html>` is from PBS and the *American Experience.* This site contains a detailed, interactive timeline of the war, interpretive essays, and autobiographical reflections from participants.

8

Rebellion and Reaction

The 1960s had begun with President Kennedy's appeal for national renewal. He had urged young people to channel their energy and idealism into community service at home and the Peace Corps abroad. Thousands followed his lead. But after his assassination, the national scenario that unfolded for the rest of the decade featured sit-ins, marches, riots, bombings, the burning of cities, and more assassinations. Hopes for peace, prosperity, and justice for all vanished in the face of political conflict, cultural crisis, and the Vietnam War. Some Americans were temporarily radicalized by their experiences; far more Americans turned conservative or simply abandoned politics. The liberal consensus that had been forged during the 1930s, 1940s, and 1950s as a consequence of fighting the Great Depression, World War II, and the Cold War disintegrated during the 1960s.

During the early 1960s, the economy was strong, the federal budget was balanced, inflation was low, and the nation was at peace. Most Americans were better off materially than they had ever been, and optimistic about the future. Social tranquility prevailed. Prospects had never looked better for the children of affluence. By 1968, inflation riddled the economy, the people were divided over a controversial war, and race riots tore apart major cities. Political assassinations agonized everyone; students protested on college campuses and in the streets. Other radical insurgents protested historical exclusions and injustices, and demanded their fair share of the American Dream. Drugs and crime became major concerns.

As civility drained from public life, many thoughtful Americans feared that the dark forces unleashed by protest and war might rip the social fabric apart and destabilize the political order. The 1968 presidential election occurred amidst the worst backdrop of violence and disorder since the Civil War.

Young Radicals

The insurgencies that characterized the middle and late 1960s began on the campuses of some of America's leading universities, the prestigious Ivy League schools, and the great public universities such as the Berkeley campus of the University of California and the University of

Michigan at Ann Arbor. A new generation of politically committed young people had already become involved in the civil rights movement and had also tried to organize poor people at the community level. After 1965, many of these youthful insurgents, most of them from affluent middle-class families, became involved in protesting the Vietnam War. In 1960, a group of young activists organized Students for a Democratic Society (SDS). In 1962, one of its leaders, Tom Hayden, wrote a manifesto for the new organization, the Port Huron Statement. Hayden criticized the apolitical apathy of college students and attacked the military-industrial complex as a threat to democracy. He called for an end to poverty in America and for the creation of "a democracy of individual participation," in which all members subject to the authority of a government institution would participate in its decision-making processes.

The first student uprising occurred on the Berkeley campus of the University of California in the fall of 1964. A group of students, many of them civil rights activists who had spent the previous summer registering voters in Mississippi, protested university efforts to prevent their using a campus area for rallying support for off-campus political activities. Student leaders Mario Savio and Jack Weinberg, both veterans of the Mississippi "Freedom Summer," formed the Free Speech Movement (FSM) to lead the resistance. When university officials attempted to discipline leaders of the FSM, about 600 students and nonstudents occupied Sproul Hall, the university administration building. After university efforts to persuade the protesters to leave failed, Governor Edmund G. "Pat" Brown ordered state police to remove and arrest them. The forced removal of the demonstrators provoked a student strike, which was supported by a large majority of the faculty. After two months of turmoil on campus, university officials rescinded the order and permitted "free speech" on campus.

The rebellion that began at Berkeley soon spread to other campuses around the country. Insurgents attacked university complicity with racial injustice and the Vietnam War. They also attacked the universities themselves. They rebelled against receiving "assembly line educations." Protesters demanded the right to sit on governing boards with the power to veto faculty appointments. Curricula and methods of instruction came under fire. Students objected to taking "irrelevant" courses, mostly required science and language classes. They called for fewer required courses, more electives, and fewer tests and grades. Other campus protests arose over issues concerning the personal lives of students. Protesters demanded the elimination of college parietal rules, which set curfews, imposed dress codes, and regulated visiting hours for university housing.

By the mid-1960s, the stalemated Vietnam War had become the main student protest issue. Since the military draft was the prime way the war could reach young people, opposition to the draft brought thousands of new recruits into protest politics. The SDS organized a Stop the Draft Week for October 16 to 21, 1967. It staged sit-ins at army induction centers, held meetings for draft card burnings, opposed campus Reserve Officer Training Corps (ROTC) programs, demonstrated against corporations known to be prime Defense Department contractors, and harassed military recruiters.Thousands of protesters besieged the Oakland, California, Army Induction Center; hundreds sat in the street blocking buses hauling in draftees. Between 1965 and 1968, the SDS led or joined hundreds of demonstrations at over 100 colleges and universities involving about 50,000 students.

The SDS also joined a violent student uprising, which occurred at Columbia University during the first six months of 1968. The issues that sparked the conflict were two potent

Figure 8.1   Columbia 1968: Young people occupy an area of Hamilton Hall on the Morningside Heights campus in New York City.   *Source:* AP/Wide World Photos.

catalysts of student militancy—civil rights and Vietnam. Antiwar radicals and civil rights activists joined forces to attack one of the nation's most prestigious universities. The SDS sought an end to university ties with a military research institute on campus. The Black Student Union opposed university plans to construct a gymnasium on land adjacent to Harlem. Both groups occupied campus buildings to force the university to sever its ties with the military and to abandon the gym project. When negotiations between administration officials and students failed, police stormed the buildings to remove the protesters, who had barricaded doors and windows. Hundreds of students were injured, and about 700 were arrested. Following the arrests, the SDS organized a campus strike that forced the university to close early that spring.

American student protests in 1968 were part of a larger web of student and worker militant actions around the world. While students barricaded buildings at Columbia, ten million French workers went on strike, and students battled police in the streets of Paris. Mass demonstrations occurred in Sao Paulo, Brazil; the most violent street fighting in decades occurred in Italy. In London, 25,000 people protested the Vietnam War. Radical political movements of every kind convulsed the planet during one of the most transformative years of the twentieth century.

At its 1969 annual meeting, the SDS split into warring factions. Its Left-wing, calling itself the "Weathermen," went off on its own. In October, hundreds of Weathermen staged "the days of rage" in Chicago, which they intended to be the opening campaign of a new American revolution. They broke windows in buildings and smashed automobile windshields. Police arrested and jailed most of them. About 100 Weathermen went underground, forming terrorist bands that carried out sporadic bombings of public buildings and corporate headquarters during the early 1970s.

The New Left radicalized only a small portion of the millions of young people attending college during the 1960s. Most students attended class, pursued their social lives, worked part time, and sought conventional goals. They never participated in radical protests on or off campus. Student rebels were mostly clustered on the campuses of major metropolitan universities such as Berkeley and Columbia. Because they were a highly visible, articulate group that received extensive media coverage, especially television news coverage, the public's perception was that student radicalism was much more extensive than demographic data confirmed. Most of the nation's 2,300 community colleges, state universities, private liberal arts colleges, and campuses with religious affiliations, which educated the vast majority of the nation's collegians, remained quiet, orderly, businesslike places during the 1960s. The young radicals of the 1960s were mostly the children of college-educated, liberal, affluent, and often influential parents. They formed a radical elite who rebelled against some of the institutions and practices of the affluent society. But these comparatively few privileged insurgents provoked a rebellion that spread beyond politics to challenge the entire culture.

THE GREENING OF AMERICA

Far more young people who felt alienated and frustrated by the affluent liberal society of the 1960s fled from it rather than radically confronted it. These "hippies" took a path previously traveled by Bohemians during the Roaring Twenties and the Beats during the 1950s. In fact, the best of the Beat poets, Allen Ginsberg, was a prominent member of the 1960s' counterculture. The hippies embraced a new youth culture that ran counter to much that was cherished by middle-class Americans—affluence, economic growth, and high technology. The discipline of parents, schools, and jobs was abandoned for a free-flowing existence expressed by the hippie motto: "Do your own thing."

Hippies grew long hair and donned jeans, tank tops, and sandals. These refugees from the "uptight, straight" world of parents, schools, and nine-to-five jobs flocked to havens in the Haight-Ashbury section of San Francisco, the Sunset Strip in Hollywood, and New York City's East Village. They joined communes that cropped up in both urban neighborhoods and rural retreats. The appeal of the commune movement lay in a romantic urge to return to the land: to adopt a simpler life, to regain physical and mental health, and perhaps to seek spiritual renewal.

The counterculture repudiated science, systematic knowledge, and rationalism. It embraced a notion of organic, mystical consciousness in which the Self merged seamlessly with Community and Nature. Infinite "being" supplanted the linear boundaries of time and space. Feeling and intuition replaced thought and knowing. Hippies explored ancient Asian and African mystical religions. Saffron-robed skinheads on San Francisco street corners chanted the

"Hare Krishna." Others found the Age of Aquarius in astrology. Some hippies turned to witch-craft and demonology. Nature was valued as being superior to society and technology. A wide array of synthetic consumer products was rejected as artificial—"plastic." Hippies prized being natural, using nature's products, and eating natural foods. The hippie ideal was personal authenticity: to live a life free of conflict, exploitation, and alienation; a life in harmony with nature, and one's true self.

Hippies also repudiated the restrictive sexual practices of "Puritan" America. Although sexual behavior in this country had become more liberal, hippies moved far beyond middle-class proprieties and inhibitions. The freer sexuality of the hippie lifestyle became one of its main attractions and also provoked the wrath of elders. Casual sex was often tied to counter-cultural music, as flocks of teenage "groupies" sought out rock musicians. English groups, especially the Beatles and the Rolling Stones, expressed the central themes and ideals of the hippie world view. Bob Dylan was the main American countercultural bard. He composed and sang "The Times They Are A-Changing" and "Blowin' in the Wind." In San Francisco, "acid rock" appeared. Promoter Bill Graham staged concerts at the Fillmore West, featuring the psychedelic sounds of San Francisco's homegrown bands, the Grateful Dead and the Jefferson Airplane. A young white blues singer from Port Arthur, Texas, Janis Joplin, became the queen of San Francisco's psychedelic music scene. Drugs and music formed the vital center of the counterculture. "Tune in, turn on, and drop out" urged the high priest of LSD, Timothy Leary, a former Harvard psychologist who had been fired for conducting psychedelic drug experiments on his students.

Figure 8.2   The Beatles. (L-R): John Lennon, Paul McCartney, George Harrison, and Ringo Starr.   *Source:* St. Louis Mercantile Library. Used with permission.

Drugs reached into the countercultural literary scene, continuing a beat generation tradition. Ken Kesey wrote part of his best-selling first novel, *One Flew Over the Cuckoo's Nest,* under the influence of LSD. With money from the book's sales, Kesey purchased a bus and named it "Further." He painted it in psychedelic Day-Glo colors, wired it for stereo, and he and his friends, who called themselves the Merry Pranksters, toured up and down the West Coast. Everywhere they went, they conducted "acid tests," wild parties featuring LSD-spiked Kool-Aid, loud rock music, and light shows.

Marijuana use was far more widespread than LSD. "Pot" became the common currency of the counterculture and spread into mainstream society. Marijuana turned up at high school and college parties during the 1960s. Hippies experimented with other drugs as well, including mescaline and methedrine. Countercultural drug use provoked a pathetic debate over whether smoking marijuana was less harmful than smoking cigarettes or drinking alcoholic beverages. All of these substances could be harmful if used excessively, but that fact was beside the point because the debate really was about values and lifestyles.

One of the major events in the life of the counterculture occurred in the summer of 1967 in San Francisco's Haight-Ashbury district—"the summer of love." Hippies sought a cultural counterpart to SDS's proclaimed summer of protest against the Vietnam war. Just as radical politics was transforming American political life, the summer of love would transform society by creating a community of young dropouts uninhibitedly enjoying the pleasures of the flesh. The reality of what occurred was dismal. Thousands of youngsters showed up, most of them runaways from troubled homes, utterly unprepared to support themselves. Often they were reduced to panhandling, drug dealing, and prostitution to survive. Sexual promiscuity and rampant drug use led to epidemics of venereal disease and drug overdoses. Far from fleeing the social problems of the larger society, the runaways brought them with them. The writer Joan Didion, who visited the Haight-Ashbury district during the summer of 1967, in an essay, "Slouching Toward Bethlehem," famously depicted the squalor and aimlessness of hippie existence. Didion found the summer of love to be:

> the desperate attempt of a handful of pathetically unequipped children to create a community in a social vacuum. . . . They are less in rebellion against society than ignorant of it.[1]

The hippie triad of "drugs, sex, and rock music" came together at rock festivals, the most important ritual of the countercultural community. The greatest of these "happenings" occurred at Woodstock in August 1969. At a site in New York's Hudson River Valley, between 300,000 and 400,000 young people gathered to hear music, enjoy drugs, and engage in casual sex.

Intellectuals fashioned ideologies for the counterculture. Charles Reich wrote in *Greening of America* about a new consciousness that would renew America, forming the basis of another American revolution, one without tears or violence. The new order would just happen. But the counterculture's expected new utopia never arrived. Instead it turned sour and disintegrated. Hard drugs replaced marijuana. Violence, most of it connected with illegal drug traffic, destroyed much of what had been attractive in the hippie culture.

---

[1]Joan Didion, *Slouching Toward Bethlehem* (New York: Washington Square Press, 1968), p. 127.

Figure 8.3   Cheerful Hippies at Woodstock.
Source: CORBIS.

Greed and selfishness also pervaded the counterculture, contradicting its presumptions of innocence. Another rock festival, promoted by the Rolling Stones and held at the Altamont Raceway in northern California, revealed the crass commercialism of the rock music business.

The Altamont concert ended in violence when the Hell's Angels, an outlaw motorcycle gang, hired by promoters to provide security, savagely beat people and even killed a person.

The counterculture lasted for about half a decade, then it simply evaporated, quickly becoming only an exotic memory. It had sprung to life because of some special circumstances prevailing during the 1960s. The postwar baby boom had created a large population cluster of young people between the ages of fourteen and twenty-five. Such a huge youth population created, for a moment, a consciousness of a separate culture. Permissive child-rearing practices also contributed to the formation of the counterculture. These children of abundance confronted a complex world of protracted education, large-scale corporate and government bureaucracies, an intricate, powerful technology, severe social conflicts and inequities, and most of all the military draft and a controversial war in Vietnam. Young people recoiled in fear and loathing over a world that they had never made, and they became "flower children," urging others "to make love, not war."

But only a minority of young people joined the counterculture. Most went about the difficult enterprise of growing up and entering the adult world without visible alienation or protest. The greatest gap in the 1960's social fabric was not a generation gap between children and parents, but between different segments of the youth population. The more significant gap was intragenerational, not intergenerational. Value conflicts between middle-class and working-class young people were profound and occasionally violent. Upper-middle-class campus radicals scoffed at bourgeois sensibilities and burned their draft cards. Young workers, for whom middle-class respectability remained a cherished ambition, defended their way of life and patriotically supported the Vietnam War. Long-haired hippies and antiwar demonstrators infuriated working-class youth who regarded them as privileged cowards and traitors. One of the most violent riots of the era occurred in New York City when hard-hat construction workers attacked a crowd of antiwar demonstrators.

Although short-lived and engaging only a fraction of young people during the 1960's, both the New Left and the counterculture left their marks. They heightened consciousness of war and racial injustice; they called attention to the negative ecological and human consequences of technology, and they forced some people to confront the disparities between their professed ideals and the lives they lived. But the most enduring impact of the counterculture came in lifestyle realms—in diet, dress, decorative art, music, and sexual practices. People became more concerned with developing their inner selves, achieving their "human potential," than with seeking the external trappings of success.

THE FIRE THIS TIME

The civil rights movement crested in 1965 when Martin Luther King Jr. led the Selma march and Congress passed the Voting Rights Act. Five days after President Johnson signed that historic measure, the Watts section of Los Angeles went up in flames. It ushered in the first of several successive "long, hot summers." The Watts riot, a weeklong orgy of burning and looting, claimed thirty-four lives, injured 1,100 people, and destroyed $40 million worth of property. The Watts explosion dismayed civil rights reformers, because the residents of Watts generally lived much better than most African-American slum dwellers in America. Watts was not physically an inner city, since families did not live in crowded, dilapidated tenements; they lived in single, detached houses with lawns located along palm-shaded boulevards. Three African Americans sat on the Los Angeles City Council; Watts was represented by a black Congressman and two black state assemblymen. Economically, African Americans living in Watts were better off than blacks in any other large American city.

Watts revealed a depth of antiwhite bitterness and alienation that few civil rights workers of either race even knew existed. African-American progress in recent years and the promise of more to come had only raised exaggerated expectations and intensified the rage of many Watts residents. A special commission investigating the Watts upheaval warned that if the breach between the races was not healed, the riot might be a curtain-raiser for future racial blowups. The commission's warning proved prophetic. Between 1965 and 1968, hundreds of inner cities exploded into major riots.

The worst violence occurred in Newark and Detroit within the same week of July 1967. In Newark, twenty-six people died and 1,200 were injured. In Detroit, forty-three people died and another 2,000 were hurt. Fires burned out the center of the nation's fifth largest city. For two weeks that summer, Detroit was a war zone with tanks rolling through the streets and the sound of machine-gun fire piercing the air.

Detroit's riot was the most alarming, not only because of the loss of life and the extensive destruction of property, but also because it occurred in a city governed by a coalition that included extensive African-American participation. Great Society reformers had lavished extensive antipoverty and urban renewal programs on the Motor City. One-fourth of all workers employed in the automobile industry, Detroit's major business, were black; the UAW was a progressive, integrated union. About 45 percent of Detroit's African-American families owned their own homes. Analysts of the Detroit riot drew a portrait of the typical rioter—a young adult black male, a high school graduate, employed, often an auto worker and a union member, a veteran, married, and with an annual income slightly below the national median for his age group. These data suggest that the typical Detroit rioters were neither juveniles out on a spree nor despairing members of a black underclass. The rioting did not occur in the poorest neighborhoods but in black working-class neighborhoods containing a high percentage of owner-occupied homes and intact families. African-American rage and violence in Detroit were apparently provoked more by insensitive police tactics than by deprivation and despair.

Nearly all major race riots started from minor episodes, often from incidents growing out of white police arresting African Americans. Watts blew up when a crowd gathered to protest the arrest of a drunken motorist. Newark exploded after police arrested an African-American taxicab driver, John Smith, for following a police car too closely. Smith protested and was beaten by the arresting officers; news of the beating provoked the riot. Detroit erupted when police raided an after-hours bar hosting a party for two returning Vietnam veterans.

Studies revealed a pattern prevailing in the major urban riots. Most rioting occurred within inner city confines; most of the destruction was inflicted upon inner city homes and businesses; and most of the violence occurred between rioters and law enforcement personnel. Over 80 percent of the fatalities were rioters, shot either by the police or by soldiers. Studies of all major riots also suggested that the underlying causes of the uprisings were chronic slum conditions, aggravated by rough police tactics and hot, humid weather. Frustration with the slow pace of black economic progress, despite years of civil rights agitation, Great Society reforms, and the war on poverty, also fueled the rioting. The National Advisory Commission on Civil Disorders called attention to a crucial reality about black inner cities: "White institutions created it, white institutions maintain it, and white society condones it."

BLACK POWER

Urban riots were the most destructive display of black militancy. The slogan "black power" made its appearance in 1966 when James Meredith attempted to march from Memphis, Tennessee, to Jackson, Mississippi, to inspire African Americans of his native state to assert their rights. He got only ten miles into Mississippi when a sniper severely wounded him. Dr. King and other civil rights leaders quickly arrived to complete his march. Two of the marchers, young leaders of the Student Non-Violent Coordinating Committee (SNCC), began chanting "black power." Soon, most of the marchers were chanting the same slogan. Initially, "black power" was a cry of outrage and defiance. It later became political doctrine, although meaning different things to different people. For SNCC leader Stokely Carmichael, "black power" meant that African Americans should take control of the civil rights movement and develop their own institutions and instruments of power. Implicit in these actions were the rejection of integration, scorning white allies, and the approval of self-defensive violence. At the extremes, "black power" became an expression of African American separatism. Separatist doctrine traced its roots to a long tradition of black nationalism in this country.

The Black Muslims articulated the most important expression of 1960s black nationalism. Founded during the 1930s in Detroit by Elijah Poole, who called himself the Prophet, Elijah Muhammad, it remained a small, obscure religious sect with about 100,000 members until the 1960s. Black Muslims had recruited many of their followers from the bottom ranks of black society—street hustlers, drug addicts, and ex-cons. Their most famous recruit was world heavyweight boxing champion Cassius Clay, who changed his name to Muhammad Ali following his conversion to the Black Muslim sect in 1965.

The sect's most articulate spokesman was Malcolm Little, an ex-con who took the name of Malcolm X. During the early 1960s, he proffered a nationalistic alternative to civil rights. He jeered at Dr. King's tactics of nonviolent Christian love: He both angered and frightened whites with his tirades against integration with "white devils." In 1964, he was expelled from the Black Muslim organization after a dispute with Elijah Muhammad. He made a pilgrimage to Mecca in 1964 and this experience enabled him to escape from the anti-white racial nationalism espoused by the Black Muslims. He moved to New York and founded his own movement. His political ideas were still evolving in the spring of 1965. He appeared to be groping for an integrationist strategy when he was murdered. His assassination had been ordered by Elijah Muhammad, or by members of his inner circle. Malcolm X's book, written with Alex Haley, *The Autobiography of Malcolm X,* became a posthumous best-seller. Actor Ossie Davis said of the fallen leader: "Malcolm expressed what was in all our hearts; he redeemed our manhood." Malcolm X was one of the three leading figures in the struggle for African-American liberation in the twentieth century—along with Thurgood Marshall and Martin Luther King, Jr.

"Black power" also expressed African American pride; it became a celebration of African-American history and culture, of "blackness itself." African-American students in high schools and colleges demanded that courses be added to established curricula in African-American history, literature, and languages. Black hair and dress styles appeared. "Black power" encouraged young blacks to seek success and remain "black," to avoid emulating white role models. The popular soul singer James Brown sang, "Say it loud, I'm black and I'm proud."

During the late 1960s, as the civil rights movement became radicalized and fragmented. King, who remained committed to the tactic of nonviolence and to the goal of an integrated, color-blind society, remained the foremost black leader. But he found that his methods did not work in the North. He tried and failed to desegregate Chicago. Tactics that had been effective against the *de jure* segregation of southern towns could not overcome the *de facto* segregation of Northern cities. King also became increasingly involved in protesting the Vietnam War because it drained away funds for civil rights and Great Society reforms. His attacks on the war alienated President Johnson and cost him the support of the NAACP.

The civil rights movement, politically successful in the South but an economic failure in the North, was faltering by 1967. In the spring of 1968, trying to regain momentum, King prepared to lead a poor people's march on Washington. He also took time to go to Memphis to support a garbage workers' strike. Early evening on April 4, while standing on a Memphis motel balcony, King was shot and killed by James Earl Ray, a white ex-con and drifter. News of King's murder provoked 168 race riots in cities and towns across the land. The worst rioting occurred in the nation's capital. Buildings burned within a few blocks of the White House, and soldiers mounted machine guns on the Capitol steps.

Figure 8.4   Malcolm X emerged during the early 1960s as the most articulate spokesman for black nationalism.   *Source:* Bettmann Archive.

RED AND BROWN POWER

Other minorities, spurred by the example of African-American insurgents, rebelled during the 1960s. Hispanic militants made their presence felt. Latinos living within the United States were diverse. They shared a common heritage based on the Spanish language and culture, but their families had come from Mexico, Puerto Rico, Cuba, Nicaragua, El Salvador, and a dozen other nations. It was impossible to form a pan-Hispanic organization or to articulate goals that all Latinos shared. Puerto Rican students in New York demanded that courses in Puerto Rican studies be added to high school and college curricula. Mexican-American militants also waged campaigns for recognition and self-assertion. Brown power militants began calling themselves "Chicanos," turning a term of opprobrium into a badge of pride and an assertion of ethnic identity that did not depend on a relationship with the "Anglo" world.

The most prominent Chicano militant of the 1960s was labor leader Cesar Chavez. A migrant farm worker turned labor organizer, Chavez founded the National Farm Workers Association (NFWA) in 1963. The NFWA joined other farm worker unions to form the United Farm Workers Organizing Committee (UFWOC), affiliated with the AFL-CIO. Chavez organized lettuce workers and grape pickers, using techniques developed by civil rights organizers, including marches, rallies, songs, and symbols that stressed the Chicano cultural heritage. Chavez led successful strikes in California's San Joaquin Valley in the 1960s. His movement obtained crucial assistance from urban, liberal, middle-class support groups that raised funds for the strikers and staged consumer boycotts, making table grapes picked by "scab" (nonunion) labor forbidden fruit.

Native American militants demanded respect for their cultural traditions and called attention to their severe economic needs, particularly repayment for their ancestral lands that had been illegally taken from them by Europeans and their descendants. Red power militant Vine Deloria Jr. wrote *Custer Died for Your Sins,* emphasizing the historical injustices European settlers in the New World had committed against Native Americans. A group of attorneys, including Native American lawyers, formed the Native American Rights Fund to seek the return of tribal lands illegally taken from Indians and to obtain compensation for other properties confiscated by whites.

Figure 8.5   Cesar Chavez (checked shirt, right) leads striking grape pickers. Most of the pickers working the grape fields of California in the 1960s and 1970s were of Mexican descent.
Source: National Archives.

GAY-LESBIAN LIBERATION

Another expression of the 1960s' insurgent spirit was the open avowal of homosexuality by formerly closeted gays and lesbians. If people could mobilize for political action around the issues of race, ethnicity, and gender, so too could they fight for their sexual identities and preferences. A dramatic event ignited the gay liberation movement: on June 29, 1969, police raided the Stonewall Inn, a gay bar located in Greenwich Village. Instead of meekly submitting to arrest, patrons defiantly hurled bottles at the police. They sent a message: there was a new militancy and pride growing among members of the gay community; they were no longer willing to passively accept police harassment and society's condemnations.

Gay and lesbian intellectuals developed ideologies that defined homosexuality as a legitimate sexual preference; they insisted that it was not abnormal, it was not sick, and it was not perverse. Gay and lesbian theorists attacked the psychoanalytic establishment for diagnosing homosexuality as a form of mental illness. Within gay-lesbian communities, a debate occurred over whether homosexuality was innate or a consequence of socialization. Essentialists argued that individuals were born gay or lesbian; others argued that gay and lesbian identities were socially constructed. Although gays and lesbians could not resolve the debate over nature versus nurture, the gay liberation movement enabled millions of homosexuals to come out of the closet and to make their claim for acceptance into the larger society. Militant homosexuals marched in gay liberation parades chanting, "Say it loud, gay is proud." Gay and lesbian activists organized for political action, seeking an end to legislative and job discrimination against homosexuals and a diminution of massive homophobic prejudices and violent assaults.

THE REBIRTH OF FEMINISM

The social and cultural ground was being prepared during the 1950s for a rebirth of feminism. By 1960, it had become the norm for middle-class white married women to perform paid work outside of the home. By 1962, married women accounted for nearly two-thirds of the female workforce. At the same time that they were entering the paid workforce in ever-greater numbers, more and more women were going to college and earning degrees. In 1961, women received over 40 percent of all baccalaureate degrees awarded.

Despite such progress, women still entered a sex-segregated job market. They took mostly "women's jobs" such as nursing, clerical work, teaching, and domestic service, jobs that paid less than men's and offered few prospects for promotion. In 1960, the median compensation for women working in full-time, year-round employment was 61 percent of men's earnings. Traditional assumptions about the proper societal roles for men and women remained deeply ingrained. They were continuously reinforced by all of the mass circulation women's magazines, all of which were controlled by men. There was no organized feminist alternative to challenge male hegemony. The wife who worked was perceived to be helping her family achieve a middle-class lifestyle, not pursuing a career of her own. As the 1960s began, there existed an ideological lag; feminine consciousness lagged behind social reality. Even though cultural norms remained unquestioned, there was increasing evidence that many college-educated, middle-class women were unfulfilled by lives that increasingly diverged from prescribed roles.

Figure 8.6   Women protesters outside the Atlantic City, N.J., Convention Hall, where Miss America will be crowned that evening.   *Source:* AP/Wide World Photos.

Because women, as women, did not share a common social experience, they tended to view their problems as being individual rather than socially derived. It was left to the founder of the modern women's movement, Betty Friedan, author of the best-selling *Feminine Mystique* (1963), to show middle class suburban housewives that what they had previously understood to be their individual problems were in fact women's problems. They were caused not by personal inadequacies but by deeply rooted attitudes that would have to be changed before women could achieve equality and fulfillment. Friedan, giving eloquent voice to the discontent of middle-class women, called the suburban, split-level home "a comfortable concentration camp." She called attention to the "problem which has no name": feelings of emptiness, of being incomplete, of wondering, "Who am I?" She asked: What is the cause of the identity problems which bothers so many women who have ostensibly fulfilled the American dream?" She urged women to listen to that still-small voice within that demands "something more than my husband and my children and my home."[2]

Friedan's timely book defined and created the modern women's movement, but in so doing her focus on passive and frustrated suburban housewives obscured other women's realities during the 1950s. Millions of working and middle class women, of various ethnoracial backgrounds, worked outside the home, often struggling to improve working conditions.

[2]Betty Friedan, *The Feminine Mystique* (New York: Dell, 1963), passim.

Women were active in civic reform movements, trade unions, peace movements, and the civil rights struggle.

It was the civil rights struggle of the early 1960s that catalyzed a sense of grievance among women. Women often joined civil rights demonstrations. The civil rights movement also provided a model for political activity. Women made connections between black demands for freedom, equality, and dignity and their own lives; they saw possibilities for acting for themselves, of mobilizing for group political action. Women perceived that the same society that oppressed blacks also oppressed women; both groups had been assigned separate and unequal spheres and told to stay in their respective places. Any efforts at self-assertion or challenges to the status quo were considered deviant. Women reasoned that if it was wrong to deny an opportunity to one group because of skin color, it was wrong to deny it to another group because of gender.

Great Society also helped the cause of women's rights. When the bill that eventually became the Civil Rights Act of 1964 was being drafted in committee, Congressperson Martha Wright Griffiths, a powerful representative from Michigan serving on the House Ways and Means Committee, led the drive to bar discrimination on the basis of sex as well as race, religion, or national origin.

Initially, the Equal Opportunity Employment Commission (EEOC), which had responsibility for enforcing Title VII of the Civil Rights Act of 1964, did not enforce the provision against sex discrimination. In response to the EEOC's failure to enforce Title VII on behalf of women workers, Betty Friedan and other women activists formed the National Organization for Women (NOW) in 1966 to pressure the commission to take sex discrimination in hiring seriously. Other groups soon mobilized, and the women rights movement was reborn. These women's organizations were political pressure groups that sought to mobilize public opinion and obtain litigation on behalf of their cause. They sought change from within the existing structure. In part, the new feminism was a species of liberal reform. It called for equal pay for equal work and demanded that women have equal access to all professional schools and occupations. To allow women to compete equally in the job market with men, feminists demanded publicly funded child care centers for women with pre-school-aged children, and they sought legislation ending all forms of gender discrimination.

There also was a radical dimension to the emerging feminism of the 1960s that grew out of the experiences of young women in SDS and SNCC. These radical young women coined the term "sexism." Mary King and Casey Hayden, both civil rights activists within SNCC, had come to resent the arrogance of male activists who expected women to work hard, take risks, and leave policy making to the men. When women raised these issues at a SNCC convention, the male leaders responded by laughing at them. The SNCC chairman, Stokely Carmichael, quipped, "The position of women in our movement is prone."

These radical women gradually evolved a language to express their grievances. They defined the problem as "sexism," or "male chauvinism." Having diagnosed the illness, they proposed a cure—"women's liberation." While liberal feminist reformers in NOW fought for equal pay for equal work, radical feminists like King and Hayden demanded control over their own bodies. They called for wider distribution of birth control literature, tougher enforcement of rape laws, the sharing of housework and child-rearing duties with husbands, and the right to abortion on demand. They met in small groups for intense "consciousness-raising" sessions. These sessions also allowed women to understand that their personal problems were connected to the larger realms of social power, of "sexual politics." Feminist writer Robin Morgan contributed the defining slogan of the women's liberation movement: "The personal is political."

The reborn feminist movement encountered a formidable array of obstacles from the beginning. Many women as well as men rejected feminist demands. A 1970 Gallup poll showed that 70 percent of American women believed that they were treated fairly by men. Feminist leader Gloria Steinem acknowledged that she spoke for only a minority of women, but attributed that reality to cultural conditioning. She asserted that women had been brainwashed to accept their oppression; they required "consciousness-raising" sessions to ignite a sense of grievance. Many men worried about the loss of male prerogatives that had long been "givens" in the culture. Fundamentalist Christians were incensed because feminist demands violated Biblically ordained roles for women.

The most serious obstacle faced by feminists trying to build a movement based on women's common problems and concerns was the diversity of the women the movement was trying to organize. Women were differentiated on the basis of race, ethnicity, class, age, education, occupation, and sexuality. Feminists quickly discovered that they had sharp differences among themselves on many matters. There were disagreements over priorities, long- and short-term goals, and methods and tactics. Was the most pressing problem economic—an economic system that oppressed women? Or was it cultural—male chauvinism? Because of the diversity prevailing among women activists, the reborn feminist movement of the 1960s spawned a proliferation of organizations, tactics, ideologies, and goals.

BACKLASH

By 1967, it seemed as though some unspoken signal had been sent coursing through the society; the message had been received by SDS radicals, by black, brown, and red militants, and by activist women. Those who perceived themselves as oppressed, disadvantaged, and denied their full measure of freedom, equality, opportunity, and dignity, rose in rebellion. Perhaps they sensed their time had come: that the system would be more responsive to their claims of justice and inclusion in the American dream; that it would not, perhaps could not, repress them or deny them their due. These militants were no longer willing to play the game by the old rules. Never in the history of the republic had so many groups mounted such a radical assault on traditional values, mores, and institutions.

The radical insurgencies of the late 1960s provoked a furious response from the middle-class majority of Americans determined to uphold traditional American ways. The media dubbed their response the "backlash." Millions of citizens had worked hard all of their lives and played the game by the established rules. They had raised their families, attended church, worked on community projects, voted, paid taxes, obeyed the law, accumulated a modest estate, and sent their sons to fight the Vietnam War. The militant minority of blacks who rioted in the cities, students who opposed the Vietnam War and carried VietCong flags, and long-haired hippies who openly flaunted their sexuality infuriated the middle-class majority. The news media, particularly television, which pumped images of rioting blacks and protesting students into millions of living rooms on the nightly news, intensified the backlash.

White, working-class ethnics felt especially threatened by African-American militants and were galvanized into action. They had worked hard all their lives to achieve a modest piece of the American dream. To them it appeared that inner city blacks were demanding that the government give them these same things; that they were entitled to them now—without working and without a struggle. White, working-class ethnics especially resented the antipoverty programs that appeared to reward black militants while law abiding whites got nothing except higher tax bills. Middle Americans, those earning between $8,000 and $15,000 a year, who constituted the rank-and-file blue-collar and white-collar workforces of the country, generally resented the challenges posed by the insurgents.

A mix of forces drove the backlashers. In part it was simply residual antiblack racism. Many Northern white ethnics and Southern white working class people had been taught to hate and fear black people and consider them inferior. They did not want to associate with them, they did not want their children attending school with them, and they surely did not want to have to compete with them in the workplace.

Economic insecurities also drove the backlash. By the late 1960s, many Middle Americans were feeling the effects of inflation, heavy indebtedness, and declining real income. Black demands for employment, rising taxes, and expensive governmental programs appeared to be direct threats to the economic well-being of increasingly hard-pressed middle-class Americans.

Most of all, it was a sense of cultural crisis that activated the backlash response. The demands of the militants, magnified by extensive media coverage and commentary, represented an attack on the traditional American way of life and its most cherished values and institutions: patriotism, the work ethic, family, and religion. While the sons of Middle America were fighting and dying in Vietnam, the sons of upper-middle-class families were opposing the war from the safe havens of prestigious university campuses. To many parents of soldiers, and to the soldiers themselves, these antiwar protesters appeared to be a privileged corps of impudent cowards and traitors.

The rise of the backlash was another important indicator of the conservative drift that was underway in American political culture. By the late 1960s, many working-class white families had come to distrust what they had held in high regard since the 1930s, centralized government power. During the 1930s, New Dealers had used the power of the federal government to establish a lifeline for millions of Americans who were left impoverished and bewildered by the Great Depression. By the 1960s, prosperity had created a new middle class that included millions of working-class families that opposed higher taxes and many of the social programs they funded. These middle Americans also embraced traditional values and were unhappy when liberal Democratic leaders did not denounce immorality and social disorder. It also appeared to them that liberals were much too attentive to the needs of the dispossessed—the poor, minorities, and radicals—and were neglecting the needs of hard-working, patriotic, and God-fearing folks like themselves. The backlash was the most visible issue fueling the growing antigovernment mood, but it was only part of a larger revolt, a much deeper disillusionment with liberal government and the pundits who championed it.

THE ELECTION OF 1968

The radical insurgencies loose in the land, coupled with the intense backlash that they provoked, guaranteed that the 1968 election would occur against a backdrop of the worst conflict and violence within American society since the Civil War. The Democratic Party, closer to the social pulse than the Republican Party, was splintered by divisions seething within the deeply troubled nation. The antiwar candidacies of Senators Eugene McCarthy and Robert Kennedy gained momentum in the spring primaries. Party regulars backed Vice President Hubert Humphrey, a Cold War liberal supporting Johnson's Vietnam policy. It was a wide open race, with public opinion polls giving Kennedy an edge over Humphrey and McCarthy.

Although Robert Kennedy focused his presidential bid on opposing Johnson's Vietnam War policy, he appears to have also been searching for a new political vision for his troubled nation. Sensing that the liberal consensus of social reform at home and containing Communism abroad had collapsed, Kennedy groped for an alternative. He visited Native Americans on reservations, and he broke bread with Cesar Chavez in California. Robert Kennedy was the only established white politician with any credibility among black people following the assassination of Martin Luther King Jr. Kennedy also reached out to white, working-class backlashers. He stressed the importance of self-government, of citizen participation in the civic life of the nation. He sought a new community, more inclusive and more involved in the process of self-government. For the most part, he sought to revitalize and reshape liberalism, but he also picked up the growing conservatism of Middle Americans and sounded some of its themes. He criticized welfare programs because they created a class of dependents who existed on government handouts. He proposed job programs and community development programs involving local people and the private sector. His was a brave, lonely, and ultimately doomed voice, trying desperately to refashion a vision of the American nation that included everyone and thereby heal the divisions that had set class against class, race against race, and fathers against sons during those terrible years.

In the California primary, Kennedy and McCarthy waged a decisive showdown battle. Kennedy, cashing in on his remarkable ability to attract black, Hispanic, and white working-class voters, narrowly defeated McCarthy. With his California victory, Kennedy appeared to have the Democratic nomination within his grasp. But on victory night, he was fatally wounded in Los Angeles. His assassin was Sirhan Sirhan, an Arab Nationalist who hated Kennedy for his strong support of Israel. Once again, a senseless act of violence had destroyed another popular leader. Kennedy's murder appeared to remove what little civility and restraint remained in the American political culture. Once more the nation paused, hurt and saddened, to pay their final respects to a political leader struck down while trying to redeem his nation.

Robert Kennedy's murder removed any chance that antiwar forces could win at the Democratic Party's Chicago convention. The convention was a bitter affair. Humphrey won an easy first-ballot nomination. Convention delegates, after a lengthy, angry debate, adopted a pro-administration plank on the Vietnam War. The rest of the platform focused on domestic issues and reflected traditional liberal stands: consumer protection, increasing farmers' incomes, and supporting trade unions. Humphrey chose Senator Edmund Muskie of Maine, a respected party leader, as his running mate.

As the Democratic delegates gathered in Chicago to nominate a presidential candidate, some 10,000 to 12,000 antiwar radicals gathered in the Windy City to protest the war. Most came to support the efforts of antiwar Democratic politicians. More militant groups came to disrupt the convention and to provoke confrontations with the police. The demonstrators came up against Mayor Richard Daley, the convention host, who had vowed that there would be no disruptions. Ironically, Daley was a supporter of the late Robert Kennedy and a strong opponent of the Vietnam War. His forces cordoned off the convention site, and Daley deployed his police in

Figure 8.7   War in the streets of Chicago. Police battle demonstrators outside of the Democratic Convention on the night that Hubert Humphrey was nominated.   *Source:* Bettmann Archive.

the parks of Chicago, where protesters had gathered. He also had thousands of National Guardsmen and federal troops available if he felt they were needed. The total number of police, guardsmen, and federal troops outnumbered the protesters.

The night that Hubert Humphrey was nominated, violence reigned in the streets of Chicago. Protesters, attempting to march on the convention, were blocked by police. They taunted them, shouted obscenities at them, and threw rocks and bottles at them. As some of the demonstrators attempted to break through police cordons, the police attacked in force. In a frenzy of violence, some of the police, chanting "Kill! Kill!" indiscriminately clubbed and gassed demonstrators, newsmen, and bystanders. Television cameramen brought the violence into millions of living rooms. Many liberal Democrats were everlastingly horrified by the actions of the Chicago police. But millions of other Democrats in white-collar suburbs and blue-collar neighborhoods cheered the police, seeing in the radical politics and countercultural lifestyles of the youthful protesters an intolerable threat to order and traditional values. The different reactions to the televised violence reflected the profound divisions seething within the American political culture created by Vietnam, race riots, and domestic insurgencies. Hubert Humphrey emerged from the political ruins as the candidate of a profoundly divided party.

The divisive Democratic Convention and the violence in the streets of Chicago played into the hands of the Republicans, who had previously held an orderly convention in Miami. They had nominated Richard Nixon, who had made a remarkable comeback. Nixon had retired from politics following a disastrous defeat in the 1962 California gubernatorial election, but he had worked hard for Republican candidates in 1964 and 1966, building support among party regulars. He had won a series of primary victories and gathered hundreds of delegates from nonprimary states. He came to Miami the front-runner and easily repelled his only remaining serious challenger, California Governor Ronald Reagan, who was making the first of his several runs at the presidency. Nixon chose Spiro T. Agnew, the governor of Maryland, who had a reputation for talking tough on law and order issues, to be his running mate. The Republican platform called for an all-out war on crime, reform of the welfare laws, an end to inflation, and a buildup of defense forces. On the crucial Vietnam War issue, the Republicans promised to end the American war through purposeful negotiations but not to accept "camouflaged surrender." The Republicans sought peace in Vietnam but not peace at any price.

Behind the Republican platform rhetoric and the choice of Agnew for vice president lay a shrewd political strategy. Nixon perceived that Southerners had become a power within his party. He also understood that Americans had become more conservative since 1964, when Johnson had scored his landslide victory over the hapless Goldwater. Nixon cut his ties with declining Northeastern liberal Republicans to forge an alliance with conservative Southerners led by Strom Thurmond. Nixon promised Thurmond that he would never abandon the South Vietnamese government and that he would slow the pace of school desegregation. He also promised to crack down hard on demonstrators who broke the law. Nixon's "Southern strategy" stopped Ronald Reagan's bid for the presidency, which had counted on winning the votes of Southern delegates. The only reason the Southern strategy did not give Nixon the entire South was because a popular third-party candidate who had a Southern base entered the campaign.

George Wallace, governor of Alabama and leader of the American Independence Party (AIP), mounted a presidential campaign with popular appeal in all sections of the nation. Wallace, formerly a Southern populist Democrat, had become increasingly unhappy with the Democratic national policies. He left the party, formed the AIP, and chose General Curtis Lemay, formerly the chief of the Strategic Air Command, as his vice-presidential running mate.

A small, combative man with a quick wit and a folksy speaking style, Wallace articulated the frustrations and resentments of his followers, who were upset by radical disruptions in the land and by the liberal politicians and intellectuals who appeared to sanction them. Wallacites could be found in the greatest numbers within the ranks of Northern blue-collar workers and Southern lower-middle-class whites. Many of these people had also lost faith in the leadership offered by the two major political parties. Wallace told his followers that there was not "a dime's worth of difference" between the Democrats and Republicans.

His main issue was playing to white antipathy toward civil rights and antipoverty programs. He was the first prominent political leader to sense the changes in social attitudes that the pundits had labeled the backlash. Wallace possessed a remarkable talent for voicing the fears and resentments of working-class whites, especially young men. He chiefly attacked liberal intellectuals, black militants, antiwar protesters, and hippies. Although his message was never a purely racist one, most of his appeal derived from white anxieties about integration and black progress. Opposition to race-related federal initiatives was always at the heart of Wallace's message to his supporters. But he learned to soften his language; he replaced the crass, racist venom spewed by extremists with a set of coded phrases such as "law and order" and "welfare chiselers" that ignited raw racial anger without making his supporters appear or feel racist.

Wallace also championed free enterprise capitalism and traditional moral values. He also took a more hawkish stance on the Vietnam War than either Humphrey or Nixon. Polls showed that Wallace was a political force to be reckoned with. At the beinning of the presidential campaign, polls gave him 21 percent of the vote, almost as many as supported Humphrey. Had he held that 21 percent to November, he would have denied any candidate an electoral college majority and thrown the election into the House of Representatives. That was his strategy and goal—to play the role of "spoiler" and to force Nixon and Humphrey to bargain for his support to win the presidency.

Meanwhile, Nixon mounted the most expensive, sophisticated presidential campaign in American political history. His acceptance speech had sounded his principal theme, a promise to heed the voice of "the great, quiet forgotten majority—the nonshouters and the nondemonstrators." He called for unity and a lowering of voices. He pledged "peace with honor" in Vietnam. His appeal reached millions of voters yearning for an end to years of discord. It was a smooth, professional campaign. Nixon campaigned at a deliberate, dignified pace. He projected an image of maturity and inner tranquility; commentators spoke of a "new Nixon" who had replaced the fiery Red-baiter of the 1950s. His campaign featured slick television commercials and short speeches filled will patriotic generalities. Admen packaged and sold his candidacy to the electorate.

While Nixon played the role of unifier and harmonizer, his vice-presidential running mate Spiro Agnew took the offensive. His task was to battle Wallace for the backlash vote. Agnew attacked the media for promoting radicalism, and he took a hard law-and-order line. Journalists dubbed Agnew "Nixon's Nixon." Polls taken in early October showed Nixon well ahead of both Humphrey and Wallace.

Humphrey's campaign floundered along, disorganized, short of both money and campaign workers. McCarthy's followers initially refused to support Humphrey. He was hurt badly by his identification with an unpopular administration and its unpopular war. Reflecting the growing conservatism of the electorate, millions of nominally Democratic voters were turning to Nixon and Wallace.

But in October, Humphrey's campaign suddenly came to life. He distanced himself from Johnson's war policy by calling for a bombing halt. Union leaders campaigned hard for Humphrey, and many antiwar activists drifted back into his fold, preferring a flawed liberal to either the hated Nixon or the populist demagogue Wallace. McCarthy finally endorsed Humphrey on October 29. Johnson helped his chances by halting all bombing of North Vietnam and talking as though the war were about to end. Humphrey sliced into Nixon's lead. Wallace's support eroded. On election eve, pollsters said that the election was too close to call.

But Humphrey's late surge fell just short. Nixon held on for a narrow victory. He received 31.7 million votes to Humphrey's 31.2 million and Wallace's 9.9 million. Nixon received 43.4 percent of the popular vote to Humphrey's 42.7 percent and Wallace's 13.4 percent. Nixon carried thirty-two states with 301 electoral votes. Humphrey carried thirteen states with 191 electoral votes, and Wallace carried five Southern states with 46 electoral votes. The Democrats retained control of Congress with sizable majorities in both Houses.

On the surface, the electorate appeared to speak in many voices, reflecting the acute political divisions within the country. Many young, idealistic citizens and older liberals could not bring themselves to vote. The old Democratic coalition had fractured, split by civil rights issues and divisions over the Vietnam war. The huge majority of sixteen million votes that Johnson had rolled up only four years ago had evaporated. Humphrey retained urban and union voters, although in reduced strength, and he got most of the African-American vote. But his appeal was confined largely to the Northeastern industrial states. The rest of the country voted for Nixon, except for five Deep South states that went for Wallace. The 1968 election revealed that the Democratic Solid South had vanished. Humphrey received only 31 percent of the Deep South vote, mostly from newly enfranchised African Americans. About 90 percent of Southern whites voted either for Nixon or Wallace. Racial attitudes were significant vote determiners in 1968, the year of the backlash. Election results also signaled that the American electorate was moving toward the Right.

Although they cannot be certain in such a close election, most analysts believe that the Vietnam War probably gave Nixon his narrow win. In the final weeks of the campaign, Nixon attracted support with his talk of a plan to end the war, the details of which he refused to divulge because he said its prospects for success depended on its remaining secret until after the election. Analysts have suggested that Humphrey could have won had he disavowed Johnson's war policy sooner. Nixon's centrist-rightist appeal had worked. He won, liberalism was weakened, and radicalism was contained. The large "silent majority" of American voters, as political analyst Richard Scammon observed, constituted "the unyoung, the unblack, and the unpoor," and they had mostly voted for Nixon. During an election year that had featured the worst violence and turmoil since the Civil War, Middle Americans had opted for the center. American political institutions had faced their most severe test in over 100 years and had survived.

SUMMING UP THE SIXTIES

Forces that had been building for years in this country climaxed in 1968 in full-blown political and cultural crises. The Cold War consensus was fractured beyond repair. The forces of reform liberalism achieved their greatest victories with Johnson's smashing electoral victory in 1964 and the subsequent enactment of Great Society. Ironically, at its moment of triumph, Great Society unraveled. The liberal reform coalition fragmented over the controversial Vietnam War and black power militancy. Congress, faced with the mounting costs of the war, rising crime and disorder at home, and growing opposition to liberal reforms, was loath to expand the boundaries of the welfare state. Great Society expired in 1967.

By 1967, many civil rights leaders, militant students, and radical women, despairing of ever achieving the kinds of fundamental reforms that they sought within existing political structures, chose to challenge the established order and to build radical movements outside of the mainstream. These various political insurgencies provoked a counterresponse led by Northern working-class ethnics and lower-middle-class white Southerners. Beneath the surface of polarized politics, a profound cultural crisis gripped the nation in 1967 and 1968. A relatively small number of articulate radicals challenged not only established political processes, but they also attacked traditional American institutions, mores, and values. The far more numerous backlashers vociferously and sometimes violently defended those same political processes and traditional values. The majority of Americans got caught in the middle of this political and cultural warfare waged by extremists during the election of 1968.

Both the political and cultural crises peaked during the election of 1968. With the murders of Martin Luther King Jr. and Robert Kennedy, left-wing radicals were denied access to established political processes; they could only sit on the sidelines in despair or try futilely to disrupt proceedings at the Democratic Convention in Chicago. The backlashers found a tribune to champion their cause in Alabama's Governor George Wallace. The two major party candidates were men of the center. The Democrats chose Hubert Humphrey, a traditional Cold War liberal, and the Republicans nominated the reborn Richard Nixon, who returned Phoenix-like from the political ashes. In one of the closest elections in American political history, characterized by a low voter turnout, Nixon bested Humphrey, with backlasher George Wallace finishing a distant third. The radical Left was not a political factor. The election revealed above all else the strength of American political institutions and the centrist instincts of the voting majority of the American people in a time of political and cultural crisis. The centrifugal forces were contained, radicalism was defeated, and liberal reformism was weakened.

The legacies of the 1960s are various, and different people draw different lessons from those turbulent times. How one remembers the 1960s turns on questions of age, gender, race, ethnicity, class, education, and above all, political ideology. A sizable number of today's scholars in the social sciences and humanities were participants in one or more of the radical insurgencies of the late 1960s, most likely the antiwar movement. For these nostalgic academics, they remember the 1960s as a time when it appeared possible that a community of progressive forces could be forged that could bring about fundamental reforms through the established political system, reforms that would bring forth peace, prosperity, and genuine social equality for all. But these utopian dreams were smashed by violence, assassinations, backlash, and most of all by the determination of the middle-aged, middle-class voting majority to turn to centrist candidates in a time of crisis.

Most radical insurgencies did not survive the 1960s. The most important one that endured has been the women's movement. The New Left fragmented in 1969, and a small faction functioned as a terrorist underground for a few more years. The counterculture simply evaporated, much of it coopted by the mainstream culture. The civil rights movement also fragmented. Some of its most militant leaders fled into exile or were killed. Some leaders such as Jesse Jackson moved into the political mainstream and became powers within the Democratic Party. Environmentalism, a cause that would become much more important in the 1970s and 1980s, derived in part from the 1960s' upheavals. Former hippies often became environmentalist advocates, as did some former antiwar activists.

The year 1968 can also be read as a turning point in American politics. It marked the end of a period dominated by the forces of liberal reformism and the start of a conservative resurgence. The rise of black militants, radical students, and hippies and the spread of crime provoked a popular backlash against what was perceived as permissive and ineffectual liberalism, a liberalism that coddled rebels and criminals, and neglected the interests of the middle-class majority. The stalemated war in Vietnam that was inflating the economy and undermining U.S. power in the world also discredited liberalism, as did what many perceived to be the excessive costs and expansion of governmental power associated with Great Society reforms. The spreading perception that liberalism was a prescription for dysfunctional policies at home and abroad fueled a rising conservatism. Conservative forces would steadily gather strength during the 1970s and would come to power in 1980 with the election of Ronald Reagan. The upheavals of the late 1960s left liberalism discredited and in decline. These disruptions also destroyed left-wing radicalism as a viable alternative, if it ever had been one for more than a handful of visionaries. The destruction of the Left and the decline of liberalism opened the political door to the growing legions of conservatives who had first surfaced in the 1964 election as fervent support-ers of Barry Goldwater and who then turned to either Nixon or Wallace in 1968.

BRIEF BIBLIOGRAPHIC ESSAY

Scholars have found the protest movements of the 1960s and their impact on American society and culture fascinating subjects to study. David Farber's *The Age of Great Dreams: America in the 1960s* is a good survey. Clayborn Carson's *In Struggle: SNCC and the Black Awakening of the 1960s,* shows how black power militancy grew out of the experiences of civil rights activists working in the South during the early 1960s. See also William H. Chafe's *Civilities and Civil Rights: Greensboro, North Carolina, and the Black Struggle for Freedom.* The best biography we have of Dr. Martin Luther King Jr. is Stephen Oates's *Let the Trumpet Sound: The Life of Martin Luther King Jr.* A reading of *The Autobiography of Malcolm X* (co-written with Alex Haley) will provide an understanding of the sources of black nationalism during the 1960s. Peter Goldman's *The Death and Life of Malcolm X* is a sympathetic biography. For student radi-calism during the 1960s, see Irwin Unger's *The Movement: A History of the American New Left, 1959–1972.* Todd Gitlin's *The Sixties: Years of Hope: Days of Rage* is a thoughtful meditation on the 1960s by a former leader of the SDS. Another fine account of the student radicalism of the 1960s is James Miller's *Democracy Is in the Streets: From Port Huron to the Siege of Chicago.* A recent collection of essays edited by Peter Braunstein and Michael William Doyle, *Imagine Nation: The American Counterculture of the 1960s and 70s,* shows that the countercul-ture was never a social movement. It was an unstable amalgam of attitudes, tendencies, pos-tures, gestures, "lifestyles," hedonisms, and moralisms. Julian Messner's *The Superstars of Rock: Their Lives and Their Music* contains insight into the pop music of the 1960s. Tom Wolfe's *The Electric Kool-Aid Acid Test* has captured Ken Kesey's adventures and the whole "acid rock" scene in psychedelic prose. Barbara Deckard, in *The Women's Movement,* offers a fine account of the revived feminist movement. See also the relevant chapters of William H. Chafe's *The American Woman: Her Changing Social, Economic, and Political Role, 1920–1970.* Recent work on Betty Friedan such as Judith Hennessee's *Betty Friedan: Her Life* raises important issues. Friedan apparently disguised her radical activist past, engaged in faulty social criticism, and gave misleading personal testimony while writing her famous manifesto. Alfredo Mirande's *The Chicano Experience* documents militancy in the Mexican-American world. Vine Deloria Jr.'s *Custer Died for Your Sins* records centuries of white mistreatment of Native Americans. Richard Krickus, *in Pursuing the American Dream: White Ethnics and the New Populism,* features a fascinating study of blue-collar culture and its resentment of liberal welfarism, student radicals, hippies, and black militants. Evan Thomas, *Robert Kennedy: His Life,* is the best recent biography of this important political leader. Lewis Gould's *1968: The Election that Changed America* is a fine recent analysis of that significant election.

WEB SITES

For the SDS and other New Left radical organizations during the 1960s and early 1970s, see
<http://www.wikipedia.org/wike/Students_for_a_Democratic_Society>.
It's a home page with links to many related New Left issues, personalities, and actions. For the

counterculture of the 1960s and after see Hippy.com for a psychedelic trip through hippyland past and present. For the militant phase of the civil rights movement see the official web site for Malcolm X at `<http://www.cmgww.com/historic/malcolm/>`, and for the Black Panthers see `<http://www.blackpanthers.org>`. For the women's liberation movement, there is an online archival collection at Duke University, which can be accessed via `<http://scriptorium.lib.duke.edu/>`. For the struggles of Chicano militants such as Cesar Chavez, the charismatic labor organizer, see `<http://www.pbs.org/itvs/fightfields/-13k>`. It is a great site with many links, films, videos, and much more.

9

Calming Down

Throughout 1968, millions of Americans watching the nightly news felt threatened by the electronic images of war, rebellion, and violent social conflict that were beamed into their living rooms from around the world and from their own divided society. Richard M. Nixon was elected president by a narrow margin amidst the worst domestic violence and disorder in nearly 100 years. He made his top priorities restoring national unity and phasing out the U.S. war in Vietnam. He partially succeeded in calming the country, although the U.S. war continued for four more years.

Reelected by a landslide margin in November 1972, President Nixon was never able to exercise the full powers of the presidency or to achieve all of his political goals because of the enveloping Watergate scandals. Ultimately the president and his men were overwhelmed by media investigations, federal grand jury probes, special prosecutors, congressional investigations, the courts, and public opinion. Richard Nixon resigned from the presidency in disgrace on August 9, 1974, mainly to avoid impeachment, trial, and probable conviction for "high crimes and misdemeanors" that he had committed while president.

PRAGMATIC CENTRISM

Nixon came to office determined to restore the consensus politics that had prevailed in this country during the 1950s and early 1960s before being shattered by the Vietnam War, the civil rights struggle, and other domestic insurgencies. To achieve his goal, he moved in different policy directions simultaneously. His general thrust was toward the center, but he also struck out in conservative directions in pursuit of his Southern strategy, and he proposed far-reaching reforms to co-opt liberal causes. But he failed to restore the lost consensus during his first term because he could not end the U.S. war in Vietnam. His pursuit of his Southern strategy perpetuated the

Figure 9.1   In contrast to his often stormy and controversial public career, Richard Nixon enjoyed a warm family life. Here he shares a joyous moment with (from left to right) son-in-law David Eisenhower, wife Pat, and daughters Julia and Tricia.
Source: Bettmann Archive.

divisions he hoped to end. Various activists and reformers continued to press their causes, despite his efforts to co-opt or suppress them.

Like Kennedy, Nixon always considered domestic affairs secondary to foreign policy concerns. His own lack of enthusiasm, the fact that 57 percent of the voters in 1968 preferred another candidate to him for president, and Democratic control of Congress, all diminished his influence over domestic affairs. Liberal Democrats in control of Congress extended the Voting Rights Act of 1965, increased spending for food stamps, increased Social Security benefits, and increased federal aid to education. Congress also proposed the Twenty-Sixth Amendment, which was ratified in 1971, enfranchising eighteen-year-olds. The new amendment added twelve million potential voters to the rolls. Nixon was not enthusiastic about any of these measures, but he did not oppose them.

Nixon proposed policies reflecting the growing conservatism of voters who were opposed to solving social problems by expanding the powers of the federal government and spending more money on them. A major target was the welfare system. He proposed a work-incentive program to replace the costly Aid to Families with Dependent Children Program. Called the Family Assistance Plan, it guaranteed a family of four with no other income $1,600 per year plus food stamps and Medicaid. It further required that all heads of households on welfare, except for single mothers with pre-school-aged children, register for job training. Congress passed only the "Workfare" feature, requiring heads of households to register for job training. Nixon's other innovative proposal, revenue sharing, was part of what he called the "New Federalism," designed to reduce the power of the federal government and to strengthen state and local agencies. Congress enacted a revenue-sharing program to begin in 1972, when $30 billion in federal funds would be split over five years, two-thirds to local governments and one-third to the states.

Nixon had to spend much of the time that he devoted to domestic affairs trying to manage an increasingly erratic American economy. The economic difficulties stemmed mainly from the Vietnam War and former President Johnson's fiscal irresponsibility. Johnson had drastically increased spending for the war in the midst of a booming economy, without raising taxes. Prices rose 5 percent in 1968, the highest inflation rate since the Korean War. Nixon initially applied the monetarist theories of economist Milton Friedman, who claimed that prices could be lowered by reducing the money supply. The results were disastrous. The stock market suffered its worst crash since 1929. Unemployment doubled and prices continued to rise. Monetarism generated both inflation and recession, creating "stagflation."

Appalled by its results, Nixon abandoned monetarism for a new economic approach, "jawboning," which amounted to pressuring both business and trade unions to keep down prices and wages. Jawboning produced only continuing stagflation. Nixon then decided that economic decline was a greater evil than inflation. Reverting to Keynesian practices, he deliberately unbalanced the budget to stimulate demand and increase employment. Stagflation stubbornly persisted as unemployment and inflation both remained high. The U.S. economy also ran its first trade deficit since 1893.

Still searching for an effective policy, Nixon once again revamped his economic policies. On August 15, 1971, he froze wages, prices, and rents for ninety days, asked Congress for tax cuts to promote business expansion, devalued the dollar, and clamped a 10 percent tax on imports. At the end of ninety days, he replaced the freeze with more flexible guidelines, allowing annual price increases of 2.5 percent and wage increases of up to 5.5 percent. These drastic measures worked for a time. The trade deficit vanished and inflation was halved. The economy snapped out of recession and the GDP rose sharply. But within a few months, pressures from business and labor undermined the controls, and the inflation rate soared.

THE SOUTHERN STRATEGY

Despite his appeals for unity and peace, Nixon only partially succeeded in reuniting the American people. Discords inherited from the Johnson years continued and, at times, intensified. A rash of terrorist bombings damaged government and corporate buildings in various cities. Nixon's most divisive actions occurred when he implemented his Southern strategy. It aimed to outflank Wallace and secure the Middle American vote consisting of Southern whites, Northern ethnics, and suburbanites. He also sought to attract voters from the Sunbelt, the most dynamic region of the country. The Southern strategy involved stressing "law and order," phasing out most antipoverty programs, and slowing the rate of school desegregation in the South.

Nixon's efforts to slow the pace of school desegregation involved his administration in a controversy over busing to achieve school integration. The Justice Department filed suits prohibiting transporting children to desegregate public schools. The busing issue had risen in 1971 when the Supreme Court had ordered the Charlotte-Mecklenburg school system in North Carolina to use busing to achieve school integration after its efforts at voluntary desegregation had failed. Soon many other Southern school districts were under court orders to bus children to achieve school integration. It worked, and within a few years Southern public schools were largely desegregated. In one important case, the Supreme Court's ruling bolstered the Nixon administration's efforts to slow the pace of school integration. In *Milliken v. Bradley* (1974), the Burger Court rendered suburbs safe from busing. Excluding the suburbs from school integration busing programs accelerated white flight from central cities to suburbs now perceived as safe from integration.

Court-ordered busing spread to the North, where resistance was fierce and occasionally violent. The worst incidents occurred in Boston in 1974, when a federal judge ordered busing to integrate its public school system. Over half of the public schools in Boston had student bodies that were 90 percent black. White pupils boycotted South Boston High School rather than accept integration. Buses hauling in African American students were stoned, and several youngsters were injured. Racial conflict in South Boston and other Northern cities led to a flight of white students from public schools.

Administration efforts to thwart busing in order to slow the pace of school integration infuriated civil rights leaders. But the Supreme Court upheld busing, which infuriated Nixon. Despite Nixon's efforts, many Northern and Southern cities used busing to achieve desegregation. Far more schools achieved integrated student bodies during Nixon's presidency than during the

Figure 9.2   The inmates at Attica State prison raise their hands in clenched fists in a show of unity. They are observing the third anniversary of the Attica uprising, which took the lives of 40 persons during September 1971. *Source:* AP/Wide World Photos.

administrations of Johnson and Kennedy. African Americans made rapid progress in other areas as well. The size of the African-American middle class increased rapidly. Black college enrollment nearly doubled between 1968 and 1972. Thirteen African-American congressmen and eighty-one black mayors held office in 1971. The Nixon administration also promoted black capitalism and pushed to increase the number of black-owned businesses.

Nixon's Southern strategy also influenced his choices to fill Supreme Court vacancies, four of which opened up during his first term. He tried to appoint a Deep South conservative, but the Senate rejected both of his choices. His four appointees, including the new Chief Justice Warren Burger, who replaced the retired Earl Warren in 1969, were all strict constructionist conservatives. But the more conservative "Nixon Court" did not overturn any of the controversial decisions of its activist predecessor, and many of its decisions went against the Nixon administration grain. It upheld busing, the right of women to have an abortion on demand, and the publication of the *Pentagon Papers*. It struck down death penalty laws and limited Justice Department efforts at electronic surveillance. It did sustain laws banning pornography, where those statutes reflected "community standards." The Nixon court proved to be an unpredictable, politically independent agency, whose decisions often angered conservatives and Administration officials.

Nixon deployed Vice President Agnew to implement part of the Southern strategy. Agnew campaigned extensively during the 1970 midterm elections on behalf of Republican congressional candidates. During the elections, he tried to link his Democratic opponents to campus upheavals, race riots, bombings, rising crime rates, drug use, and pornography. Agnew's verbal onslaughts had little noticeable impact on the elections. Republicans gained two Senate seats, but lost nine seats in the House. The Democrats remained entrenched in Congress.

As part of its law-and-order campaign, the Justice Department prosecuted antiwar activists. The most important trial occurred in Chicago in 1971, involving a group of radicals known as the "Chicago Seven." The trial turned into a farce because of the disruptive antics of the defendants and the extreme bias against them of the judge, Julius Hoffmann. Six of the seven activists were convicted of various charges stemming from their roles in organizing demonstrations at the 1968 Democratic Convention in Chicago. All of the convictions were overturned on appeal because of Judge Hoffmann's procedural errors and bias.

Along with its efforts to prosecute antiwar activists, the Nixon administration also took a hard line on crime and drug use. During his 1968 presidential campaign, Nixon had blamed the rise in street crime and drug use on "liberal permissiveness" and had promised a crackdown on both if elected. In 1969 and 1970, Nixon proposed tough anticrime legal reforms. The Democrat-controlled Congress responded by enacting a series of anticrime laws. The main effect of the new laws was to increase penalties for federal crimes. In 1972, the Nixon administration declared war on drugs, particularly on heroin. The President created a new agency called the Office for Drug Abuse and Law Enforcement (ODALE) to spearhead the assault on heroin dealers. A few celebrities joined the war on drugs, including Sammy Davis Jr. and Elvis Presley. Neither crime rates nor drug use showed appreciable drops during Nixon's presidency, but his strenuous efforts on behalf of these issues paid political dividends. Nixon campaigned for reelection in 1972 as a champion of law and order and as a leader concerned with diminishing the contagion of violence and drug use in America.

In one important civil rights area, the Burger Court moved far beyond its more liberal predecessor; that area involved discrimination based on gender. Frequently using the provisions

Figure 9.3   Norma McCorvey, the Dallas mother whose desire to have an abortion was the basis for a landmark Supreme Court decision, takes time from her job as a house painter to pose for a photograph in Terrel, Texas. To legal scholars, she is simply "Jane Roe," the fictitious name McCorvey used when her two attorneys filed her historic lawsuit. Photo by Bill Jenscha. *Source:* AP/Wide World Photos.

of the Civil Rights Act of 1964 that prohibited gender-based segregation, the Court struck down many laws that had in various ways made women subordinate to men. In *Phillips v. Martin Marietta* (1971), the Burger Court nullified corporate hiring practices that discriminated against women with small children. In an important 1973 decision, *Frontero v. Richardson,* the Court ruled that the U.S. armed forces had to provide the same fringe benefits and pensions for female veterans as they did for males.

In 1973, the Supreme Court went far beyond questions of equal pay and employment rights for women. In *Roe v. Wade,* the justices struck down all state laws restricting abortions. Feminist attorneys had challenged a Texas law that made any abortion a felony, on behalf of a poor single woman, Norma McCorvey, who could not afford to raise the impending child properly. Associate Justice Harry Blackmun, who wrote the majority decision, anchored the right of a woman to have an abortion in a right to privacy, which, while not explicitly stated in the

Constitution, according to Blackmun's reading of that document, could be inferred. The decision granted women an absolute right to obtain an abortion during the first trimester of pregnancy, because medical experts all agreed that the fetus was not viable during that phase of pregnancy. During the second trimester, when fetus viability was possible, states could regulate abortions. During the third trimester, according to *Roe v. Wade,* states could prohibit abortions.

Roe v. Wade was the most controversial Supreme Court decision since the Warren Court's famed 1954 *Brown* decision that had outlawed segregation in public schools. *Roe v. Wade* immediately provoked an angry outcry from Catholics, from the Protestant religious Right, from prominent conservative politicians, and from many others. For the next thirty-plus years, the waters of public life in this country would be frequently roiled by controversy over *Roe v. Wade.* The issue proved impossible to compromise politically, because it involved two absolutist moral views that flatly contradicted each other. As conservative political forces steadily built up their strength during the 1970s, attacking *Roe v. Wade* became one of their most powerful rallying points.

Although it was certainly true that an integral part of Nixon's southern strategy was to try to slow the pace of school integration in order to court white southern voters and civil rights activists regarded the Nixon administration as opposing African-American efforts to achieve equality in American life, some of the Nixon administration actions helped black people and other minority groups make significant progress in many important arenas during the 1970s. Nixon strongly believed that African Americans and other groups ought to be given a chance to compete fairly. He supported affirmative action, expanded set-aside programs for minority-owned companies, aided historically black colleges, championed Native American tribal self-determination, backed bilingual programs for Hispanic children, and was the first president to specifically include the aged and the disabled in executive orders prohibiting bias in education and employment.

ACTIVISTS AND REFORMERS

The women's movement gained momentum as more women opted for many new career choices.The number of women in medical schools, law schools, and graduate business programs doubled between 1970 and 1974. Representative Edith Green introduced legislation, Title IX of the Education Amendment of 1972, to achieve gender equity in college sports. It cleared Congress and was signed into law by President Nixon. New magazines devoted to women's issues emerged. The most successful of these publications was *Ms.,* edited by Gloria Steinem. *Ms.* focused on the emotional and political needs of women, explored the frustrations of working women, and gave liberated women a forum of their own. The women's movement of the 1970s continued to be divided between liberal reformers in NOW who sought equality before the law, no-fault divorces, equal pay for equal work, child care centers, and abortion rights; and radical feminists who sought to achieve women's liberation through fundamental changes in the structure of society and changes in sexual identity.

Political opposition to feminism in the 1970s came from an antifeminist conservative leader, Phyllis Schlafly, head of the Eagle Forum. Schlafly led an effort to defeat the Equal Rights Amendment (ERA). She insisted that its passage would not help women and would take

Figure 9.4   Native Americans standing guard at Wounded Knee.   *Source:* CORBIS.

away rights that they already had, such as the right to be supported by a husband, the right to be exempted from conscription, and the right to special job protections. Schlafly succeeded when the ERA fell three votes short of the thirty-eight needed for ratification.

While feminists organized for action, so did Native Americans. Militant Indians occupied Alcatraz Island in San Francisco Bay in November 1969. The protesters wanted to highlight their demand that the Bureau of Indian Affairs respond more effectively to a myriad of Native American social problems. One of the prominent supporters of the Indian cause was the popular movie actress Jane Fonda, who soon moved on to become involved in radical anti-Vietnam War activities. In 1973, the most important militant Native American group, the American Indian Movement (AIM), seized the South Dakota town of Wounded Knee, the site of an 1890 massacre of Lakota Sioux Indians by U.S. soldiers. AIM activists wanted to call attention to the misery of the poverty-stricken Native American inhabitants of Wounded Knee and to the hundreds of Indian treaties broken by the federal government. Armed federal agents reclaimed the town, killing an AIM member in the process. In negotiations that followed, government officials agreed to examine conditions among the Indians and their treaty rights. The Second Battle of Wounded Knee signaled that a new era of Indian activism had arrived.

Hispanic organizations also were active in the early 1970s. Young Chicanos formed a militant organization that called itself the Brown Berets. The Brown Berets were active in the Midwest and Southwest. Some Chicano activists also joined the antiwar movement. Spokesmen called attention to Chicano casualty rates in Vietnam that were proportionally higher than those of the Anglo population. Aware of the political activity of some Mexican Americans, President Nixon set out to win their support, offering them political appointments and programs. The effort paid off; in the 1972 election, Nixon received 31 percent of the Mexican American vote, which helped him carry California and Texas. In 1974, the Supreme Court responded to another Chicano concern when it ruled that public schools had to meet the learning requirements of youngsters with limited English language skills. That decision led to the federal funding of bilingual education programs.

ECOLOGY AND CONSUMERISM

Environmentalism was another movement that emerged during the 1960s and grew rapidly during the early 1970s. The origins of the modern ecology movement lay in a book written by Rachel Carson called *Silent Spring* (1962). When there was almost no concern about ecological issues, Carson wrote about environmental damage caused by chemical pesticides, particularly DDT. Her writings spawned a cause that grew into a movement. The Great Society contained an important environmentalist component. By 1970, a broad-based, diverse environmentalist movement was active on a variety of fronts.

During the Nixon presidency, Congress responded to growing environmental concerns. Legislators enacted the Water Quality Improvement Act in 1970, tightening existing safeguards against threats to water quality. The National Air Quality Standards Act required automakers to reduce exhaust emission pollutants significantly by 1975 and the federal government to establish air quality standards. The Resource Recovery Act provided $453 million for resource recovery and recycling systems.

In 1971, Congress created the Environmental Protection Agency (EPA), which combined federal agencies concerned with pesticides, nuclear radiation, auto exhaust emissions, air and water quality, and waste disposal under a single Cabinet-level department. Nixon appointed William Ruckelshaus to head the new agency. Under Ruckelshaus's aggressive leadership, the EPA quickly initiated action on several fronts. It provoked a reaction from Detroit automakers, who insisted that EPA emission and safety standards were too expensive and beyond their technological capabilities. Nixon's Secretary of the Interior Walter Hickel, a conservative, self-made oil millionaire, also turned out to be an energetic environmentalist who protected the public domain.

Ecology was not a major Nixon priority, and at times he opposed the environmentalists. Nixon vetoed a mammoth $24.7 billion measure to clean up America's polluted rivers and lakes. He claimed that it was much too costly, but Congress enacted the law over his veto. Environmentalism was a political issue that cut across party, class, and ideological lines. Most everyone endorsed in principle the need for clean air and clean water and the protection of natural resources, scenic landscapes, and wilderness areas. But not everyone was willing to pay the high costs of environmental safeguards. At times, environmentalists clashed with vested economic interests.

Related to the ecology movement and sometimes overlapping with it, a strong consumer movement developed during the early 1970s that concerned itself with protecting consumers from unsafe, shoddy products and with making the business community more responsive to consumers' interests. Ralph Nader, whose attacks on the auto industry during the mid-1960s had led to the enactment of federal safety laws, headed the consumer movement of the 1970s. Operating out of a small office in the nation's capital, Nader organized task forces of volunteers called "Nader's Raiders," who examined many industries and governmental agencies and followed up these investigations with critical reports and with proposals for their reform.

Nader's Raiders attacked governmental regulatory agencies for being more protective of the businesses that they were supposed to regulate than of the consumers who used the products made by these businesses. These latter-day Muckrakers also attacked the multi-billion-dollar processed food industry, accusing it of serving American consumers a "chemical feast" of harmful food additives. They also attacked agribusiness for its use of chemical fertilizers and pesticides that harmed the environment and put toxic substances into the nation's food supplies. In their most radical finding, they reported on the adverse economic impact of land-use monopoly in some states. As a consequence of the growing consumer movement, millions of Americans became much more concerned about product safety and quality, and more assertive of their rights as consumers.

THE ELECTION OF 1972

The Democratic Party was still in disarray from the upheavals of 1968, and its members remained deeply divided over emotional issues such as the Vietnam War and busing. Nevertheless, many Democrats sought their party's nomination at the outset of the 1972 campaign. They included Senators Edmund Muskie, Hubert Humphrey, and George McGovern, who was an outspoken critic of the Vietnam War. After these contenders came two formidable possibilities, Senator Edward "Ted" Kennedy and George Wallace. Kennedy's appeal had been tarnished by his behavior following an auto accident in which a young woman had died; but he still retained the vote-getting magic of the Kennedy name. George Wallace, returned to the Democratic fold, also remained a major player.

Muskie flamed out early, in part the victim of Watergate "dirty tricks," as the nation would discover a year later. A would-be assassin eliminated Wallace by wounding him severely and forcing him out of the campaign in May. With Muskie and Wallace eliminated, McGovern moved strongly ahead. He won a series of primary victories, including California, where he beat Humphrey, and he rolled on to a first-ballot nomination. State delegations at the Democratic Convention in Miami contained high proportions of women, blacks, and young antiwar activists. These insurgent practitioners of a "new politics" took control of the convention and forged McGovern's victory. His supporters drafted a platform calling for an "immediate and total withdrawal of all American forces in Southeast Asia." It also supported busing to achieve school integration, full employment, tax reform, and various social reforms.

Meeting in Miami after the Democrats, the Republicans unanimously chose Nixon and Agnew to run again. The Republican platform staked out a clear strategy. It called for a "new American majority to repudiate McGovern's program." It also called for arms limitations with the Soviets, full employment, and tax reform. It opposed busing. On the crucial war issue, Republicans insisted that the United States could not honorably withdraw from Vietnam until all of the U. S. prisoners of war had been returned.

The presidential campaign turned out to be boring and one-sided. McGovern never had a chance, and most Americans quickly lost interest in the contest. The Democrats remained divided. Most Wallace supporters and about half of Humphrey's followers voted for Nixon. Organized labor, the strongest power bloc within the party, refused to endorse McGovern.

Nixon possessed formidable political assets that made him practically unbeatable. The president had achieved impressive diplomatic victories, capped by detente with the Soviets and the opening to China. The American war in Vietnam was winding down, and most U.S. troops had been withdrawn. At home, the economy was reasonably strong and the society had calmed. Nixon also stood foursquare against all of those features of American life that so upset Middle Americans and had given liberalism a bad name during the late 1960s and early 1970s—busing, hippies, the coddling of criminals and welfare chiselers, antiwar activists, drug use, and sexual permissiveness. He also employed, it was later revealed, an undercover army of political hirelings, using their arsenal of "dirty tricks" to sabotage the Democratic campaign.

There was a potential chink in Nixon's political armor—corruption. McGovern called Nixon's administration "the most morally corrupt in history." He cited several seamy deals where corporations and trade associations had given the GOP large campaign donations in exchange for political favors. The most blatant case of corruption involved a break-in at Democratic Party national headquarters at Watergate Towers in Washington on June 17, 1972. Five men, including two former White House aides and a member of the Committee to Re-elect the President (CREEP), had been caught trying to photograph and steal documents and install electronic bugging equipment. Two others, G. Gordon Liddy and E. Howard Hunt, who had directed the operation, were also arrested. It appeared that members of the Republican campaign organization and even members of the President's staff had engaged in espionage against their opponents. But news of the burglary produced little public concern at the time, and the prominent mass media exhibited little sustained interest in the bizarre event after a day or two of sensational headlines. Republicans denied all of McGovern's charges and dismissed the Watergate break-in. McGovern failed to generate much voter interest in Watergate or the corruption issue. Within less than a year it would turn out that McGovern had touched only the tip of the corruption iceberg.

In November Nixon scored his predicted landslide victory, carrying forty-nine of fifty states and rolling up an electoral vote of 521 to 17. He swept the South and even got a majority of the urban vote. The "silent majority, whom the president had courted—middle- and lower-middle-class whites, blue-collar voters, ethnics, Sunbelt inhabitants, and Westerners—all voted for him. The 1972 election was the first in which eighteen- to twenty-one-year-olds could vote. McGovern spent much of his time campaigning for their vote, considering the youth vote his secret weapon. Only one-third of these young people voted, and half of them opted for Nixon.

Despite Nixon's sweep, Democrats retained control of Congress, even gaining two seats in the Senate while losing twelve seats in the House. Such ticket-splitting suggested that millions of voters had cast their ballots for Nixon because they could not abide McGovern. Clearly the political climate had become more conservative by 1972; however, except for the South, the results gave no indication that political realignment was occurring, or that a new Republican majority was emerging. American voters mainly repudiated a candidate whom they saw as lacking in leadership qualities, and they chose to keep the incumbent, whom they perceived as a successful leader.

WATERGATE

President Nixon began his second term in January 1973, convinced that his landslide victory was a mandate for moving in more conservative directions. His new budget cut spending for welfare and education. He removed all remaining controls from the economy and impounded billions of dollars appropriated by Congress for purposes he opposed. Nixon also began reorganizing the federal government to make the bureaucracies more efficient and more responsive to his authority. His attitude toward the Democratic Congress was belligerent and contemptuous. He believed that the large majority of American citizens supported him and his agenda; he also believed that the tides of history were flowing in the direction he wanted to take the country. Richard Nixon was riding high that spring of 1973. Then his administration began to self-destruct. A process of disintegration was set in motion that ultimately brought him down.

Watergate, latent since the break-in, suddenly erupted with a rash of disclosures and confessions that made it one of the most serious political scandals in American history. Watergate activities fell into two categories—those occurring before the June 17, 1972, break-in and those following. The break-in turned out to be only one event in an extensive dirty-tricks campaign developed by CREEP and White House staffers to prevent news leaks, to spy on radicals, and to ensure Nixon's reelection. Investigators eventually unearthed an astonishing web of criminal activities and abuses of power that had begun early in Nixon's presidency. These activities included illegal wiretaps placed on government bureaucrats and journalists suspected of leaking embarrassing information about administration policies to the press, using the IRS to harass political opponents, and raising millions of dollars in illegal campaign funds.

The burglars caught inside of Democratic Party National Headquarters had previously tried unsuccessfully to break into McGovern's campaign headquarters. Other dirty tricksters circulated literature slandering Democratic candidates and disrupted their meetings. All dirty tricks were cleared with the president's top advisers. Nixon's defenders argued that many of the dirty tricks had been used by previous administrations and were traditional parts of the American political process. That contention was true, but the extent of Nixonian dirty tricks vastly exceeded any previous administration's efforts. More seriously, these practices flowed from a mind-set that was contemptuous of law and fair play, viewed politics as war, and saw political opponents as enemies to be destroyed.

Dirty tricks proved to be only the beginning. The Watergate burglars had been caught red-handed. CREEP officials and White House staffers who sent them in could have confessed and resigned. Such actions would have embarrassed the Nixon administration, but the president would still have been reelected easily. But White House officials instead chose to cover up its and CREEP's complicity; the cover-up began immediately following the Watergate arrests. White House aides moved to destroy all evidentiary links between the burglary, themselves, and CREEP, and to concoct denials and alibis.

An FBI investigation of the break-in and testimony before a federal grand jury were carefully limited so that they could not uncover any tracks leading to CREEP or the White House.

The cover-up began immediately after White House officials learned that the burglars had been caught. President Nixon was directly involved in the cover-up activities from the start. He put White House Counsel John Dean in charge; at times, Nixon himself directed the cover-up activities. From the moment the cover-up efforts began, a process was set in motion that would strain the constitutional system of government, cause many American citizens a great deal of anguish, provide some of the most bizarre political theater in American history, and eventually destroy Nixon's presidency.

The cover-up orchestrated by Nixon, Dean, and other top White House aides succeeded for a time. In September 1972, the federal grand jury indicted only the seven men involved in the burglary. The cover-up also held through the November election. The cover-up was still holding as the trial of the seven burglars opened in March 1973. Meanwhile, it was business as usual for the president and his men, who were confident that they had contained the incident and remained in the clear.

But too many people were involved in the cover-up. Too many connections among the burglars, CREEP, and White House survived. Too many investigators were looking for answers to puzzling questions. The *Washington Post* had assigned two young reporters, Carl Bernstein and Bob Woodward, to find answers. They were able to trace some of the illegal campaign funds to CREEP. The Senate created a Select Committee on Presidential Campaign Activities, soon to be known as the Watergate Committee, chaired by Senator Sam J. Ervin, to investigate the burglary and other dirty tricks that may have influenced the outcome of the 1972 election. Federal prosecutors, continuing the federal grand jury probe, continuously investigated the burglary, other dirty tricks, violations of campaign spending laws, and the cover-up. The Watergate trial judge, John J. Sirica, who did not believe the burglars when they told him that they alone had planned the break-in, pressured them to tell the truth.

The cover-up began to come unglued when one of the convicted burglars, James McCord, hoping to avoid a long prison term, wrote a letter to Judge Sirica implicating CREEP and prominent White House officials in the planning of the Watergate burglary. After McCord cracked, the whole cover-up edifice crumbled. The accused officials hired lawyers and promptly implicated other prominent officials in the hope of getting immunity from prosecution or a lighter sentence. Federal prosecutors often entered into plea bargaining arrangements with accused lesser officials to gather evidence against the ringleaders, including President Nixon.

In April, Nixon was forced to fire several senior advisers implicated in the cover-up— L. Patrick Gray III, acting director of the FBI, and John Erlichman, H. R. "Bob" Haldeman, and John Mitchell, the director of CREEP. Nixon also fired John Dean for telling the Watergate Committee staffers that the president had been involved in the cover-up from the beginning. President Nixon maintained publicly that he had only learned about the cover-up from Dean in March 1973, and since then he had done everything he could to cooperate with investigators, get out the truth about Watergate, and punish wrongdoers. Nixon tried to discredit Dean by suggesting that he had directed the cover-up without the president's knowledge. To reinforce the image of a president concerned with getting to the bottom of the scandal, Nixon appointed a Special Prosecutor, Harvard law professor Archibald Cox, a liberal Democrat, to continue the Justice Department's investigation of the Watergate cover-up.

On May 17, 1973, public interest in the scandal increased dramatically when the Senate Watergate Committee began holding televised hearings that ran through the summer. The committee started with low-level hirelings, CREEP minions who did the dirty work and delivered illegal payments. Gradually they worked their way up the chain-of-command in CREEP and in the Nixon White House. On the way up, the millions of American citizens who watched the proceedings daily got a fascinating and appalling tour through the dark underside of American politics. They learned about political dirty tricks such as shredding documents, blackmail, bribery, forgery, perjury, and "laundered money." They also learned about the misuse of government agencies, including the FBI and the IRS. And they learned about fund-raising techniques that violated election laws and often amounted to blackmail. The televised hearings made a folk hero out of the committee's chairman, seventy-nine-year-old Sam Ervin. Ervin's folksy manner and good humor cloaked a keen intellect and a fierce moral outrage at the steady parade of criminals and corrupt politicians who appeared before his committee.

By mid-June, as a result of the committee's investigations, the key question had become whether President Nixon had been involved in the Watergate cover-up: in the words of the committee's vice chairman, Tennessee Republican Howard Baker, "What did the president know and when did he know it?" On June 25, John Dean appeared before the committee. For two days he read a lengthy 250-page statement describing the details of the cover-up. He detailed President Nixon's role in the cover-up: Nixon knew all about it, had approved it, and indeed had played a central role in it from the outset. Despite efforts by the White House to discredit Dean's testimony, the fired counselor came across as credible to members of the committee and to the large television audience. He knew too much; he had too many details at his command. The testimony of Nixon loyalists before the committee further damaged the president's position. Men

Figure 9.5   In May 1973, the Senate Watergate Committee began holding televised hearings. For months, fascinated television audiences were treated to exposures of corrupt political practices that pervaded the Nixon presidency.
Source: Bettmann Archive.

such as Haldeman, Erlichman, and Mitchell often gave rambling, incoherent, evasive answers to direct questions.

But Dean's testimony, while sounding authentic, was legally inconclusive. It depended entirely on his ability to recall the events and conversations that he described before the Committee. He had no corroborative evidence or documents to substantiate his testimony. Only Dean had implicated President Nixon in the cover-up activities. The President had denied all of Dean's accusations and fired him. Dean himself was a suspect source. He was deeply involved in the cover-up. All of the Nixon loyalists who had appeared before the committee had insisted on the President's innocence, and they all accused John Dean of being the evil mastermind of the cover-up. They also accused Dean of trying to pin the blame on an innocent President in order to save his own skin.

Decline and Fall

On July 16 came a sensational discovery. The assistant counsel for the Watergate committee, Fred Thompson, found out from Alexander Butterfield, an assistant to Haldeman, that President Nixon had recorded White House conversations and phone calls on a secret tape-recording system installed in the Oval Office in 1970. If the disputed conversations between Dean and Nixon were on tape, it would be possible to find out which one of them was telling the truth and if the president had been involved in the cover-up. From that date on, the Watergate drama focused on the tapes and the prosecution's efforts to obtain them from the President, who was determined not to surrender them.

Immediately both the Watergate Committee and the Special Prosecutor subpoenaed the tapes of the Nixon–Dean conversations. Nixon rejected both subpoenas. Both investigators then asked Judge Sirica to force Nixon to honor their subpoenas. Nixon's attorneys defended his right to refuse to surrender the tapes on the grounds of "executive privilege." Judge Sirica rejected the argument and ordered Nixon to release the tapes. Nixon's attorneys appealed his ruling. The appeals court upheld the ruling, saying that "The president is not above the law's commands."

While the battle for control of the tapes was raging, another White House scandal surfaced, unrelated to Watergate, involving Vice President Agnew. Justice Department investigators learned that Agnew, when governor of Maryland during the 1960s, had taken bribes from construction companies in return for favorable rulings on their bids. He had continued to receive payments while serving as vice president. In August 1973, Agnew was charged with bribery, extortion, conspiracy, and income tax evasion. Nixon, convinced of his guilt, pressured Agnew to resign. To get rid of him, Nixon offered him a deal: resign and plead "no contest" to a single count of tax evasion for not reporting or paying taxes on the bribes, and the other charges would be dropped. The other charges and evidence sustaining them would be published so people would know why Agnew resigned. Knowing that the federal prosecutors had hard evidence against him, Agnew accepted the offer. Otherwise, he knew that he would go to prison. He resigned, was fined $10,000, and was given three years' unsupervised probation. The evidence released to the public showed that the case against Agnew amounted to fifty indictable offenses. Even so, Agnew, displaying considerable gall, toured the country, making speeches and appearing on talk shows. Everywhere he insisted on his innocence, and he argued that he only resigned to avoid embarrassing the embattled president.

Shortly after Agnew's forced resignation, President Nixon chose House minority leader Gerald R. Ford of Michigan to succeed the fallen vice president. Ford was a conservative, a Nixon loyalist, and was popular with his colleagues. Further, there were no political or personal scandals in his life. This last factor was crucial, because many Senators who voted to confirm Ford knew that if the tapes substantiated Dean's charges, Nixon was not only selecting a vice president, he was choosing his successor. Ford had to be squeaky clean.

Meanwhile, Archibald Cox and the Watergate Committee were pressing the Nixon administration for tapes of key conversations with his top aides pertaining to the Watergate cover-up. The release of these tapes posed a mortal danger to the president, which he knew better than anyone. Nixon decided on a bold move to avoid surrendering them: unless a compromise was arranged, permitting the president to keep custody of the tapes, Nixon would dismiss Cox and prepare his own summaries of the tapes for Judge Sirica. Efforts to forge a compromise failed. On Saturday evening, October 20, Nixon ordered Attorney General Elliot Richardson to fire Cox. The attorney general refused and resigned. Nixon then directed Deputy Attorney General William Ruckelshaus to fire Cox. Ruckleshaus also refused, and Nixon fired him. Finally, the third-ranking officer at the Justice Department, Robert Bork, dismissed Cox. Nixon also abolished the Special Prosecutor's office and ordered the FBI to seal all of the office files.

Journalists dubbed these resignations and the firing of Cox the "Saturday Night Massacre." The firings provoked a dramatic outpouring of public protest. During the next forty-eight hours, over one million letters, telegrams, and phone calls poured into Senate and Congressional offices, nearly all of them denouncing the Saturday Night Massacre. Eight resolutions of impeachment were introduced into the House of Representatives. Nixon's approval rating in the polls dropped to 27 percent. Polls also revealed that most Americans suspected that the President was trying to hide his involvement in criminal activities. In addition to his Watergate actions, Nixon also came under attack for questionable financial dealings involving his real estate holdings in California and Florida. He was accused of charging the government for making improvements to both properties, which were primarily for his personal use, that enhanced their value considerably. The IRS also investigated Nixon for tax evasion.

Nixon tried hard to repair the largely self-inflicted damage with a public relations campaign. He agreed to release the original tapes ordered by Judge Sirica. He replaced Cox with another Special Prosecutor, Leon Jaworski, a Houston corporation lawyer. Nixon met with Congressmen and Senators to reassure them of his innocence. He released a detailed financial statement to dispel doubts about his personal finances. He went on a national speaking tour to reclaim his lost reputation. Before an audience of newspaper publishers, he insisted that he was "not a crook." His efforts failed. Except for hard-core loyalists, the public, the media, and Congress remained skeptical of Nixon's efforts at reassurance. The president's lingering credibility was further undermined when White House officials admitted that two of the nine subpoenaed tapes, covering important conversations with Dean, did not exist. Even worse, an eighteen-and-one-half-minute segment of a crucial conversation between Nixon and Haldeman, held three days after the break-in, had been erased. Calls for Nixon's impeachment grew louder.

With the failure of his public relations campaign, Nixon grew defiant. He refused Jaworski's requests for more tapes. On March 1, 1974, the grand jury indicted several key players in the cover-up, including Erlichman, Haldeman, and Mitchell. It would have indicted Nixon as well if Jaworski had not told them that under the law a sitting president was not indictable. Nixon's legal status became "an unindicted co-conspirator." At about the same time the grand jury issued its indictments, the House Judiciary Committee began impeachment proceedings against the president. When its staff sought tapes and documents from the White House, Nixon refused its requests as well. Both Jaworski and the House Judiciary Committee then issued subpoenas to obtain the desired evidence and to overcome the president's "stonewalling" tactics.

Nixon was caught in a serious bind. He knew that refusal to comply with subpoenas would not work; the courts would not sustain his efforts. He also knew that conversations on several of the requested tapes would ruin him if released. He came up with one more big play to try to escape the trap. He decided to release edited transcripts of the requested tapes. In a speech to the American people, delivered on April 29, dubbed by the media "Checkers II," he made a final effort to retrieve his failing political reputation. He told his vast audience of his intent to release the transcripts. "These materials will tell all," he said. The next day, the transcripts were published in full.

The public response to Nixon's ploy was again emphatically negative. House Judiciary Committee members, comparing the edited versions with tapes already released, discovered many discrepancies. They refused to accept the edited versions and told the president that as far as they were concerned, he had refused to comply with the committee's subpoena for the tapes. The contents of the edited tapes were even more damning to the President's cause because of the impression they conveyed of Nixon's conduct of the presidency: crude, vulgar language; the voicing of racial and ethnic stereotypes; and the complete lack of scruples or morality. Nixon evidently failed to understand that the inner workings of his government could not stand public exposure. Conservatives as well as liberals were appalled by Nixon's way of governing. Senate Republican leader Hugh Scott said that the transcripts revealed a "deplorable, disgusting, shabby, and immoral performance" by everyone recorded on the tapes. House Republican leader John Rhodes of Ohio called upon Nixon to resign. Both the House Judiciary Committee and Jaworski continued their demands for more tapes from the White House. Nixon refused all of their requests. Jaworski subpoenaed sixty-four additional tapes. Nixon tried to quash the subpoena, but Judge Sirica upheld it and ordered Nixon to release the tapes.

When the White House announced that it would appeal the ruling, Jaworski asked the Supreme Court to decide the matter. It agreed to do so. The question before the Court was clear: who had the final authority to decide whether a president had to obey a subpoena, the subpoenaed president himself or the courts? The Court heard arguments by both sides in July. Nixon's attorneys argued that the president had the right to decide; the only way the law could be applied to the president was through the impeachment process. Jaworski countered with the argument that if the president decides what the Constitution means, "if he is wrong, who is there to tell him so?"

In the case of *United States of America v. Richard M. Nixon,* the Supreme Court ruled unanimously that Nixon had to surrender the subpoenaed tapes to Judge Sirica. On the same day the Court announced its verdict, the House Judiciary Committee began voting on articles of impeachment against the president. Within a week, it voted to send three articles of impeachment to the full House. Article I accused the president of obstructing justice for his involvement in the cover-up of the Watergate break-in. Article II accused the president of abusing power by his involvement in efforts to harass his political opponents. Article III accused the president of unconstitutionally refusing to honor the Committee's subpoenas. Two other proposed impeachment articles were defeated. If the full House of Representatives adopted at least one of the three approved articles, Richard Nixon would become the second president in U.S. history to be impeached. Nixon would then be tried in the Senate, who would sit as a jury of 100 members. The Senators would decide whether Nixon would be removed from office for "high crimes and misdemeanors" or be allowed to continue serving as president.

The evidence that completed the destruction of Nixon's presidency was a tape released on August 5, 1974, of a conversation between Nixon and Haldeman, held on July 23, 1972, six weeks after the Watergate burglars had been caught: Nixon can be heard ordering Haldeman to tell the CIA to fabricate a national security operation to keep the FBI from pursuing its investigation of the burglary. Here was the "smoking gun," proof of a criminal act—conspiring to obstruct justice. The taped conversation also proved that Nixon had been lying about his Watergate involvement. He had known of the cover-up and had been involved in it from the beginning. Nixon, in a written statement, conceded that the tape was "at variance with certain of my previous statements." With the release of the "smoking gun" tape, remaining congressional support for the president collapsed.

For several days, Nixon wavered between resigning and fighting the impeachment process. On August 7, Republican Congressional leaders called on Nixon at the White House. They told the President that he faced certain impeachment, conviction, and removal from office. Some of the president's advisers worried about his mental health; they felt that he had been broken by the stresses of the long Watergate ordeal. Both Secretary of Defense James Schlesinger and White House Chief of Staff Alexander Haig informed all American military commanders around the world to check with them before carrying out any unusual orders that might come from President Nixon. Henry Kissinger urged a distraught Nixon to resign before the crisis seriously damaged American foreign policy. That night, the President decided to resign.

On the evening of August 8, President Nixon spoke to the American people for the last time. He told the nation that everything he had done he believed had been done with the best interests of the country in mind. He expressed regret for any harm that he might have done others. He admitted to making "errors in judgment." He could not bring himself to admit to breaking the law or to any wrongdoing. He claimed that he was resigning only because he had lost his political base and could no longer govern effectively. On the morning of August 9, he made a rambling, incoherent, and often emotional farewell speech to his White House staff. His resignation became effective at 12:00 noon that day. At that point in time, Nixon was aboard the Spirit of '76, flying over "Middle America" en route to "exile" in Southern California. At noon, Gerald R. Ford took the oath of office as the thirty-eighth president of the United States. The new president began his short acceptance speech by saying "our long national nightmare is over."

Ford was right; Watergate had been a long national nightmare, its impact accentuated by extensive media coverage for over a year. Americans reacted differently to the Watergate scandals. For well-informed citizens who understood that the integrity of the American system of constitutional governance was at stake, the events of Watergate were the stuff of high drama. For less well-informed people, the revelations of Watergate appeared confusing and perhaps much ado about not very much. For millions of Middle Americans who had voted for Nixon in 1972 in good faith, Watergate was a series of painful disillusionments. For young people especially,

Figure 9.6   President Nixon resigns.   *Source:* CORBIS.

Watergate was traumatic. Many of these youngsters sought refuge in a pathetic cynicism. They shrilly insisted that Watergate was what all politicians did; Nixon and his minions merely got nailed. And even to the bitter end, Nixon retained many defenders. These stalwarts insisted that the only mistake Nixon made was to not burn the tapes. It was the tapes that had ruined him, because they made him vulnerable. The tapes had given his enemies among the liberal political and media establishments, the people who hated Nixon because he had proven them wrong so often, the opportunity to destroy him. And then there were the Nixon haters. They rejoiced in their long-time political adversary's humiliation and fall from power. For them, his disgrace was richly deserved and poetic justice. They pointedly observed that Watergate only revealed aspects of the man that they had known were there all along.

Thoughtful analysts searched out the multiple causes of the Watergate scandals. Some found the springs of Watergate within the personality and approach to politics of Richard M. Nixon. Relentlessly ambitious, intensely partisan, insecure, and perhaps even paranoid, Nixon was willing to use or countenance ruthless, even criminal, means to advance his career, to achieve his policy goals and destroy his enemies. Some analysts located Watergate in the institution of the presidency itself, in the rise of an "imperial presidency" since the 1940s. The presidency dominated the federal government, particularly in the realms of national security and foreign policy. All modern presidents wielded awesome powers and came to be regarded as special people, above the restraints of the Constitution and the claims of morality. Other analysts saw the rise of a Cold War mentality as contributing to the Watergate syndrome. In a struggle for survival against ruthless and powerful adversaries, it is sometimes necessary to employ the same ruthless methods that the Communists used, and to employ them more extensively than they. It was necessary to enter an Orwellian world where undemocratic methods were required to preserve democracy. Still others saw the Watergate scandals as deriving from an ethic that held that winning was so important that there were no limits on what could be done to achieve victory. This do-whatever-it-takes-to-win attitude also reflected the political ethics of the many *nouveau riche* Sunbelt politicians who rode to power on Nixon's coattails. Nixon was the leader of this dangerous new political class that did not play the game of politics by the traditional establishmentarian rules. It therefore had to be destroyed.

George McGovern was right when he labeled Nixon's administration the most corrupt in U.S. history. But the corruption of the Nixon White House, Agnew excepted, was not the commonplace corruption of crooks, thieves, bribers, grafters, chiselers, and influence peddlers that infested past presidencies. It was a more dangerous kind of corruption that threatened the integrity of the American system of government. It threatened to replace a government based on constitutional law with the rule of a powerful leader heading a staff of loyalists, whose highest calling was to do his bidding and vanquish his enemies. His list of enemies included Democratic Party leaders, prominent journalists, bureaucrats, antiwar protesters, black militants, celebrities, and hippies, who posed threats to the leader's personal authority, which he equated with national security. Their threat would be contained by any means necessary, including wiretapping, surveillance, burglary, blackmail, political sabotage, and intimidation. President Nixon and his men, for a time, posed a serious threat to American constitutional governance and democratic political processes.

But they failed. A constitutional crisis was resolved. Arbitrary power was thwarted. Eventually due process ran its course. Three hundred seventy-eight officials, including three former Cabinet members and several top-level White House aides, either pleaded guilty or were convicted of Watergate-related offenses. Thirty-one went to prison. It is probable that only President Ford's pardon kept Nixon from prison. Assisted by some good fortune, the system of checks and balances established by the Founding Fathers eventually worked. The system met its gravest challenge. A free press sounded alarm bells. Various investigations exposed the culprits. The Supreme Court firmly established the principle that no one, including the President, is above the law. Congress, spearheaded by the Senate Watergate Committee and the House Judiciary Committee, overrode efforts at executive usurpation. The forces of democracy united to purge a would-be tyrant and his lackeys from office.

Watergate left a mixed legacy. Paradoxically, it revealed both the terrible vulnerability and the underlying strength and resiliency of the American democratic political system. The abuses of power by the president and the president's men were finally checked. But it took an agonizingly long time for the mainstream media to get involved, for the public to become aroused, and for Congress to take action. Suppose the tapes had not been discovered? Or suppose that Nixon had ordered them destroyed? Watergate's outcome provided no guarantee that the system would be able to contain a subsequent president's abuses of power. Watergate, along with the Vietnam War, made Americans skeptical, even cynical, about politics and politicians. Watergate reminded thoughtful Americans of what the Founding Fathers knew to be the chief threat to republican government: that power can corrupt fallible leaders. Within the psyches of political leaders, the grubby demons of greed and lust for power compete with desires to serve and to do good. And sometimes the demons prevail. Above all, Watergate reaffirmed the oldest lesson of our political heritage: eternal vigilance is the price of liberty.

Brief Bibliographic Essay

James T. Patterson's *Grand Expectations: The United States, 1945–1974* is a comprehensive survey of the first three decades of post–World War II U.S. history that includes virtually every major development that marked American life during those years. Several major studies of Richard Nixon have been undertaken in recent years. The best of these works is Stephen E. Ambrose's three-volume biography: Volume 1 is entitled *Nixon: The Education of a Politician, 1913–1962;* Volume 2 is entitled *Nixon: The Triumph of a Politician, 1962–1972;* and Volume 3 is entitled *Nixon: Ruin and Recovery.* Roger Morris, a scholar who worked for the National Security Council staff under both Johnson and Nixon, has written a major study of Nixon covering the years of his life and political career up to 1952, entitled *Richard Milhous Nixon: The Rise of an American Politician.* Another fine study is Garry Wills's *Nixon Agonistes.* A recent study by Anthony Summers, *The Arrogance of Power: The Secret World of Richard Nixon,* treats issues associated with Nixon's aberrant personality, whether he suffered from serious psychological disorders. Summers notes that at times Nixon consulted with a psychiatrist and his associates feared that he might suffer a nervous collapse. The former president is himself the author of several books, the best of which is his autobiography, *RN: The Memoirs of Richard Nixon,* one of the finest presidential memoirs ever done. The best historical study of the Watergate crisis is Stanley I. Kutler's *The Wars of Watergate.* Kutler sees Watergate as a reflection of the essence of Nixon's political career and presidency. Kutler has also edited *Abuse of Power: The New Nixon Tapes.* These newly released tapes fill in some of the remaining gaps in the Watergate story and provide more evidence of criminal behavior by the president and the president's men. See also the two books by *Washington Post* reporters Carl Berstein and Bob Woodward, *All the President's Men* and *The Final Days.* The two best of many books written by men involved in the Watergate scandals are Harry R. Haldeman's *The Ends of Power* and John Dean's *Blind Ambition.* Kevin B. Phillips's *The Emerging Republican Majority* is an important theoretical tract that influenced Richard Nixon's domestic political strategies. Allen J. Matusow's *Nixon's Economy: Booms, Busts, Dollars, and Votes* is a recent study of Nixonomics. The author charges Mr. Nixon with pursuing economic policies primarily to win reelection in 1972 that did serious harm to both the U.S. economy and the developing world economy. Dean J. Kotlowski's *Nixon's Civil Rights: Politics, Principle, and Policy* argues that, despite the southern strategy, Nixon generally pursued progressive civil rights policies. Melvin Urofsky's *The Continuity of Change: The Supreme Court and Individual Liberties, 1953–1986* contains a good section on the Burger Court.

Web Sites

For those who are concerned about exploring the life and political career of Richard Nixon, see <www.POTUS.com/rmnixon.html>. It is a rich site containing a wealth of data about the thirty-seventh president of the United States, his wife and family, his presidency, and his political associates. Includes primary source documents, video and audio resources. For Watergate, see <http://www2.cnn.com/ALLPOLITICS/1997/gen/resources/watergate/

site/html> done by CNN in 1997 on the occasion of the twenty-fifth anniversary of the break-in. It contains a myriad of data pertaining to Watergate and also includes a catalogue of all related Web sites. The Social Security Agency controls a special collection of Nixon papers and hundreds of hours of the White House Tapes recorded secretly by the President. You can access the collection at <http://www.ssa.gov/history/Nixon/cabinetgen.html>. For Native American issues, see <http://www.nativeweb.org>. It is a comprehensive site for Native American studies. See <http://www.lib.utk.edu/refs/ecology> maintained by the University of Tennessee at Knoxville, which includes selected Web sites for persons interested in ecology and environmental science with links and access to databases.

10

Detente, China, and Vietnam

Richard Nixon assumed office amidst the gravest political and cultural crises in modern American history. He had won a narrow plurality of votes, in part by appealing to the vast unhappiness of millions of citizens with the costs and consequences of America's global foreign policy, particularly the seemingly interminable Vietnam War, which the Johnson administration could neither win nor terminate.

Aware that America's Vietnam entanglement was dividing the nation, sapping its strength, and diverting it from full pursuit of its global rivalry with the Soviet Union, the new president made phasing out the Vietnam War his top foreign policy priority. Aware also that the world was rapidly changing in the early 1970s, Nixon, aided by his most prominent foreign policy adviser, Henry Kissinger, sought to change American relations with the major Communist powers, with the turbulent nations of the Middle East, and with America's major allies in Western Europe. As they forged the nation's foreign policy, Nixon and Kissinger sought three major goals: to bring America's foreign policy commitments in line with the nation's ability to meet them more effectively; to ensure that the United States continued to play the central role in world affairs; and to erect a structure of peace that would last a generation. During Nixon's presidency, significant changes occurred in all facets of American diplomacy, including a dramatic opening to China, the relaxation of tensions with the Soviet Union, and the eventual phaseout of the Vietnam War. Nixon proved to be a bold, innovative diplomatist who achieved the respect of other world leaders. However, many of his and Kissinger's foreign policy achievements turned out to be short lived. Relations between the Soviet Union and the United States deteriorated in the late 1970s, as the Cold War heated up.

DETENTE

Nixon applied most of his considerable political talents to the conduct of U.S. foreign policy. The president, who had built his political reputation as a hardline cold warrior, with help from Henry Kissinger, launched a new era of detente with the Soviet Union, built on a relaxation of tensions and realistic diplomacy. The development of new relations with the Soviets reversed the direction American foreign policy had taken since 1945. A glimmer of detente had surfaced in 1963 in the aftermath of the missile crisis with the signing of the Nuclear Test Ban Treaty. However, relations between the United States and the Soviet Union were strained at the time of Nixon's accession to office, and ongoing efforts at arms control negotiations were unproductive.

Since the beginning of the Cold War, U.S. foreign policy had been premised on the necessity of responding to threats to American interests posed by expansionist Communist states. Both Nixon and Kissinger knew that the model of a world dominated by a bipolar struggle between Communism and the Free World had been rendered obsolete by the late 1960s. They understood that power now flowed along a pentagonal axis representing the United States, Western Europe, the Soviet empire, China, and Japan.

Nixon and Kissinger understood that U.S. power had suffered relative decline since the late 1950s. America no longer dominated its major allies. They realized that the unity of the Communist world had been fatally sundered. In early 1969, the most serious international conflict pitted the two major Communist states, the Soviet Union and the People's Republic of China, against each other. Kissinger and Nixon perceived that, in the case of the quarreling Communist giants, questions of conflicting national interests overrode their ideological kinship. Nixon and Kissinger set out to use this rift between the two Communist powers to improve U.S. relations with both, and to enhance American power in the world.

Nixon and Kissinger had many reasons for seeking detente with the Soviets. They hoped to persuade the Soviets to help them achieve a satisfactory peace in Indochina by linking Soviet willingness to persuade the North Vietnamese to accept U.S. terms with improved relations between the two superpowers. They also expected detente to enable the United States to maintain influence over its NATO allies, who had recently shown a tendency to make deals of their own with the Soviets and with the Eastern Bloc countries. Prosperous and no longer fearful of Soviet aggression, the French and West Germans had been pursuing their own detentes with the Communists. Another powerful motive for detente was the desire of U.S. industrial and financial interests to move into Soviet and eastern European markets. Powerful U.S. agricultural interests saw the Soviets as major customers for their wheat and other commodities. Most important, Nixon and Kissinger had to be concerned by the ever-present danger of nuclear war arising from the spiraling arms race.

In 1969, Nixon signed a Nuclear Non-Proliferation Treaty with the Soviets. At Nixon's initiative, U.S. and Soviet delegates began strategic arms limitation talks (SALT) in April 1970 at Helsinki and Vienna. At the same time, Kissinger began talks with the Soviet ambassador to the United States, Anatoly Dobrynin. Nixon wanted nuclear weapons agreements with the Soviets to be the key to detente and to an expanding network of agreements with the Soviets. As he pushed for SALT to begin, Nixon expanded America's nuclear arsenal, believing that the United States must always negotiate from a position of strength with the Soviets. At the time, both nations possessed roughly equal nuclear arsenals, and both were refining and expanding their nuclear weapons systems. Nixon wanted to add two new weapons systems to the U.S. arsenal, an anti-ballistics missile (ABM), which would protect U.S. missiles from a possible first strike, and a multiple, independently targeted reentry vehicle (MIRV), which would make it possible for multiple nuclear warheads to be fired from a single missile in flight at several targets simultaneously. The Soviets also had begun work on ABMs and MIRV missiles.

Nixon also began a phased reduction of U.S. conventional military forces. These military cutbacks coincided with a general scaling back of U.S. global commitments. In August 1969, the president proclaimed a new Asian policy, the Nixon Doctrine. According to this new doctrine, America would no longer provide direct military protection in the Far East. Asian nations must henceforth assume greater responsibility for their strategic security. The United States could furnish economic and technical assistance, and logistic support, but not troops. There would be no more Vietnams or Koreas. The Nixon Doctrine also had applications for other regions and other conflicts outside of Southeast Asia. The new doctrine also signaled that a new dynamic U.S. policy of negotiation and maneuver was supplanting the essentially static policy based on military containment of Communism.

While SALT negotiators representing both sides grappled with the intricate technical questions involved in controlling the asymmetric nuclear weapons systems of the United States and the Soviet Union, other negotiators concluded a series of important economic agreements. In November 1971, representatives of both governments signed agreements whereby the United States would sell the Soviets $136 million worth of wheat and $125 million worth of oil drilling equipment. Arrangements also were concluded on a joint venture, the building of a large truck factory within the Soviet Union. These and many other smaller deals led to a threefold increase in U.S.–Soviet trade over the next three years.

In March 1972, Nixon sent Kissinger to Moscow to make preparations for a summit meeting between the U.S. president and Leonid Brezhnev, general secretary of the Soviet Communist Party. Nixon later journeyed to Moscow where he and Brezhnev met for a series of talks. Three major agreements signed by both leaders in May 1972 came from these talks. The first agreement limited each country to two ABM sites and also set a ceiling on the number of ABM's per site. The second agreement, an interim one called SALT I, froze the number of strategic missiles in both arsenals at the 1972 levels for five years, but it put no limit on MIRVs, which both sides continued to build. Neither the ABM treaty nor SALT I ended the thermonuclear arms race, but the arms agreement did bring a measure of stability welcomed by both powers. The third agreement, "Basic Principles of U.S.–Soviet Relations," committed both sides to accept strategic parity as the basic premise for future arms control negotiations. Americans no longer sought nuclear superiority over the Soviets; they had accepted sufficiency. Congress subsequently approved all three agreements by large bipartisan majorities. These breakthrough agreements fundamentally altered U.S.–Soviet relations and constituted the bedrock of the new superpower relationship founded on detente.

Other significant diplomatic agreements between the United States and the Soviet Union were concluded. The Berlin question, a recurring flash point in the Cold War, was resolved. Both sides signed the Berlin Agreement of 1971, which clearly defined the political status of Berlin and created mechanisms for the peaceful resolution of any conflicts that might arise. The next year, the two German states normalized relations and America recognized East Germany as a legitimate state.

All of these agreements forged during the most productive era in U.S.–USSR relations following World War II did not make the two superpowers allies. But detente had created the opportunity for realistic agreements between the two countries, which stabilized the arms race, reduced the risk of nuclear war, and resolved several long-standing political problems that had divided them. Competition and rivalry between the superpowers would continue, especially in the Third World, but "peaceful coexistence" had become a reality.

The Nixon and Kissinger policy of detente with the Soviet Union came under attack from Democratic Cold Warriors who controlled Congress. Senator Henry "Scoop" Jackson, from the state of Washington, emerged as the leader of the Democratic opposition to detente. Jackson attacked SALT I as giving the Soviets a dangerous advantage over the United States, because it allowed them to keep more land-based ICBMs. Jackson ignored the fact that the United States relied for strategic deterrence on a triad of land-based missiles, submarine-launched missiles, and strategic bombers. The Soviets, lacking equivalent submarine and bomber forces, required additional ICBMs to offset the U.S. advantage. Jackson also criticized the Nixon administration for its tolerance of Soviet human rights violations, particularly Moscow's refusal to let Soviet Jews emigrate.

Jackson's criticism was valid, although the Soviets liberalized their emigration policy and permitted 30,000 Jews to leave the country during 1973, the largest number ever. Jackson, who harbored presidential ambitions, helped push the Jackson-Vanik Amendment through Congress, which denied the Soviet Union "most favored nation" trading status with the United States, until they stopped human rights abuses and allowed unlimited emigration. The Jackson-Vanik Amendment effectively prevented Washington from granting equal trading rights to the Soviet Union, hindered the developing commerce between the two nations, and weakened detente.

OPENING CHINA

Nixon's most dramatic foreign policy achievement was the famed opening to China. Since the Chinese revolution in 1949, U. S. officials had insisted that Jiang Jieshi's regime on Taiwan was the legitimate government of China and had refused to recognize the government in Beijing. For over twenty years, the United States and China had had no commercial, diplomatic, or cultural relations, and the United States had prevented China from joining the United Nations. Americans were forbidden to travel to China. The United States also maintained a trade boycott and loan ban against China, and it attempted to prevent other nations from trading with the Chinese. When Nixon took office in 1969, China was emerging from years of upheaval caused by Mao Zedong's "Cultural Revolution." Chinese leaders, worried about threats to China's security posed by conflicts with the Soviets, sought contacts in the West. Mao was hopeful that friendly relations could be developed with the United States, a country he had long admired.

Beijing sent friendly signals to Western nations. Nixon, sensing possibilities for rapprochement with the People's Republic, responded positively. Trade and travel restrictions between the two countries were eased. In April 1971, the Chinese invited an American table tennis team to visit China to play against Chinese athletes. This "ping pong gambit" preceded the major breakthrough that came in July when Henry Kissinger secretly visited China. Nixon then stunned the American people when he announced on July 15 that Kissinger had made arrangements for him to visit China in early 1972.

Nixon sought improved relations with China for many reasons. Most of America's European allies had long since normalized relations with China, and he knew that the U.S. policy of nonrecognition no longer worked. Nixon also knew pressures were mounting within the United Nations to evict Taiwan and seat China in its stead. Further, Nixon expected to use friendly relations with China as a diplomatic weapon against the Soviets; he wanted to be able to play the

Figure 10.1   President Nixon's most significant diplomatic achievement was the opening to China, achieved when he journeyed to that great country in 1972. Here he meets Mao Zedong at his apartment. *Source:* National Archives.

"China card" to incline the Soviets to conclude arms control and other agreements with the Americans. Improved relations with China also were part of Nixon's and Kissinger's strategy for removing the United States from its Vietnam entanglement. They hoped that Chinese leaders would be helpful in persuading Hanoi to negotiate a settlement of the war that Washington could accept. Normal relations with China would also help the United States reassert its power in Southeast Asia and develop a wider network of interests in that important region. Nixon knew that his impeccable anti-Communist credentials protected him from right-wing attacks about his being soft on Communism. He also knew that media coverage of the China trip would boost his political stock at home during an election year.

The announcement that Nixon was going to China was greeted with tremendous enthusiasm by nearly all Americans, regardless of their political leanings. Many Democratic political leaders put aside their usual criticisms of Nixon's and Kissinger's diplomacy to praise both men effusively. Kissinger returned to China in November 1971 to finalize the arrangements. While he was in Beijing, the United Nations expelled Taiwan and awarded its seat on the Security Council to China. Some critical voices, mostly on the Republican Right, were raised in protest over Washington's quick abandonment of its longtime ally.

President Nixon arrived in China on February 22, 1972, accompanied by advisers and an army of journalists. Back in America, millions of fascinated viewers watched spectacular live television coverage of Nixon's arrival at the Beijing airport, his journey into the Forbidden City, and many other highlights of his five-day visit. Nixon's party were the first Americans to go to

China officially in over twenty years. The video images beamed back to America through a communications satellite were the first live U.S. television coverage ever shot in China. Nixon met with Premier Jou En-lai several times for hours of discussion. Nixon and Kissinger also had a lengthy meeting with Mao Zedong. The U.S. delegation was the guest of honor at a lavish banquet hosted by the Chinese leaders inside of the Great Hall of the People.

At the conclusion of the historic visit, Nixon and Jou En-lai issued a joint statement, the Shanghai Communique, which defined the terms of the new U.S.–Chinese relationship. Each country agreed to open a legation in the other's capital. America removed its restrictions on trade and travel to China, and it acknowledged that Taiwan was part of China. Both sides attacked the Soviet Union.

There was no agreement on the Vietnam War. Both China and the United States reaffirmed support for their respective sides in that ongoing war. But the joint communique itself, the fact that it was being promulgated jointly by former adversaries, signaled that the United States was moving beyond the Vietnam war toward a larger role in Southeast Asia. U.S.–Chinese relations would go forward regardless of the Indochina War. Within a year of Nixon's visit, American travelers flocked to China. Trade between the two nations increased dramatically. Both countries exchanged diplomatic missions. The China opening was the high point of Nixon's presidency and the most significant diplomatic achievement of any modern American president.

A WAR TO END A WAR

The most urgent problem confronting Nixon was extricating the United States from Vietnam. He tried new approaches to end the war, including implementing the plan announced during his presidential campaign. But his policies suffered from the same flaw as Johnson's. Nixon still sought to achieve an independent non-Communist South Vietnamese state, which the North Vietnamese refused to accept; thus the war went on.

Even though Hanoi had consistently rejected any settlement that would leave a non-Communist government in the South, Nixon and Kissinger believed that they could compel Hanoi to accept one. They planned to use the improved relationship between the United States and the USSR by linking increased trade and arms agreements with the Soviets to their willingness to pressure Hanoi into accepting U.S. terms in Vietnam. Nixon also escalated the war by removing the limits Johnson had placed on the use of military force in Southeast Asia. In the spring of 1969, Nixon ordered a bombing campaign to begin against VietCong and North Vietnamese sanctuaries in Cambodia. Because Cambodia was a neutral nation, the bombing was illegal. It was kept secret from Congress and from the American people. In addition, Nixon, through Soviet intermediaries, offered the North Vietnamese more realistic peace terms. He proposed withdrawing both U.S. and North Vietnamese troops from the South and reinstituting the demilitarized zone as the boundary between North and South Vietnam. At the same time, to please American public opinion that had turned against the war, Nixon announced a phased withdrawal of U.S. combat troops from Vietnam.

But Hanoi was neither intimidated by threats nor lured by concessions into changing its terms. The Paris talks remained deadlocked. Hanoi continued to demand the unilateral withdrawal of all U.S. forces from South Vietnam and the installation of a coalition government in the South, excluding General Thieu. Nor did the Soviets cooperate. The linkage strategy proved to be a failure in 1969.

Nixon faced a dilemma; unable to extract the slightest concession from Hanoi, he had to choose between a major escalation of the war or a humiliating withdrawal. Unwilling to make concessions and unable to use greater force because he did not want to arouse domestic opponents of the war and because of doubts about its effectiveness, Nixon offered what Secretary of Defense Melvin Laird called "Vietnamization." The United States would continue gradually to withdraw its troops while building up South Vietnamese forces. The South Vietnamese forces would become strong enough to prevent a Communist takeover following the U.S. pullout. At the time Nixon announced his Vietnamization plan, it had already been in place for a year. He had inherited it from Johnson and given it a new label. While U.S. forces battled the North Vietnamese and the VietCong, U.S. advisers built up the South Vietnamese armed forces. Pacification and rural development programs accelerated. In March 1970, President Nixon announced that 150,000 U.S. combat troops would be withdrawn that year.

In neighboring Cambodia, neutralist leader Prince Sihanouk was suddenly overthrown by his pro-American Prime Minister, Lon Nol. Nixon, fearing that the North Vietnamese might take over Cambodia following the coup, and responding to a U.S. Army request to attack North Vietnamese sanctuaries in that country, ordered U.S. troops into an area of Cambodia about fifty miles northwest of Saigon. The Cambodian incursion produced mixed results. It relieved pressure on Saigon and bought more time for Vietnamization. It also widened the war and provoked Hanoi into a full-scale support of Cambodian insurgents fighting Lon Nol's forces. The United States now had two fragile client states in Southeast Asia to defend against insurgents backed by North Vietnam and China. The Vietnam War had been widened; it had become an Indochina war. The Cambodian campaign proved to be the last major campaign of the Indochina War involving U.S. ground combat forces.

Nixon did not anticipate the furious domestic reaction to the Cambodian invasion. College campuses across the land exploded at the news of an unexpected widening of a war that he had promised to phase out. At Kent State University, tragedy occurred when Ohio National Guardsmen opened fire into a crowd of student protesters, killing four of them and wounding nine others. Following these shootings, hundreds of student strikes forced many colleges to shut down. More than 100,000 demonstrators gathered in Washington to protest the Cambodian invasion and the "Kent State Massacre." The Cambodian initiative also caused the most serious congressional challenge to presidential authority to conduct the war. The Senate repealed the Gulf of Tonkin resolution and voted to cut off all funds for Cambodia. But the fund cutoff failed to clear the House. Both the North Vietnamese and the VietCong broke off negotiations, confident that political pressure would eventually force U.S. withdrawal from both Cambodia and South Vietnam.

To appease Dovish critics at home, the president accelerated the timetable for troop withdrawals in 1971. He expanded the air war by ordering more bombing missions into Cambodia and along the Laotian panhandle. He also authorized an ARVN raid into Laos to disrupt enemy supply routes and staging areas, but the raid failed to achieve most of its objectives. Within the United States, Doves attacked another widening of the Indochina War.

During the spring and summer of 1971, two events at home shocked the war-weary nation. On March 29, a military court convicted Lieutenant William Calley of multiple murders and sentenced him to life imprisonment for ordering his infantry platoon to kill hundreds of

Figure 10.2   Tragedy struck Kent State University on May 4, 1970. Troops of the Ohio National Guard fired into a crowd of student protesters, killing four. This photo shows a young woman reacting to the death of one of the students.   *Source:* CORBIS.

Vietnamese civilians at a hamlet called My Lai. Calley's men had been brought in to destroy the hamlet suspected of harboring VietCong. But instead of evacuating the population beforehand or eliminating the village with long-range artillery and bombs, Calley's men had massacred the villagers at close range with pistol, machine gun, and automatic rifle fire.

Calley claimed that he only followed orders. U.S. Army attorneys insisted that Calley had misunderstood his orders. No one else was convicted of war crimes. Many Americans felt sympathy for Calley and his men; a public opinion poll showed that a majority of Americans blamed the media for reporting the incident, which had exposed the Army's efforts to cover up the affair. Responding to the angry outcry over Calley's conviction, President Nixon reduced Calley's sentence. Some Americans wondered how many other My Lai-type massacres had gone undetected. Others found cold comfort in the fact that VietCong and South Vietnamese army forces had murdered thousands of civilians. There also was the troubling inconsistency of convicting one young junior officer for mass murder in a war where long-range artillery fire and aerial bombing had killed thousands of villagers since the Americanization of the war in 1965.

No sooner had the uproar over Calley's conviction subsided than the *New York Times* began publishing excerpts from the *Pentagon Papers*, secret government documents pertaining to the Vietnam War stolen from files of the RAND Corporation by a former employee, Daniel Ellsberg. The papers revealed that U.S. leaders had deliberately escalated the war, had ignored peace offers, and had often lied to the public about their actions. These revelations further undermined the credibility of government officials and weakened support for the war.

An increasingly frustrated president fought back against the mounting opposition to his war policy. He ordered that wiretaps be placed on National Security Council staffers and journalists suspected of leaking secret information to the media. He ordered illegal surveillance of antiwar groups by both the FBI and the CIA. He accused congressional Doves of encouraging the enemy and prolonging the war. Administration lawyers tried to prevent the *New York Times* from publishing the *Pentagon Papers* by securing a court injunction against their publication on the grounds that their release compromised national security. An appellate judge quashed the injunction and the Supreme Court sustained his ruling. Blocked by the U.S. Supreme Court, the president approved the creation of a special White House undercover unit, the "Plumbers," to prevent leaks from within the government and to discredit Ellsberg. Under extreme pressure, Nixon had developed a siege mentality, feeling beset by enemies in Congress, the media, the bureaucracies, and the streets, all of whom, he believed, were working to undermine his authority to govern. These paranoid attitudes, which drove him to order his men to commit illegal acts, were one of the prime causes of the Watergate scandals.

By the summer of 1971, polls showed that public support for Nixon's war policies had dropped to 31 percent. Another survey revealed that two-thirds of Americans approved of the withdrawal of all American troops from Vietnam by the end of the year, even if that meant a Communist takeover in the South. Twice the Senate passed resolutions setting a deadline for withdrawal of all troops as soon as North Vietnam released U.S. prisoners of war. Nixon responded to those signs of war-weariness by making new, secret peace proposals to Hanoi: In exchange for the release of American prisoners, the United States would withdraw all of its troops within six months and would no longer insist that Hanoi withdraw its troops. These new U.S. concessions started the first serious negotiations since talks had begun in 1968, but deadlock continued because Washington insisted that Thieu remain in power in the South, whereas Hanoi insisted that his removal was a precondition of any settlement.

The war entered its final phase in 1972. Knowing that there were only 6,000 U.S. combat troops remaining in the South, North Vietnam launched its largest offensive of the war. 120,000 North Vietnamese regulars struck directly at ARVN forces across several fronts. Simultaneously, VietCong guerrillas resumed their attacks in rural areas to disrupt pacification efforts. The U.S. retaliated with massive B-52 bombing raids against targets in the Hanoi-Haiphong area. Tactical bombers pounded the North Vietnamese invaders and their supply lines. The North Vietnamese and VietCong continued to press their attacks. Nixon then carried out his boldest escalation of the war. He ordered a naval blockade of North Vietnam and the mining of Haiphong Harbor; he also escalated the bombing campaigns. In addition to his military responses, Nixon also approached the Soviets again about persuading Hanoi to accept a diplomatic settlement of the war.

Nixon's decisive response to the North Vietnamese assault received strong support at home. The bombing and blockade sufficiently disrupted North Vietnamese supply lines to enable the hard-pressed ARVN forces to stabilize their lines around Hue and Saigon. The North Vietnamese offensive had stalled by summer. South Vietnam managed to survive the assaults because of the strong response by the United States. Both the Soviets and the Chinese, while loudly condemning the U.S. response publicly, privately exerted pressure on Hanoi to end its war with the United States. Detente with the two Communist powers at last bore fruit and helped Nixon bring the U.S. war in Southeast Asia to an end.

With the onset of the summer rains in 1972, the war stalemated once more. The North Vietnamese had expected its spring offensive, combined with the approaching U.S. election, to force Nixon to accept their terms and remove Thieu. But the president's powerful response had neutralized their assault and inflicted heavy losses. Soviet and Chinese pressures on Hanoi pushed the North Vietnamese toward a diplomatic settlement. George McGovern, the Democratic challenger for the presidency in 1972, proved to be an ineffectual candidate who posed no threat to Nixon. A combination of military losses, economic strains, and diplomatic isolation forced Hanoi to seek a settlement with the United States, as long as it did not conflict with their long-range goal of achieving a unified Vietnam under Communist control.

Secret negotiations resumed in Paris. Hanoi dropped its demand that Thieu must go before any settlement could be reached. By October 11, 1972, Kissinger and the North Vietnamese emissary, Le Duc Tho had forged an agreement: within sixty days, after a cease-fire, America would remove all of its remaining troops, and North Vietnam would release the U.S. POWs. The Thieu government would remain in power, pending a political settlement in the South. North Vietnamese troops would remain in the South, and the National Liberation Front, now known as the People's Revolutionary Government (PRG), would be accorded political status in southern Vietnam.

But General Thieu refused to accept the agreement. Nixon supported Thieu. The North Vietnamese, believing themselves betrayed, angrily broke off negotiations. The October agreement was placed on hold and the war went on. Nixon, reelected by a landslide, tried to secure peace terms that were more favorable to the South Vietnamese government. He ordered air attacks on North Vietnamese targets in the vicinity of Hanoi and Haiphong. There ensued the most powerful attack in the history of aerial warfare. This "Christmas bombing" lasted from December 18 to 29. Nixon was determined to pound Hanoi into resuming negotiations. At the same time he turned the U.S. Air Force loose on the North, Nixon significantly increased U.S. aid to South Vietnam and told Thieu to accept U.S. peace terms or the United States would settle without him.

The Christmas bombing provoked worldwide criticism and a storm of protest at home. Congress moved to cut off all funding for the war. With time running out on his options, Nixon told the North Vietnamese that if they agreed to resume negotiations, he would halt the bombing. The battered North Vietnamese accepted his offer, and the talks resumed. Kissinger and Tho reached an agreement signed by all parties on January 27. The January agreement was similar in all major provisions to the suspended agreement of October 11. This time Nixon imposed the agreement on Thieu, who signed reluctantly. In order to make the treaty more palatable to Thieu, Nixon pledged in writing that the United States "would respond in full force" if North Vietnam violated the agreement.

Although Nixon insisted that the peace agreement had brought "peace with honor" to Indochina, the January accords represented a disguised defeat for the United States, which permitted the Americans to extricate themselves from a war that they no longer believed in and to retrieve their POWs. It also permitted North Vietnamese forces to remain in the South, and it granted the PRG political legitimacy. It allowed the Thieu regime to survive in the South for a time. The major question over which the war had been fought for nearly a decade, who would govern in the South, was deferred, to be resolved by political means in the future. But the political provisions of the treaty proved unworkable in practice, so that question would finally be settled by force of arms in two years during the presidency of Gerald R. Ford.

THE MIDDLE EASTERN DILEMMA

As they maneuvered to realign U.S. relations with the major Communist powers and sought to extract the United States from the stalemated Indochina War, Nixon and Kissinger had to cope with another crisis in the Middle East. Since the 1967 Six Day War, a state of simmering hostility between Arabs and the Jewish state had prevailed; no progress toward resolving their serious differences had been made. Israel refused to surrender any of the Arab territories that it had seized during the Six Day War—East Jerusalem, the West Bank, the Golan Heights, and the Sinai. The Arabs, for their part, adamantly refused even to meet with Israeli representatives or to accord the Jewish state the right to exist. Sporadic border skirmishes between Israeli and Egyptian troops occurred in 1969 and 1970. It was a war of nerves between two bitter enemies. In the fall of 1970, Gamal Abdul Nasser, the Arab Nationalist leader, suddenly died, to be replaced by his key assistant Anwar Sadat. Sadat, in time, found the tense state of relations between his country and Israel intolerable; he plotted with his ally Syria to stage another attack on Israel. The ground was prepared for another bloody Middle Eastern war.

On October 6, 1973, the fourth Arab–Israeli war began. Choosing Yom Kippur, the holiest day of the year for Jews, the Egyptians and Syrians launched surprise attacks on Israeli positions in the Sinai and along the Golan Heights. Egyptian forces captured hundreds of Israeli soldiers. To the north, Syrian forces regained territory in the Golan Heights region and threatened to slice Israel in two. Caught off guard by the surprise Arab attacks, Israeli Prime Minister Golda Meir appealed to Washington to send the Israelis more planes, tanks, and ammunition. The United States responded promptly with an airlift of war materiel to their beleaguered ally.

Washington's decision to resupply the Israelis had unanticipated economic consequences for the American people, because it provoked Saudi Arabia to impose an oil embargo against the United States as reprisal for its support of Israel. The oil embargo, although it proved to be of brief duration, destabilized world oil markets. It also created the first of a series of "energy crises" in the United States, an energy crunch that had devastating impacts and far-reaching consequences. Unemployment rose, as did the rate of inflation. The stock market dropped sharply and the U.S. economy went into a steep recession. "Stagflation," a condition of high unemployment, stagnant economic growth, and a high rate of inflation, worsened.

Amply resupplied by their American patrons, Israeli armor counterattacked in force both in the Sinai and Golan Heights regions. They drove the Syrians from the Golan Heights and chased them back towards Damascus, the Syrian capital. In the Sinai, Israeli tanks halted the Egyptian offensive and drove them back toward the Suez Canal. A frightened Sadat now turned to his ally, the Soviet Union, for help, a move that alarmed Washington because it appeared to threaten detente. On October 20, Nixon dispatched Kissinger, now Secretary of State as well as

National Security Adviser, to Moscow to meet with Brezhnev. The U.S. envoy told the Soviet leader not to send forces to the Middle East. Kissinger also rejected a Soviet proposal that the United States and the Soviet Union jointly impose a cease-fire. Meanwhile, Israeli armor crossed the Suez, enveloped large numbers of Egyptian troops, and placed troops on Egyptian soil. Egypt's situation was growing desperate, and the Soviets were growing more nervous as Sadat's situation deteriorated.

The anxious Soviets warned the Israelis not to continue their war or else risk Soviet military reprisals. On October 25, Nixon responded to the Soviet threat to Israel by ordering U.S. forces around the world to go on full military alert. The next day, the President announced that intelligence sources had evidence that the Soviets were preparing to airlift combat forces to the Middle East. The worst crisis in U.S.–Soviet relations since the Cuban Missile Crisis was at hand. Another eyeball-to-eyeball confrontation between the two superpowers appeared a distinct possibility.

But the crisis passed quickly. The Soviets, if they had ever intended to send troops, quickly made it clear that they would not. A United Nations peacekeeping force that excluded both U.S. and Soviet troops was dispatched to the region. Kissinger, shuttling back and forth between Cairo and Jerusalem, persuaded the Egyptians and Israelis to accept a cease-fire that left the Israelis in control of more territory than when the Yom Kippur War had begun, but it permitted the Sadat regime to survive.

The cease-fire was the first of a series of Middle Eastern agreements facilitated by Kissinger's "shuttle diplomacy." Subsequently, the Suez Canal was reopened, and the Arabs lifted their oil embargo. Egypt and Syria resumed diplomatic relations with the United States. In June 1974, not long before he was forced to resign the presidency, President Nixon traveled to the Middle East. He went both to Cairo, where he was cheered by huge throngs, and to Jerusalem, where he received a more restrained reception by the Israelis, who were still recovering from the effects of the Yom Kippur War. That junket to the Middle East was President Nixon's last hurrah as world leader and peacemaker.

Paralleling their fervid diplomacy vis-à-vis the seemingly intractable Arab–Israeli conflict, Nixon and Kissinger sought to strengthen U.S. relations with Iran. Washington wanted to involve Iran in U.S. efforts to contain Soviet expansionism into the Middle East. More important, Nixon and Kissinger intended to use Iran as a stabilizing force within that turbulent region to enable the United States to distance itself from the chronic Arab–Israeli disputes. Washington tapped Iran, led by the Shah, whom the CIA had helped reclaim his throne in 1953, to become the major U.S. ally in the Persian Gulf region.

The United States began importing more oil from Iran, and in May 1972, in effect, it gave Iran a blank check to buy conventional weaponry from U.S. arms manufacturers. Iran quickly became the preeminent military power in the region and the leading purchaser of U.S. arms. With help from Washington, relations improved between Saudi Arabia and Iran, who historically had been rivals. The rapprochement between the Saudis and Iranians strengthened the Organization of Oil Exporting Countries (OPEC), an emerging consortium of leading oil exporters that challenged the power of the Western oil companies, which had hitherto controlled the world's oil markets. Washington's opening to Iran had sacrificed the interests of the major oil companies to the larger goals of Nixon's and Kissinger's Middle East diplomacy. These goals included

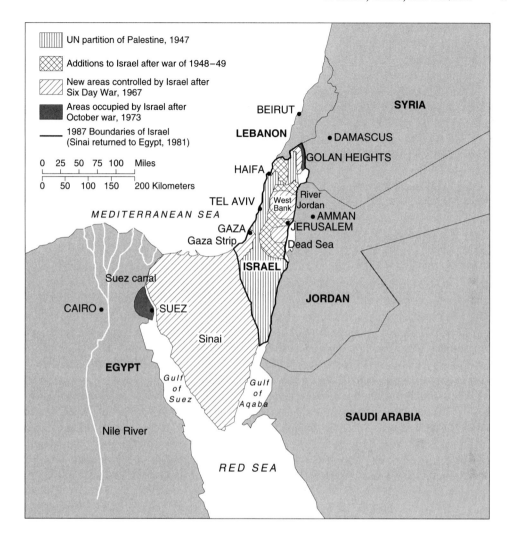

UN partition of Palestine, 1947

Additions to Israel after war of 1948–49

New areas controlled by Israel after
Six Day War, 1967

Areas occupied by Israel after
October war, 1973

1987 Boundaries of Israel
(Sinai returned to Egypt, 1981)

0   25 50 75 100   Miles

0   50 100 150   200 Kilometers

SYRIA

BEIRUT

LEBANON

•DAMASCUS

GOLAN HEIGHTS

HAIFA

MEDITERRANEAN SEA

TEL AVIV

West
Bank

River
Jordan

•AMMAN

GAZA

JERUSALEM

Gaza Strip

Dead Sea

ISRAEL

Suez canal

JORDAN

CAIRO •

SUEZ

Sinai

EGYPT

Gulf
of
Suez

Gulf
of
Aqaba

SAUDI ARABIA

Nile River

RED SEA

Figure 10.3   The Middle East, 1947–1981.   *Source:* U.S. State Department.

keeping the Soviets out, stabilizing the region, ensuring Israel's security, maintaining good relations with moderate Arab regimes, and neutralizing the effects of (if not eliminating) the zero-sum game known as the Arab–Israeli conflict. Nixon's and Kissinger's grand design for the Middle East would come a cropper in 1978, when the Shah of Iran was overthrown by anti-Western Islamic fundamentalists.

Further to the east, the United States became embroiled in a regional dispute between India and Pakistan. The cause of the conflict was Pakistani efforts to suppress a Nationalist rebellion in its East Bengal territory. India intervened in the civil war on behalf of the Bengali rebels. Nixon and Kissinger decided to support Pakistan to prevent the Indians from going to war against the Pakistanis. The Soviets backed the Indians and the rebels; the Chinese, fearful of a Soviet–Indian alliance, supported the Pakistanis, making the Americans and the Chinese, in effect, allies. The United States suffered a diplomatic setback when the Bengalis, assisted by the Indians and Soviets, won their independence from Pakistan and became the new state of Bangladesh. The Soviets gained enhanced prestige and influence in the region, strengthening their ties with the Indians and the new country of Bangladesh.

CHAOS IN CHILE

Nixon's and Kissinger's foreign policy focused on the nations of the northern tier; they were relatively unconcerned about the affairs of most Pacific island, African, and Latin American countries located in the Southern Hemisphere of the planet. One significant exception to this general pattern of neglect of much of the Third World was Chile. In 1970, Chile's national congress elected a Marxist, Salvador Allende Gossens, as Chile's president, even though he had received only a third of the popular vote.

Upon his election to office, Allende quickly moved to nationalize U.S.-owned enterprises in Chile, including two copper mining companies and telephone companies. He also established friendly relations with China, the Soviet Union, and Cuba. Under Allende's leadership, Chile was traveling the road to socialism. In response to Allende's socialist agenda, Washington declared economic war on Chile. U.S. banks no longer loaned Chile money. Washington also prevented international agencies such as the International Monetary Fund and the World Bank from providing Chile with financial assistance. All military assistance programs to Chile's armed forces were suspended. The AFL-CIO also played a key role in the U.S. campaign to destabilize Chile. The American Institute for Free Labor channeled millions of dollars to right-wing unions and political parties opposing Allende's socialist agenda. According to a 1975 report, issued by a Senate committee that investigated CIA activities in Chile during the early 1970s, CIA agents worked to destabilize Chilean politics and plotted to overthrow Allende. They bankrolled the opposition press and the main opposition party, the Christian Democrats. They also supported a teamsters strike that paralyzed the nation's economy and deprived the urban populations of food.

By the summer of 1973, the Chilean economy was in ruins and the newly impoverished middle classes were in revolt. With the CIA's support, on September 11, 1973, a junta of disgruntled army officers, led by General Augusto Pinochet, overthrew Allende, who was killed or who committed suicide during the coup d'etat. Pinochet instituted a reign of terror that resulted in the deaths of hundreds of Allende supporters, the torture and imprisonment of thousands more, and the forced exile of additional thousands. Soon after taking power, Pinochet restored the U.S. properties to their former owners. The United States quickly lifted all restrictions on economic and military assistance to Chile. Pinochet established a military dictatorship and ruled Chile for the next sixteen years. The CIA did not overthrow the Allende regime, perhaps his government would have been overthrown without U.S. involvement; but the hostile actions of the Nixon administration helped to create the economic and political conditions within Chile that provoked the coup.

TROUBLES IN EUROPE

When Nixon came to the presidency, a number of political, strategic, and economic factors were creating serious strains between the United States and the three major powers of Western Europe—Great Britain, France, and West Germany. All three nations were asserting greater autonomy from the United States. Both Nixon and Kissinger perceived the danger in this West European trend to their carefully crafted strategy of detente with the Soviet Union. Detente could never realize its full potential unless the NATO nations as well as the Eastern bloc nations remained subservient to their respective superpower patrons.

In response to the growing assertiveness of the Western European nations, Washington sought a new relation with its major allies, one that superseded the costly commitments assumed early in the Cold War to provide for Western Europe's defense and its economic reconstruction. At the same time, they hoped to hold the evolving new relationship somewhat short of full autonomy for Great Britain, France, and West Germany. Washington wanted the new relationship to be characterized by limited autonomy within the Atlantic community, which was still firmly tied to the United States. It hoped to find ways to use Western Europe's new power and wealth globally but at the same time to keep the major Western nations from asserting their independence from American world leadership. But Washington failed to achieve most of its goals in Western Europe during Nixon's tenure. It was perhaps Nixon's and Kissinger's gravest diplomatic failure. NATO retained its traditional structure, organization, and strategic goals, but West Germany, France, and Great Britain continued to draw away from the United States.

By 1970, West Germany was beginning to reassert its traditional national identity. The nation lay at the economic heart of a prospering Western Europe. In 1969, Social Democrat Willy Brandt became Chancellor, the leader of a coalition of the Social Democratic Party (SDP) and the Free Democratic Party (FDP), a liberal party committed to policies promoting the interests of big business and free enterprise. Quickly Brandt implemented his *Ostpolitik,* the most serious challenge to U.S. hegemony in Western Europe since the end of World War II. At its core, *Ostpolitik* was an economic strategy that entailed opening up the markets of Eastern Europe and the Soviet Union to West German high-tech exports. *Ostpolitik* also entailed investments, loans, and joint ventures with East bloc nations and the Soviets and served as a kind of West German detente with the Soviets, breaking through the barriers of traditional anti-Communism that had dominated West German foreign policy for twenty years. Finally, *Ostpolitik* represented an assertion of Germany's sovereignty that ran counter to Washington's goals for the nations of Western Europe.

The British and French also began a series of collaborations that ran counter to U.S. expectations and interests. First, the French, under the leadership of Georges Pompidou, dropped their long-standing opposition to British membership in the European Economic Community (EEC), also known as the Common Market. The French apparently were alarmed by the growing economic power of the Germans and sought closer ties with the British to offset it. The

British, for their part, now appeared ready to join the EEC. Reduced tariffs would enable them to sell their exports on the lucrative continental market, and a recent devaluation of the pound sterling made their goods more competitive. After a bruising debate in the House of Commons in September 1971, the British Parliament voted by a large majority to join the EEC.

The British and French also began a series of military and technological collaborations. The most spectacular achievement of the new Anglo-French togetherness was to form a consortium to construct a new supersonic airplane capable of flying across the Atlantic Ocean at twice the speed of sound. It was designed to compete with a planned American supersonic aircraft called the Supersonic Transport (SST). The new French–British plane, called the Concorde, had British engines and a French air frame. It flew its maiden transatlantic flight in 1976. Meanwhile, the Democratic-controlled Congress had killed the SST project, despite intense pressure from the Nixon White House to go ahead with it, because congressional leaders viewed it as too expensive and too noisy. The United States has never built a supersonic civilian airliner.

THE EMERGENCE OF JAPAN

By the early 1970s, Japan was the most important nation in the American Far Eastern economic and strategic system. It also was increasingly a major player in the growing world economy of the 1970s. Yet, from Washington's perspective, Japan posed some serious problems. Like the prosperous nations of Western Europe, Japan exhibited some of the same tendencies to take a foreign policy tack more independent of Washington. The Japanese also contributed a minuscule fraction of their gross domestic product to their own national defense. They happily continued to rely on the American nuclear umbrella for their strategic security. Washington had been annoyed that the Japanese had not supported the U.S. effort in Vietnam with any enthusiasm, even though one of the reasons the United States had intervened in the Indochina War was to protect Japanese economic and strategic interests in that region. The Japanese in turn were annoyed at the United States for Nixon's peaceful overtures to China. Further, the Japanese, with their rebuilt modern economy, were increasingly selling cars, television sets, and cameras in American markets during the early 1970s, hurting U.S. domestic industries in these crucial high-tech fields.

Nixon and Kissinger hoped to rein in the high-flying Japanese and make them pay more of the costs of their own defense. Washington also wanted to slow the penetration of American markets by Japanese exporters. In 1971, Nixon erected a 10 percent surcharge on all imports from Japan, which was aimed primarily at Japanese automakers. In addition, the OPEC oil embargo engineered during the fall of 1973 by the Saudis badly hurt the Japanese economy, because it was 100 percent dependent on imported oil.

DIPLOMACY IN PERSPECTIVE

Nixon and Kissinger's diplomacy was a complex mix of policies that had many successes and also knew many failures. During the years that Nixon and Kissinger worked together to forge and implement American foreign policy, journalists and other analysts tended to write favorably about Kissinger's diplomatic performances. Kisssinger was skilled at cultivating the media and often appeared on talk shows. He sometimes implied that he had provided most of the ideas that composed the grand design of American foreign policy; his concepts seemed to determine its structure and shape. Foreign policy analysts often assumed that this was so. Such views were unwarranted and unfounded. Nixon conceived America's foreign policy during his presidency. He was a shrewd and experienced statesman, in charge conceptually as well as officially. It was Nixon's grand design that unfolded during his presidency. Kissinger was, in the last analysis, sophisticated hired help and an errand boy. Capable, intelligent, learned, and shrewd—Kissinger was adviser, envoy, and confidante to the president. Together they forged and implemented the most successful U.S. foreign policy since Harry Truman had initiated the policies that contained Soviet expansionism in Europe during the formative years of the Cold War.

Nixon's greatest success came with changing U.S. relations with the major Communist powers, the Soviet Union and the People's Republic of China. Nixon and Kissinger were less successful in Indochina. It took considerably longer than they had expected to phase out the U.S. Indochina War. The 1973 Paris Accords that they managed to arrange after four years of effort failed to save South Vietnam from a Communist takeover two years later. But in the aftermath of the failed Vietnam enterprise, America made important gains in its East Asian and Southeast Asian relations. Outside of Indochina, no more dominoes fell to Communist "wars of national liberation." Since 1975, most of the nations of Southeast and East Asia, such as Thailand, Malaysia, and South Korea, have become more stable, strong, and prosperous, enjoying friendly ties and strong commercial relations with the United States.

The foreign policy analyst Franz Schurman has written about the development of a world economic system during the 1970s, by which he meant the emergence of an international economic system within which the national economies of most countries are inextricably interlinked in numerous ways. Trade has been integrated, a global monetary system has arisen, and capital markets are interdependent. Political links have likewise arisen through networks of political leaders, civil servants, and senior military officials. The appearance of a world economy suggests, among other things, that the traditional distinctions between foreign policy and domestic affairs have been breaking down. During the Nixon administration, foreign and domestic policy, especially economic policy, became inseparable. Nixon's frequent efforts to try to fix the U.S. economy involved changing U.S. foreign economic policies that were influencing trade, tariff rates, and exchange rates.

Nixon's foreign policy, by reducing the threat of war with the major Communist powers and by bringing them, at least to a limited extent, into the evolving world economic system, which is essentially a world capitalist system, ensured the further development of the world system. His grand design also ensured that the United States would continue to occupy the central place in that world system, because the prosperous Western European nations accepted America's central role, perceiving that their own future prosperity was inextricably linked to the United States. In broad historical perspective, Nixonian diplomacy is best understood as capping the end of a thirty-year era that began with Truman in 1945 rather than viewed as a guide to future U.S. foreign relations of the 1980s and 1990s.

But there were many failures in Nixonian diplomacy during the early 1970s. The Iranian revolution, in time, destroyed all of his plans for the Middle East. His neglect of the poor nations of the Southern Hemisphere in Africa and Latin America ensured political instability and mass immiserization in those important parts of the world during the 1980s. The Nixon Doctrine, which was supposed to be a post-Vietnam politico-military strategy for dealing with insurgencies in the Third World, failed to work effectively. Most of all, Nixon's grand goal, a generation of peace, proved unattainable. Much of his foreign policy demonstrated a short-term brilliance, but it lacked staying power. By the late 1970s, detente was discredited, and Jimmy Carter revived the Cold War. If one of the purposes of Nixon's foreign policy was ultimately conservative and counterrevolutionary, that is, as an effort to stem the Marxist revolutionary tide in the Third World, it also must be counted as mostly a failure. Communism did ultimately fail, but its failure did not derive from any clever diplomatic, strategic, or economic maneuvers by Nixon and Kissinger.

BRIEF BIBLIOGRAPHIC ESSAY

Most helpful in understanding Nixon's conduct of foreign policy are the relevant chapters in the second volume of Stephen E. Ambrose's magisterial three-volume biography entitled *Nixon: The Triumph of a Politician, 1962–1972*. After his forced retirement from the presidency, Mr. Nixon wrote several books about world affairs. The best of these books was his first, his memoirs, entitled *RN: The Memoirs of Richard Nixon*. This book contains extensive treatments of his foreign policies. There are several fine analyses of the Nixon administration's foreign policies, including Henry Brandon's *The Retreat of American Power*. A critical view of Nixon's and Kissinger's foreign policies can be found in Tad Szulc's *The Illusion of Peace: Foreign Policy in the Nixon Years*. See also Herbert Parmet's *The World and Richard Nixon* for a friendlier treatment of Nixon's foreign policy. Franz Schurman, in *The Foreign Politics of Richard Nixon,* offers an original analysis of the politics of Nixon's and Kissinger's diplomacy. For detente with the Soviet Union, see the relevant chapters of William G. Hyland's *Mortal Rivals: Superpower Relations from Nixon to Reagan*. The first book-length scholarly study of Nixon's Vietnam policies, Jeffrey Kimball's *Nixon's Vietnam War,* promises to become the definitive account. Arnold Isaacs's *Without Honor: Defeat in Vietnam and Cambodia,* is a scathing critique of Nixon's and Kissinger's Indochina policy. For Nixon's Middle Eastern diplomacy, see the relevant portions of Daniel Yergin's *The Prize*. Henry Kissinger, Nixon's able foreign policy adviser, has analyzed their foreign policies in two important books: *The White House Years* and *Years of Upheaval*. Seymour Hersh, in *The Price of Power: Kissinger in the Nixon White House,* has written an extremely negative critique of Kissinger's foreign policy roles.

WEB SITES

See <http://www.cnn.com/SPECIALS/cold.war/episodes/16/>. It is an excellent site with audio and video materials, historical documents, essays, study questions and guides, and much more, all pertaining to President Nixon's conduct of foreign policy focusing on his dealings with the Soviet Union and its leader, Leonid Brezhnev.

11

Era of Limits

Vietnam and Watergate ushered in a time of trouble for Americans. They experienced years of ineffective presidential leadership, partisan squabbling, continuing social divisions, severe economic dislocations, energy crises, and international disorders. All of these difficult problems were compounded by a massive loss of faith in politics and politicians, especially among young people. They feared that the American system would not be able to maintain affluence at home, and they worried about declining American influence in the world. A social malaise settled over the land. Americans experienced a crisis of confidence, fearful that their leaders and institutions could not find solutions to their many, complex, and often interrelated problems. Many lost faith in themselves, in their institutions, and in the future.

A FORD, NOT A LINCOLN

The new president was as different as possible from the driven, tormented man he succeeded. Gerald Ford was friendly, warm, and outgoing. A nation that was weary of war and political scandal appreciated his personal charm, modesty, and integrity as he reminded his fellow citizens that, "I am a Ford, not a Lincoln." Ford had represented Michigan's Fifth District for thirteen consecutive terms, until he was appointed vice president in 1973. He had risen through the ranks of the seniority system to become House Minority Leader in 1965. As president, Ford retained many of Nixon's advisers and vowed to continue his policies.

Sensing the malaise of the nation in the wake of war and Watergate, Ford made "binding up the nation's wounds" and restoring national confidence his top priorities. But a month after he took office, Ford granted former President Nixon a "full, free, and absolute" pardon for any crimes he may have committed while in office. Ford apparently had a mix of reasons for granting the pardon. The most important were to refocus the nation's attention on the urgent problems of the day—the faltering U.S. economy and the ongoing Cold War with the Soviet Union. He also wished to spare the nation the divisive spectacle of putting a former president on trial. He insisted that there was no advance understanding between himself and Nixon.

Whatever his intent, Ford's decision to pardon Nixon backfired, ruining his chances for receiving bipartisan support for his policies from the Democratic-controlled Congress. Despite his denials, many Americans suspected that Ford and Nixon had made a deal—Nixon had chosen Ford to replace Agnew, with the understanding that if Nixon resigned or was removed from office, Ford would pardon him. Furthermore, it was patently unfair to send underlings to jail for their parts in Watergate while the leader whose directives they followed went free. Most Americans believed that if Nixon had broken the law, he should have to face trial like any other citizen. Ford's pardon of Nixon perpetuated the suspicions and resentments of Watergate that the new leader was trying to dispel, tied his presidency to that of his despised predecessor's, hurt his party in the 1974 elections, and may have cost him the 1976 presidential election.

Ford generated further controversy when he established an amnesty program for the thousands of young men who had violated draft laws or deserted from the military during the Vietnam era. According to its terms, if they agreed to perform public service for one to two years, their prison terms were waived or reduced. Hawks condemned the plan as being too lenient; Doves denounced it as punitive. Another of Ford's efforts to bind up national wounds had had the opposite effect of reopening them.

The 1974 midterm elections took place amidst an atmosphere of continuing political controversy and public mistrust, much of which had been inadvertently perpetuated by Ford's own actions. The Democrats gained forty-three seats in the House and four seats in the Senate, increasing their margins to 291 to 144 in the House and to 61 to 38 in the Senate. More voters than ever before called themselves "Independents," and only 38 percent of those eligible to vote went to the polls.

Shortly after the midterm elections had taken place, a Senate committee investigating CIA operations discovered that over the years it had been involved in numerous assassinations or attempted murders of foreign leaders, including Fidel Castro. A commission headed by Vice President Nelson Rockefeller found that the CIA had routinely kept citizens under surveillance and had conducted drug experiments on unwitting victims. The CIA also had engaged in illegal domestic espionage and compiled files on dissenters. Other investigations revealed that the FBI also had engaged in a variety of lawless actions, including wiretapping, spying, burglary, blackmail, and sabotage. Former FBI director J. Edgar Hoover had conducted a personal vendetta against civil rights leader Martin Luther King Jr. FBI agents spied on King and his associates, read his mail, tapped his phones, bugged his hotel rooms, and blackmailed him.

These discoveries of official lawlessness, most occurring during Nixon's presidency, confirmed that the CIA and the FBI, in their obsessive pursuit of internal security, had repeatedly violated the constitutional rights of numerous American citizens. In response, President Ford issued new directives providing for greater congressional oversight of CIA activities and restricting its covert operations. The Justice Department issued new guidelines for the FBI. Ford also helped restore credibility to the CIA by appointing a new director in late 1975, George H. W. Bush.

ECONOMIC AND ENERGY WOES

While Americans learned more about official wrongdoing in Washington, their economy deteriorated. The inflation rate soared beyond 10 percent in 1974, spurred by wage hikes, increased consumer demand, budget deficits, and competition from the surging Japanese and western

European economies. The Ford administration attacked inflation by slowing down the economy with tight money policies. Tight money brought the worst downturn since the Great Depression of the 1930s. Some traditional U.S. mass-production industries with inefficient methods of production and high payroll costs struggled to compete with manufacturers in Europe and the Pacific Rim. U.S. multinational corporations relocated their manufacturing facilities overseas to take advantage of lower costs, tax breaks, and cheap labor. U.S. auto makers lost a sizable portion of their domestic market to Japanese and German imports. Unemployment climbed to 7 percent by year's end and reached 9 percent in 1975, the highest since before World War II.

In October 1973, an alarming new factor disrupted American economic life—the energy crisis. It appeared suddenly when OPEC embargoed oil shipments to the United States. The oil cutoff was initiated by Saudi Arabia and other Arab members of OPEC to protest U.S. support of Israel in its recent war with Egypt and Syria and to force a settlement of the war favoring the Arabs. Americans experienced shortages of heating oil and power "brownouts." Impatient motorists formed long lines at the gas pumps.

The energy crisis had been building for years; the OPEC embargo triggered it. American postwar growth and prosperity had been founded on cheap energy. U.S. domestic oil production began declining in 1969, while demand continued to rise. By 1970, America, with only 6 percent of the world's population, used over one-third of the world's energy. To meet the ever-increasing demand for oil, U.S. oil companies bought more and more imported oil. Daily consumption of imported oil rose from 12 percent in 1968 to 36 percent by 1973. During the winter of 1972–1973, homeowners in New England experienced heating oil shortages, a harbinger of more serious problems to come. An increasing proportion of imported oil came from OPEC nations, and two-thirds of OPEC oil came from the Middle East. U.S. oil companies became the mechanisms for maintaining the OPEC cartel, since they refined the oil for U.S. markets. When OPEC shut off oil in October 1973, these companies made huge profits from the rapid rise in oil prices.

The OPEC embargo was short-lived. Arab countries removed it after a few months, and oil supplies returned to normal. But gasoline prices rose from 30 cents to 70 cents a gallon during that period and they stayed there. Much higher energy prices became a permanent fact of U.S. economic life. Higher oil prices sent an inflationary jolt coursing through all facets of the American economy, because oil had seeped into the fabric of American life. Oil heated homes; it was synthesized into fibers and plastics; farmers used it for fertilizer, pesticides, and fuel; and it was crucial to all forms of transportation. Rising energy prices struck hardest at the older industrial centers of the Northeast and the Great Lakes region, because they had to import most of their energy. Cutbacks in federal spending fell hardest on cities in these regions, given their shrinking tax bases, declining industries, and expensive social services.

Before he was forced to resign, Nixon had battled the energy crisis. He created the Federal Energy Office to formulate a national energy policy and to promote conservation. He proposed a plan called "Project Independence" to make America energy-independent by 1980. The plan called for increasing domestic oil production by tapping Alaskan oil fields and accelerating offshore drilling; producing more natural gas, coal, and nuclear energy, extracting oil from shale deposits; and developing renewable energy sources. Project Independence made little progress. With the lifting of the embargo and the return of normal supplies of oil, most people forgot about the energy crisis, although motorists complained about the high price of gasoline.

Figure 11.1   Energy crisis USA. Motorists line up to get gas at a service station in Los Angeles.   *Source:* National Archives.

Ford tried to continue Nixon's energy program, but he encountered much opposition. Environmentalists opposed many of its features. Antinuclear groups opposed building additional nuclear power plants. Ford tried to deregulate domestic oil and natural gas prices, only to be blocked by the Democratic majority in Congress, who believed that deregulation would hurt low-income families and aggravate inflation. Congress enacted legislation in 1975, giving the president standby authority to ration gasoline, to create a strategic petroleum reserve, and to set mandatory fuel economy standards for new cars. Three years later, the United States imported 40 percent of its daily oil requirements.

Partisan conflicts between the Republican president and the Democratic-controlled Congress hampered government effectiveness during Ford's tenure. He vetoed sixty-six bills enacted by Congress, including federal aid for education, a heath care measure, a housing measure, and a bill to control strip mining. During Ford's presidency, Congress extended the Voting Rights Act of 1965 and increased Social Security benefits.

EXTENDING DETENTE

Henry Kissinger, whom Ford inherited from former President Nixon, doubled as Secretary of State and head of the National Security Council, and had a major part in shaping U.S. foreign policy. The new President, who did not have an extensive foreign policy background background, was happy to give Kissinger the leading role in conducting his administration's foreign policy. Ford and Kissinger tried to improve relations with China and the Soviet Union, but they had little success. Ford visited China in 1975, but Washington's support of Taiwan prevented him from forging closer ties.

Efforts to extend detente and to achieve additional arms control agreements with the Soviets failed. Negotiators got bogged down in technical details as advances in nuclear weapon technologies outstripped their efforts to impose political controls. In November 1974, Ford met Soviet President Leonid Brezhnev in the Siberian port of Vladivostok. There the two leaders signed an agreement for an arms control treaty that would be known as SALT-II, but the agreement never evolved into a full-fledged treaty. SALT-II never happened, because American domestic opponents of detente, led by Senator Henry Jackson, refused to accept any agreement that allowed the Soviets to maintain a large advantage in land-based ICBMs, even though the United States had more manned bombers and missile-launching nuclear submarines.

Another effort to extend detente brought Ford and Soviet leader Leonid Brezhnev together with European leaders at the Conference on Security and Cooperation in Europe, held in Helsinki, Finland, in August 1975. Both sides agreed to recognize the political boundaries dividing Eastern and Western Europe since the end of World War II. For the first time, the United States officially recognized the legitimacy of Communist rule in Eastern Europe. The Helsinki conference brought forth a declaration of human rights supporting basic freedoms, such as the right to emigrate, free speech, and religious freedom. For his part, Brezhnev agreed to ease restrictions on the right of Soviet Jews to emigrate. Kissinger's overtures to the Communists outraged conservatives within the Republican Party, such as presidential hopeful Ronald Reagan, who denounced both detente and Kissinger for trafficking with the Reds.

VIETNAM: THE END

Between 1973 and 1975, Congress restricted the president's power to involve the United States in the continuing Indochina War. Congress also reduced the amount of aid going to Saigon. The War Powers Act, which was passed over President Nixon's veto in 1973, required that the president consult with Congress before sending American forces into a foreign war. When North Vietnam mounted a spring offensive in 1975, South Vietnam suddenly collapsed. The invaders overran its territory. President Ford wanted to honor U.S. commitments to intervene, but given the lack of Congressional and popular support, he could do nothing. On April 23, President Ford told a cheering audience at Tulane University that the Vietnam War "is finished as far as America is concerned," thereby making U.S. abandonment of the South Vietnamese government official. Saigon fell to the Communists six days later. About a month after the fall of Saigon, Cambodian Communists seized an American merchant ship, the *Mayaguez,* which was cruising near the Cambodian coast. On May 12, Ford sent in a detachment of 350 marines to rescue the ship and crew. Most Americans applauded the president's determined show of force at a time when Americans were feeling pushed around in Southeast Asia.

The twenty-five-year-long American effort to prevent a Communist takeover in southern Vietnam had ended in disaster for the United States and the people it had tried so hard for so long to help. The Indochina War had been the longest, least popular war in U.S. history. It had divided Americans more than any other conflict since their own Civil War. It was the first major war that Americans had ever lost. Its aftermath refuted every Cold War assumption upon which American involvement had been based. American security was not threatened. American alliances elsewhere were not weakened, nor were American allies disheartened by the outcome. American power and prestige in the world community was not significantly diminished.

There was no unified Communist takeover of Southeast Asia, because the victorious Communist states fell to warring among themselves. A vicious Marxist regime, which overthrew Lon Nol in Cambodia at about the same time the North Vietnamese conquered Saigon, was responsible for the death of more than one million of its own people. Communist Vietnam invaded Cambodia, now called Kampuchea. China, supporting the Kampuchean regime, attacked Vietnam. The Soviet Union backed Vietnam in these intramural Communist wars. The United States, which had gone to war in Southeast Asia, ostensibly to stop the spread of Chinese Communism, found itself quietly backing Chinese efforts to contain Vietnamese expansionism. Southeast Asian national interests turned out to be a stronger force than Marxist ideology in determining their behavior. There was no bitter "who lost Vietnam" debate in the United States and no resurgence of McCarthyite Red-baiting. Instead, amnesia set in; no one wanted to talk about Vietnam for years, much less indulge in recriminations over it.

The harm done to the United States and Vietnam by the long, losing war was severe and lasting. George Kennan, the principal theorist of containment, called the Vietnam War "the most disastrous of all America's undertakings over the whole 200 years of its history." The war killed perhaps 2 million Vietnamese and turned one-fourth of its population into refugees. It left 58,000 Americans dead and another 300,000 seriously wounded. There were few parades for returning Vietnam veterans. Except for the POWs, they were not welcomed home. A people who

Figure 11.2   A young American soldier assisting a family fleeing Vietnam as the Communists take over on April 30, 1975. *Source:* U.S. Army photograph.

had carelessly sent them off to fight in Vietnam for a cause they no longer believed in were embarrassed by their presence and sought to ignore them, or worse, to denounce them.

The war experience for many veterans had been an ordeal. In addition to facing the ravages of war, many soldiers returned home disillusioned over their combat experiences. To these veterans, the war appeared futile and pointless. The rejection of the war by the civilian population made it more difficult for many soldiers to justify their efforts or to derive any meaning from them. Most returning veterans were neither war criminals nor victims. They did not suffer from drug or alcohol addiction nor did they have acute psychological or physical disabilities. But many veterans struggled to come to terms with their war experiences, to readjust to civilian routines, and to reintegrate into American life. Most succeeded; the typical Vietnam veteran has been more successful in life than his or her non-veteran counterpart. The stereotype of the typical Vietnam veteran as a loser or a drugged-out violent wacko is demonstrably false, a product of sensational television shows and movies. Whatever their politics or view of the U.S. war policy, most Vietnam veterans served with pride. They went to Vietnam, did their duty, and returned home to get on with their lives, just as most soldiers who have fought in previous U.S. foreign wars have done.

In addition to the human costs of the war, the economic costs also were high. The Vietnam War cost $167 billion, more than any other war in U.S. history except World War II. President Johnson's efforts to finance both the Great Society and the war ignited inflation. His refusal to trim domestic spending, to raise taxes, or to apply economic controls because he was trying to hide the costs of war from the American people brought economic decline to millions of American households.

The war also undermined public faith in the competence and honesty of elected officials. Military service was discredited for years. The war shattered the bipartisan ideological consensus that had guided U.S. foreign policy since the late 1940s. The losing war also proved that American technology and wealth could not defeat a poor Third World nation determined to prevail, nor could the United States support forever an ineffective regime. Americans discovered that there were limits to U.S. power, and that there were limits to the burdens that Americans were willing to bear in pursuit of Cold War foreign policy aims. For the first time since the Cold War began, many Americans questioned the validity of their global mission to contain Communism. The ordeal of Vietnam also marred the American spirit. The ultimate domino was America's vision of itself as a powerful, benevolent nation. That lofty self-image perished in the jungles, swamps, and rice paddies of Vietnam.

THE ELECTION OF 1976

As the 1976 election approached, Ford appeared to be politically vulnerable, having achieved the office of the president only through the grace of Nixon's appointment. He faced a powerful challenge from within Republican ranks from Ronald Reagan, the leader of a growing conservative movement. A large field of Democratic contenders sought their party's nomination including Senators Henry Jackson and Frank Church, Governors George Wallace and Jerry Brown, and Morris Udall, an Arizona congressman. The surprise of the 1976 Democratic race proved to be the sudden emergence of Georgia Governor James Earl Carter, Jr., who called himself "Jimmy," who was unknown outside his native state.

Carter beat them all to capture the Democratic nomination. He won a series of primary victories in both the North and the South. His major pitch was the need for a leader untainted by the corruptions of Washington, an outsider who could restore integrity to government. When the Democratic convention opened in New York, Carter had more than enough votes to ensure a first-ballot nomination. He chose a Midwestern liberal for his running mate, Senator Walter Mondale, from Minnesota, and they ran on a platform attacking Ford's "government by veto" and Kissinger's "manipulative" foreign policy. Carter's capturing of the Democratic Party nomination in 1976 was one of the most remarkable achievements in modern American political history. His victory could only have happened within the context of post-Vietnam, post-Watergate massive disillusionment with politics as usual in this country.

Ford, meanwhile, was locked in a fierce struggle for the Republican nomination with Ronald Reagan, leader of the resurgent Republic Right. Ford adopted a centrist stance, projecting an image of a moderate leader healing the nation's wounds, promoting economic recovery, and keeping the nation at peace. His strategy worked initially. He beat Reagan decisively in the early primaries. When the Sunbelt primaries came up in the spring, Reagan ran off a string of victories, surging ahead of Ford in the delegate count. Ford rallied with victories in several Northern industrial states. Reagan countered with a big win in California. When the Republican Convention assembled in Kansas City, the two candidates were so close that the winner would be the one who captured a majority of the few uncommitted delegates. Ford managed to win a close first-ballot nomination, but the Reaganites influenced the drafting of a conservative platform. Ford chose a sharp-tongued conservative, Kansas Senator Robert Dole, to replace Rockefeller, who chose not to run again. Although Reagan endorsed Ford, many of his supporters did not. Ford led a divided party into battle against a Democratic Party united behind the candidacy of the centrist Jimmy Carter.

The presidential campaign turned out to be rather dull and unenlightening. Neither man made much impact on a wary electorate. Neither candidate stood out in a series of three televised debates. Ford ran on his record, which was unimpressive. Carter conducted a vaguely liberal, populist, and moralistic campaign. He promised to tame Washington's bloated bureaucracy, and he pledged to craft a government that was "as good and honest as are the American people."

Carter scored a narrow victory, receiving forty-one million votes to Ford's thirty-nine million. His winning margin in the electoral vote was 297 to 241. Carter carried the South, several border states, and some Northern industrial states. He lost most of the Midwest and carried no state west of the Mississippi River. Black votes provided his margin of victory in the South. He also did well among traditional Democratic voters—labor, urban, Jewish, liberals, and intellectuals. Carter's party ran much better than he did. Democrats retained their large majorities in both houses of Congress.

Carter's victory suggested that a majority of voters shared his revulsion over abuses of power by Washington-based professional politicians. They were willing to entrust the reins of government to an inexperienced outsider from a Southern village. Given a choice between "fear of the known and fear of the unknown," the citizenry opted for a fresh, new face who promised to tell them the truth.

Carter's winning the Democratic nomination before the convention signaled an important new political reality; most states were now holding presidential primaries. The primary process opened up the nominating process to the mass of voters and reduced the importance of political parties. It also lengthened the campaigns, greatly increased their costs, and enhanced the role of television. Ford and Carter both accepted $22 million of federal funds to finance their fall campaigns, and both renounced private fund-raising. They were the first presidential candidates to use new federal spending laws that were enacted following the Watergate disclosures of fund-raising abuses.

Mr. Carter Goes to Washington

One of Carter's most valuable political assets proved to be his wife Rosalyn, who was attractive, strong, and politically shrewd. She made a dynamic First Lady, going well beyond the usual roles of hostess, ornament, and goodwill ambassador. She was her husband's principal adviser on many issues, a member of his inner circle. Not since Eleanor Roosevelt had a First Lady achieved such power in her own right.

Carter came to office knowing that millions of Americans were still deeply suspicious of the political system. He strove from the outset to "de-imperialize" the White House and to restore popular faith in national politics. He also brought many previously excluded groups into the higher levels of the federal government. Out of his 1,195 full-time federal appointments, 12 percent were women, 12 percent were black, and 4 percent Hispanic, far more coming from these historically disadvantaged backgrounds than any previous president's appointees. But Carter's populist campaign style contradicted his managerial and technocratic approach to governing. Carter was the most conservative Democratic president since Grover Cleveland. His top priority became slashing the size and cost of the government.

Carter's policies also reflected the conservative mood that increasingly gripped the country by the late 1970s. More and more Americans repudiated 1960s-style liberalism, which they associated with foreign policy failures, inflationary domestic policies, oversized government, high taxes, and a generalized permissiveness and moral decay. The antigovernment, antispending inclinations of voters were expressed dramatically in California's 1978 election. An elderly real estate lobbyist, Howard Jarvis, led a successful taxpayer's revolt that slashed property taxes by two-thirds. A 1978 poll revealed that conservatives outnumbered liberals by a ratio of more than two to one.

When Carter took office, the inflation rate stood at 6 percent and the unemployment rate at 8 percent. Carter had gotten political mileage during his campaign against Ford by attacking the incumbent's failure to solve these serious economic problems, labeling the combined total of inflation and unemployment rates the "misery index." He called the "misery index" of fourteen intolerable and promised to reduce it drastically. Carter first tried stimulating the economy to reduce unemployment by implementing Keynesian "pump priming" programs. Congress enacted a $6 billion local public works bill, an $8 billion public service jobs bill, tax cuts, and an increase in the minimum wage. Unemployment declined to 6 percent in two years.

But the inflation rate rose rapidly, back to 7 percent in 1977 and 10 percent in 1978. It zoomed to 12 percent in 1979 and 13 percent in 1980, the worst two years since World War I. Confronted with runaway inflation, Carter radically shifted his economic focus. He concentrated on attacking inflation, adopting fiscal restraints similar to Ford's. In 1979, Carter appointed Paul Volcker to be chairman of the Federal Reserve Board. Volcker immediately imposed severe monetary restrictions on the economy that drove interest rates to historic highs, pulling the economy into a recession without immediately curbing inflation. The ensuing "stagflation" of 1979 and 1980 was far worse than it had ever been under either Nixon or Ford. In 1980, the "misery index" had reached 21, a figure that Carter's Republican opponent, Ronald Reagan, would use against him with devastating effectiveness.

Declining productivity signaled another kind of economic rot that beset Americans. Productivity had increased an average of 3 percent per year between 1945 and 1965. During the 1970s, productivity only rose at an annual rate of 1 percent. As late as 1968, the American economy had been the most productive in the world; by 1980, it had slipped to twentieth place. Energy problems added to America's economic difficulties. Despite the 1973 energy crisis, Americans continued to use more oil and to import a high proportion of their daily requirements throughout the 1970s. Domestic oil production continued to decline. In April 1977, Carter developed a comprehensive energy plan that he called "the moral equivalent of war (MEOW)." His plan sailed through the House but got bogged down in the Senate. MEOW faded from view but not before late-night comedians had a field day with Carter's acronym. Congress later passed a watered-down version of Carter's original energy proposals.

In 1979, a second oil crisis hit the deteriorating U.S. economy when the new Islamic revolutionary government of Iran cut off its oil exports after toppling the Shah. Gasoline shortages again forced angry motorists to line up at the pumps. Carter responded to this second crisis by implementing a phased deregulation of domestic oil prices to spur production. Oil deregulation immediately raised gasoline prices by 50 percent (from 70¢ to over $1 a gallon) and increased oil company profits, some of which the government siphoned off as excise taxes.

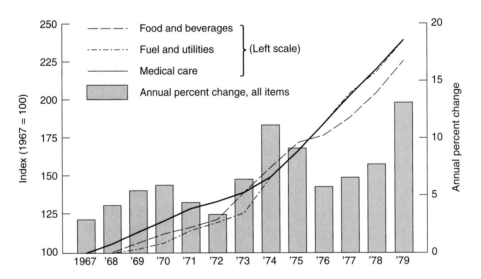

Figure 11.3   Inflation was the most serious economic problem afflicting the American people during the 1970s. Note that the cost of living, as measured by the Consumer Price Index, increased nearly 250 percent between 1967 and 1979.   *Source:* Statistical Abstract of the United States.

President Carter, baffled by the failures of Americans to solve their serious economic and energy problems, invited 130 leaders from all walks of life to Camp David for ten days of meetings to determine what was wrong with the nation. From these intensive discussions, the president concluded that the nation was facing "a crisis of the spirit." In what proved to be his finest speech, he told Americans that they faced a crisis of confidence that posed a fundamental threat to American democracy—they had lost faith in themselves and their institutions; they had lost faith in the future.

Critics of the Carter administration suggested that the major problem facing the nation was failed presidential leadership. Carter never firmly grasped the reins of government and never established effective liaison with Congress. He failed to develop a consistent approach to public policy. He mastered the details of problems, but he could never project a broad national vision or a sense of direction. His presidency was a perpetually floundering government that ultimately lost the trust and respect of many citizens. He never communicated effectively with the press or with the American people. Another aspect of Carter's presidency that weakened his leadership and undermined his efforts to stake out the moral high ground on issues were some of his friends and family. They were a colorful cast of characters including his younger brother Billy. Billy was an alcoholic given to tactless and ribald commentary about people and issues, which proved a continual embarrassment to the strait-laced chief executive.

A few weeks after his "malaise" speech, President Carter suddenly purged his cabinet, confirming the public view of a directionless administration. A poll taken shortly after his cabinet purge put his popular approval rating at 26 percent, one of the lowest ever recorded for a sitting president. The Liberal journalist Tom Wicker called Carter's administration the greatest failure since Herbert Hoover's performance during the Great Depression.

THE DECLINE OF DETENTE

Carter came to office with a limited background in foreign affairs. His only previous international experience came from his having served on the Trilateral Commission, an association of businessmen, bankers, politicians, and intellectuals gathered from the United States, Japan, and European countries, committed to strengthening economic ties among major Free World nations. Carter recruited his two top foreign policy advisers from the commission, his Secretary of State Cyrus Vance, a Wall Street lawyer, and his National Security Adviser Zbigniew Brzezinski, a professor of international relations at Columbia.

Carter initially tried to steer U.S. foreign policy in new directions. He announced at the outset of his administration that he would make human rights the distinctive theme of his foreign policy; he said that human rights would be "the soul of our foreign policy." The new President's emphasis on human rights expressed both his Wilsonian idealism and his desire to move beyond the realm of Nixon–Kissinger realism. He wanted to reclaim the ideological high ground in the ongoing Cold War competition with the Soviet Union. Human rights espoused traditional American ideals and a noble cause but proved in practice to be difficult to implement. Carter was also a born-again Christian and his religious beliefs informed his commitment to human rights. He was the most devout and moralistic president since Woodrow Wilson.

Carter's greatest diplomatic triumph occurred in the Middle East, where he played a major role in achieving peace between Egypt and Israel. He built upon a foundation laid by Kissinger's shuttle diplomacy and the extraordinary actions taken by Egyptian leader Anwar Sadat. Sadat, perceiving that Egyptians could never dislodge the Israelis from the Sinai by force, offered them peace in exchange for the return of Egyptian lands. Sadat electrified the world when he went to Jerusalem in the fall of 1977. He told Israelis that any permanent agreement between Egypt and Israel must include an Israeli withdrawal from the West Bank and the Golan Heights, a homeland for Palestinian Arabs, and a recognition of the Palestine Liberation Organization (PLO) as the government of the Palestinians.

Israeli Prime Minister Menachem Begin was willing to strike a bargain with Egypt on the Sinai, but he balked at the Palestinian issues. Negotiations between the two countries reached an impasse after six months. President Carter then invited both leaders to Camp David for conferences. After two weeks of intense negotiations in which Carter was fully engaged, they achieved what he called "a framework of peace for the Middle East." Egypt agreed to a separate peace with Israel, and the Israelis agreed to return the Sinai region to Egypt. The Palestinian issues were left vague. Both sides agreed to a "self-governing" authority for the people inhabiting the West Bank, with their specific political status to be worked out in subsequent negotiations. Sadat and Begin signed the historic peace agreement, which ended more than thirty years of war between their countries, on March 26, 1979, in Washington. Egypt and Israel then proceeded to normalize their relations.

Figure 11.4   The signing of the Camp David Accords. President Carter looks on as Israeli Prime Minister Begin (to Carter's left) and Egyptian President Anwar Sadat (to Carter's right) sign the historic pact on March 26, 1979, at a formal ceremony held on the North Lawn of the White House.   *Source:* National Archives.

President Carter hoped that these Camp David Accords would launch a new era of peace in the Middle East, but insurmountable obstacles persisted. No other Arab nation followed Egypt's lead. Negotiations on the Palestine question went nowhere. Israel refused to recognize the PLO or any other Palestinian political organization, and these groups all refused to recognize the results of any negotiations excluding them. The Palestine issue was further complicated by the outbreak of civil war in Lebanon between Muslim and Christian factions over PLO camps in southern Lebanon. These camps served both as staging areas for terrorist raids into Israel and as targets of Israeli reprisals.

Carter also achieved diplomatic successes in Latin America. In April 1978, he persuaded the Senate to ratify two treaties turning the Panama Canal over to Panama by 2000. These treaties permitted the gradual phasing out of the last vestiges of U.S. colonialism in Central America. The United States reserved the right to intervene to keep the canal open, and it also retained priority of passage in the event of a foreign crisis. The treaties protected U.S. interests and removed a source of resentment for Panamanians and other Central American Nationalists. The treaties proved popular in Panama and elsewhere in Latin America; they were taken as a sign that the Carter administration genuinely wanted to treat Latin American people as equals. Within this country, the Panama treaties drew fire from outraged conservatives. California Senator S. I. Hayakawa said that the United States should never return the Canal Zone to Panama because "we stole it fair and square."

Elsewhere in Latin America, Carter changed U.S. policies, usually in the name of human rights. He withdrew support for the tyrannical Pinochet dictatorship in Chile, which Ford and Kissinger had backed. In February 1978, he cut off military and economic aid to Nicaraguan dictator Anastasio Somoza. Deprived of aid, Somoza was soon overthrown by revolutionaries calling themselves Sandinistas. The United States promptly extended a $75 million aid package to the new Sandinista government, which included Marxist elements. In El Salvador, Marxist guerrillas, assisted by the Sandinistas, began a civil war against the government. The Rightist government fought back brutally. The United States suspended aid to the Salvadoran government after government troops murdered three American nuns.

In the Far East, Carter completed the process that Nixon had begun with his historic opening to China in 1972. Since Nixon's visit, both the United States and China had been moving toward normalizing relations. Carter, trying to continue the strategies of Nixon and Kissinger, wanted to use good relations with China as a lever to pry cooperation out of the Soviet Union. American businessmen eagerly anticipated tapping into China's consumer economy of 1 billion people. The two nations established normal relations with an exchange of ambassadors in 1979.

United States relations with sub-Saharan Africa improved during Carter's tenure. He appointed Andrew Young, a black minister and former civil rights activist, as the U.S. Ambassador to the United Nations. Young was able to dampen much of the rhetorical fire that Third World delegates to the UN routinely directed at the United States. President Carter made a successful trip to Liberia and Nigeria in 1978. Good relations with Nigeria were especially important. It was the richest, most populous black African nation and the second largest foreign supplier of oil to the United States.

Detente had already begun to decline under Ford and Kissinger, and it continued to decline during Carter's presidency. Carter's diplomatic efforts toward the Soviet Union were hindered badly by his inexperience. He was influenced initially by Secretary of State Vance, who took a conciliatory approach to the Soviets. Carter sent what he intended to be a friendly signal to the Soviets when he announced his intention to withdraw U.S. troops from South Korea. Far from responding in kind, the Soviets took Carter's friendly words and gestures as signs of weakness; the Soviets became more aggressive. Escalating their arms buildup, they extended their influence in Africa, using Cuban soldiers as proxies, and they increased their military forces stationed in Cuba.

The president had hoped to achieve quick ratification of SALT-II, but he surprised and angered the Soviet leaders at the outset of his presidency by proposing additional deep cuts in the two nations' strategic arsenals. His talk of human rights and his granting of full diplomatic recognition to China further annoyed the Soviets. It took more than two years before SALT-II negotiators could complete their work. When finished, the treaty limited both sides to 2,400 nuclear launchers and 1,320 MIRVs. If implemented, it would have further stabilized the arms race.

But when the SALT-II treaty was finally sent to the Senate in 1979, it encountered strong opposition. The chief senatorial critic was Nixon and Kissinger's old opponent, the nemesis of detente, Henry Jackson. Jackson insisted that the proposed agreement allowed the Soviets to retain strategic superiority in several categories of weapons. He also was upset by the expansion of the Soviet presence in Africa. More moderate critics of SALT-II were uncomfortable with the fact that the treaty acknowledged that the Soviets had achieved nuclear parity with the United States, a reality that they interpreted as confirming the relative decline of U.S. strategic power. Some liberal senators were unhappy with SALT-II because it did not eliminate key weapons systems, such as the huge Soviet land-based ICBMs and the new American cruise missiles.

Carter himself lost faith in SALT-II and withdrew it from consideration before the Senate could vote it down. Instead, he took a tougher stance toward the Soviet Union. He accepted a controversial West German request to station new intermediate-range Pershing II missiles in Western Europe to counter the SS-20 missiles that the Soviets were installing in Eastern Europe. Carter also pressured all NATO members to significantly increase their military spending. Installing these weapons in Europe represented a major escalation of the nuclear arms race. As Carter made the transition from conciliation to a tougher stance vis-à-vis the Soviets, he relied more and more on foreign policy advice from the hawkish Zbigniew Brzezinski, and he no longer paid much attention to the dovish Vance.

Suddenly, in December 1979, 85,000 Soviet troops invaded Afghanistan to suppress a Muslim rebellion against a faltering Marxist regime backed by the Soviet Union. Alarmed, President Carter reacted strongly, calling the Soviet invasion "the most serious threat to world peace since the Second World War." Carter canceled grain shipments to the USSR, suspended the sale of high-tech equipment to the Soviets, and ordered American athletes to boycott the summer Olympic games, scheduled to be held in Moscow during the summer of 1980. The President also increased U.S. military spending and removed restrictions on CIA covert operations. He proclaimed the Carter Doctrine for Southwest Asia. Calling the Persian Gulf a vital U.S. interest, he declared that the United States would repel "by any means necessary" an attack in that region by outside forces. Carter's reaction to Soviet aggression and his adoption of a hard line toward Moscow reversed U.S. policies toward the Soviet Union that went back to the Kennedy years. The man who began his presidency espousing kind words for the Soviets killed detente and revived the Cold War.

DEBACLE IN IRAN

The United States suffered a major foreign policy disaster in the Persian Gulf region that humiliated President Carter and contributed to his defeat in the 1980 election. Nixon and Kissinger had made Iran America's major ally in the Persian Gulf area. It had played a key role in containing the Soviet Union. It was a major supplier of top-grade oil, and Iranians annually purchased billions of dollars worth of American arms. The Shah, whom a CIA covert operation had helped restore to power in 1953, permitted the intelligence agency to station electronic surveillance equipment along Iran's border with the Soviet Union. Tens of thousands of Iranian students attended American colleges and universities. American oil companies supplied the state-owned Iranian oil industry with equipment and technicians, and shared in its profits. Iran was a vital U.S. interest, much more important than Vietnam had ever been. On the surface, Iran and America were best friends when Carter took office.

Beneath the surface, Iran in the late 1970s seethed with anti-Shah and anti-American fervor. Only the Shah and a powerful ruling elite were genuinely pro-American. Carter, in contradiction of his human rights policy and unaware of the tensions in Iran, traveled to Iran in late 1977 to pay tribute to the Shah. At a state banquet held in his honor, President Carter called Iran "an island of stability in one of the most troubled areas of the world." The CIA station chief in Teheran issued a report in 1978 stating that Iran was not even near a revolutionary situation. American intelligence operatives were blind to the faults of the Shah's corrupt, oppressive regime, and equally blind to the existence of revolutionary forces poised to destroy it.

The assault on the Shah was led by fundamentalist Islamic clergy intent on replacing Iran's modern, Westernized state with an Islamic republic. The revolutionaries were led by aged religious leader, Ayatollah Ruholla Khomeini. From exile in France in 1978, Khomeini ordered his legions to demonstrate, to disrupt the economy, to do anything to create chaos—to force the Shah to abdicate. Carter initially dismissed Khomeini's revolution, assuming that the Shah would suppress it. Carter watched in disbelief as Iran's oil production stopped and its economy ground to a halt. The Iranian army, forbidden by the Shah to fire upon the rioters for fear that it would ruin the chances of his son succeeding him, was demoralized. On January 16, 1979, the Shah fled his country. Khomeini returned to Iran to a frenzied hero's welcome from revolutionary crowds. One of the most bizarre events of modern times had occurred. A virtually unarmed people led by clergymen had overthrown one of the world's most powerful rulers and defeated one of the world's largest, best-equipped military forces, without firing a shot!

U.S. leaders, thinking in conventional Cold War terms, did not know how to deal with a man who denounced both the United States and the Soviet Union with equal vehemence. Fearing Soviet intrusion into Iran and the loss of a crucial source of Western oil, Carter tried to establish normal relations with the new Iranian government, which proved impossible. Khomeini, who called the United States the "Great Satan," refused all American overtures.

Meanwhile, President Carter allowed the Shah, who was suffering from terminal cancer, to enter the United States for medical treatment. On November 4, 1979, Iranian militants overran the U.S. Embassy in Teheran and took fifty-three Americans hostage. Khomeini approved the action, which violated the principle of diplomatic immunity observed by all nations. Carter retaliated for this outlaw act by ordering the 50,000 Iranian students within the United States to report to the nearest immigration office. Any students found to be in violation of their visas were deported. He also froze billions of dollars worth of Iranian assets in the United States. He further suspended arms sales and placed a boycott on all U.S. trade with Iran.

Carter made the return of the hostages his number one priority, which it remained for the rest of his presidency. The hostage crisis dominated American foreign policy for the next fourteen months. The crisis also dominated American television screens. Each night, when the most popular news program, the CBS Evening News with Walter Cronkite, would sign off, the viewing public would be reminded of just how many days of captivity the hostages had endured. The popular late-night television news show Nightline originated as a series of special reports on the Iranian hostage crisis. As the crisis wore on, day after day, Carter had to watch his own popularity plummet to new lows. For months, U.S. officials negotiated futilely for release of the hostages with a series of Iranian governments, but no Iranian leader could acquire the necessary authority to make a binding agreement.

Five months after the hostages were taken, Carter severed diplomatic relations with Iran and authorized a military operation to attempt a rescue. He had previously resisted any suggestions to use force to attempt a rescue, because he feared that the hostages would be killed. On

Figure 11.5   Carters most serious setback and the nation's greatest humiliation occurred in 1979 when Iranian militants occupied the U. S. embassy in Iran and took Americans hostage. Here their captors put blindfolded hostages on display soon after taking them prisoner. *Source:* Bettmann Archive

the night of April 24, 1980, three helicopters transporting the rescue team suffered mechanical failures. At a staging area in an Iranian desert north of Teheran, a fourth chopper crashed into a C-130 transport plane, killing eight soldiers and severely burning five more. For days following these accidents, the news media bombarded Americans with sickening pictures of the wreckage and charred corpses. Each photo and television image reinforced the notion that the United States was not what it used to be. They also reinforced the popular image of Carter as an irresolute bumbler. The failed rescue attempt also symbolized the impotence of the United States; a once-powerful and feared power, now apparently unable to protect its citizens against terrorism from revolutionary outlaws.

Prospects for resolving the hostage crisis improved in late 1980. The ailing Shah died in July. On September 22, Iraq suddenly invaded Iran, intending to take advantage of Iranian political instability to annex territories, and provoked a full-scale war between the two nations. In October, President Carter offered to release frozen Iranian assets and to resume normal relations and trade with Iran in exchange for the release of the hostages. On November 4, Ronald Reagan was elected President. Khomeini responded to Carter's offer. He needed money for the war with Iraq, and he now had another cause around which to rally support for the revolution. He also feared that the new president might take stronger action against his regime. On January 21, 1981, Carter's last day in office, Iran agreed to release the hostages in exchange for the return of $8 billion of Iranian assets. The hostages finally came home after 444 days in captivity.

THE ELECTION OF 1980

As the 1980 election approached, Carter was clearly in serious political trouble. His "misery index," the sum of the rate of inflation plus the unemployment rate, was much higher than when he had run against Ford in 1976. And there was the daily embarrassment of the hostages. Carter had also to fight off a primary challenge from Senator Edward "Ted" Kennedy. Kennedy's old-fashioned liberal philosophy was out of sync with the times, and Carter easily deflected his challenge.

The Republicans entered the 1980 presidential race brimming with confidence. Many candidates entered the race for the Republican nomination, but from the outset, the clear choice of most of the party faithful was the old right-wing war horse Ronald Reagan. Of the others, only George Bush showed any strength in the primaries. Reaganites controlled the Republican Convention and pushed through a conservative platform, calling for deep tax cuts, a balanced budget, large increases in defense spending, constitutional amendments banning abortions and restoring prayer in public schools, and opposition to the Equal Rights Amendment. Reagan chose Bush for the vice presidential slot after failing to get former President Ford for the position.

A third-party candidate joined the race, John Anderson, running as an Independent. He had no organization, constituency, or particular issues that set him apart from the major candidates. He offered the electorate his self-proclaimed integrity and competence. He qualified for federal election funds, and his campaign received extensive media coverage. Anderson attracted mainly Democratic voters who were turned off by Carter's performance, although his candidacy did not affect the outcome of the election.

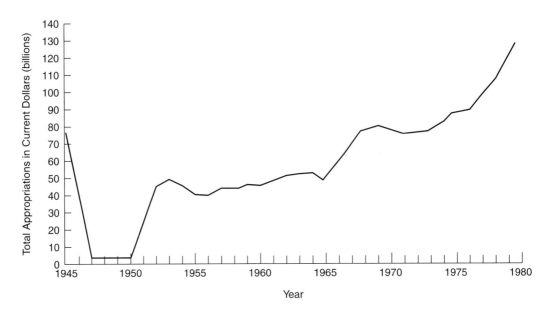

Figure 11.6   National Defense Outlays, 1945–1980. During the 1980 election, Ronald Reagan accused Carter of neglecting the nation's defenses and allowing the Soviet Union to forge ahead of the United States. Actually, defense spending increased substantially during Carter's presidency, as this graph demonstrates.   *Sources: Historical Statistics of the United States: Colonial Times to 1970, and Statistical Abstract of the United States, 1980.*

Reagan was favored to win when the presidential campaign began in August. But he made several erroneous statements concerning important issues, which conveyed the impression that he might be dangerously out of touch with the times. Within a month, Carter had caught up. Sensing an advantage, Carter attacked Reagan personally. He accused him of racism and war-mongering, and he raised the question of his age. At sixty-nine, Reagan was the oldest major party candidate ever to seek the presidency. But Carter's attacks backfired, because voters resented them. Polls taken at the end of September showed Reagan back in the lead.

Reagan attacked Carter's handling of the economy at a time of historically high "stagfla-tion." He attacked his handling of foreign policy at a time when the world was especially unstable and when the hostages were in Iranian hands. Carter, hoping to salvage his failing campaign, challenged Reagan to debate him on television. Carter was confident that his detailed knowledge of the issues would expose Reagan as a windy fraud. Reagan agreed to one debate, which took place at Cleveland's Convention Center on October 28 just a few days before the election.

It was the best of all of the televised presidential debates. The panelists chose excellent questions about major issues. The candidates were evenly matched through the early rounds of questioning. Then Carter, responding to a question about nuclear arms control, said that he had consulted with his thirteen-year-old daughter Amy about the important issues of the campaign. His answer unintentionally suggested to the vast television audience that the President of the United States relied on the advice of a child when considering important policy matters. Reagan scored impressively when he responded to Carter's attacks on his record on Medicare. Using his actor's skills, Reagan shook his head ruefully, saying, "There you go again"; then, in the manner of a parent correcting an erring child, he firmly set the record straight.

In terms of content, the debate was a draw. On image and personality, Reagan won decisively. In ninety minutes, he had erased the image of himself that Carter had been projecting throughout the campaign, the image of Reagan as a combination scrooge and mad bomber. During the debate, Reagan came across as a firm, genial leader who would never push the nuclear button in panic or anger. He sealed Carter's fate when be closed the debate by asking the huge television audience a series of rhetorical questions: Are you better off than you were four years ago? Is America as respected throughout the world as it was four years ago? Are we as strong as we were four years ago?

Reagan had turned a close contest into a rout. He received 44 million votes to Carter's 35 million and Anderson's 5.7 million. Reagan swept the election with 489 electoral votes to Carter's 49, with zero for Anderson. The Republicans gained thirty-three seats in the House. The most surprising outcome of the 1980 election was the Republican reconquest of the Senate for the first time since 1954. Republicans gained twelve senatorial seats, giving them fifty-three, the largest Republican total since 1928. Reagan carried blue-collar voters, middle income voters, the Catholic vote, the ethnic vote, and the Southern vote. He carried all the populous Northern industrial states. He brought an important new class of voters into the Republican fold, "Reagan Democrats." He got a third of the Hispanic vote. Only African American voters remained faithful to Carter.

The vote revealed two cleavages among voters. African Americans voted 90 percent for Carter; whites voted 56 percent for Reagan. For the first time in the sixty years since women had achieved the vote, a gender gap appeared in the electoral results. Whereas 56 percent of men voted for Reagan and only 36 percent for Carter, only 47 percent of women voted for Reagan and 45 percent for Carter. Reagan's opposition to abortion and the ERA, plus his aggressive foreign policy rhetoric and initiatives, alienated women voters. Many working women, struggling to cope with precarious economic circumstances, perceived that Reagan did not represent their interests and they feared that he might call for Congress to eliminate governmental programs upon which they and their families depended.

Some analysts read the 1980 election as a harbinger of a new conservative Republican majority coalition. More saw it as the rejection of an ineffective leader who could not control inflation or retrieve the hostages. The main issue apparently was Reagan himself. Could he be a safe replacement for the discredited incumbent? Many people thought Reagan too old, too conservative, and too dangerous—until the debate. Reagan's adept performance in that forum turned a close election into a landslide.

Jimmy Carter was not a particularly successful or popular president, and he suffered a humiliating reelection defeat at the hands of Ronald Reagan in November 1980. However, since the end of his presidency, after more than two decades of tireless work as a practicing Christian and elder statesmen, Jimmy Carter has achieved a stature and respect from his fellow citizens that he never attained while he was in the White House. He established the Carter Center near his presidential library in Atlanta as a place where the parties to the world's most stubborn political conflicts could come together and try to find solutions.

He also set himself up as a crusader for world peace. He supervised elections and guaranteed their legitimacy in Panama and Nicaragua. He inserted himself into dangerous confrontations in Haiti and North Korea to head off conflict. In May 2002, Carter journeyed to Cuba to meet with Fidel Castro and also a small group of Cuban dissidents. He spoke to the Cuban people in Spanish and, with Castro attending, called for democratic reforms. He also called for improved relations between the United States and Cuba. Even though it was contrary to the policies of the President George W. Bush, Carter also called for an easing of the U.S. economic boycott of Cuba. Carter was not a great president, but since his presidency he has achieved the stature of a world statesman and an indefatigable advocate of world peace and reconciliation. Carter was awarded the prestigious Nobel Peace Prize for 2002 in recognition of his decades of effort to resolve conflicts.

A TIME OF TROUBLES

In the aftermath of the upheavals of the late 1960s, the disastrous outcome of the Vietnam War, the Watergate scandals, and the revelations of wrongdoing by the CIA and FBI, millions of Americans lost faith in politicians and in political institutions. During the era of limits, both Gerald Ford and Jimmy Carter did not provide effective leadership. They confronted challenges, conditions, and problems beyond their capacities to control or master. Ford never had a realistic chance to lead. An unelected president who lacked a political base, he was chosen to serve out the unfinished term of the disgraced Nixon. Carter, elected on a wave of public disenchantment with politics as usual, appeared initially to represent the aspirations of millions of ordinary citizens who wanted to make a clean, fresh start in politics. He was a tribune of all of those who yearned for honesty and decency in politics. But the inexperienced Carter could never transcend his outsider status and take hold of the levers of power. Within a few years, his bumbling, directionless presidency demonstrated that good intentions were insufficient for governing a complex society experiencing a series of crises.

Serious economic problems appeared greater than the leaders who tried to solve them. Soaring inflation coupled with high unemployment, "stagflation," did not yield to Ford's and Carter's efforts to manage them, and the misery index continued to rise. Purchasing power and living standards for millions of families were eroded. Productivity declined. Major manufacturing industries lost large market shares to efficient foreign competitors. Periodic energy crises exacerbated economic woes and added an element of uncertainty to an already clouded future.

In the larger world outside of American boundaries, the United States appeared to be a declining entity. An aggressive Soviet Union appeared to be gaining an upper hand in the Cold War. Prosperous Western European nations increasingly asserted their independence from American initiatives, and the Japanese had become formidable commercial rivals. The Iranian hostage crisis was a daily reminder of American fecklessness in world affairs.

By the time of the 1980 election, pundits, reflecting views widely shared by millions of Americans, were writing that the United States had become an ungovernable nation of dysfunctional institutions and demoralized citizens. They feared that the presidency had grown too large and too complex for any one person to control. They feared that America no longer worked; its economy was in decline, its society was fragmented, and its political system was controlled by incompetent leaders who lacked both vision and practical solutions to pressing problems. Americans turned, perhaps in desperation, to an aging former actor and television personality who promised to revitalize the American system, to reassert American primacy in the world, and to restore the American Dream. A large majority of Americans believed that Reagan could hardly do worse than his predecessors, and they hoped he might do better.

BRIEF BIBLIOGRAPHIC ESSAY

One of the most important general studies of U. S. history from 1945 to the mid-1970s has been done by Godfrey Hodgson in *America in Our Time.* Peter N. Carroll, in *It Seemed Like Nothing Happened,* offers a general political and social history of the 1970s. Both President Ford and President Carter have written their memoirs. Ford's is called *A Time to Heal;* Carter's is entitled *Keeping Faith: Memoirs of a President.* The best account of the election of 1976 is Jules Witcover, *Marathon: The Pursuit of the Presidency, 1972–1976.* John R. Greene's, *The Presidency of Gerald R. Ford,* is a solid work. See also Robert T. Hartmann's *Palace Politics: An Insider Account of the Ford Years.* Burton Kaufman, *The Presidency of James Earl Carter, Jr.* is also very good. Clark Mollenkoff in *The President Who Failed: Carter Out of Control* is a critical account. A. James Reichley, in *Conservatives in an Age of Change,* is an interesting account of the rising conservative cause throughout the 1970s. Peter Steinfels's *The Neo-Conservatives* is a critical account of the emergence during the 1970s of a neo-con intelligentsia, many of them formerly Leftist radicals. A lively account of the rise of the Sunbelt region to political prominence is Kirkpatrick Sale's *Power Shift: The Rise of the Southern Rim and Its Challenge to the Eastern Establishment.* Stanley Hoffmann's *Primacy and World Order* is a critical assessment of the Ford administration's foreign policy. Barry Rubin, in *Paved with Good Intentions: The American Experience in Iran,* has the best study of the Iranian fiasco. A good study of the energy crises of the 1970s is Richard Victor's *Energy Policy in America Since 1945.* CIA abuses of power are portrayed in Victor Marchetti's and John D. Marks's *The CIA and the Cult of Intelligence.* David Halberstam, in *The Reckoning,* offers a good account of the decline of the American auto industry during the 1970s.

WEB SITES

`<http://www.ford.utexas.edu/library.htm>` is the homepage of the Ford Presidential Library located in Ann Arbor, Michigan maintained by the University of Texas. The Ford library collects, preserves, and makes accessible to the public important historical resources pertaining to the Ford presidency, 1974–1977. It has links to many other sources and sites. A guide to the library holdings can be downloaded using Microsoft Word format.

`<http://www.turnerlearning.com/cnn/coldwar/freeze/frze_ttl .html>` covers the Carter–Brezhnev years of the Cold War, 1977–1981, aka "decline of detente" (see Episode 19).

12

The American People in the 1970s

The decade of the 1970s was characterized by a series of significant social and cultural transformations that confirmed both the pluralism and volatility of American life. These changes often reflected and paralleled underlying technological, economic, and demographic developments that rapidly altered the contours of American society and changed the ways most Americans lived and worked. New attitudes toward sex, family, and work changed the nature of many important American institutions. Many members of two important groups, African Americans and women, maintaining the momentum generated by the movements of the 1960s, made dramatic gains during the 1970s in education and income. But at the same time that thousands of women and African Americans were taking advantage of new opportunities to achieve middle-class status, many other women and blacks remained locked into low-paying, low-status jobs, or slipped even further into the ranks of welfare dependency and poverty.

The most important development of the 1970s represented a historic shift in the direction of the American economy. The longest boom in American history, which had kicked in during World War II and had continued, with occasional recessions, for thirty years, came to a halt during the early 1970s. The seemingly perpetual American prosperity—fueled by a high growth rate, job creation, federal spending, innovative technology, and most of all, consumerism—stalled. The boom was replaced by the double whammy of "stagflation," business stagnation and inflation, which eroded purchasing power and lowered living standards for millions of American families. The apparent end of economic progress frustrated and bewildered Americans. Stagflation undermined their morale and robbed them of their sense of control over their destinies.

A DEMOGRAPHIC PROFILE

There were 205 million Americans in 1970 and 227 million by 1980. Regionally, Southern and Western states accounted for 90 percent of that population increase. Many Northeastern and Midwestern states showed little or no growth, and several lost population. Population trends that had first appeared in this country soon after World War II continued. The Sunbelt regions, stretching from South Carolina to southern California, contained the dynamic centers of the nation's technological innovation, economic growth, and population increase.

Two additional demographic shifts with profound social implications occurred during the 1970s—the birthrate fell sharply, and human longevity increased significantly. Twentieth-century birthrates peaked in 1947, at 26.6 live births per thousand, and tumbled to 18.1 per thousand in 1975. Low birthrates meant that adults were not bearing enough children to replace themselves, and that only expanded immigration prevented long-term U.S. population decline. Increasing longevity derived from advances in medicine and nutrition. But the most important causes of rising longevity were reductions in the infant mortality rate and the childhood death rate. By 1975, median longevity in America had reached 73.1 years. The fastest-growing age group consisted of people age seventy-five and older. The median age of the U.S. population reached thirty years on April 1, 1980, making America one of the older societies in the world.

The traditional American household comprising a nuclear family of four declined sharply during the 1970s. Nearly half of the households added in the 1970s consisted of persons living alone or with nonrelatives. Declining birthrates, declining marriage rates, high divorce rates, households occupied by unmarried couples, households occupied by single-parent families, and the existence of millions of men and women living alone all suggested that household arrangements in America increasingly reflect the sociological diversity that has become America's most salient characteristic.

By the late 1970s, one of the most rapidly growing population segments comprised the thirty-somethings, the advance wave of baby boomers. This group received much media attention, particularly the better-educated "yuppies." Yuppies were upwardly mobile, affluent young Americans earning $40,000 or more a year. Having few or no children, yuppie couples often held two high-paying jobs. Businesses and advertisers catered to their large disposable incomes and lifestyle preferences based on buying expensive homes, cars, and clothes, dining in upscale restaurants, and taking costly vacations.

But yuppies did not represent the boomer norm. Of the seventy-eight million baby boomers, only 5 percent had incomes of $40,000 or more in the late 1970s. The median income for baby boomers in 1977 was $16,000, below the national average. Too many boomers were chasing too few educational and economic opportunities. Opportunities for baby boomers also were curtailed by the energy crisis and the high inflation of the late 1970s and early 1980s. Furthermore, the annual growth rate of the American economy averaged a sluggish 1.6 percent per annum during the 1970s, and long-term unemployment rates were the highest since the 1930s. Baby boomers as a whole were less upwardly mobile than their parents, the first such group in America since the generation that came of age during the Great Depression of the 1930s.

ECONOMIC STASIS

During the thirty-year boom cycle lasting from the early 1940s to the early 1970s, the majority of Americans families had enjoyed unprecedented prosperity. Real per capita family income doubled, and the GDP more than doubled during those three decades of strong economic growth. The steadily expanding economy and rising living standards over a long period of time convinced most Americans that prosperity was perpetual. But during the early 1970s, stagflation replaced perpetual growth and created a set of economic circumstances that eroded the prosperity that middle class Americans had taken for granted for decades.

During the early 1970s, the declining U.S. economy also was showing the effects of strong foreign competition. Rebuilt after having been destroyed during World War II, the industrial economies of West Germany and Japan were more productive than the older U.S. industries. U.S. shares of many world markets declined. Within America, many industries lost large shares of the domestic market to their foreign competitors. In 1970, about 10 percent of new cars sold in America were imported; by 1980, that figure had reached 30 percent.

Inflation, deficits, and loss of both domestic and export markets combined to create a serious balance of payment problem by 1972, which threatened to undermine the value of the dollar. When the Nixon administration devalued the dollar by severing it from gold, this action unleashed an orgy of gold speculation in the world that drove the price of gold from $35 an ounce to over $800 an ounce and added to the inflationary burden of American consumers.

In geopolitical terms, the U.S. defeat in Vietnam signaled that U.S. hegemony in the world had eroded. In economic and financial terms, the declining U.S. position in the world economy likewise signaled that the era of American dominance had ended. The OPEC embargo that kicked in during October 1973 compounded American economic difficulties, added to the inflation rate, and highlighted the dangers of continued dependency on foreign sources of oil. Yet, during the 1970s, America became more dependent on foreign sources of oil. The bill for oil imports in 1970 was $5 billion. By 1980, it was in excess of $90 billion. The huge rise in the cost of imported oil was another dramatic sign of American economic decline in the world. It also served as a potent reminder that America no longer controlled its own economic destiny. The U.S. economy had become increasingly connected to the emerging global economic order.

The struggles of millions of American families for economic survival during the 1970s were exacerbated by structural trends that weakened the economic foundations of American middle-class society. As the economy became increasingly based on high-tech service and information-oriented industries, the number of jobs that provided middle-class incomes declined. A service economy employs millions of clerical workers, salesclerks, waiters, bartenders, cashiers, and messengers. Wages for these jobs are comparatively low. While millions of new service-sector jobs were created during the 1970s, the number of higher-paying manufacturing jobs decreased.

The 1970s were devastating for union and nonunion workers. Millions of factory jobs disappeared because of declining productivity, cutbacks in capital spending, and because production work became increasingly automated. Trade unions lost hundreds of thousands of members to automation and to declines caused by foreign competition in the steel, rubber, auto, and other manufacturing industries. The manufacturing jobs that disappeared during the 1970s tended to be skilled jobs from middle income spectra. These displaced workers usually could not find alternative employment that offered comparable pay and fringe benefits. Their options were early retirement, if they could afford it, or they could take jobs in the rapidly expanding service sectors of the economy.

But most of these service jobs were low-paying jobs with minimal opportunities for advancement or for a career. In any case, most of these new service sector jobs went to women, minorities, and youngsters. The fastest-growing sector of the service economy in the 1970s, which carried into the 1980s, was the fast food industry. McDonald's became the nation's largest employer. During the 1970s, the fast food industry added workers faster than manufacturing lost them. These "Mcjobs" paid one-third as much and came with far fewer benefits, especially health care.

There were other signs of economic decline during the 1970s. Real income declined 15 percent from 1973 to 1980 in this country. By 1980, working-class family purchasing power had fallen back to 1960 levels. Meanwhile, the inflation engine drove housing and new car prices upward. The median price of new homes doubled during the decade. The 1970s appeared to reverse the social and economic trends of the 1940s, 1950s and 1960s. There was a wholesale loss of faith in economic progress; during the 1970s, millions of families faced what they had been led to believe could never recur—economic retrogression, the first since the 1930s.

For generations, Americans had been sustained by their belief in economic individualism: talent, initiative, and hard work generated upward mobility and economic security, enabling men and women to provide for their families and ensuring that their children would have better lives than they. But during the 1970s, faith in the work ethic was eroded. Millions of Americans could not find steady work in the 1970s. Those who worked often found not affluence but subsistence. For many young people, the struggle was not to reach the top, but to not to fall any lower. They could not realistically expect to earn as much, to own as much, and to be as successful in their work as their parents. At a time when racist and sexist barriers to advancement were crumbling, economic obstacles were growing stronger.

CARS AND COMPUTERS

Despite stagflation and energy crises, Americans during the 1970s continued their longtime love affair with the automobile. The car culture was alive and well in America during the 1970s. Automobile registrations reached 90 million in 1970 and 118 million in 1980 Americans accounted for about one-third of all of the cars owned in the world in 1975. Millions of Americans purchased automobiles manufactured in Europe and Japan during the 1970s. High performance sports cars, small trucks, and vans became more popular. Consumers became more value conscious and safety conscious. Manufacturers responded by offering their customers a far greater choice of vehicles than had been previously available. The application of new technologies meant that 1970s' automobiles were more aerodynamically designed, more fuel efficient, safer, and much easier to handle than the cars of the 1950s and 1960s had been. Automobiles of the 1970s also were much more expensive and, especially the American-made cars, much more prone to breakdown and costly repairs.

Automobiles continued to be the primary means of intercity travel in the United States during the 1970s, although commercial airlines did increase their share of the travelers' market, from about 5 percent to 10 percent. Despite sizable increases in their business, most domestic airlines found themselves in serious financial difficulties during the late 1970s. Most of these difficulties derived from the deregulation of the airline industry, implemented during the Carter presidency. Several well-known airlines went out of business, including Eastern and Braniff.

Deregulation of the airlines probably created more problems than it solved. In the short term, passengers obviously benefited from the far greater variety of flights offered at lower

Figure 12.1   Computer Science Professor Leonard Kleinrock, points out, Thursday, September 2, 1999, that the microprocessor in his watch is more powerful than that of the IMP (Interface Message Processor), left, the first network switch. Kleinrock, whose research into "packet switching" provided the technological foundation upon which the Internet was built, is on hand to celebrate the thirtieth anniversary of the Internet, which began with IMP on September 2, 1969. The IMP's processor is the item that is pulled out below. Photo by Mark J. Terrill.   *Source:* AP/Wide World Photos.

prices generated by a new era of cutthroat competition. In the long run, deregulation created conditions in the airline industry that were reminiscent of the era of cutthroat competition in the railroad industry of 100 years ago: Weaker competitors were driven to bankruptcy and either forced to shut down or be absorbed by the stronger airlines. Serious questions of reliability and safety also arose. As a result, as happened in railroading, a cry went up from customers and consumer advocates for a return to at least a measure of regulation to the airlines.

The most dramatic technological innovations of the 1970s were all connected to the computer revolution. America was computerized during the 1970s. There were approximately 6,000 computers in use in this country in 1972; by 1980, there were millions. The agent of revolution was the microcomputer. The use of microcomputers vastly enhanced the abilities of individuals working in a wide variety of fields to calculate and retrieve information. Individuals using computers also could build statistical models and process words. The key invention that brought forth the microcomputer was the microprocessor, or computer chip, perfected by Ted Hoff in 1972. Hoff was a young engineer on the staff at Intel Corporation when he designed the world's first microprocessor, which started the revolution in electronic technology. The computer revolution made possible the information revolution of the 1970s and 1980s, which transformed the way America worked.

The first personal computers were marketed in the mid-1970s. In California's "Silicon Valley," a suburban area located about forty miles south of San Francisco, dozens of small computer companies found themselves on the cutting edge of technological revolution. In 1976, two young men, Steven Wozniak, a computer genius, and Steve Jobs, an entrepreneurial visionary, opened a small business in a garage they had rented for $50 a month. Wozniak designed, and Jobs sold small, inexpensive personal computers. They called their fledgling company Apple. Sales were slow at first; no one appeared to be interested in a small, cheap personal computer. However, sales picked up in the late 1970s, and in 1985, Americans bought six million of these machines. By the mid-1980s, Apple had become a multi-billion-dollar business; Wozniak and Jobs had become rich. The editors of *Time,* catching the spirit of the times, instead of designating a "Man of the Year," as they had done annually for decades, in 1982 designated the computer as "Machine of the Year."

NEW IMMIGRANTS

Because the Immigration Act of 1965 abolished the discriminatory national origins system dating back to the 1920s, there occurred both a huge increase in immigration and a significant shift in the sources of immigrants. Once again, large-scale immigration to the United States became a vital part of the American experience. Most of the millions of immigrants who came to the United States in the 1970s and 1980s were Asians and Latin Americans. Mexico furnished the most immigrants. Along with Mexicans came Cubans, Puerto Ricans, and Central Americans, particularly people from El Salvador and Nicaragua. Some of these new arrivals were fleeing religious and political oppression, but most of them came for the same reasons that have always attracted newcomers to America—opportunities for a better job and a better life for their families.

The United States, true to its ancient heritage, remained one of the few countries in the world to freely welcome these millions of newcomers from foreign lands. But many native-born Americans were alarmed by the flood of poor immigrants arriving annually, especially the "illegals" who came mostly from Mexico through a porous membrane called the United States-Mexico border. They feared that these people would take jobs from native-born workers, lower wages and living standards, overload the welfare and school systems, and become a permanent underclass of poor people amidst an affluent society.

Their fears were exaggerated and based upon dubious assumptions and misperceptions. Studies have shown that most immigrants take jobs at pay levels that most native-born Americans scorn, and they pay more in taxes than they ever collect in government services. Many of these immigrants also strive to become law-abiding, hard working, and productive citizens.

Another problem posed by elements in the Hispanic-American population, fueled by large-scale immigration from Mexico and other Hispanic countries, is the ancient question of assimilation. Hispanics often have formed their own communities, or "barrios," where they can get along quite well without having to speak or write English. Some Hispanics have also insisted that their children be taught in bilingual school and the Supreme Court has authorized bilingual instruction in public schools.

Spokesmen for the native-born population have argued that the existence of large, Spanish-speaking populations clustered in southern California, southern Florida, the Southwest, and sections of New York and Chicago pose a threat to national unity and to the political cohesiveness of the American system. Hispanic spokesmen insist on their rights to have their children educated as they see fit. They also insist on retaining their language and cultural identity as a distinct ethnic group within a pluralistic society.

A prominent Mexican American journalist, Richard Rodriquez, has written about the need for Mexican Americans and all other Spanish-speaking citizens of the United States to learn English in order to realize their full opportunities, and he accepts, as a painful necessity, the loss of some parts of the traditional Hispanic culture and the comfort it provided. It is the price exacted for full participation in American life, a price he believes individuals from all immigrant groups have paid historically and must continue to pay.

After Hispanics, Asians have furnished the largest supply of newcomers. They have come mainly from Hong Kong, Taiwan, China, Vietnam, Korea, India, and the Philippines. Between 1970 and 1980, the Filipino population within the United States more than doubled, from 343,060 to 774,652. Two-thirds of the additional Filipino population were new immigrants. By 1980, Filipino Americans were the third largest Asian-American group after Chinese Americans and Japanese Americans.

Their numbers boosted by large-scale immigration, the Asian-American population has doubled in the past decade, from two million people to more than four million. Asians are among the most upwardly-mobile population groups within American society. Seventy-five percent of Asian Americans have graduated from high school. One-third of Asian American adults have four or more years of college, twice the rate for Americans of European descent. In the economic sphere, data from the 1980 Census show that the Asian-American median annual income was more than $2,000 above the national median annual income.

Success has not come easily for Asian Americans. Historically, they have been the victims of exclusion, prejudice, discrimination in various forms, and violent assaults. And not all

Figure 12.2   Mr. and Mrs. Van Ngo Vu stocking shelves in their family grocery store. Vu's Market opened in 1987. *Source:* National Archives.

Asians have achieved success in America. Many recent Asian immigrants remain mired in poverty, alienated from the mainstream of American life, and tempted by vice and crime. Many struggle to fathom a mysterious language and culture that is neither open nor friendly to them. Incidents of violence against Asian immigrants abound. Many recent arrivals from Vietnam, Cambodia, and Laos, the "boat people," refugees from oppression in their homelands, have encountered only grief and failure in this country. But there also is the saga of Jean Nguyen. Nguyen, at age eleven, escaped from Vietnam with her family by boat when Saigon fell to the Communists in 1975. She spoke no English upon her arrival in America that same year. In 1981, she graduated number one in her high school class, and in May 1985, she graduated from the U.S. Military Academy at West Point, receiving a commission as a second lieutenant in the U.S. Army. President Reagan paid tribute to Nguyen in his 1985 State of the Union Address, calling her "an American hero."

AFRICAN AMERICANS: A DUAL SOCIETY

For millions of African-American families, the decade of the 1970s was one of significant progress. Institutionalized racism and other obstacles to black achievement crumbled. Affirmative action programs, spawned by the civil rights movements of the 1960s, paid off for middle-class African Americans in the 1970s and carried into the 1980s. The greatest progress for African Americans came in education. By 1980, more than one million black people had enrolled in colleges, and thousands attended the finest universities and professional schools in the country. Thousands of young African-American men and women became doctors, lawyers, college professors, government bureaucrats, and business executives. The size of the African-American middle class increased rapidly, and black per capita income rose appreciably. African-American couples married, had children, and bought homes in the suburbs, their lifestyles much like that of their white counterparts in similar circumstances. Many young black professionals, reared and educated in the North, flocked to the Sunbelt cities to live and work. Many black Americans found urban life in Atlanta, Houston, and New Orleans offering more opportunities for ambitious careerists than the supposedly more liberal Northern cities. African American political participation in Southern states also far outstripped that in the North.

Despite significant gains for many, millions of African Americans lost ground during the 1970s. Affirmative action admissions programs were challenged by the Bakke case. Allen Bakke, a white applicant to the University of California at Davis Medical School, sued the university when his application was rejected. He showed that his qualifications were superior to several minority candidates who were admitted as "disadvantaged students" under a special quota reserved for them. The state supreme court ruled in his favor, as did the U.S. Supreme Court in a 1978 5 to 4 decision. The Supreme Court held that Bakke's rights to equal protection under the Fourteenth Amendment had been violated, and it nullified the school's affirmative action program based on racial quotas. But by a similar 5 to 4 decision, the Court upheld the right of the university to use race as "one element" in its effort to recruit medical students. Meanwhile, Davis had admitted Bakke to its medical school, and he went on to become a physician. The university also continued an affirmative action admissions program without explicit quotas for minority group students. The Supreme Court, despite its confusions and ambiguities, appeared to be saying that limited affirmative action policies could continue if they did not rely on numbers or if they did not try to do too much too fast.

The plight of poor inner-city blacks worsened during the 1970s. Unemployment among African Americans remained high, about twice the national average, averaging 14 percent to 15 percent. Unemployment among African-American teenagers skyrocketed to the 40 percent to 50 percent range by 1980. Black median family income was $12,800 in 1980, only about half that of whites. Ironically, African-American income was proportionately higher in 1950, when Jim Crow was still intact and antiblack racism was nearly universal and before the modern civil rights movement, civil rights legislation, and affirmative action programs had appeared.

Among poor inner-city African Americans, statistics revealed a frightening pattern of intertwined social pathologies—rising drug usage, delinquency, vice, and crime; rising school dropout rates and unemployment rates; and rising numbers of illegitimate births and households headed by an unmarried female parent. A permanent underclass was being forged within black America, without the possibility of its integration into the American mainstream. People within the underclass had no chance of personally fulfilling lives.

According to the sociologist William J. Wilson, one of the nation's most eminent scholars, the fundamental cause of the social misery and disorganization afflicting the black inner city was economic. Factories and businesses providing good jobs at good wages have disappeared from most of the black inner cities of America. Most prosperous black working-class and middle-class families have long since exited once-thriving neighborhood communities. Without the prospect of good jobs and without positive role models to set good examples, many of the inner-city

Figure 12.3   Boys play in a garbage-strewn vacant lot. Photo by Bayer.   *Source:* Monkmeyer Press.

dwellers were deprived of opportunities to seek productive, and meaningful lives. Wilson believed that without the economic and moral anchor of respectable employment, there was little chance of solving the interrelated, nearly intractable social problems of the black inner cities.

Within America, African Americans have forged a dual society—on the one hand, a thriving middle class that has achieved a place for itself in recent years that is roughly equal to white America, and, on the other hand, a declining underclass rotting on the mean streets of inner cities.

WOMEN: CHANGING ATTITUDES AND ROLES

Of all of the movements born during the upheavals of the 1960s, the one that retained its momentum and had the greatest impact during the 1970s was the women's movement. Feminists challenged men and women to refashion their identities, to abandon traditional notions of masculinity and femininity. Women exhorted their "sisters" to demand an end to second-class citizenship, to class discrimination, and to sexual exploitation. Other activists encouraged women to no longer confine themselves to domesticity, to seek fulfillment in new roles and statuses beyond those of mother, wife, and homemaker.

Because the women's movement in this country during the 1970s was so diverse and decentralized, it suffered from serious internal conflicts. Lesbian and straight women often discovered that they did not share the same goals and priorities. Radical feminists called for fundamental changes in the social and political structures; liberal reformers sought to achieve their goals by working within the system. Feminist intellectuals often engaged in ideological controversies that divided women into hostile camps. More serious conflicts of interest often divided women along the fault lines of class and race. Middle-class white women found, for example, that they had little in common with black working women, nor did they share the same perceptions, beliefs, and values.

The women's movement also encountered much opposition and resistance from groups within the larger society. Women antifeminists like Phyllis Schlafly and Anita Bryant successfully campaigned against the Equal Rights Amendment. They also attacked the gay rights movement and fought to repeal the right of women to have an abortion on demand, as sanctioned by the Supreme Court. Antifeminists won an important victory in 1980, when the Supreme Court upheld the constitutionality of a congressional law prohibiting federal funding of abortions for poor women. Antifeminists also charged the women's movement with being responsible for the spiraling divorce rate and the breakdown of family life in America.

Many men felt threatened by the women's movement. They perceived that their power and privileges were under assault, that many women expressed hostility toward men *qua* men. Some men responded negatively to the women's movement and abandoned their traditional roles as financial providers and authority figures for their families. Many women who had devoted their lives to being good mothers, wives, and homemakers felt that feminists judged them as victims and failures.

Despite its internal conflicts and weaknesses, and despite encountering powerful and widespread opposition, the women's movement of the 1970s helped bring about major social and cultural changes. Attitudes toward gender roles in this country changed dramatically during the 1970s. When a Gallup Poll in 1962 asked women if they believed they were discriminated against, two-thirds said no. In 1974, two-thirds of women responded yes to the same question, and they also indicated that they favored efforts to improve their status. The women's movement had its greatest influence on young college-educated women during the 1970s, many of whom were movement activists. Surveys showed that a majority of women graduating from college

Asked of those who said they had
heard of or read about the Equal Rights
Amendment: Do you favor or oppose this amendment?

Favor	58%
Oppose	24%
No Opinion	18%

By Sex

Male

Favor	63%
Oppose	22%
No Opinion	15%

Female

Favor	54%
Oppose	25%
No Opinion	21%

Interviewing Date 3/7–10/1975, Survey#925-K

Figure 12.4   Gallup poll taken on the Equal Rights Amendment, 1975. By 1973, thirty of the thirty-eight states required to ratify the ERA had done so. Although the amendment ultimately failed to achieve ratification and died in June 1982, public support was strong. In the 1976 presidential campaign, the platforms of both Democratic and Republicans included planks favoring its passage. Note that a higher proportion of men than women favored enactment of the ERA. *Source:* The Gallup Poll, 1975.

during the 1970s believed that a career was as important to a fulfilling life as a good marriage. These women believed that women and men were born with the same talents and potentials. These same women also stated that they expected equality in their sexual relations. Surveys revealed that three-fourths of college women had engaged in premarital sex, and that college women were more active sexually than college men.

Such attitudinal changes were reflected in the accelerated pace of women's entry into the workplaces of America during the 1970s. Since 1945, the rate of employment for women had risen steadily. By 1970, over half of women with children over age six worked full time or part time outside of the home. But during the 1970s, a major change occurred in women's employment patterns. The proportion of younger women with children who worked increased dramatically. By 1980, more than half of the mothers with children under age six found themselves in the labor force. For many women, the notion of work had been redefined during the 1970s. Work for women had become a life vocation. Women expected to work for most of their lives, with a few years off for childbearing and child rearing. They expected to have careers of their own. This new concept of work as career for young women of the 1970s contrasted dramatically with their mothers' concept. For the older generation of women, work came after child rearing; it was defined primarily as helping the family enjoy a more affluent lifestyle, not as an opportunity to have a career.

Female enrollment in colleges, graduate schools, and professional schools expanded rapidly during the 1970s. The proportion of women entering law school increased fivefold. Some entering classes at medical schools were 30 percent to 40 percent women. Women earned 25 percent of all doctoral degrees awarded during the 1970s. Women also entered the corporate world in ever-increasing numbers. Roles for some women television stars changed during the 1970s. The *Mary Tyler Moore Show* depicted an ambitious television studio executive, economically independent, who remained single. Other shows featured women as tough, aggressive, and violent in *Charlie's Angels* and the *Bionic Woman.* Working-class women continued to join unions, to enter the skilled trades, and to increase their numbers in previously all-male occupations. Both federal and state laws were enacted that helped women obtain credit, start their own businesses, and buy homes. Other women made their way in politics. Several were elected state governors and U.S. Senators. At the same time women flooded into professional fields hitherto exclusively or overwhelmingly male, the proportion of women entering the traditionally feminine fields of nursing, library work, and elementary school teaching declined sharply.

Figure 12.5   Office staff talking at desk. Photo by Richard Hutchings.   *Source:* Photo Researchers, Inc.

But despite their many impressive successes, women continued to encounter barriers in their struggle to overcome historical disadvantages and to achieve genuine equality in contemporary American society. "No-fault divorces," initially hailed as a great victory for women, proved to be a two-edged sword, because equality before the law did not bring equality in the marketplace. Compounding their economic difficulties, many divorced women, who had obtained custody of their children, found that their former husbands defaulted on child support payments. The courts were often lax in forcing ex-husbands to pay.

Sophisticated postfeminist analysts faulted the liberal leaders of the women's movement for being too concerned with achieving legal and political equality and thereby neglecting fundamental economic pressures that women faced in a society where male economic domination remained a continuing reality. They also criticized feminists who were obsessed with getting middle-class women into previously all-male professions and occupations, while neglecting the interests of the more numerous working-class women mired in low-paying occupations traditionally reserved for women.

Harsh economic realities during the 1970s limited opportunities for women. For every glittering career success scored by ambitious, capable, upwardly mobile women, many more women worked in low-paying jobs, which offered few opportunities for promotion or substantial pay increases. Occupational segregation, in which women remained concentrated in low-paying positions while men earned much higher incomes for their work, remained a persistent problem for women during the 1970s. Most of the new jobs created in the service sectors of the economy were taken by women, and these jobs invariably paid less than manufacturing or professional jobs. In the mid-1970s, women earned only 60¢ for every dollar earned by men. The 60¢ represented an improvement over previous decades, but it fell far short of economic parity with men. Women also were the victims of the "superwoman syndrome." Early feminist leaders proffered an idealized image of the woman who could have it all—career, home, husband, and family—a life of perfect equality and complete fulfillment. In practice, having it all often meant doing it all: women worked full time all day outside of the home, just like men, then they came home to continue working—doing all of the cleaning, cooking, and caring for their children, while men watched *Monday Night Football* with their neighbors, drank beer, listened to music, and played with the family dog.

During the 1970s, the divorce rate rocketed upward. By 1980, more than 40 percent of marriages ended in divorce. The median length of a first marriage fell to seven years. The median length of a second marriage fell to four years. The number of households headed by a single parent, almost always a female, climbed rapidly during the 1970s. The large majority of women entering the workforce during the 1970s did so because they had to support themselves or because they headed a single-parent household. They were not college-educated professionals choosing a career; they were working women who had to find work to survive economically within the American system. Inflationary pressures during the 1970s also drove many women into the workforce to ensure that their families could still enjoy a middle-class lifestyle no longer affordable on a single income. Many women slipped into the ranks of the working poor during the 1970s as a result of being divorced and saddled with child-rearing duties. The feminization of poverty and the fact that millions of children were growing up poor were two ominous socioeconomic realities directly affecting the status of women that first surfaced during the 1970s.

EDUCATION

In 1975, an estimated ten million students were enrolled full time or part time in the nation's 2,500 institutions of higher learning. Americans continued to spend far more on post–high school education than any other people, and America possessed 100 of the world's finest universities. Distinguished university faculty members continued to do important research and to publish their findings. American scholars led the world in many disciplines, especially the sciences. Each year, several U.S. scientists usually won Nobel Prizes in physics, chemistry, medical research, and economics. America's great universities were the vital centers of the nation's flourishing intellectual life.

In contrast to the turbulent 1960s, college campuses were mostly tranquil places in the 1970s. Students, reverting to historical norms, were much more interested in preparing for well-paying careers than they were in protesting public issues or trying to make society better. Yet some students could still respond to issues of conscience. Thousands of students joined protests against the nuclear arms race and called for universities to divest themselves of securities issued by companies doing business with the repressive apartheid regime in South Africa. Others continued to express concern about ecological and social issues.

But for most students, it was business as usual—attending classes, playing sports, perhaps working part time, and enjoying an active social life. College students of the 1970s were much less interested in the humanities and social sciences than they had been a generation earlier. Students of the 1970s flocked to majors in math, economics, finance, business, engineering, and computer science. Many students, including the brightest ones, demonstrated deficiencies in verbal skills, ignorance of history and literature, and a general decline in cultural literacy. A generation of technocratic "wannabes" had no time to pursue the traditional goal of a broad liberal arts education.

While colleges flourished, in many cities, American public schools deteriorated. Scholastic aptitude scores declined during the 1970s, and the high school dropout rate increased. About one in three eighteen-year-olds in this country were declared functionally illiterate in 1980. At a time when competition for jobs and all of the accouterments of the American-style good life were intensifying, when the economic and social life of the nation was becoming more complex and demanding, and when employers were demanding brighter and better educated employees, the public school system increasingly failed to meet individual and national needs. In May 1983, the National Commission on Excellence in Education reported that

> if an unfriendly foreign power had attempted to impose on America the mediocre educational performance that exists today, we might well have viewed it as an act of war.[1]

Many culprits were blamed for the dismal performance of the public schools during the 1970s. Television has been cited for keeping youngsters from reading books and for fostering boredom in the classroom. Indifferent parents, who neither set a good example nor encouraged their children to do well in school, were part of the problem. Popular entertainers and professional athletes whose riches and fame derived from talent rather than study in schools

---

[1]Quote is taken from *Report of the National Commission on Excellence in Education,* May 1963, p.1.

were accused of setting bad examples and of leading youngsters astray. In addition, the best and brightest college graduates rarely went into elementary and secondary teaching. Entry-level salaries were low, and teaching commanded little prestige as a profession. Americans once believed that education could solve all social problems; by the 1970s, to many social critics, the schools had become a social problem. One study found that 10 percent of teachers were incompetent; they could neither teach nor keep order in the classroom. Another 20 percent were considered only marginally qualified to teach youngsters in any subject.

There were signs in the early 1980s that educators were trying to turn their public schools in the direction of excellence. Polls showed that people were willing to pay more taxes to improve their schools. California and other states implemented legislation lengthening the school day and year, strengthening the curriculum, raising teachers' salaries, and requiring new teachers to pass competency tests. The fundamental question raised by the public school issue is one of cultural value. How highly does the nation prize learning? How highly do parents prize learning, and how much are they willing to pay for good public schools?

THE RISE OF THE RELIGIOUS RIGHT

The United States in the 1970s remained the most religious nation in the Western world. Nearly all Americans espoused a belief in God, and 60 percent of the population claimed membership in a church in 1976. Members of the more liberal Protestant churches and Reformed Jews became more accepting of divorce, homosexuality, birth control, and women clergy. The ministers and rabbis of these groups often urged their congregants to work for a more humane and just social order. American Catholics in the 1970s and 1980s were concerned with the continuing consequences of Vatican II, the church council that had met in the early 1960s to bring the church more into accord with modern life. After Vatican II, the liturgy was given in English, and the laity sang hymns during services. Priests were allowed more latitude in their interpretations of the Bible, and they sought ecumenical dialogues with Protestant ministers and rabbis. Catholics recognized the legitimacy of non-Catholic and non-Christian faiths and condemned anti-Semitism.

Church leaders spoke out on issues. In 1983, American Catholic bishops condemned nuclear war and urged the superpowers to disarm. In 1985, the bishops criticized the American capitalist economy for not meeting the needs of the millions of disadvantaged Americans. Many educated, liberal, middle-class Catholics welcomed the changes induced by Vatican II. But many traditionalists felt betrayed and were disturbed by these changes. They continued to adhere to the church's traditional teachings on sex, birth control, abortion, homosexuality, and a celibate, male priesthood.

Evangelical Christians formed one of the most powerful elements within the ranks of the growing conservative movement of the late 1970s and early 1980s. These fervent souls emphasized the personal responsibility of each individual believer. A sinner could be redeemed only by being "born again," that is, by confessing his or her sins, accepting Jesus Christ as a personal savior, and thereafter living a righteous life. Books by evangelical authors became best-sellers. "Christian Yellow Pages" appeared in many large cities. Millions of schoolchildren attended Christian elementary, middle, and high schools, where subjects were taught from an evangelical

Figure 12.6   In the aftermath of the *Roe v. Wade* **decision in 1973, the televangelist Jerry Falwell became increasingly political in his sermons on** *The Old-Time Gospel Hour***. He declared a "war against sin" by opposing abortion, gay-lesbian rights, pornography, and crime.**   *Source:* Magnum Photos, Inc.

perspective. In Christian nightclubs, patrons could order fruit juice cocktails and listen to gospel singers. As the 1970s ended, over 1,500 radio stations were owned by evangelical Christians.

Television quickly became the prime conduit for spreading the evangelical message and promoting its conservative social and political agenda. Pat Robertson started the 700 Club, aired over his Christian Broadcasting network. One of the regulars on his show, Jim Bakker, spun off to create his own program, the PTL (Praise the Lord) Club, starring his wife Tammy Faye Bakker, formerly a country-and-western singer. Bakker's show combined sermons, faith healing, inspirational stories, and musical entertainment, often featuring his wife joining the choir or doing a solo number. The PTL Club quickly became the most widely viewed television program on the planet. By 1980, Bakker's organization was taking in $25 million a year in contributions.

Born-again Christians frequently attacked what they called "secular humanism," the world view that held all truths to be relative, all moral values to be situational, and all ethical judgments to be necessarily tentative. They supported the "right to life" movement, denounced *Roe v. Wade,* and condemned abortion as murder. They opposed most feminist demands and the Equal Rights Amendment. They declared war on pornography and insisted that homosexuality was "unnatural" and sinful. Evangelical Christians sought to reintroduce school prayer and to have "creation science" taught in public schools as an alternative to the theory of evolution.

An evangelical leader, Jerry Falwell, became a prominent political activist. Falwell, for many years the pastor of the Thomas Road Baptist Church in Lynchburg, Virginia, had attracted a constituency of thousands. He also had his own television show *The Old-Time Gospel Hour.* In July 1979, Falwell formed the Moral Majority. Combining old-time religion with the latest computer-age technology, Falwell's organization targeted potential contributors and kept scorecards on how politicians voted on key issues such as the ERA, school prayer, and public funding for abortions.

For the 1980 elections, Falwell's Moral Majority activists developed a "hit list" of liberal Senators and Congressmen, then they mailed out more than one billion pieces of campaign literature to selected voters gleaned from their computerized mailing lists. Falwell's organization played a major role in bringing about the Republican takeover of the Senate in January 1981. The Moral Majority also threw all of its considerable resources into campaigning for Ronald Reagan. Reagan consolidated his hold on the Religious Right when he appointed Robert Billings, Executive Director of the Moral Majority, as his campaign's religious adviser. Reagan also incorporated the Moral Majority's social and political agenda into his successful campaign for the presidency in 1980.

In 1987, Pat Robertson announced that he would seek the Republican nomination for president in 1988. He was instantly a serious candidate with a potential electorate of millions. That same year, scandal rocked the Fundamentalist world when Jim Bakker was forced to resign his ministry because of sexual improprieties and financial irregularities.

THE "ME" DECADE

While some Americans carried the activist reform spirit of the 1960s into the 1970s, many more turned inward. They wanted to change themselves, not the external world of politics and society. They incorporated many of the elements from the hippie countercultural rebellion into their lifestyles—drug use, permissive sexuality, and above all, the "consciousness revolution." Participants included mostly young, middle-class professionals who prized affluence and professional attainment but who defined success primarily in psychological rather than material terms. It was more important to them to fulfill their "human potential" than to accumulate as much wealth as possible.

The cutting edge of the consciousness revolution could be found in California, home of the new lifestyles based on developing one's inner resources. Facilities like the Esalen Institute at Big Sur offered weekend encounter sessions for seekers wanting to "get in touch with themselves." Another entrepreneur of the human potential movement offered Erhard Seminars Training (est), built around marathon encounter sessions in which participants were encouraged to confront their most powerful inner feelings. Journalist Tom Wolfe labeled these people "psychonauts of inner space," the "Me" generation, and he compared their movement to a religious revival. According to Wolfe, the whole effort was aimed at remaking "one's very self," to strip away the artificial elements of personality that had been added by society "in order to find the Real Me."

As millions of Americans joined the consciousness revolution to seek salvation in narcissistic self-absorption, others sought refuge from the stresses of secular society by joining religious cults. Some of these religious orders embraced Eastern mystical religious practices such as Transcendental Meditation (TM) or Zen Buddhism. One cult, led by Indian holy man Bhagwan Rajneesh Mahareshi Yogi, established a flourishing colony near Antelope, Oregon. Thousands of people, attracted by the Bhagwan's message of spiritual rebirth combined with permissive sexuality, lived and worked in apparently joyous harmony for a time. But the cult disintegrated in 1986 because of internal dissension among its leaders. The Rajneesh fled Oregon for India to avoid prosecution on several federal charges.

The most prominent of these religious cults was the Unification Church, founded by Korean businessman and preacher Sun Myung Moon, who relocated to the United States. Moon, trained as a Presbyterian minister, developed his own brand of religion. He claimed to be the son of God and to receive divine revelations. His movement was controversial. His disciples were accused of kidnapping and brainwashing some of their teenage recruits. Reverend Moon also ran afoul of the law and was convicted on several counts of income tax evasion. Another cult came to a horrible end in November 1978, when its insane leader, Jim Jones, led the cult members from California to Guyana and later convinced more than 700 members to engage in a ghastly ritual mass suicide by drinking a poisoned fruit drink.

POPULAR CULTURE

America calmed in the early 1970s; the era of limits also was an era of comparative civic and social tranquility. In the words of historian John Wiltz, during the 1970s, "the national society became more mellow." No more fiery urban riots or militant campus protests convulsed the nation. Gone was the strident rhetoric of youthful radicals denouncing government policies at home and abroad and challenging traditional American values, mores, and institutions.

Several factors accounted for the calming down of American during the 1970s. The end of the Vietnam War removed the single most powerful source of dissidence. The decline of the economy, stagflation, and energy crises shifted the attention from political troubles to more fundamental economic and financial dysfunctions. The victories and partial victories of many of the 1960s movements led some of their participants to cease their activism in the 1970s with a sense of having accomplished their missions. Some radicals, suffering from moral and political exhaustion, abandoned their futile efforts to refashion American politics and society, retreating into a sullen personalism. Some joined the "me generation," redirecting their reformist energies away from the world and toward their own personalities. Others, reaching adulthood, made an accommodation with the system that they had previously spurned. Many hippies and campus radicals abandoned their countercultural ways, discarded their tie-dyed tank-tops and sandals, shaved their beards, trimmed their hair, donned three-piece suits, and became yuppies.

As the society calmed down in the 1970s, Americans, retreating into private realms, embraced a variety of fads and activities. Disco dancing, which had begun in the underground gay, black, and Latino night clubs, became enormously popular. Couples, often fueled by cocaine, danced the night away beneath pulsating lights in one of the hundreds of nightclubs that sprung up across America in the mid 1970's. Discos also were places where marginalized groups such as racial minorities and gay men could interact with white middle class Yuppies. The most famous disco was New York's Studio 54. An attractive African American soul singer, Donna Summer, became the "Queen of Discoland"; her records sold millions of copies during the years of the disco craze. A powerful film, *Saturday Night Fever,* starring John Travolta, with its electrifying dance sequences, popularized disco dancing; and also captured some of the emptiness and hopelessness of the 1970s.

During the 1970s, millions of Americans became more diet-conscious. People reduced their salt and cholesterol intake. Others stopped drinking alcoholic beverages and caffeinated drinks. Closely related to dieting and part of the new health consciousness, millions of people embraced the so-called fitness revolution. They became avid weight lifters as well as weight watchers. They swam, jogged, and rode bicycles; they joined health clubs, played racquetball, and performed aerobic exercises. Millions of people abandoned smoking cigarettes. By the end of the 1970s, approximately 30 percent of the adult population smoked, the lowest percentage since the 1920s.

If Americans were smoking fewer cigarettes during the 1970's, they were drinking more alcoholic beverages, especially beer. The per capita alcoholic consumption increased from twenty-two gallons in 1970 to twenty-seven gallons in 1980. Televised sporting events invariably featured numerous beer commercials associating good times with their products. Directing their ads mainly toward single young men, breweries strove to link beer drinking with male fantasies about sexy young women.

During the late 1970s alcohol abuse among teenagers and college students became a serious national issue. Studies found that thousands of high school students were alcoholics. In 1975, out of the approximately 45,000 Americans killed in traffic accidents, more than half died in accidents in which at least one of the drivers had been drinking. Auto accidents were one of the leading killers of young people between the ages of fifteen and twenty-five. Another survey found that at least ten million Americans were alcohol abusers.

Figure 12.7   An aerobics class.   *Source:* Monkmeyer Press.

Americans used other drugs besides ethanol in increasing amounts during the 1970s. The use of marijuana ("pot"), which had become a potent symbol of the youth revolt during the turbulent 1960s, expanded in the 1970s. Pot farming became a major underground industry in many parts of the country. Surveys showed that nearly half of the nation's college students during the 1970s used marijuana. Because most experts believed that the effects of the drug were comparatively mild if used in moderation, the federal government and most states reduced the legal penalties for possession of small amounts of pot from felonies to misdemeanors. A far more serious drug problem arose when the nation discovered that it had nearly a million heroin addicts on its hands by 1975.

Americans during the 1970s discovered the microwave oven, and they consumed a record number of frozen dinners annually. American families also dined out much more often than ever before, especially at fast food places. The major cause of the 1970s' eating-out phenomenon was the fact that more than 50 percent of married women with children now worked full time outside the home. The new dining-out patterns attested to a major cultural change that had occurred: the great American dinner was being redefined for families with children. Dinner was no longer a private familial activity; it had increasingly become a public activity.

The movie industry flourished during the 1970s. Hollywood turned out many fine films, some of which set box-office records. In 1972, a brilliant young director, Francis Ford Coppola, made the *The Godfather,* starring Al Pacino, Marlon Brando, and Diane Keaton. Based on a novel by Mario Puzo, the film was an epic about a powerful Mafia family making it in America. In 1973 came the occult classic, *The Exorcist,* starring a talented child actress, Linda Blair. Based on a novel by William Blatty, the film dealt in dramatic fashion with demonic possession and the valiant efforts of a Roman Catholic priest to exorcise the devil from the body of the child. The techno-thriller *Jaws* was released in 1975, produced by another brilliant young filmmaker, Steven Spielberg. It was a terrifying account of a killer great white shark attacking swimmers. The star of the film turned out to be Jaws himself, the technological monster that terrorized a New England town: it was shown devouring swimmers in gruesome detail. *Jaws* had the largest box office gross of any film ever made.

Jaws' record take at the box office was broken in 1977 by *Star Wars,* the first of a brilliant series of science-fiction films by George Lucas, another major filmmaking talent that burst on the Hollywood scene in the 1970s. Set in the distant past, *Star Wars* was essentially a child's fantasy, a fairy tale about high-tech adventures in space, starring Mark Hamill as Luke Skywalker, Harrison Ford as Hans Solo, and Carrie Fisher as Princess Leia. They were supported by a charming cast of bizarre-looking but gentle aliens and humanlike machines called androids. The plot was a simple morality tale, of the good guys triumphing over the bad guys, who controlled the evil Galactic Empire. Lucas reasserted the pleasures of straightforward storytelling, along with accessible, two-dimensional characters whose adventures ended happily. Much of the appeal of *Star wars* lay in the fact that it had no message, no sex, and only the mildest of violence. It could be enjoyed by "kids" of all ages. It relied on a dazzling array of special effects and technological wizardry to mesmerize its audience. One critic called it a Wild West adventure in outer space. Another analyst, pondering the deeper meanings of *Star Wars,* suggested that it pointed the way toward a new American mythology in the wake of the disillusionment with the Vietnam War, which destroyed the American frontier myth. *Star Wars* represented a creative effort to reclaim lost American innocence.

Surveys revealed that Americans watched more television shows than ever before during the 1970s. New technologies significantly enhanced the range and capabilities of the electronic medium. Communication satellites in geosynchronous orbits hundreds of miles in space enabled television news to provide live, instantaneous coverage of news events from anywhere on the planet. The 1970s also featured the beginning of cable television. Viewers were freed from having to rely on the three major networks that controlled prime time programming and the few shows that were worth watching, generated by local independent stations. By the late 1970s, because of the advent of cable utilizing the VHF channels, viewers who signed on for their services had a choice of twenty to thirty stations to watch. During the 1980s, cable television grew exponentially, and viewers could receive up to eighty channels. The most important new television technology of the 1970s was the introduction in 1975 of the videocassette recorder, or VCR. Because the early versions of VCRs were difficult to use and rather expensive, they were slow to catch on. Sales boomed in the 1980s and wrought another revolution in the nation's television and movie-viewing habits.

Because so many sporting events were televised during the 1970s, commercial spectator sports became a more important part of popular culture than ever before. Major professional spectator sports flourished, especially the National Football League (NFL), the National Basketball Association (NBA), and Major League baseball. Due in large part to television, professional football became the most popular national sport. Pro football is a fast-paced, complex, fiercely competitive, violent game played by tough, smart, and highly skilled athletes. Some analysts have linked its powerful hold on fans to the fact that pro football was a microcosm of the corporate economy that America had become in the 1970s. Pro football is also like the Internet economy—endlessly innovative and disruptive. Football coaches routinely revolutionize the game with new strategies and formations. One year the St. Louis Rams' offense featuring multiple deep passing formations carried them to a Super Bowl victory. The next year the Baltimore Raven's defensive formations featuring zone blitzes carried them to the championship.

College sports, particularly football and basketball, grew rapidly in popularity largely because of television. The growth of these major college sports was tinged with scandals. Some schools recruited athletes who were simply not equipped to succeed academically. Unless they were among the very few elite athletes who went on to successful careers as professional athletes, most left school after their athletic eligibility was expended without degrees and without the prospect of professional careers of any kind.

Other scandals that plagued college football and basketball programs included illegal payments to "amateur" athletes by alumni boosters, drug use, and other criminal behavior among some athletes. The National Collegiate Athletic Association (NCAA) exercised a rather ineffectual policing function over intercollegiate athletics. From time to time, they would investigate collegiate athletic programs, find illegalities, and impose penalties. One had a sense that the NCAA sporadically discovered the tip of a scandalous iceberg.

Amidst the commercialism and scandals of collegiate sports, there was one positive innovation. Women athletes demanded parity with men at the nation's colleges and universities. Although most schools fell far short of achieving gender equality in their sports programs, scholarship support for female athletes significantly increased. Several college women's sports flourished, including basketball, volleyball, swimming, and softball; these breakthroughs for women athletes represented another victory for the powerful women's movement of the 1970s.

A DISMAL DECADE

The 1970s was a dismal decade for millions of Americans. The economic growth cycle that had sustained the affluent society for thirty years stalled. U.S. power and prestige in the world declined. Politicians failed to provide effective leadership at home or abroad. The failure of the U.S. war in Vietnam filled most Americans with shame. The revelations of the Watergate scandals filled most Americans with disgust. Revelations of wrongdoing by the CIA and the FBI enraged most Americans. The Iranian hostage crisis humiliated most Americans.

For many citizens, 1970s' America no longer worked in accordance with traditional ideals and expectations. Young people coming of age during the 1970s enjoyed fewer opportunities than their parents. Double-digit inflation undermined real per capita income. For the first time in over 100 years, the average workweek lengthened, reversing a long-running historic trend. Millions of Americans had to work harder for less money during the 1970s. With more and more married women with children having to work or choosing to work, family life often deteriorated. People had less leisure time and fewer satisfying or fulfilling ways of using it. Those with disposable incomes threw themselves into a mindless consumerism.

Americans of the 1970s faced a plethora of serious problems, many of which proved to be interrelated and intractable. The debate over legalized abortion generated enormous strife and anguish. The country's growing dependence on expensive foreign oil remained a worrisome issue. The decline of America's manufacturing industries in the face of fierce foreign competition, and the decisions of American-based multinational corporations to export manufacturing operations presaged a bleak economic future for millions of American workers. Rising deficits in international trade balances and the federal budget made America the world's leading debtor nation. The failing public school system suggested that young people would be poorly prepared for good jobs that were fast disappearing. Social problems abounded: medical care was too expensive for the millions of working-class families who did not have health insurance coverage. There were serious shortcomings in the care available for people with disabilities, the very elderly, and the terminally ill. An epidemic of drug use swept the nation in the 1970s. There was a rising tide of crime, especially serious and violent crime. Massive poverty continued, as did discrimination against racial minorities, women, and gay and lesbian people, despite the significant gains that these groups had made during the 1960s. Continuing serious ecological problems fouled the air and poisoned the environment.

It is little wonder that the American people turned to an aging former film actor in 1980 who promised to restore American primacy in world affairs and revitalize the American economy. Even more important, Ronald Reagan promised to restore the American dream and make Americans feel good about themselves once again.

BRIEF BIBLIOGRAPHIC ESSAY

Recently, some substantial books have been written about the 1970s and historians are acquiring a broader appreciation of an era that until now has not fared well in scholarly hands. One of these new studies in Bruce J. Schulman's *The Seventies: The Great Shift in American Culture, Society, and Politics.* Schulman argues that the political, social, and cultural transformations occurring during the 1970s gave birth to the America we now inhabit. The implications of recent demographic shifts are discussed in Joseph J. Spengler's *Population and America's Future.* Two important books on the 1970s' economic crises are Robert L. Heilbroner's *An Inquiry into the Human Prospect* and Lester Thurow's *The Zero Sum Game.* U.S. economic decline during the 1970s is charted in Barry Bluestone's and Bennett Harrison's *The Deindustrialization of America.* A fine recent study, edited by Michael A. Bernstein and David E. Adler, *Understanding American Economic Decline,* is the best analysis that we have of the economic downturn that began in the early 1970s. A good study of the impact of computer technology on American society and culture is Tracy Kidder's *The Soul of a New Machine.* For a study of African Americans in the 1970s, read Ken Auletta's *The Underclass* and William J. Wilson's *The Declining Significance of Race.* Wilson also published another important study, *When Work Disappears: The World of the New Urban Poor. Today's Immigrants: Their Stories* is a recent study by Thomas Kessner and Betty Caroli. David M. Reimore's *Still the Golden Door: The Third World Comes to America* dramatically shows that the immigrant experience in America did not end with the 1920s. It may prove to be the case that the period from 1930 through the 1960s was the exception, the only time when immigration to America from most countries was banned or severely restricted.There is an extensive and generally excellent literature on women during the 1970s and 1980s. See Winifred D. Wandersee's *On the Move: American Women in the 1970s.* Mary Ann Mason's *The Equality Trap,* offers a perceptive study of the limitations of liberal feminism and its failure to cope with the economic plight of divorced working women. Christopher Lasch's *The Culture of Narcissism: American Life in the Age of Diminishing Expectations* catches many of the anxieties and discontents of the American people during the era of limits. Gillian Peele, in *Revival and Reaction: The Right in Contemporary America,* offers a study of current religious and political conservatism. Current education trends are analyzed in Sanford W. Reitman's *Education, Society, and Change.* Movie buffs will want to read Robert Bookbinder's *The Films of the 1970s.* Students of popular culture may want to read John-Manuel Andriote's *Hot Stuff: A Brief History of Disco.*

WEB SITES

The 1970s were the first decade of large-scale Asian immigration in the twentieth century. See <http://goldsea.comAAD/PARSING/parsing3.html> for a site that focuses on the experiences of Vietnamese Americans and Filipino Americans.

Through <http://besthistorysites.net/ushistory_women.shtml> you can reach many sites devoted to women's history. One topic of particular interest to women's history during the 1970s is The Dawn of the New ERA, and why the ERA failed of passage in the 1970s despite strong popular and bipartisan support.

Another important site is <http://www.anb.org/main_aa.html>, which is concerned with how African Americans adapted to the waning of the civil rights movement during the 1970s. Many more middle-class blacks than previously took advantage of enhanced educational and career opportunities. Many of these young professionals, reared in the North, moved South, where opportunities for careers in business and politics were more promising.

<http://www.uta.fi/FAST/UST/REF/pclinks.html> is a portal for U.S. popular culture links, many of which are pertinent to the 1970s popular culture.

13

America Revived

When President Ronald Wilson Reagan addressed the nation on inauguration day on January 20, 1981, it marked the coming to power of a resurgent conservatism. Newly empowered conservatives did not form a monolithic political movement; rather, they represented a diverse collection of people unhappy with the results of what they saw as nearly fifty years of liberal misgovernment. There was no essential conservative philosophy accepted by all politicians who called themselves conservatives. They formed no consensus and often bickered among themselves. Libertarians and the religious rightists often locked horns over fundamental principles and the use of governmental power. In reality, a miscellany of ideas, policy proposals, and programs were melded together under the marketing label "conservative."

In the early 1970s, conservatives of various stripes voiced their vehement opposition to many liberal public policies that they believed were bringing about too much social change too quickly. Many conservative whites in both the North and the South attacked what they called "forced busing" to integrate the public schools. They also denounced affirmative action programs that guaranteed minorities, particularly African Americans, equal opportunity in their quest for schooling and employment. Antifeminist conservatives opposed the Equal Rights Amendment and helped defeat it. They also opposed efforts to protect the rights of gays and lesbians. Most conservatives opposed all gun control measures and favored the restoration of capital punishment. They were outraged when the Supreme Court issued its controversial *Roe v. Wade* (1973), which granted women the right to an abortion on demand during the first trimester of a pregnancy. Conservatives also attacked Supreme Court rulings made during the 1970s that outlawed prayer in the public schools and appeared to strengthen the rights of criminals at the expense of law enforcement personnel. Evangelical Christians stressed the cruciality of tradition, religion, and family values. Most conservatives attacked welfare programs, and high taxes, and they deplored the erosion of wave-the-flag patriotism. Traditional business conservatives championed free-enterprise capitalism, criticized government regulation of economic activity, and attacked trade unions.

286

New Right conservatives, whose chief national leaders were Barry Goldwater and Ronald Reagan, believed that Soviet leaders were the personification of evil and responsible for all that had gone wrong in the world since 1945. They insisted that America must maintain an arsenal of thermonuclear and conventional weapons to contain the aggressive tendencies of the Kremlin and its clients. These conservatives lamented over the decline of U.S. power and prestige in the world, symbolized by the Vietnam debacle and the Iranian hostage crisis.

The varied groups that called themselves conservative, led by Ronald Reagan, brought about a remarkable transformation in the way the American people viewed conservatism. Since the New Deal era of the 1930s, the term *conservative* had been a political epithet; conservatism connoted selfishness, anti-intellectualism, and most of all, an irrational clinging to traditional ways in the face of novel, unprecedented challenges. But since the 1970s, with the Democratic Party and especially its liberal wing under siege as the icons of discredited and dysfunctional policies, conservatives have stepped forward as dynamic agents of change. Carter appeared to be the inept defender of the status quo in the face of Reagan's dynamism and calls for renewal. In the election of 1980, to a large majority of voters, the conservative Republican combination of evangelical Christianity, family values, supply-side economics, and a hard-line, anti-Soviet foreign policy looked quite like a much-needed reform program to revitalize and redeem America. His coalition during the 1980s received support from a large majority of the American people and it buried the old liberal consensus that had prevailed from the 1930s through the 1960s.

THE ADVENT OF REAGANOMICS

Reagan grounded his program for economic recovery in "supply-side" economic theory. Contradicting the long-prevailing Keynesian theory, which relied on government spending and tax cuts to boost consumer demand, supply-siders favored cutting both federal spending and taxes at the same time. According to supply-siders, high taxes siphoned capital that otherwise would be invested in productive enterprises. They believed that the private sector, freed from shackles imposed by government regulation and high taxes, would increase its investment in productive enterprises, thereby generating economic growth and creating millions of new, well-paying jobs. Economic growth also would cut inflation and generate increased tax revenues, despite the lower tax rates. Government expenditures would be trimmed by shrinking government benefits. Spending cuts, coupled with the projected economic expansion, would bring in a balanced budget.

The president brought a mixed group of senior advisers to Washington. He appointed James A. Baker as his chief of staff. Baker urged Reagan to move quickly on his two key issues—tax cuts and the military buildup. At the Treasury Department, he installed Donald Regan, a securities broker. David Stockman became director of the Office of Management and Budget. Stockman, who was a supply-side zealot, carried to Congress Reagan's program of cutting spending and reducing taxes. While Stockman overhauled the federal budgetary process, Paul Volcker, a Carter holdover and chairman of the Federal Reserve Board, kept tight reins on the money supply with high interest rates.

Stockman made cutting federal spending the Reagan administration's top priority. He slashed $41 billion in social spending for food stamps, public service jobs, student loans, school lunches, urban mass transit, and welfare payments. Social Security was exempted, and Reagan also left what he called a "safety net for the truly needy." At the same time he was cutting back social spending, Reagan increased military spending sharply.

Reagan persuaded many Sunbelt Democratic congressmen to support his programs. These "boll weevils," led by Representative Phil Gramm of Texas, were crucial in getting his program through the Democratic-controlled House. Reagan made a dramatic personal appearance before a joint session of Congress to plead for his budget only a few weeks after being seriously wounded during an attempt on his life. Even Democrats who opposed his budget and could not abide Reagan's conservative political philosophy were on their feet applauding the gallant old actor. He had built up a strong bipartisan coalition in the House and won a commanding 253 to 176 victory. His winning margin in the Senate was even more impressive, 78 to 20. Many liberal Democrats were skeptical that supply-side economics could work, but they lacked an alternative program that had any popular appeal.

Congress quickly enacted the key element of Reagan's economic policy—tax cuts. The Economic Recovery Tax Act of 1981 was the most significant legislation of the Reagan Era. Based on a proposal by Senator William Roth and Congressman Jack Kemp, the across-the-board tax cuts reduced basic personal income tax rates by 25 percent over three years. It also in-dexed tax brackets, which kept tax rates constant when incomes rose solely because of inflation. Congress wrote additional tax concessions into an omnibus bill. Capital gains, inheritance tax, and gift taxes also were reduced. Business tax write-offs were enhanced.The Reagan tax cuts, with congressional sanction, were the most generous tax reductions in the nation's history.

Reagan also sought to reduce federal regulation of the economy. He appointed men and women to federal regulatory agencies who shared his views that markets, not governmental agencies, ought to direct the national economy. He appointed Anne Gorsuch Burford, who op-posed air quality and toxic waste regulations, to head the EPA. During her tenure, the EPA bud-get was slashed and all of its enforcement efforts were weakened. Reagan's most controversial appointment was James Watt, to head the Department of the Interior. Watt had directed an antienvironmentalist legal action group before his appointment to the Interior Department. He supported strip-mining and favored opening up public lands to private developers, including off-shore oil-drilling sites. Reagan tried to eliminate the Department of Energy; failing to do that, he settled for severe cuts in its budget and operations. He persuaded Congress to cut federal spending for elementary and secondary education. Much of the responsibility, and the costs, of regulatory activity was shifted to the states.

Drew Lewis, Reagan's secretary of transportation, removed many of the regulations to re-duce pollution and increase driver safety that had been imposed on the U.S. auto industry during the 1970s. He also persuaded the Japanese to voluntarily restrict automobile imports to the United States. Lewis opposed an illegal strike by an air traffic controller's union (PATCO) in the summer of 1981. President Reagan fired the 11,500 striking workers, decertified the union, and ordered Lewis to train and hire thousands of new air controllers to replace them. The destruction of the air traffic controller's union was the most devastating defeat for organized labor in mod-ern times. It demoralized a labor movement already reeling from the decline of American manu-facturing and loss of political clout.

By the end of the summer of 1981, "Reaganomics" was in place. The new leader had as-serted a popular mandate, seized the political initiative, redefined the public agenda, and got most of his program implemented. *Time* magazine observed that, "No President since FDR had done so much of such magnitude so quickly to change the economic direction of the country." Reaganomics amounted to a radical assault on the liberal welfare state erected during the previous fifty years.

Aware that few African Americans had voted Republican, the Reagan administration was unresponsive to black concerns. Federal support for civil rights weakened. Reagan opposed affirmative action hiring programs. His Attorney General, Edwin Meese, opposed busing to achieve school desegregation. The number of African American officials appointed to major government positions declined. Both the staff and budget of the Civil Rights Division of the Justice Department were cut.

Reagan's record for appointments of women was better than his record for African Americans. He appointed a few highly visible women to top government positions. He fulfilled a campaign pledge and made a major symbolic gesture to women when he appointed Sandra Day O'Connor to the Supreme Court, the first women jurist ever chosen. He appointed Jeane Kirkpatrick as the U.S. Ambassador to the United Nations. Several women served in his cabinet. Reagan opposed the Equal Rights Amendment, and he was an outspoken foe of abortion, denouncing *Roe v. Wade.*

Figure 13.1   Sandra Day O'Connor.   *Source:* Supreme Court Historical Society.

RECESSION AND RECOVERY

After a year, it was evident that Reaganomics had not brought about an economic revival but instead had brought forth a recession. Unemployment exceeded 9 percent, the highest rate since 1941. Business bankruptcies rose to depression levels. Steep interest rates priced homes and cars beyond the reach of millions of families and plunged those two major industries into depression. The nation was mired in its worst slump since the Great Depression. Manufacturing output declined, and the construction industry slumped. In Detroit, unemployment reached 20 percent. A class of "new poor," not seen since the 1930s, appeared on the streets: homeless, unemployed workers and their families.

Supply-side economics did not work as advertised. A combination of deep tax cuts, steep hikes in military spending, and drastic economic shrinkage drove the federal budget deficit to over $100 billion, the highest ever. The one bright spot in an otherwise dark economic picture was declining inflation. It dropped from 13 percent in 1980 to 9 percent in 1981, and fell to 5 percent in 1982. The short-term failure of Reaganomics derived from two fiscal realities: the failure of the tax cuts to stimulate increased business investment and continuing high interest rates that put a crimp in both business spending and consumer purchases. The recession worsened throughout 1982. Toward the end of the year, unemployment reached 10 percent; over 11 million Americans were out of work.

The 1982 midterm elections took place amidst the worst economic conditions the country had seen in over forty years. The election amounted to a referendum on Reaganomics. The Democrats picked up twenty-five House seats, but the Republicans held on to the Senate. When the new Congress convened in January 1983, Reagan lost his bipartisan majority coalition that had pushed through Reaganomics. House Speaker Thomas "Tip" O'Neill, the leader of the opposition to Reaganomics, forced the president to accept budget compromises in 1983. Cuts in social spending were lessened, and increases in military spending were reduced.

The economy recovered strongly in 1983, and the surge continued in 1984. The GDP rose by 6.8 percent in 1984, the largest one-year gain since the Korean War. Unemployment and interest rates declined. Housing starts and new car sales picked up. The rate of inflation dropped to 4 percent for both years, the lowest since the late 1960s. Personal income rose; consumer and business confidence soared. Abundant world oil supplies were an important cause of the drop in the rate of inflation. By the end of 1984, OPEC was in disarray and world oil prices were plummeting. The economic expansion that began in 1983 continued into the early 1990s. Economic growth generated 18 million new jobs and tripled the price of stocks by 1990.

Despite the strong rebound in 1983, serious problems continued to plague the American economy. Tax cuts combined with large increases in military spending to generate record federal deficits. The nation's international trade deficit reached a record $108 billion in 1984. The main causes of the soaring international debt were the nation's continuing thirst for foreign oil and imported manufactures, such as autos, VCRs, cameras, and stereos. By the end of his first term, Reagan had managed to double the national debt. Amidst the economic revival, over 7.5 million Americans remained out of work. The Census Bureau reported that the nation's poverty rate reached 15.2 percent in 1983, the highest since 1965. There were thirty-five million poor people in America, six million more than when Reagan assumed office.

Figure 13.2   Pro-life demonstrator and a pro-choice demonstrator exchange barbs outside Faneuil Hall in Boston, where pro-life forces held their 11th annual Assembly for Life.   *Source:* CORBIS.

THE COLD WAR REVIVED

Because he made reviving the economy his top priority, Reagan relied heavily on advisers both for designing and implementing U.S. foreign policy. For the new president, the traditional verities of the Cold War still prevailed: America and its allies were locked in a life-or-death struggle for survival with a ruthless, expansionist Soviet empire. Reagan repudiated previous efforts at detente and announced his intention to challenge the Soviets around the globe. He launched a rapid buildup of military power and he also announced what came to be known as the "Reagan Doctrine." The United States would help anti-Communist resistance movements wherever they cropped up in the world. Reagan was the first president to take the offensive both ideologically and strategically against Communism.

Reagan also made clear that he intended to make major use of the CIA as an instrument of American foreign policy, especially its covert paramilitary operations. He freed U.S. arms sales from the restrictions imposed by the Carter administration and scrapped Carter's human rights policies. Reagan viewed the Cold War between the United States and the Soviet Union as fundamentally a moral conflict. He denounced the Soviet Union in a speech before the United Nations in 1982, charging that Soviet agents were working everywhere in the world, "violating human rights and unnerving the world with violence." Addressing a convention of evangelical Christians in Orlando, Florida, in May 1983, he called the Soviet Union "an evil empire" and declared that the Soviet leaders were "the focus of evil in the modern world."

Secretary of Defense Casper Weinberger proposed a $1.2 trillion defense buildup over five years, which Reagan strongly supported. Weinberger insisted that during Carter's presidency the Soviets had achieved strategic superiority over the United States. A "window of vulnerability" existed for American land-based missiles that could tempt the Soviets to try a "first strike" nuclear attack. Reagan and Weinberger spoke of being able "to prevail" in the event of a nuclear war with the Soviets. Such rhetoric, yoked to the gigantic increases in military spending, frightened millions of Americans, who feared that Reagan was preparing for a nuclear war with the Soviets.

In the early 1980s, Washington successfully hindered Soviet efforts to crush Afghanistan's *mujahadin* rebels. The CIA shipped arms to Pakistan, which were then smuggled into Afghanistan. The Soviets soon found themselves bogged down in a Vietnam-like quagmire. The Soviets also tried to interdict the movement of arms and supplies from Pakistan and threatened the Pakistanis if they did not desist, all to no avail. The *mujahadin,* despite absorbing heavy casualties, maintained a determined resistance to Soviet efforts to pacify them. The application of the Reagan Doctrine in Afghanistan succeeded. During these efforts in Afghanistan, CIA officials worked with Islamic militants including al-Qaeda, a terrorist group led by a young Saudi national, Osama bin Laden.

Reagan succeeded in implementing Carter's 1979 initiative to place 572 intermediate-range cruise and Pershing II missiles in western Europe that could strike targets in the western regions of the Soviet Union. These missiles would counter Soviet SS-20 missiles already deployed and aimed at NATO countries. This initiative provoked an angry response from the Soviets, who tried to stop it. It also aroused opposition from peace groups in Europe and from a "nuclear freeze" movement in the United States. In the spring of 1982, nearly a million nuclear freeze supporters gathered in Central Park, the largest political rally in U.S. history.

To offset European and domestic opposition to his plan, Reagan offered two new arms control initiatives. The first, called the "zero option," offered to cancel the proposed deployment of cruise and Pershing missiles in exchange for Soviet removal of their SS-20 missiles. Second, at a new series of arms talks between U.S. and Soviet negotiators in Geneva, called START, the United States proposed that both sides scrap one-third of their nuclear warheads and permit land-based missiles to have no more than half of the remaining warheads. The Soviets did not take these proposals seriously. They had no incentive to remove missiles already in place in exchange for cancellation of weapons not yet deployed. They rejected the second offer because 70 percent of their warheads were on land-based missiles, compared to about one-third for the United States. However, these U.S. arms control proposals reassured nervous Europeans and slowed the nuclear freeze movement. When the new missiles began arriving in Great Britain and West Germany in 1983, the Soviets broke off the START talks.

The United States escalated the arms race in 1983, when Reagan ordered the Pentagon to develop a Strategic Defense Initiative (SDI). The SDI was an immensely complex antimissile defense system that used high-powered, space based lasers to destroy enemy missiles in flight. The SDI was quickly dubbed "Star Wars" by its critics. Many scientists expressed skepticism that the SDI could work. If it could be built, they estimated that it would take years and cost $1 trillion.

If it proved successful, the defense system would destabilize the arms race because it would force the Soviets to build more missiles and develop an SDI of their own. Reagan strongly backed the SDI, assuming that it could be built and would free the world from the deadly trap of deterrence based on mutually assured destruction. He clung to his vision of a world free from the threat posed by the nuclear arms race. Whatever his public image or the views of his critics, Ronald Reagan was at heart a passionate antinuclear idealist. His overriding goal was to escape the awful dilemma of Mutually Assured Destruction (MAD) that had kept both sides feverishly building more efficient weapons of mass destruction and had also kept both societies in a state of perpetual angst.

The costly and dangerous nuclear arms race between the two superpowers roared on. Both sides continued to develop new weapons systems and to refine existing ones. Although both sides observed the unratified SALT II agreement, it placed few curbs on their activities. The death of Russian leader Leonid Brezhnev, followed by two short tenures of old and sick successors, created a succession crisis for the Soviets. It also made any efforts at negotiations between the Soviets and the Americans difficult. According to some scholars, in November, 1983, the Soviets, alarmed by Reagan's harsh anti-Soviet rhetoric and the rapid U.S. arms buildup, convinced themselves, mistakenly, that the United States might be planning to launch a pre-emptive strike against the Soviet Union. Soviet forces began to prepare for a retaliatory strike before the crisis subsided. The Soviet misinterpretation of U.S. intentions coupled to their own preparations for a nuclear strike against the United States, sobered President Reagan. He toned down his anti-Soviet rhetoric and began to explore possibilities for improving relations with Soviet leaders and seeking ways of reducing the nuclear threat that imperiled both superpowers.

In March 1985, a dynamic new leader emerged in the Soviet Union, Mikhail Gorbachev. Future negotiations on arms control between the two superpowers again became possible. Although he had escalated the arms race, and intensified the Cold War, Reagan's efforts against the Soviets did restore a measure of American pride and self-confidence. Reagan showed that he had no fear of the Soviet Union and exuded confidence that America would eventually win the Cold War. His great insight, derived at a time when few defense experts and Sovietologists shared his views, was that the Soviet Union was both evil and weak, and that it could be beaten if Americans kept the faith and increased defense spending.

THE PACIFIC RIM

The Reagan administration also gave much attention to U.S. foreign policy interests in the Far East. Many experts believed that Asia was destined to become the center of U.S. diplomatic concerns by the dawn of the twenty-first century. The most important nations were China, home to a quarter of the planet's six billion inhabitants, and Japan, a nation that had become an economic powerhouse by the 1970s. The economies of South Korea, Taiwan, Hong Kong, Maylasia, and Singapore also were thriving in the early 1980s, their prosperity in large measure fueled, like Japan's, on the sale of manufactures to the United States and western Europe.

Washington did not have good relations with China initially, mainly because of Reagan's efforts to bolster the military forces of Taiwan, which the Chinese considered part of their country. In 1984, Sino-American relations improved when Premier Zhao Zivang of the PRC visited the United States and signed agreements pledging cooperation between China and the United States in such crucial areas as industry, science, and technology. Reagan later visited China and signed pacts, pledging renewed cultural exchanges between the two countries.

Diplomacy with Japan was the Reagan administration's prime Asian concern. Two major problems strained Japanese-American relations in 1981. The first concerned efforts by the Reagan administration to get Japan to pay a larger share of its defense costs rather than continue to rely on the nuclear shield provided by U.S. taxpayers. The Japanese subsequently increased their defense outlays.

The second, more serious problem concerned the growing imbalance in U.S.-Japanese trade that increasingly favored the Japanese. The imbalance had reached $10 billion in 1980 and $16 billion in 1981. The largest part of the imbalance derived from the sale of Japanese cars to U.S. consumers. In 1981, Japanese automakers sold almost two million cars to American buyers, hurting domestic automakers, who had lost 25 percent of their market to the Japanese in a decade. U.S. negotiators persuaded the Japanese to reduce voluntarily auto shipments to America for 1982 and to reduce barriers to the importation of U.S. agricultural commodities. Despite these concessions, the trade imbalance continued to grow in favor of Japan, reaching $20 billion in 1983 and $35 billion in 1984.

DISASTER IN LEBANON

In the Middle East, the Reagan administration tried to continue the peace process established by Carter, of providing Israel with strategic security and giving the Palestinians a homeland on the West Bank. The larger goal of U.S. Middle Eastern policy continued to be containing Soviet influence in that strategic region. While trying to implement its policies, the United States became embroiled in a civil war going on in Lebanon. In June 1982, in an effort to destroy the PLO, Israeli forces invaded Lebanon and besieged West Beirut, where refugee camps contained thousands of Palestinians had provided a base for PLO fighters. The PLO and other Muslim factions in Lebanon turned to Syria to counter the Israeli forces.

Even as it supported the Israeli invasion, the Reagan administration employed an envoy of Lebanese descent, Philip Habib, who arranged for the Israelis to lift their siege while a UN force supervised the removal of PLO forces. Following the removal of the PLO, the Israelis reoccupied West Beirut. On September 17, 1982, Lebanese Christian militia, working closely with Israeli forces, entered two Palestinian refugee camps and slaughtered hundreds of people in reprisal for the murder three days earlier of a Christian leader. Following the massacre of the Palestinians, the United States sent in troops to try to restore peace in Beirut.

But the U.S. forces came under siege themselves as civil war raged in the streets of Beirut between Christian and Muslim militias. Syrian forces, backed by the Soviets, occupied eastern Lebanon and controlled most of the Muslim factions. Iranian militants also provided support

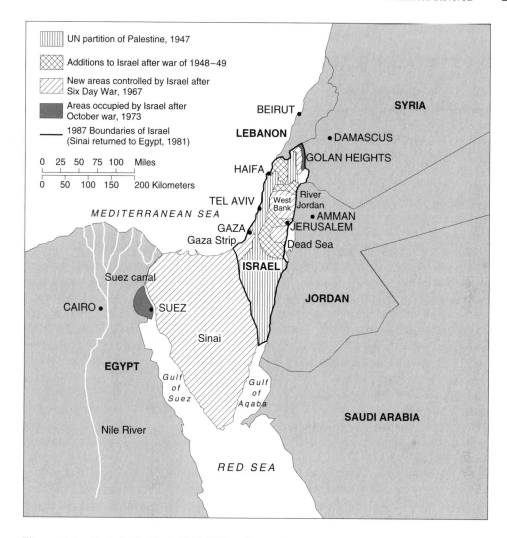

Figure 13.3   The Middle East, 1947–1981.   *Source:* U.S. State Department.

and helped to train the militias. Israeli troops remained in southern Lebanon. The 1,500 U.S. Marines, isolated at the Beirut airport were perceived by the Muslims and their foreign supporters to be aligned with the Christian forces.

The United States tried unsuccessfully to restore order to Lebanon and to arrange for the Syrians and Israelis to withdraw from that battered country. Early on the morning of October 23, 1983, a yellow Mercedes truck, loaded with explosives and driven by a Muslim terrorist, slammed into the U.S. Marine compound near the Beirut airport. The powerful blast killed 241 Marines who were sleeping inside. Reagan was forced to withdraw the remaining U.S. forces in February 1984, which terminated the U.S. military presence in Lebanon. Lebanon became a fertile source of kidnappings and terrorist attacks on U.S. citizens. Moderate Arab states refused to support U.S. Middle East policy, and the peace process appeared hopelessly stalled. Lebanon was a humiliating defeat for the Reagan administration, and the slaughter of the Marines constituted the worst U.S. military disaster since Vietnam. The developing Islamic terrorist war against the United States and Israel, going on since the late 1970s, had escalated.

POLICING THE WESTERN HEMISPHERE

Reagan committed himself to removing the Sandinista government in Nicaragua. The Sandinistas were friendly with Marxist leaders in Cuba and the Soviet Union, but they were not Communists. Reagan accused the Sandinistas of suppressing democratic elements within Nicaragua and aiding Marxist rebels in nearby El Salvador. Reagan viewed the Sandinista regime as a serious threat in Central America that must be contained; otherwise it could become another Cuba. He feared that the Sandinistas would use Nicaraguan military bases as staging areas to export Marxist-Leninist revolution to neighboring countries. The CIA estimated that there were approximately 500 Cuban, Soviet, and east European military advisers, technicians, and intelligence operatives in Nicaragua in 1981.

In the spring of 1982, Reagan approved the use of CIA operations to interdict arms shipments from Nicaragua to El Salvador and to overthrow the Sandinista regime. Washington's chosen instrument for deposing the Sandinistas was to be a "Contra" military force recruited from various groups of anti-Sandinista Nicaraguans, including former supporters of the deposed dictator, Anastasio Somoza Debayle.

Congress enacted the Boland Amendment in December 1982, which forbade the CIA or the Pentagon to provide any funds or training to anyone for the purpose "of overthrowing the government of Nicaragua." Reagan appealed to Congress in 1983 for funds to "hold the line against externally supported aggression" in Central America. Congressional Democrats accused him of exaggerating the Cuban and Soviet threats, of relying too heavily upon military solutions, and of ignoring serious social and economic problems within Central American countries that bred rebellion. Public opinion polls showed that a majority of Americans opposed U.S. military involvement in Central America and feared being drawn into another Vietnam. Congress rejected Reagan's request for $80 million to support CIA covert operations against Nicaragua; later, it approved $24 million for covert operations against the Sandinistas.

Meanwhile, Contra forces, trained by the CIA at bases in neighboring Honduras, began operations inside Nicaragua. Other CIA-trained forces attacked various port installations at several sites. In early 1984, helicopters flown by CIA-trained operatives mined three of Nicaragua's harbors. When Congress learned that CIA-trained forces had mined Nicaraguan harbors and damaged merchant ships, it cut off all U.S. aid for the Contras. The World Court later ruled that the United States had violated international law and that Nicaragua could sue America for damages.

With funding of its secret war in Nicaragua cut off by Congress, Washington made a deal with the Saudi Arabians, whereby the United States sold the Saudis 400 Stinger aircraft missiles, in return for which they agreed to provide the Contras with $10 million. The administration also persuaded Israel to aid the Contras, and wealthy Americans also chipped in money.

The Iran-Contra scandal originated in these efforts at creative financing to circumvent the will of Congress and keep Washington's proxy war in Nicaragua going.

In El Salvador, the war between left-wing guerrillas and the government continued. Carter had cut off U.S. aid to the government following the murder of three American nuns by government forces. The Reagan administration restored U.S. assistance and sent in forty-five U.S. military advisers to help government forces. Washington backed a government headed by a moderate democrat, Jose Napoleon Duarte. Duarte defeated the candidate of the extreme Right, Roberto d'Aubisson, in a 1984 election and began a reform program. He also tried to curb the excesses of right-wing "death squads" that had murdered thousands of civilians since the war began. But Duarte's forces could not defeat the rebels.

While the Reagan administration pursued its proxy war against the Sandinistas in Nicaragua and backed the Duarte government in El Salvador, it also fought a brief miniwar for control of Grenada, small island located in the eastern Caribbean. Early in the morning of October 25, 1983, 1,900 U.S. Marines and Army paratroopers stormed the shore. The U.S. forces invaded Grenada ostensibly to rescue several hundred American citizens studying medicine there.

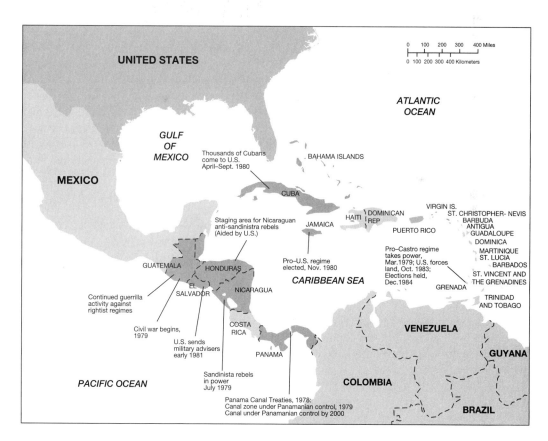

Figure 13.4   The United States in Central America, 1978–1990.   *Source:* Public Domain Map.

The main purpose of the invasion was to overthrow a Marxist regime, which had recently come to power. What most concerned the Reagan administration was the construction of an airport at Point Salines, which could serve as a refueling station for Soviet aircraft ferrying weapons to the Sandinistas. Within four days, U.S. forces had overwhelmed the small Grenadian army and deposed the Marxist regime.

Washington installed a friendly interim government pending elections and granted it $30 million in military and economic assistance. UN spokesmen and some liberal media pundits and politicians within the United States denounced the Grenada operation. Public opinion polls showed that Reagan's actions enjoyed broad popular support. By staging a brief, dramatic, and low-casualty rescue operation only two days after the Marines were blown up in their barracks in Beirut, the Grenada miniwar diverted attention from that horrible event.

THE ELECTION OF 1984

During his first term especially, liberal pundits frequently savaged Ronald Reagan. The historian John Wiltz called Reagan "the least cerebral" of modern presidents. They portrayed him as a kind of ceremonial president: while he looked and acted the part, an inner circle of advisers made policy and ran the country. Reagan tended to disengage himself from the details of his day-to-day administration. On occasion, he dozed off at cabinet meetings while his advisers debated policy options. He often appeared dependent on his wife Nancy for advice and guidance, and the First Lady was fiercely protective of her husband's image. Reagan sometimes confused events that had transpired in the celluloid world of Hollywood films with political reality. He often was given to misstatements. During his presidency, Reagan's staffers became adept at damage control, at putting the proper "spin" on his more ludicrous remarks. At times, Reagan appeared to be an old actor playing the role of president rather than functioning as chief executive.

His liberal detractors, who ridiculed his intellectual and administrative shortcomings, underrated Reagan's remarkable political talents. Intellectuals might have scoffed at the old actor's simplistic ideas, but Reagan understood that average American citizens could not care less whether the president of the United States possessed a powerful mind or was a policy wonk. They wanted a leader who had a clear vision of the direction in which he wanted to move the country. Reagan was determined to reverse the fifty-year trend whereby the federal government assumed increasing responsibility for underwriting the general welfare of the population. Reagan wanted to slash taxes and eliminate government regulations that he believed had shackled the entrepreneurial energies of the American people for a half-century. He also was determined to restore U.S. military primacy in the world and to contain Soviet expansionism as Americans had done in the 1940s and 1950s, before the Vietnam debacle sapped their will. And if he could, he would win the Cold War.

In response to a succession of failed presidencies, it had become part of the conventional wisdom to assert that the presidency had grown too large, that contemporary problems had become too complex for any mortal to master. Reagan's performance in office disproved such notions. He strengthened the office of the presidency. He reasserted influence over Congress. He centralized the budget-making process, and brought the bureaucracies under heel.

He confronted the dilemma that faced all conservative reformers committed to downsizing government at all levels. They first had to achieve power and assert strong leadership to make government less intrusive and expensive.

Reagan largely succeeded in moving Congress and the American people in accordance with his conservative vision. He retained the trust and affection of a large majority of his fellow citizens for most of his presidency. The social service state was pared down and the social contract was attenuated. The economy, after enduring a bitter recession in 1982, rebounded strongly. Inflation was brought under control, and long-term stable growth for the rest of the decade of the 1980s ensured national prosperity. Reagan strengthened the armed forces; Americans were treated with a new respect in the world by both friends and foes. Reagan's stirring speeches helped lift the malaise that had fastened itself on the nation during the era of limits. Most Americans became more optimistic about both their prospects and future of the nation.

But there was a dark side to the Reagan record. While yuppies prospered, the number of poor Americans increased. Ronald Reagan presided over a major redistribution of national income. Median family income for African Americans and for people of Hispanic origin declined during Reagan's presidency. Over half of the new jobs created during the 1980s were low-wage entry level jobs that could not sustain a family. The rich became richer, while the poor became poorer. The Reagan administration had scant interest in civil rights or ecological concerns. Drugs poured into the country and crime rates soared.

Reagan's landslide reelection victory on November 6, 1984, reaffirmed his personal popularity. His forty-nine-state sweep expressed voter approval of the strong economic recovery and the country's powerful military buildup. Reagan received 525 electoral votes, the largest total in history. Walter Mondale, the Democratic party candidate, carried only his home state of Minnesota and the District of Columbia. Reagan got 52.7 million votes to 36.5 million for Mondale. The Republicans gained thirteen seats in the House and won seventeen of thirty-three Senatorial elections, retaining a 54 to 46 majority.

Reagan's smashing reelection victory crossed all regional and most demographic lines. The Democrats appeared to have no remaining regional base of support. In the once-Solid South, every state went for Reagan by decisive majorities. In the West and Southwest, Reagan won easily. The Northeast, once the stronghold of both moderate Republicans and liberal Democrats, also voted for Reagan. He swept the industrial states of the Great Lakes and the Midwestern farm belt, despite continuing economic problems in both of those regions. All age groups voted for him. He did especially well among young, first-time voters, ages eighteen to twenty-one. Baby-boomers voted 2 to 1 for Reagan. Half of union members voted for Reagan, even though Mondale's chief backers were the AFL-CIO leadership. Class and ethnic differences were visible in the voting returns. Middle-class and wealthy voters overwhelmingly supported Reagan. Less affluent voters generally supported Mondale. Ninety percent of blacks voted for Mondale, as did 60 percent of Hispanics. Election results showed Hispanics to be an emerging political force, comprising large voting blocs in populous states such as California, Texas, and Florida.

At the outset of the election campaign, Reagan had appeared vulnerable to charges that Reaganomics unfairly favored the rich and hurt the poor. His Middle East policy had failed in Lebanon. His Central American policy was controversial, and the Soviets had broken off arms control talks. There had been several scandals involving Administration members. But Reagan

Figure 13.5   The Democratic Party made history in 1984 when delegates chose Geraldine Ferraro, a member of Congress, as its first female vice-presidential candidate.   *Source:* AP/Wide World Photos.

mounted a buoyant and an energetic campaign. His reelection bid used slick television commercials that emphasized the restoration of the national economy and national pride, while avoiding specific issues. His commercials stressed the themes of redemption, family values, and wave-the-flag patriotism. One of his speech writers, Peggy Noonan came up with the best line of his reelection campaign, which highlighted the spirit of renewal: "America is back. It's morning again."

Mondale tried to focus the campaign on issues, but he never found one that enabled him to cut into the president's huge lead. Public opinion polls showed that voters disapproved of many of Reagan's specific policies, but they were voting for him because they liked and trusted the man. Mondale also hurt whatever chance he might have had to win by announcing bluntly to American voters at the outset of his campaign that he intended to raise taxes if he won.

In defeat, the Democrats made history twice. Jesse Jackson, the first serious black candidate for president, conducted a spirited primary campaign, winning 373 delegates to the Democratic Convention. Mondale's running mate, Representative Geraldine Ferraro, the first woman vice presidential candidate on a major party ticket, conducted a historic campaign.

CENTRIST CONSERVATISM

President Reagan began his second term by reorganizing his White House staff with not entirely happy results. His chief of staff, James Baker, switched jobs with Secretary of the Treasury Donald Regan. Regan never developed the rapport with the president that Baker had enjoyed, nor did he have the ability to protect Reagan from his shortcomings as had Baker. Worst of all, he did not get along with Nancy Reagan. Two other personal advisers also departed: Michael Deever and Edwin Meese, who along with Baker had formed a "Troika" that was responsible for much of the Reagan administration's legislative successes during the first term. Deever formed a public relations firm to cash in on his White House connections; he promptly ran afoul of laws forbidding influence peddling. Meese became attorney general, where he managed to establish the lowest ethical standards for the nation's top law enforcement office since the days of Warren G. Harding.

Reagan made tax reform his top legislative priority for his second term. The federal tax system had become exceedingly complex over the years as Congress had factored in a great many exemptions and loopholes favoring corporations and wealthy individual taxpayers. Bipartisan support for tax revision gradually emerged in Congress, led by Democratic Congressman Daniel Rostenkowski and Republican Senator Robert Packwood. In the summer of 1986, Congress passed the Tax Reform Act, which brought the first fundamental overhaul of the modern federal income tax system since its inception during World War II. The act simplified the tax code by eliminating many tax shelters and deductions. It reduced multiple tax brackets on individuals to just three, at rates of 15, 28, and 33 percent. It removed six million low-income Americans from the federal tax rolls and lowered the tax burden for a majority of taxpayers. The new law shifted some of the tax burden to the business community by closing loopholes and eliminating write-offs and exemptions.

Reagan shared another major achievement when his administration supported a landmark immigration bill passed by Congress in October 1986. The bill revamped the 1965 act, offering legal status to millions of aliens living illegally in the United States. It also required employers to ask for identification, verifying the citizenship of job applicants, and it levied fines on employers who hired illegal aliens.

Another pressing problem to which Reagan was slow to respond was acquired immune deficiency syndrome (AIDS). An AIDS epidemic swept the country during the mid-1980s and each year killed thousands, predominantly gay males. For years, the administration refused to publicly acknowledge AIDS, and it was, at least in the eyes of those most concerned about fighting the disease, painfully slow to support increased AIDS research and study. Administration officials mainly called for the mandatory testing of categories of people thought to be at risk, or those who held positions of public responsibility. Meanwhile, the disease continued to wreak devastation. AIDS became a world-wide epidemic, and it struck with a special fury among the people of Central and East Africa.

Reagan had come to Washington in 1981, committed to waging a war on drugs and bringing the international drug trade under control. Drug traffic in marijuana, cocaine, and heroin flourished in the mid-1980s. America was the world's major consumer of illicit drugs. The immense costs of America's gargantuan drug habit included thousands of deaths annually, health problems for millions, huge increases in urban crime, corruption in the criminal justice system, and loss of productivity. Efforts to enforce drug laws and U.S.-financed efforts to eradicate drug crops at their sources in Asia and Latin America continued to be ineffective. One of the major reasons for the failure of the Reagan administration's war against drugs, popularized by First Lady Nancy Reagan, was its inability to slow the great American appetite for drugs. All efforts to curtail the supply side of the drug problem were doomed to fail until a measure of control could be imposed on the demand side.

Figure 13.6   AIDS awareness. This poster by David Lance Goines uses the image of the serpent in the Garden of Eden to warn of the dangers of AIDS. By 1985, the year that this poster appeared, 12,500 Americans had already died of AIDS, and the country had begun to confront the epidemics staggering human and medical costs.   *Source: David Lance Goines.*

After years of activity and having spent $3 billion, Reagan announced early in 1988 that the war against drugs had been won. His claim was preposterous. According to contemporary surveys, twenty-five million Americans regularly used marijuana, six million regularly used cocaine, particularly "crack," and another million were heroin addicts. Public opinion polls showed that Americans considered the drug epidemic to be the nation's number one domestic problem. Washington's policy of criminalizing drug use and interdicting the supply, either at the source or at the point of entry into this country, was failing as Reagan's presidency ended. Experts suggested that an alternative policy, one that focused on educating people, especially young people, about the hazards of drug use, and one that relied on therapies, counseling, and community support groups to wean people from drug dependencies, promised better results over the long term.

THE GO-GO ECONOMY

The economy continued to perform strongly through Reagan's second term. Inflation remained low and oil supplies were plentiful. Growth rates averaged 3 percent to 4 percent per annum; many corporations enjoyed record sales and profits, and continually expanded their production. The stock market continued to push through record highs as the Great Bull Market of the 1980s roared on. Consumer spending and consumer confidence remained high.

Despite the economy's strong performance, individual and corporate indebtedness increased rapidly. The takeover mania that had gripped Wall Street during the 1980s continued. Most of these corporate buyouts were severely "leveraged"; that is, they were financed by consortia of bankers and brokerage houses that often sold huge portfolios of "junk bonds" (high-yield, high-risk securities issued by companies with low credit ratings) to raise the vast sums of capital needed to buy out shareholders at above-market prices.

Leveraged buyouts (LBOs) often left companies in serious debt, with no funds for research or the development of new products. Toward the end of Reagan's presidency, investigations exposed some of the financial wizards who had brokered corporate takeover deals as criminals who had violated laws against insider trading. The two biggest names were high-fliers Ivan Boesky and Michael Milken, both of whom served years in jail and paid millions of dollars in fines.

Budget deficits continued to grow, exceeding $200 billion in 1986. During Reagan's presidency, the national debt tripled—from $1 trillion to $3 trillion. Paying the annual interest due on the national debt became the third largest item in the federal budget, after Social Security and defense. The massive indebtedness came about as a result of a tacit agreement between the Reagan White House and the Democrats in Congress. They agreed to support large increases in military spending, modest cuts in social spending, and deep tax cuts.

The national debt became so large during Reagan's presidency that servicing it absorbed much of the net savings accrued by individuals and businesses each year. Pressures on interest rates were eased, because foreign investors, particularly the Germans, Japanese, and Saudi Arabs, bought up about 20 percent of the U.S. debt each year. Even so, the federal government had to take so much money from the private capital markets to fund the debt each year that the money available for investment in research, product development, new technologies, and increased productive capacity was significantly curtailed. Long-term interest rates remained high. There was a link between the huge federal indebtedness and declining American competitiveness in the world's marketplaces. Both the federal government and the private sector became dependent on large annual infusions of foreign capital.

In December 1985, Congress enacted the Gramm-Rudman Act, a measure that required automatic annual reductions in the budget deficit if the president and Congress failed to agree on cuts. The following year, the Supreme Court nullified the law, and the deficit for 1986 came in at a record $226 billion. Congress then enacted a modified version of Gramm-Rudman, but the White House and congressional legislators agreed to accounting procedures that effectively gutted the law. Several large spending programs were declared "off-budget" and not included when figuring the deficit in order to evade Gramm-Rudman limits. It took a record crash of the stock market on October 19, 1987, and fears of an impending recession, to force Reagan and Congress to reduce the budget deficit.

Trade deficits also had expanded rapidly between 1980 and 1985, as imports increased 41 percent while exports decreased slightly. Every week during the Reagan presidency, American consumers spent about $1 billion more buying imported goods than foreigners spent buying American-made products. To offset that imbalance in international trading, huge amounts of American securities, real estate, and factories were purchased by foreign investors who had to recycle their surplus dollars. By the end of Reagan's presidency, U.S. assets in foreign lands totaled less than the U.S. assets owned by foreigners. Until the early 1970s, America had been the world's leading creditor nation. By the end of the Reagan presidency, it had become the world's leading debtor.

Increasing numbers of U.S. manufacturing concerns moved their operations overseas to get away from unionized workers and high taxes, and they took thousands of good jobs with them. At the same time, foreign investors continued buying up U.S. assets. By the end of Reagan's presidency, foreign corporations owned American banks, investment houses, fast food restaurants, motion picture studios, landmark skyscrapers, thousands of acres of farm land, publishing firms, and supermarket chains.

While foreigners continued to buy up U.S. properties, other foreign competitors steadily increased their share of American domestic markets for autos, electronic products, cameras, textiles, and shoes. Many of these developments reflected a new reality, that the economic lives of nations were increasingly intertwined. By the mid-1980s, the American economy was intricately plugged in to a global economic system.

Other financial disasters were entirely homegrown. The savings and loan debacle was an unintended consequence of bipartisan good intentions. Under the influence of supply-side economic theory, federal agencies relaxed or abolished regulations affecting the operations of a wide range of American industries. One of these was savings and loan (S & L) banks. Historically, S&Ls loaned money to individuals to buy homes in local areas where the banks were located. Home mortgages tended to be low-risk, low-profit investments.

At the urging of the Reagan administration, Congress deregulated the savings and loan industry in 1982. Consequently, S&Ls could offer a much wider range of loans; they could invest depositors' funds in commercial real estate, undeveloped land, in fact just about any kind of high-risk project imaginable. They also could loan funds for national and even international projects. Even if these high-risk operations went bust and the banks collapsed, the existence of the Federal Savings and Loan Insurance Corporation (FSLIC) meant that the bankers would not incur personal liabilities and that the depositors would get back their money from the government.

In many parts of the nation, especially in the Southwest and West, the new era of deregulation in the S&Ls attracted a generation of incompetent and crooked buccaneers into the banking industry. They proceeded to invest billions of dollars of depositors' funds in a bewildering variety of dubious projects, knowing that they might reap huge profits from their high-risk undertakings but ran no risk of incurring personal responsibility for any losses because of the existence of the FSLIC. Deregulation of the savings and loan industry eventually reaped a financial disaster that left taxpayers saddled with a tab that ran into hundreds of billions of dollars.

Although the economic expansion of the "go-go" years of the 1980s was real, it also could be selective and spotty. The chief regional beneficiaries of the Reagan boom years were the Northeast and California. Both regions were on the cutting edge of the computer revolution, and both had extensive military and aerospace industries. In these areas, good jobs at good salaries abounded; real estate prices for both residential and commercial properties shot upward.

But in the states of the upper Midwest, the site of the traditional smokestack industries, economic conditions deteriorated. Agricultural and energy-producing states also slumped during the 1980s. While the Northeast and the West Coast boomed, much of the rest of the country was mired in a decade-long stagnation and recession. Real wages, adjusted for inflation, continued to stagnate in many parts of the country during the 1980's. Real take-home pay for factory workers declined slightly from 1975 to 1987.

Figure 13.7   Some of the many street people who live on the top of the steam vents of the Philadelphia sidewalks get comfortable for the night. The moist air of the vents provides warmth but also prevents cuts and ulcers from healing. Photo by Putsy Kennedy. *Source:* AP/Wide World Photos.

Revenue-sharing with state and local governments, enacted by Richard Nixon in 1972, was cut during the Reagan years. Infrastructure repairs to roads and bridges were neglected. Cities, strapped for funds by shrinking tax bases and increasingly needy populations, were especially hard hit by these losses of federal funds. Social services deteriorated.

During the 1980s, income differentials between upper-income and lower-income families widened. The number of poor women and children increased. One of the main reasons poverty was increasingly feminized was because of a sharp increase in the number of unwed mothers; the rate of children living with a never-married mother increased threefold during the 1980s. By the end of the 1980s, one-fourth of the children born in the United States was born to a never-married mother. The Reagan administration made matters worse for them by cutting funds for the Women-Infants-Children program (WIC), which provided both prenatal and postnatal care to low-income women.

During the 1980s, the poverty rate in America regressed to approximately where it had been in the mid-1960s, to about 15 percent. But poverty in America had changed by the mid-1980s. Whereas the elderly had comprised a majority of the poor people of America in the mid-1960s, by the mid-1980s, most of the poor consisted of single mothers, children, and young men with low educational and job skills. A sizable proportion of the 1980s poor worked full or part-time at minimum-wage levels.

Homeless people constituted a growing proportion of the 1980s poor population. Home-less people came from many backgrounds: the unemployed, the mentally ill, drug and alcohol abusers, people with serious medical problems, including AIDs victims, racial minorities, run-aways, dysfunctional Vietnam veterans, and women fleeing abusive husbands. Many of the homeless struggled to survive, living on the streets of large cities and begging for food and money. If prospering yuppies represented the glittering successes of the Reagan era, the home-less represented the abject failures. In the new Gilded Age, the homeless were the prime victims of recrudescent Social Darwinism. Nobody knew exactly how many homeless there were in America in the 1980s. Estimates ranged from a low of 200,000 up to more than a million. Presi-dent Reagan, while expressing his personal sympathy for the plight of the homeless, proposed no new federal programs to alleviate their suffering or to get them off of the streets. The assis-tance that existed for the pathetic armies of the homeless came mostly from local governments, private charities, churches, and compassionate individuals. Most Americans, embracing individ-ualistic values, apparently oblivious to the socioeconomic causes of destitution, in Barbara Ehrenreich's words, "relieved their consciences by vilifying the destitute."

JUDICIAL CONSERVATIVES

President Reagan had long opposed most civil rights laws and supported a constitutional amendment outlawing busing to achieve school integration. The Supreme Court in 1983 blocked attempts by the Justice Department to restore tax benefits to segregated private schools and colleges. When the 1965 Voting Rights Act was up for renewal, Reagan advised Congress to kill it. Congress ignored Reagan's advice and renewed it by large majorities.

In the field of civil liberties, Reagan, like most conservatives, believed that the court sys-tem favored the rights of accused criminals over law-abiding citizens who were often victims of violent crimes. During the 1980s, both the Congress and the states, responding to widespread popular concerns, took a stronger law-and-order line. Longer, mandatory sentences were im-posed for many crimes. Many states reinstituted the death penalty for heinous crimes. By the end of the 1980s, over a million Americans were incarcerated, the highest rate of incarceration for any country in the world. Each year during the 1980s, many more new prisons were con-structed than new schools.

Over the course of his presidency, Reagan appointed over 400 federal judges; these jurists constituted about 60 percent of all sitting federal judges in 1989. The president also appointed a chief justice and three associate justices to the Supreme Court. The administration searched for strict constructionists whose constitutional views also could incorporate right-wing social agenda, including opposition to affirmative action programs, abortion, pornography, and harsher sentences for convicted criminals. Conservative judges also were expected to support efforts to restore prayer in the public schools and to favor the death penalty.

The president's appointments to the Supreme Court allowed him to gradually reshape it. In 1981 he had appointed Sandra Day O'Connor and in 1986 he had selected Antonin Scalia to be associate justices. Both O'Connor and Scalia were conservatives. Reagan also had replaced retiring Chief Justice Warren Burger with Associate Justice William Rehnquist, the most conservative member of the Court. Reagan's efforts to add a third justice to the High Court in July 1987 proved embarrassing. His first nominee, Appellate Judge Robert Bork, was rejected by the Senate because of his extreme views concerning First Amendment rights. Reagan's second choice, Douglas Ginsburg, had to withdraw his name from consideration after revealing to the press that he had smoked marijuana when he was a student in the 1960s. Reagan's third choice, also a judicial conservative, Anthony Kennedy, was unanimously confirmed by the Senate in February 1988.

Gradually, the Reagan appointees on the Supreme Court shifted its decisions in a conservative direction. The Reagan court also put some restraints on government affirmative action policies. In *City of Richmond v. J. A. Croson Company* (1989), the Court nullified a government set-aside program that reserved a proportion of government contracts for minority groups.

CONTAINING TERRORISM

During Reagan's second term, global financial crises threatened as Third World nations sank deeper into debt. The collective debt of Argentina, Brazil, and Mexico approached $250 billion, most of it owed to U.S. and European banks. The possibility of these countries ever repaying their debts appeared nil, and default, which could derange international financial transactions and do serious harm to major U.S. banks, remained a constant danger.

International terrorism was another mounting problem. Between 1981 and 1986, thousands of people were kidnapped, injured, or killed by terrorist attackers. The State Department estimated that approximately 700 major terrorist assaults occurred in the world in 1985. Many terrorists had their roots in the bitter conflicts in Lebanon between Christian and Arab factions, and in the continuing war between Israelis forces and PLO fighters. Arab terrorist organizations, dedicated to the destruction of Israel and to attacking its Western supporters, frequently targeted Americans. In June 1985, Lebanese Muslim terrorists hijacked an American jetliner and held thirty-nine Americans hostage for seventeen days. In October 1985, four members of the PLO seized an Italian cruise ship, the *Achille Lauro,* killing a disabled elderly American. In April 1986, U.S. military installations in West Germany were bombed by Palestinian terrorists supported by Libya. In retaliation, U.S. bombers attacked targets in and near the Libyan capital of Tripoli.

In South Africa, a racist, white minority continued its rule over black, Asian, and mixed-race groups that comprised 86 percent of the population. Washington, following a policy it called "constructive engagement" toward the South African apartheid regime, refrained from public criticism and tried to nudge it toward democracy. The policy produced few results, and South Africa was racked by violence in the mid-1980s as government security forces violently repressed black demonstrators. Angry and frustrated blacks retaliated with terrorist attacks of their own.

Critics of "constructive engagement" believed that only economic pressure could force the South African government to dismantle apartheid. Fourteen states and forty-one cities passed divestiture laws restricting or prohibiting the investment in South Africa of pension funds and requiring the selling off of current holdings in South Africa securities. Some universities ordered partial or full divestment. In October 1986, Congress, overriding a presidential veto, imposed economic sanctions on South Africa, including a boycott of South African products and a ban on new U.S. loans and investment in that country. Some U.S. corporations sold off their South African operations.

Washington also had to confront a crisis in the Philippines, the former territory and long-time ally of the United States. For years, a corrupt military dictator, whom Washington had supported, Ferdinand Marcos, had been losing power. Communist rebels were gaining strength in several regions of the country. Pressure from U.S. officials forced Marcos to permit elections that had been suspended since he took office. In February 1986, he was challenged by Corazon Aquino, the widow of an assassinated political opponent of Marcos. Both sides claimed victory in an election marked by violence and fraud. U.S. officials, worried about the declining Philippine economy and the rising Communist insurgency in a strategically important country, pressured Marcos to resign. He fled Manila in March 1986, and Aquino assumed office. She worked to restore political democracy, revamp the economy, maintain friendly relations with the United States, and suppress the Communist threat.

THE IRAQI–IRANIAN WAR

The continuing Iraqi–Iranian war reached menacing proportions in 1987. The stalemated war spilled into the Persian Gulf and threatened vital oil shipments that flowed daily from the Gulf oil fields to Europe, Japan, and the United States. Iraq attacked Iran's oil-export terminals and also struck at Iranian tankers carrying oil from the Gulf. Iran could not strike at Iraqi oil shipments directly because Iraq's oil traveled through pipelines to terminals on the Mediterranean and Black Seas, but the Iranians undertook reprisals by attacking ships hauling oil from Kuwait, a small, oil-rich Arab emirate that was bankrolling Iraq's war against Iran.

Soviet entry into the Gulf, along with both Iraqi and Iranian threats to Gulf oil shipping, caused the United States to send a large fleet of naval vessels to the region and provide escorts for oil convoys. In what amounted to armed intervention into the shipping war, Washington agreed to reflag and escort tankers carrying oil produced by Kuwait. In the summer of 1987, a U.S. guided-missile frigate, stationed in the Gulf, was attacked, apparently by accident, by an Iraqi plane, resulting in the loss of thirty-eight lives. On July 3, 1988 a U.S. destroyer, the USS *Vincennes,* fired a missile that brought down an Iranian airliner, killing all 290 people aboard. Crewmen aboard the U.S. destroyer apparently thought that it was an Iranian fighter closing in on their ship for an attack.

Washington feared that a victory by either Saddam Hussein's secular Iraqi regime or Khomeini's Islamic fundamentalist Iranian government would make the winner the dominant power in the Persian Gulf. To prevent either side from winning the war—a victory that could threaten the political stability of Saudi Arabia, Kuwait, and other moderate Arab regimes, and disrupt the flow of oil to the United States and its allies—America, behind an official facade of neutrality, secretly aided whichever side appeared to be losing. In the early years of the war, Washington helped Iran, but after 1986, the United States aided Saddam. There had been several incidents involving attacks on merchant shipping by Iranian speedboats, and several ships had been damaged by mines lain by Iranians. U.S. ships and helicopter gunships had retaliated for some of the Iranian attacks, sinking speedboats and damaging an Iranian oil platform in the Gulf. In April, 1988, U.S. and Iranian naval units clashed repeatedly. Iran and the United States were engaged in an undeclared naval war.

The Iraq–Iran war ended suddenly in August 1988 when Ayatollah Khomeini accepted a UN-proposed cease-fire. At the time, Iraq had gained the upper hand. Although he had seized the initiative, Saddam, weary of the long war, readily consented to the cease-fire. Mutual exhaustion had brought an end to war. During the war, the Iraqis had used poison gas against the Iranians and were feverishly working to develop nuclear weapons. Despite the ominous indicators, the Reagan administration continued to back Iraq, considering it a necessary counterforce to the Iranians. Washington's support of Saddam in the late 1980s is one of the background causes of the 1991 Persian Gulf War.

As the war between Iraq and Iran ended, the Arab-Israeli conflict took another violent turn. Palestinians living in the West Bank and Gaza took to the streets to protest the continuing Israeli occupation of the two territories. Roving bands of Palestinian youths, armed with rocks and Molotov cocktails, clashed with Israeli army squads. This Palestinian *intifida* (uprising) continued intermittently through 1988 and 1989, resulting in the deaths of hundreds of Palestinians and a dozen Israeli soldiers. The Israeli government, headed by Prime Minister Yitzhak Shamir, refused to consider any resolution of the conflict that established a Palestinian state in the territories. He also refused to meet with Yasir Arafat and the PLO, the only organization that represented a majority of the Palestinians. The Reagan administration backed the Shamir government's refusal to meet with PLO leaders, but did favor some kind of political arrangement in the occupied territories that would give the Palestinians autonomy.

CENTRAL AMERICA

The Reagan administration continued its support of the Contra rebels fighting to overthrow Nicaragua's Sandinista regime. In the summer of 1985, Congress narrowly approved $100 million in support of the Contras. Public opinion polls showed a majority of Americans opposed to Contra aid and fearful that U.S. troops would be sent to fight the Sandinistas if the rebels failed.

A peaceful alternative to war in Nicaragua surfaced late in 1987, when President Oscar Arias Sanchez of Costa Rica, proposed a plan calling for an end to U.S. military backing of the Contras, the restoration of democracy in Nicaragua, and negotiations between the Sandinista government and Contra leaders leading to a cease-fire. U.S. officials agreed to let Arias try to implement his plan, and Nicaraguan leader Daniel Ortega Saavedra appeared willing to accept some of the proposals. In April 1988, both sides agreed to a temporary cease-fire and Congress voted $48 million for humanitarian aid for the Contras. In El Salvador, efforts to get negotiations going between the Duarte government and the Marxist rebels continued to fail, and the civil war in that tormented country went on.

IRAN-CONTRA

President Reagan's personal popularity remained high through the first half of his second term. But two weeks after the midterm elections in November 1986, the worst political scandal since Watergate erupted in Washington. Americans were shocked to learn that the Reagan administration had entered into secret negotiations with Iranian officials that involved selling them arms in exchange for the release of American hostages held captive in Lebanon by Muslim terrorists. Two weeks after Americans had learned of the arms-for-hostages deals with Iran, Attorney General Edwin Meese told a stunned press conference audience that his investigators had discovered that profits from the Iranian arms sales had been sent to Contra rebels fighting in Nicaragua, even though Congress had enacted legislation forbidding U.S. military aid to the rebel fighters.

President Reagan denied that he had authorized trading arms for hostages, and he insisted that he had no knowledge of any such transactions. He claimed that an operative with the National Security Council, Marine Lieutenant Colonel Oliver North, was mainly responsible for both the dealings with Iran and the Contra arms sales, and that only North's immediate superior, National Security Adviser, Vice Admiral John Poindexter, knew of his activities. For the first time in his presidency, Reagan's integrity and competence were seriously questioned by the citizenry. His public approval rating dropped precipitously, from 67 percent to 46 percent.

The origins of the Iran-Contra scandals went back to 1981 when President Reagan ordered CIA Director William Casey to organize an anti-Sandinista force among Nicaraguan exiles living in Honduras. Over the next several years, these Contra forces waged a guerrilla war against the Sandinista forces. Congress, enacted the Boland Amendment, which forbade the use of any U.S. funds for the purpose of trying to overthrow the Sandinista government. Reagan, committed to the goal of overthrowing the Sandinistas, instructed the CIA, the National Security Council, and the Pentagon to circumvent congressional restrictions on aiding the Contra forces. Casey, National Security Adviser Robert McFarlane, and one of McFarlane's aides, Colonel North, persuaded Israel, South Africa, Saudi Arabia, South Korea, and Taiwan to provide funds for the Contras.

While Reagan and his subordinates were violating the Boland Amendment by continuing the war in Nicaragua, the administration also began an involvement with Iran aimed at freeing U.S. hostages being held in Lebanon by pro-Iranian Muslim terrorists.

In July 1985, an Iranian arms dealer, Manucher Ghobanifar, who claimed to represent a moderate faction within the Iranian government that wanted to improve relations with the United States met with McFarlane. Ghobanifar proposed to McFarlane that Washington, working through Israeli middlemen, arrange for the delivery of TOW antitank missiles to Iran that the Iranians needed for their ongoing war with Iraq. In return, the moderates would work to arrange the release of some of the American hostages. A few months later, Reagan authorized the sale of 100 TOW missiles to Iran. At the time he authorized the sale of the weapons, Reagan clearly understood that the United States was trading arms for hostages. He also knew that it was against the law and contrary to U.S. policy to sell weapons to Iran because of its support of international terrorism.

No hostages were freed after this transaction. Ghobanifar told McFarlane that the Iranians wanted an additional 400 missiles in exchange for the release of a single hostage. McFarlane arranged for the missiles to be sent, and on September 15, 1986, one of the American hostages, Benjamin Weir, was set free. In November, Ghobanifar was back with another deal: send Iran 100 HAWK surface-to-air missiles and five American hostages would be freed. In December, President Reagan signed a secret document, called a "finding," which approved the proposed sale. The finding described the transaction as an arms-for-hostages deal.

Even though the several arms sales to Iran had yielded only one released hostage, Poindexter, who replaced McFarlane as National Security Adviser in December 1985, working through North, arranged for another shipment of arms to Iran. This time, 3,000 TOW missiles and another 100 HAWKs would be sent in exchange for the remaining six Americans who were still held captive by terrorists in Lebanon. Both Secretary of State George Schultz and Secretary of Defense Casper Weinberger opposed the arms-for-hostages transactions because they were illegal and did not serve the national interest.

Oliver North came up with the plan to divert the profits from the sale of arms to the Iranians to the Contras. Did President Reagan direct North to send the money to the Contras? Later, in sworn testimony, Reagan could not remember if he had approved the funds; Poindexter testified under oath that the president approved the funds. In February 1986, a sale of 1,000 TOW missiles to the Iranians netted a profit of about $8 million. North gave the money to retired Air Force Major General Richard Secord to buy arms for the Contras. No hostages were released, but two more Americans in Lebanon were taken hostage. After four arms shipments to the Iranians, more Americans than ever were held hostage.

On July 26, Iran arranged for the release of another American hostage. Another shipment of missiles was sent to Iran, but it resulted in no further prisoners being freed. On November 2, just before the midterm elections, a final arms shipment was sent to Iran, which resulted in the release of another hostage, David Jacobsen.

On October 5, 1986, a plane hauling weapons to the Contras was shot down and the Sandinistas captured an air crewman, who confessed to his captors that he was part of a secret U.S. program to aid the Contras. On November 1, the Lebanese magazine *Al Shiraa* ran a story about the U.S. arms-for-hostages deals with Iran, which Iranian officials quickly confirmed. Three weeks later, Edwin Meese made his stunning announcement that money from the sale of arms to Iran had been diverted to the Contra war effort against the Sandinistas.

The fallout from the Iran-Contra scandal was worse than Watergate. It severely damaged U.S. foreign policy. The U.S. policy of taking a hardline against terrorism had been compromised. The Saudis and other moderate Arab states felt an acute sense of betrayal over the news that U.S. officials had sold antitank and antiaircraft missiles to Khomeini's government in the hope of securing the release of seven Americans being held hostage in Lebanon At home, there was widespread condemnation for conducting a clandestine foreign policy in Central America against the expressed wishes of Congress, contrary to public opinion, and in violation of the law. The essence of the Iran-Contra scandal involved officials within the Reagan administration selling weapons to an outlaw regime to raise money for illegal purposes. Constitutional scholars saw an important principle at stake. By circumventing the congressional ban on aid to the Contras, the architects of the Iran-Contra scandal also had circumvented Article 1 of the Constitution, which vested all control over public moneys in Congress.

There were several investigations of the details of trading arms for hostages and aiding the Contras. A federal court appointed an independent counsel to investigate the scandals. President Reagan appointed a commission headed by former Senator John Tower to investigate the affair. Congress also appointed committees to examine the scandals. The Tower Commission's report was made public in March 1987. It portrayed Reagan as an out-of-touch president who had surrounded himself with irresponsible advisers pursuing ideologically driven policies that did harm to the national interest.

Reagan responded with a speech to the American people on March 4. He acknowledged responsibility for the Iran-Contra affair, but he insisted that it was not his intent to trade arms for hostages and that he knew nothing about using some of the money obtained from Iran to buy arms for the Contras. Reagan's speech failed to restore public confidence.

Following the Tower report, the combined congressional committees began holding televised hearings that ran through the summer of 1987. At times, the hearings evoked memories of Watergate as congressmen tried to follow the money trail, find out how the profits from arms sales to Iran were channeled to the Contras, and discover who profited from all of these weird transactions.

Two of the witnesses appearing before the committees, General Secord, who had been recruited by Colonel North to run the Contra weapons supply system, and former National Security Adviser Robert McFarlane, who had arranged the Iranian arms sales, implicated the president in their testimonies. They insisted that Reagan was repeatedly briefed about the arms sales to Iran and approved of the efforts to get the hostages released. They also implicated the late CIA Director William Casey, who may have been the mastermind behind the Iran-Contra operations.

The two key witnesses to appear before the Committees, Colonel North and Admiral Poindexter, both insisted that they had kept President Reagan uninformed about the details of the Iranian negotiations and that they never told him of the government's involvement in shipping arms to the Contras. They also admitted that they had deliberately misinformed Congress and the press about their actions. Colonel North passionately defended his actions as being moral and patriotic, even though they did defy Congress and break the law.

The committee hearings were seriously flawed. They were hastily conducted, and investigators lacked crucial documents that would have enabled them to discover more of the truth about the Iran-Contra scandals. Key witnesses lied or gave evasive answers. The investigating committees clearly did not have the stomach to press their investigation too close to Reagan, nor to consider the possibility of impeaching him, even though they possessed evidence suggesting that he had knowingly and deliberately broken laws and harmed U.S. foreign policy interests. Committee members knew that most Americans could not care less whether funds from arms sales were diverted to the Contras. While resenting the arms sales to Iran, many Americans also could see Reagan's good intentions: he was trying to free the hostages, even though the means chosen were dubious. Lawmakers also feared political reprisals at the hands of the people if they stood guilty once again of regicide. Besides, there was no "smoking gun" in the Iran-Contra scandals that irrefutably implicated the president.

The committees issued a joint 450-page report on November 18, 1987, that was scathingly critical of the president. The report bluntly accused Reagan of not obeying his oath to uphold the Constitution and the laws of the land, and it said he bore "the ultimate responsibility" for the wrongdoing of his aides. The congressional report also provided the most accurate accounting to date of how nearly $48 million raised from the arms sales had been distributed. The report stated that the Iran-Contra affair was "characterized by pervasive dishonesty and inordinate secrecy." It also voiced the suspicion that Reagan knew more about the arms sales and Contra funding efforts than he acknowledged and it challenged the credibility of Colonel North's and Admiral Poindexter's testimony. Without citing specific individual actions or naming specific laws, the report asserted that "laws were broken" in the Iran-Contra affair. Public opinion polls revealed that a majority of Americans believed that the president knowingly traded arms for hostages and he knew about the government's involvement in the Contra arms shipments.

Figure 13.8   Lt. Col. Oliver North. Photo by Lana Harris.   *Source:* AP/Wide World Photos.

In March 1988, independent counsel Lawrence Walsh issued grand jury indictments to Colonel North and Admiral Poindexter. They were charged with multiple offenses, including conspiracy, fraud, theft, perjury, and covering up illegal operations. At his trial in 1990, Poindexter repudiated his testimony previously given before the congressional committees. He stated that Reagan was in charge of the Iran-Contra operations from the beginning and had ordered him, North, and others to break the law.

The former president was called to testify at Poindexter's trial. In answers to 127 questions put to him by prosecutors, Reagan frequently gave confused and vague answers. Often he could not recall the names of subordinates or their activities. He reiterated that he was not involved in any wrongdoing and that he did not know what his subordinates were doing, or that they traded arms for hostages or diverted the profits to the Contras. It was a humiliating performance by Reagan. Some observers believed that he was exhibiting the early signs of Alzheimer's disease, which he later contracted. Poindexter was convicted of five felonies, including perjury. North was convicted of obstructing Congress and destroying confidential documents. The trials of the Iran-Contra conspirators concluded this shabby episode that marred the reputation and undermined the popularity and power of President Reagan. Years later, Poindexter's and North's convictions were overturned on appeal.

THE SLEAZE FACTOR

While Iran-Contra investigations raised troubling questions about the integrity and competence of high government figures, other scandals rocked the Reagan administration. In December 1987, former White House adviser Michael Deaver, who operated a political consulting service, was convicted on three counts of perjury for denying that he improperly used his White House connections to help clients. In February 1988, Attorney General Edwin Meese was accused of having a conflict of interest stemming from his alleged financial relations with a small company that received a defense contract. He came under further attack for his alleged awareness of a proposal to bribe Israeli officials to guarantee that they would not attack a planned oil pipeline construction project in the Middle East. Further problems for Meese developed at the Justice Department when several top officials resigned in April 1988 because they believed that Meese's mounting problems prevented him from exerting strong leadership of the Department.

In addition to these revelations of wrongdoing and improprieties at high levels in the White House came another startling disclosure through the memoirs of Donald Regan, Reagan's former chief of staff. Regan revealed that the president, following the attempt on his life, had permitted his wife Nancy, who had consultations with an astrologer, to influence his scheduling. By the end of Reagan's presidency, allegations of illegal and unethical activities tarnished the reputations of more than 100 current and former White House officials.

Reagan administration officials were not the only politicians to be plagued by scandal in 1987 and 1988. The leading contender for the Democratic presidential nomination, Gary Hart, had to abandon his campaign for seven months when a newspaper reporter disclosed that Hart had spent a weekend with an attractive model. When Hart belatedly reentered the race in 1988, he found that he had lost all of his organization and most of his popular support, and he had to abandon his candidacy. Another Democratic presidential hopeful, Senator Joseph Biden of Delaware, had to withdraw when reporters learned that he had frequently plagiarized the speeches of other politicians and had padded his academic record.

THAWING THE COLD WAR

The United States and the Soviet Union urgently needed to stabilize the nuclear arms race. Ronald Reagan alarmed most of his conservative supporters when he softened his hard-line approach to the Soviet Union and authorized the resumption of arms negotiations. A dramatic moment in world history occurred when Soviet leader Mikhail Gorbachev and President Reagan met in Geneva from November 24 to November 27, 1985, the first Summit conference since Carter had journeyed to Moscow in 1979. But their six hours of private talks were inconclusive. They achieved no major agreements on arms control. The major block was Reagan's insistence

Figure 13.9   On December 8, 1987, President Reagan and General Secretary Mikhail Gorbachev signed the INF Treaty to eliminate an entire class of nuclear weapons, intermediate-range missiles.   *Source:* National Archives.

that the United States would continue its development of the SDI. Gorbachev demanded that the United States abandon the SDI before he would sign any arms control agreements.

Although it was an exercise in global public relations by both sides, the Summit was also an important breakthrough, giving further diplomacy a needed impetus. A budding friendship between the two world leaders was the main consequence of the meetings. President Reagan toned down his anti-Communist rhetoric, saying Gorbachev was a man with whom he could do business. In the controlled Soviet press, a new image of Reagan as a man who could be reasoned with had replaced a version in which he had often been compared to Hitler. At a hastily called summit meeting held in Reykjavik, Iceland, in October 1986, Gorbachev and Reagan almost reached major agreements on nuclear arms control. For one extraordinary moment at Reykjavik, both leaders flirted with the idea of ELIMINATING ALL NUCLEAR WEAPONS. Only a disagreement over Star Wars and the Anti-Ballistic Missile treaty prevented Reagan and Gorbachev from possibly ridding themselves of these monstrous weapons.

During the next year, Reagan replaced many of his hard-line anti-Communist advisers with a new breed of more pragmatic bureaucrats. Frank Carlucci replaced Weinberger at Defense. Army General Colin Powell became the new head of the National Security Council. Senator Howard Baker replaced Donald Regan as the president's chief of staff. These men favored reaching arms control agreements with the Soviets. First Lady Nancy Reagan, concerned about her husband's place in history in the aftermath of the Iran-Contra scandal, urged him to seek a major arms control agreement with Gorbachev. She wanted an accommodation with the Soviet Union to be the chief legacy of a Reagan presidency.

A year after Reykjavik, joint arms control efforts finally resulted in a major agreement between the two superpowers. Gorbachev journeyed to the United States, where he and Reagan signed a historic treaty in December 1987. The treaty eliminated an entire class of weapons, intermediate range thermonuclear missiles, which had been located mostly in Europe. Both sides had, in effect, accepted the "zero option" originally proposed by Reagan in 1983. The agreement, known officially as the Intermediate Nuclear Forces (INF) Treaty, was the first nuclear arms control agreement ever reached that required the destruction of deployed nuclear weapons systems. It also provided for inspectors of both nations to observe the dismantling and destruction of the intermediate-range missiles. The INF Treaty and the return of cordial relations with the Soviet Union represented President Reagan's most significant diplomatic achievements. The old Cold Warrior was thawing the Cold War.

The signing of the INF Treaty and the return of detente with the Soviets also held out the promise of future agreements cutting strategic weaponry on both sides. Negotiators from both countries continued to work on a Strategic Arms Reduction Treaty (START). The Soviets also announced that they were ending their costly, futile war in Afghanistan. In addition to phasing out the Afghan adventure, Gorbachev undertook a worldwide scaling back of Soviet diplomatic activity. He indicated that the Soviets might end their economic and military support of the Sandinistas. He urged the PLO to recognize Israel's right to exist. He pressured Hanoi to pull its troops out of Kampuchea. He pulled Soviet forces back from the Sino-Soviet border regions, and he urged the Soviet satellites in eastern Europe to reform their economies and become more involved with the nations of western Europe.

The sudden and quite remarkable turnabout in U.S.–Soviet relations culminated in Reagan's triumphant visit to Moscow in June 1988. He spoke to the Soviet people on television and embraced his friend Mikhail Gorbachev at the site of Lenin's tomb. After such acts of reconciliation, no one appeared to care that both nations still had thousands of thermonuclear warheads on hair-trigger alert aimed at each other.

THE ELECTION OF 1988

As both parties geared up for the 1988 elections, the race for the presidency appeared wide open. For the Republicans, the major contenders included Vice President George Bush, Senate Republican leader Robert Dole, and former "televangelist" Pat Robertson. For the Democrats, the major candidates included Congressman Richard Gephardt of Missouri, senator Albert Gore of Tennessee, Governor Michael Dukakis of Massachusetts, and the charismatic black leader Jesse Jackson.

When the lengthy and costly primary process ran its course in June, the winners were Vice President Bush and Governor Dukakis. Jesse Jackson finished a strong second in the primary balloting to Dukakis. Dukakis chose an elderly conservative senator from Texas, Lloyd Bentsen, to be his vice-presidential running mate. George Bush selected youthful Senator J. Danforth Quayle of Indiana as his.

The Republicans conducted an amply financed and efficient campaign. The Bush campaign easily won what media analysts have called the "battle of the sound bites," those punchy

**Figure 13.10   The Reverend Jesse Jackson
campaigning for the presidency in 1988.**   *Source:*
St. Louis Mercantile Library. Used with permission.

ten- to twenty-second pronouncements uttered daily by the candidates as they campaigned across the nation that would be picked up on the evening television news programs and beamed into millions of living rooms nightly until Election Day. Bush also found most of the "hot" electoral buttons to push during the contest with Dukakis. He projected a vision of a "kinder, gentler nation," and he encouraged Americans to help one another and shine forth from "a thousand points of light." He pledged "no new taxes," and when questioned about his commitment, he responded á la a popular Clint Eastwood movie character with "read my lips."

Bush also waged a relentless assault on Dukakis as an exemplar of all that was wrong with contemporary liberalism. He charged that Dukakis was weak on foreign policy and national security matters. The most notorious attack commercial pandered to racist fears by including a mug shot of Willie Horton, a black convicted murderer and rapist who committed another murder while on a weekend furlough from prison. The commercial implied that Dukakis, who was governor when Horton was serving time in a Massachusetts prison, was soft on crime.

Dukakis disdained negative campaigning, and he refused to even respond to the Bush attack commercials. Dukakis tried to focus his campaign on the issues. His approach failed, and his campaign never caught fire. He never found a telling issue or a rousing theme that resonated among the voters.

On Election Day, the Bush–Quayle ticket buried Dukakis and Bentsen, winning 54 percent of the popular vote to 46 percent, 48,000,000 votes for the Republicans to 41,000,000 for the Democrats. Bush carried forty of the fifty states and had a 426 to 112 advantage in the electorate vote. Dukakis's defeat could be attributed in part to the continued flight of white voters, who comprised over 80 percent of the electorate. Since 1948, the only Democratic presidential candidate to receive a majority of the white vote was Lyndon Johnson. Dukakis got about 38 percent of the white vote in 1988. The once solidly Democratic South was now solidly Republican, as was most of the Midwest and the West. Millions of blue-collar workers, once a Democratic mainstay, voted for Bush.

Despite being beaten in the presidential vote, the Democrats retained control of both houses of Congress, two-thirds of state governorships, and thirty-six state legislatures. Although they had lost five of the last six presidential elections, the Democrats in 1988 retained considerable political power at the local, state, and Congressional levels.

Bush won in 1988 primarily because he was Reagan's heir apparent. The elderly leader had lost some of his luster in the wake of the Iran-Contra scandal. As he neared the end of his presidency, Reagan clearly showed the effects of failing health, mental deterioration, and fatigue. Dukakis and other Democratic leaders also called attention to a long list of national problems that eight years of conservative Republicanism had either created or neglected: gigantic federal budget deficits, millions of additional poor people, indifference to civil rights, environmental degradation, scant interest in consumer protection or safety in the workplaces of America, the decline of unions, the decline of the public schools, and the fact that one-third of American families lacked adequate health insurance. The Democrats also raised a basic question of fairness. They charged that Reaganomics had favored the rich and affluent classes at the expense of the middle classes, working classes, and poor. Democrats also called attention to a series of Reagan foreign policy failures in Central America and the Middle East.

But the majority of voters in 1988 no longer supported liberal programs, nor did they look to the Democrats for presidential leadership on either domestic or foreign policy. For most Americans, talk of national debts involved incomprehensibly large numbers that had no relevance to their daily lives. Most voters in 1988 were not poor or members of a minority, and they did not appear very concerned about the folks who were. Eight years of Reagan's rule had coincided with the longest sustained period of economic growth in U.S. history.

Even though he had numerous failures and shortcomings, Ronald Reagan remained by far the most popular man in public life. He presided over a peaceful, prosperous America. Relations with the Soviet Union were better than at any time since World War II. The 1988 election amounted to a referendum on the Reagan presidncy. A large majority of the electorate concluded that George Bush was more likely than Michael Dukakis to keep the nation at peace and to keep the good times rolling.

BRIEF BIBLIOGRAPHIC ESSAY

A sizable historical and journalistic literature has already accumulated for the 1980s. F. Clifton White's *Why Reagan Won: A Narrative History of the Conservative Movement, 1964–1981* tells the story of the conservative movement from the Goldwater debacle to Reagan's successful bid for the presidency in 1980. In an important recent book, *The World Turned Right Side Up,* Godfrey Hodgson sees the conservative ascendancy as a consequence of conservatives assuming the mantle of reformers and supplanting liberals who came to be seen by a majority of Americans as defenders of a discredited status quo. Haynes Johnson's *Sleepwalking Through History: America in the Reagan Years* is a critical look at the Reagan era. The most informed account of the Reagan presidency is Lou Cannon's *President Reagan: The Role of a Lifetime.* The best biography of Reagan is Edmund Morris's recently published, *Dutch: A Memoir of Ronald Reagan.* Morris, the official Reagan biographer, was allowed access to President Reagan for several years. His book is controversial because he has used fictional devices to illuminate Ronald

Reagan's life. President Reagan has written a solid memoir, *An American Life.* A fine recent study is Stephen Vaughn's *Ronald Reagan in Hollywood: Movies and Politics,* explores the important relationships among Reagan's film and political careers. Two important books that interpret the public career of Ronald Reagan are Garry Wills's *Reagan's America: Innocents at Home* and Michael P. Rogin's *Ronald Reagan: The Movie.* A good account of the early years of the Reagan presidency is Laurence I. Barrett's *Gambling with History: Reagan in the White House.* P. C. Roberts's *The Supply-Side Revolution* defends Reaganomics. T. B. Edsall's *The New Politics of Inequality* challenges the president's economic policies. Strobe Talbott's *Deadly Gambit* is a lucid and fascinating analysis of the arcane complexities of arms control. Edward N. Luttwack's *Making the Military Work* is a critical study of 1980s military policies. Frances Fitzgerald's fascinating (and frightening) *Way Out There in the Blue: Reagan and Star Wars and the End of the Cold War* has an account of that moment when the Soviets, fearful that the United States was about to launch a preemptive strike, began to prepare a retaliatory strike. Peter Schweizer, in *Reagan's War: The Epic Story of His Forty-Year Struggle and Final Triumph Over Communism,* says the Soviet leaders did not take the threat of a U.S. preemptive strike seriously. The most thorough account of the Iran-Contra scandal that rocked the Reagan administration in 1986 and 1987 is Theodore Draper's *A Very Thin Line: The Iran-Contra Affairs.* Seth P. Tillman's *The United States and the Middle East: Interests and Obstacles* is a balanced treatment of American policy in that troubled region. Stansfield Turner's *Terrorism and Democracy* is a thoughtful study of one of the most serious problems that U.S. presidents have had to deal with since the 1970s. Michael Mandelbaum's *Reagan and Gorbachev* is a good account of their personal diplomacy. Roy Gutman's *Banana Diplomacy,* is a critical study of U.S. foreign policy in Nicaragua and El Salvador in the 1980s. Michael Schaller's *Reckoning with Reagan: America and Its President in the 1980s* is a fine study of the Reagan presidency.

WEB SITES

<http://www.cusd.claremont.edu/~rcrosby/rr.html> contains a scholarly discussion of Reaganomics. <http://www.cnn.com/coldwar_Episode 22> is an excellent site that covers the Cold War foreign policy of President Ronald Reagan, 1980–1988.

14

Going Global

The opening of the Berlin Wall on November 9, 1989, was the first in a series of stunning events that culminated in the collapse of the Soviet Union and the end of the Cold War that had been the focus of American foreign policy for nearly a half century. As the world's only remaining superpower, the United States suddenly found itself incontestably the most powerful nation on the planet. But Americans quickly learned that living in the richest and most powerful nation in the history of the planet did not insulate them from the dangers of an increasingly unstable world order or even allow them to feel safe and secure within their own county.

At the same time Americans sought new strategic roles in the post–Cold War world, they also found themselves intricately enmeshed in the rapidly evolving world economy. The contagion of bankruptcies and currency devaluations that collapsed the booming economies of Thailand and Korea during the summer of 1997, spread to other Pacific Rim countries, and then engulfed Russia, and Brazil, highlighted not only the interconnectedness of economic relations, but also the volatility of the new global economy in which loan money could be quickly put into and then pulled out of markets around the world.

As Americans struggled to adapt to the new realities of the global economy, at home they had to deal with rapidly changing demographics, a fragmented social order, culture wars, and increasingly ideologized politics.

During the early 1990s, Americans suffered a mild economic recession. The economy recovered by 1993 and began a sustained period of growth that reached to the end of the decade. The longest and strongest bull market in U.S. financial history carried stocks to record levels. Unemployment and inflation remained low. However, as the U.S. economy became increasingly integrated into the global economy, the terms of competition were fiercer. Competitive pressures kept prices and wages down, and people had to work harder than ever to keep their jobs. Despite record prosperity, the gap between rich and low-income Americans continued to widen.

THE DEMOGRAPHICS OF DIVERSITY

During the decade of the nineties, the nation's population grew from 247,000,000 in 1990 to 281,000,000 in 2000. The decennial increase of 34,000,000 people was the largest ever. One-third of the nation's population growth during the decade of the 1990s came from the influx of immigrants. Most of the immigrants emigrated from a Hispanic country within the Western Hemisphere or from a Pacific-Island or an Asian nation. The new immigrants flocked to the big cities, but they also spread into all regions of the country. Millions lived and worked in towns and small cities. As the Nineties ended, there were 56 million Americans who were either immigrants or the children of immigrants, the largest number in U.S. history.

In New York, Los Angeles, San Francisco, Chicago, and other great cities, the new Hispanic and Asian populations settled into ethnic neighborhoods. They brought their distinctive cultures, languages, cuisine, dress, music, and styles. America's big cities became home to the most culturally diverse populations in world history.

While cultural diversity brought energy and vitality, and made America's big cities the most vibrant urban centers in the world, it also brought tensions and serious social problems. The huge influx of new people during the 1990s triggered an upsurge of nativism. In 1994, California voters approved Proposition 187, a ballot initiative that barred undocumented aliens from access to public schools, health clinics, and all other social services. Federal courts declared most of the initiative's provisions unconstitutional, and it was never enforced.

In addition, the 2000 census reflected the growing variety of household living arrangements in America. Nuclear families comprised less than one-fourth of the nation's households; just as many households were made up of a person living alone. The number of single mothers heading a household increased rapidly during the decade, especially among minority populations. In 1999, there were nearly fourteen million single-parent families, most headed by a woman who had never married. Approximately 15 percent of American households were poor, about the same proportion that could be found in this country in 1965. The large increase in poor, single-parent families during the 1990s had ominous implications for millions of America's poorest children.

BUST, BOOM, AND BUST

Many intertwined economic problems, exacerbated by the recession that struck during the early 1990s, vexed the American people. The annual trade deficit ranged between $40 billion and $60 billion. Annual federal deficits continued to run up huge amounts of red ink. The national debt reached $4 trillion in 1992 and was approaching $5 trillion in 1995. That year, annual interest payments on the national debt consumed 16 percent of all federal spending. During the recession, about 9,000,000 workers were without jobs. Housing starts, new car sales, and business investment plummeted. The Federal Reserve Board slashed interest rates to thirty-year lows, but the economy did not pick up.

More importantly, the long-term structural weaknesses of the U.S. economy that had first appeared during the early 1970s persisted into the 1990s. The most serious one that eroded the economic underpinnings of millions of families has been the slow rate of economic growth. From 1890 to 1970, the U.S. economy grew at an annual rate of 3.5 percent, adjusted for inflation. That rate of economic growth, sustained over much of the twentieth century, more than any other single factor created a prosperous middle-class society. Since 1973, including the boom years of the 1980s and 1990s, the annual rate of growth has averaged 2.2 percent. This sharp decline in growth rates had devastating impacts on millions of middle-class families. Both real income and the annual share of national income earned by the middle classes declined.

By the mid-1990s, the U.S. economy had fully recovered from recession. From 1995 through 1999, the economy grew at an annual rate of 3.4 percent. By 1996, American industry once again led the world in productive efficiency. U.S. automakers dominated the markets for popular minivans, light trucks, and off-road vehicles. In 1998 and 1999, American-made, powerful, and expensive sports utility vehicles were the vehicles of choice for those who could afford them.

The stock market soared to record highs in the late 1990s, with high-tech stocks leading the way. The Dow Jones Index of thirty industrial stocks rose from 3900 in 1992 to a peak of 11,600 in May 1999. The volume of shares traded on the New York Stock Exchange rose exponentially during the nineties, exceeding a billion shares on many trading days. Profits were extraordinarily large for some of the leading-edge companies; in some years they earned returns on investment exceeding 20 percent. Microsoft became the largest corporation in the world, primarily because of its virtual monopoly of Windows platforms. Bill Gates, the CEO of Microsoft and its largest individual stockholder, became the world's richest person, with a personal fortune exceeding $60 billion in 1999. Gates, who personified the new high-tech economy of the 1990s, became an iconic figure. An estimated eighty million people owned stocks often through mutual funds or retirement portfolios managed by professionals. Thousands of employees of aggressive high-tech firms became "instant millionaires" on paper by acquiring stock options of the companies they worked for.

There was a down side to the high-flying economy of the late 1990s. Corporate managers enjoyed unprecedentedly high incomes while blue collar workers of the same companies struggled to earn a living wage and sustain their families. Many companies resorted to downsizing to increase profits or to survive in a more competitive environment. IBM laid off over half its workforce in the 1990s. Savings rates for Americans reached historic lows during the late 1990s. Millions of prosperous families reported a negative savings rate and consumer debt rose rapidly. Many of these people proved to be vulnerable to bankruptcies when a downtown began in 2000.

During the peak years of the new economy, a ten-by-thirty-mile strip of Santa Clara County, California, located about forty miles south of San Francisco, a region that until the 1960s had been noted for the luscious fruits and vegetables it produced, became the center of the microelectronics industry. The consumer electronics revolution that had originated in the 1970s created a vast web of hundreds of high-tech firms that manufactured, distributed, or "processed" new information technologies.

Silicon Valley attracted extensive media attention, which reinforced its popular image as a place where brilliant, hard-driving entrepreneurs founded companies that churned out technological marvels and accumulated great personal fortunes. America had not seen anything like this generation of electronic buccaneers since the industrial revolution of the 1880s and 1890s. Silicon Valley and the other regions within the United States where high-tech companies flourished were also plugged into the rapidly expanding global economy. U.S. companies competed fiercely with their rivals in Japan, Taiwan, and Korea. Silicon Valley also reflected the growing multiculturalism of American society; perhaps one-third of the engineers and technical personnel developing the software and hardware driving the new economy were people of Chinese or South Asian descent, many of them immigrants.

In the summer of 1997, Thailand, Hong Kong, South Korea, Indonesia, and several other Asian countries experienced turmoil in their financial markets that abruptly reversed years of robust economic growth and rising prosperity. Asian financial disasters drove stock values down and devalued currencies. It also brought many large banks and corporate conglomerates to the verge of bankruptcy. Several nations received financial assistance from the International Monetary Fund and were forced to implement harsh austerity programs to try to stop the financial hemorrhaging. In Indonesia, mass unrest in the wake of economic decline forced the aging autocrat, Suharto, to resign.

These financial and economic crises deepened the long recession that had already engulfed Japan and threatened to slow the Chinese juggernaut. In September 1998, Russia verged on financial collapse. Even the U.S. powerhouse felt the effects of the Asian meltdown and the Russian collapse. During the summer of 1998, the growth rate of the U.S. economy slowed; businesses that sold goods and services on Asian markets were hurt. U.S. farmers who sold grain and beef to Asians were especially hard hit.

Figure 14.1   Aerial view of the Oracle campus in Silicon Valley.   *Source:* CORBIS.

TV AND CYBERSPACE

The electronic technologies of the late twentieth century changed the way most Americans lived and worked. The revolution in telecommunications created the global information superhighway. The arrival of cable and satellite television in the nineties offered viewers vastly expanded programming choices. VCRs allowed viewers to schedule program watching around their schedules. Hollywood studios began releasing films direct to video rental stores. By the mid-nineties, the rental and sale of movie videos to home viewers had become the main source of profit for the movie studios.

Television dominated political campaigning in the 1990s. Politicians raised and spent huge sums of money advertising themselves, their parties, and their programs—and attacking their opponents. They hired staffs of consultants who focused intensely on their candidates' television images. Cosmetic concerns and catchy slogans prevailed over substantive issues. A new generation of wealthy telegenic candidates sought election as governors of large states, senators, and presidents. The chief prerequisites for many political offices came to be: Can he/she project a positive, voter-friendly image? and Can he/she raise the big bucks required for seeking important political offices?

The most significant electronic development was the creation of that fluid world called cyberspace. Cyberspace is that conceptual region occupied by people linked via computer networks within the country and around the world. It originated in the early 1970s when the Department of Defense created ARPANET. When inexpensive personal computers came online in the 1980s that were capable of linking to the worldwide telecommunications network, the number of people entering cyberspace rapidly expanded. Researchers and scholars linked themselves to the Internet, the successor to ARPANET. The creation of the World Wide Web (WWW, often simply called the Web) and the development of inexpensive browser technologies in 1994 made the information superhighway accessible to millions and created a communication medium with global dimensions.

By the end of the century, more than half of all U.S. households had at least one computer and most public schools were online. At work, the typical American spent 20 hours per week online and at home about ten hours per week online. Most users of the Internet and the Web gained access from independent service providers such as America Online (AOL) and Earthlink. There were over 300 million web sites. These new information technologies created a global media community that ignored national boundaries. Telecommunications had become an essential part of the global economy, which required instant access to the information super highway

BLACK AND WHITE, BUT NOT TOGETHER

Festering ethnic tensions exploded in May 1992, when a California jury acquitted four white police officers charged with savagely beating an African-American suspect, Rodney King. A bystander had videotaped the incident, and portions of the tape were repeatedly broadcast. To nearly all who observed the gruesome sequences, the television camera presented compelling images of police brutality. The verdict to acquit the four policemen, rendered by a politically conservative suburban jury containing no African American members, ignited the most violent race riot in the nation's history. As it swept through South Central Los Angeles, thousands of businesses were looted and many of them were burned. Fifty-four people were killed and thousands were injured. Property losses reached $850 million. The Los Angeles police, poorly led and confused, were initially slow to respond to the riot, and events got out of control. National Guard troops were rushed to Los Angeles to quell the rioters. Before order was restored and peace returned, approximately 12,000 people were arrested for looting and arson, most of them young black and Hispanic males.

The riot was reminiscent of the 1965 Watts upheaval, but there were significant differences. The 1965 riot had pitted blacks against whites. The 1992 riot had much more complex ethnic dynamics, reflecting the ethno-racial diversity of the nation's second largest city. One observer called it the nation's first "multicultural riot." Blacks attacked other blacks as well as whites. Hispanics attacked whites. Blacks and Hispanics both attacked Asians. Gangs of African American and Hispanic thugs also engaged in violence and looting. These violent actions exposed the deep divisions and animosities among various groups. The division was sharpest between whites and various minorities. An affluent West Side white woman stated, "We don't know and don't care about the problems of the inner cities . . . most of us don't even know where South Central is . . ." The King verdict obviously triggered the riot, but the underlying

Figure 14.2   A city police officer holds a shotgun on two young suspects as a California state police officer puts handcuffs on them during the riot in South Central Los Angeles.   *Source:* AP/Wide World Photos.

causes appeared to be a potent mix of ethno-racial antagonisms, poverty, and neglect, all exacerbated by a severe economic recession that hit poor people, working-class people, and small businessmen especially hard.

In 1995, an ironic sequel to the Rodney King case played out. From January to October, a former star athlete turned TV sportscaster and film actor, O. J. Simpson, stood trial for the murder of his former wife, Nicole Brown Simpson, and her friend, Ronald Goldman. After a lengthy trial, a jury acquitted Simpson of all charges.

Because of the political and cultural contexts in which the trial occurred, it acquired a significance that far transcended the guilt or innocence of one prominent individual. All of the major media provided constant coverage of the trial for months. Cable TV watchers could catch analyses and perspectives on the trial from ex-prosecutors and ex-defense lawyers. Millions of Americans became personally involved. Attorneys for both sides and the judge, Lance Ito, often played to the ever-present television cameras. Due process became judicial theater and Hollywood showbiz. A brutal double murder became prime-time entertainment.

In the eyes of a substantial majority of viewers and expert commentators, prosecutors presented a strong case based on physical evidence that implicated Simpson beyond a reasonable doubt in the two murders. The fact that Simpson, whose resources matched those that Los Angeles County could allocate for the trial, hired a battery of high-priced attorneys to mount a successful defense proved to many Americans that he was immune to the justice system. Simpson's acquittal also reinforced the widely held notion that there was one standard of justice for the rich and another, harsher standard for the poor. The antics of the attorneys on both sides, the often erratic behavior of Judge Ito, and most of all, the outcome of the trial suggested to many observers that the criminal justice system had produced a terrible miscarriage of justice. The trial also raised an ominous question: maybe the traditional jury system could not work in a racially polarized society?

Looming over the trial was the ugly reality of racism. Because the murder victims, Nicole Brown Simpson and Ronald Goldman, were white, and because Simpson was a black celebrity, racial attitudes in this country became central to the outcome of the trial and how people viewed that outcome. The jury, consisting of nine African Americans, eight of them women; a Hispanic male; and two white women, reached a verdict of acquittal within four hours. The jurors rushed to judgment without seriously considering the evidence, much of it quite complex and technical, presented by 133 witnesses who testified during the long trial. Polls showed that 87 percent of black Americans agreed with the jury's verdict; 65 percent of whites believed Simpson to be guilty as charged.

The black-white racial chasm that existed in this country was highlighted on October 4, 1995, when the clerk of the court read the jury's verdict. Around the country, wherever crowds of black Americans had gathered to hear the verdict, they cheered loudly and hugged each other at what appeared to them to be a triumphal deliverance. Wherever crowds of whites had gathered to hear the verdict, they stared in disbelief at what appeared to them to be an egregious miscarriage of justice. These differential responses dramatically revealed that white and black Americans stared uncomprehendingly at each other from across a vast cultural divide.

Seemingly lost in all of the furor over the verdict of acquittal was the fact that Simpson still faced civil suits brought by the families of the murder victims accusing him of the "wrongful deaths" of Nicole Brown Simpson and Ronald Goldman. On February 4, 1997, in subsequent civil trials conducted in a West Los Angeles courtroom before a mostly white, middle-class jury that did not include a single African American, in which a tough old judge excluded the television cameras and kept a rigid order, Simpson was convicted of being responsible for the "wrongful deaths" of Nicole Brown Simpson and Ronald Goldman. The survivors were awarded a total of $33.4 million in compensatory and punitive damages, vastly more than Simpson's severely depleted resources could cover. There was far less media coverage of the civil trial and little noticeable public reaction to the verdicts.

The publicity generated by the beating of Rodney King, the riot, and O. J. Simpson's first trial all highlighted the continual ethno-racial divide. They also called attention to some troubling aspects of the American criminal justice system. More than six million people were either on probation or serving time in 1999, triple the number in 1980. Ethnic and racial minorities accounted for more than two-thirds of the inmates, even though they made up 25 percent of the total population. The huge increase in the number of people on probation and in prison was mostly attributed to the stepped-up war on drugs. Even though studies showed that 80 percent of cocaine users were white and blacks constituted perhaps 12 percent of drug users, African Americans made up over 50 percent of all people arrested for drug possession.

A FRAGMENTED SOCIETY

In 1999, more than two million people identified themselves as Native Americans, more than twice the 1970 total. This figure reflected not only a rapid natural increase in the Amerindian population but also the growing numbers of people of mixed-race ancestry eager to affirm their ethnic roots. A network of tribal-controlled colleges and universities provided Native Americans with relevant educations and cultural sustenance. Many tribes energetically pursued various business ventures, from growing wild rice to operating profitable gambling casinos. In August 1998, near New London, Connecticut, on Mashantucket Pequot Tribal Nation land, the 550 surviving Pequots, grown rich on profits from their Foxwood Casino complex, proudly unveiled a magnificent museum and research center. The museum, built at a cost of nearly $200 million, celebrated the resurrection of a once-powerful Native American people who had struggled for centuries to survive at the margins of the dominant European society that had nearly obliterated them during the seventeenth century.

Fed by continuing high rates of immigration, the Asian-American and Pacific Islander populations continued to grow rapidly during the decade of the 1990s. People from South Korea, the Philippines, Vietnam, and China continued to come to the United States in large numbers. Strengthened by family cultures and prizing academic success, Asian Americans showed high rates of college attendance and upward mobility. However, Asian-American communities experienced generational tensions as young people got caught between the tug of traditional ways and the lure of American popular culture.

In the mid-1990s, African Americans remained divided along class lines. At one end of the social spectrum, a large and growing class of black professionals and businesspeople enjoyed affluent lifestyles. In 1998, 12 percent of college students were black, roughly equal to their ratio of the general population. In 1998, nearly half of African Americans in the workforce held white-collar, middle-class jobs. At the other end of the spectrum could be found the impoverished inner-city blacks, representing one-third of the African-American population. The poorest of the poor, representing perhaps 10 percent of the African-American population in 1998, comprised the "underclass."

Although intact families, thriving churches, and other strong institutions could be found in the inner city, this culture of decency often was overwhelmed by a staggering array of social pathologies. As factory jobs once open to urban workers disappeared, inner-city unemployment rates soared. With good jobs no longer available locally, young people faced life on mean streets or held marginal service-sector jobs in car washes or fast food restaurants. Inner-city patholo-gies such as high crime rates, drug abuse, welfare dependency, and teenage pregnancies derived from more fundamental problems: lack of good educational and job opportunities.

In 1998, the nation's 23,000,000 Hispanics represented America's fastest- growing minor-ity. Hispanic Americans were themselves a diverse group; they included sixteen million Mexi-can Americans concentrated in California and in the American Southwest; one million Cuban Americans mostly living in south Florida; and between one and two million immigrants from the Caribbean region and Central America, living mostly on the East Coast or in California. The Hispanic American population also included two million Puerto Ricans, who are American citi-zens by birth.

Most Hispanics, regardless of their national origins, emigrated to America in search of a better life for themselves and their families. Millions have found success. Family, church, and cultural institutions have sustained hard-working people making it in America. But life re-mained harsh for millions of Hispanic families. In 1998, 20 percent of Mexican Americans and one-third of Puerto Ricans lived in poverty. Hispanic communities often were devastated by al-cohol and drug abuse, soaring crime rates, and high rates of school dropouts and teenage pregnancies.

As American society grew more fragmented in the 1980s and 1990s, the ideal of a com-mon national culture proved to be ever more elusive. Americans appeared to share only con-sumerist cultural experiences, such as shopping at malls and watching prime-time television programs and sporting events. To many immigrant families, becoming an American was defined primarily in residential and economic terms: reside in the country, get a good education, and then get a well-paying job. Make money, buy a home in the suburbs, purchase an SUV, and enjoy the good life based on consumerist values. Questions of politics and culture were ignored or downplayed. Futurists predicted that America would become the world's first post-national political entity in which cultural identities would replace traditional nationalistic identities.

CULTURE WARS

In the public arena, debate erupted, as hitherto marginalized groups demanded cultural as well as political equality. The multiculturalism controversy took many forms. High school and col-lege course offerings became contested arenas. Newly empowered advocates for women, African Americans, Hispanic Americans, Asian Americans, Native Americans, gays and les-bians, and fundamentalist religious groups demanded that high schools and colleges revise their curricula. Multiculturalists challenged course reading lists that continued to privilege DWEMs (dead white European males). Literary scholars revised reading lists to include works by

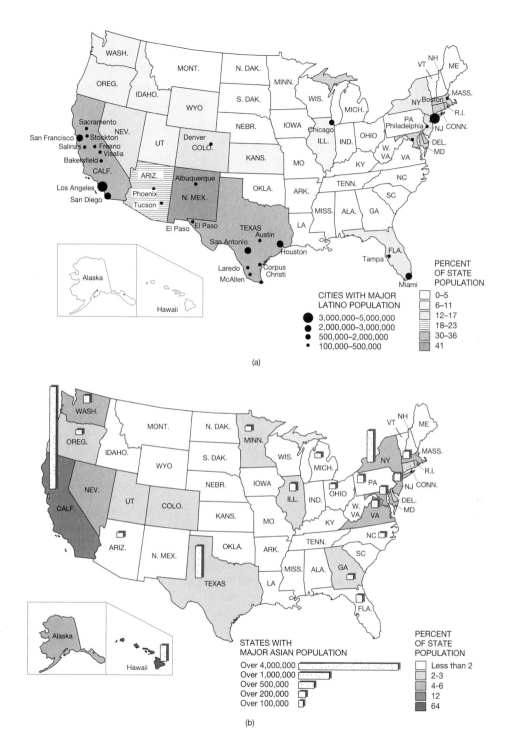

Figure 14.3 **(a) Distribution of Hispanic population in the United States. (b) Distribution of Asian population in the United States.** *Source:* Public Domain Map.

329

women, persons of color, and Third World writers. Historians hastened to rewrite textbooks to include previously neglected or excluded groups. Some professors and teachers expressed dismay at working in repressive environments in which newly empowered champions of multiculturalism and "politically correct" speech imposed a new bureaucratic orthodoxy that stifled academic freedom and encouraged an aggressively litigious culture of victimization.

Culture wars raged on other fronts as well. Congressional conservatives tried to eliminate federal funding for the arts, humanities, and public television. The National Endowment for the Arts and the National Endowment for the Humanities survived the onslaught, but with drastically reduced budgets. The Corporation for Public Broadcasting survived without severe funding cuts.

The multiculturalist reforms provoked a backlash. For many conservatives, multiculturalism replaced Communism as the nation's most dangerous enemy. They insisted that these efforts at more inclusive scholarship eroded any sense of a shared national identity. Critics insisted that all of that counting by race, ethnicity, gender, sexual preference, age, and religious affiliation could lead to a balkanization of American society. They worried lest a heedless rush to multiculturalism destroy the basic unity of the most successful pluralistic society in world history.

Another dimension of the culture wars of the 1990s was the controversy over the legal recognition of marriage for same-sex couples. In May 1993, The Supreme Court of Hawaii ruled that the law barring marriages between same-sex couples was unconstitutional. Responding to the court's decision, Republican Congressmen, fearing that if any state recognized same-sex marriages, all the other states would be forced to recognize these marriages as legal, sponsored federal legislation that would deny recognition of these unions. In 1996, President Clinton signed the Defense of Marriage Act, which defined marriage to be a union of one woman and one man. It also specified that gay couples would be ineligible for spousal benefits. Over thirty states, including Hawaii, enacted similar legislation. Vermont, alone of the fifty states, recognized "civil unions" between same-sex couples, allowing them to receive most of the legal benefits of marriage.

A number of voices resisted all efforts to polarize Americans into warring factions and insisted that multiculturalism's many positive contributions could be retained, while rejecting its extremist claims. In this view, the cultures carried by ethnically and racially defined communities could be appreciated without expecting individuals to define themselves narrowly as members of the descent-based community into which they were born. David Hollinger, one of the nation's most eminent historians, distinguished sharply between biology and culture, complaining that multiculturalists too often assumed that a person's values and tastes flowed from skin color or facial shape. In a brilliant and timely little book, *Postethnic America: Beyond Multiculturalism,* Hollinger offered his cosmopolitan and inclusive vision of a dynamic, pluralistic society, embracing all people of whatever descent:

> Postethnicity prefers voluntary to prescribed affiliations, appreciates multiple identities, pushes for communities of wide scope, recognizes the constructed character of ethno-racial groups, and accepts the formation of new groups as part of the normal life of a democratic community.[1]

---

[1]David A. Hollinger, *Postethnic America: Beyond Multiculturalism* (New York: Basic Books, 1995), p. 116.

WOMEN AND WORK

By the late-1990s, women had smashed through many sexist barriers to higher education and in the workplace. In many fields that were long virtually closed to women, such as medicine, law, engineering, and business management, large numbers of women energetically pursued productive careers. There also were huge increases in the number of women holding public office in the 1980s and 1990s. In 1996, the number of working mothers with children exceeded the number of mothers with children not working outside of the home. In 1998, one-fourth of all doctors and lawyers were women. By 1999, women constituted almost half of the total work force.

But as increasing numbers of women moved into formerly male-dominated occupations and professions, disparities continued in the pay women received for performing comparable work. Women who worked full time in 1999 earned about 73 cents for every dollar a man earned. Many working-class women still confronted a segregated job market in the late 1990s. Sixty percent of working women held "pink collar" jobs.

Many women who had reached managerial positions in business in the late 1990s felt that they were paying too high a personal price for their professional successes. Others complained

Figure 14.4   From left, Cindy Tsingis, Jennifer Almirol, Anna Detzner, and Angela Saucier stand on the rooftop of a construction project overlooking Oakland, California. The women, at work on the city's new federal building, make up eight percent of the workforce, which is considered well above normal and an indicator of the growing numbers of women building careers in construction. Photo by Olga Shalygin.   *Source:* AP/Wide World Photos.

that they could not fulfill family obligations at home and perform their jobs at the highest levels. Felice Schwartz, the head of a research institute that studied women in business, suggested that these woman might pursue a slower career track in business to have more time for family responsibilities. But feminists claimed that Schwartz's so-called "mommy track" perpetuated the very second-class status of women in business that they were trying to surmount.

Long-term structural changes in the economy adversely affected working women. The rise of service industries and the implementation of new technologies created millions of new jobs for women but also created new limits and liabilities. Automated offices were the sweatshops of the 1990s. Many businesses, to cut costs, hired part-time and temporary clerical workers. These contingent workers typically received less pay and fewer benefits than full timers.

Cultural changes also have accompanied the advent of women into the workplaces of America. Most notable is the change in women's consciousness. Many women in the 1990s felt that they were equal to men in the market place and had greater ambitions and expectations than previous generations of women. But traditional values and stereotypes also exhibited strong staying powers. Advertisers no longer celebrated domesticity as a woman's only appropriate realm but still insisted that the busy career woman had to keep her weight down and be attractive. Women spent far more of their incomes on clothes, beauty aids, and diets than men.

The Good Earth

American environmentalists had much to celebrate during the mid-1990s. Many of the nation's rivers, lakes, and waterways were cleaner than they had been since the advent of the American Industrial Revolution. Air pollution had been reduced by one-third. Lead emissions from gasoline had been practically eliminated. Many bird species that had been on the verge of extinction, including the magnificent bald eagle, the peregrine falcon, and the California condor, made amazing comebacks. Americans annually recycled billions of dollars worth of metals, glass, plastics, wood, and paper products. When Congressional Republicans in 1995 tried to freeze or roll back environmental initiatives, they had to retreat in the face of strong public disapproval of their anti-environmental stance.

However, despite much progress on several fronts, environmentalists perceived that much remained to be done. Millions of Americans continued to breathe dirty air every day of their lives. Many rivers and lakes remained unsafe for fishing and swimming. Toxic waste dumps abounded, some of them near residential areas and parks where children played.

It also was clear during the 1990s that environmentalists had to take an increasingly international approach to what were now understood as global problems. The first major international action on an environmental issue occurred in 1987, when delegates from thirty-four nations met in Montreal to sign an agreement to phase out ozone-damaging fluorocarbons. Among other consequences, the Montreal protocol amounted to a death sentence for aerosol spray cans. In 1991, the United States signed a treaty banning all development in Antarctica for fifty years. The following year, Americans signed an international agreement on global warming, according to environmental scientists the most pressing of the world's environmental problems. The world's growing concern about global warming was highlighted in 1998 with the advent of the worst El Niño in twenty years. Record rainfall totals, severe flooding, the worst droughts in decades, and destructive storms in the minds of concerned environmentalists foreshadowed the greater global disasters that were inevitable unless the trend toward global warming was reversed

THE PRESIDENCY OF GEORGE H. W. BUSH

Bush's presidency was dominated by two overriding concerns: the savings and loan crisis and the reduction of huge federal deficits. Bush proposed a rescue plan to either close or sell the bankrupt S&Ls and repay depositors. Congress created a new agency, the Resolution Trust Corporation (RTC), to sell off the assets of the failed thrifts to solvent banks. At the same time, the FSLIC was folded into the Federal Deposit Insurance Corporation (FDIC) to provide the billions needed to bail out depositors.

In the spring of 1991, Bush, under heavy pressure from Congress to reduce the federal debt, conceded the need to accept some new taxes. His concession promptly outraged his conservative supporters and many citizens who had voted in good faith for Bush and his no-new-taxes promise. This sense of betrayal felt by conservatives contributed to Bush's electoral defeat in 1992. In October 1991, the Bush administration and the Democratically-controlled Congress finally agreed on a combination of tax hikes and budget cuts that promised modest reductions in the budget deficits over the next four years. Meanwhile, the economy slipped into a recession, the first in nearly a decade. The recession seriously undermined Bush's popularity with the voters.

Bush also inherited a host of serious social problems. The most feared pathology was the ongoing AIDS epidemic. By 1990, the disease had claimed over 110,000 lives, and an estimated 1.5 million people had tested HIV-positive. Most of the AIDS-infected cases involved gay males, but in the early 1990s, the proportion of AIDS cases among African American and Hispanic American intravenous drug users grew rapidly. The number of women infected with the AIDS virus also increased. Despite the huge sums of money spent on research, there appeared to be no prospect for an early cure or even the development of an effective vaccine. However, progress occurred in the development of drugs and therapies that suppressed or delayed the onset of AIDS symptoms. In 1990, while the nation devoted vast resources to waging a war against AIDS, Congress enacted one of the most important legislative acts of the Bush presidency, the Americans with Disabilities Act.

Bush continued the war on drugs begun during Reagan's years. He pushed for more stringent drug testing in the workplaces of America, better enforcement of existing drug laws, and additional measures taken to interdict the flood of illicit drugs pouring into the country from Mexico, Peru, and Colombia. Despite stepped-up efforts on all three fronts, drugs, especially "crack" cocaine, remained widely available within the United States. There also was a connection between widespread crack use and the rising level of violent crime amidst the inner cities of America. Even though the Bush administration spent billions of dollars on its war on drugs, it failed to curb the great American appetite for drugs or significantly slow the illicit traffic.

THE SUPREME COURT IN THE 1990S

By the late 1980s, the Supreme Court had taken a conservative turn. In *Webster v. Reproductive Health Care Services* (1989), the Court, by a five-to-four majority decision, sustained a Missouri statute that restricted abortions. In *Planned Parenthood v. Casey* (1992), the Court, by a five-to-four decision, upheld a Pennsylvania law requiring a twenty-four-hour waiting period and informed consent before an abortion could be performed. Although the conservative Supreme Court placed restrictions on women's access to abortion, they never challenged *Roe v. Wade,* which established that women have a constitutional right to seek an abortion.

With the retirement from the Court in 1990 and 1991 of William Brennan and Thurgood Marshall, two elderly liberal associate justices, Bush had opportunities to add additional conservative jurists to the Supreme Court. His first appointment, David Souter, an obscure federal judge from New Hampshire, was quickly confirmed by the Senate with little opposition. Bush's second appointee, Clarence Thomas, a conservative African American jurist, was narrowly confirmed by the Senate in October 1991 by a fifty-two-to-forty-eight vote.

Judge Thomas had to survive challenges from many senators who were dissatisfied with his evasive answers to their questions concerning his views on abortion and other issues. In dramatic televised hearings before the Senate Judiciary Committee, Thomas also had to refute charges brought by an Oklahoma University law professor, Anita Hill, that he had sexually harassed her when she had worked for him at two federal agencies in 1982 and 1983. The nation witnessed three days of often sexually explicit testimony. The close Senate vote to confirm

Figure 14.5   University of Oklahoma law professor Anita Hill, who accused Supreme Court nominee Clarence Thomas of sexual harassment. *Source:* Getty Images, Inc.

Thomas was not appreciably affected by the hearings; nearly all of the negative votes were cast by senators who would have voted against Thomas, had Hill never made her charges.

The controversy attending Thomas's confirmation hearings brought to the fore the troubling matter of sexual harassment of women in the political system. The hearings also made people more aware of the seriousness of the problems women face in the workplaces of America.

The insensitive treatment accorded Hill by some male senators bent on discrediting her testimony revived the feminist political movement. Patricia Ireland, a spokeswoman for the National Organization for Women (NOW), vowed that women would seek to replace male office holders with qualified women. Using as their rallying cry, "they still don't get it," woman entered mainstream politics in unprecedented numbers during the 1992 elections.

ENDING THE COLD WAR

The advent of the Bush presidency coincided with dramatic developments occurring in international affairs that brought about the most fundamental changes in American foreign policy since World War II. The most important of these developments was the decline of Communism, as evidenced by the disintegration of the Soviet empire in eastern Europe and then the collapse of the Soviet Union itself. The Cold War, which had been the dominant reality of international life for nearly a half century, suddenly ended.

It is impossible to know exactly what role President Reagan's policies played in the Soviet Union's downfall. Conservative spokesmen were quick to say that the rapid American military buildup in the 1980s, especially Reagan's commitment to the Strategic Defense Initiative, along with the Reagan Doctrine, and Reagan's bold rhetorical attacks on Communism brought about the demise of the Soviet Union. To many Sovietologists, it appeared that Communism had imploded, the internal collapse hastened by Gorbachev's bumbling efforts to reform Communism, which led to consequences that could not be foreseen by him much less any U.S. officials. Washington's aggressive anti-Soviet strategies and the pressures of trying to compete with the Americans probably hastened the Soviet collapse.

The sudden demise of Communism caught official Washington by complete surprise. No one appears to have seen the collapse coming. Neither the CIA, nor any of the other American intelligence agencies, nor any of the myriad of experts inhabiting prestigious U.S. strategic institutes and think tanks had the slightest inkling that the Soviet system was on the verge of collapse until it disintegrated.

Mikhail Gorbachev inadvertently destroyed the Soviet Union while trying to save it. He understood that the Achilles heel of the Soviet empire was its stagnating economy and lagging technology, especially in the areas of computer technology and information processing. By the mid-1980's, Gorbachev perceived that the Soviet Union could no longer maintain the arms race with the United States and feed its own people. In an effort to revive a failing system, Gorbachev proclaimed an era of *perestroika* (economic restructuring) and *glasnost* (openness). Economic controls were loosened and censorship was lifted. A civic awakening occurred. An elected parliament supplanted party *aparatchiks*.

Although Soviet politics were reformed, the economy continued to deteriorate. Continuing economic rot forced Gorbachev to pull Soviet troops out of Afghanistan, ending a nine-year war in that country. In July 1989, Gorbachev repudiated the Brezhnev doctrine that had given Soviet troops the right to intervene in eastern European countries. He cut loose from client governments in Poland, Czechoslovakia, East Germany, Hungary, Bulgaria, and Romania. Once the people of these countries understood that Soviet tanks no longer protected their rulers, they promptly overthrew all of those hated regimes. The dominoes toppled in rapid succession.

The most dramatic event heralding the collapse of the Soviet empire in Eastern Europe occurred on November 9, 1989, when the Berlin Wall that had so long served as a hated symbol of the impasse between East and West, was breached. Hundreds of thousands of East Germans rushed into West Berlin. With the borders between East and West Germany fully open, the Communist government of East Germany collapsed. A democratic government quickly replaced it, and on October 3, 1990, East Germany reunited with West Germany. The reunited Germany remained in NATO, and the Warsaw Pact disintegrated. Since disputes over Germany between the Soviets and Americans were the major causes of the Cold War that originated during the mid-1940s, it was historically appropriate that the reunion of Germany signaled the beginning of the end of the long conflict.

Presidents Reagan and George Bush supported the Gorbachev revolution. Many U.S. corporations quickly penetrated the Soviet Union. McDonald's opened a large restaurant just off of Red Square. But it was the Germans who led the drive to penetrate Soviet markets in the immediate aftermath of the Cold War. Gorbachev and the West Germans cut a deal: the Germans would provide about $30 billion to prop up the Soviet economy, and in return Gorbachev would accept speedy German reunion and the end of the Warsaw Pact. On August 19, 1991, Stalinist reactionaries among the Red Army, the KGB, and the bureaucrats who controlled the Soviet economy attempted a military coup. It failed because 40,000 citizens of Moscow defied the *putschists* and rallied around the courageous leadership of Boris Yeltsin.

The death of the Soviet Union was officially proclaimed on December 21, 1991, by Boris Yeltsin who announced the formation of a new federation of sovereign states. The former USSR had rapidly mutated into an eleven-republic Commonwealth of Independent States, three independent Baltic nations, and an independent Georgia. On December 26, major European powers and the United States officially recognized the Russian republic under Yeltsin's leadership as the *de facto* successor to the defunct Soviet Union.

Following its reappearance as a nation, Russia's economy stagnated; it lacked the institutional base or competitive strategy required to develop a dynamic capitalistic economy. Exogenous factors, such as falling world commodity prices, particularly for oil, and turmoil in Asian financial markets, hurt Russia. The results were all ruinous. The nation was in a 1930s-style depression that continued into the new millennium. Real GDP had fallen 40 percent to 50 percent since 1990; investment shrunk by 80 percent. Eighty percent of the 150,000,000 Russian people lived in poverty.

The Russian economy and government were controlled by a corrupt capitalist elite, many of them former Communist bureaucrats, who acquired ownership of formerly state-owned enterprises for a fraction of their value. This coterie of billionaires concealed income, evaded taxes, and removed an estimated $200 billion in assets offshore. Since 1991, Russia has dropped into the ranks of a Third World exporter of raw materials.

POST–COLD WAR DIPLOMACY

As the Soviet Union receded from the world stage, Europe, led by a reunified Germany, moved to form a European community free of tariffs, travel restrictions, and monetary impediments. Eleven nations with a population of about 350 million constituted the world's richest market. The euro was launched January 1, 1999; it promised to transform the transatlantic relationship for good by placing Europe on an equal economic footing with the United States.

Figure 14.6   Post–Cold War Europe, 1992.   *Source:* U.S. State Department.

Along the Pacific Rim, Japan suffered a series of financial and economic setbacks in the 1990s. America's Asian and Pacific trade in 1998, over half of it with Japan, was much larger than its trade with Europe. China, its economy freed from Communist shackles, had the world's fastest-growing major economy. By January 1999, the Chinese GDP had reach an estimated $1.6 trillion, making it the world's third largest economy.

U.S. foreign policy in Latin America also benefitted from the end of the Cold War. Gorbachev announced that Soviet aid to prop up the Cuban economy, which had been running at $5 billion per annum, would be drastically curtailed. In the post–Cold War era, Castro appeared to be only an aging *caudillo* clinging to power in an impoverished insular backwater within a hemisphere that had abandoned dictatorship of either the leftist or rightist variety and had turned instead to U.S.-style free markets and political democracy.

In Nicaragua, the Sandinistas also felt the impact of the end of the Cold War. The Soviet Union, which had subsidized the Sandinistas to the tune of $500 million a year, turned off the aid spigot. In early 1990, the Sandinistas permitted free elections to take place in Nicaragua. To their dismay, a coalition of anti-Sandinista forces, led by Violetta Chamorro, won. Cut off by their former Soviet patron and repudiated by the people of Nicaragua, the Sandinistas surrendered their power. Chamorro became Nicaragua's first freely elected president in more than sixty years.

While supporting the spread of democracy in Nicaragua, the United States also settled some scores in Panama. In December 1989, the United States sent military forces into Panama to overthrow dictator Manuel Noriega and to install a pro-American government. Noriega had previously worked with the CIA. He later broke with the Americans, supported the Sandinistas, and became rich as a drug trafficker for the Medellin cartel. Previously, U.S. federal grand juries had indicted Noriega for drug smuggling, gun running, and money laundering. He was captured and brought to the United States for trial. Public opinion polls showed that the Panamanian intervention, which was of dubious legality since Panamanian officials had not requested U.S. assistance, was overwhelmingly popular with Americans.

China also felt the impact of rising anti-Communism. In April 1989, thousands of Chinese students and intellectuals gathered in Beijing's Tiananmen Square to demand democracy for China. The pro-democracy movement spread rapidly, and soon demonstrations sprouted in Nanjing, Shanghai, and other Chinese cities. Americans strongly supported the pro-democracy forces. For a time, Chinese authorities appeared uncertain about how to respond to the challenge because of the extensive media coverage the pro-democracy movement received in the world's press. But on the morning of June 4, 1989, the Chinese army crushed the drive for democracy. A brutal massacre claimed the lives of at least 1,000 people. Dissident democrats were hunted down and jailed *en masse*. The nascent pro-democracy movement was violently suppressed. President Bush publicly condemned the Chinese regime's slaughter of its own people; however, he would take no actions that might jeopardize the friendly relations carefully cultivated between the Chinese and American governments since Richard Nixon's historic journey to Beijing in 1972.

While Communist regimes were collapsing in eastern Europe, rightist authoritarian regimes also were succumbing to the world democratic revival. In Chile, General Pinochet's regime gave way to a democratically elected government. In South Africa, Frederick DeKlerk became prime minister in August 1989. Within a few months, he released African National

Conference leader Nelson Mendela from prison, where he had languished for more than twenty-five years. In 1991, as DeKlerk began dismantling apartheid, President Bush lifted American sanctions. In April 1994, there occurred one of the most thrilling moments in modern world history: South Africa held its first elections in which *all* South Africans could vote. Mandela was elected president, and a multiracial parliament was chosen. Democracy had trumped apartheid.

Elsewhere in Africa, famine threatened millions of people, especially in Somalia, where years of civil war had destroyed any semblance of government. In December 1992, when warring Somali factions diverted UN-sanctioned food relief shipments to black markets, Washington sent in 30,000 U.S. troops to protect food deliveries. Under President Clinton, the U.S. mission expanded to include restoring order and state-building. Eighteen U.S. Special Forces were killed in fighting the forces of Somali warlord Mohammed Farah Aidid. Yielding to public pressure to bring the troops home, Clinton withdrew all U.S. forces from Somalia in 1994.

WAR IN THE PERSIAN GULF

During January and February 1991, the first major military action of the new post-Cold War era occurred when America and its allies fought a war in the Persian Gulf against Iraq. The war had a long preparation time, and it derived in part from previous U.S. Middle Eastern diplomatic policies and priorities. During the Iraq-Iranian war, the United States often aided Iraq to prevent an Iranian victory that Washington feared could threaten the oil-rich Saudis. During the late 1980s, America sent the Iraqis nearly a billion dollars' worth of agricultural, economic, and technical aid.

Soon after Iraq's war with Iran ended in a draw under the terms of an agreement brokered by UN representatives, Kuwait, which, along with Saudi Arabia, had bankrolled Iraq's war with the Iranians, increased its production of oil in violation of OPEC rules. World oil prices dropped, hurting Saddam Hussein's government, already deeply in debt and dependent on oil revenues for sustaining the Iraqi economy. Saddam also was angered by the Kuwaitis and the Saudis over their refusal to forgive Iraq's huge indebtedness to them. He asserted claims to Kuwaiti territory based on maps predating the 1919 political settlement that had created the modern nation-state of Iraq out of the decaying Ottoman Empire.

Even as Iraq prepared for war, U.S. leaders did not anticipate military action in the region. Washington was preoccupied with the historic events that brought the Cold War to a sudden end and its policies in the Gulf region still turned on the notion that Iraq was the major counterweight to Iranian revolutionary aggression. On the eve of Iraq's invasion of Kuwait, the U.S. ambassador to Baghdad, April Gillespie, told Saddam that the United States would not become involved in regional disputes, although America would defend its vital interests. Saddam either interpreted Gillespie's ambiguous remark as a green light for aggression or calculated that he could defeat any U.S. military intervention.

On August 2, 1990, Iraqi forces occupied Kuwait and threatened neighboring Saudi Arabia, possessor of 25 percent of the world's proven oil reserves. Bush, determined to protect the Saudis and to force Saddam Hussein to withdraw his forces from Kuwait, forged an international coalition under United Nations auspices to thwart Iraqi aggression. Bush also persuaded Soviet leader Mikhail Gorbachev to abandon his former Iraqi clients and support the UN initiative.

The UN promptly enacted Resolution 661, authorizing a trade embargo against Iraq. The international community clamped a tight economic boycott on Iraq and deployed a military force of some 250,000 troops to defend Saudi Arabia from possible attack. Most of these forces, dubbed OPERATION DESERT SHIELD, were U.S. troops under the command of U.S. Army General Norman Schwarzkopf. Schwarzkopf's forces also included a sizable representation from Great Britain, France, and several Arab countries, including Saudi Arabia, Egypt, Syria, and the United Arab Emirates.

Initially, Bush appeared willing to use military force defensively, to protect Saudi Arabia and other possible Iraqi targets from attack and to let economic pressures force Saddam out of Kuwait. But almost from the beginning of Gulf military operations, Pentagon planners were preparing for offensive military action. Bush soon became convinced that the boycott would not work. During November, 580,000 soldiers representing some twenty countries gathered in and near Saudi Arabia.

Many liberal Democrats opposed military action against Iraq. They believed that the economic boycott ought to be given a chance to work, and they also did not want America to go to war without congressional approval. The UN enacted Resolution 629 on November 29, which set January 15, 1991, as a deadline for Iraqi withdrawal from Kuwait. It authorized the use of force to drive the Iraqis from Kuwait if they did not leave by that date. On January 12, both the House and the Senate narrowly enacted resolutions formally approving the use of U.S. military force in the Gulf.

On January 16, 1991, after a last-minute UN peace mission failed, President Bush ordered an Allied air assault on Kuwaiti and Iraqi targets. OPERATION DESERT STORM had begun. Deploying an impressive arsenal of high-tech weaponry, America and its allies waged a destructive 42-day air war against the Iraqis.

On February 23, 1991, General Schwarzkopf sent his forces, now 700,000 strong, into Kuwait and southern Iraq. Two hundred thousand American, British, and French armored forces roared across the undefended Iraqi border with Saudi Arabia 200 miles to the west of Kuwait. They smashed into the elite Republican Guard forces and quickly demolished them. Within four days, Allied forces had overwhelmed the Iraqis, whose fighting capabilities had been seriously eroded by the air attacks that preceded the invasion. President Bush offered a ceasefire and the Iraqis quickly accepted it. At war's end, the Allied forces occupied Kuwait and held southern Iraq.

Only 184 Americans were killed and 467 wounded during the short war, but an estimated 100,000 Iraqi soldiers and civilians died. The Persian Gulf war cost $60 billion, of which 80 percent of the tab for the war was picked up by wealthy U.S. allies who did not send combat forces.

Americans erupted in a frenetic celebration of a victory that had been achieved so quickly and at such a low cost. Parades and celebrations, the likes of which had not been seen since 1945, welcomed home the conquering heroes. President Bush's approval ratings soared beyond 90 percent. In the first major crisis of the post–Cold War era, America had boldly asserted its leadership, and the Soviets had followed the U.S. lead.

American home audiences followed the war around the clock on the Cable News Network (CNN). But the U.S. military tightly controlled television reportage, and American TV viewers

Figure 14.7   Some of the men and women serving in the U.S. Army during OPERATION DESERT STORM.   *Source:* SUIPA Press.

saw only a censored version of the war. Reporters were allowed in the field only with military escorts who limited what they saw and whom they interviewed. Focusing on the marvels of U.S. high-tech warfare, reporters dubbed the conflict, the "Nintendo War."

The immediate U.S. goal in the Persian Gulf War was liberating Kuwait. Larger U.S. strategic goals included keeping the vast Middle Eastern oil reserves in friendly hands and destroying Saddam Hussein's capacity to wage offensive war or achieve paramountcy in the Persian Gulf region.

Critics observed that even though the Allied coalition succeeded in driving the Iraqis out of Kuwait, it failed to bring down Saddam Hussein. Bush encouraged ethnic Kurds and Shiite Muslims within Iraq to rebel, but when they did, Washington allowed Saddam to destroy them. Bush's reluctance to continue the war derived from Saudi fears that if Saddam were deposed, Iraq would disintegrate. The Saudis preferred a defanged Saddam presiding over a stable Iraq than chaos and civil war on their border. They also feared Iranian hegemony in the region in the wake of an Iraqi collapse.

The short war had a negligible impact on the American economy. Domestic oil prices briefly spiked and the economy remained mired in recession. Bush's high approval ratings at the time of the war dissipated during the next six months as the U.S. economy remained in the doldrums. There was a poignant aftermath to the war. Hundreds of U. S. Persian Gulf veterans developed symptoms, including fatigue, nausea, joint pain, and memory loss, after serving in the

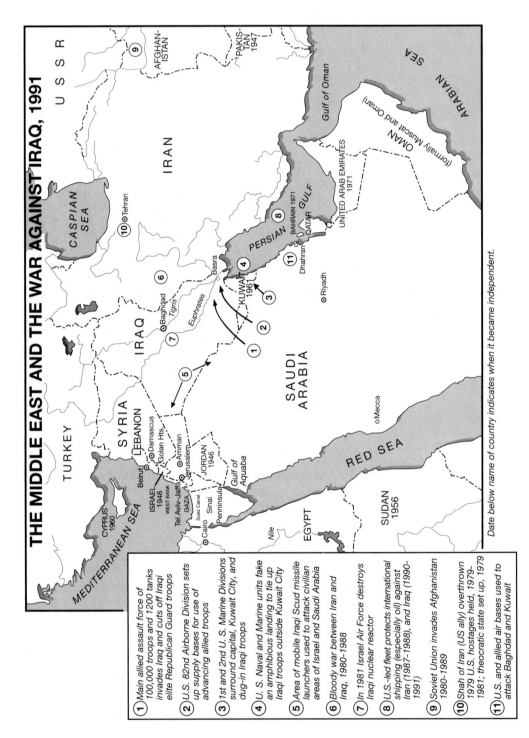

Figure 14.8   The Middle East and the war against Iraq, 1991.   *Source:* Public Domain Map.

combat zone. Medical experts believed that many of these veterans were suffering from the effects of having been exposed to chemical and biological agents released when Allied forces destroyed Iraqi poison gas storage facilities.

Because of the Soviet collapse and the smashing Iraqi defeat, Israel felt more secure than at any other time since the Jewish state was founded. Responding to U.S. pressures, Israeli leaders agreed to participate in an international conference convened in Madrid in December 1991 to try to resolve the Palestinian issue and to achieve a comprehensive Middle East peace treaty. Delegates from several Arab nations and representatives of the Palestinians engaged in dialogues with Israeli envoys. In the spring of 1993, the talks were placed on indefinite hold as Israeli security forces fought with Palestinian militants in the occupied territories.

THE ELECTION OF 1992

In the summer of 1990, the economy slid into a recession, the first downturn in eight years. Although the recession was not severe, the economy's slow recovery from it put the Republican hold on the White House in jeopardy. The state of the economy and jobs for the people became the dominant issues in the 1992 elections.

Reminiscent of Jimmy Carter in 1976, a political unknown emerged to capture the Democratic presidential nomination in 1992. He was William Jefferson "Bill" Clinton, the young, energetic governor of Arkansas. Clinton had been critical of both conservative Republican economic policies and of what he called liberal Democratic "tax-and-spend" alternatives. He had served as chairman of the Democratic Leadership Council, a group of moderate Democrats intent on winning control of the national party. In a crisp acceptance speech, Clinton pronounced an end to spendthrift liberalism and special-interest politics. He called for welfare reform, affordable health care for all Americans, a tax cut for the middle class, higher taxes for rich people, tax breaks for small businesses, large reductions in budget deficits, and sharp reductions in military spending.

A strong third-party candidate, billionaire populist H. Ross Perot, entered the 1992 campaign. While Bush and Clinton battled their way through the primaries, Perot's electronic grass-roots campaign was fueled by citizen outrage at a political system that could not address the myriad of problems facing ordinary Americans. By May, Perot was outpolling both Clinton and Bush in some national surveys. In mid-July, Perot abruptly announced that he was withdrawing from the race and threw his support to Bill Clinton, whom, Perot claimed, had taken up his issues.

During the fall campaign, Clinton attacked what he called the "trickle-down" economic policies of the Reagan and Bush administrations. He portrayed himself as "an agent of change" to appeal to "Perotistas." Clinton called for welfare reform to obtain the votes of Reagan Democrats. He repeated his proposals made at the Democratic Convention—affordable health care for all Americans, raising taxes on the rich, and tax breaks for the middle class.

Bush made a strenuous bid for reelection. He tried to run on his foreign policy record, but in 1992, in the post–Cold War era, the American people considered foreign policy issues secondary or peripheral. Bush blamed the Democratically controlled Congress for political gridlock, the lingering recession, and the runaway deficits. Mostly he concentrated his fire on Bill

Clinton. He charged him with being a tax-and-spend liberal disguised as a moderate. He questioned Clinton's character and his judgment. He challenged Clinton's patriotism for being a draft avoider, and he even questioned his loyalty for having visited the Soviet Union.

In the final month of the campaign, Perot leaped back into the ring. Once again, the election became a three-way contest. The election results confirmed the lead that Clinton had long maintained in the polls. He received 43.7 million votes to 38.1 million for Bush and 19.2 million for Perot. He garnered a total of 370 electoral votes to 168 for Bush and 0 for Perot. For the first time since 1977, the Democrats won control of both the White House and Congress.

Clinton's moderate campaign partially restored the old Democratic coalition that had been ripped to shreds by Nixon and Reagan. Clinton retained the African American vote. Hard times and Bush's failed policies brought a lot of Reagan Democrats home to Clinton, especially in the Midwestern industrial states. Clinton probably won the election by carrying Ohio, Illinois, Michigan, and Pennsylvania—all of which had gone to Bush in 1988. Clinton also got a majority of the women's vote and the youth vote. Clinton and Al Gore, his vice-presidential running mate, both moderate Southerners, also chipped away at the Solid South, which had been solid for Republicans in recent presidential elections.

Although the shift in relative strength of the major parties was slight, 1992 represented a year of upheaval in congressional voting. Elections for the House were held for the first time under the reapportionment brought about by the 1990 census. Demographic trends underway since World War II continued to prevail. Sunbelt states like California, Arizona, Texas, and Florida were the big winners, gaining many additional seats. The Northeastern states and the old industrial states of the upper Midwest continued to be the big losers, losing the seats that the Southern Rim states gained. Women, African Americans, Asian Americans, and Hispanics were elected to the House in record numbers. In the Senate women scored a major breakthrough; five women, all of them Democrats, won seats. Carol Moseley Braun, from Illinois, became the first African American woman to serve in the Senate. California sent two women to the Senate, Diane Feinstein and Barbara Boxer. Colorado sent a Native American, Ben Nighthorse Campbell.

RETURN OF THE DEMOCRATS

As in 1960, the 1992 election brought both a change of party in the White House and a generational shift along the corridors of power. With Clinton and Gore in office, and over 100 new members of Congress in place, the Baby Boomers assumed national leadership. Clinton made good on his pledge to diversify the upper echelons of the executive branch by selecting many women and minority candidates. Women headed the Environmental Protection Agency and the Council of Economic Advisers. Janet Reno was picked to be the first woman attorney general. Clinton's determination to select women for important offices also reflected the influence of his wife, Hillary Rodham Clinton, an attorney, who became the most powerful First Lady since Eleanor Roosevelt.

The new president quickly got embroiled in a controversy with the Pentagon over his proposal to allow openly gay and lesbian people to serve in the armed forces. In July 1993, Clinton announced a compromise policy that had the support of the Joint Chiefs of Staff: The military would no longer ask prospective recruits questions about their sexual orientation and would no

Figure 14.9   Baby boomers in the White House. President Bill Clinton and First Lady Hillary Rodham Clinton. *Source:* The White House Photo Office.

longer employ security forces to hound suspected gays and lesbians out of the armed forces. But gays and lesbians serving in the military could not engage in overt homosexual behavior on or off military duty stations; also, open acknowledgment of gay or lesbian preferences would be grounds for dismissal from military service. This "don't ask, don't tell, don't pursue" compromise failed to satisfy gay and lesbian activists, who vowed to continue their campaign to achieve equality within the armed forces. It also angered those who opposed any change in the anti-gay-and-lesbian policies of the military services. Military security forces continued to harass suspected gay and lesbian personnel despite the new policy.

Although the recession was over in the spring of 1993 and the economy was growing again, the high rate of unemployment remained fixed at 7 percent. Thirty-six million Americans lived in poverty and more Americans than ever before were receiving food stamps. In the post–Cold War era, cuts in military and aerospace spending brought massive layoffs at prime defense contractors such as Boeing, McDonnell-Douglas, and Lockheed. American businesses both large and small were forced to become more efficient to meet the rigors of world economic competition in the 1990s. They laid off workers and mid-level managers to become more cost-effective operations. Companies replaced human workers with computers and computer-driven machines to increase production and cut costs.

Millions who continued to work had to work harder and longer than ever before. Pressures on workers to be more productive were unrelenting, and they intensified. Record numbers of workers filed disability claims in the 1990s, their disabilities linked to stress or to disabling injuries caused by spending too many hours on computer terminals. Millions of workers and their families in the cutthroat 1990s suffered serious declines in the quality of their lives. They worked harder than their parents, endured more stress, and were often less well compensated.

The continued decline of trade unions also contributed to the deteriorating status of working people. In 1999, scarcely 15 percent of American workers belonged to unions, down from a high of 35 percent reached during World War II. Beset by corporate downsizing, the wholesale transfer of jobs overseas, harsh union-busting tactics, and increasingly conservative Congresses that were indifferent or hostile to trade union interests, unions have been powerless to lift the wages of most workers or even to protect their jobs. Adjusted for inflation, wage levels in unionized industries have been stagnant for over twenty years, as corporate profits have soared.

In August 1993, a Democratic Congress enacted a five-year economic renewal program that incorporated some of Clinton's proposals. It raised the top marginal income tax rates from 31 to 36 percent, eased taxes on low-income families, and provided funding for education, retraining, and apprenticeship programs aimed at upgrading workers' skills. The program also brought about modest reductions in the deficits which continued to exceed $200 billion annually in 1994 and 1995.

Clinton also signed the North American Free Trade Agreement (NAFTA). Negotiated by the Bush administration, NAFTA incorporated Mexico into a free-trade zone already created by Canada and the United States during Reagan's presidency. NAFTA aroused both strong support and fierce opposition. Liberal Democrats and trade union leaders led the opposition. With strong support from Republicans, NAFTA carried Congress, giving Clinton a political victory over the liberal wing of his own party.

Congress also approved a new round of tariff reductions on manufactured goods under the General Agreement on Tariffs and Trade (GATT), which had been in place since the end of World War II. In 1994, Clinton followed these victories by reducing trade barriers with major Pacific Rim nations. In 1995, he became embroiled in a nasty trade dispute with Tokyo over its refusal to allow American companies to sell automotive spare parts to the Japanese. Only after Clinton threatened to impose sanctions that would have severely hurt sales of Japanese luxury automobiles to the United States did the Japanese make concessions.

Polls taken during the 1992 election showed that public concern about the rising tide of crime, especially violent crime, was second only to economic worries. Congress, in 1993, enacted the Handgun Violence Prevention Act. In 1994, it enacted the most costly, far-reaching crime bill in American history. It provided $30 billion to fund increased law enforcement, crime prevention, and prison construction. It extended the death penalty to fifty additional federal crimes, and it banned the sale of certain kinds of assault rifles.

In October 1993, following the lead of Hillary Rodham Clinton, the Clinton administration moved to implement health care reform. Their complex plan had three main goals: to provide coverage for the forty-five million Americans who had no health insurance, to hold down costs, and to preserve the high quality of available health care for all Americans. The plan would have drastically restructured the existing health care system. All Americans would be enrolled into large regional health alliances. Individuals could enroll in either a fee-for-service plan, enabling them to choose their own physicians, or in less expensive health maintenance organizations (HMOs), where they would see doctors on the HMO staffs. Employers would pay 80 percent of workers' health insurance costs. Self-employed workers would buy their own insurance, and Medicaid would continue to cover the poor. To cover the plan's estimated $100 billion in added costs, Congress would enact large tax increases on tobacco products.

The administration's health-care reform proposal instantly attracted legions of critics but had relatively little support. After six grueling months of hearings, the administration conceded defeat on health care reform and settled for some token reforms to contain costs. The big losers were the Americans who had no health insurance in 1994. These working-class families represented one fifth of the U.S. population under age sixty-five.

A REPUBLICAN EARTHQUAKE

The 1994 midterm elections amounted to a popular referendum on Clinton's performance during his first two years in office. A sizable majority of voters used the occasion to voice their dissatisfaction with the first yuppie president. Fears about rising crime rates, unresolved social issues, cultural conflicts, and continuing economic insecurities produced one of the most significant transformations in recent political history. The 1994 midterm elections completed the political transition that had begun with Ronald Reagan's electoral victory in 1980.

The elections brought a Republican Congress to power, the first since 1952. The shock troops leading this Republican political "earthquake" were a group of seventy-three mostly young conservative reformers, many of whom had strong ties to the religious Right. The new Speaker of the House of Representative, Newt Gingrich, was the leader of the Republican revolt. He quickly became the second most powerful politician in Washington.

Gingrich read the election results as a mandate for implementing his "Contract with America," a conservative agenda for the 1990s, with its top priorities being a balanced budget, the phasing out of welfare, and deep tax cuts. Following Gingrich's lead, the 104th Congress set out to downsize the federal government and to dismantle the welfare state. In 1995, the most activist Congress in decades enacted legislation that weakened affirmative action programs, cut foreign aid, cut Medicare, cut taxes, and reduced budget deficits.

As the Republicans seized the legislative initiative, President Clinton was forced to adopt a defensive political strategy. He tried to fend off Republican efforts to cut deeply or destroy liberal programs whenever he sensed that he had public opinion on his side, and of trying to position himself to win reelection within an increasingly conservative political environment.

Twice in the fall of 1995, Republican enthusiasm for deep tax cuts and achieving a balanced budget by 2002 caused a partial shutdown of the federal government. When Clinton vetoed an appropriations bill, some national parks and museums were forced to shut down, and some recipients reported delays in getting Social Security and Medicare payments. Public anger focused mainly on Republicans, who viewed them as ideological zealots whose refusal to compromise created problems for ordinary American citizens. Gingrich's and Congress's approval ratings plummeted, while Clinton's soared.

In 1996, both President Clinton and the Republican-controlled Congress sought a centrist middle ground that produced several important new programs and policies. The minimum wage was increased. A major telecommunications bill replaced government regulation of the industry with open competition among telephone and cable TV companies. Congress also established a program that over seven years would gradually remove restrictions on farmers and phase out subsidy payments going back to the New Deal era of the 1930s.

The most important legislation enacted by Congress ended the federal welfare program that also dated back to the New Deal. The Welfare Reform Act of 1996 returned the program to the states. According to its provisions, many aid recipients were required to find work and be off of welfare within two years. It also restricted eligibility for welfare to five years during a person's lifetime. The defederalizing of welfare was the most significant downsizing of the federal government in modern times and further attenuated the social contract that was at the heart of what remained of the federal welfare state.

THE ELECTION OF 1996

Several prominent Republicans sought their party's presidential nomination in 1996, but Bob Dole, the Senate majority leader, emerged as the party's nominee by capturing a block of key Southern primaries. He ran on a platform intended to attract all Republican factions: deep tax cuts, deregulation, economic growth, a balanced budget, and continued derogation of social programs to the states.

Bill Clinton ran a well funded, smoothly orchestrated centrist campaign tailored to appeal to middle-class suburban voters. He went after the "soccer mom" vote, suburban women whose political concerns focused on families and children. Clinton also attracted strong support from powerful segments of the business community—particularly Silicon Valley, Hollywood, telecommunication, and multimedia companies. He and Vice President Gore promoted education, job training, and computer literacy as building bridges to the twenty-first century Information Age.

Dole tried to raise the character issue. He called attention to the Whitewater scandals, which involved a failed real estate development and a defunct savings and loan bank that occurred in Arkansas when Bill Clinton was governor. Because there was no smoking gun, irrefutable evidence of wrongdoing or law-breaking by either Bill Clinton or Hillary Rodham Clinton, Dole got little political traction out of raising those issues. Another scandal occurred during the final weeks of the campaign when evidence surfaced that the Clinton campaign had illegally raised campaign funds from foreign sources, including Chinese officials.

Clinton and Gore nevertheless coasted to an easy victory. They got 49 percent of the vote to 41 percent for Dole and 8 percent for maverick Ross Perot, back for another run but this time providing only a colorful footnote to a lackluster campaign. The Democrats won the electoral vote 379 to 159. The Republicans retained control of both branches of Congress, but by reduced majorities.

The election took place within a generally conservative climate of opinion, reminiscent of the 1920s. Citizen apathy about politics prevailed, especially among younger citizens, who viewed the political process with a mixture of amused contempt and horror. Despite saturation multimedia coverage, scarcely half of the people eligible to vote bothered to do so on election day. It simply did not matter to millions of Americans whether Bill Clinton was reelected or replaced by Bob Dole.

A PRESIDENT IMPEACHED

Political gridlock characterized the first two years of Bill Clinton's second term of office. The Republican reformers, outmaneuvered by the president, lost momentum. Clinton was content to propose modestly plotted programs to help the middle classes, none of which Congress enacted.

Congress also failed to enact a $368 billion settlement against Big Tobacco to recover the costs of treating smoking related illnesses. The one significant achievement of both Congress and the White House came in May 1997, when they reached an agreement on a balanced budget. The federal government produced a balanced budget for the fiscal year 1998, the first in nearly thirty years.

Most of the news out of Washington concerning Clinton's second term focused on a myriad of scandals that plagued the president and at times implicated several cabinet members and Vice President Al Gore. Many of the scandals stemmed from illegal fund-raising practices during the 1996 presidential campaign. In July 1997, the Senate convened a special investigating committee, chaired by Republican Senator Fred Thompson of Tennessee, to hold hearings into potentially illegal fundraising practices relating to both the 1994 and 1996 electoral campaigns.

In January 1998, the fund-raising scandals were relegated to the back pages by sensational discoveries that President Clinton had had an eighteen-month-long sexual relationship with Monica Lewinsky, a young White House intern from Beverly Hills. The affair attracted the attention of Independent Counsel Kenneth Starr, who for three years had been conducting an investigation into possible illegal activity by both Bill Clinton and Hillary Rodham Clinton, going back to the days of Whitewater and including several White House scandals. On January 27, Star formally convened a grand jury inquiry to look into the Lewinsky affair.

Figure 14.10   Former White House intern Monica Lewinsky and her attorney William Ginsburg. *Source:* AP/Wide World Photos.

President Clinton quickly went on television to deny that he had had a sexual liaison with Lewinsky. Looking the American people squarely in the eye and wagging his right index finger, he emphatically stated, "I did not have sexual relations with that woman, Ms. Lewinsky." Thereafter, he stonewalled the matter.

While Star's team of experienced prosecutors methodically subpoenaed witnesses and compiled evidence, the President ostentatiously went about conducting the public's business. Behind the scenes, Clinton's legal advisers and political operatives did everything they could to discredit Star's investigation. Clinton's lawyers repeatedly tried to find legal grounds to prevent Secret Service agents and senior aides from testifying before the grand jury. The courts kept quashing the legal arguments and witnesses continued to be compelled to testify. Clinton's power and room for maneuver eroded.

As the investigation went forward, polls showed that Clinton's approval rating remained high. The economy remained strong and prosperous, and the nation was at peace. A majority of Americans did not think having a sexual relationship with an intern and lying about it, even if proven true, were grounds for impeachment.

On July 17, prosecutors issued a subpoena compelling the President's testimony before the grand jury pursuant to a criminal investigation in which he was a suspect. Star withdrew the subpoena on July 29 when the President agreed to testify from the White House with his lawyers present. On August 6, Lewinsky, granted immunity from prosecution, testified before the grand jury. She told prosecutors that she had had a sexual relationship with the President.

Clinton testified on August 17. Later that evening, he spoke briefly to the American people. During his four-minute speech, he admitted that he had had "a relationship that was inappropriate" with Lewinsky. He insisted that he had not committed perjury when he denied under oath that he had had sexual relations with Lewinsky, although he acknowledged that his testimony was misleading. But half his speech was devoted to an angry attack on Kenneth Star. The speech not only failed to end the matter, it ensured its indefinite perpetuation. Mainstream media editorialists and leading Democratic senators condemned the President's behavior and his attempts over the past seven months to deceive both Congress and the American people about it.

On September 9, Star delivered his report to the House of Representatives. He had gathered evidence showing that Clinton may have committed perjury, tampered with witnesses, obstructed justice, and abused the power of his office. Star's report set the stage for high political drama reminiscent of the days of Watergate when a Senate committee discovered that President Nixon had secretly taped recorded White House conversations. The report posed the threat that President Clinton could be removed from office. That evening the Star Report went out over the Internet. The next day both the electronic and print media presented the Star report to the public in its entirety or in edited form with extensive commentary. On September 21, a videotape of the president's testimony to the grand jury was broadcast to the nation. Clinton's political fate was now in the hands of Congress and the American people.

After the release of the Star Report, polls showed that two-thirds of Americans still thought Clinton was doing a good job as president and did not want him to be impeached, but his personal ratings had sunk to new lows. Clinton the president was praised for a job well done; Clinton the fallible human was condemned for immoral behavior and for degrading the revered office of the presidency.

The Republican Party leadership in the House set the impeachment process in motion. On October 5, by a strict party-line vote, the House Judiciary Committee recommended that the House of Representatives open a formal investigation into grounds for impeaching President Clinton. Three days later, the Congress voted 258 to 176 to authorize a formal impeachment inquiry. Thirty-one Democrats joined with the Republican majority in authorizing the impeachment inquiry. For only the third time in American history, the House Judiciary Committee began hearings to see if there were grounds for impeaching a president.

On November 3, as the House Judiciary Committee prepared to hold impeachment hearings, the 1998 midterm elections took place. Given the dramatic contexts in which these elections occurred, they would amount to a referendum on the impeachment process. The results surprised the experts and confounded the Republican Right that was determined to destroy Clinton if it could. After almost a year dominated by scandals that put the White House in jeopardy and put the Democrats on the defensive, the Democrats made unexpected gains on election day. They picked up five seats in the House and broke even in the Senate. The Republicans retained control of Congress, but by a smaller majority.

Revealing of the disconnect between the American people and the Washington political culture was the fact that only 36 percent of those eligible to vote turned out on election day. In many states, the turnout was less than 20 percent. The percentage of young people (ages eighteen to twenty-nine) voting was also less than 20 percent. Despite the fact that there were six news stories about the scandal for every news story about electoral politics, exit polls revealed that the scandals were not a factor in determining how they voted.

The election amounted to a victory for incumbents and the status quo. What hurt Republicans the most was their capitulation to Clinton on federal spending priorities. Fearful of being blamed if another governmental shutdown occurred, the Republican Congress enacted all of Clinton's budget proposals during the congressional session that ended three weeks before the election. Lacking bold leaders and alternative issues, many Republican voters stayed home on election day. Following the election, Newt Gingrich was forced to resign the Speakership of the House. The man who had orchestrated the attacks on Clinton was himself consumed by the fires that he had ignited.

On November 18, the House Judiciary Committee formally convened the impeachment inquiry. On December 11 and December 12, the House Judiciary Committee approved four articles of impeachment; The first two articles charged Clinton with perjury, the third article charged Clinton with obstruction of justice, and the fourth article charged Clinton with abuse of power.

The drama built as the full House of Representatives opened formal impeachment hearings on December 18. On the next day, December 19, William Jefferson Clinton became only the second president in American history to be impeached. The House passed two articles of impeachment: Article 1 charged that Clinton had committed perjury in his grand jury testimony of August 17. It passed by a vote of 228 to 206. Article 2 charged that the president obstructed justice. It passed by a vote of 221 to 212.

On January 7, 1999, the Senate impeachment trial of President Clinton opened, presided over by Chief Justice William Rehnquist, with the Senators themselves impaneled as a 100-person jury to hear the case and render a verdict. From January 14 to January 16, the impeachment managers from the House presented their cases. From January 19 to January 21, a battery of lawyers representing the president presented their defenses. The impeachment managers argued that Clinton should be convicted on both articles and removed from office. Clinton's defense team presented a dual line of defense: the president was not guilty of either charge, and even if he were, they did not rise to the level of impeachable offenses under the Constitution.

As the five-week-long trial in the Senate ran its course, polls consistently showed that two-thirds of Americans did not want President Clinton convicted and removed from office. Virtually all of the nation's most influential newspapers, led by the *New York Times, Washington Post,* and the *Los Angeles Times,* opposed conviction and removal from office.

On February 12, 1999, The Senate voted to acquit Clinton. The Senate rejected the perjury charge, 55 to 45, and it split 50–50 on the obstruction of justice charge. Many moderate Republican and Democratic Senators were clearly uncomfortable with their votes for acquittal, because they believed that there was considerable evidence to substantiate the charges of perjury and obstruction of justice against President Clinton brought by the House, and by their votes they were acquitting him of all charges. However, they had no choice because they did not want to remove him from office. They were voting to save the presidency, not the man whom many despised.

Public opinion probably saved Clinton's presidency. Most Americans believed that he was guilty of both the perjury and obstruction of justice charges as did many of the senators who voted for acquittal. Clinton would probably have been removed from office had public opinion been running 2:1 for conviction as it had against Richard Nixon in 1974 just before he resigned the presidency. Once the threat of removal had passed, Clinton's popularity and job approval ratings both dropped sharply.

The impeachment scandals amounted to a prolonged Constitutional crisis that seemed to have no impact outside the cocooned world of Washington politics. While the President and the Republican majority in Congress were locked in mortal combat, most Americans happily went about their business. The news media gave the crisis saturation coverage from start to finish, yet most Americans could not care less, or so they said, and denounced the news media for their obsessive devotion to tabloid politics.

CLINTONIAN DIPLOMACY

For Clinton, internal affairs took priority over foreign policy issues. In the conduct of foreign affairs, Clinton was handicapped by his lack of experience and his failure to appoint strong leaders to key positions. In the post–Cold War era, Clinton also faced the daunting task of developing and implementing effective foreign policies in a new environment without precedents and without guidelines to follow.

Because Clinton and his foreign policy advisers lacked clear objectives and did not have a consistent set of criteria to apply, Washington could never decide when or how much U.S. power to commit in situations that did not involve vital national interests. A pattern of *ad hoc* responses to crises as they arose characterized Clinton's approach to foreign policy. He tried to downplay international politics and the use of military force. He focused U.S. foreign policy on promoting free trade and human rights. In the area of foreign economic policy, he had major achievements. He supported NAFTA, normalized relations with Vietnam, and negotiated trade agreements with Pacific Rim nations.

The shortcomings of the Clinton approach to foreign affairs were evident in Bosnia and Herzegovina, where the largest war in Europe since World War II raged on. Vicious ethnic fighting among the Serbs, Bosnian Muslims, and Croats had killed over 100,000 people and generated over 3.5 million refugees. The Bosnian Muslims were clearly the victims of aggression and atrocities, and they were hindered in their efforts at self-defense by an arms embargo. Even so, Washington appeared more concerned with avoiding significant military involvement and confining the conflict to the petty successor states of the now-defunct Yugoslav federation than with aiding the struggling Bosnians. Despite feeble UN efforts to broker a cease-fire and negotiate a settlement that would have divided Bosnia and Herzegovina into a patchwork of ethnic regions, the war raged on in 1994 and 1995.

In the fall of 1995, Assistant Secretary of State Richard Holbrooke acted. He understood that the United Nations and the Europeans were incapable of effective action in Bosnia. He brought the leaders of the three warring factions to Dayton, Ohio, in December, brokered a ceasefire, and worked out a complex political settlement to be implemented gradually. The settlement involved sending a NATO force of 60,000 troops, 20,000 of which were U.S. combat soldiers, to police the ceasefire and allow the political settlement to gradually take hold. A vocal majority in Congress and among the American public opposed sending U.S. forces to Bosnia. The ceasefire held. However, one year later, the date that Clinton had scheduled for the withdrawal of all U. S. troops, the political settlement had not been implemented. Bosnia-Herzegovina had, in effect, been partitioned and the U. S. forces settled in for a long campaign.

WAR IN KOSOVO

While Bosnia-Herzegovina endured an uneasy peace, ethnic conflict erupted into war in nearby Kosovo, a Yugoslav province inhabited by 1.8 million ethnic Albanians, 90 percent of the region's population. The conflict had been building for years. In 1989, the Yugoslav leader, Slobodan Milosevic, revoked the autonomy that the Kosovars had enjoyed since 1974. As the Belgrade regime became more repressive, the Kosovars, following the moderate leadership of Ibrahim Rugova, attempted to create a parallel government that would permit at least a semblance of autonomy within the Yugoslav federation. In 1991, militant Kosovars founded the Kosovo Liberation Army (KLA); its leaders were committed to achieving independence from Yugoslavia and one day uniting with Albania. KLA terrorists attacked Serbian soldiers and police stationed in Kosovo. The Serbs retaliated, trying unsuccessfully to eliminate the KLA and its supporters. In the spring of 1998, the KLA began a full-scale rebellion against Serbian authority. Milosevic responded by escalating the violence against the Kosovars. NATO, led by the United States, attempted unsuccessfully to impose a settlement along the lines of the Dayton Accords.

On March 24, 1999, NATO, commanded by U. S. Army General Wesley Clark, began an aerial war against the Milosevic government to induce him to sign the agreement that he had rejected. Clark had assumed that a few days of precision bombing would quickly return Milosevic to the bargaining table. Instead, he escalated his campaign of "ethnic cleansing" against the Kosovars.

Figure 14.11   Ethnic Albanian Kosovar refugees wait to be placed in a tent after crossing into Macedonia at a refugee camp near the village of Blace, 25 km northwest from Skopje, Saturday, April 24, 1999.   *Source:* AP/Wide World Photos.

Within a few weeks, NATO confronted a humanitarian catastrophe of biblical proportions. An estimated 800,000 Kosovars were forced into exile in neighboring Macedonia, Albania, and the Yugoslav province of Montenegro. The presence of these refugees threatened to destabilize these small multiethnic countries and draw them into the conflict. Another 600,000 Kosovars were driven from their homes and villages, but remained inside the province, hiding in mountain forests and canyons. Thousands of Kosovars, mostly young men, were slaughtered. Another 100,000 were unaccounted for. Hundreds of villages, towns, and cities had been razed. NATO, the United Nations, and numerous international aid agencies rushed to provide food, clothing, shelter, and medicines to the Kosovars driven from their own country by the barbarous assaults.

NATO's gradually escalating air war, OPERATION ALLIED FORCE, seriously damaged the Serbian infrastructure and degraded its industrial capacity. But it also allowed Milosevic to consolidate his control over Serbia. Further, the bombing could not stop the ethnic cleansing. Hawkish critics of the air war, such as Senator John McCain, doubted that bombing alone could defeat Milosevic. He called for sending U.S. ground combat forces to Kosovo. However, President Clinton ruled out sending in ground forces.

Public support for the war was lukewarm from the outset and the American people gradually disengaged from the war despite mostly favorable media coverage. On April 30, six weeks into the war, and with the plight of the Kosovars worse than ever, the Republican controlled Congress defeated a resolution of support for the air war. Within the nation, there were signs of growing antiwar sentiment.

The war ended after seventy-eight days of bombing. Milosevic signed an agreement that differed little from the one that he had previously rejected. Diplomatic isolation and the increasingly effective bombing campaign convinced him that the NATO offer was the best he was likely to get. Besides, he had accomplished his major goals: he had consolidated his power in Serbia and and he had rid Kosovo, at least temporarily, of much of its Albanian population.

NATO troops, including 7,000 U.S. soldiers, were deployed as peace keepers in Kosovo as the Serbian troops exited that ravaged land. NATO's postwar goals were to assist the Kosovars as they returned. But a lot of these traumatized people did not want to return to Kosovo; they did not feel safe. Others discovered that they had no homes, farms, or businesses to return to. Many Kosovars, radicalized by their experiences, turned to the KLA. These people would accept nothing less than independence for Kosovo. But the agreement did not support independence for Kosovo, even as a distant goal.

Secretary of State Madeleine Albright characterized the Balkan interventions as humanitarian and strategic victories. But the price was steep: an estimated 300,000 people killed, three million more displaced, and the *de facto* partitions of countries. Western protectorates of indefinite duration involving thousands of U.S. forces were created at a cost of $30 billion. Slobodan Milosevic also paid a high price for his ruthless policies. His country lay in ruins and he was voted out of office. He became the first head of state to be tried for war crimes and crimes against humanity when he was extradited to the custody of the United Nation's International War Crimes Tribunal in The Hague, Netherlands. The NATO goal of peaceful multiethnic democratic nations living in harmony with one another and fully integrated into Europe appeared unattainable and divorced from harsh and enduring Balkan realities.

TERRORISM ABROAD AND AT HOME

The war against terrorism that reached back into the 1970s continued during the 1980s and 1990s. In 1988, Pam AM Flight 103 en route to New York exploded over Lockerbie, Scotland, killing all 259 people on board. Years later, a Libyan terrorist was convicted of having planted a powerful plastic explosive on the plane.

In February 1993, a small group of terrorists associated with Osama bin Laden bombed the World Trade Center in New York City, killing five people and injuring scores of others. Taken in retaliation for U.S. policies in the Middle East; the bombing was the most destructive act of terrorism committed in the United States to date. In 1995, following a dramatic trial, a militant sheik and four of his Shiite fundamentalist followers were convicted of the bombing. Despite increased surveillance of terrorist groups by the FBI and CIA, bin Laden's group struck again. On August 7, 1998, two powerful car bombs exploded within minutes of each other outside U.S. embassies in Nairobi, Kenya, and Dar es Salaam, Tanzania, killing 225 people and injuring more than 5,000.

On April 19, 1995, Americans discovered to their horror that they did not have to import terrorists when a truck bomb of tremendous explosive power utterly demolished a nine-story federal building in Oklahoma City, killing 168 people, many of whom were children. The FBI soon arrested Timothy McVeigh and Terry Nichols, who were charged with the crime. Both men had loose ties with the militia movement, an extreme rightwing fringe group that viewed efforts to impose a measure of gun control as part of a conspiracy by the federal government to extinguish freedom in America. Both were convicted of mass murder. McVeigh was sentenced to die for his crimes, and Nichols was given a life sentence without the possibility of parole. McVeigh was executed by lethal injection, June 11, 2001, in Terre Haute, Indiana.

Previously, on February 28, 1993, FBI agents, working with agents of the Federal Bureau of Alcohol, Tobacco, and Firearms (ATF), had conducted a raid on the compound of the Branch Davidians, an obscure religious sect led by David Koresh. The federal agents suspected Koresh of stockpiling illegal weapons and ammunition in the compound located near Waco, Texas. A short battle ensued in which four ATF agents and six members of the Branch Davidian sect were killed. On April 19, federal agents assaulted the compound where the Branch Davidians had barricaded themselves. A fire, either deliberately or accidentally set, quickly consumed the buildings, killing seventy-six members of the sect, including twenty-one children. Both the FBI and ATF were criticized from many quarters for what appeared to be a lethal operation carried out against a small group of religious sectarians. Rightist groups such as the National Rifle Association (NRA) were outraged, likening the federal agents to 'Hitler's storm troopers." Spokesmen for the militia movement vowed revenge. Two years later to the day, April 19, McVeigh and Nichols bombed the federal building in Oklahoma City.

Acts of domestic terrorism continued. Medical clinics that provided legal abortion services to women became a prime target of terrorists. There were nineteen bombings and burnings of abortion clinics in 1992 and forty-two murders of abortion providers in 1994.

In March 1996, FBI agents, acting on a tip from his brother, arrested fifty-three-year-old Theodore Kaczynski, as the suspected Unabomber, a serial killer who had waged a campaign of terror-bombing since 1979 that had killed three people and injured twenty-three others in 16 separate attacks. In 1998, after a trial in federal court held in Sacramento, California, Kaczynski, who admitted that he was the Unabomber, was sentenced to life imprisonment without the possibility of parole.

Homegrown terrorist assaults reached new levels of horror in 1998 and 1999, when troubled schoolboys gunned down fellow students and teachers in a rash of schoolground massacres that took place in various cities across the country. The worst slaughter occurred at Columbine High School in Littleton, Colorado, a suburb of Denver. On Tuesday morning, April 20, 1999, Eric Harris and Dylan Klebold arrived on campus armed with an arsenal of high-powered weaponry consisting of automatic pistols, automatic rifles, sawed-off twelve-gauge shotguns, and dozens of pipe bombs. They murdered twelve students and a teacher, and wounded dozens more of their classmates. Then they took their own lives. In the aftermath, bewildered, terrified, and grieving survivors struggled to cope with the inexplicable tragedy.

BRIEF BIBLIOGRAPHIC ESSAY

An extensive historical literature on the decade of the 1990s is not yet available. However, many fine books and collections of essays dealing with many of the major historical issues of the nineties have been written. Those interested in the serious world environmental problems of the

1990s will want to read Peter Borrelli, ed., *Crossroads: Environmental Priorities for the Future.* Kevin Phillips, a conservative political analyst, has written *The Politics of Rich and Poor,* which is concerned about the social inequities deriving from contemporary economic policies. For the matter of women's pay issues, see Sara M. Evans's and Barbara J. Nelson's, *Wage Justice: Comparable Worth and the Paradox of Technocratic Reform.* One of the best books about AIDS is Randy Shilts's *And the Band Played On.* On contemporary drug problems plaguing Americans, see Erich Goode's, *Drugs in American Society.* Ellis Cose's *The Rage of a Privileged Class: Why Are Middle-Class Blacks Angry?* is an important and disturbing book. See William Wei's *The Asian American Movement* for study of a large, diverse group of Americans who are making rapid gains in education, wealth, and influence. There is a growing literature on all the historic changes occurring in Eastern Europe and the former Soviet Union. See Robert O. Crummey, ed., *Reform in Russia and the USSR* and William E. Griffith, ed., *Central and Eastern Europe: The Opening Curtain.* Two American Sovietologists, Robert Jervis and Seweryn Bailer, present diverse looks at the post–Cold War world in *Soviet-American Relations After the Cold War.* For American-Japanese relations, Akira Iriye and Warren I. Cohen, eds., *The United States and Japan in the Postwar World* is very good. Judith Miller's and Laurie Mylorie's *Saddam Hussein* is an informative study that sheds light on the motivations of the Iraqi leader and the genesis of the Persian Gulf crisis.

WEB SITES

There are some excellent Internet resources for the major historical developments of the 1990s. Using the portal `<http:www.besthistorysites.net/index.html>`, go to the hyperlink U.S. History. Click on Post Cold War Era. Go to Global Connections, which contextualizes events within a world historical framework. See The Gulf War, which views the events of that war from the perspective of its participants. And see War Against Terror, which creates a historical framework for understanding the events leading up to 9/11/01. For the Clinton presidency, there is The Clinton Years, a PBS analysis, and there is Clinton Accused, a *Washington Post* report that covers the impeachment scandal with photos, documents, and articles.

15

The New Millennium

The United States entered the new millennium as the most powerful nation on earth. Furthermore, the disparity in power between the United States and the other major powers was greater than at any time in world history. One Carrier Battle Group (and the United States had twelve, with two more being developed) carried more firepower than had been used in all of history's previous wars. In addition to the "hard" economic and strategic power that the American colossus could project around the globe, U.S. "soft" power in the form of fast foods, fashions, television programming, movies, computer games, and pop music also had a global reach. For the first time in human history, high-tech telecommunication systems and a global economy plugged Americans and the rest of the inhabitants of the global village into an intricate web of economic, social, political, and cultural relations. A new transnational world order had taken shape, and it had the potential of casting nation-states into the ash heap of history.

At home, Americans struggled to cope with social processes that they scarcely comprehended. Nearly all Americans paid lip service to egalitarian social values yet American society was more stratified than ever along class and ethno-racial lines. Within the United States, the disparity of wealth between the very rich and the growing legions of the dispossessed had never been greater. The new economy, service-oriented and high-tech, transformed the way most Americans lived and worked. That new economy, which had sustained an astonishing decade-long boom during the 1990s, suddenly went slack as the new millennium opened. The Silicon Valley bubble burst, the stock market crashed, unemployment shot up, and bankruptcies multiplied while millions of Americans struggled to climb out of a recession. After three years of recession and stagnation, the economy rebounded strongly in the latter half of 2003. In December, the Dow Jones average of thirty bellwether industrial stocks reached the psychologically significant 10,000 level. As 2004 dawned, all important macroeconomic indicators were positive. The economy was growing at a robust 6 percent per annum as consumer spending and business investment remained strong.

358

The only constant appeared to be ceaseless change. Omnipresent visual advertising media, the most intrusive ever, bombarded consumers daily with hundreds of commercials. Consumers, driven by advertising and their own materialistic values, plunged ever deeper into debt as they tried to buy all the "stuff" required for the good life as defined by consumerist values. The velocity of history appeared to be accelerating and many Americans had the sense that they lived in a society in perpetual motion, a social order without solid institutional foundations, enduring values, or any clear direction. Americans were traveling faster than ever into a future that they both feared and welcomed.

The leaders of the world's only "hyperpower" discovered that they could not unilaterally impose American solutions on the world's vast array of dire problems. AIDS pandemics ravaged the countries of sub-Saharan Africa and threatened to spread to China and India, the world's two most populous countries. Russia appeared to be a perpetual basket case, a pathetic shadow of its former Soviet self. Japan found itself mired in permanent recession. The latest Palestinian-Israeli war raged on with no peaceful resolution of their fundamental conflicts in sight. North Korea appeared determined to build nuclear weapons and develop long-range missiles that could strike targets in North America. India and Pakistan, both of which possessed weapons of mass destruction, threatened to go to war with each other over the Vale of Kashmir. International terrorism was a persistent threat, culminating in the horrors of September 11, 2001. As 2004 dawned, the United States was locked into an apparently interminable war against terrorism, which involved fighting wars in Afghanistan, Iraq, and perhaps other nations that U.S. leaders perceived as strategic threats to the United States

THE 2000 CENSUS

According to the 2000 census, 281,421,906 people inhabited the fifty states comprising the United States of America. For the first time ever, the population increased in all fifty states. The populations of both the largest cities and rural America also showed increases, reversing long-running trends. The South and the West showed the greatest population growth, continuing trends established during World War II. Nevada, because of its robust economy and because it served as a haven for many white middle-class people fleeing the multicultural diversity of California, showed the greatest population growth of all the states, a whopping 66 percent.

According to the census, the number of foreign-born residents and children of immigrants in the United States had reached fifty-six million, the highest level in history, and up from thirty-four million in 1980. One country, Mexico, accounted for more than one quarter of the foreign born. The foreign-born population was heavily concentrated in a few populous states—California, New York, Florida, and Texas. California, with 26 percent, had the highest percentage of foreign-born residents. Los Angeles, with 30 percent of its residents foreign-born, led all U.S. cities. The Asian population in America grew by nearly 50 percent during the 1990s. The number of Chinese, Vietnamese, and Indians doubled or more than doubled during the decade.

The 2000 census also revealed the growing diversity of household living arrangements in the United States. For the first time ever, fewer than 25 percent of all households were made up of nuclear families, married couples with children. During the 1990s, the number of single parent families headed by women who had children grew five times faster than the number of married couples with children. The number of unmarried couples doubled in the 1990s, from three million in 1990 to just under six million in 2000. The decades-long decline in the number of households with children continued into the new millennium. The number of nonfamily households, which consisted of either people living alone or with people who were not related, made up 35 percent of all households, the largest proportion ever.

The new census also showed that people were marrying later, if they married at all. The median age for the first marriage for men reached twenty-seven, and for women it increased to twenty-five. Both these ages were the highest ever recorded. While 14.1 percent of non-Hispanic whites were age sixty-five or older, only 7.9 percent of African Americans fell into that group. In 2000, there were about twenty-one million women age sixty-five or older compared with 14.5 million men, or seventy men for every 100 women. That ratio kept dropping at higher-aged groups among the elderly.

The median age of the country increased to 35.3, the highest it has ever been. The median age for non-Hispanic whites, who comprised about 70 percent of the nation's population, reached 37.3 in 2000. However, the median age for African Americans was 29.5 and for Hispanics it was 25.8. Census data also showed that there were six million more women than men comprising the national population. Women made up 50.94 percent of the population; men made up 49.06 percent. However, men were narrowing the gap, partly because of improved health care and greater health awareness, and because death rates were rising for women due to increased smoking and increased job stresses.

Men also closed the median life expectancy gap. In 1990, women could expect to live 78.8 years and men could expect to live 71.8 years, a seven-year differential favoring women. In 2000, women could expect to live 79.5 years and men could expect to live 73.8 years, a differential of 5.7 years. These longevity statistics were the highest ever recorded for Americans. Demographers also noted that U.S. infant mortality rates dropped to their lowest levels ever.

The 2000 census also surveyed the health of the American people, and found both progress and decline. Infant mortality, child mortality, and deaths from breast cancer all diminished. There was a 35 percent drop in heart disease cases and a remarkable 65 percent drop in the number of people afflicted with strokes. But there was an alarming increase in the number of new asthma cases, especially among young people, and a similar increase in the number of people afflicted with adult-onset diabetes.

The number of Americans who were overweight reached record highs. According to surveys, 56 percent of the American population was overweight. The number of overweight young people rose rapidly through the 1990s and in 2000 registered 30 percent. The dramatic increase in the numbers of overweight people occurred even though Americans spent over $30 billion annually on dieting products and services. Medical experts most often linked the rise in obesity to diet, nutrition, and sedentary life styles. People, especially younger people, were eating ever-larger portions of foods high in saturated fats and drinking ever-larger amounts of soft drinks loaded with sweeteners. Supersized french fries and Big Gulps appeared irresistible to a nation of young junk food junkies.

The rapid increase in the number of obese American youngsters was also linked to the public schools they attend. Many schools, in order to cut costs and to provide greater choices, have signed contracts with corporate fast-food providers. Youngsters, offered a choice between fresh vegetables and french fries, in 90 percent of the cases, chose the french fries. Also, most young people did not get adequate physical exercise. A major cause of this was the sharp decline in high school offerings of physical education classes. Nearly three-fourths of the nation's high schools no longer offered physical education courses in 2000, having either dropped them to save money or else have replaced them with academic subjects. Many young people spent many more hours playing Nintendo games than they did playing games and sports that involved vigorous physical activity.

ECONOMIC DISPARITIES

In the wake of the collapse of the dot-com bubble and the crash of the Great Bull Market of the 1990s, the economy suffered its first recession in over a decade. The recession, lasting from March through November 2001 was one of the mildest and shortest in recent U.S. history. During the recession, consumer confidence remained high and sales of "big ticket" items such as homes and SUVs remained strong as buyers took advantage of historic low interest rates.

But there were worrisome aspects of the New Economy, including a sharp rise in bankruptcies, increased private indebtedness, and a jobless recovery from recession. Worse, even though the economy rebounded quickly from the short-lived recession and by the fall of 2003 grew at the rate of 6 to 8 percent per annum, jobs continued to disappear. From March 2001 through August 2003, over 2,500,000 jobs vanished, most of them from the manufacturing sectors. The unemployment rate, which had dropped to 4 percent in early 2000, climbed to 6.4 percent during the summer of 2003. Worst of all, the disparity between rich and poor Americans widened steadily.

Despite two decades of sustained prosperity, the share of national income received annually by the poorest 10 percent of the population declined from 4.1 percent to 3.6 percent. Median household income also declined as did per capita income. Over the same stretch of time, the share of national income going to the top 5 percent of income earners rose substantially—from 43 percent to 49.5 percent. More dramatically, by mid-year 2003, the number of millionaire households in the United States grew to their highest levels ever recorded—3.8 percent, up from 3.3 percent in 2002. During the same period, the number of Americans living in poverty increased substantially, reaching 35,000,000. Approximately 18 percent of the nation's children lived in poor households in 2003.

Many factors accounted for this widening gap between the best-off and worst-off American families. There were real-wage gains adjusted for inflation at the top end and real-wage losses at the bottom end of the income spectrum. As the economy shifted away from an industrial economy toward a service economy, and in recent years to an information-processing service economy, education became increasingly crucial. According to the 2000 census, the median annual income for individuals with bachelor's degrees or advanced degrees was $67,000. The median annual income for individuals who had only high school diplomas or less, was below $25,000. The rise in the number of single parent households and non-family households, which tend to have lower incomes than households headed by married couples, also contributed to the growing disparities of wealth and income.

Gender and ethno-racial variables continue to play a role. The gap continued to widen despite the significant gains made by women and minorities in recent decades. According to data derived from the 2000 census, median annual household income in the United States was $41,000. For households headed by women, it was $26,000. For African Americans, median household income was $29,000 and for Hispanic households, $28,000. Perhaps most discouraging of all, the real wages of women, African Americans and Hispanic Americans, adjusted for inflation, declined relative to those of non-Hispanic white males. A survey conducted in March 2003 found that women were less likely to reach higher salary brackets and more likely to live in poverty than men. Older women were twice as likely as older men to live in poverty.

According to a recent report issued under the auspices of the United Nations, globalization also compounded the gap between rich and poor nations. Globalization was also intensifying American dominance of the world's economic and cultural markets. The report focused on the spread of the Internet and computer technology. The United States dominated the new global telecommunications marketplaces. English was the language of choice for over 80 percent of the world's 322 million Web sites. Nearly 25 percent of Americans used the World Wide Web, whereas only 3 percent of Russians and less than 0.1 of 1 percent of people in Arab countries used the Web. The Ford Motor Company, the world's fourth-largest industrial corporation with sales of $181 billion in 2000, generated more income annually than did Saudi Arabia. The forecast is for disparities between the globally well-connected and the unconnected people of the world to grow even faster given the continued explosive development of new telecommunication technologies and the continued U.S. dominance of the industry.

A MULTICULTURAL SOCIETY

Because of its history as a haven for diasporic populations and because of the huge upsurge in immigration in recent decades, the United States was home to the most diverse population on the planet. Multicultural diversity reached virtually into every town and region of the country, but it was in the great cities of the land where America's diverse peoples were concentrated. New York, Chicago, and Los Angeles, America's largest metropolitan centers, were where people from virtually every nation and culture on earth chose to live and work.

As America headed into the new millennium, the news from black America was both good and bad. In many important ways, African Americans were thriving. Millions of well-educated middle-class black professionals were thriving. Black home ownership and employment both were up. More young African Americans were attending America's finest colleges and universities than ever before. Nearly 90 percent of young black adults have completed high school or its equivalent. The percentage of black families living below the poverty line was at its lowest point since the federal government began keeping black poverty statistics. Fewer black families were on welfare than ever before. Once desolate inner cities such as Chicago's North Lawndale area have become prosperous and vibrant neighborhoods. Thousands of black political leaders were elected to office at all levels of government. Two African American leaders, Condoleeza Rice and Colin Powell, held powerful positions in President George W. Bush's administration. Clarence Thomas sat as an Associate Justice on the Supreme Court. Polls showed that more

African Americans than whites were optimistic about their personal futures. Confident young black people expected to succeed in twenty-first-century America.

However, millions of black families continued to struggle to survive and to overcome serious obstacles. If millions of blacks were thriving, millions were not. Many inner-city neighborhoods offered neither good jobs nor good schools, and did not foster hope in young people. Among many African-American students from middle and upper middle-class families, there remained a persistent achievement gap compared with white and Asian students.

Shaker Heights, an affluent suburb of Cleveland, was noted for its integrated public high school that consistently ranked as one of the nation's finest. African-American students comprised about half of the school's population; however, they accounted for less than 10 percent of those at the top of the class and for 90 percent of those at the bottom. Black students who took the College Board Scholastic Aptitude Tests (SAT), when class and cultural factors were controlled, consistently scored about 100 points lower on both the verbal and math parts of the test than did white and Asian students. No one has satisfactorily explained the persistent differential in scores. It may be at a subtle level, that many black students simply did not believe that they could excel even if they tried. It may be that they did not prize learning as much as their white counterparts. It may be that their parents did not push them hard enough or did not expect high achievement from them. And it may be that some black students consider excelling academically to represent a renunciation of their black identities

Since the 1980s, Hispanic people have been the fastest growing ethnic group within the United States. In 2003, Hispanic people, nearly forty million of them, made up the nation's largest minority group. Hispanics, who could be of any race, were placed into four main groups. By far the largest of these groupings were people of Mexican descent. They accounted for 60 percent of Latinos within the United States. The second largest group consisted of people who came from Central and South American countries. They represented the fastest growing of the major Hispanic groups. Their population doubled during the 1990s, from five million to about ten million people. The next two groups included 3.5 million Americans of Puerto Rican descent and 1.2 million people of Cuban descent. Assuming current growth rates continue for the ensuing decade, there will be an estimated fifty million Americans of Hispanic descent out of a total population of approximately 312 million when the 2010 census is taken.

The booming Hispanic population carried significant political consequences, especially for the states in which Hispanic populations were concentrated: Florida, New Mexico, Arizona, Nevada, Colorado, New Jersey, and especially Texas and California. In 2003, half the Hispanic population within the United States lived in Texas and California. In California and Texas, Hispanic political leaders have won election to important city and state offices. In Los Angeles, Antonio Villaraigosa, the former speaker of the California Assembly, narrowly lost his bid to become mayor of the nation's second largest city. In the 2003 California gubernatorial recall election, Lieutenant Governor Cruz Bustamente finished second to action hero movie star Arnold Schwarzenegger.

Hispanics tend to favor a liberal economic agenda and a majority of politically active Latinos are Democrats. The only Hispanics by group who leaned toward the Republican Party were the Cuban Americans clustered in south Florida. However, at least one-third of Hispanic voters declined to identify with either party. Further, many middle-class Hispanics are religious, and tend to have traditional social and family values. Polls also show that Hispanic immigrants and their children are more optimistic about their new country and their prospects within it than native-born non-Hispanic whites

The Asian-American population has changed dramatically in the past decade to include more people from all over Asia, not just East Asians, who for much of the twentieth century made up the bulk of that ethno-racial group within the United States. The immigration explosion of Asian Indians has fueled most of the change. The Asian-Indian population more than doubled during the 1990s, from less than one million to nearly two million, becoming the third largest Asian ethnic nationality within the United States. Asian Indians also constituted the largest group who immigrated to America with H-1B visas, which identified high-tech workers.

The large influx of Asian Indians has forced Americans to reconceptualize what the label "Asian American" represents. Historically, for most Americans, "Asian" has meant people of Chinese, Filipino, and Japanese descent. However, with the advent of Asian Indians, and with the prospect of millions more South Asians from India, Pakistan, Bangladesh, and Sri Lanka coming to America in the twenty-first century, a broader definition of "Asian American" will be required.

America's two largest Asian groups, the Chinese and Filipinos, also posted large population gains during the decade. The Asian population within the United States grew almost 50 percent during the decade of the 1990s and continued to increase during the first years of the twenty-first century. In 2003, approximately twelve million Asian Americans lived in the United States. The Asian population boom has stimulated a rapid increase of new communities filled with businesses and services catering to immigrants who want to do business in their own languages.

Figure 15.1   Young Asian-Indian businessman.
Photo by LWA-Sharie Kennedy.   *Source:* CORBIS.

Children of the New Millennium

Most Americans cherish their children and the country is filled with child-centered families. Parents often make great personal sacrifices to ensure that their children get the best educations possible and have the best opportunities to develop any special talents, skills, or interests they may have. Many parents try hard to function as positive role models for their children to help prepare them for entering the adult world as confident, responsible and productive citizens. Every year thousands of young adults graduate from some of the finest colleges and universities in the world.

But the numbers from the 2000 census often tell a different, darker story. They reveal how America's children are doing relative to American history and to young people in other lands. Too often, American society's performance falls well short of its stated goals. U.S. child poverty rates are the highest in the world for developed countries. Child poverty in America is linked to the prevalence of single parent households invariably headed by women that are poorer than other households (women earn about 73¢ for every dollar earned by men). This problem is compounded by the fact that single parent households in the United States are relatively much worse off than single parent households in other developed countries because of the curtailed U.S. welfare state. Cuts in various programs supportive of single parent households enacted during the 1990s by conservative Republican-controlled Congresses and signed by Centrist Democrat President Bill Clinton have exacerbated the already severe problems of many poor children in America.

Americans, citizens of the richest nation on the planet, spend proportionately less money for primary and secondary education than do most other developed nations. In 2000, Americans spent approximately 3 percent of the U.S. GDP on public schooling. Sweden, Israel, Canada, and France spent almost twice as much proportionately as the United States. Child mortality rates were higher in the United States than in any other developed nation. As a rough indicator of how young people in the United States handled the stressful transition from childhood to young adulthood, suicide rates were higher for that age group than at any time in the nation's history. Young people in America also killed themselves more frequently than did youngsters in most developed countries.

Election 2000

Voters were not given much of a choice between the major party presidential candidates during the 2000 election. Both were fifty-something, non-Hispanic white males with Ivy League educations. Democratic Party candidate Al Gore, a Harvard graduate, was the son of a former leader of the Senate; Republican Party candidate George W. Bush, was a Yale graduate, and the son of a former president. Within the prevailing conservative political climate, both men campaigned as moderate Centrists, Bush from the Right side and Gore from the Left side of a narrowed political spectrum. For the increasing factions of voters unhappy with the ideologically neutered campaigns conducted by the mainstream candidates, they could choose between the Green Party candidate Ralph Nader, who ran as an "Old Liberal" critic of money-driven politics; and the Reform Party candidate Pat Buchanan who ran as an unreconstructed nativist vowing to close down America's relatively open immigration policy. The disciples of Adam Smith, true believers in free enterprise capitalism, could vote for the Libertarian Party candidate, Harry Browne.

Even though Election 2000 was the longest and most expensive political campaign in American history and received saturation multimedia coverage for its entirety, it failed to generate much enthusiasm among the people. Most Americans, better-off economically than ever before, and living in peace, paid scant attention to national politics or to the presidential campaigns.

Perhaps the strangest aspect of the rather dull 2000 election was that Al Gore lost an election that he clearly could have won. According to the conventional wisdom, pocketbook issues determined who has won and who has lost presidential elections. Al Gore entered the campaign with apparently overwhelming advantages. As Clinton's capable high-profile vice president for eight years, he was the heir-apparent of the 1990s prosperity binge. He was much better known to the American public than the relatively obscure governor of Texas who bore a famous name. Polls consistently showed that most Americans regarded the economy and their own prospects as "excellent" or "good." For fiscal 2000, the federal budget showed a hefty surplus of $400 billion. Polls also demonstrated that Bill Clinton, despite the impeachment scandal, remained popular. Had the twenty-second Amendment not barred him from seeking a third term, he could easily have won the 2000 election.

According to many of the pundits who covered the presidential campaign from start to finish, Al Gore and his cadre of advisers lost Election 2000 because they chose not to exploit Clinton's popularity or to take credit for the good times. Gore would not even allow the popular incumbent to campaign for him lest he provoke some kind of moralistic backlash. Apparently Gore did not understand that the only voters likely to react that way were already committed to voting for Bush. According to the historian Douglas Brinkley, had Al Gore campaigned all-out for prosperity and embraced Clinton's administration with no apologies for any personal failings the president may have exhibited, he would now be sitting in the White House. George W. Bush, commenting after the election had been held, said that he was surprised that he won given that he was running against "peace, prosperity, and a popular incumbency."

When the campaign opened with the New Hampshire primaries in February 2000, Al Gore defeated his one serious challenger, former Senator Bill Bradley. On the Republican side, maverick Arizona senator John McCain defeated Bush. McCain also won some of the other early primaries, running on his single issue of campaign finance reform. McCain's sudden emergence as a serious presidential candidate was the major surprise of election 2000. McCain quickly became the darling of political reporters covering his campaign because of his open, personal style. But Bush, by shoring up his standing with conservative Republicans, quickly stopped McCain's upstart challenge. Bush also succeeded in branding McCain as just another professional politician who would keep the people's money in Washington rather than returning some it to them in the form of a tax cut, which Bush promised to do. Gore and Bush had the nominations sewed up by the end of March.

Bush and his running mate Dick Cheney also carefully distanced themselves from some of the pet issues of social conservatives, reinforcing the moderately conservative image, which they consistently projected. Bush spoke of a "compassionate conservatism" and made improving public schools his top domestic priority. Bush and Cheney virtually ignored the religious

Right. Bush refused to agree to appoint only anti-abortion jurists. Cheney did not rule out same-sex marriages, leaving that issue to the states to decide.

There were three televised debates during the campaign. Going into the debates, the Gore camp confidently assumed that their candidate would win them all. Gore was a policy wonk, much more cerebral and articulate than Bush. He was the author of many articles and a book about environmental issues. Bush, on the other hand, had provided late-night comedians with many hilarious examples of mangled syntax. Some observers wondered if George W. Bush might be dyslectic or perhaps suffered from a brain disorder. He seemed to be surprisingly uninformed about major international issues, and he did not appear much interested in learning about them.

But Gore managed to lose all three debates. In the first one, he came across as arrogant and rude. In the second, trying to correct the impression he had created in the first debate, he came across as smarmy and insincere. In the third debate, Gore made a serious error when he invaded Bush's physical space. Bush, sensing an advantage, gave Gore a little nod of derision. The debates significantly influenced the campaign. Gore did not overwhelm Bush. Bush came across as knowledgeable enough to do the job and as a "regular guy." Gore came across as something of a bumbler and bully, who was not as smart as he thought he was.

As election day approached, all the polls gave Gore a tiny, shrinking lead. The presidential election was going to be close. The approximately 49 percent of eligible voters who bothered to vote on election day produced one of the closest elections in U. S. history. Gore won the popular vote, 50,996,064 to Bush's 50,456,167, even though Bush carried thirty states. Gore also led in the in the electoral votes 266 to 249, not counting Florida (the winner required 270). Ralph Nader garnered 2,882,897 votes, and may have siphoned off enough potential Gore votes in four states, including Florida, to give those states' electoral votes to Bush. Many Gore supporters bitterly accused the Nader camp of costing them the election, overlooking the inconvenient fact that Gore's inept campaign probably cost him an election that he should have won. The Reform Party candidate Pat Buchanan polled only 448,392 votes and the Libertarian Party candidate Harry Browne polled a scant 384,439 votes. Republicans lost seats in both the Senate and the House of Representatives. Their majority in the House shrank to twelve, and in the new Senate had fifty Democrats and fifty Republicans.

THIRTY-SIX DAYS

The closeness of the presidential election created serious problems for the TV networks. The spotlight was on Florida, where the outcome of the election was going to be decided. Early Tuesday evening, on election night, all of the TV news anchors declared Al Gore the winner in Florida. By 2:15 A.M. on Wednesday morning, they had reversed themselves and declared Bush the likely winner. Two hours later, they reversed themselves again, declaring Florida "too close to call," even though Bush was leading by about 1,700 votes.

Network confusion about the outcome of Election 2000 set the stage for the most extraordinary thirty-six days in the history of U.S. presidential elections. The American political classes went to war over who would win Florida's twenty-five electoral votes and with them the presidency of the United States. While the politicians and their lawyers battled furiously, most

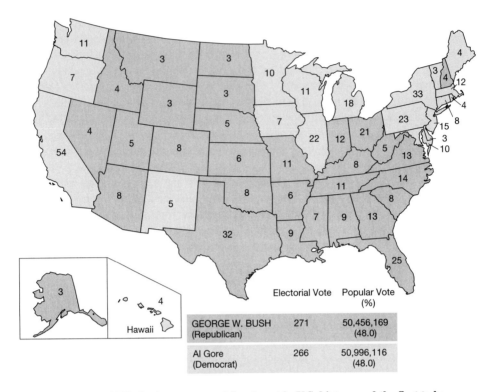

Figure 15.2   The 2000 election was one of the closest in U.S. history and the first to be decided by a decision of the Supreme Court.   *Source:* Public Domain Map.

Americans, and much of the rest of the world, watched from the sidelines as the spectacle unfolded. For once, it appeared, every vote did count.

The thirty-six-day political war, which unfolded in Florida following the inconclusive election, raised a plethora of significant issues. Civil rights leaders accused Florida election officials of deliberately disfranchising black voters. The controversy also exposed the antiquated voting technologies and the patchwork of local practices in place for recording and counting votes. To many observers, the election exposed the electoral college for the eighteenth-century anachronism that it was, and they demanded that America elect presidents directly like all the other modern democracies did. Above all, the dispute raised questions about to what extent, if at all, should state and federal courts involve themselves in elections.

But the most immediate issues involved recounting votes, and which ones to recount. There were two main categories of votes to be recounted. Some ballots had apparently misled some Gore voters into voting for Pat Buchanan. The larger category of disputed votes were "under votes," votes that the voting machines did not tabulate because voters had not punched their choices completely through on the punch card ballots. Some of the nation's top legal talents argued with one another over if and how they would evaluate dimpled chads, hanging chads, and pregnant chads (Chads were the bits of cardboard punched out of the cards by voters, or, as in the case of the "under votes," the bits of cardboard not completely punched out.) Gore, trailing in the vote, demanded recounts in those counties where he calculated they would gain him enough votes to win. The Bush people, narrowly ahead in the vote, insisted that there be no recounts. Florida's Secretary of State Katherine Harris, an appointee of Governor Jeb Bush, the Republican presidential candidate's brother, halted the recount process on November 27 and declared George W. Bush the winner by 537 votes. Harris insisted that her actions were dictated by the Florida electoral codes. Gore than appealed to the Florida State Supreme Court, comprised of mostly Democratic appointees, who overruled Harris and ordered the recounts to continue.

Bush eventually appealed to the U.S. Supreme Court. Late on the night of December 12, the Supreme Court, deeply divided along partisan and ideological lines, in *Bush v. Gore,* decided by a 5 to 4 decision, that the equal protection clause of the Fourteenth Amendment required that all ballots must be counted the same way, and since time did not permit a statewide hand recount, all recounts must cease immediately. The four dissenting justices all filed strongly worded opinions. One of them, Justice Stephen Breyer, a Clinton appointee, wrote that the Court's majority opinion was clearly a political one that "runs the risk of undermining the public's confidence in the Court itself." The disputed election of 2000 was resolved when five Supreme Court justices, by ordering all recounts to cease while Bush still retained his 537-vote lead, awarded Florida's twenty-five disputed electoral votes to him. The next day, an embittered Al Gore conceded the election; George W. Bush became the forty-third president of the United States.

COMPASSIONATE CONSERVATISM

George W. Bush took the oath of office as president of the United States on January 20, 2001. Mindful of the close, controversial election that had brought him to the White House via a 5–4 decision of the Supreme Court and of the partisan acrimony that had characterized Washington politics in recent years, Bush's brief inaugural address focused on the themes of civility, tolerance, and what he called "compassionate conservatism." He promised to consult with Democratic leaders of Congress and to work with them to solve the myriad of problems facing the American people. The new president observed that America's grandest ideal is that "everyone belongs, that everyone deserves a chance, that no insignificant person was ever born."

Concerned to shed the Republican Party's image as the party of, by, and for white men, Bush appointed the most diverse cabinet in U.S. history. Spencer Abraham, a Lebanese American, became Secretary of Energy; Norman Mineta, a Japanese American, became Secretary of Transportation; Elaine Chao, a Taiwanese immigrant, became Secretary of Labor; and Mel Martinez, a Cuban immigrant, became Secretary of Housing and Urban Development. In addition to Chao, two other women were appointed to cabinet positions—Gale Norton as Secretary of the Interior and Ann Veneman as Secretary of Agriculture. Two African Americans were also appointed to the new Cabinet—Roderick Page as Secretary of Education and Colin Powell as Secretary of State. Although the new president received only 6 percent of the black vote, he appointed two African Americans to two powerful foreign policy advisory positions—the aforementioned Colin Powell at State and Condoleeza Rice as his National Security Adviser. Powell and Rice became the two most powerful black political leaders in the nation's history.

During the first months of the Bush presidency, the White House pushed through Congress its two top priorities—educational reform and tax cuts. The Leave No Child Behind Act, the new administration's most important education reform was noteworthy mainly for establishing a larger federal presence in the nation's public schools, and for implementing a testing regimen whereby schools would be held accountable for what they taught, or failed to teach, their pupils. Schools failing to show progress after two years could lose their federal funding, or, in extreme cases, could be closed. Bush's educational reforms did not work as well as proponents hoped, mainly because Congress failed to provide adequate funding for their full implementation.

On May 26, 2001, Congress, controlled by Republicans, approved by large majorities a $1.35 trillion tax cut spread over ten years. One provision of the tax measure provided for immediate tax relief in the form of $300 rebates to all single workers and $600 to those filing joint returns. The new law also provided for lowering every tax bracket except the 15 percent bracket in stages until 2006. By 2006, the top bracket would have dropped from 39.6 percent to 35.6 percent. The new tax law gradually reduced the estate tax and then phased it out altogether after ten years. It also raised the child credit in stages and allowed increased contributions to Individual Retirement Accounts (IRAs) and 401(k)-type plans. Finally, taxes for couples would be adjusted downward to eliminate the so-called marriage penalty.

Democratic critics of the Bush tax cuts claimed that most of the tax savings went to rich people while the middle classes and working classes received only token reductions in their taxes. Democrats also argued that significantly reducing taxes while the U.S. economy was weak was fiscally irresponsible because it risked rising deficits and imperiled the solvency of the Social Security system. The debate over the tax cuts highlighted a basic fiscal reality that neither conservative Republicans nor liberal Democrats acknowledged—the federal government was increasingly dependent on income taxes collected from taxpayers in the upper income brackets.

The Bush presidency also made a series of decisions that provoked criticism from many environmentalists. On March 13, President Bush announced that he would not regulate carbon dioxide emissions from power plants. On March 20, the President announced that he was canceling a last-minute Clinton administration decision to reduce the amount of arsenic traces allowed in drinking water. On March 27, Bush removed the United States from the Kyoto Protocol, the 1997 Treaty that required the United State to cut greenhouse gas emissions by one-third over a fifteeen-year period. Many European leaders as well as American environmentalists strongly condemned Bush's decision. Since American industries were responsible for the production of more than 25 percent of the emissions, Bush's unilateralist decision to pull the United States out of the Kyoto agreement nullified international efforts to control greenhouse gas emissions. Nearly all environmental scientists believed that greenhouse gases such as carbon dioxide were a major cause of global warming. To all the critics of his anti-environmentalist actions, President Bush had the same rejoinder: He would take no actions that harmed the American economy.

President Bush's prospects for getting most of his pro-business conservative agenda enacted by Congress suddenly were reduced significantly on June 5, 2001, when Republican Senator Jim Jeffords of Vermont announced that henceforth he would be an Independent. Jeffords defection from the Republican Party gave the Democratic Party a 50–49 majority in the Senate and thus control of that branch of the federal legislature. Democrat Tom Daschle of South Dakota became the new Senate Majority Leader replacing Trent Lott, a Republican from Mississippi. Democratic Senators became the chairs of major committees and the Democrats also acquired voting majorities on them.

JUDICIAL WARFARE

Probably the most important domestic political battle being waged between the Administration and the Democratic minority in the Senate was over how many and what kind of judges would President Bush appoint to the federal judiciary. The stakes were high in a political culture in which federal judges not only interpret and refine the laws, but increasingly make laws that have important programmatic and policy impacts. Further, because judges have life tenures and serve beyond the reach of electorates, Bush's judicial appointments were destined to have a long-term influence on the political life of the nation.

President Bush repeatedly made it clear during his campaign for the presidency in 2000 and reaffirmed it often since assuming office that one of his primary goals was to bring about an ideological transformation of the federal judiciary, which include 675 district judges, 179 appellate judges, and nine Supreme Court Justices. Through the fall of 2003, he had nominated over 200 federal judges, many of whom were approved by the Senate, although Senate Democrats were able to prevent the appointment of a few of his most controversial nominees.

These battles over Bush's judicial nominees presaged the more significant battle that will ensue when a Supreme Court justice retires and the administration has its first opportunity to nominate a candidate to the High Court. Hanging over the next Supreme Court nominee is the possibility that *Roe v. Wade* (1973), the controversial Court decision that legalized abortion, could be severely restricted or even overturned. Court watchers believe that only a 5–4 majority is currently supportive of *Roe v. Wade;* President Bush appears determined to nominate an opponent of abortion whenever he gets the opportunity.

Meanwhile, one of the most conservative Supreme Courts in recent U.S. history issued two landmark decisions that delighted liberals and confounded conservatives. In a remarkable final week of its 2002–2003 term, the Court preserved affirmative action in University admissions, then found that the Constitution's due process clause guaranteed that gays and lesbians be accorded dignity and respect for their private sexual behavior. In *Grutter v. Bollinger* (2003), the Court, by a 5–4 ruling, upheld the University of Michigan law school's use of race as a factor when considering an individual's eligibility for admission. In *Lawrence v. Texas* (2003), the Court, also by a 5–4 majority, struck down a law that criminalized sexual behavior between gays. These two historic decisions, neither of which President Bush endorsed, strengthened his resolve to continue nominating conservative jurists to serve on federal courts.

9/11/01 AND THE WAR ON TERRORISM

On the morning of September 11, 2001, at 8:45 A.M. local time, American Airlines Flight 11, a Boeing 767, ripped into the North Tower of the World Trade Center (WTC). Twenty minutes later, United Airlines Flight 175, also a Boeing 767, slammed into the South Tower. Ninety minutes later, both of the 110-story structures had collapsed into gigantic mounds of burning rubble. Buried among the wreckage were over 2,700 people, dead and dying, including 350 firefighters who had rushed into the giant buildings just before they collapsed. Located at the southern end of Manhattan, the twin towers of the WTC, the financial and commercial nerve center of the global economy, had been potent symbols of America's wealth and power, and of its dominant role in international financial relations. All who saw the televised images of the second plane crashing into the tower must have felt as if they were witnessing an unimaginable horror, a nightmare from which there could be no awakening.

At almost the same time the WTC was destroyed, a third airliner, probably aiming for the White House, slammed into the Pentagon. A fourth aircraft, diverted from its intended target by a band of courageous passengers, crashed into a field not far from Pittsburgh, Pennsylvania. Informed observers speculated that the fourth airliner was probably headed for the Capitol Building in Washington, D.C. All 246 people on board the four aircraft perished. The four planes had been hijacked by highly trained operatives, members of Osama bin Laden's al-Qaeda terrorist network. They had turned the aircraft into flying bombs to carry out the most destructive terrorist acts against the United States in its history.

What made the horror worse on that dreadful day, and for many days afterward, was the fear that more attacks were imminent. How many other planes might have been turned into flying bombs? What other weapons of mass destruction would terrorists unleash on vulnerable Americans—chemical, biological, even crude nuclear weapons? What other symbolic or strategic targets would be hit? How many more Americans would die? National Guardsmen were hastily mobilized and assigned to guard duties all over the country. The skies over America's great cities and other potential targets were filled with Air Force fighters and refueling aircraft. A nation which had been attacked braced itself for perhaps many more attacks.

Searching for historical parallels, media pundits were quick to compare the terrorist attacks with Pearl Harbor. But the attacks at Pearl Harbor had been carried out by Japanese Naval aviators, who attacked only U.S. military targets and personnel. The terrorist attacks of September 11 were carried out by members of a shadowy, decentralized terrorist network that represented no nation or state. They deliberately targeted innocent civilians who were guilty only of having gone that morning to their usual places of work. The terrorists justified their attacks by espousing an extremist religious ideology that was premised on hatred of the United States foreign policy, its culture, and its people.

The 9/11 attacks were best understood as the most recent and by far the most destructive terrorist assaults on the United States; they were the latest episodes in an ongoing terroristic war against U.S. interests at home and abroad that had originated in the late 1970s. If one needed a historic parallel, it was the murder of John F. Kennedy on November 22, 1963. No event since the assassination of President Kennedy has scarred the American consciousness in the way that the events of September 11, 2001, did.

President George W. Bush spoke to the American people on the evening of September 12. Speaking with a tone of controlled anger, he called the deadly attacks "acts of war" and vowed to hunt down and bring to justice all those found responsible for "the dastardly and cowardly attacks." He blamed bin Laden's terrorist organization for the attacks and also ordered the Taliban rulers of Afghanistan, who had long protected bin Laden, to turn him over to U.S. authorities or face military attack. He also condemned the vigilante attacks on Middle Easterners that

Figure 15.3   A hijacked jet airliner is caught on camera an instant before it crashed into the South Tower of the World Trade Center. (AP Photo/Carmen Taylor).   *Source:* AP/Wide World Photos.

occurred in a few American cities. The president warned any nation that harbored terrorists to expect the full consequences of their treachery. Secretary of State Colin Power bluntly announced to all nations, "You're either with us or against us." Congress, with one dissenting vote, granted the President the power to take whatever actions he found necessary to protect the security of the American nation and its people. The President also called for the creation of a new Cabinet-level agency, the Office of Homeland Security, to coordinate the activities of over forty state and federal agencies charged with protecting U.S. internal security.

After quickly forging an unwieldy alliance that included NATO countries, Russia, China, Indian, Egypt, Saudi Arabia, and Pakistan, the United State launched a retaliatory war against the Taliban and the al-Qaeda terrorist networks within Afghanistan. President Bush provided strong national and international leadership in a time of crisis. Most Americans responded positively to what many of them regarded as the defining moment of Bush's presidency. His public approval ratings soared, reaching 90 percent. 88 percent of Americans said that they supported the war against terrorism in Afghanistan.

A surge of old-fashioned patriotism swept across the nation. American flags were proudly flown from front porches and vehicles. Red, white, and blue quickly became the colors of choice for patriots from eight to eighty. Tens of thousands of sports fans stood in stadia to sing the "Star Spangled Banner" and "America the Beautiful" with renewed pride and spirit. Strangers hugged, cried together, and vowed to respond in whatever ways they could to meet the challenges posed by the horrible events of 9/11. Money, commodities, and people poured into New York to aid the victims and to help with the massive cleanup operations. Prayer vigils were held in churches, synagogues, and mosques as well as in public parks and buildings. Rudolph Guiliani provided inspired leadership and became a national hero in his final days as mayor of New York. Ground Zero, the site of the ruined towers, became the scene of the most massive cleanup job in the nation's history. Ground Zero also became sacred ground, consecrated by the blood of heroes who died doing their jobs in the prime of their lives.

Beyond the instant loss of life and property, the deadly assaults did serious damage and inflicted considerable financial and economic pain on America. An official report, issued a year after the fiery destruction of the WTC towers placed the overall cost to New York City at $95 billion. The sluggish economy, declining tax revenues, plunging stock prices, which were exacerbated by an epidemic of corporate scandals, along with increased spending on national defense and homeland security, combined to transform a federal budget surplus of $127 billion for fiscal 2001 into a deficit of $157 billion for fiscal 2002.

Federal tax revenues suffered their largest one-year percentage drop in over fifty years and expenditures showed their most rapid increase since the early 1980s. Wall Street, already reeling in the wake of the collapse of the Silicon Valley dot-com bubble, suffered its worst one-week loss since the Great Crash of 1929. Forty-six of the fifty states reported budget shortfalls for fiscal 2002. California, the nation's most populous state, reported a budget deficit of $22 billion. Unemployment rose as over a million workers lost their jobs in the wake of the attacks. By the end of the year, the unemployment rate had reached 5.8 percent, the highest in seven years. The attacks probably pushed a teetering economy into its first recession in a decade. Many airlines, already operating in the red, faced bankruptcy in the aftermath of the attacks and a ruinous falloff in business. Only a quick $15 billion bailout from Congress temporarily halted the disastrous decline of the airline industry.

Nearly all Americans united to help New York rebuild and restore the nation's shattered confidence. The federal government made $40 billion available to help New York clear out the rubble, aid the survivors of the victims, and rebuild the area. Nearly all Americans closed ranks to wage the war on terrorism. Extremists on the far Left and far Right dissented. From the Right, the Reverend Jerry Falwell, founder and leader of the Moral Majority, called the attacks God's punishment for Americans' sins of liberalism, secularism, abortion, and homosexuality. From the Left, Noam Chomsky, wrote a short book, *9/11,* which became an improbable best seller, in which he blamed imperialistic America for provoking the attacks. He argued that Islamic fundamentalists like Osama bin Laden were retaliating for numerous terrorist acts committed by the United States against Islamic peoples.

Months after the attacks, it became evident that the government had failed to anticipate or adequately prepare for the terrorist attacks on September 11. The FBI and CIA failed to heed the numerous warning signs and red flags. One missed opportunity occurred when a FBI field agent noted that a large number of young males of Middle Eastern descent were enrolling in flight schools to learn to fly jet airliners. The report was filed in the FBI's Central Office and not read until after the attacks had occurred. According to Coleen Rowley, a lawyer working out of

Minneapolis, Minnesota FBI office, who testified before a Congressional investigating committee, another missed opportunity occurred when FBI agents from Washington, D.C., refused to allow Minnesota agents to search the computer of Zacarias Moussani, an alleged co-conspirator arrested in August 2001, three weeks before the 9/11 attacks occurred. Congressional investigators, after a thorough study, concluded that there had been enough warning signs for the federal agencies charged with protecting the security of the United States to fear that a terrorist attack was imminent and to take aggressive steps to heighten security at airports. There also were warnings that terrorists were considering using airplanes by converting them to flying bombs.

There also were systemic failures. The CIA and FBI did not coordinate counter terrorist activities nor exchange intelligence. The FBI had a policy of not sharing intelligence data with CIA operatives in order to protect its bureaucratic turf. The most blatant deficiency was the CIA's inability to gather human intelligence. It had failed for nearly ten years to penetrate the al-Qaeda network. Few CIA operatives were fluent in Arabic languages or knew anything about Islamic cultures or traditions. Most CIA field officers assigned to Middle Eastern countries appeared to be more comfortable working within U.S. embassies. They rarely traveled into the countryside or met with people. They saw nothing and they learned nothing about the impending attack.

The air war, and later a limited ground war, that the United States waged against the Taliban and al-Qaeda networks in Afghanistan in the wake of the 9/11 attacks, reshuffled the world's diplomatic deck. Not only had the Cold War era ended, so had the relatively brief post-Cold War era. Russia, which had been humiliated when it fought a losing war in Afghanistan ten years earlier, opened its airspace for U.S. warplanes. Vladimir Putin, the Russian leader, moved Russia closer to an alliance with the United States and closer to the nations of western Europe. Washington ceased its criticism of Russia's ongoing war against the break-away republic of Chechnya.

The Muslim members of the U.S.-led coalition were ambivalent about their roles. The most ambivalent one was also the most essential. Pakistan, led by a military dictator, General Pervez Musharraf, allowed Americans to mount attacks on the Taliban from bases in Pakistan after the United States provided billions of dollars of aid and canceled an embargo that had been clamped on Pakistan after it had exploded a nuclear weapon.

Egypt and Saudi Arabia were even more reluctant allies. The Saudis had contributed millions of dollars to support the Taliban and Osama bin Laden while they were driving the Soviets out of Afghanistan in the 1980s. bin Laden, who was a Saudi citizen of Yemeni descent, the son of one of the richest men in Saudi Arabia, was himself enormously wealthy and used his personal wealth to fund many of al-Qaeda's anti-Soviet operations. The CIA had also funneled weapons and money into Afghanistan to aid the Taliban and al-Qaeda in the war against the Soviets. Ironically, the United States and bin Laden had been de facto allies in the war against the Soviet occupation of Afghanistan.

The air war in Afghanistan began on October 7, 2001, when United States and Great Britain launched a powerful assault against Afghanistan using strategic bombers, tactical bombers, fighter planes, and cruise missiles. Within a few days, the U.S.-led coalition had established control of the air. They pounded al-Qaeda training camps and Taliban military strongholds. The Americans also provided aid to the opposition Northern Alliance within Afghanistan, which quickly went on the offensive.

The Islamic fundamentalist Taliban regime led by Mullah Muhammad Omar, which had sheltered bin Laden and his al-Qaeda network, collapsed under the pressure of U.S. bombs and attacks by the rebel armies of the Northern Alliance. One by one, key cities fell to the advancing Northern Alliance forces. On November 13, Northern Alliance forces rolled into Kabul, the capital of Afghanistan, where they were enthusiastically greeted by the people, who were delighted to be liberated from the severe Taliban regime. Within a month, most of the country was under the control of the Northern Alliance and other anti-Taliban forces. Mullah Omar abdicated on December 6 and fled Kandahar, the Taliban religious capital, for the mountainous eastern region bordering Pakistan.

Prodded by the Americans, Afghan leaders began forming an interim coalition government representative of all major factions in the strife-torn country, including, for the first time in Afghanistan's history, women. On December 17, the United States reopened its embassy in Kabul for the first time since 1989. On December 20, the UN Security Council approved placing a British-led security force in Afghanistan, which would consist of 4,500 peacekeepers representing seventeen nationalities. On December 22, an interim government headed by Hamid Karzai, a Pashtun tribal leader and relative of Zahir Shah, Afghanistan's exiled king, was installed in Kabul. On June 10, 2002, delegates to a *loya jirga* (grand council) assembled in Kabul to create a constitutional framework for a permanent government. The interim coalition leader Hamid Karzai was elected president and a new cabinet was sworn in.

Figure 15.4   The interim Afghani government meeting in Kabul in December, 2001.   *Source:* CORBIS.

While Afghan leaders were working to establish a functioning government for the battered and impoverished people of Afghanistan, U.S. and British commandos searched for the elusive bin Laden and his top lieutenants in mountainous caves near the Pakistani border. Even though the Allied forces used powerful bombs and explosive charges to destroy many of the caves, and they killed or captured hundreds of al-Qaeda fighters, bin Laden, most of his top aides, and many al-Qaeda fighters survived.

However, hundreds of Taliban and al-Qaeda fighters captured during the war were flown to the U.S. Naval base at Guantanamo Bay, Cuba. The first contingents arrived January 11, 2002. They were housed, fed, clothed, and given medical attention. Many were interrogated intensively. International human rights organizations quickly raised questions concerning their treatment and the refusal of the United States to consider them prisoners of war. A U.S. congressional investigating committee visited the base and reported that the prisoners were being treated humanely. U.S. Secretary of Defense Donald Rumsfeld called them "unlawful combatants" not entitled to POW status under the Geneva Convention. Later, President George W. Bush announced that the Taliban fighters interned at Guantanamo would be treated as POWs, but not the al-Qaeda prisoners since they were not fighting as citizen-soldiers of a sovereign state with which the United States was at war.

Civil libertarians worried that some of the security measures taken by the U.S. government in the wake of the 9/11 terrorist attacks to protect the American people might involve unacceptable invasions of the privacy of individual citizens. Of particular concern was the USA Patriot Act, passed by Congress and signed by President Bush on October 26, 2001. Enacted at the request of Attorney General John Ashcroft, the Patriot Act gave local police added powers to wiretap telephones, monitor Internet and e-mail use, and to search the homes of suspected terrorists without having to first obtain search warrants. Citizens feared that in their zeal to protect citizens from danger, lawmakers had created an Orwellian monster: Big Brother is watching you. The new law also permitted authorities to detain any foreigner suspected of terrorism for seven days without formally charging him with any crime.

As the war in Afghanistan wound down and the Karzai government struggled to take hold, Americans went to the polls to elect a new U.S. Congress. The polls leading up the election all pointed to a close election. Could the Democrats retain the Senate and regain control of the House of Representatives? Could the Republicans regain control of the Senate and widen their majority in the House? Few issues separated the parties and nearly all incumbents were re-elected, often by majorities of 60 percent or more. As the party associated with patriotism and national defense, Republicans benefited from a policy agenda that put foreign policy issues in the forefront. The war on terrorism upstaged social spending issues such as Medicare and Social Security where the Democrats could have had an advantage. The Democrats also failed to get much political traction out of criticizing President Bush's failure to jump start the weak economy and to restore prosperity.

From top to bottom, Election 2002 resulted in Republican victories. They regained control of the Senate and widened their majority in the House of Representatives. Additionally, Republicans won control of a majority of state governorships, including four of the six most populous states. And, for the first time in half a century, they won control of a majority of state legislatures. President Bush strengthened his power with Congress by involving himself extensively in various campaigns. He worked hard for Republican candidates for the Senate, the House, and for several gubernatorial candidates. Nearly all of the candidates that President Bush campaigned for emerged victorious. The Republican achievements went against the historical tradition of midterm elections, which normally produced sizeable losses for the presidential party. It was a Republican sweep that strengthened President Bush and gave his party control of both the Congress and the White House for the first time since 1954. The Republican party appeared to have consolidated its status as the majority party.

Underlying the campaigning and hoopla of the elections, a few enduring realities suggested that the American political system was severely flawed. Despite months of frenetic campaigning, the vast majority of American citizens evinced little interest in the election or its outcome. Scarcely a third of eligible voters bothered to vote. Pundits suggested that it was not disillusionment with politics and politicians so much as simply a lack of interest, especially among younger and working-class citizens. Money was still key to success in electoral politics. The money, nearly a billion dollars raised in 2002, was mostly spent on 1.5 television commercials, many of them attack commercials that denigrated opponents and often included personal attacks. Whatever their ethical implications, political operatives employed attack commercials because they worked. They rallied the faithful and brought them to the polls on election day.

THE IRAQ WAR

By the summer of 2002, the war on terrorism, which the United States had energetically launched following the attacks of September 11, 2001, appeared to have lost both its momentum and focus. Osama bin Laden and most of his top associates had neither been killed nor captured. They were believed to be hiding in Afghanistan's remote mountain ranges and the lawless tribal areas that straddle the border with Pakistan. Although some of its networks and funding sources had been disrupted, and several top al-Qaeda officials had either been killed or captured, U.S. counterterrorist experts believed that al-Qaeda sleeper cells were still functioning, probably some of them within the United States. CIA director George Tenant stated that the threat of attacks by al-Qaeda was as great as it was before September 11, 2001. Whenever Americans traveled by air, the extensive security procedures in place at all major airports were quick reminders of the continuing state of uncertainty and fear lurking just below the threshold of everyone's consciousness.

The Bush administration also broadened the war on terror to incorporate what the President termed "rogue nations" and other terrorist organizations, some with links to al-Qaeda. President Bush spoke of an "axis of evil" running from Iraq through Iran to North Korea. Senior officials in the Bush administration, including Vice President Dick Cheney, Secretary of Defense Donald Rumsfeld and Assistant Secretary of Defense Paul Wolfowitz, wanted to remove the Iraqi dictator Saddam Hussein from power.

They advised President Bush to incorporate "regime change" in Iraq into the expanding war on terrorism for many reasons: It would eliminate the security threat Saddam posed to his neighbors, to core U.S. allies, and ultimately to the United States itself. It would provide an opportunity to bring liberal democracy to an important Arab country, which in time could spread to other Middle Eastern countries. It would increase the chances of a peaceful resolution of the interminable Arab–Israeli conflict. It could provide U.S. access to Iraqi oil, which could drive down world oil prices and ease American dependency on Saudi Arabian oil. Most of all, it would signal to terrorists and to nation's that sponsored or harbored terrorists that Washington possessed the political will and military power to take preemptive actions to eliminate perceived threats to U.S. interests wherever they were found to exist. And The United States would act unilaterally if necessary.

On August 21, 2002, President Bush stated publicly that the United States was considering "regime change" in Iraq, but he indicated that no final decision had been made and that he was keeping all of his options open. Sanctions imposed on Iraq in 1991 in the wake of the Gulf War had required Iraq to destroy all of its weapons of mass destruction (WMDs), including any chemical, biological, or nuclear weapons that it retained or was developing. The sanctions regime also required Saddam Hussein to allow UN inspectors unfettered access to all the sites where WMDs might be manufactured or stored. U.S. officials maintained that Saddam Hussein had failed to cooperate with United Nations weapons inspectors and that Iraqi scientists continued to develop and stockpile weapons of mass destruction.

In a speech that he delivered to the UN General Assembly on September 12, President Bush promised to work with the Security Council to meet the challenge posed by Iraq's defiance, but he also stressed that the international community must act decisively to end the threat posed by Iraq's possession of weapons of mass destruction. On October 10, the House of Representatives, by a 296–133 vote, and on October 11, the Senate, by a 77–23 vote, enacted a measure sought by the White House backing President Bush's use of military force against Iraq if it did not comply fully with the UN WMDs inspectors. Two weeks later, the U.S. delegate to the United Nations introduced a resolution to the Security Council calling for military action against Iraq if all of its weapons of mass destruction were not eliminated. On November 8, the Security Council voted unanimously, 13–0, to give Iraq "a final opportunity" to comply with all the previous UN disarmament resolutions and established a strict timetable for compliance. A few days later, acceding to the threat of force, Iraq agreed to allow UN inspections to resume, while insisting that it did not possess any WMDs. The first cadre of UN weapons inspectors arrived in Baghdad November 25.

For the next several weeks UN inspectors led by Hans Blix searched sites throughout Iraq, but could find no weapons of mass destruction. However, inspectors did find evidence that indicated WMDs had been previously stored at some sites. Iraqi documents also failed to account for large numbers of weapons of mass destruction that had been discovered during past inspections and had supposedly been destroyed. On December 19, Secretary of State Colin Powell declared that Iraq was in "material breach" of UN resolutions and risked war if it continued its pattern of lying, deception, and noncompliance. On January 7, 2003, Hans Blix issued a report in which he accused Iraq of failure to cooperate with UN weapons inspectors in accounting for and removing chemical and biological weapons. The United States moved closer to war with Iraq a few days later when Secretary of Defense Donald Rumsfeld signed orders deploying 62,000 U.S. troops to the Persian Gulf region. Great Britain announced that it was joining the U.S. military buildup and sent an aircraft carrier and 26,000 troops to the Gulf.

As the United States and Great Britain, ratcheted up the military pressure on Iraq, a worldwide debate on the merits of the impending war intensified. Colin Powell appeared before the UN Security Council on February 5 to make his case for a UN endorsement of a war against Iraq. Citing various intelligence sources, Powell accused Saddam Hussein's regime of removing evidence from various sites and intimidating Iraqi scientists in efforts to deceive UN weapons inspectors. He also accused the Iraqi leaders of maintaining ties with al-Qaeda and harboring their own terrorist cells. Following his presentation, ten East European countries, led by Poland, voiced their strong support for the United States; however, France, Russia, and China all opposed taking any military action against Iraq. Their leaders all insisted that Powell had failed to prove conclusively that Iraq retained weapons of mass destruction, had ties with al-Qaeda, or posed an imminent threat to U.S. security. They demanded that the UN inspections should be given more time. They also maintained that UN sanctions against Iraq had worked well enough to contain Saddam Hussein's aggressive tendencies.

As it became increasingly obvious that the United States and Great Britain were positioning their forces for an invasion of Iraq, millions of people opposed to the war demonstrated in cities around the world. In London an estimated 750,000 people and in Rome an estimated 600,000 people protested the impending war. There were huge antiwar rallies in New York and San Francisco. Responding to the outpourings of antiwar sentiment, President Bush stated that his decisions would not be swayed by protesters; he also maintained that the allied coalition did not need another UN resolution authorizing an attack. However, Powell and other U.S. diplomats continued to try to get a second resolution through the Security Council supporting the use of military force against Iraq.

On March 5, Hans Blix stated that the weapons inspectors needed more time. China issued a statement declaring that the inspections required more time. France, Germany, and Russian announced that they would oppose a draft resolution submitted to the UN Security Council by the United States, Great Britain, and Spain declaring that Iraq had missed its last chance to disarm peacefully.

All of the protests and all of the diplomatic efforts failed to avert war. On March 6, Colin Powell stated that the United States would lead a "coalition of the willing nations" that would disarm Iraq with or without UN authority. On March 17, when it was apparent that the Security Council would not approve the resolution, the three co-sponsors withdrew it. President Bush told Saddam Hussein that he and his two sons must leave Iraq within 48 hours. Saddam rejected Bush's ultimatum. The U.S.-led military offensive to oust the regime of Saddam Hussein got underway on the evening of March 19, 2003 when U.S. aircraft and Tomahawk cruise missiles attacked targets located in the southwest sector of Baghdad in response to intelligence information that Saddam Hussein was meeting with other high Iraqi officials in a house located in that part of the city. This effort to decapitate the regime at the outset of the war failed because Hussein did not show up. In a television address to the nation, President Bush announced the onset of a military campaign named OPERATION IRAQI FREEDOM. The Iraq War had begun.

Units of the Army's 3rd Infantry Division and elements of the 1st Marine Expedition Force quickly moved northward from staging areas in Kuwait toward Baghdad. In an aerial bombardment, which the Pentagon dubbed its "shock and awe" campaign, carefully coordinated with ground combat elements, U.S. aircraft and cruise missiles rained lethal punishment on selected targets in Baghdad and various Iraqi military units trying to defeat the invading U.S. ground forces. The aerial campaign was covered live by the U.S. media, particularly the major television all-news channels, CNN, CNBC, and Fox News. Television coverage of the war was supplemented by reports from journalists, many of them veterans, "embedded" with the

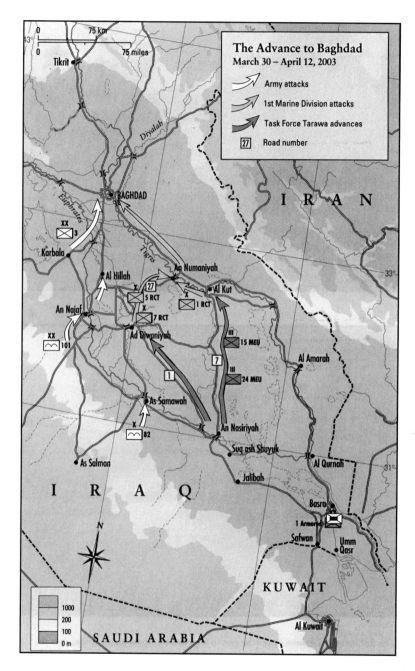

Figure 15.5   The Advance to Baghdad, March 30–April 12, 2003.   *Source*:
U.S. Army Map.

advancing ground forces. These media resources provided Americans with the most extensive coverage of a major war in human history.

Within a week, during which U.S. forces continuously surprised, outmaneuvered, and destroyed the Iraqi troops trying to fight back, the Americans had reached the approaches to Baghdad. Never had a large military force combined the elements of movement, flexibility, and lethality of precision weapons so effectively in combat. Never had an invading army moved so quickly so deeply into enemy territory. While the U.S. forces moved rapidly toward Baghdad, British forces in the south moved more slowly toward Basra, Iraq's second largest city.

Then the lightening U.S. advance hit several snags simultaneously. Fierce sandstorms called *shamals,* that raged for days, impeded progress. Attacks by *fedayeen,* Iraqi irregulars, who made up for their lack of military skills with a willingness to martyr themselves for a cause in which they devoutly believed, threatened to slow the U.S. advance by attacking overextended supply lines. Another complicating factor was the refusal of the Turkish government to allow coalition forces to invade Iraq from the north as had been planned. The northern campaign would have forced the Iraqis to disperse their forces to meet simultaneous threats from the north and south.

Critics of the war, who had opposed it from the outset, seized on these delays to make their case that coalition forces had tried to achieve victory with inadequate forces and were now facing a Vietnam-like "quagmire." Public opinion polls taken at the time showed a narrow majority in England supported coalition forces and President Bush enjoyed the support of a large majority of his countrymen for the war effort.

After a few days of delay, in the most sophisticated and effective military campaign ever waged, coalition forces consisting almost entirely of U.S. and British troops crushed the Iraqi military in two weeks of hard fighting. On April 4, the U.S. Army and Marine forces met on the outskirts of Baghdad after both had to quash some last-ditch resistance by elite Republican Guard units and the *fedayeen.* The next day, elements of the 3rd Infantry Division reached the city center. On April 8, the regime of Saddam Hussein simply collapsed and melted away, becoming part of the detritus of history. In the north, fighting continued for a few more days. On April 10, Kurdish forces captured Kirkuk a large city near the northern oil fields. The next day, Marines occupied Tikrit, Saddam Hussein's hometown. On April 14, President Bush declared that the fighting was over, Saddam was finished, and the Coalition of the willing had won the war. Coalition forces suffered few casualties. Because of their use of precision weapons, particularly Global Positing System (GPS) ordnance and Laser Guided Bombs (LGBs), there was comparatively light collateral damage inflicted on the hapless Iraqis.

All celebrations of victory by Coalition forces were muted because they understood that Saddam Hussein's hopelessly politicized dysfunctional military culture had lacked the resources necessary to field effective military forces. They had lacked command and control capabilities, effective air defenses, mobility, training, discipline, and commitment. Their artillery, armor, and air force were mostly obsolete. The grim real-world, choices facing Iraqi soldiers were to surrender, desert, or be slaughtered. Celebrations were also muted by the realization that now that the conventional phase of the war had ended, the occupying Coalition forces faced the daunting tasks of reconstruction and of suppressing a bitter guerrilla resistance mounted by diehard supporters of the deposed dictator. Further, they would have to rebuild a country filled with angry people who, while they expressed gratitude for the overthrow of a brutal regime, resented the occupiers of their country who had killed thousands of their countrymen, caused serious damage to

Figure 15.6   Captain Kim Campbell examines the damage inflicted on her A-10 Warthog over Baghdad on April 7, 2003. Among fixed-wing aircraft, the Warthog, flying at low altitude and providing close air support, bore the brunt of Iraqi anti-aircraft fire.   *Source:* U.S. Air Force Photo.

the Iraqi infrastructure, battered an economy already weakened by years of UN sanctions, and brought anarchic conditions in which neither life nor property were secure.

Futurists concerned about the fate of the small planet located in an obscure corner of the universe that we inhabit fear that rapid world population increases and severe environmental degradation pose far more serious long-term threats to our living standards and general sense of well-being than do political and economic crises. On January 1, 2003, the world's estimated population reached 6.3 billion people. Demographers predict that by 2025, the world's population will have reached eight billion people and, by 2050, the world's population will have soared to over nine billion people. In 2050, the population of the United States will have surpassed 400 million people. The next two generations of population growth will add three billion people, a 50 percent increase in the world's population in fifty years.

The consequences of such population growth will mostly be dire. Mass immiseration, especially in developing countries, will breed extremist political and religious movements that will ensure a turbulent future. Surging populations will use up huge quantities of the earth's finite resources, wipe out millions of acres of rain forest needed to cool and purify the planet, and extinguish thousands of species of plants and animals. The world's supply of arable farm land and fresh water will continue to diminish. Global warming looms as a serious danger.

The futurist Robert D. Kaplan foresees an American future that will arrive before the twenty-first century has run its course: A land in which the dominant culture is an internationalized one. A society so diverse that ethno-racial markers have ceased to have any meaning. A political order in which national identities have eroded to a point where the only political units that matter are confederations of city-states; in which loyalty is understood primarily in economic terms. The primary function of the nation state will be to provide military protection for U.S. interests that are inextricably linked with global strategic and economic relations.

Americans, increasingly enmeshed in a global network of strategic, economic, political, and cultural relations, will face many challenges that will test the adaptability of their values and the strength of their social characters. As the velocity of history continuously accelerates, Americans, in order to survive and possibly flourish, must remain committed to finding new ways of coping with the fundamental changes that are exploding among them at an accelerating rate.

BRIEF BIBLIOGRAPHIC ESSAY

There has already accumulated a sizeable literature concerning the major events occurring in the first few years of the twenty-first century. Books that students seeking additional information on particular subjects might want to read include: *Fat Land: How Americans Became the Fattest People in the World,* by Greg Critser; *2000 Presidential Election Crisis,* a collection of articles written by correspondents of the *New York Times,* with an introduction by Douglas Brinkley; and *The Vanishing Voter: Public Involvement in an Age of Uncertainty,* by Thomas E. Patterson, which explains why more and more citizens have simply tuned out politics and politicians. *Bush at War,* by Bob Woodward, is the best account of the 100-day campaign to oust the Taliban from Afghanistan and to send the remnants of al-Qaeda's forces fleeing into the mountains of eastern Afghanistan and the border area that country shares with Pakistan; *The Cell,* by John Miller, Michael Stone, with Chris Mitchell, is the best of several books explaining why the FBI and CIA failed to stop the 9/11 plot. *The Threatening Storm: The Case for Invading Iraq,* by Kenneth M. Pollack, a military analyst for the CIA and the National Security Council, who has immersed himself in the Persian Gulf region for a decade, makes the best possible case for an invasion of Iraq. Robert Kagan's timely essay, *Of Paradise and Power,* argues that Americans and Europeans are fundamentally different and becoming more so. He provides important insights into why so many Europeans opposed the American-led military intervention in Iraq. An excellent Brief history of the Iraq War is Williamson Murray and Major General Robert H. Scales, Jr. *The Iraq War: A Military History. Faster: The Acceleration of Just About Everything,* by James Gleick, is a nimble, readable, and fast-paced account of the speeding up of all aspects of American life and its many consequences.

WEB SITES

For those readers who wish to explore the 2000 census data more broadly and deeply, start with the U.S. Census homepage at `<http://www.census.gov>`. Using the portal `<http://www.besthistorysites.net/index.html>`, students can access *America Remembers,* a site containing pictures, videos, and articles not only of the events of 9/11/01, but also of the days that followed. Also see *War Against Terror,* which is part of the CNN.com archives. Those interested in the Allied Coalition's war against Iraq should consult `<http://www.strategypage.com>`. It is a comprehensive summary of military news, analyses, historical perspectives, maps, orders of battle, and much more. It features many links covering a vast array of military topics. For the futurists among us, there is *The Next Millennium: Now What?* CNN.com asks fourteen experts to outline their visions of the next 1,000 years.

Appendix A

The Declaration of Independence

When in the Course of human events, it becomes necessary for one people to dissolve the political bands which have connected them with another, and to assume among the Powers of the earth, the separate and equal station to which the Laws of Nature and of Nature's God entitle them, a decent respect to the opinions of mankind requires that they should declare the causes which impel them to the separation.

We hold these truths to be self-evident, that all men are created equal, that they are endowed by their Creator with certain unalienable Rights, that among these are Life, Liberty and the pursuit of Happiness. That to secure these rights, Governments are instituted among Men, deriving their just powers from the consent of the governed, That whenever any Form of Government becomes destructive of these ends, it is the Right of the people to alter or to abolish it, and to institute new Government, laying its foundation on such principles and organizing its powers in such form, as to them shall seem most likely to effect their Safety and Happiness. Prudence, indeed, will dictate that Governments long established should not be changed for light and transient causes; and accordingly all experience hath shown, that mankind are more disposed to suffer, while evils are sufferable, than to right themselves by abolishing the forms to which they are accustomed. But when a long train of abuses and usurpations, pursuing invariably the same Object evinces a design to reduce them under absolute Despotism, it is their right, it is their duty, to throw off such Government, and to provide new Guards for their future security.—Such has been the patient sufferance of these Colonies; and such is now the necessity which constrains them to alter their former Systems of Government. The history of the present King of Great Britain is a history of repeated injuries and usurpations, all having in direct object the establishment of an absolute Tyranny over these States. To prove this, let Facts be submitted to a candid world.

He refused his Assent to Laws, the most wholesome and necessary for the public good.

He has forbidden his Governors to pass Laws of immediate and pressing importance, unless suspended in their operation till his Assent should be obtained; and when so suspended, he has utterly neglected to attend to them.

He has refused to pass other Laws for the accommodation of large districts of people, unless those people would relinquish the right of Representation in the Legislature, a right inestimable to them and formidable to tyrants only.

He has called together legislative bodies at places unusual, uncomfortable, and distant from the depository of their public Records, for the sole purpose of fatiguing them into compliance with his measures.

He has dissolved Representative Houses repeatedly, for opposing with manly firmness his invasions on the rights of the people.

He has refused for a long time, after such dissolutions, to cause others to be elected; whereby the Legislative Powers, incapable of Annihilation, have returned to the People at large for their exercise; the State remaining in the mean time exposed to all the dangers of invasion from without, and convulsions within.

He has endeavoured to prevent the population of these States; for that purpose obstructing the Laws of Naturalization of Foreigners; refusing to pass others to encourage their migration hither, and raising the conditions of new Appropriations of Lands.

He has obstructed the Administration of Justice, by refusing his Assent to Laws for establishing Judiciary powers.

He has made Judges dependent on his Will alone, for the tenure of their offices, and the amount and payment of their salaries.

He has erected a multitude of New Offices, and sent hither swarms of Officers to harass our People, and eat out their substance.

He has kept among us in time of peace, Standing Armies without the Consent of our legislature.

He has affected to render the Military independent of and superior to the Civil power.

He has combined with others to subject us to a jurisdiction foreign to our constitution, and unacknowledged by our laws; giving his Assent to their acts of pretended Legislation:

For quartering large bodies of armed troops among us:

For protecting them, by a mock Trial, from punishment for any Murders which they should commit on the Inhabitants of these States:

For cutting off our Trade with all parts of the world:

For imposing taxes on us without our Consent:

For depriving us in many cases, of the benefits of Trial by Jury:

For transporting us beyond Seas to be tried for pretended offences:

For abolishing the free System of English Laws in a neighbouring Province, establishing therein an Arbitrary government, and enlarging its Boundaries so as to render it at once an example and fit instrument for introducing the same absolute rule into these Colonies:

For taking away our Charters, abolishing our most valuable Laws, and altering fundamentally the Forms of our Governments:

For suspending our own Legislature, and declaring themselves invested with Power to legislate for us in all cases whatsoever.

He has abdicated Government here, by declaring us out of his Protection and waging War against us.

He has plundered our seas, ravaged our Coasts, burnt our towns, and destroyed the lives of our people.

He is at this time transporting large Armies of foreign Mercenaries to complete the works of death, desolation and tyranny, already begun with circumstances of Cruelty & perfidy scarcely paralleled in the most barbarous ages, and totally unworthy of the Head of a civilized nation.

He has constrained our fellow Citizens taken Captive on the high Seas to bear Arms against their Country, to become the executioners of their friends and Brethren, or to fall themselves by their Hands.

He has excited domestic insurrections amongst us, and has endeavoured to bring on the inhabitants of our frontiers, the merciless Indian Savages, whose known rule of warfare, is an undistinguished destruction of all ages, sexes and conditions.

In every stage of these Oppressions We have Petitioned for Redress in the most humble terms: Our repeated Petitions have been answered only by repeated injury. A Prince, whose character is thus marked by every act which may define a Tyrant, is unfit to be the ruler of a free people.

Nor have We been wanting in attention to our British brethren. We have warned them from time to time of attempts by their legislature to extend an unwarrantable jurisdiction over us. We have reminded them of the circumstances of our emigration and settlement here. We have appealed to their native justice and magnanimity, and we have conjured them by the ties of our common kindred to disavow these usurpations, which, would inevitably interrupt our connections and correspondence. They too have been deaf to the voice of justice and of consanguinity. We must, therefore, acquiesce in the necessity, which denounces our Separation, and hold them, as we hold the rest of mankind, Enemies in War, in Peace Friends.

We, therefore, the Representatives of the United States of America, in General Congress, Assembled, appealing to the Supreme Judge of the world for the rectitude of our intentions, do, in the Name, and by Authority of the good People of these Colonies, solemnly publish and declare, That these United Colonies are, and of Right ought to be Free and Independent States; that they are Absolved from all Allegiance to the British Crown, and that all political connection between them and the State of Great Britain, is and ought to be totally dissolved; and that as Free and Independent States, they have full Power to levy War, conclude Peace, contract Alliances, establish Commerce, and to do all other Acts and Things which Independent States may of right do. And for the support of this Declaration, with a firm reliance on the protection of divine Providence, we mutually pledge to each other our Lives, our Fortunes and our sacred Honor.

Appendix B

Amendments to the United States Constitution Since 1945

THE TWENTY-SECOND AMENDMENT

The Twenty-Second Amendment, a belated slap at Franklin D. Roosevelt by a Republican-dominated Congress, limits the president to two terms in office. Amendment XXII [1951]

No person shall be elected to the office of the President more than twice, and no person who has held the office of President, or acted as President, for more than two years of a term to which some other person was elected President shall be elected to the office of the President more than once.

But this Article shall not apply to any person holding the office of President when this Article was proposed by the Congress, and shall not prevent any person who may be holding the office of President, or acting as President, during the term within which this Article becomes operative from holding the office of President or acting as President during the remainder of such term.

THE TWENTY-THIRD AMENDMENT

The Twenty-Third Amendment allows residents of the District of Columbia to vote in presidential elections.

Amendment XXIII [1961]

Section 1. The District constituting the seat of Government of the United States shall appoint in such manner as the Congress may direct:

A number of electors of President and Vice President equal to the whole number of Senators and Representatives in Congress to which the District would be entitled if it were a State, but in no event more than the least populous State; they shall be in addition to those appointed by the States, but they shall be considered, for the purposes of the election of President and Vice President, to be electors appointed by a State; and they shall meet in the District and perform such duties as provided by the twelfth article of amendment.

Section 2. The Congress shall have the power to enforce this article by appropriate legislation.

THE TWENTY-FOURTH AMENDMENT

The Twenty-Fourth Amendment prevents the states from making payment of a poll tax a condition for voting. Common at the time among Southern states, the poll tax was a capitation (poll, or head) tax on individuals. A poll tax receipt was often required in order to vote. It was designed to prevent uneducated people, especially blacks, who were unaccustomed to saving receipts, from voting.

Amendment XXIV [1964]

Section 1. The right of citizens of the United States to vote in any primary or other election for President or Vice President, for electors for President or Vice President, or for Senator or Representative in Congress, shall not be denied or abridged by the United States or any State by reason of failure to pay any poll tax or other tax.

Section 2. The Congress shall have the power to enforce this article by appropriate legislation.

THE TWENTY-FIFTH AMENDMENT

The Twenty-Fifth Amendment, inspired by President Eisenhower's heart attack and President Johnson's abdominal surgery, provides for the temporary replacement of a president who is unable to discharge the duties of the office.

Amendment XXV [1967]

Section 1. In case of the removal of the President from office or his death or resignation, the Vice President shall become President.

Section 2. Whenever there is a vacancy in the office of the Vice President, the President shall nominate a Vice President who shall take the office upon confirmation by a majority vote of both houses of Congress.

Section 3. Whenever the President transmits to the President pro tempore of the Senate and the Speaker of the House of Representatives his written declaration that he is unable to discharge the powers and duties of his office, and until he transmits to them a written declaration to the contrary, such powers and duties shall be discharged by the Vice President as Acting President.

Section 4. Whenever the Vice President and a majority of either the principal officers of the executive departments, or of such other body as Congress may by law provide, transmit to the President pro tempore of the Senate and the Speaker of the House of Representatives their written declaration that the President is unable to discharge the powers and duties of his office, the Vice President shall immediately assume the powers and duties of the office of Acting President.

Thereafter, when the President transmits to the President pro tempore of the Senate and the Speaker of the House of Representatives his written declaration that no inability exists, he shall resume the powers and duties of his office unless the Vice President and a majority of either the principal officers of the executive departments, or of such other body as Congress may by law provide, transmit within four days to the President pro tempore of the Senate and the speaker of the House of Representatives their written declaration that the President is unable to discharge the powers and duties of his office. Thereupon Congress shall decide the issue, assembling within 48 hours for that purpose if not in session. If the Congress, within 21 days after receipt of the latter written declaration, or, if Congress is not in session, within 21 days after Congress is required to assemble, determines by two-thirds vote of both houses that the President is unable to discharge the powers and duties of his office, the Vice President shall continue to discharge the same as Acting President; otherwise, the President shall resume the powers and duties of his office.

THE TWENTY-SIXTH AMENDMENT

The Twenty-Sixth Amendment corrected a historic injustice: young men could be drafted and sent to war at age eighteen but were not allowed to participate in the nation's democratic processes until they were twenty-one. It extended the vote to eighteen year olds.

Amendment XXVI [1971]

Section 1. The rights of citizens of the United States, who are 18 years of age or older, to vote shall not be denied or abridged by the United States or any state on account of age.

Section 2. The Congress shall have the power to enforce this article by appropriate legislation.

THE TWENTY-SEVENTH AMENDMENT

The Twenty-Seventh Amendment has a curious history. It was originally proposed as part of the Bill of Rights to allay citizen fears that politicians would vote themselves fat pay raises while in office. It lay quiet for two centuries until congressional scandals forced Congress in 1992 to quickly resuscitate it. It was speedily ratified and became law on May 7, 1992.

Amendment XXVII [1992]

No law, varying the compensation for the services of the Senators and Representatives, shall take effect, until an election of Representatives shall have intervened.

Appendix C

Presidential Elections Since 1944

Year	Candidates Receiving More Than One Percent of the Vote (Parties)	Popular Vote	Electoral Vote
1944	FRANKLIN D. ROOSEVELT (Democratic)	25,606,585	432
	Thomas E. Dewey (Republican)	22,014,745	99
1948	HARRY S. TRUMAN (Democratic)	24,179,345	303
	Thomas E. Dewey (Republican)	21,991,291	189
	J. Strom Thurmond (States' Rights)	1,176,125	39
	Henry Wallace (Progressive)	1,157,326	0
1952	DWIGHT D. EISENHOWER (Republican)	33,936,234	442
	Adlai E. Stevenson (Democratic)	27,314,992	89
1956	DWIGHT D. EISENHOWER (Republican)	35,590,472	457
	Adlai E. Stevenson (Democratic)	26,022,752	73
1960	JOHN F. KENNEDY (Democratic)	34,226,731	303
	Richard M. Nixon (Republican)	34,108,157	219
1964	LYNDON B. JOHNSON (Democratic)	43,129,566	486
	Barry M. Goldwater (Republican)	27,178,188	52
1968	RICHARD M. NIXON (Republican)	31,785,480	301
	Hubert H. Humphrey (Democratic)	31,275,166	191
	George C. Wallace (American Independent)	9,906,473	46
1972	RICHARD M. NIXON (Republican)	45,631,189	521
	George S. McGovern (Democratic)	28,422,015	17
	John Schmitz (American Independent)	1,080,670	0
1976	JAMES E. CARTER, JR. (Democratic)	40,274,975	297
	Gerald R. Ford (Republican)	38,530,614	241
1980	RONALD W. REAGAN (Republican)	42,968,326	489
	James E. Carter, JR. (Democratic)	34,731,139	49
	John B. Anderson (Independent)	5,552,349	0
1984	RONALD W. REAGAN (Republican)	53,428,357	525
	Walter F. Mondale (Democratic)	36,930,923	13
1988	GEORGE H. W. BUSH (Republican)	47,917,341	426
	Michael Dukakis (Democratic)	41,013,030	112

(*continued*)

Year	Candidates Receiving More Than One Percent of the Vote (Parties)	Popular Vote	Electoral Vote
1992	WILLIAM JEFFERSON CLINTON (Democratic)	43,682,624	370
	George H. W. Bush (Republican)	38,117,331	168
	H. Ross Perot (Independent)	19,217,213	0
1996	WILLIAM JEFFERSON CLINTON (Democratic)	47,401,185	379
	Bob Dole (Republican)	39,397,469	159
	H. Ross Perot (Independent)	8,845,294	0
2000	GEORGE W. BUSH (Republican)	50,459,211	271
	Albert Gore (Democrat)	51,003,894	266
	Ralph Nader (Green)	2,834,410	0

Appendix D

Population of the United States Since 1940

1940	132,164,569
1950	151,325,796
1960	179,323,175
1970	203,302,031
1980	226,542,203
1990	246,709,873
2000	281,421,906
2004	294,000,000 (est.)

Index

Aaron, Henry (Hank), 63

ABM. *See* Missiles

Abortion, 205, 206–7, 289

Abraham, Spencer, 369

Acheson, Dean, 37–38, 47, 49, 72, 74

Adams, Sherman, 118

Adenauer, Konrad, 42

Advertisers, 22–23

AEC. *See* Atomic Energy Commission

The Affluent Society (Galbraith), 94

Afghanistan, 254, 292, 335–36, 373–77

AFL. *See* American Federation of Labor

AFL-CIO, 82, 187, 236, 299

Africa, 26, 37–38, 132, 253

African American(s), 3–4. *See also* Black
    power
  athletes, 63
  in government, 145, 289, 369–70
  households, 85–86, 183–84, 205, 269–72,
    299, 328, 362
  militants, 191–92
  during postwar, 62–65, 101
  racism and, 9–12, 21, 108–9, 270–71
  students, 107
  voters, 63, 66, 129, 145, 156–57, 159, 248,
    259

  women, 8, 24
  during WW II, 9–12, 21

African National Conference, 338–39

AFSCME. *See* American Federation of State,
    County, and Municipal Employees

Age of Aquarius, 180

Agent Orange, 169

Agnew, Spiro, 195–96, 205, 215–16

Aid to Families with Dependent Children
    Program, 202

Aidid, Mohammed Farah, 339

AIDS (acquired immune deficiency syndrome),
    301, 333

AIM. *See* American Indian Movement

AIP. *See* American Independence Party

Airlines, 265–67

Alabama, 65, 108–9, 145–47, 159

Alabama National Guard, 147, 159

Albania, 353

Albright, Madeleine, 355

Alcatraz Island, 208

Alcohol, 281

Ali, Muhammad, 185

Allen, Gracie, 95

Allende Gossens, Salvador, 236

Alliance for Progress, 132, 152

al-Qaeda, 373–77

Altamont concert, 181

AMA. *See* American Medical Association

"America the Beautiful," 1, 374

America Online (AOL), 324

American Communist Party, 71

American Express, 79

American Federation of Labor (AFL), 6, 60

American Federation of State, County, and
    Municipal Employees (AFSCME), 83

American Independence Party (AIP), 195

American Indian Movement (AIM), 208

American Institute for Free Labor, 236

American Medical Association (AMA), 68,
    158

American University, 138

Amos 'n Andy, 22

Anderson, John, 257, 259

Anderson, Rudolph, 137

Antelope, Oregon, 279–80

Appalachian Regional Development Act, 157–58

Apple, 267

Aquino, Corazon, 308

Arab-Israeli conflicts, 116–18, 163–64, 233–34,
    252–53, 309

Arafat, Yasir, 309

Arbenz, Jacob, 115–16

Arden, Eve, 95

Area Development Act (1961), 143

Arizona, 82

Arkansas, 107, 162

Arms race, 224–25

Army of the Republic of Vietnam (ARVN), 172,
    174, 229

Arnaz, Desi, 95

Arness, James, 95

ARPANET, 324

ARVN. *See* Army of the Republic of Vietnam

Asia, 26, 111, 132, 293–94. *See also* Southeast
    Asia; Southwest Asia

Asian Americans, 268–69, 329, 359, 363
    racism and, 13–17, 21
    during WW II, 13–17

Asian Indians, 364

Astronauts, 141

Aswan Dam, 117

ATF. *See* Federal Bureau of Alcohol, Tobacco,
    and Firearms

Atlanta, Georgia, 86, 144–45

Atlanta University, 144

Atomic Age, 35–36

Atomic bomb, 31–34, 36. *See also* Manhattan
    District Project

Atomic Energy Act, 35

Atomic Energy Commission (AEC), 35

Australia, 113

Automakers, 62, 79–80, 210, 243

Automobiles, 77, 79–80, 159–60, 265, 281

The Autobiography of Malcolm X (Haley), 185

Axis power, 1–2, 7, 10

Baby and Child Care (Spock), 89

Baez, Joan, 147

Baghdad Pact, 117

Baker, Howard, 214, 315

Baker, James A., 287, 300–301

Baker v. Carr, 162–63

Bakke, Allen, 270

Bakker, Jim, 278–79

Bakker, Tammy Faye, 278

Ball, Lucille, 95

Bandung, Indonesia, 114–15

Bangladesh, 236, 364

Bao Dai, 46

Barnett, Ross, 146

Baruch, Bernard, 35

Baseball, 20, 283

"Basic Principles of U.S.-Soviet Relations," 225

Batista, Fulgencio, 120

Battle of Britain, 22

Bay of Pigs, 131–32
Baylor University, 38
Beatles, 180
Beats, 99, 179
Begin, Menachem, 252–53
Benny, Jack, 95
Bentsen, Lloyd, 316–17
Berle, Milton, 95
Berlin, 30
    Agreement, 225
    Airlift/blockade, 133
    Khrushchev and, 122, 133–34, 152
    Wall, 132–34, 152, 320
    West, 122, 133–34, 336
Bernstein, Carl, 213
Berry, Chuck, 98
Bhagwan Rajneesh Maharishi Yogi, 279–80
Biden, Joseph, 314
Big Three, 27
Bikini atoll, 36
Bill Haley and the Comets, 97
Billings, Robert, 279
bin Laden, Osama, 355, 372–73, 378
Bionic Women, 274
Birmingham, Alabama, 146–47
Black, Hugo, 146
Black Muslims, 185
Black power, 185–87
Black Sea, 37
Blackmun, Harry, 162, 206–7
Blair, Linda, 282
Blatty, William, 282
Blix, Hans, 379, 380
Blough, Roger, 143
"Blowing in the Wind," 180
"Blue Suede Shoes," 98
Blythe, California, 1
Boeing, 345
Boesky, Ivan, 303
Bogart, Humphrey, 22

Bolshevik Revolution, 27
Bond, Julian, 161
Bond v. Floyd, 161
Books, 20, 99–100
Boone, Pat, 98
Boone, Richard, 95
Bork, Robert, 216, 307
Bosch, Juan, 164–66
Bosnia, 353–55
Boston, 204
Boy Scouts, 71
Boyer, Paul, 36
Braceros (laborers), 12
Bradley, Bill, 366
Bradley, Omar, 51
Branch Davidians, 356
Brando, Marlon, 282
Brandt, Willy, 237
Brannan, Charles F., 68
Brave Men (Pyle), 20
Brazil, 178
Brennan, William, 334
Breyer, Stephen, 369
Brezhnev, Leonid, 225, 234, 245, 293
Bridges, Styles, 45
Brinkley, Douglas, 366
Brinkmanship, 111
Brown Berets, 208–8
Brown, James, 186
Brown, Jerry, 247
Brown power, 187
Brown v. the Board of Education of Topeka,
    107–8
Browne, Harry, 366, 367
Bryant, Anita, 272
Brzezinski, Zbigniew, 251, 254
Buchanan, Pat, 365–67, 368
Buddhism, 140, 279
Bulganin, Nikolai, 115
Bulgaria, 29

Bunche, Ralph, 116
Bundy, McGeorge, 130
Burford, Anne Gorsuch, 288
Burger, Warren, 205, 307
Burma, 139
Burns, George, 95
Bush, George H. W., 242, 316–18
    Persian Gulf War and, 339–43
    presidency of, 333–43
Bush, George W., 157, 260, 365–69
    presidency of, 362, 369–84
Bush, Jeb, 369
Bush v. Gore, 369
Businesses, 17–19
Busing, 203–6, 289
Bustamente, Cruz, 363
Butterfield, Alexander, 215
Byrnes, James F., 5

Cable News Network (CNN), 340, 380
Caen, Herb, 99
Caesar, Sid, 95
California, 1, 87–88, 156, 176–79, 270, 321
    consciousness revolution in, 279
    elections in, 249
    industries, 82, 187
    population of, 3–4, 12, 13, 78, 359, 363
    Silicon Valley in, 267, 322–23, 374
    Southern, 3–4, 12
    during WW II, 3–4
Calley, William, 229–30
Cambodia, 113, 228–30, 246, 269
Camelot, 150–52
Camp David Accords, 252–53
Camp Poston, 1
Campfire Girls, 71
Canada, 41, 70, 144, 172
Cape Canaveral, 141
Capitalism, 23
Capra, Frank, 21

Caribbean, 164–65
Carle, Frankie, 20
Carmichael, Stokely, 185, 190
Carnegie Endowment for International Peace, 71
Carney, Art, 95
Carson, Rachel, 209
Carter, Amy, 258
Carter Center, 259
Carter Doctrine, 254
Carter, James Earl, Jr. (Jimmy), 248–49, 257–60
    foreign policies of, 251–60
    on Iran, 255–57
    presidency of, 249–51
Carter, Rosalyn, 249
Casablanca (movie), 22
Casey, William, 310
Cassius Clay. See Ali, Muhammad
Castro, Fidel, 120–21, 130–31, 242
Catcher in the Rye (Salinger), 99–100
Catholic Church, 68, 140
    Legion of Decency, 21
Catholics, 127, 129, 158, 277
CBS, 94–95
CBS Evening News, 256
CCC. See Civilian Conservation Corps
CEA. See Council of Economic Advisers
Censorship, 21, 22–23
Central America, 115–16, 296
Central High School, 107
Central Intelligence Agency (CIA), 39, 115–16,
    374–75
    operations, 131–32, 166, 236, 242, 296
Chafe, William, 91
Chambers, Whittaker, 72
Chamorro, Violetta, 338
Chao, Elaine, 369
Charles, Ray, 98
Charlie's Angels, 274
Charlotte-Mecklenburg school system, 203
Chavez, Cesar, 187

Cheney, Dick, 366–67, 378

Chevrolet, 80

Chicago, 1, 3, 193–94, 362

Chicago Seven, 205

Child care centers, 9

Children, 9, 365

Chile, 236–37, 253

China, 5, 21, 293–94, 380

    civil war in, 37, 44–46

    Communism in, 37, 44–47, 166, 224

    Cultural Revolution in, 226

    Eisenhower on, 113–15

    Korean War and, 48–53

    Lobby, 45–46

    Nationalists in, 37, 44–45, 48, 113

    U.N. and, 226–27

    U.S. and, 113–15, 226–28, 338

    Vietnam and, 47

    White Paper, 44–45

    during WW II, 26–27, 31

Chinese Americans, 16–17, 364. *See also* Asian

    Americans

Chinese Exclusion Act, 17

Chomsky, Noam, 374

Christian Broadcasting network, 278

Christians, 191, 253, 277–79, 286–87

Church, Frank, 247

Churches, 92

Churchill, Winston, 27–30, 34–35, 111

CIA. *See* Central Intelligence Agency

CIO. *See* Congress of Industrial Organizations

Cities, 3–4, 11, 158, 204–5

City of Richmond v. J. A. Croson Company,

    307

Civil rights, 191–92

    movement, 183–92

    in U.S., 62–65, 67, 106–9, 144–48

Civil Rights Act of 1957, 109, 145

Civil Rights Bill of 1964, 157

    Title VII of, 190

Civil Rights Commission, 109

Civil unions, 330

Civilian Conservation Corps (CCC), 17

Clark, Wesley, 353–54

Clean Air Act, 159

Cleveland, 363

Cleveland, Grover, 249

Clifford, Clark, 173–74

Clinton, Hillary Rodham, 344, 346, 348

Clinton, William Jefferson (Bill), 69, 330

    impeachment of, 348–52

    as president, 344–48, 352–56

CNBC, 380

CNN. *See Cable News Network*

Coca, Imogeen, 95

Cocaine, 301

Cold War, 18, 23. *See also* Korean War; Marshall

    Plan; Truman Doctrine

    during 1960s, 163–66

    consensus, 53–54

    domestic, 69–75, 101

    in Europe, 122

    Germany and, 27

    Japan and, 27, 30, 42, 239

    nuclear arms race during, 35–37, 58, 115

    origins of, 26–37

    post, 335–39

    revived, 291–93, 314–16

    Soviet Union and, 27–35, 40–42, 47, 49,

        51–54, 69–75, 109–11, 122, 239,

        254–55

College Board Scholastic Aptitude Tests (SAT),

    363

Colleges, 87, 276–77

Colonizations, 26, 37

Columbia University, 96, 177–79

Columbine High School, 356

Committee on Civil Rights, 63–64

Committee to Re-elect the President (CREEP),

    211–14

Communism, 24, 26. *See also* McCarthy, Joseph;
        Red Scare; Soviet Union
    anti-, 56, 69–75, 106, 224–26
    in Asia, 111
    in China, 37, 44–46, 166, 224
    CIA and, 116
    containment of, 39, 42, 45–46, 53–54
    New Look and, 109–11
    threat of, 37–39
    unions and, 60–61
Communist parties, 26, 39, 70
Computers, 265–67, 362
Concorde, 238
Confederacy, 107
Conference on Security and Cooperation in
        Europe, 245
Congress of Industrial Organizations (CIO), 6,
        11, 19, 71. *See also* Political Action
        Committee
Congress of Racial Equality (CORE), 145
Connally, John, 149
Connally, Nellie, 149
Connecticut, 162
Connor, Eugene (Bull), 146
Conservatives, 155, 160, 287, 347–48
Consumerism, 7, 209–10, 262, 264
Contras, 296, 309–14
Copacabana, 20
Coplon, Judith, 72
Coppola, Francis Ford, 282
Corporations, 17
Costa Rica, 309
Council of Economic Advisers (CEA), 57
Counterculture, 179–83
Cox, Archibald, 213, 216
Credit, 79
CREEP. *See* Committee to Re-elect the President
Croats, 353
Cronkite, Walter, 256
Crosby, Bing, 21
Crusade in Europe (Eisenhower), 103

Cuba
    Eisenhower on, 120–21
    Guantanamo Bay, 377
    missile crisis and, 134–38
    Soviets and, 121, 134–38
    U.S. and, 120–21, 134–38, 260
Cuban Americans, 363
Cushing, Richard Cardinal, 150
Custer Died for Your Sins (Deloria), 187
Cyberspace, 324
Czechoslovakia, 29, 40, 164

Daley, Richard, 193–94
Dallas, 148–50
Dallek, Robert, 140
Danang, 167–68
Dar es Salaam, 355
Dardanelles, 37
Darien, port of, 28
Dasmascus, 233
Day, Doris, 90
de Gaulle, Charles, 163
Dean, John, 213–15
Deaver, Michael, 301, 314
Defense of Marriage Act, 330
DeKlerk, Frederick, 338–39
Deloria, Vine, Jr., 187
Democratic Convention
    in Chicago, 193–94, 205
    of 1948, 65
Democratic Party, 19, 363, 371
    during 1946, 59–60
    during 1948, 65–67
    during 1982, 290
    Dixiecrats in, 65, 66
    liberalism in, 58, 104
    National Headquarters, 212
    in 1970s, 210–11, 242, 247–49
    in 1960s, 126, 130, 141, 156–57,
        192–97
    Southern, 17, 64–65, 148, 156–57

Democratic Socialist Republic of Germany. *See*
    East Germany

Dental care, 4

Des Plaines, Illinois, 88

Detente, 140, 152, 223–26
    decline of, 251–55
    extension of, 244–45

Detroit, 3, 11
    automakers, 79–80
    riots, 184

Dewey, Thomas E., 18–19, 65–67

Dewitt, John, 13

Dien Bien Phu, 111

Dies, Martin, 69

Diners' Club, 79

Discrimination. *See also* Racism
    in federal government, 64–65
    gender, 8–9, 205–8
    labor, 12
    against women, 205–7, 272–75

Disney, Walt, 88

Disneyland, 88

Divorces, 275

"Do the Job HE Left Behind," 8

Dobrynin, Anatoly, 137, 224

Doby, Larry, 63

Dole, Robert, 248, 316, 348

Dominican Republic, 164–65

Domino, Fats, 98

Domino theory, 37–38, 141

Dorsey, Tommy, 20

"Double V" campaign, 11

Douglas, Helen Douglas, 74

Douglas, William O., 162

Doves, 171–72, 242

Dow Chemical, 80

Dow Jones Index, 322

Drugs, 180–83, 205, 301–2, 333

Du Pont, 80

Duarte, Jose Napoleon, 297

Dubinski, David, 58

Dukakis, Michael, 316–18

Dulles, John Foster, 103, 105, 109, 113

Dutch, 26, 37, 115

Dylan, Bob, 180

Eagle Forum, 207

Earthlink, 324

East Germany (Democratic Socialist Republic of
    Germany), 28, 41, 133, 336

East Village, 179

Eastern Bloc, 224

Ecology, 209–10

Economists, 57

Ed Sullivan Show, 98

Eden, Anthony, 115

Education Amendment of 1972, Title IX, 207

EEC. *See* European Economic Community

EEOC. *See* Equal Employment Opportunity
    Commission

Egypt, 117–18, 163–64, 233–34, 243, 252–53

Eisenhower, Dwight D., 18, 52
    adminstration of, 101–4, 111–13, 118–20,
        122–24, 133
    on China, 113–15
    on Cuba, 120–21
    elections of, 65, 101–3

El Salvador, 187, 253, 296–97, 309

Elementary and Secondary Education Act (1965),
    158

Ellsberg, Daniel, 230

Employment, 57, 264–65, 273
    during WW II, 3–4, 5–6, 7–9

Employment Act (1946), 57

Energy crisis, 243–44, 250

Engel v. Vitale, 162

England, 6

Enola Gay, 32

Environmental Protection Agency (EPA), 209

Environmentalism, 24, 244, 332–33

Equal Employment Opportunity Commission
    (EEOC), 190

Equal Rights Amendment (ERA), 207–8, 257, 289

Erhard Seminars Training (est), 279

Erlichman, John, 213, 215, 217

Ervin, Sam J., 213

Esalen Institute, 279

Europe, 116, 122, 144, 226

    Central, 37

    Eastern, 27, 30, 34–37, 40, 109

    economies of, 40

    Jews in, 116, 226, 245

    post WW II, 26–37, 39–40

    Soviet Union and, 34–35, 224

    U.S. and, 37–40, 237–38

    Western, 24, 27, 43

European Common Market, 144, 237, 337

European Economic Community (ECC), 237–38

The Exorcist, 282

Face the Nation, 72

Fair Deal, 68–69, 160

Falwell, Jerry, 278–79, 374

Family Assistance Plan, 202

Far East, 26, 34, 47, 253

Farming, 6, 81–82, 304

Farnham, Marynia, 90

Fascism, 53

Father Knows Best, 97

Faubus, Orville, 107

Faure, Edgar, 115

FBI. *See* U.S. Federal Bureau of Investigation

FCC. *See* Federal Communications Commission

FDP. *See* West Germany

Federal Bureau of Alcohol, Tobacco, and
    Firearms (ATF), 356

Federal Communications Commission (FCC), 95

Federal Energy Office, 243

Federal Republic of Germany. *See* West Germany

Federal Reserve Board, 82, 249, 287

Federal Savings and Loan Insurance Corporation
    (FSLIC), 304

Federal Trade Commission, 143

Feminine Mystique (Friedan), 189–90

Feminism, 9, 62, 188–91, 207–8

FEPC. *See* President's Fair Employment
    Practices Committee

Ferraro, Geraldine, 300

Fighting Seabees (movie), 21

Filipino Americans, 268, 364. *See also* Asian
    Americans

Fillmore West, 180

Finland, 245

Fisher, Carrie, 282

Flanders, Ralph, 105

Flesch, Rudolf, 119

Florida, 3, 78, 82, 120, 141

    2000 election in, 367–69

Florida State Supreme Court, 369

Flying Tigers (movie), 21

Fonda, Henry, 20

Fonda, Jane, 208

Food stamps, 202

Forbidden City, 227

Ford, Gerald R., 216, 220, 233, 248–49

    economic policies of, 242–44

    foreign policies of, 244–47

    presidency of, 241–42, 260

Ford, Mary, 97

Ford Motor Company, 130, 362

Formosa, 47, 49, 113. *See also* Taiwan

Fort Knox, 34

Fort Monmouth, 105

The Fountainhead (Rand), 20

442nd Regimental Combat Engineers, 15

Fox News, 380

France, 21, 117, 224, 380

    Communist Party in, 26

    post WW II, 26–28, 38, 39–40

    Vietnam and, 46–47, 111–13

Fred Korematsu v. the United States, 13–15, 16

Freed, Allen, 97

Freud, Sigmund, 90
Friedan, Betty, 189
Friedman, Milton, 203
Frontero v. Richardson, 206
FSLIC. *See* Federal Savings and Loan Insurance
    Corporation
Fuchs, Klaus, 33, 75
Fulbright, William, 171

Gable, Clark, 20
Gagarin, Yuri, 140
Galbraith, John Kenneth, 94
Gates, Bill, 322
Gays, 21, 188, 330, 344–45
Gaza Strip, 117
General Motors, 58–59, 82
Geneva Accords, 112–13, 138, 154
Geneva summit conference, 115
Georgia, 144–45
Georgia House of Representatives, 161
Gephardt, Richard, 316
Germany, 20, 24, 337. *See also* East Germany;
    West Germany
    Cold War/U.S., 27–30
    industries in, 243
    occupation of, 27, 40–41
    post WW II, 26–28, 37–38
    reparations by, 28, 30–31
    surrender by, 33
Ghobanifar, Manucher, 310
G.I. Bill of Rights, 11, 12, 19, 57
Gideon, Clarence, 162
Gideon v. Wainwright, 162
Gillespie, April, 339
Gingrich, Newt, 347
Ginsberg, Allen, 99, 179
Ginsburg, Douglas, 307
Gleason, Jackie, 95
Glenn, John H., Jr., 141
Global positing system (GPS), 382

Globalization, 362
Goals for Americans, 123
Godfrey, Arthur, 95
The Godfather, 282
Golan Heights, 163–64, 233, 252
Gold, Harry, 33, 75
Goldberg, Arthur, 143
Golden State. *See* California
Goldman, Ron, 326–27
Goldwater, Barry, 128, 156–57, 199, 287
Goodman, Paul, 94
Gorbachev, Mikhail, 293, 314–16, 335–36, 340
Gore, Albert, 316, 344, 365–69
GPS. *See* Global positing system
Grable, Betty, 21
Graham, Bill, 180
Gramm, Phil, 288
Gramm-Rudman Act, 303
Grand Alliance, 23–24, 27, 30
Grateful Dead, 180
Gray, L. Patrick, III, 213
Great Britain, 5, 21, 75, 115, 375–77, 379–82
    colonies of, 37, 117
    post WW II, 26–27, 30, 34, 39–40
    Vietnam and, 112–13
Great Bull Market, 302, 361
Great Crash, 5
Great Crash of 1929, 5, 374
Great Depression, 2, 6–7, 17, 23
Great Society, 68, 154–74
Greece, 37–39, 54
Green Party, 365
Green, William, 61
Greenglass, David, 33, 75
Greenhouse gases, 370
Greening of America (Reich), 181
Greensboro, North Carolina, 144
Greenwich Village, 99
Grenada, 297–98
Griswald v. Connecticut, 162

Groves, Leslie, 31
Growing Up Absurd (Goodman), 94
Grutter V. Bollinger, 371
Guatemala, 115–16, 131–32
Guiliani, Rudolph, 374
Gulf coasts, 3
Gulf of Tonkin, 166, 168
Gunsmoke, 95

Habib, Philip, 294
Haig, Alexander, 218
Haight-Ashbury district, 181
Haiti, 260
Haldeman, H.R. (Bob), 213, 215, 217–18
Haley, Alex, 185
Hamill, Mark, 282
Hanoi, 170
Hare Krishna, 180
Harlem, 11, 178
Harriman, Averill, 30, 138
Harrington, Michael, 161
Harris, Eric, 356
Harris, Katherine, 369
Harrison, Ford, 282
Hart, Gary, 314
Have Gun Will Travel, 95
Hawaii, 16, 330
Hawks, 171–72, 242
Hayden, Casey, 190
Hayek, Friedrich, 20
Hayworth, Rita, 21
Health care, 4, 78, 346–47
Health maintenance organizations (HMOs), 346
"Heartbreak Hotel," 98
Helsinki, Finland, 245
Herbicides, 169
Heroin, 301
Hersey, John, 20
Herzegovina, 353–55
HEW. *See* U.S. Department of Health, Education, and Welfare

Hickel, Walter, 209
Hideki Tojo, 27
Highway Trust Fund, 104
Hill, Anita, 334
Hippies, 179–83, 283
Hirohito (Emperor), 32
Hiroshima, 31–32, 115
Hispanic American(s), 3, 267–68. *See also* Brown Berets; Brown power
    households, 85, 299, 328, 362–64
    voters, 159, 209, 259
    during WW II, 12
Hiss, Alger, 71–72
Hitler, Adolf, 27, 38
HMOs. *See* Health maintenance organizations
Ho Chi Minh, 46, 113, 168
Hodgson, Godfrey, 101
Hoff, Ted, 267
Hoffman, Julius, 205
Holbrooke, Richard, 353
Hollinger, David, 330
Hollywood, 20–23, 179
    Ten's, 70–71
Holocaust, 116
Homosexuality, 21, 188
Honduras, 296
The Honeymooners, 95
Hong Kong, 268
Hood, James, 147
Hoover, Herbert, 251
Hoover, J. Edgar, 242
Hope, Bob, 21
"Hound Dog," 98
House Committee on Un-American Activities (HUAC), 69–72
Housing and Home Finance Agency, 145
Hudson River Valley, 181
Human rights, 251
Humphrey, George, 103
Humphrey, Hubert, 127, 193–97, 210
Hungary, 29, 118, 336

Hunt, E. Howard, 211
Hussein, Saddam, 308, 339–43, 378–82
Huston, John, 21

I Love Lucy, 95
IBM. *See* International Business Machines
ICBM. *See* Missiles
ICC. *See* Interstate Commerce Commission
ILGWU. *See* International Ladies' Garment
    Workers' Union
Illinois, 4, 88
IMF. *See* International Monetary Fund
Immigration Act (1965), 158–59, 267–69
"In God We Trust," 92
India, 37, 139, 235–36, 268, 364
Indians, Lakota Sioux, 208
Individual Retirement Accounts (IRAs), 370
Indochina, 37
Indochina War, 111, 113, 238, 239, 245–47
Indonesia, 114–15
Industrial Revolution, 23
INF. *See* Intermediate Nuclear Forces
Inflation, 6–7, 58, 262
    rate of, 79, 242–43
Intel Corporation, 267
Intermediate Nuclear Forces (INF) Treaty, 316
Internal Revenue Service (IRS), 214
International Business Machines (IBM), 81, 322
International Ladies' Garment Workers' Union
    (ILGWU), 58
International Monetary Fund (IMF), 35
International Telephone and Telegraph (ITT), 79
Interstate Commerce Commission (ICC), 145
Interstate Highway Act, 104
Iran, 115, 117, 234–35
    Iraq and, 257, 308–9
    U.S. and, 255–57
Iran-Contra scandal, 296–97, 309–14
Iraq, 117
    Iran and, 257, 308–9
    war with, 339–43, 378–84

IRAs. *See* Individual Retirement Accounts
Ireland, Patricia, 334
Iron Curtain, 35, 43
IRS. *See* Internal Revenue Service
Islam, 118
Israel, 309, 343
    Egypt and, 117–18, 163–64, 233–34,
        252–53
    Soviet Union and, 116–18
    Syria and, 163–64, 295
    U.S. and, 116–18, 243, 252–53
Italy, 38
ITT. *See* International Telephone and Telegraph
Ives, Burl, 71
Ivy League, 176

Jackson, Henry (Scoop), 226, 245, 247
Jackson, Jesse, 300
Jackson-Vanik Amendment, 226
Japan, 47, 139, 293–94
    atomic bomb and, 31–34
    Cold War/U.S. and, 27, 30, 42, 239
    industries in, 243, 338
    post WW II, 26–27
    surrender by, 1, 23, 32, 51
    during WW II, 2, 13, 28, 31
Japanese Americans, 1, 3, 268. *See also* Asian
        Americans
    restitution for, 16
    during WW II, 13–17, 18, 21
Jarvis, Howard, 249
Jaworski, Leon, 216–17
Jaws, 282
Jefferson Airplane, 180
Jeffords, Jim, 370–71
Jews, 21, 31
    European, 116, 226, 245
Jiang Jieshi, 44, 50
Jobs, Steve, 267
John Birch Society, 155
Johnson, Claudia (Lady Bird), 159

Johnson, Lyndon, 106, 119
    foreign policies of, 163–66
    Great Society and, 157–61
    1964 election of, 155–57
    presidency of, 148–49, 152–53
    as Senate majority leader, 109, 127
    on Vietnam, 166–74
Joplin, Janis, 180
Jordan, 118, 163–64
Jou En-lai, 115, 228
Judd, Walter, 45
Judges, 306–7

Kaczynski, Theodore, 356
Kampuchea. *See* Cambodia
Kaplan, Robert D., 384
Karzai, Hamid, 376
Kazan, Elia, 71
Keaton, Diane, 282
Kemp, Jack, 288
Kennan, George, 38, 246
Kennedy, Anthony, 307
Kennedy, Edward (Ted), 257
Kennedy, Jacqueline Bouvier, 152
Kennedy, John F., 49, 60
    assassination of, 148–50, 372
    Bay of Pigs and, 131–32
    as cold warrior, 130
    elections and, 126–30
    missile crisis and, 134–38
    presidency of, 140–52
    on Vietnam, 138–40
Kennedy, Robert, 83, 193, 197
    as attorney general, 130, 131, 135–37
Kent State Massacre, 229
Kenya, 355
Kerouac, Jack, 99
Kesey, Ken, 181
Keynes, John Maynard, 6
Khomeini, Ayatollah Ruholla, 255–57

Khrushchev, Nikita, 117, 120
    Berlin and, 122, 133–34, 152
    missile crisis and, 134–38
Kim Il-Sung, 48
Kimball, Penn, 85
King, Martin Luther, Jr., 108–9, 129, 152, 197
    SCLC and, 144–48, 185–86
    surveillance of, 242
King, Mary, 190
King, Rodney, 324–27
Kinsey, Alfred, 99
Kirkpatrick, Jeanne, 289
Kissinger, Henry, 218, 223–26, 233–36, 239–40
    Ford and, 244–45
KLA. *See* Kosovo Liberation Army
Klebold, Dylan, 356
Knoxville, Tennessee, 156
Kokura, 32
Korea, 32, 47, 268. *See also* North Korea; South
    Korea
Korean War, 47–48
    38th parallel and, 49–50
    China during, 48–53
    U.S. and, 48–53, 64–65
Koresh, David, 356
Kosovo, 353–55
Kosovo Liberation Army (KLA), 353, 355
Kroc, Ray, 87–88
Krug, Julius, 59
Ku Klux Klan, 148
Kurile Islands, 28
Kuwait, 339–41
Kyoto Protocols, 370

Labor, 6, 58–59, 82–83
Labor Management Relations Act. *See*
    Taft-Hartley Act
Ladies' Republican Club of Wheeling, 72
Laird, Melvin, 229
Lamour, Dorothy, 21

Landrum-Griffin Act in 1959, 83

Laos, 113, 138, 269

Laser Guided Bombs (LGBs), 382

Latin America, 121, 131–32, 253, 338

Latin Quarter, 20

Lattimore, Owens, 73–74

Lawrence v. Texas, 371

LBOs. *See* Leveraged buyouts

Le Duc Tho, 232

Leary, Timothy, 180

Lebanon, 294–96, 307

Lemay, Curtis, 195

Lenin, Vladimir, 27

Lesbians, 21, 188, 272, 330, 344–45

Letter from Birmingham (King), 147

Leveraged buyouts (LBOs), 303

Levitt, William, 85

Levittowns, 85

Lewinsky, Monica, 349–50

Lewis, Drew, 288

Lewis, John L., 59

LGBs. *See* Laser Guided Bombs

Liberia, 253

Libertarian Party, 366

Libertarians, 286

Liddy, G. Gordon, 211

Life, 90, 122

Lippmann, Walter, 39

Little, Malcolm. *See* Malcolm X

Little Richard, 98

Littleton, Colorado, 356

Lockheed, 345

Lon Nol, 229

London, 28, 178

Lonely Crowd (Riesman), 93

Long Island, 85

Longsworth, Alice Roosevelt, 19

Los Alamos, New Mexico, 31

Los Angeles, 94, 324–27, 359, 362

Los Angeles Times, 352

Lost Weekend (movie), 22

LSD, 180–81

Lublin, 28

Lucas, George, 282

Lucky Strike Hit Parade, 22

MacArthur, Douglas, 27, 32, 48–51

MAD. *See* Mutually Assured Destruction

Magazines, 19–20

Malaysia, 239, 293

Malcolm X, 150, 185

Male chauvinism, 190

Malone, Vivian, 147

Manchuria, 28, 31

Mandela, Nelson, 339

Manhattan District Project, 31–33

Manpower Retraining Act (1962), 143

The Man in the Gray Flannel Suit (Wilson), 93

Mao Zedong, 44–45, 226–28

Marcos, Ferdinand, 308

Marijuana, 181, 282, 301–2

Marriages, 275, 330, 360

Marshall, Burke, 145

Marshall, George C., 40, 44

Marshall Plan, 39–40, 42–43, 54

Marshall, Thurgood, 107, 109, 145, 185, 334

Martin, Joseph, 51

Martinez, Mel, 369

Marx, Groucho, 95

Mary Tyler Moore Show, 274

Maryland, 215

Mayaguez, 245

McCain, John, 354, 366

McCalls, 92

McCarran Internal Security Act (1950), 74

McCarthy, Joseph, 46, 60, 72–75, 102, 104–5

McClellan, John, 83

McCord, James, 213

McCorvey, Norma, 205

McDonald, Dick, 88

McDonald, Mac, 88

McDonald's, 88, 265

McDonnell-Douglas, 345

McFarlane, Robert, 310, 312

McGovern, George, 210–11, 220, 232

McGrath, J. Howard, 74

McNamara, Robert S., 130, 132–33, 135–37, 167, 173

McVeigh, Timothy, 356

Meany, George, 82

Media, 174, 191, 239, 380–82

Medicaid, 158, 160, 202

Medicare, 158, 160, 259

Mediterranean, 37

Meese, Edwin, 299, 300, 311, 314

Meir, Golda, 233

Memphis, Tennessee, 156

Men, 2–3, 9–12, 360

MEOW. *See* Moral equivalent of war

Meredith, James, 145–46, 185

Mexican-Americans. *See* Hispanic Americans

Mexico, 187, 268

Michigan, 4

Microprocessors, 267

Microsoft, 322

Middle East, 26, 37–38, 154

accords, 252–53

dilemma, 233–36

Milken, Michael, 303

Milland, Ray, 22

Milliken v. Bradley, 204

Mills, C. Wright, 94

Milosevic, Slobodan, 353–54

Mineta, Norman, 369

Miranda, Ernesto, 162

Miranda v. Arizona, 162

MIRV. *See* Missiles

Missiles

anti-ballistics (ABM), 224, 225

Cruise, 292

intercontinental ballistics (ICBM), 118, 133, 226

multiple, independently targeted reentry vehicle (MIRV), 224, 225

Pershing II, 254, 292

Mission to Moscow (movie), 21

Mississippi, 65, 145–46

Freedom Summer, 177

Missouri gang, 56

Mitchell, John, 213, 215, 217

Modern Woman: The Lost Sex (Farnham), 90

Molotov, V. M., 29

Mondale, Walter, 299–300

Monday Night Football, 274

Mongolia, 28

Monroe, Marilyn, 90

Montgomery, Alabama, 108, 145, 159

Moral equivalent of war (MEOW), 250

Moral Majority, 278–79

Morgan, Robin, 191

Moss, George Donelson, 1–2

Mossadegh, Mohammed, 115

Moussani, Zacarias, 375

Movies, 19–20, 20–22, 90, 282

Ms. (magazine), 207

Mumford, Lewis, 85

Mundt, Karl, 105

Murphy, Frank, 15

Murrow, Edward R., 22

Musharraf, Pervez, 375

Muskie, Edmund, 193, 210

Muslims, 253, 294–96, 353

Mutually Assured Destruction (MAD), 293

My Lai massacre, 229–30

NAACP. *See* National Association for the Advancement of Colored People

Nader, Ralph, 159–60, 210, 365, 367

NAFTA. *See* North American Free Trade Agreement

Nagasaki, 32, 115

Nagy, Imre, 117

Nairobi, 355

NASA. *See* National Aeronautics and Space Administration

Nasser, Gamal Abdul, 117, 163–64, 233–34

National Advisory Commission on Civil Disobedience184-185

National Aeronautics and Space Administration (NASA), 120, 140

    Mercury and, 141

    Project Apollo and, 141

National Air Quality Standards Act, 209

National Association for the Advancement of Colored People (NAACP), 11, 63–65, 107, 109

National Association of Manufacturers, 9

National Basketball Association (NBA), 284

National Collegiate Athletic Association (NCAA), 283

National Commission on Excellence in Education, 276

National Defense Education Act (NDEA), 119

National Endowment for the Arts, 330

National Endowment for the Humanities, 330

National Farm Workers Association (NFWA), 187

National Football League (NFL), 284

National Goals Commission, 122–24

National Housing Act, 68

National League, 63

National Liberation Front (NLF), 167, 170, 232

National Organization of Women (NOW), 190, 207, 335

National Press Club, 172

National Rifle Association (NRA), 356

National Security Act (1947), 39

National Security Council (NSC), 39, 47, 231

    Document Number 68 (NSC-68), 47, 49

National Wilderness Preservation Act, 159

Native American Rights Fund, 187

Native Americans, 1, 13, 21, 208, 327. *See also* Red power

NATO. *See* North Atlantic Treaty Organization

Nazi Party, 27

NBA. *See* National Basketball Association

NBC, 22, 94–95

NCAA. *See* National Collegiate Athletic Association

NDEA. *See* National Defense Education Act

New Deal, 5–6, 104

    coalition, 66

    policies/reforms, 4, 17–18, 60, 160

    Second, 60

New Dealers, 65

New Federalism, 202

New Frontier, 68, 141–43, 154

New Hampshire, 366

New Jersey, 85, 86, 184

New Left, 179, 183, 198

New Look, 109–11

New Right, 155–56

New York, 1, 4, 359, 362

New York City, 3, 179

New York Metropolitan Opera, 22

New York Stock Exchange, 322

New York Times, 122, 230–31, 352

New York Times Magazine, 85

New York Times v. Sullivan, 161–62

New Zealand, 113

Newark, 86, 184

Newspapers, 19–20

NFL. *See* National Football League

NFWA. *See* National Farm Workers Association

Ngo Dinh Diem, 113, 138–40, 166

Nguyen, Jean, 269

Nguyen Van Thieu, 169, 232

Nicaragua, 187, 259, 296–97, 309, 338

Nichols, Terry, 356

Nigeria, 253

Nightline, 256

Nixon Doctrine, 224–26, 240

Nixon, Richard, 46, 60, 74
   foreign policies of, 223–40
   HUAC and, 70, 72
   in 1960s, 126–30, 194–99
   pardon of, 241–42
   presidency of, 201–20
   resignation of, 69
   southern strategy of, 203–7
   as vice-president, 102–3
   Watergate and, 212–20
NLF. *See* National Liberation Front
Noonan, Peggy, 300
Noriega, Manuel, 338
North American Free Trade Agreement
   (NAFTA), 346, 353
North Atlantic Treaty Organization (NATO),
   40–44, 54, 122
   allies, 163, 224, 237, 353–55, 373
North Carolina, 129, 144, 203
North Carolina Agricultural and Technological
   College, 144
North Korea, 47–53, 260
North, Oliver, 310–14
North Vietnam, 113, 166–74, 228–33
Norton, Gale, 369
NOW. *See* National Organization of Women
NRA. *See* National Rifle Association
NSC. *See* National Security Council
NSC-68. *See* National Security Council
Nuclear Non-Proliferation Treaty, 224
Nuclear Test Ban Treaty, 224
Nuremberg trials, 27

Oakland, California, 177
OAS. *See* Organization of American States
O'Connor, Sandra Day, 289, 306
ODALE. *See* Office for Drug Abuse and Law
   Enforcement
OECD. *See* Organization of Economic Coopera-
   tion and Development
Office for Drug Abuse and Law Enforcement
   (ODALE), 205

Office of Economic Stabilization, 5
Office of Management and Budget, 287
Office of Price Administration (OPA), 6, 58
Office of Strategic Services (OSS), 69–70
Office of War Information (OWI), 8, 21
Ohio, 4
Oil, 115, 243–44, 264
   production, 115
Okinawa, 47
Oklahoma City bombing, 356
Old Time Gospel Hour, 278
Omar, Mullah Muhammad, 376
On the Road (Kerouac), 99
One Flew Over the Cuckoo's Nest (Kesey), 181
O'Neill, Thomas (Tip), 290
OPA. *See* Office of Price Administration
OPEC. *See* Organization of Oil Exporting
   Countries
Open Skies, 115
OPERATION ALLIED FORCE, 354–55
OPERATION DESERT SHIELD, 340–43
OPERATION IRAQI FREEDOM, 380
Operation ROLLING THUNDER, 167–68
Oppenheimer, J. Robert, 31
Oregon, 13, 279
Organization Man (Whyte), 93
Organization of American States (OAS), 121, 131
Organization of Economic Cooperation and
   Development (OECD), 144
Organization of Oil Exporting Countries (OPEC),
   234, 243
Ortega Saavedra, Daniel, 309
OSS. *See* Office of Strategic Services
Oswald, Lee Harvey, 149
The Other America (Harrington), 161
Our Miss Brooks, 95
OWI. *See* Office of War Information

PAC. *See* Political Action Committee
Pacific coasts, 3
Pacific Rim, 293–94, 338
Pacino, Al, 282

Packwood, Robert, 301
Page, Roderick, 369
Paige, Satchel, 63
Pakistan, 113, 117, 235–36, 292, 364, 375–76
Palestine, 37, 116, 164, 309
Palestine Liberation Organization (PLO), 252–53, 294
Palmer raids, 69
Panama, 253, 259, 338
Panama Canal, 253
Parent-Teacher Association (PTA), 71
Paris Accords, 239
Paris talks, 228–29, 232
Parkland Hospital, 149
Parks, Rosa, 108
PATCO (air controller's union), 288
Patel, Marilyn Hall, 16
Paterson, Thomas G., 38
Paul, Les, 97
Peace Corps, 132, 152, 176
Peale, Norman Vincent, 92
Pearl Harbor, 2, 16, 23, 372
Pennsylvania, 4, 85
Pentagon Papers, 205, 230–31
People's Revolutionary Government (PRG), 232
Peress, Irving, 105
Pesticides, 209
Philadelphia, 3
Philippines, 47, 113, 139, 268, 308
Philips v. Martin Marietta, 206
Pinochet, Augusto, 236, 338
Planned Parenthood v. Casey, 334
Pledge of Allegiance, 92
PLO. *See* Palestine Liberation Organization
Poindexter, John, 310–14
Poland, 28–30, 117, 336
Political Action Committee (PAC), 58
Pompidou, Georges, 237
Poole, Elijah, 185
Port Arthur, 28
Postdam conference, 30–31

Postethnic America: Beyond Multiculturalism (Hollinger), 330
Poverty, 7, 77
    anti, 157–58, 161
    at mid-century, 83–84
    in U.S., 83–84, 157–58, 161, 290, 305–6
Powell, Colin, 315, 362, 369–70, 373, 379–80
Powers, Francis Gary, 122
The Power Elite (Mills), 94
The Power of Positive Thinking (Peale), 92
President's Fair Employment Practices Committee (FEPC), 11
Presley, Elvis, 96, 98
PRG. *See* People's Revolutionary Government
Proctor and Gamble, 23
Progressive Party, 65, 67
Prohibition, 7
Project Independence, 243
Prophet, Elijah Muhammd. *See* Poole, Elijah
Protestants, 130, 158
PTA. *See* Parent-Teacher Association
PTL (Praise the Lord) Club, 278
Puerto Rico, 187, 328
Putin, Vladimir, 375
Puzo, Mario, 282
Pyle, Ernie, 20, 21

Quayle, J. Danforth, 316–18
Quemoy-Matsu crisis, 114–15

Racism, 3, 9–11
    African American and, 9–12, 21, 108–9, 270–71
    Asians and, 13–17, 21
    ethnicity and, 85–86
    in movies, 21
    postwar, 62–65
    riots and, 11, 12, 183–85, 324–27
    during WW II, 1, 9–11, 12, 13–17
Radicals, 176–79, 197–98
Radio, 19–20, 22–23
Rand, Ayn, 20

RAND corporation, 230

Randolph, A. Philip, 11

Ray, James Earl, 186

Rayburn, Sam, 106

Reagan, Nancy, 298, 301, 314

Reagan, Ronald, 16, 21, 70, 88, 155, 195
  economic policies of, 287–90, 302–6
  election of, 257–60, 279, 286–87, 298–300
  foreign policies of, 291–98, 307–16

Reagonomics, 287–89, 299–300

Reconstruction Finance Corporation (RFC), 69

Red Army, 32, 41

Red power, 187

Red Scare, 69

Reform Party, 365

Regan, Donald, 287, 300–301, 314

Rehnquist, William, 307, 351

Reich, Charles, 181

Reiner, Carl, 95

Religions, 77, 92–93

Religious right, 277–79

Reno, Janet, 344

Republican Convention (1952), 102

Republican National Committee, 102

Republican Party, 45, 347–48, 363, 370–71,
    377–78
  during 1946, 59–60
  during 1948, 65–67
  during 1952, 75, 101–3
  during 1982, 290
  Eastern, 156
  in 1970s, 210–12, 242, 247–49
  in 1960s, 126–27, 130, 155–57, 193–97
  Northern, 17

Reserve Officer Training Corps (ROTC), 177

Resource Recovery Act, 209

Reuther, Walter, 58

RFC. *See* Reconstruction Finance Corporation

Rhodes, John, 217

Rice, Condoleeza, 362, 370

Richardson, Elliot, 216

Richmond, 86

Rickey, Branch, 73

Ridgway, Matthew, 50

Riesman, David, 93

The Road to Serfdom (Hayek), 20

Roaring Twenties, 179

Robertson, Pat, 278–79

Robinson, Jackie, 73

"Rock Around the Clock," 97

Rock 'n' roll, 97–99, 181–83

Rockefeller Foundation, 130

Rockefeller, Nelson, 128

Roe v. Wade, 205–6, 286, 289, 334, 371

Rolling Stones, 180, 182–83

Roosevelt, Franklin D., 6, 11
  elections of, 18–19, 58, 66
  policies of, 13, 17–18, 23, 32
  at Yalta, 27–30

Rosenberg, Ethel, 75

Rosenberg, Julius, 33, 75

"Rosie the Riveter," 8

Rostenkowski, Daniel, 301

ROTC. *See* Reserve Officer Training Corps

Roth v. United States, 162

Roth, William, 288

Rowe, James, 66

Rowley, Coleen, 374–75

Ruby, Jack, 149

Ruckelshaus, William, 209, 216

Rugova, Ibrahim, 353

Rumania, 29

Rumsfeld, Donald, 377, 378

Rusk, Dean, 130

Sadat, Anwar, 233, 252–53

SAG. *See* Screen Actors Guild

Sahkalin Island, 28

Saigon, 46

SALT. *See* Strategic arms limitation talks

San Bernardino, California, 87–88

San Francisco, 1, 51, 99, 179–82

San Joaquin Valley, 187

Sanchez, Arias, 309

Sandinistas, 253, 296–97, 309, 338

The Sands of Iwo Jima (movie), 21

Sao Paulo, Brazil, 178

SAT. *See* College Board Scholastic Aptitude Tests

Saturday Night Fever, 280

Saturday Night Massacre, 216

Saudi Arabia, 233, 238, 243, 296–97, 339

Savings and loans (S&Ls), 304

Scalia, Antonin, 306

Scammon, Richard, 197

Schlafly, Phyllis, 155, 207–8, 272

Schlesinger, James, 218

Schools, 78, 176, 207, 276–77

    busing and, 203–6, 289

Schwarzenegger, Arnold, 363

Schwarzkopf, Norman, 340–43

SCLC. *See* Southern Christian Leadership Council

Scott, Hugh, 217

Screen Actors Guild (SAG), 70

SDI. *See* Strategic Defense Initiative

SDP. *See* West Germany

SDS. *See* Students for a Democratic Society

SEATO. *See* Southeast Asia Treaty Organization

Second Battle of Wounded Knee, 208

Secord, Richard, 310–14

Segregation, 9–12, 63–65

    de, 101, 145, 204–5

    de jure, 186

    U.S. Supreme Court on, 61, 71, 106–9, 161–63

Select Committee on Presidential Campaign Activities, 213

Selma march, 183

Serbs, 353

Sergeant Bilko, 95

700 Club, 278

Sex, 21, 99, 180–83

Sexism, 190

Sexual Behavior in the Human Female (Kinsey), 99

Sexual Behavior in the Human Male (Kinsey), 99

Sexuality, 21, 188

Shah (of Iran), 234–45, 255

Shaker Heights, 363

Shamir, Yitzhak, 309

Shanghai Communique, 228

Shaw, Irving, 20

Shepherd, Alan B., Jr., 141

Sherman Adams scandal, 18–69, 126

Shore, Dinah, 80

The Show of Shows, 95

Shuttle diplomacy, 234, 238

Siberia, 28

Sihanouk (Prince), 229

Silent Spring (Carson), 209

Silvers, Phil, 95

Simpson, Nicole Brown, 326–27

Simpson, O.J., 326–27

Sinai, 164, 2333

Sirica, John J., 213, 216–17

Six Day War, 164, 233

$64,000 Question, 96

Skelton, Red, 95

Smith Act, 69

Smith, John, 184

SNCC. *See* Student Nonviolent Coordinating Committee

Social Security, 18, 82, 156, 158, 370

    benefits, 57, 84, 244, 288

Somalia, 339

Somoza, Anastasio, 253

Sousa, John Philip, 1

South Africa, 276, 307–8, 338–39

South Carolina, 3

South Korea, 47–53, 239, 293

South Pacific, 20, 36

South Vietnam, 113, 138–40, 228–33

    during 1960s, 166–74

    fall of, 239

Southeast Asia, 111, 139

Southeast Asia Treaty Organization (SEATO), 113

Southern Christian Leadership Council (SCLC), 144–47

Southern Manifesto, 107

Southwest Asia, 254

Soviet Communist Party, 225

Soviet Union, 5, 21, 380. *See also* Sputnik
  in Afghanistan, 254, 292, 335–36
  client states of, 29–30, 234
  Cold War/U.S. and, 27–35, 40–42, 47, 49, 51–54, 69–75, 109–11, 122, 239, 254–55
  Cuba and, 121, 134–38
  economy of, 30
  European expansion of, 34–35, 224
  Hungary and, 118
  Israel and, 116–18
  missile crisis and, 134–38
  NATO and, 41–42
  post WW II, 26, 34, 40
  SALT and, 224–25, 245, 254, 293
  spies, 33–34
  Vietnam and, 47, 228, 246
  WW II and, 23–24, 28–30

Space Council, 141

Spain, 380

Spielberg, Steven, 282

Spock, Benjamin, 89

Sputnik, 118–20, 141

Sri Lanka, 364

SST. *See* Supersonic Transport

St. Louis Rams, 283

Stagflation, 203

Stalin, Joseph, 23–24, 27–30, 33, 53

Standard Oil, 22

"Star Spangled Banner," 374

Star Wars, 282

Starr, Kenneth, 349–50

"Stars and Stripes Forever," 1

START. *See* Strategic Arms Reduction Treaty

"The Star-Spangled Banner," 1

Steinem, Gloria, 191, 207

Stevenson, Adlai, 102, 106, 122, 127

Stewart, Jimmy, 20

Stimson, 31

Stockman, David, 287–88

Stop the Draft Week, 177

The Story of GI Joe (movie), 21

Strategic arms limitation talks I (SALT I), 224–26

Strategic arms limitation talks II (SALT II), 245, 254, 293

Strategic Arms Reduction Treaty (START), 292, 316

Strategic Defense Initiative (SDI), 292–93, 315

Student Nonviolent Coordinating Committee (SNCC), 145, 185, 190

Students, 176–79, 190, 197

Students for a Democratic Society (SDS), 177–79, 190

Studio 54, 280

Suez Canal, 116–18, 233–34

Sullivan, Ed, 95

Summer, Donna, 280

Sun Myung Moon, 280

Sunbelt, 3, 77, 263, 288

Sunset Strip, 179

Superbowl, 283

Supersonic Transport (SST), 238

Sutton, Marjorie, 90, 91

Sweden, 172

Symington, Stuart, 105, 127

Syngman Rhee, 48, 52

Syria, 163–64, 233–34, 243, 294–95

Taft, Robert, 54, 60–61, 68, 101

Taft-Hartley Act, 60–61

Taiwan, 113–14, 226–27, 268, 293. *See also* Formosa

Taiwan Strait, 114

Taliban, 373–77

Tanzania, 355

Tax Reform Act (1986), 301

Taylor, Maxwell, 135

Technology, 130, 322–23
    computer, 265–67, 362
    space, 140–41, 143
    telecommunications, 362

Television, 19–20, 80–81, 276–77, 324
    at mid-century, 94–97, 283
    quiz show scandals in, 96–97
    westerns in, 95–96

Tenant, George, 378

Tennessee, 156

Tennessee Valley Authority (TVA), 156

Terrorism, 307–8, 355–56
    9/11/01, 371–78

Tet Offensive, 172–74

Texaco, 22

Texas, 3, 129
    population of, 12, 78, 359, 363
    tragedy in, 148–50

The Texaco Comedy Hour, 95

Thailand, 113, 139, 239

Third Reich, 53

Third World, 26, 240
    countries, 130, 132, 253
    emergence of, 114

Thomas, Clarence, 334–35, 362

Thomas Road Baptist Church, 278

Thompson, Fred, 215

Thurmond, Strom, 195

Time, 267, 289

"The Times They Are A-Changin'," 180

Tinian, 31

TM. *See* Transcendental Meditation

"To Secure These Rights," 63

Togetherness, 92

Tokyo, 27

Tower, John, 311

Trade Expansion Act (1962), 144, 152

Transcendental Meditation (TM), 279

Travolta, John, 280

Trujillo, Rafael, 164

Truman Doctrine, 37–39, 42–43, 54

Truman, Harry S., 19. *See also* Fair Deal
    on atom bomb, 31–33
    on civil rights, 63–65, 67
    corruption and, 68–69
    Korean War and, 47–53
    presidency of, 29–30, 37–41, 45, 47, 53,
      56–59
    re-election of, 59–60, 65–67, 70–72

Tuchman, Barbara, 45

Turkey, 37–39, 117

TVA. *See* Tennessee Valley Authority

Twenty-One, 96

Tydings Committee, 73–74

Tydings, Joseph, 73–74

UAW. *See* United Auto Workers

Udall, Morris, 247

UFWOC. *See* United Farm Workers Organizing
    Committee

U.N. *See* United Nations

Unabomber, 356

Unions, 71
    communism and, 60–61
    membership in, 61
    trade, 17, 58, 83, 264, 345–46

United Auto Workers (UAW), 58–59, 82

United Farm Workers Organizing Committee
    (UFWOC), 187

United Fruit Company, 115–16

United Nations (U.N.), 23
    China and, 226–27
    creation of, 27–28, 71
    General Assembly, 28, 379
    Korean War and, 48
    Security Council, 48–49, 227, 376,
      379–280
    U.S. and, 26–27, 137

United Nations War Crimes Tribunal, 355

United States (U.S.), 23–26, 77, 122–24, 260–61, 284. *See also* Korean War; Marshall Plan; Truman Doctrine
allies of, 1, 5, 21, 27–30, 131
anti-communism, 56, 69–75, 106, 224–26
Asian Americans in, 13–17, 18
China and, 113–15, 226–28, 338
cities/regions of, 3–4, 158, 204–5
civil rights in, 62–65, 67, 106–9, 144–48
class/status in, 86–87
counterculture in, 179–83
Cuba and, 120–21, 134–38, 260
culture in, 19–20, 79–80, 87–88, 280–83, 328–30
deficits, 143–44, 203, 303, 321
demographics of, 3–5, 9, 78, 262–63, 321, 359–61, 362–64
economy, 5–7, 17–18, 34, 56–59, 78–79, 82–83, 143–44, 176, 203, 242–44, 249–50, 263–65, 287–90, 302–6, 320–23, 374
education in, 158, 207, 274, 276–77
elections in, 18, 56–59, 65–67, 126–30, 192–97, 210–12, 247–49, 257–60, 290, 316–18, 343–44, 347–48, 365–69
entertainment in, 20–23
Europe and, 37–40, 237–38
federal government, 5–7, 17–18
foreign aid/policies, 37–40, 142, 163–66, 223–40, 244–47, 251–60, 291–98, 307–16
Germany and, 27–30
health care in, 4, 78, 346–47
Hispanic Americans in, 12
immigration, 267–69
income/income taxes in, 4–5, 143, 299, 304–5, 361–62
industries in, 79–80
Iran and, 255–57
Israel and, 116–18, 243, 252–53
Japan and, 27, 30, 42, 238
labor, 58–59, 82–83
middle-class in, 77
military, 2–3, 9–10, 12, 15–18, 56–57, 132–33, 344–45, 358
Native Americans in, 13
in new millennium, 358–84
nuclear power of, 31–36, 44, 115
occupation by, 27, 40, 133
politics, 17–19, 56–58, 60–61, 101–6
post WW II, 26–27, 35–37
poverty in, 83–84, 157–58, 161, 290, 305–6
rationing in, 6–7, 58
rebels in, 99–100
rock 'n' roll in, 97–99, 181–83
rural, 3–5
social critics in, 93–94
social reform in, 141–43
Soviets and, 27–35, 40–42, 47, 49, 51–54, 79–75, 109–11, 122, 239, 254–55
spy satellites of, 122
suburbia in, 84–86
Suez Canal and, 116–18
taxes in, 4–5, 143, 249, 288, 374
television in, 94–97
U.N. and, 26–27
Vietnam and, 111–13, 138–40, 166–74, 228–33, 245–47
women in, 2–3, 7–9, 24, 61–62, 89–92, 272–75
United States of America v. Richard M. Nixon, 217–18
United States Steel (USS), 143
Universities, 18, 78, 87
University of Alabama, 147
University of California at Berkeley, 176–79
University of California at Davis, 270
University of Michigan, 176
University of Mississippi, 145–46
Unsafe at Any Speed (Nader), 160

U.S. Air Force, 136, 167

U.S. Army, 31, 58, 105, 146, 165
    Induction Center, 177
    Special Forces, 139

U.S. Army Air Corps, 10, 20–21

U.S. Army Forces, 57, 64–65

U.S. Army Green Berets, 139

U.S. Bill of Rights
    Fifth amendment, 162
    First amendment, 142, 162
    Fourteenth amendment, 163
    Sixth amendment, 162
    Twenty-Second amendment, 60, 126
    Twenty-Sixth amendment, 202

U.S. Bureau of Indian Affairs, 208

U.S. Bureau of Labor Statistics, 83

U.S. Census Bureau, 290
    2000 Census, 359–61

U.S. Coast Guard, 7

U.S. Congress, 16–19, 205, 370
    acts of, 35, 39, 58, 92, 159–60, 167, 209
    80th, 37, 39, 60–61, 66
    81st, 68
    hearings, 51
    of 1962, 141–42
    taxes and, 5, 58

U.S. Congressional Medal of Honor, 12

U.S. Department of Defense, 39, 324

U.S. Department of Energy, 288

U.S. Department of Health, Education, and
    Welfare (HEW), 103

U.S. Department of Labor, 60

U.S. Department of Transportation, 159–60

U.S. Executive Order No. 9066, 13–15

U.S. Federal Bureau of Investigation (FBI), 18,
    212–14, 218, 242, 374–75

U.S. House of Representatives, 59–60
    Judiciary Committee, 217–18, 351–52
    Rules Committee, 142

U.S. Joint Chiefs of Staff, 39, 48

U.S. Justice Department, 63–64, 71
    Civil Rights Division, 145

U.S. Marine Corps, 7, 10, 12, 21, 165

U.S. National Guardsmen, 107, 194, 372

U.S. Navy, 57, 136

U.S. Pentagon, 18, 49, 372

U.S. Revenue Acts of 1942/1943, 5

U.S. Secretary of Defense, 39

U.S. *See* United States

U.S. Senate, 17, 59, 73–74, 352
    Armed Services Committee, 51
    Foreign Relations Committee, 38, 51

U.S. Seventh Fleet, 113

U.S. State Department, 105

U.S. Supreme Court, 13–15, 16, 18
    during 1960s, 161–63, 205
    during 1990s, 334–35
    justices, 306–7, 371
    rulings, 61, 71, 217, 220, 231, 270, 369
    on segregation, 61, 71, 106–9, 161–63,
        203–7

USA Patriot Act, 377

USO (United Service Organization), 9

USS Maddox, 166–67

USS Missouri, 32

USS. *See* United States Steel

USS Turner Joy, 166

USS Vincennes, 308

Van Doren, Charles, 96–97

Vance, Cyrus, 251

Vandenberg, Arthur, 38, 40

Vaughn, Harry, 56, 69

"Vaya Con Dios," 97

VCRs. *See* Videocassette recorders

Veneman, Amy, 369

Vermont, 330

Videocassette recorders (VCRs), 283

Viet Minh, 46, 111–13

VietCong, 114, 169–72, 228–31

Vietnam, 123, 191. *See also* Army of the Repub-
  lic of Vietnam; National Liberation Front;
  North Vietnam; South Vietnam
  amnesty, 242
  beginnings of, 46–47, 111–13
  China and, 47
  end of, 245–47
  France and, 46–47, 111–13
  Great Britain and, 112–13
  Great Society and, 154–74
  Johnson, Lyndon, on, 166–74
  Kennedy, John F., on, 138–40
  Soviet Union and, 47, 228, 246
  Tet-68 and, 172–74
  U.S. and, 111–13, 138–40, 166–74, 228–33,
    245–47
Vietnamese, 37
Vietnamization, 229
Villaraigosa, Antonio, 363
Vo Nguyen Giap, 46
Volcker, Paul, 249–50, 287
Voting Rights Act of 1965, 159, 183, 202, 244

WACS (Women's Auxiliary Army Corps), 7
Wallace, Henry A., 18–19, 39, 54, 147
  as candidate, 65, 195–97, 198–99, 247
War Labor Board, 6
Warner Brothers, 20–2
Warren Commission, 149–50
Warren, Earl, 13, 106–7, 149, 163–64, 205
Warsaw Pact, 41, 117–18
Washington, 13
Washington, D.C., 18, 86
  march, 147–48
Washington, George, 123
Washington Post, 213, 352
Water Quality Act, 159
Water Quality Improvement Act (1970), 209
Watergate Committee, 123, 213–18, 220
Watergate Towers, 211

Watkins, Arthur, 105
Watt, James, 288
Watts riot, 183–84
WAVES (Women Accepted for Voluntary
    Emergency Service), 7
Wayne, John, 21
Weapons of mass destruction (WMDs), 379
Weathermen, 179
Weaver, Robert, 145
Webster v. Reproductive Health Care Services,
    334
Weinberger, Caspar, 292
Welch, Joseph, 105
Welfare Reform Act of 1996, 347–48
West Bank, 164, 233, 252
West Berlin, 122, 133–34, 336
West Coast, 3, 13
West Germany (Federal Republic of Germany),
    237, 307, 336
  economy of, 41, 224
  Free Democratic Party (FDP) in, 237
  Ostpolitik in, 237
  Social Democratic Party (SDP) in, 237
West Virginia, 72
Westmoreland, William, 167–72
Wheeler, Earle, 172
Wheeling, West Virginia, 72
White, Theodore, 150
Whites, 66–67, 86, 192
Why Johnny Can't Read (Flesch), 119
Whyte, William, 93
Wicker, Tom, 251
Wilder, Billy, 22
Wilson, Charles E., 103
Wilson, Sloan, 93
Wilson, William J., 270–71
Wilson, Woodrow, 251
Wisconsin, 60
WMDs. *See* Weapons of mass destruction
Wolfe, Tom, 279

Wolfowitz, Paul, 378
Women
   athletes, 283
   discrimination against, 205–7, 272–75
   employment of, 7–9, 62, 84, 273–74
   feminism and, 188–91, 207–8
   at mid-century, 89–92
   in U.S., 2–3, 7–9, 24, 61–62, 89–92, 272–75
   work and, 331–32
   during WW II, 2–3, 7–9, 24
Women's Political Council, 108
Woodstock concert, 181
Woodward, Bob, 213
Work Progress Administration (WPA), 17
Workers, industry, 6
World Bank, 35
World Series, 20
World Trade Center (WTC), 371–74
World War I (WW I), 10
World War II (WW II), 1, 26–37

World War III (WW III), 41, 118, 135
World Wide Web (WWW), 324, 362
Wounded Knee, South Dakota, 208
Wozniak, Steven, 267
WPA. *See* Work Progress Administration
WTC. *See* World Trade Center
Wyman, Jane, 22

Xerox, 81

Yalta conference, 27–30
Yeltsin, Boris, 336
Yom Kippur War, 234
Young, Andrew, 253

Zahir (Shah), 376
Zen Buddhism, 279
Zoot suits, 12
Zwicker, Ralph, 105